THE PAPERS OF

WOODROW WILSON

VOLUME 31

SEPTEMBER 6–DECEMBER 31, 1914

SPONSORED BY THE WOODROW WILSON
FOUNDATION
AND PRINCETON UNIVERSITY

# THE PAPERS OF

# WOODROW WILSON

ARTHUR S. LINK, *EDITOR*

DAVID W. HIRST, *SENIOR ASSOCIATE EDITOR*

JOHN E. LITTLE, *ASSOCIATE EDITOR*

PHYLLIS MARCHAND AND MARGARET D. LINK,
*EDITORIAL ASSISTANTS*

Volume 31
September 6 – December 31, 1914

PRINCETON, NEW JERSEY
PRINCETON UNIVERSITY PRESS
1979

*Note to scholars*: Princeton University Press
subscribes to the Resolution on Permissions of
the Association of American University Presses,
defining what we regard as "fair use" of copyrighted works. This Resolution, intended to encourage scholarly use of university press publications and to avoid unnecessary applications
for permission, is obtainable from the Press or
from the A.A.U.P. central office. Note, however,
that the scholarly apparatus, transcripts of
shorthand, and the texts of Wilson documents
as they appear in this volume are copyrighted,
and the usual rules about the use of copyrighted materials apply.

Publication of this book has been aided by a
grant from the National Historical Publications
and Records Commission.

Printed in the United States of America
by Princeton University Press
Princeton, New Jersey

# INTRODUCTION

THE beginning of this volume finds Wilson still in deep depression over the death of Ellen Axson Wilson. As he wrote to Mary Allen Hulbert, in the first letter printed herein: "I am lamed and wounded more sorely than any words I have could describe. I never dreamed such loneliness and desolation of heart possible."

Wilson, as he often writes, finds salvation in his work; perhaps fortunately for him, the daily tasks multiply. Having already laid the foundations of American neutrality, he works with Secretary of State Bryan and Counselor Lansing to protect American overseas trade against ever tightening British restrictions. Wilson carries on long and futile negotiations aimed at persuading the British government to adopt with some modifications the Declaration of London as the code to govern maritime warfare. Then, falling back upon traditional law, he asserts those rights forcefully in a note to the British government on December 26, 1914.

No sooner does the war break out than talk of peace begins, and Wilson soon finds himself in the center of conversations which come to nothing as Germany and Great Britain try to throw the onus for rejecting Wilson's mediation offer on each other. Moreover, all through these months Mexico remains a daily concern as the revolutionary forces divide, civil war breaks out between Carranza and Villa, and Wilson tries without success to bring the rival forces together. As this volume ends, Wilson is profoundly concerned by growing evidence that Japan is moving to take advantage of the war in Europe to extend her control over China.

Congress is still in session as this volume opens, and Wilson is deeply involved in the rewriting of the Clayton Antitrust bill in order to bring it into harmony with the objectives of the Federal Trade Commission bill.

## "VERBATIM ET LITERATIM"

In all volumes of this series we have said something like the following: "All documents are reproduced *verbatim et literatim*, with typographical and spelling errors corrected in square brackets *only* when necessary for clarity and ease of reading." We think that an explanation of our textual methods and review procedures is long overdue, and we present the following explanation with apologies to our readers for its lateness.

We should say in the beginning that we have never and do not intend to print critical, or corrected, versions of documents. We print them exactly as they are, with a few exceptions which we have always noted. We never use the word *sic* except when words are repeated in a document; in fact, we think that a succession of *sics* simply defaces a page.

As we have said, we repair words in square brackets only for clarity and ease of reading. Our general rule is to do this when we ourselves cannot read the word without stopping to determine its meaning. Jumbled words and names misspelled beyond recognition of course have to be repaired. However, we are usually able to correct the misspelling of a name in the footnote identifying the person.

However, when an old man writes to Wilson saying that he is glad to hear that Wilson is "comming" to Newark, or a semiliterate farmer from Texas writes phonetically, we see no reason to correct spellings in square brackets when the words are perfectly understandable. We do not correct Wilson's misspellings. For example, for some reason he insisted upon spelling "belligerent" as "belligerant." Nothing would be gained by correcting "belligerant" in square brackets.

We think that it is very important for several reasons to follow the rule of *verbatim et literatim*. Most important, a document has its own integrity and power, oftentimes particularly when it is not written in perfect literary form. There is something very moving in seeing a Texas dirt farmer struggling to express his feelings in words, or a semiliterate former slave doing the same thing. Second, in Wilson's case it is crucially important to reproduce his errors in letters that he typed himself, as he always typed badly when he was in an agitated state. Third, since style is the essence of the person, we would never correct grammar or make tenses consistent, as one correspondent has urged us to do. Fourth, we think that it is obligatory to print typed documents *verbatim et literatim*. For example, we think that it is very important that we print exact transcripts of Charles L. Swem's copies of Wilson's letters. Swem made many mistakes (we correct them in footnotes from a reading of his shorthand books), and Wilson let them pass. We thus have to assume that Wilson did not read his letters before signing them, and this, we think, is a significant fact. Bryan had one abominable stenographer. In letters in the next volume, he spells the name of the steamship *Falaba* as *Fabala* and "principle" as "principal." (We did not correct these and similar errors.) We think that it tells us a great deal about Bryan, who was himself a sloppy speller and writer, that he should have let such letters go to the President of the United States. Finally, printing letters and typed documents *verbatim et literatim* tells us a great deal about the educational level of the stenographical profession in the United States during Wilson's time.

We think that our series would be worthless if we produced unreliable texts, and we go to some effort to make certain that the texts are authentic.

Our typists are highly skilled and proofread their transcripts carefully as soon as they have been typed. The Editor sight proofreads documents once he has assembled a volume and is setting the annotation. The editors who write the notes read through documents several times and are careful to check any anomalies. Then, once the manuscript volume has been completed and all notes checked, the Editor and Senior Associate Editor orally proofread the documents against the copy. Every comma, dash, and character is read. Every absence of punctuation is noted. Every nearly illegible word in written documents is carefully studied.

Once this process of "establishing the text" is completed, the manuscript volume goes to our editor at Princeton University Press, who checks the volume carefully and sends it to the printing plant. The volume is set by linotype by two typographers who have been working on the Wilson volumes for years. The galley proofs go to the proof room, where they are read orally against copy. And we must say that the proofreaders at the Press are extraordinarily skilled. Some years ago, before we found a way to ease their burden, they used to query every misspelled word, absence of punctuation, or other such anomalies. Now we write "O.K." above such words on the copy.

We read the galley proofs three times. Our copyeditor gives them a sight reading against copy to look for remaining typographical errors and to make sure that no line has been dropped. The Senior Editor and the Senior Associate Editor sight read them against documents and copy. We then get the page proofs, which have been corrected at the Press. We check all the changes twice. In addition, we get *revised* pages and check them twice.

This is not the end. Our indexer of course reads the pages word by word. Before we return the pages to the Press, she comes in with a list of queries, all of which are answered by reference to the documents.

Our rule in the Wilson Papers is that our tolerance of error is zero. No system and no person can be perfect. We are sure that there are errors in our volumes. However, we believe that we have done everything humanly possible to avoid error; the chance is remote that what looks at first glance like a typographical error is indeed an error.

We are indebted to Katharine E. Brand, John Milton Cooper, Jr., and William H. Harbaugh for reading the manuscript of this volume with great care and to Judith May, our editor at Princeton University Press, for continuing assistance.

THE EDITORS

*Princeton, New Jersey*
*March 7, 1979*

# CONTENTS

## Collateral Materials

# ILLUSTRATIONS

Following page 298

Wilson and Tumulty in the Oval Office
*Library of Congress*

Wilson and House at Cornish, September 1914
*Archives of the* Washington Star

The President and the Secretary of State
*Library of Congress*

Sir Edward Grey
*Library of Congress*

Sir Cecil Arthur Spring Rice
*Princeton University Library*

Francisco Villa
*Library of Congress*

Venustiano Carranza
*Library of Congress*

William Monroe Trotter
*Boston Public Library*

# ABBREVIATIONS

| | |
|---|---|
| ALI | autograph letter initialed |
| ALS | autograph letter signed |
| CC | carbon copy |
| CCL | carbon copy of letter |
| CCLS | carbon copy of letter signed |
| CLS | Charles Lee Swem |
| CLSsh | Charles Lee Swem shorthand |
| CLST | Charles Lee Swem typed |
| EBW | Edith Bolling Wilson |
| EMH | Edward Mandell House |
| FR | *Papers Relating to the Foreign Relations of the United States* |
| FR-LP | *Papers Relating to the Foreign Relations of the United States, The Lansing Papers* |
| FR-WWS 1914 | *Papers Relating to the Foreign Relations of the United States, 1914, Supplement, The World War* |
| Hw | handwriting, handwritten |
| HwLS | handwritten letter signed |
| JPT | Joseph Patrick Tumulty |
| JRT | Jack Romagna typed |
| MS | manuscript |
| RG | Record Group |
| RL | Robert Lansing |
| T MS | typed manuscript |
| TCL | typed copy of letter |
| TL | typed letter |
| TLI | typed letter initialed |
| TLS | typed letter signed |
| TS | typed signed |
| WHP | Walter Hines Page |
| WJB | William Jennings Bryan |
| WGM | William Gibbs McAdoo |
| WW | Woodrow Wilson |
| WWhw | Woodrow Wilson handwriting, handwritten |
| WWsh | Woodrow Wilson shorthand |
| WWT | Woodrow Wilson typed |
| WWTLI | Woodrow Wilson typed letter initialed |
| WWTLS | Woodrow Wilson typed letter signed |

## ABBREVIATIONS FOR COLLECTIONS
## AND REPOSITORIES

### Following the National Union Catalog of the Library of Congress

| | |
|---|---|
| A-Ar | Alabama Department of Archives and History |
| AGO | Adjutant General's Office |
| CtY | Yale University |
| CtY-D | Yale University Divinity School |

| | |
|---|---|
| CSt-H | Hoover Institution on War, Revolution, and Peace, Stanford University |
| DLC | Library of Congress |
| DNA | National Archives |
| FFM-Ar | French Foreign Ministry Archives |
| FO | British Foreign Office |
| GFO-Ar | German Foreign Office Archives |
| JFO-Ar | Japanese Foreign Office Archives |
| MB | Boston Public Library |
| MH | Harvard University |
| NcD | Duke University |
| NHpR | Franklin D. Roosevelt Library, Hyde Park |
| NjP | Princeton University |
| NNC | Columbia University |
| NRU | University of Rochester |
| PRO | Public Record Office |
| RSB Coll., DLC | Ray Stannard Baker Collection of Wilsoniana, Library of Congress |
| ScCleU | Clemson University |
| SDR | State Department Records |
| WC, NjP | Woodrow Wilson Collection, Princeton University |
| WDR | War Department Records |
| WHi | State Historical Society of Wisconsin |
| WP, DLC | Woodrow Wilson Papers, Library of Congress |

## SYMBOLS

| | |
|---|---|
| [Sept. 8, 1914] | publication date of a published writing; also date of document when date is not part of text |
| [*Oct. 7, 1914*] | composition date when publication date differs |
| [[Oct. 20, 1914]] | delivery date of speech if publication date differs |
| * * * * | elision by author of document |

THE PAPERS OF
WOODROW WILSON

VOLUME 31
SEPTEMBER 6–DECEMBER 31, 1914

# THE PAPERS OF
# WOODROW WILSON

---

## To Mary Allen Hulbert

Dearest Friend,          The White House 6 September, 1914.

Mr. McAdoo sent for Mr. Wallace and asked him to serve on the advisory board which is to oversee the new Bureau of Marine Insurance. I believe he accepted and is at work already. I have not seen him yet, but hope I shall very soon. I am heartily glad if this is like what he wished, and shall look forward with genuine pleasure to welcoming him to the service of the government.

It comforts and steadies me to think of other people and try to serve them, when I understand them and really care. I found that the most comforting part of your last letter (but one) was not the sweet sympathy and comprehension of my loss (somehow sympathy from those who really care as yet, while it warms my heart and gives me the strength that companionship always gives, does not in any literal sense *comfort*) so much as the cheering things you told me about yourself and Allen, the news that you were well and that the affection of your neighbours was beginning to form about you for your support and pleasure and that the boy was doing what you had hoped and prayed for, and that you were getting once again the sort of faith in God's providence that sustains more than anything else can. I think I should go mad without it! Thoughts of you, especially comfortable ones, taking the place of long anxiety, took me away from myself and taught me once again, what we are so slow to comprehend, that happiness lies, not in *anything* that you can get out of thinking about yourself, but always in being glad about others and living outside yourself in the free atmosphere of God's big world. How profoundly happy I am that the world grows brighter and sweeter to you, and that, in the midst of loneliness, your love of what is around you is working once more the miracle of healing! I have much that is delightful now to think about!

In God's gracious arrangement of things I have little time or chance to think about myself. The day's work and responsibilities exhaust all the vitality I have and there is none left to spend on pity for myself. I am lamed and wounded more sorely than any words I have could describe. I never dreamed such loneliness and desolation of heart possible. I suffer all the time a sort of dumb agony of longing. But I *must* spend every energy of my brain on the matters which touch the life of this dear nation, entrusted for the time to my guidance. I *dare* not expend the least part on myself. The very magnitude and fatefulness of the tasks I have every day to face dominates me and holds me steady to my duty. Nothing less great, I imagine, could. The world itself seems gone mad, and there is a sort of grim pleasure, and stern compulsion to keep sane and self-possessed amidst the general wreck and distemper. And so I fare well enough from day to day; and this letter is not written of myself but of you, in heartfelt gratitude that God has been good to you and brought you health and cheer and courage again.

My little household unites with me in affectionate messages.
Your devoted friend   Woodrow Wilson

WWTLS (WP, DLC).


## To Nancy Saunders Toy

My dear Friend,          The White House 6 September, 1914

How selfish I have been, how absorbed in my own anxieties, how thoughtless of you and of yours! For five months, nearly, I saw my dear one go slowly, slowly down the hill, a great fear growing darker and darker in my heart, the burden more and more nearly intolerable to my heart, while I tried to command myself for the great tasks which *had* to be performed, and performed with a clear head and an attentive conscience, if I was to be faithful to the trust a great nation had imposed upon me; and while I staggered to keep my feet I heard of your great loss, of the death of that wonderful lady[1] whom you had made me admire and even love by the glimpses you gave me of her wonderful mind and great heart; I knew what it meant to you, and yet I was dumb! It was as if I *could* not speak. It was as if, should I speak to you at all about the fears that had come true to *you* my own fear would overcome me. I feared to open the floodgates in my own soul. Or else my own grief overtopped everything. I do not know. It seemed to me that I stood looking at you, and was unable to speak, trusted that you would somehow see in my eyes what I was not able to utter. But I see now how selfish that was, and beg that you will forgive me! How were you to know what I was *thinking* of you, or how my heart went out to you in your loss? How were you to know that that, too, made the world a little darker for me?

I do not see the light yet; but it is not necessary for me to see it: I know that it shines, and I know *where* it shines, as your dear mother did. All that I need do now is to go straight ahead with the near duty, and lean on that to be steadied: for it comes from where the light does. And how thankful and happy I am that I have such friends as you are, and that you write me such letters of cheer, to let me know that you are thinking of me! Else I would feel as if I stood alone in the world, with my incomparable one gone, gone beyond recall, when I needed her most and was sustained by her love and comradeship from day to day when the days meant most and were hardest!

Most of my dear ones are at Cornish, by my wish. I am well. Please give my warmest regards to Mr. Toy; and please graciously accept my heartfelt sympathy, deep and filled with a real knowledge of what you have suffered and are suffering. I feel as if I, too, in her death had lost a truly great friend.

Your devoted friend,   Woodrow Wilson

Please do not think this dictated to a stenographer. This machine is my familiar pen.

WWTLS (photostat in RSB Coll., DLC).
  1 Her mother, Mary Toomer (Mrs. R. M.) Saunders, had died on July 24, 1914. See Nancy S. Toy to WW, Aug. 28, 1914, ALS (WP, DLC).

## From Edward Mandell House

Dear Governor:      Prides Crossing, Mass. September 6th, 1914.

Last night I had a conference with the Austrian Ambassador. He talked very indiscreetly and if one will sit still, he will tell all he knows. I sat very still.

I learned that the Germans were making a mighty effort to gain a decisive victory in France and that when that was accomplished, they would be ready to consider overtures for peace.

I also learned that their great fear was starvation. Austria is fairly self-sustaining and because of her close proximity to Roumania, she would not unduly suffer, but Germany faces famine if the war continues.

England, it seems, lets no ship pass into neutral ports without first ascertaining whether or not it contains foodstuffs and when it does, she exercises her right to purchase it.

What Dumba particularly wants is for the American ships to defy England and feed Germany. He also wants them to take German and Austrian reservists over. He says the only way they can cross now is to become stokers and get over in that way, or in other disguises.

It is his purpose to talk with you about these matters later, but he asked me to communicate this part of his conversation to you. He said it seemed quite certain that Germany would have a large number of Allies as prisoners and then it would be clearly up to the Allies whether they desired these prisoners to starve, that self-preservation would compel Germany to feed her own people first. He wondered whether this country would permit widespread starvation in order that the Allies might win.

He spoke of England's enormous power and said Germany's military power was not to be compared with that England exercised over the entire world because of her navy. He forgot to add that England is not exercising her power in an objectionable way for it is controlled by a democracy.

He strongly deprecated the war and said if he had been Foreign Minister in Austria it would never have occurred. He intimated that Germany and Austria felt that Russia would have been prepared in 1915 and therefore it was necessary to anticipate her.

He spoke as if he knew that I was fully conversant with Germany-Austria-Russia conditions, having been on the ground so recently.

He deprecated the use of bombs.

Your very affectionate,   E. M. House

TLS (WP, DLC).


## From Walter Hines Page

Dear Mr. President:                    London. Sepr. 6. 1914.

In those rushing days of a month ago when nobody here had time to catch one's breath, of course I knew event after event as they transpired—many events before they happened. There was no time to make a record or to write even to you, and of course you have been as much occupied as I have been—and more. I do not know, therefore, how closely you have kept informed of the causes of the war, of the case of each bellig[er]ent, and of the inner meaning of it all.

I have given the general subject of the German-English rivalry, which has fast become Prussian hatred and English distrust these ten years—I have given it as serious study as I could since I was here and (for a brief time) in Germany six years ago. A war between them has ever since then seemed to me inevitable—an early war, a war within my life-time—except in moods when I shared the feeling of most men, that perhaps the terrible modern engines of destruction would, at the last moment, cause every nation to desist. As I became acquainted with some of the literature of Prussian militairism, I recall I wrote down several years ago in a fitful diary that I have kept, the conviction that Italy, Spain, France, Holland, and England had each had its day of primacy in Europe, and that Prussia would not content itself till it, too, tried. Then, after I came here and began to get some glimpses into the way great national policies were made, this definite Prussian determination became clearer; and little by little I got knowledge of the Prussian beauracracy's methods—got glimpses from other than British sources. Their recent diplomacy has been—simply a lie, all bent on making ready themselves and on keeping other nations from getting ready. Their "publicity" campaign throughout the world has become clear to all men who know the publishing and newspaper work of the world. I know an American whom the Prussian Foreign Office sought deliberately to bribe to affect public opinion in the United States.

When House's plan first came to me, I wrote him a letter to show the utter futility of his idea. The next day I wisely burnt it, because it was foolish, perhaps wicked, to discourage any such effort made by anybody; and I sent him another letter instead.

Sir Edward Grey never told me in so many words that he regarded it as his life-work to prevent such a war; but as events have unfolded themselves this has become plain. And it is equally plain to me that for years he has worked with a diminishing hope. Not only English soldiers—men like Roberts[1] and Kitchener[2] —and English sailors—men like Jellicoe[3] and Fisher[4]—but both English and American and French students of modern history and modern politics—men like the late Professor Camb[5] of the University of London—have seen no way to avoid it.

The "cult of valour"—a sort of religion of military force, captured Prussia, scholars and all. It makes one revise one's values of sheer scholarship.

I have tried in my own mind to detach myself from the English and from the English point-of-view. Well, of course, the French have been aware of the danger. So have the Belgians and the Dutch. A distinguished and thoughtful Dutch man told me six years ago almost what has happened this past month.

I believe it literally true that the "cult of valour," which is the modern name of sheer force—force that really believes that might, however brutal, is right—is driving these militairists mad: their incomprehensible and incalculable big-head is sheer madness. It is another case of Napoleon—even more brutal: a dream of universal conquest. Sir Edward remarked to me the other day that if this thing succeeds, Europe will become a place in which life will not be worth living: "the only place worth living will be the United States—till it attacks that, as it would." That seems to me literally true.

I see no hope of the world's going on towards ends and ideals that we value except on the hypothesis that Prussian militairism be utterly cut out, as surgeons cut out a cancer. And the Allies will do it—must do it, to live. It would dash our Monroe doctrine to the ground. It wd. even invade the U. S. in time.

There are many objectionable things that will accompany its defeat under present circumstances, such as the prominence of Russia as one of the victors—itself a menace in the future— and the continuance of the warlike spirit in Japan, and the acquisition by England of still more colonies. But these are all lesser or less immediate evils.

Every revelation of German methods as the war goes on confirms all my fears and solidifies all my convictions about Prussian militairism and a war-lord monarchy. The terror and the danger of it are not even yet fully or generally realized.

Yours very heartily,   Walter H. Page

Sir Edw. Grey's Speech[6]  ⎫ make the whole
The British 'White Paper'[7] ⎬ case very clear.
The German 'White Paper'[8] ⎭

London, 8. Sep. '14.

P.S. I see by this morning's papers that the Allies' declaration, that none of them will make peace without the consent of all, is understood by the American press. As I regard it, this makes the result of the war certain—there will be no compromise with the German system. England will fight and starve the Germans out if it takes years to do it—to a complete defeat. The war-spirit, which was hard to awaken, is now completely aroused here. The German Empire and its military system are doomed. The only open question is the cost. It will cost hundreds of thousands of men and most of the treasure of Europe. This side of the world will be bankrupt but free.   W.H.P.

ALS (WP, DLC).
    [1] Frederick Sleigh Roberts, 1st Earl Roberts (1832-1914).
    [2] Field Marshal Horatio Herbert Kitchener, 1st Earl Kitchener of Khartoum, at this time Secretary of State for War.
    [3] Admiral Sir John Rushworth Jellicoe, commander in chief of the Grand Fleet.
    [4] Admiral of the Fleet John Arbuthnot Fisher, 1st Baron Fisher of Kilverstone, soon to become First Sea Lord of the Admiralty.

[5] John Adam Cramb (1862-1913), late Professor of Modern History, Queen's College, London. His posthumous book, *Germany and England* (London and New York, 1914), appeared in June.

[6] Grey's speech of August 3, 1914, in the House of Commons justifying the declaration of war. *Parliamentary Debates*, 5th Ser., LXV, cols. 1809-27.

[7] Identified in E. W. Gosse to WW, 1914, n. 2, Vol. 30.

[8] [Germany. Foreign Office.] *The German White-Book (Only Authorized Translation): How Russia and her Ruler Betrayed Germany's Confidence and Thereby Caused the European War* (Berlin, 1914). Several editions of this work appeared in 1914 under differing titles in both German and English.

## Count Johann Heinrich von Bernstorff to the German Foreign Office

Washington, den 7. September 1914

Oskar Strauß sondierte mich hinsichtlich einer amerikanischen Vermittelungsaktion in Form einer Botschafterkonferenz in Washington. Er meint, der Augenblick hierzu sei gekommen, da Frankreich besiegt wäre und es sich empfehle, die Zerstörung von Paris zu verhindern. Da Herr Wilson und Bryan die Sache gleich darauf mit mir aufnahmen, handelte Strauß vermutlich in deren Auftrag.

Hier wünscht jedermann den Frieden, weil die Vereinigten Staaten schwer unter dem Krieg leiden.[1] Ich verhielt mich daher nicht ablehnend, da ich das Odium der Ablehnung unseren Feinden überlassen wollte. Ich habe aber Herrn Bryan bestimmt gesagt, daß von einem Waffenstillstand keine Rede sein könnte, weil ein solcher ausschließlich unseren Feinden nützen würde. Auch müsse ich gegebenenfalls Wiederherstellung des Kabels verlangen, damit ich regelrecht mit meiner Regierung in Verbindung treten könnte.

Nach Lage der hiesigen Verhältnisse fühle ich mich verpflichtet die Annahme des Wilsonschen Vorschlages, der Euerer Exzellenz durch Gerard übermittelt werden wird, zu empfehlen, weil die hiesige öffentliche Meinung, die schon stark von England beeinflußt wird, sich unbedingt gegen denjenigen wenden wird, welchen sie für die Verlängerung des Krieges verantwortlich hält. Bernstorff.

T telegram (Russland 104, No. 2, No. D934791, GFO-Ar).

[1] In a dispatch to Berlin on September 6, Bernstorff wrote: "I found the attitude here just about as I had expected. The government is definitely neutral. It would have to be even if it did not want to be neutral. President Wilson told me, 'We definitely have to be neutral since otherwise our mixed populations would wage war against themselves.'" J. H. von Bernstorff to T. von Bethmann Hollweg, Sept. 6, 1914, T telegram (Russland 104, No. 2, D934862, GFO-Ar).

TRANSLATION

Washington, September 7, 1914.

Oscar Straus felt me out about an American mediation action by way of an ambassadorial conference in Washington. He believes the moment for it has come, since France has been defeated, and it would be advisable to prevent the destruction of Paris. Since Mr. Wilson and Bryan took up the matter with me immediately thereafter, Straus acted presumably on their order.

Here everyone desires peace, for the United States suffers heavily because of the war. I, therefore, did not reject the offer, since I wanted to leave the odium of rejection to our enemies. But I definitely said to Mr. Bryan that there could be no talk of an armistice, since it would be useful exclusively to our enemies. Also, I would have to demand in that case the re-opening of the cable, so that I could have a regular connection with my government.

As I see the situation here, I feel obliged to recommend the acceptance of Wilson's propositions, which he will convey to Your Excellency through Gerard, because public opinion here, which has already been strongly influenced by England, will unquestionably turn against the belligerent whom they hold responsible for prolonging the war.            Bernstorff.

## To Edward Mandell House

My dear Friend:          The White House September 8, 1914

I have your letters of September fifth and sixth. I have sent your letter to Herr Zimmerman to the German Ambassador with the request that he forward it.

I have read your letter to Page with entire approval.

What you tell me of your conversation with the Austrian Ambassador is little less than amazing but it is immensely useful as a cross light.

In haste      Affectionately yours,   Woodrow Wilson

TLS (E. M. House Papers, CtY).

## A Proclamation[1]

[Sept. 8, 1914]

WHEREAS great nations of the world have taken up arms against one another and war now draws millions of men into battle whom the counsel of statesmen have not been able to save from the terrible sacrifice;

AND WHEREAS in this as in all things it is our privilege and duty to seek counsel and succor of Almighty God, humbling ourselves before Him, confessing our weakness and our lack of any wisdom equal to these things;

AND WHEREAS it is the especial wish and longing of the people of the United States, in prayer and counsel and all friendliness, to serve the cause of peace;

THEREFORE, I, Woodrow Wilson, President of the United States of America, do designate Sunday, the fourth day of October next, a day of prayer and supplication and do request all God-fearing persons to repair on that day to their places of worship there to unite their petitions to Almighty God that, overruling the counsel of men, setting straight the things they cannot govern or alter, taking pity on the nations now in the throes of conflict, in His mercy and goodness showing a way where men can see none, He vouchsafe His children healing peace again and restore once more that concord among men and nations without which there can be neither happiness nor true friendship nor any wholesome fruit of toil or thought in the world; praying also to this end that he forgive us our sins, our ignorance of His holy will, our wilfulness and many errors, and lead us in the paths of obedience to places of vision and to thoughts and counsels that purge and make wise.

In witness whereof I have hereunto set my hand and caused the seal of the United States to be affixed.

Done at the city of Washington this eighth day of September in the year of our Lord one thousand nine hundred and fourteen and of the independence of the United States of America the one hundred and thirty-ninth.

(SEAL)                                         Woodrow Wilson.

T MS (WP, DLC).
1 There is a WWsh draft of the following proclamation in WP, DLC.

## To Dudley Field Malone

[The White House] September 8, 1914.

Confidential. I feel extremely reluctant to have the administration as such constructively associated with the primary campaign[1] because that would be so glarlingly inconsistent with position taken in other states. Hope you will think it best not to take part as campaigner. You will inevitably be considered

my spokesman because of our close personal relationship which
I so much prize.                          Woodrow Wilson.

T telegram (Letterpress Books, WP, DLC).
  ¹ In New York. Wilson was replying to D. F. Malone to WW, Sept. 3, 1914,
TLS (WP, DLC), arguing that he (Malone) should provide "an active, though
dignified, support" of the anti-Tammany candidacies of John A. Hennessy for
governor and Franklin D. Roosevelt for United States senator in the forthcoming Democratic primary campaign.


## To the *Houston Chronicle*

[The White House] September 8, 1914

Please enter me as a subscriber for a bale of cotton.¹
                                   Woodrow Wilson.

T telegram (Letterpress Books, WP, DLC).
  ¹ About the panic in the cotton market and the buy-a-bale campaign, see
Arthur S. Link, "The Cotton Crisis, the South, and Anglo-American Diplomacy,
1914-1915," in Arthur S. Link, *The Higher Realism of Woodrow Wilson and
Other Essays* (Nashville, Tenn., 1971), pp. 309-29. Wilson bought several bales.


## From Charles Jenkinson¹

Sir:                        Washington, D. C. September 8, 1914.

I have the honor to enclose, herewith, an original letter in
Spanish dictated and signed by General Emiliano Zapata,² the
leader of the revolution in the south of Mexico, which he has
asked me to hand to you as setting forth the reasons, purposes
and objects actuating his army.

I also have the honor to enclose an original letter, in Spanish,
from General Zapata,³ in which he asks me to inquire of you
whether you would receive a commission of his representatives
if they come to Washington, to discuss the Zapata movement
with you.

For your information, I also enclose a printed copy of the plan
of Ayala, a printed copy of the ratification thereof, and a dictated
and signed memorandum containing comments by the author of
the plan.⁴

I also enclose an original memorandum in Spanish dictated
and signed by General Amador Salazar,⁵ the second in command
of Zapata's army. These papers were handed to me while I was in
the States of Morelos and Mexico with General Zapata, at whose
request I had gone to Cuernavaca to discuss with him the
economic situation within his lines, as there are at the present
time approximately two hundred and fifty thousand non-

combatants in the states of Mexico, Morelos, Guerrero and Puebla actually starving to death.

I am, of course, at your orders for any further information you may desire upon this subject.

General Zapata has also asked me to speak to you about a Mr. Hall,[6] of Cuernavaca, who has stated that he represents General Zapata.

As of possible interest to you, I also enclose copy of a personal letter addressed to me by General Zapata[7] in appreciation of the work done by me in the name of the American Red Cross among his people.          Very respectfully,   Charles Jenkinson

TLS (WP, DLC).
   [1] Director of the Atlantic Division, American National Red Cross.
   [2] E. Zapata to WW, Aug. 23, 1914, TLS (WP, DLC).
   [3] E. Zapata to C. Jenkinson, n.d., TLS (WP, DLC).
   [4] "Plan de Ayala," Nov. 28, 1911, printed broadside; "Acta de ratificación del Plan de Ayala," July 19, 1914, printed broadside; Otilio E. Montaño, Aug. 23, 1914, TS memorandum, all in WP, DLC.
   [5] A. Salazar, Aug. 23, 1914, TS memorandum (WP, DLC).
   [6] Hubert L. Hall, about whom see WJB to WW, May 19, 1914, n. 1, Vol. 30.
   [7] E. Zapata to C. Jenkinson, n.d., TLS (WP, DLC).


## To Belle Dunton Westcott Harper

My dear Mrs. Harper:          [The White House] September 8, 1914

Your letter of August twenty-fourth touched me very deeply. I find that I cannot trust myself yet to speak about Mrs. Wilson's death, but I know how you loved her and I know how she loved you. Your words of sympathy, therefore, come to me with a peculiar touching quality and I am sincerely your debtor.

I hope that you are not suffering a too painful inconvenience from the present distressing circumstances and that you are all of you well.

With warmest regard,
          Cordially and sincerely yours,   Woodrow Wilson

TLS (Letterpress Books, WP, DLC).


## Sir Cecil Arthur Spring Rice to Sir Edward Grey

My dear Sir Edward          Washington. September 8 1914

. . . The feeling of nearly everyone with whom I speak is very friendly but then the friends I have here are those who would naturally be friendly. Still there seems no doubt at all that the mass of the people dislike the Germans more than they dislike us. In 1870 the feeling was overwhelmingly German so there has been a great change. I think that there is a wide-spread belief (to quote you) that Prussian militarism is the question at issue and that if it triumphs in Europe America will have to defend itself. The President said in the most solemn way that if that cause succeeds in the present struggle The United States would have to give up its present ideals and devote all its energies to defence which would mean the end of its present system of Government. He is a great student of Wordsworth and when I alluded to the sonnets at the time of the great war especially "It is not to be thought of that the flood" and "we must be free or die who speak the tongue etc" he said he knew them by heart and had them in his mind all the time. I said "You and Grey are fed on the same food and I think you understand." There were tears in his eyes. I am sure we can at the right moment depend on an understanding heart here.

Yours ever    Cecil Spring Rice

TLS (E. Grey Papers, FO 800/84, PRO).

## James Watson Gerard to the German Foreign Office

### Memorandum.

Berlin, September 8, 1914.

The Ambassador is informed that at a dinner in Washington Count Bernstorff said to Mr. Oscar Strauss, in answer to a question as to whether he thought His Imperial Majesty would favorably consider an offer of mediation, if extended, that he believed, although he had had no recent word from his Government, from statements made to him by the Chancellor before his return to America, that His Imperial Majesty would accept mediation if the other nations involved would do the same. The Ambassador is informed that Count Bernstorff confirmed this conversation to the President and that he agrees that this matter should be reported to the German Government and that the Ambassador ask that the Imperial Foreign Office state to His Imperial Majesty, on behalf of the President of the United States that, upon receipt of a favorable reply to the question as to whether mediation will be entertained, the President of the United States will cause similar inquiry to be made of the other Governments involved, and that if the President shall be the means of bringing the nations into conference with a view to the adjustment by them of their differences he will be much gratified.

T MS (Russland 104, No. 2, No. D934790, GFO-Ar).

# Jean Jules Jusserand to the French Foreign Ministry

Washington le [8 septembre, 1914]

298. Le Comte Bensdorff a confirmé au secrétaire d'État que son Gouvernement acceptait une médiation américaine. Il n'en a pas indiqué les bases et est (parti) le même jour pour New York sans avoir vu le Président par crainte des journalistes qui pullulent devant la Maison-Blanche. M. Bryan a téléphoné la substance de la conversation à M. Wilson. On attend la réponse de l'Ambassadeur américain à Berlin qui doit vérifier les dispositions exactes de l'Empereur Guillaume.

Cette démarche ne me paraît (plus) pouvoir être interprétée que comme un aveu d'anxiété et nous y devons puiser un surcroît de confiance dans le succès de notre résistance (devant se) poursuivre avec une énergie redoublée.

Je n'ai pas caché à M. Bryan que les chances de réussite de l'intervention envisagée étaient infinitésimales, chaque jour allongeant la liste des crimes allemands (aujourd'hui la destruction de Dinant) et accroissant l'indignation universelle. Comme à un moment il avait fait allusion à un retour au statu quo, je lui ai répondu que nous l'accepterions quand les Allemands pour le rétablir rendraient la vie à nos morts.

Les journaux de New York malgré toutes les précautions ont soupçonné le but du brusque voyage de l'Ambassadeur Allemand. Le Secrétaire d'État dément [démit] les rumeurs qu'ils publient.

Jusserand.

T telegram (Guerre 1914-1918, États-Unis, Vol. 489, FFM-Ar).

T R A N S L A T I O N

Washington [Sept. 8, 1914]

298. Count Bernstorff has confirmed to the Secretary of State that his government would accept an American mediation. He has not indicated the bases of it and left the same day for New York without having seen the President for fear of the journalists milling around in front of the White House. Mr. Bryan telephoned the substance of the conversation to Mr. Wilson. They await the response from the American Ambassador in Berlin who must verify the exact dispositions of Emperor William.

This démarche seems to me capable of being interpreted as only a sign of anxiety, and we should be able to gain from it an increase of confidence in the success of our resistance, enabling us to pursue it with redoubled energy.

I did not conceal from Mr. Bryan that the chances of success of the intervention envisaged were infinitesimal, each day adding to the list of German crimes (today the destruction of Dinant) and growing universal indignation. As at one moment he had made allusion to a return to the status quo, I replied to him that we would accept it when the Germans, in order to re-establish it, could give us back the lives of our dead ones.

The newspapers of New York, in spite of all the precautions, have guessed the objective of the quick trip of the German Ambassador. The Secretary of State denies the rumors that they publish.                                        Jusserand.

## To Grace Elizabeth Titus[1]

My dear Miss Titus:        [The White House] September 9, 1914

Knowing as I do how glad Mrs. Wilson would have been to continue paying your tuition at Drexel, I take pleasure in enclosing my check for five hundred dollars. There goes with it my most earnest good wishes for you and all your family.

Sincerely yours,   Woodrow Wilson

TLS (Letterpress Books, WP, DLC).
  [1] Of 17 Alexander St., Princeton, N. J.

## From William Jennings Bryan, with Enclosure

My Dear Mr President,                     [Washington, Sept. 9, 1914]

I enclose 1st dispatch from Emperor William. It is fortunate that it comes at this time. There can be no impropriety in receiving a communication from the Belgians if the Emperor can send a protest

2 newspaper clipping giving an interview with Turkish Ambassador[1] He goes beyond the bounds it seems to me in his reference to our own and other countries.

3d Given Mr Lansings views[2] at to what can be done with the Belgians I have asked the Belgian Minister to let me know what his countrys representatives desire. With assurances of respect I am my dear Mr President    Yours truly   W. J. Bryan

ALS (WP, DLC).
  [1] Clipping from the *Washington Post*, Sept. 8, 1914. It was a statement issued by the Turkish Ambassador to the United States, Ahmed Rustem Bey. He charged that the British, by raising the specter of a massacre of Christians in Turkey, were attempting to induce the United States to send warships into Turkish waters in order to foment a war between Turkey and the United States. He admitted that he could not deny that there had been massacres in Turkey, but he asserted that Armenians and Maronites had suffered at the hands of

Moslems, "not as Christians, but as political agitators engaged in undermining the Ottoman state." After charging Britain, France, and Russia with various barbarities, he remarked that it was hardly fitting for Americans, who lynched blacks "daily" and had subjected Filipinos to the water cure, to criticize Turks for acts of savagery committed under far greater provocation. The statement is also printed in *FR-LP*, i, 70-71.

² R. Lansing to WJB, Sept. 8, 1914, TLS (WP, DLC). Lansing concluded that Wilson should receive the Belgian delegates personally in any case, but that he should receive them officially and hear any statement or communication they had to make only if they bore credentials as special ambassadors or a letter from the King of the Belgians addressed to the President of the United States.

## E N C L O S U R E

Berlin, via Copenhagen, Sept. 7, 1914.

Number 53. September 7. I am requested to forward the following telegram from the Emperor to the President:

"I feel it my duty, Mr. President, to inform you as the most prominent representative of principles of humanity, that after taking the French fortress of Longwy, my troops discovered there thousands of dumdum cartridges made by special government machinery. The same kind of ammunition was found on killed and wounded troops and prisoners also on the British troops. You know what terrible wounds and suffering these bullets inflict and that their use is strictly forbidden by the established rules of international law. I therefore address a solemn protest to you against this kind of warfare which owing to the methods of our adversaries has become one of the most barbarous known in history. Not only have they employed these atrocious weapons but the Belgian Government has openly encouraged and since long carefully prepared the participation of the Belgian civil population in the fighting. The atrocities committed even by women and priests in this guerrilla warfare, also on wounded soldiers medical staff and nurses (doctors killed), hospitals attacked by rifle fire, were such that my generals finally were compelled to take the most drastic measures in order to punish the guilty and to frighten the blood-thirsty population from continuing their work of vile murder and horror. Some villages and even the old town of Loewen [Louvain] excepting the fine hotel De ville had to be destroyed in self defense and for the protection of my troops. My heart bleeds when I see that such measures have become unavoidable and when I think of the numerous innocent people who lose their home and property as a consequence of the barbarous behavior of those criminals. Signed. William, Emperor and King."                    Gerard.

T telegram (SDR, RG 59, 763.72116/27, DNA).

## From William Jennings Bryan, with Enclosure

My Dear Mr President,         [Washington, c. Sept. 9, 1914]

This dispatch from Fuller would indicate that Caranza not only resents our interest [in] Villa but virtually demands the retirement of our soldiers. Shall be pleased to confer with you on the subject at such time as you may designate. With assurances of regard I am my dear Mr President

Very truly yours   W. J. Bryan

ALS (WP, DLC).

## ENCLOSURE

## John Reid Silliman to William Jennings Bryan

Mexico City, September 8, 11 p.m.

Following transmitted for Mr. Fuller: ["]Second interview with Carranza alone. Stated hope that plan by Villa and Obregon would be carried out. Asked him to explain decree of yesterday revoking previous order of Governor of District requiring order of First Chief, Governor or Post Commander and written complaint before arrest. Many arrests made last night and refusal of passports has encreased alarm approaching a panic throughout the city. Carranza explained that earlier degree prescribing safeguards had not been submitted to him who alone had the right to make it and therefore he had revoked it; that existing laws were sufficient for protection and police should have the right to arrest without complaint. Brazilian Minister's[1] intercession for a passport to Iturbide[2] was denied. Carranza stated that he had directed that passport be refused as case must wait the determination to be reached in regard to all political offenders.

He then broached the subject of evacuation of Vera Cruz and said that the continued occupation was entirely unjustifiable and not to be tolerated. Occupation was directed against act of Huerta and moreover present duration was ample reparation; that present Government was organized and in operation and entitled to surrender of the place without delay; that presence of American troops might at any moment lead to friction and conflict; that he [had] no excuse to offer in answer to inquiries as to why the Government permitted foreign troops to remain in possession and expected United States to accede to wishes of Mexican Government. Understood that my mission gave me no power to determine the question but desired me to communicate his wishes to the President. At this point Foreign Secretary Fabela entered and inquired of Carranza whether he had spoken of the subject on which they previously conferred. He then added that editor of the paper EL LIBERAL advised him that he was [in] daily receipt of complaints against the continued occupation and the attitude of the Government in permitting it and that this dissatisfaction would culminate in revolution. As Mr. Silliman lingered a moment to say that after I left he would be alone and hoped for a continuance of the present pleasant personal relations here. Carranza replied that if Silliman thought what he had said to me was not sufficient to bring about the evacuation of Vera Cruz it would be well for Silliman to accompany me; that he expected my mission to have to do with the most important of international questions, namely evacuation of Vera Cruz, and not to be merely a talk about the international questions of Villa and Zapata and domestic pacification with which he was competent to deal.

Have arranged interview with Obregon for tomorrow at ten."

Silliman.

T telegram (WP, DLC).
  [1] José Manuel Cardoso de Oliveira.
  [2] Eduardo Iturbide, former governor of the Federal District of Mexico.


## To Mahlon Pitney

My dear Mahlon:          [The White House] September 10, 1914

Thank you very much for the little book, "The Mystery of Golf."[1] I shall read it with a great deal of interest. The mystery is certainly deep enough and I hope that this book will afford some clue to it. I come away from my game every time I play wondering why Nature made me so stubbornly awkward and so incapable of following perfectly plain rules.

With warmest regard,

Faithfully yours,    Woodrow Wilson

TLS (Letterpress Books, WP, DLC).
  [1] Theodore Arnold Haultain, *The Mystery of Golf*, 2d edn. (New York, 1910). The book is in the Wilson Library, DLC.


## To William Jennings Bryan

[The White House]

My dear Mr. Secretary:          September 10, 1914

I have the important things you sent me yesterday and am giving myself a little time to let them settle in my comprehension before I form a judgment about them.

But there is one about which I am very clear. The Turkish Ambassador has clearly exceeded all bounds. I think it would be well if a report of what he is alleged to have said were laid before him and he were asked to state whether the report was correct or not and, if not correct, courteously to let us know what he did say. After learning from him what it was that he actually said we ought then to consider whether we could longer entertain him as *persona grata*.[1]

Cordially and faithfully yours,   Woodrow Wilson

TLS (Letterpress Books, WP, DLC).
  [1] He left a short time later, unrepentant. About this episode, see Arthur S. Link, *Woodrow Wilson: The Struggle for Neutrality* (Princeton, N. J., 1960), pp. 68-69.

## To Frank Trumbull[1]

Dear Mr. Trumbull:          [The White House] September 10, 1914

Since you read it to me yesterday, I have read again the statement[2] you made me on behalf of the committee of railroad presidents[3] whom I had the pleasure of meeting and conferring with at my office. It is a lucid statement of plain truth.

You ask me to call the attention of the country to the imperative need that railway credits be sustained and the railroads helped in every possible way, whether by private cooperative effort or by the action, wherever feasible, of governmental agencies; and I am glad to do so, because I think the need very real. I cannot say that I entertain any deep anxiety about the matter, except, of course, the general anxiety caused by the unprecedented situation of the money markets of the world; because the interest of the producer, the shipper, the merchant, the investor, the financier, and the whole public in the proper maintenance and complete efficiency of the railways is too manifest. They are indispensable to our whole economic life, and railway securities are at the very heart of most investments, large and small, public and private, by individuals and by institutions. I am confident that there will be active and earnest cooperation in this matter, perhaps the one common interest of our whole industrial life. Undoubtedly, men both in and out of official position will appreciate what is involved and lend their aid very heartily wherever it is possible for them to lend it.

But the emergency is in fact extraordinary, and where there is a manifest common interest we ought all of us to speak out in its behalf and I am glad to join with you in calling attention to it. This is a time for all to stand together in united effort to comprehend every interest and serve and sustain it in every legitimate way. The laws must speak plainly and effectively against whatever is wrong or against the public interest and these laws must be observed; for the rest and within the sphere of legitimate enterprise, we must all stand as one to see justice done and all fair assistance rendered, and rendered ungrudgingly.

Cordially and sincerely yours,    Woodrow Wilson[4]

TLS (Letterpress Books, WP, DLC).
 1 Chairman of the board, Chesapeake & Ohio Railway Co.
 2 "Conference Between the President and Railroad Executives," Sept. 9, 1914, T memorandum (WP, DLC).
 3 Samuel Rea, Daniel Willard, Fairfax Harrison, Edward Payson Ripley, and Hale Holden.
 4 There is a WWsh draft of this letter, with the composition date of Sept. 10, 1914, in WP, DLC.

## To Charles Allen Culberson

My dear Senator:        [The White House] September 10, 1914

May I not have the privilege of expressing my admiration of the way in which you have handled the trust bills? I read your report[1] with genuine admiration and it has been the greatest comfort to me to feel that the whole matter was in such hands from beginning to end.

Cordially and sincerely yours,    Woodrow Wilson

TLS (Letterpress Books, WP, DLC).
 1 The Senate Judiciary Committee's report on the Clayton bill, submitted on July 22. 63d Cong., 2d sess., Senate Report No. 698.

## Walter Hines Page to William Jennings Bryan

London, September 10, 1914.

636 Confidential.

Referring to your telegram of September 8, 4 p.m.[1] I have on my own account had an informal conference with Sir E. Grey about possible mediation. He reminded me that he exhausted every honorable means to keep peace and that every government involved showed a disposition to meet some of his proposals except Germany. She had deliberately planned and prepared for a war. Still he is willing to come to any honorable arrangement for peace now or at any time but everything will depend on the terms. The war has already revealed two great facts, first that all Europe has been living on the brink of a precipice and second that Germany has done a grievous and irreparable wrong to Belgium. No peace can be concluded that will permit the continuance of or the recurrence of an armed brute power in central Europe which violates treaties to make war and in making war assaults the continuity of civilization. Any terms that England will agree to must provide for an end of militarism forever and for reparation to ruined Belgium.[2]

The foregoing was Grey's wholly private talk to me not to be quoted to anybody nor made public. It was personal and must be regarded as inviolably secret.

The following is the practically universal view held here. They regard the German Emperor and the system of government that he stands for as they regarded Napoleon, a world pest and an enemy of civilization, and that there can be no permanent peace till he and his system are utterly overthrown.

All the Allies must agree on peace terms before any one can consent. They would all regard it as a part of the German propaganda if the Emperor should now make an impossible offer so that on its rejection the peace advocates in the United States would say that the Allies are to blame for the continuance of the war. That is precisely what the Emperor is playing for.

I send you this as the opinion universally held here. Such a move has been openly discussed here in the press and is expected. The feeling here is that there can be no peace now on any terms that the Emperor will propose, and that he knows this and if he proposes anything now he will propose it only to affect public opinion in America. If our government try to bring out any premature or inadequate proposal, this action may prejudice us as possibly successful mediators later.

American Ambassador,<br>London.

T telegram (WP, DLC).

[1] WJB to the Ambassadors in Great Britain and France, Sept. 8, 1914, T telegram (SDR, RG 59, 763.72119/20b, DNA), printed in *FR-WWS 1914*, p. 99. This telegram informed Page and Herrick about Straus's conversation with Bernstorff, in which the latter said that he had reason to believe that the Kaiser would accept mediation if the other belligerents were also willing to do so. Bryan added that he had confirmed the accuracy of Bernstorff's statement in a conversation with the Ambassador; and that he had sent a telegram on September 7 at the President's direction to Berlin reporting the conversation, asking for the Emperor's views, and saying that if he responded favorably a similar inquiry would be addressed to the other belligerents. Bryan continued: "We do not know, of course, what reply the German Emperor will make but this war is so horrible from every aspect that no one can afford to take the responsibility for continuing it a single hour. The British and French Ambassadors fear that Germany will not accept any reasonable terms but even a failure to agree will not rob an attempt at mediation of all its advantages because the different nations would be able to explain their attitude, the reasons for continuing the war, the end to be hoped for and the terms upon which peace is possible. This would locate responsibility for the continuation of the war and help to mold public opinion. Will notify you as soon as answer is received from Bernstorff."

[2] Grey's telegram reporting on this conversation was E. Grey to C. A. Spring Rice, Sept. 9, 1914, T telegram (FO 371/2223, No. 48451, pp. 65-67, PRO). There is no significant difference between the two reports.

## To Thomas Riley Marshall

[The White House]

My dear Mr. Vice President:          September 11, 1914

I have refrained from telling you how warmly I appreciated as a generous expression of your confidence in me what you are reported to have said the other day with regard to the choice of a Democratic candidate for the Presidency in 1916[1] only because I hesitated to risk misrepresenting myself by seeming to be thinking of my own political fortunes. But I am not at liberty to belie myself by seeming ungrateful for such confidence as you have expressed merely because of such a delicacy of scruple. I am sure you will believe me when I say that the performance of my duties is not connected in my mind in the least degree with calculations as to my own political future. I am willing to let that take care of itself. I should be especially chagrined if my fellow-countrymen were to think that such personal matters played a part in my thoughts in these critical times when duty should be purged to the utmost of every thought of oneself, of every thought except the country's welfare and advantage. But since you have spoken so generously I cannot be churl enough not to tell you how grateful I am to be so believed in and supported.

With warmest regard,

Cordially and sincerely yours,     Woodrow Wilson[2]

TLS (Letterpress Books, WP, DLC).

[1] Marshall issued the following statement on September 2:

"The Democratic Party will have but one candidate for President in 1916, and his name happens to be Woodrow Wilson. He will have the entire and unqualified and united support of his party. Fair-minded Democrats will recognize that he is entitled to a chance for a second term to prove the utility of his policies.

"Lightning rods already up may as well be taken down and preserved for future use; Democratic lightning will not strike a rod in 1916." *New York Times*, Sept. 3, 1914.

[2] There is a WWsh draft of this letter, with the composition date of Sept. 11, 1914, in WP, DLC.

## From William Jennings Bryan

My dear Mr. President:     Washington September 11, 1914.

I beg to enclose herewith, for your information, a copy of a confidential report just received from the American Consul at Matamoros, Mexico,[1] in which the Consul dwells at some length on the uneasiness exhibited by Mexicans in various parts of the Mexican republic, as a result of the continued presence of American forces at Vera Cruz. Other American Consuls in Mexico have also reported strong feeling against Americans in their districts.

The Vice Consul at Tampico[2] has reported the publication, very recently, of inflammatory articles at Victoria, Tamaulipas, and he ascribes these publications to the fact that the Mexicans resent the presence of our forces at Vera Cruz. The Department has already telegraphed to him to make suitable representations, to the end that the printing of such articles be not permitted in the future.

I am, my dear Mr. President,

Sincerely yours,   W. J. Bryan

TLS (WP, DLC).
  [1] J. H. Johnson to WJB, Sept. 3, 1914, TLS (SDR, RG 59, 812.00/13812, DNA).
  [2] Neill E. Pressley.

# From Thomas Watt Gregory, with Enclosure

Dear Mr. President:        Washington, D. C. September 11, 1914.

As the conference committee on the anti-trust legislation is likely to conclude its labors very shortly, permit me to call your attention to what seems to me to be a very important feature of both the House and Senate Bills, as indicated by enclosed memorandum.

I have taken no steps whatever in the matter except to send you this letter and memorandum.

Faithfully yours,   T. W. Gregory

TLS (WP, DLC).

## ENCLOSURE

### MEMORANDUM

Section 5 of the Senate Bill, page 8 (substantially the same language appearing in Section 7 of the House Bill) is as follows:

That the labor of a human being is not a commodity or article of commerce. Nothing contained in the antitrust laws shall be construed to forbid the existence and *lawful*[1] operation of labor, agricultural, or horticultural organizations, instituted for the purposes of mutual help, and not having capital stock or conducted for profit, or to forbid or restrain individual members of such organizations from lawfully carrying out the legitimate objects thereof; nor shall such organizations, or the members thereof, be held or construed to be *in & of themselves* illegal combinations or conspiracies in restraint of trade, under the antitrust laws.

I am not sure whether or not it is the purpose of the bill to make lawful the doing of acts by labor or agricultural organizations and the members thereof which would be unlawful if done by others. If it is the purpose to bring about this result, the language should be clear and explicit. If this is not the intention of the bill, then the language should be equally explicit.

I consider it peculiarly difficult to construe the above language, but undoubtedly a very strong argument can be made to the effect that these organizations are not only to be construed as legal in and of themselves, but that they and the members thereof are to be absolutely immune from any prosecution under the terms of the Sherman Act.

To illustrate, it seems to me that the section is fairly open to a construction which would permit those engaged in agriculture to form associations for the purpose of limiting production, fixing prices and dividing territory. It could be argued that such associations are instituted for the purpose of mutual help, and that since they have no capital stock and are not conducted for the profit of the associations, they would fall directly within the exemption.

In case the bill goes through in its present shape, this Department will be almost immediately called upon to determine whether or not labor and agricultural organizations and the members thereof can any longer be prosecuted; and it will have to determine the question one way or the other, and, no matter which course it pursues, there will be a perfect storm of protest and denunciation from those who take the other view.

If the purpose of the section is only to prevent such organizations from being dissolved because they or their members had committed unlawful acts, and to recognize the organizations as being in and of themselves lawful, but not to grant them entire immunity from prosecution under the antitrust law then why leave the matter to doubtful construction?

The insertion of five words will probably accomplish what I assume is desired and make it fairly plain. I have inserted in pencil the words suggested and refer this to you for such consideration as you may think it deserves.

The insertion of these words, together with the addition at the end of the following proviso, would place the matter beyond all question:

Provided, however, that nothing in this section contained shall be construed as sanctioning associations or organizations for the purpose of limiting the production or fixing the price of any article of commerce, or of restricting the territory in which the members of such associations or organizations may sell any article of commerce.

T MS (WP, DLC).
   1 The words in italics were penciled in by Gregory.


## From Frank Trumbull

Dear Mr. President:          New York, September 11, 1914.

It is a great privilege to thank you most cordially for the very gracious reception and the considerate hearing which you gave our Committee on Wednesday; also for your letter of the 10th instant. We thank you, not only for what you have done and said, but also for the promptness with which you have done it—for "He who gives quickly gives doubly."

It has fallen to the lot of few men to do in eighteen months so many really constructive things as you have done. I hope that some time when the pressure upon you is somewhat relieved, I may have the opportunity of talking with you about a constructive railroad program for our common country, which I believe would appeal to you. In the meantime, we are deeply grateful to you and I am, with high regard,

Very sincerely and cordially yours,   Frank Trumbull

TLS (WP, DLC).


## Walter Hines Page to William Jennings Bryan

London Sept. 11, 1914.

Six hundred forty-four.

CONFIDENTIAL TO THE PRESIDENT.

Stories of horrors so naturally come with every war that for weeks I discredited the unspeakable tales that were brought from the continent, and many are told which yet seem incredible. But American and other neutral witnesses of German atrocities in France and especially in Belgium now make doubt impossible about some of the most barbarous acts in human annals. Man after man and woman after woman tell of very young girls whom they have seen that were violated by German soldiers. They tell of Belgian boys the tendons in whose arms and legs were cut with swords. I am told by two persons who have seen him, of a physician whose hand was cut off while he was dressing a Belgian soldier's wounds. I am told by a trustworthy woman that there are wounded English soldiers now in an English hospital whose noses were cut off while they lay wounded on the field. Hundreds of such stories are told by apparently credible persons.

The violators of the Belgian treaty, the sowers of mines in the open sea, the droppers of bombs on Antwerp and Paris to kill anybody they may hit, have taken to heart Bernhardi's doctrine of the glorious enjoyment of war.[1] It is impossible longer to doubt the wholly barbarous conduct of the Prussians.

This conviction is helping to increase the number of English volunteers enormously and is producing a silent, grim determination to make an end forever of the military system that has produced such men.       American Ambassador, London.

T telegram (SDR, RG 59, 763.72/838, DNA).
 [1] About Friedrich Adam Julius von Bernhardi and British use of his book, *Deutschland und der nächste Krieg* (Stuttgart and Berlin, 1912), as propaganda, see David Wayne Hirst, "German Propaganda in the United States, 1914-1917" (Ph.D. dissertation, Northwestern University, 1962), pp. 197-205.


## From Florence Stevens Hoyt, with Enclosures

Dear Cousin Woodrow,       Tamworth, N. H. Sept. 12, 1914.

Mary wrote me that you wanted words of Cousin Ellen's. I am sure that she can give you what you want much better than I can, but these few that I am enclosing are words that I should hate to be without. She may not have said just these to Mary. I want you to have them. I wish I could give her exact words more surely. But they need most the look and the personality that you have with you to give them all their dearness.
                         With great love,   Florence.

ALS (WP, DLC).


E N C L O S U R E S

"I wonder how any one who reaches middle age can bear it if she cannot feel on looking back that, whatever mistakes she may have made, she has on the whole lived for others & not for herself. I cannot see how those who believe that life is only for development of the self can look at their past years when they get older & have a more sober point of view."

✧

(After Ed's death[1] when she had seemed not well.)
"I have learned one thing. You try & try with all the strength that is in you to help a person & you can't. Suddenly you find

that you can help in your weakness as you can't in your strength. Woodrow had been so far from well, so discouraged, and despondent. I had tried and tried to give no sign of weakness, to be strong to help him. I seemed to have lost all the power. Then I was all weakness & that helped him as nothing else could have done. He has been wonderful. He has dropped everything & bent every energy to help me. And it has brought him up out of all his own gloom. He seems really to have improved physically."

❖

(At the little house in Princeton when I was convalescing there)

She told me of her religious difficulties. "Carlyle helped me with his doctrine of work. I thought that was the best way, to go on with your work and wait for the solution to come. I think now that it was a poor way. You can let things alone too long. If you have the courage to take the question up you can find the way. I had always supposed I was not intelligent enough to read Kant & Hegel. But they were quite comprehensible." Then she told me a great deal about her reading on that line & of the happiness it had brought to her. We had a great deal of conversation at that time about Hegel, Caird, Campbell's "The Atonement"—all of the books to which she led me.

❖

(After about a year of the Governorship)

She had been telling me how wonderful you had been. I remarked that you were not the only one that seemed to me wonderful. She asked in great surprise what I meant. I spoke of its not being easy for her to give up much of the life that she cared for—to become public, be occupied with functions, & waste no time regretting.

I shall never forget her amazement at my point of view. She fairly burst out, "But when Woodrow is being so wonderful I couldn't be so low as to give a thought to anything but to how I could help him!"

❖

(After the first of Stock's really dreadful times.[2]) She had been telling me the details.

"I used to think that it didn't matter if you gave way if no one knew. Now I know that every time you let yourself go weakens you. I have not dared to give way a minute. Both Stock and Woodrow needed me to be strong all the time. I got so I didn't need the periods of weakness. I am sure that it is the way to grow strong—to act all the time as if you were strong."

✧

(At Prospect)
"I am afraid my besetting sin is my resentful nature. I find it hard to forgive injuries. I have to pray for strength. Oh, I don't mean injuries to myself! I don't know that there have been any— I never notice. I mean to those I love. Some of the unkindnesses to Papa and now to Woodrow."

✧

She had been telling me all about her alley work in Washington.
"The women are so grateful that it is embarassing. How they have worked years & years & could get nothing. I have done so little—only been interested. Do you remember Wordsworth's 'Simon Lee'? I think of that line, 'The gratitude of man hath oftener left me mourning.' "

Hw MSS (WP, DLC).
1 About the tragic death of Edward Axson and all his family, see WW to R. Bridges, April 28, 1905, n. 1, Vol. 16.
2 With depression and other mental troubles.

## To Thomas Watt Gregory

Cornish, N. H.,
My dear Mr. Attorney General: September 14, 1914
I feel as you do the questionable interpretation and the grave importance of the labor sections of the Clayton bill, but they have been gone over so often and worked at so conscientiously that I really feel we must risk them as they are. You may be sure if I get a chance I will speak again about them, however.
Thank you for your thoughtful kindness in sending me the excellent memorandum about them.
Cordially and sincerely yours, [Woodrow Wilson]

CCL (WP, DLC).

## To Walter Hines Page

My dear Page: Cornish, N. H., September 14, 1914
I cannot tell you how chagrined both the Secretary of State and I are that the leaks should have occurred of which your dis-

tressed cable of the other day[1] spoke. We have for some time been trying to trace them, for they have occurred frequently, and we are now all but convinced that our code is in the possession of persons at intermediary points. We are going to take thoroughgoing measures.

My thought and sympathy have gone out to you every day along with my genuine admiration for the admirable way in which you have handled an infinitely difficult set of circumstances. I have read your latest group of letters, August ninth and August twenty-fifth,[2] and have made a number of notes with regard to what I shall try to do to make things go easier for you.

I am writing in haste but with the most genuine concern and appreciation and with gratitude for your letters.

Cordially and faithfully yours,   Woodrow Wilson

TLS (W. H. Page Papers, MH).
[1] WHP to WW, Sept. 11, 1914, T telegram (WP, DLC), complained that his report to Bryan of September 10 had appeared in Washington dispatches to London newspapers and indicated that he would have to tell Grey "the truth— that the State Department leaks."
[2] WHP to WW, Aug. 9, 1914, Vol. 30, and WHP to WW, Aug. 25, 1914, ALS (WP, DLC).

## To Arthur W. Tedcastle

My dear Tedcastle:          Cornish, N. H., September 14, 1914

I received your letter of September eleventh[1] and it made a great impression on me. I have discussed several times with the members of the House and Senate Committees the point you make in the letter, and I left Washington Friday hoping that the Conference Committee would so change the bill as to meet the difficulty.[2]

In haste, with warmest regard from us all,

Faithfully yours,   Woodrow Wilson

TLS (WP, DLC).
[1] A. W. Tedcastle to WW, Sept. 11, 1914, TCL (WP, DLC). Tedcastle was concerned about the tying contract section of the Clayton bill (about which see W. A. Copeland to WW, Aug. 18, 1914, n. 2, Vol. 30), which had recently been restored to the bill at the demand of agrarian radicals in the Senate. Tedcastle warned that many small manufacturers of shoes, as well as distributors like himself, would go out of business if the United Shoe Machinery Co. was prohibited from continuing its present leasing system substantially unchanged.
[2] The conference committee on the Clayton bill did so change the tying contract section by amending it to prohibit such contracts where their effect was "to substantially lessen competition or tend to create a monopoly in any line of commerce." See "Antitrust Legislation: Conference Report on H.R. 15657," 63d Cong., 2d sess., Senate Doc. No. 585, p. 4.

## From John Philip White and Others

Dear Sir:                    Indianapolis, Ind., September 14th, 1914.

With feelings of personal esteem we reply to your favor of September 5th.

We have weighed well and thoughtfully both the sentiments expressed in your personal letter and the proposed tentative basis for the adjustment of the coal mining strike in Colorado, the acceptance of which you urge "with very deep earnestness."

We are profoundly impressed with what you say and fully conscious of the fact that in submitting this basis of settlement you are actuated only by feelings of public concern and inspired by motives both lofty and patriotic.

The organization which we have the honor to represent stands for industrial peace. We favor the establishment of right relations between employers and employees to the end that strikes may be rendered unnecessary. Having proper regard for these aims we sought in the beginning to avoid an industrial conflict in Colorado. We repeatedly asked for a meeting with the mine owners with the object in view of entering into contractual relations with them so that peace might prevail. Had this been done, we are confident that the awful industrial struggle which has been going on in Colorado could have been avoided; instead of bloodshed, bitterness, industrial strife and economic waste, there could have been established throughout the coal fields, peace prosperity and harmonious co-operation. It is our judgment that employers and employees through their chosen representatives ought to meet and settle their differences by mutual agreement. A direct, working agreement entered into in a friendly spirit, makes for abiding permanent industrial peace. This, we believe ought to be done by the miners and operators of Colorado. However, we are mindful of the suffering and waste which this strike has thus far imposed and the additional sacrifice which will be made if it continues.

Feeling keenly therefore our responsibilities, as the representatives of our organization, we accept your proposed basis of settlement of the Colorado strike subject of course to the approval of the miners of Colorado. A Convention of the representatives of the miners of Colorado will be held at Trinidad, Colo. Tuesday September 15th, at which time action will be taken thereon.

We sincerely appreciate the personal concern which you have manifested in the Colorado strike. Speaking as you do in the names of all the people of our great nation we feel it our duty to respond to your earnest wish.

We do so therefore as we trust in the true spirit of American citizenship.

Very sincerely,    John P. White President,
Frank J. Hayes Vice-President,
Wm. Green Secretary-Treasurer.

TLS (WP, DLC).

## From Willard Saulsbury

Dear Mr. President:            [Washington] September 14, 1914.

I thought I would write you regarding the Emergency Revenue Bill.[1]

I believe the feeling is almost universal among those Senators who are willing to express an opinion, that a stamp tax along the lines of the Spanish War Tax Act would be much preferable to the freight tax proposed. The NEW YORK WORLD editorial to-day expresses generally the situation as I view it and find it from talking with Senators. The people are somewhat accustomed to stamp taxes, and a tax on beer, wines and the brandies used for reinforcing wines would probably be much more satisfactory than any other form of taxation I have heard mentioned. My feeling is that if you can confine our new taxes to those the Republicans levied during the Spanish War, we can readily answer any criticisms; otherwise we will have to defend our position by the logic of the situation without an easy answer.

I think your position against an increased income tax at this time has been most popular and right, and that we should adjust ourselves to the present income tax before utilizing the income tax as a means of additional revenue.

I am glad you have taken up the Rustem Bey matter and think wholesome discipline in this case might be a desirable intimation to the local Diplomatic Corps that they should not resort to the newspapers for notoriety.

I trust you had a pleasant trip to N. H.

Yours very truly,    Willard Saulsbury

TLS (WP, DLC).
[1] About the struggle over the provisions of the emergency revenue bill, see Link, *Struggle for Neutrality*, pp. 102-104.

## A Draft of a Reply to William II

[Sept. 15, 1914]

I received Your Imperial Majesty's important communication and I have read it with the gravest interest and concern. I am honored that you should have turned to me for impartial judgment as the representative of a people truly disinterested as respects the present war and truly desirous of knowing and speaking the truth.

3rd paragraph of the reply to the Belgians.[1]

I speak thus frankly because I know that you will expect and wish me to do so, and as one friend should to another, and because I feel sure that such a reservation of judgment until the end of the war, when all its events and circumstances can be seen in their entirety and in their true relations, will commend itself to you as a true expression of a sincere neutral.[2]

Transcript (WC, NjP) of WWsh (WP, DLC).
[1] Remarks to the Belgian commissioners, printed below.
[2] This message was sent on September 16, 1914, and is printed in *FR-WWS 1914*, p. 797.

## To Lindley Miller Garrison

[The White House]
My dear Mr. Secretary:                          September 15, 1914

Following out our conversation of this morning, I write to ask if you will not issue order and make preparation for the immediate withdrawal of the troops from Vera Cruz. In view of the entire removal of the circumstances which were thought to justify the occupation, it seems to me that the presence of the troops there is no longer necessary.

Cordially and sincerely yours,   Woodrow Wilson

TLS (Letterpress Books, WP, DLC).

## Remarks to the Belgian Commissioners[1]

September 16, 1914.

Permit me to say with what sincere pleasure I receive you as representatives of the King of the Belgians, a people for whom the people of the United States feel so strong a friendship and admiration, a King for whom they entertain so sincere a respect; and to express my hope that we may have many opportunities of earning and deserving their regard. You are not mistaken in believing that the people of this country love justice, seek the true paths of progress, and have a passionate regard for the rights of humanity. It is a matter of profound pride to me that I am permitted for a time to represent such a people and to be their spokesman, and I am honored that your King should have turned to me in time of distress[2] as to one who would wish on behalf of the people he represents to consider the claims to the impartial sympathy of mankind of a nation which deems itself wronged.

I thank you for the document you have put in my hands containing the result of an investigation made by a judicial committee appointed by the Belgian Government to look into the matter of which you have come to speak.[3] It shall have my most attentive perusal and my most thoughtful consideration.

You will, I am sure, not expect me to say more. Presently, I pray God very soon, this war will be over. The day of accounting will then come when I take it for granted the nations of Europe will assemble to determine a settlement. Where wrongs have been committed, their consequences and the relative responsibility involved will be assessed. The nations of the world have fortunately by agreement made a plan for such a reckoning and settlement. What such a plan cannot compass the opinion of mankind, the final arbiter in all such matters, will supply. It would be unwise, it would be premature, for a single government, however fortunately separated from the present struggle, it would even be inconsistent with the neutral position of any nation which like this has no part in the contest, to form or express a final judgment.

I need not assure you that this conclusion, in which I instinctively feel that you will yourselves concur, is spoken frankly because in warm friendship and as the best means of perfect understanding between us, an understanding based upon mutual respect, admiration, and cordiality. You are most welcome and we are greatly honored that you should have chosen us as the friends before whom you could lay any matter of vital consequence to yourselves in the confidence that your course would be understood and met in the same spirit in which it was conceived and intended.[4]

CLST MS (SDR, RG 59, 763.72116/44, DNA).

[1] Wilson received the Belgian commissioners in the Blue Room of the White House at 2:15 P.M. on September 16.

[2] The commissioners presented Albert to WW, Aug. 30, 1914, HwLS (WP, DLC), as their letter of introduction.

[3] This document cannot be found in SDR, DNA.

[4] There is a WWsh draft of this statement, with the composition date of Sept. 15, 1914, in WP, DLC.

## To Count Johann Heinrich von Bernstorff[1]

My Dear Mr. Ambassador:    [Washington] September 16, 1914.

Replying to the note of your Government's Charge dated July 25th, 1914,[2] regarding the matter of Customs control in Haiti, I beg to say that the Government of the United States recognizes the large part which German merchants and German bankers have played in the development of the trade and enterprise of

Haiti and wishes to make this correspondence the occasion for expressing the pleasure with which it witnesses the employment of German capital and the activity of German men of affairs in this hemisphere; but represents to the Government of his Imperial Majesty that German interests are not the only interests which have played a conspicuous and highly influential part in the development of the Haitian Republic and that the Government of the United States is well known to have taken for many years and without variation of policy the position that neither foreign mercantile influences and interests, nor any other foreign influence or interest proceeding from outside the American hemisphere, could with the consent of the United States be so broadened or extended as to constitute a control, either wholly or in part, of the government or administration of any independent American state.

The Government of the United States cannot depart from that policy and feels confident that the Government of his Imperial Majesty will not expect it to do so.

Probably a participation of the Government of his Imperial Majesty in any method which might be agreed upon by which the Government of the Republic of Haiti should be assisted in the orderly, efficient, and economical administration of its customs revenues did not present itself to his Imperial Majesty's Government as a departure from the traditional policy of the Government of the United States when its note of July 25th was drafted. But this Government would regard such a participation as a very serious departure from that policy alike in principle and in practice. The Government of the United States regards it as one of the grave possibilities of certain sorts of concessions granted by governments in America to European financiers and contractors and of certain sorts of contracts entered into by those governments with European banking houses and financiers that the legitimate and natural course of enforcing claims might lead to measures which would imperil the political independence or, at least, the complete political autonomy of the American states involved, and might issue in results which the Government of the United States has always regarded it as its duty to guard against as the nearest friend and natural champion of those states whenever they should need a friend or champion.

Whatever the Government of the United States might deem it friendly and wise to agree to with the Government of the Republic of Haiti by way of assisting her to make good her obligations and excape the risks of default or disorder to her finances would be done without intending to serve the interest of any citizen of the

United States or the interest of the Government of the United States in preference to the interest of the citizens or government of any other country. It would be planned for the benefit of all concerned and upon a basis of absolute neutrality. This government does not regard its insistence upon an exclusive privilege in matters of this kind, therefore, as a course dictated by selfishness, but, on the contrary, as a course clearly dictated by a desire for peace and the exclusion of all occasion of unfriendliness with any nation of the other hemisphere. It is willing to give any pledges of disinterest and impartiality that may reasonably suggest themselves, but thinks that its best pledge is the course which it has, in fact, invariably pursued in matters and in circumstances of this kind. Its declared purpose in this case, should the Republic of Haiti desire a convention with regard to the administration of her customs revenues, would, as always, be made frankly and without reservation of any kind, and this it would deem the best evidence of its friendship and respect for the Government of Germany and the rights of German citizens wherever American influence may touch them. This is the way of peace and of mutual accommodation.

Accept, Excellency, the renewed assurances of my highest consideration. W. J. Bryan

CCL (SDR, RG 59, 838.51/354, DNA).
[1] There is a WWsh draft of the following document in WP, DLC, and a CLST draft in the C. L. Swem Coll., NjP.
[2] E. Haniel von Haimhausen to W. Phillips, July 25, 1914, TLS (SDR, RG 59, 838.51/354, DNA), insisting that the German government participate in any arrangement for the control of the customs of Haiti.

## To George McLean Harper

My dear Harper: [The White House] September 16, 1914

Your letter of September sixth[1] brought me the comfort and renewal which always come with the words of a real friend who understands and knows, and you may be sure that it was valued at its full worth. I cannot trust myself to speak of her yet, but some day you and Mrs. Harper and I can have a talk about her that will recall the old days of happiness.

I am very much interested to know that you are going to carry out your plan of spending the next ten months in London. They will be intensely interesting and vital months. You may be sure that we are eagerly watching for any opportunity that may present itself to serve the cause of peace.

With affectionate greetings to you all,

Faithfully yours, Woodrow Wilson

TLS (Letterpress Books, WP, DLC).
¹ G. M. Harper to WW, Sept. 6, 1914, ALS (WP, DLC).

## From William Jennings Bryan

My dear Mr. President:      Washington September 16th, 1914.

I am enclosing despatch just received giving the Chancellor's reply¹ to our telegram of last Sunday week.

You will notice that after laying the blame for the war upon England, France and Russia, the Chancellor says it is up to the United States "to get our enemies to make peace proposals" and then proceeds to propose conditions.

The next sentence would seem to indicate that they did not accept the offer of mediation for they say that to accept it *now* would be interpreted as a sign of weakness.

I do not know what answer you will feel like making to this, shall call you up by telephone between seven and eight o'clock or at such other time as you may like, and go over the matter with you.

With assurances of high esteem I am, my dear Mr. President,
                    Yours very truly,   W. J. Bryan

TLS (WP, DLC).
¹ J. W. Gerard to the Secretary of State, Sept. 14, 1914 (SDR, RG, 59, 711.673/35, DNA), printed in *FR-WWS 1914*, p. 104. Bryan summarizes it below.

## From Frank J. Hayes and Others

Trinidad, Colorado, September 16, 1914.

The Colorado Mine Workers in Convention Assembled have carefully considered your proposal for a settlement of the coal strike and after calm and deliberate thought we have this day decided to accept the proposition you submit. The delegates to this Convention convey to you their abiding faith in your integrity and your earnest and patriotic desire to be helpful in the present strike situation. Upon notice of the acceptance of your proposition by the coal operators we will immediately terminate the strike and return to work.
                    Frank J. Hayes,
                    John R. Lawson,
                    John McLennan,
                    E. L. Doyle,
                         Policy Committee,
                    Representing Colorado Mine Workers.

T telegram (WP, DLC).

## To Robert Lansing, with Enclosure

My dear Mr. Lansing:      The White House September 17, 1914

Will you be kind enough to suggest the sort of reply I should make to President Poincare's telegram to me which I enclose? I should very much like a suggestion from you.

Cordially and sincerely yours,    Woodrow Wilson

TLS (SDR, RG 59, 763.72116/411/2, DNA).


E N C L O S U R E

Bordeaux, September 10, 1914. 7:25 p.m.

Monsieur Le Président je suis informé que le gouvernement allemand a cherché à surprendre la bonne foi de votre excellence en alléguant que des balles dum dum auraient été fabriquées dans un atelier de l'état Français et utilisées par nos soldats    cette calomnie N'est qu'une audacieuse tentative d'interversion des rôles    l'allemagne a depuis le commencement de la guerre employé des balles dum dum et commis de quotidiennes violations du droit des gens    dès le 18 août et à plusieurs reprises depuis lors nous avons eu l'occasion de signaler les attentats à votre excellence et aux puissances signataires de la convention de la haye    l'allemagne qui a connu nos protestations cherche aujourdhui à donner le change et à se ménager des prétextes mensongers pour se livrer à de nouveaux actes de barbarie    au nom du droit méconnu et de la civilisation outragée j'envoie à votre excellence une protestation indignée.

Raymond Poincaré.

T telegram (SDR, RG 59, 763.72116/31, DNA).


T R A N S L A T I O N

Bordeaux, September 10, 1914.

Mr President: I am informed that the German Government has tried to impose on Your Excellency with a claim that dumdum bullets were made in a French Government shop and used by our soldiers. This calumny is but a bold attempt to shift responsibilities. Since the beginning of the war Germany has been using dumdum bullets and committing [daily] breaches of international law. As early as August 18, and repeatedly thereafter, we have had occasion to renounce [report] outrages to Your Excellency and to the powers signatory of The Hague Convention. Germany aware of our protests is now trying to divert attention and to lay up mendacious pretexts for indulging in fresh atrocities. In the name of slighted right and outraged civilization I send to Your Excellency an indignant protest.          Raymond Poincaré

Hw translation (SDR, RG 59, 763.72116/31, DNA).

## To Robert Lansing

My dear Mr. Lansing:       The White House September 17, 1914
I entirely approve of the enclosed suggestions and rules[1] and would be very much obliged indeed if you would send them with my approval and as by my request to the Departments of the Treasury and of Commerce.
          Cordially and sincerely yours,   Woodrow Wilson

TLS (SDR, RG 59, 763.72111/1742, DNA).
[1] Concerning the treatment of armed merchantmen in American ports. The memorandum is printed in FR-WWS 1914, pp. 611-12.

## To John Pierpont Morgan, Jr.

My dear Mr. Morgan:       [The White House] September 17, 1914
Your letter of September fourth, though unanswered, has by no means been overlooked. I have read it with the closest attention.
I am sincerely sorry that you should be so blue about the situation. I believe that being blue is just the wrong thing, if you will permit me to say so. It is a situation which requires nothing more, in my judgment, than courage and the kind of intelligence which our bankers and men of affairs have shown themselves equal of applying to any circumstances that have yet arisen, and my judgment differs radically with yours with regard to the pending legislation. Some features of the bills passed will, I hope, be changed in conference, because they seem to me to involve a risk of injustice as well as of disturbance. But, essentially, they attack nothing but practices which it has been generally agreed should be abandoned in the interest of sound and honest business, and my own judgment (which I pray may be verified by experience) is that the clearing of the air and the removal of the doubt as to what legislation is to be passed will be beneficial, not detrimental.
I may be mistaken in all these things, of course, but I have sought to take as wide a view as possible and to be guided by the net result of my observation and information,—information

drawn from many quarters,—and my own confidence in the result is considerable.

I need not tell you that I value your frank letters, not only for information, but also because I sincerely want to consider the judgment of men in the midst of affairs and whose judgments are based upon actual contact with business.

Cordially and sincerely yours,   Woodrow Wilson

TLS (Letterpress Books, WP, DLC).


## To the Policy Committee of the Colorado Mine Workers

[The White House] September 17, 1914.

Allow me to acknowledge the receipt of your telegram conveying to me the action of the Colorado Mine Workers in convention assembled and to express my deep appreciation. The action does honor to the convention, and the spirit in which the action was taken is a fine prophecy of the conclusion of the trouble.

Cordially and sincerely yours,   Woodrow Wilson.

T telegram (Letterpress Books, WP, DLC).


## To John Philip White and Others

My dear Sirs:          [The White House] September 17, 1914

Allow me to acknowledge with deep appreciation your letter of September fourteenth. Your acceptance, so far as you yourselves are concerned, of the basis for a three year's truce in the mining trouble in Colorado does you honor, the more so because of the spirit in which it is accepted.

Cordially and sincerely yours,   Woodrow Wilson

TLS (Letterpress Books, WP, DLC).


## To John R. Mott, with Enclosure

My dear Doctor Mott:    The White House September 17, 1914

I need not tell you with what pleasure I send you the enclosed letters. I hope sincerely that they will answer the purpose you have in mind.[1] My thoughts and prayers will go with you.

Cordially and sincerely yours,   Woodrow Wilson

TLS (J. R. Mott Coll., CtY-D).

[1] In addition to the enclosure here printed, Wilson provided Mott with letters to the American ambassadors and ministers in Great Britain, France, Germany,

Switzerland, and the Netherlands. Mott conferred with Wilson at the White House from 12 to 12:35 P.M. on September 16 about his forthcoming trip to Europe, the purpose of which was to study ways and means of providing religious and social services to the men in arms and prisoners of war of all countries. Mott's cryptic notes of the interview make it clear that the discussion was wide-ranging. Wilson commented on his interview with the Belgian delegation of the same day and on his exchange of correspondence with William II regarding dumdum bullets. He stressed his "strong desire" to preserve American neutrality so that, at the right time, the United States would be able to mediate. He quoted a remark attributed to Napoleon near the end of his career: "No lasting peace [was] ever secured by force." He also quoted a remark of Bryan to the Japanese Ambassador: "Nothing is final between friends." J. R. Mott, Hw notes of interview, Sept. 16, 1914 (J. R. Mott Coll., CtY-D).

### E N C L O S U R E

The White House
To Whom It May Concern:          September 17, 1914

The bearer of this letter is Dr. John R. Mott. Doctor Mott is a trusted friend of mine. He is traveling upon a mission which concerns nothing except the spiritual interests of Christians throughout the world. He is associated with men active in religious matters throughout the world and is seeking to cooperate with them in matters which concern only religious and personal conduct. He is seeking in this time of general anxiety and disturbance to confer with such men wherever it is possible to do so. I commend him to the courtesy and highest consideration of all with whom he may come in contact and give my personal assurance that his errand is consistent with the most complete and conscientious neutrality.

Sincerely,   Woodrow Wilson

TLS (J. R. Mott Coll., CtY-D).

## From John Charles Floyd[1]

Washington, D. C.
My dear Mr. President:          September 17, 1914.

Having suggested, in our conversation over the telephone, certain amendments to Sections 2 and 4 of the House Bill, I desire to make plain my position in regard to the proposed amendments.

Sections 2 and 4, as originally prepared, were criminal provisions, describing offenses for which a penalty was attached. It was proposed, and tentatively agreed upon in conference, to restore Sections 2 and 4 of the House Bill, omitting the penalties. In order to harmonize these two Sections as restored with Section 8 of the holding companies provision of the Bill, my suggested amendment to Section 2 is to the effect that the words, "with the purpose or intent thereby to injure or wrongfully injure the business of a competitor of either such purchaser or seller," be stricken out, and that the following words be inserted in lieu thereof, "where the effect of such discrimination may be to substantially lessen competition, or to create a monopoly in any line of commerce."

And my suggested amendment to Section 4 is to insert after the word "seller" in the last line, the following words, "where the effect of such condition, agreement or understanding may be to substantially lessen competition, or to create a monopoly in any line of commerce." If these two sections are to be retained in the Bill, I think the language proposed in the amendment to Section 2 preferable to that in the original section, which related to criminal offenses. I also think that the addition of the language proposed as a amendment to Section 4, as reported to the Senate Committee, would be a great improvement upon that section, and would give the Trades Commission a wider discretion in the administration of the same, and would harmonize this Section, and also Section 2, with the principle laid down in Section 8 of the Bill.

In justice to myself, I felt that I ought to explain my position to you, and my object in proposing the amendments. I desire further to state that while it is my personal view that it would be better for Sections 2 and 4 to remain in the Bill in this modified form under all the circumstances, yet, if you deem it best to omit them altogether, and leave the practices involved to the determination of the Trades Commission, I, as one of the House conferees, desire to express a perfect willingness to yield my personal views to your judgment in the premises.[2]

I herewith enclose Senate report, and call your attention to Pages 55 and 56, where my amendments are set out at the proper places.

I desire further to state that I am strongly opposed to Section 25 of the Bill, as reported to the Senate,[3] for the reason that I think it would be unwise to curtail or restrict the powers of the courts in dealing with such important and intricate matters as are involved in the dissolution of trusts and combinations.[4]

Very respectfully,  J. C. Floyd

TLS (WP, DLC).

[1] Democratic congressman from Arkansas.

[2] Sections 2 and 4 (renumbered 3 in the final version) did remain in the Clayton Act with the modifications suggested by Floyd. See the parallel texts of the House bill, the Senate bill, and the final version agreed to by the conference committee, printed in 63d Cong., 2d sess., Senate Doc. No. 584, pp. 4-5.

[3] Section 25 of the Senate version of the Clayton bill provided that, when a

corporation was found to be a monopoly or combination in restraint of trade, the court rendering the judgment was to order its dissolution, appoint receivers, and cause all of its assets to be sold "in such manner and to such persons as will, in the opinion of the court, restore competition as fully and completely as it was before said corporation or combination began to be formed." Moreover, the court was to reserve jurisdiction over the assets sold "for a sufficient time to satisfy the court that full and free competition is restored and assured." *Ibid.*, pp. 26-27.

⁴ The conference committee struck Section 25 from the final version of the bill.

## From Charles Creighton Carlin

Washington, D. C.
My dear Mr. President:            September 17, 1914.

I am writing to advise you that I have seen the amendments proposed to Sections 2 and 4 by Mr. Floyd, and they are perfectly acceptable to me, *provided they meet with your approval.* I have, however, advised my associate conferees of my willingness to omit the Sections from the Bill, believing that the Trades Commission has full power under the law to declare as unfair practices, every evil at which they are aimed.

I am also strongly of the opinion that Section 25 ought not to be retained in the Bill in any form, and am urging that it be stricken out.            Sincerely yours,   C. C. Carlin

TLS (WP, DLC).

## Jesse Floyd Welborn to Joseph Patrick Tumulty

Denver, Colo., Sept. 17, 1914.

Will the President consent to receive on or after next Tuesday a small committee of operators including myself to discuss the Colorado strike situation.            J. F. Welborn.

Yes, on Wed. next, the 23rd.   W.W.

T telegram (WP, DLC).

## To William Jennings Bryan

My dear Mr. Secretary:   The White House September 18, 1914

Thank you sincerely for having let me see the enclosed.[1] All fingers seem to point in the same direction.

Cordially and sincerely yours,   Woodrow Wilson

TLS (SDR, RG 59, 812.00/13812, DNA).
[1] J. H. Johnson to WJB, Sept. 3, 1914, printed as an Enclosure with WJB to WW, Sept. 11, 1914.

## To Jenny Davidson Hibben

My dear Mrs. Hibben,     The White House 18 September, 1914.

Your letter of August fifteenth reached me only yesterday. I sincerely and warmly thank you for it. In these days when the darkness has settled about me thoughts of those old days in Princeton "when we were young and happy" flash in upon me with peculiar brightness, despite the sadness that inevitably follows them. I have memories to live upon such as few men have had to make their hearts rich, and the dear lady who is gone has left nothing but what is bright and pure and beautiful to remember,—it is only that the world is so empty without her!

Thank you again, and please thank your daughter and President Hibben, for your thought of me in my distress. I dare not think much of myself, but I am glad and very grateful that others should think of me and lend me their gracious sympathy.

Sincerely Yours,   Woodrow Wilson

WWTLS (photostat in WC, NjP).

## To Emilie Isabel Wilson Barrington[1]

[The White House]

My dear Mrs. Barrington:                September 18, 1914

I was very much touched by your letter of sympathy of September sixth.[2] In the midst of the great strain and anxiety to which you and your sister must be put in the present circumstances it was peculiarly kind of you to think of me in my deep personal distress and suffering. I am deeply pleased that you should pay me the compliment of regarding me as a personal friend and I hope that some day I may have the great pleasure of meeting both you and Mrs. Bagehot[3] to talk intimately of the man I have so much admired and by whom my own thought has been so deeply affected and so much enriched. May I not express personally and as your friend my deep sympathy for you in the circumstances through which the English Empire is now passing?

With warmest appreciation and regard,

Sincerely yours,   Woodrow Wilson

TLS (Letterpress Books, WP, DLC).

[1] Mrs. Russell Henry Barrington, author and artist, best known as the biographer (1914) and editor of the collected works (1915) of her brother-in-law, Walter Bagehot.

[2] Emilie I. W. Barrington to WW, Sept. 6, 1914, ALS (WP, DLC).

[3] Eliza Wilson (Mrs. Walter) Bagehot, sister of Mrs. Barrington.

## From Edward Mandell House

Dear Governor— New York, Sept. 18, 1914.

Bernstoff came to see me this afternoon. I suggested that he meet Sir Cecil here at dinner. He is willing. I am writing Sir Cecil asking if it would be convenient to come to New York within the next day or two, but making no mention of my conference with Bernstoff. If we can get these two together we can, at least, make a start. For the moment England dominates her allies. Later she may not. She would probably be content now with an agreement for general disarmament and an indemnity for Belgum. Germany, I think, would be glad to get such terms. Shall I go on, or shall I give Sir Cecil some satisfying reason for wanting to see him? Now that I am in touch with Bernstoff I hope to persuade him to close his mouth for awhile. He promises that no human shall know of these negociations. The world expects you to play the big part in this tragedy, and so indeed you will, for God has given you the power to see things as they are. Affectionately yours, E. M. House

ALS (WP, DLC).

## From William Cox Redfield

My dear Mr. President: Washington September 18th, 1914

I beg respectfully to return H.R. 15613, an Act to create a Federal Trade Commission, to define its powers and duties, and for other purposes, and to say that I know of no objection to its approval.

I venture, however, to take this occasion to lay before you certain suggestions which seem of urgent importance at this time.

Section 2 of the so called Clayton Bill, as passed by the Senate, which replaces section 4 of the same bill as passed by the House, is now before the conferees. It relates to the forbidding of exclusive contracts for domestic selling agencies. The Senate confines the prohibition to patented articles; the House makes it wide. Either prohibition, in my judgment, contains the serious error of closing the door to the small manufacturer while leaving it wide open to the wealthy one who by reason of his power needs no exclusive agent but can open his own establishment which the small man cannot do. This I have already dealt with in writing and it is needless to go over it again.[1]

The Federal Trade Commission, however, affords a way out. I earnestly ask, therefore, your consideration of the suggestion that instead of an absolute prohibition in either of the above, this matter be placed within the scope of the Federal Trade Commission, allowing them to decide whether the proposed action is or is not monopolistic in character. If time permitted, I should myself be glad, if you wished it, to state the case to you again or to the conferees. The suggestion I now make has the approval of the Commissioner of Corporations and has the merits of flexibility upon the one hand and of safety and supervision upon the other.[2]

In like manner I earnestly recommend that the Federal Trade Commission be by current legislation empowered to permit and to supervise collective action by American exporters in foreign markets. As matters now are the large American manufacturer is the only one who can individually enter in any efficient way into the foreign field. He alone can afford the means and can take the time requisite to establish and build up a foreign trade, which sometimes requires years. Witness the Standard Oil Company and the United States Steel Corporation. No small manufacturer can do this. Today, to my certain knowledge, many small American manufacturers are anxious to enter the foreign field for which a peculiar opportunity exists but are forbidden to do so because there is no permissible form of cooperation known to the law. This matter has had the thoughtful attention of the Foreign Trade Advisers of the State Department, and on the 15th inst. Mr. Robert F. Rose, Foreign Trade Adviser, submitted to the Secretary of State a recommendation from which I quote:

"Because of conditions resulting from the European war, the subject which the Trade Commission Bill thus left for future legislation has become immediately urgent.

This office, therefore, recommends to you and, through you, to the President of the United States that a bill be immediately introduced, empowering the Federal Trade Commission to permit and to supervise collective action by American exporters in foreign markets in such instances and on such conditions as the Commission upon investigation shall determine.

Such a bill is entirely in line with the provisions of the Trade Commission Bill and with the recommendations of the Committee of the House of Representatives on Merchant Marine and Fisheries in its recent report upon shipping combinations in foreign trade, and with the bill which it recently reported, permitting collective action by shipping lines in foreign trade, subject to the supervision and control of the Interstate Commerce Commission.

This office considers this a matter of such importance and of such urgent necessity that it would be pleased to secure your views and those of the Honorable President of the United States on the subject at as early a date as possible."

I concur in the above. The present condition is one that has seriously restricted many whole industries from obtaining a normal foreign outlet. It is so with lumber, with chemicals, with steel, with many others. The National Foreign Trade Council, on the 16th inst., made the following statement on this subject:

"The security and orderly development of foreign trade, under the encouragement of comprehensive national policies, depends upon the participation of an increasing proportion of small manufacturers. The way should be opened, through some organization, for small manufacturers confidently and successfully to enter the great foreign markets. Cooperative foreign selling organizations appear to offer the only escape from heavy expense beyond the small manufacturer's means. If, as certain legal authorities hold, the Sherman Law applies to foreign trade, this door may be closed to the small manufacturer."

The above, I think, is true. Indeed, I may say from my own experience both in small and in large manufacturing concerns that the present law stands as a block in the way of the small manufacturer and puts a premium in favor of the one with large means. There thus exists in very truth the very kind of discrimination the law professes to prohibit, and a discrimination in favor of the powerful concerns and against the weak in a market of great and increasing importance and of particular urgency at this moment. This, if I may be permitted to say so, is of far greater importance than ships. Without it, there will be far less for ships to do.

I therefore urge your consideration of this matter in the hope that it may be so placed within the scope of the Federal Trade Commission that the recognized danger of utilizing such combinations in the American markets wrongfully may be avoided through their supervision, and that the shackles may be taken off from our manufacturers of small and moderate size who desire to enter the foreign field and are often unable to do so.[3]

Yours very truly,   William C. Redfield

TLS (WP, DLC).
    1 W. C. Redfield to WW, April 15, 1914, Vol. 29.
    2 As has been previously noted, the conference committee amended this section so as to prohibit such contracts only where their effect was substantially to lessen competition or to tend to create a monopoly. See WW to A. W. Tedcastle, Sept. 14, 1914, n. 2.
    3 Such legislation—the Webb Act—was finally enacted in April 1918.

## From Jesse Floyd Welborn, with Enclosure

My dear Mr. President: Denver, Colorado. September 18, 1914.

I beg to thank you for your courtesy in agreeing to receive several of the coal operators of Colorado next Wednesday. I shall come as representing The Colorado Fuel & Iron Company, and in addition there will be one or two others whose names I will forward later.

You will find enclosed, on behalf of our company, a formal report of progress in directions suggested in the plan of truce proposed in your open letter to the operators, dated September 5. I hope you will feel that we are sincerely trying to co-operate in improving conditions, and concerning any point in the case which may or may not be covered in my letter I shall be more than glad to give you all the information we have. The perplexities of the situation are very great, and it will be a real help to us to have the benefit of a personal consultation with you concerning them.

In view of the fact that the responses of the leaders of the men who quit work have been published, and of the popular expectation that we make our position clear to the public, I feel sure you will not regard it as a discourtesy if I give a copy of the enclosed letter to the press after you have had time to receive it.

I am, with great respect,

Faithfully yours,    J F Welborn

TLS (WP, DLC).

E N C L O S U R E

## From Jesse Floyd Welborn

My dear Mr. President:    Denver, Colorado. September 18, 1914.

Permit me to express my sincere appreciation of your letter of September 5 and your evident purpose to lend us the benefit of your good offices in the amelioration of industrial conditions in Colorado. We have ourselves keenly realized the danger to our common welfare involved in a failure to allay distrust and to establish healthy relationships. From the very beginning of the present trouble we have done everything we could in good conscience, first to prevent and then to heal the breach.

When this agitation first started I assured the Governor of Colorado that so confident were we that our men already enjoyed all the so-called conditions of peace, other than recognition of the United Mine Workers of America, that we were willing to accept the decision of the Governor himself as to whether this were not so at our mines. If it were not so, we told him we would make it so. At no time have we desired a triumph merely through superior strength or endurance, and we have been peculiarly sensitive of the popular misunderstanding that we have been unwilling to yield anything or to consider terms of accommodation.

Some of the incidents of this dispute have been most painful to us all, and we have felt a profound responsibility to take steps which would if possible create a condition permanently satisfying to all concerned. It is a pleasure, therefore, for us to accept those portions of the plan you have endorsed which can form a sound basis for permanent progress. We cannot but regret, however, that the plan is, in form and effect, a truce, for that implies a possible renewal of hostilities—an eventuality we are supremely anxious to avoid.

In order that you may understand the situation in which we now find ourselves, we feel impelled to set forth certain controlling factors which distinguish this from the usual industrial dispute:

1. Before this agitation began, our employees had not manifested dissatisfaction with their conditions, and had not asked us to change them.

2. This breach was instigated by an organization financed and controlled outside this State, and of which but few of our employees were members. A careful inquiry at the most critical stage of the agitation a year ago disclosed almost unanimous opposition on the part of our men to the proposed cessation of work.

3. Only a fraction of our men responded to the call to lay down their tools, many of those took them up almost immediately, and today our production of coal is over 70 per cent of the usual output, and fully 90 per cent of the demands of the trade.

These conditions prevail in spite of a most aggressive propaganda of persuasion, incendiary appeal, and intimidation. The effectual collapse of this campaign and the refusal of most of our men to respond to the appeals made to them, is the best testimony we can offer to their very real satisfaction with the way they have been and are being treated.

At the moment, this is the situation: There is no likelihood that the supply of Colorado coal, of which our Company produces but 35 per cent of the total, will be inadequate, or that the price will be unusual. More than 9,500 men—nearly all old employees—are peaceably at work in Colorado coal mines, receiving the highest wages paid to that class of labor anywhere in the United States. In our own mines a larger number of men are at work today than at any time for a year past.

It is unfortunately true that a substantial number of men still decline to work, and it is generally agreed that without an effective restraining influence, some of these men might become a menace to the peace. This danger does not arise from our own employees, who as a class are peaceable, desiring only to be allowed to work unmolested. If the Federal troops should be withdrawn, no one seriously fears that any of our men—none of whom are armed—would create disturbance.

It must be, therefore, that the only necessity for the continued presence of the troops is to prevent violence by that small group of non-workers who have been taught to believe themselves justified in taking forcible means to accomplish their purposes.

Many of those still idle would, we are informed, willingly return to work but for fear or [of] intimidation. It is also a matter of common knowledge that the labor leaders have made their men understand that while Federal troops were in Colorado there must be no disorder. If these same leaders should earnestly co-operate with the agencies of the State as they have done with those of the Nation, the troops might with perfect safety be withdrawn.

A proclamation issued April 22 (a copy of which is enclosed), and signed by leading State officers of the United Mine Workers of America, calling upon the workmen of the State to take up arms and fight, was an overt declaration of rebellion and insurrection. At the convention of the non-workers at Trinidad, Colorado, on the 15th instant, held to consider the proposed plan of truce, one of the leaders is publicly reported to have said in a speech: "God only knows what would happen if the troops were withdrawn." That was in effect an announcement that the rebellious attitude of those men toward the State has not been modified.

We are thus in the unique position of having to consider what measures we may take to induce a small coterie of misguided non-workers to agree to keep the peace!

The problem is complicated by the fact that so large a number of these men are of foreign birth, many of whom do not understand our language, many more of whom do not understand the meaning of a government of laws. It is unfair, therefore, to judge the conduct of such men by the same standards as we apply to the acts of American citizens. This has made us all the more eager to make any reasonable concession which might so enlighten the minds of these men as to our real attitude and purposes, that a healthy condition of peace and security might be realized.

Nevertheless, if men are determined to attain their ends by violence, it is axiomatic that government cannot make concessions of principle merely to induce such men to refrain from riot. The United States government refused to purchase peace with Huerta in Mexico at the expense of sound political morality; for a similar reason no surrender, merely for temporary peace, should be made to those who incited and directed the lawlessness which has taken place in Colorado. To make such surrender would but sow the wind against inevitable whirlwind.

We have given most earnest thought to the specific plan of truce, proposed to you by Messrs. Davies and Fairley. With the following provisions in that plan we are in hearty accord:

"The enforcement of mining and labor laws of the State."

We must challenge, however, the inference in this proposition that we had not already been obeying these laws. For The Colorado Fuel & Iron Company, I can state unequivocally that during the seven and one-half years I have been its president, we have not knowingly violated a single constitutional law of the State. The 1913 coal mining statute of Colorado merely crystallized into law many of the practices to insure health and safety which had been previously adopted by the larger companies. On this point it will be informative to quote from the last biennial report of the State Coal Mine Inspector, James Dalrymple, himself a member of the United Mine Workers of America. Mr. Dalrymple said.

"I believe it is fair to give credit to those operators who have cooperated with this department in making improvements recommended beyond the requirements of the present mining law. In acknowledging the concessions made by them, it must be further added that there is no authority embodied in the law by which these conceded improvements could have been enforced, no matter how essential they were to protect the life and health of the employees. The Colorado Fuel & Iron Company ranks first in making improvements not compulsory or demanded by the law; it complied cheerfully with most of our recommendations."

"Intimidation of union and non-union men strictly prohibited."
The wisdom of this provision is beyond question.

"Current scale of wages, rules and regulations of each mine to be printed and posted."

Upon receipt of your letter we took steps to give effect at our mines to this suggestion.

If we agreed, as is further proposed, to re-employ "all striking miners who have not been found guilty of violation of the law," we should be subject to serious difficulties. We have not now enough work available to provide new places for all the men who left our employ. We are also a large iron and steel manufacturer, and many of our employees alternate between the steel works and the mines. Owing to the depressed state of the steel industry, we feel that we should offer work available at our mines to such of our iron and steel workers as might be thrown out of employment because of reduced production. Indeed we are now faced with the possibility that through having to curtail our steel production, with the consequent effect upon coal and coke operations, work will not be available for all the miners even now employed.

You will understand, too, that a great deal of ill feeling has been engendered between some of the men who quit and those who have remained at or returned to work. We are very sure you would not urge that we re-instate former employees who although not actually found guilty of violating the laws, have to our knowledge given overt indications of hostility toward our men. The inside of a coal mine at best is attended with hazards not common to other operations. It is, therefore, peculiarly a place where we should not assign men peaceably inclined, to work alongside of other men who had been instructed to accomplish their ends, if necessary, by violent means and who were now restrained by nothing more than an agreement by their leaders to suspend hostilities.

We are prepared to re-employ upon work which may be available, any man who so far as we know has not shared in responsibility for acts of violence or overt hostility. In fact, we are daily taking back such men into our service. Our company bears no ill will toward those the limit of whose offending was that they left its employ. Our desire is to make our terms of employment so attractive that we can obtain at all times the very best class of workmen.

But our paramount and immediate responsibility must be to the men still at work, men who for nearly a year have labored under most trying difficulties. For thirty years past this company has assured its every employee that its mines were "open shops," where any good workman might obtain employment irrespective of whether he was a union or non-union man. The very high wages paid and these conditions of freedom are, we believe, the reasons which have attracted to our employ a large percentage of our men. We feel now, as we have always felt, that we must stand by these men in defense of the right we have promised them to defend, of every workman to labor how, where and for whom he pleases.

The particular plan of a grievance commission which Messrs. Davies and Fairley propose, while desirable in purpose, is not, as we see it, applicable in essential details to our conditions. For example, the proposal that mines could not be closed down more than six consecutive days except by permission of the proposed commission would make us dependent upon the views of the commission rather than upon our knowledge of mercantile conditions.

The proposal that the commission assess penalties for violation of any feature of the scheme is not equitable. Penalties might be imposed on operators, but obviously no penalties could be enforced against the miners. They would be free, without practical recourse, to reject any decision of the commission.

The plan that the men should pay half the cost of the commission would commit our employees to an expense to which they have not agreed, and which we do not believe they want. This is precisely the sort of exaction from which the promise of an "open shop" entitled our men to expect exemption.

For many years past our company has made systematic efforts to promote the welfare and happiness of its men. We fully recognize that the interests of stockholders and employees are really the same; neither can prosper permanently unless the just rights of both are conserved. Since this agitation was started, we have sought more than ever to ascertain the nature of whatever grievances the men have had, and to adjust them. We have always been quite prepared to meet committees of our men and discuss with them affairs of our common interest. Our problem is complicated by violent racial jealousies among some of the men, and other difficulties incident to the employment of a large number of foreign-born workmen. Our coal operations are also closely inter-related with iron and steel production, and any plan of dealing between the men and the management, should in fairness apply to all classes of employees alike. A plan to secure harmonious relations in some industries or sections of the country would not necessarily apply to our peculiar conditions. We are now developing an even more comprehensive plan, embodying the results of our practical experience, which will, we feel confident, result in a closer understanding between ourselves and our men. This plan contemplates not only provision for the redress of grievances but for a continuous effort to promote the welfare and the good will of our employees.

We shall be glad at all times to relate to you the outlines of our progress in this direction. In the promotion of our purpose we shall welcome suggestions not only from yourself but from every agency of social welfare. We, therefore, bespeak your confidence and continued co-operation.

With great respect, we are,

Faithfully yours,    J F Welborn[1]

TLS (WP, DLC).

[1] Other letters from coal owners and operators in Colorado to Wilson, not printed, are W. F. Oakes to WW, Sept. 17, 1914, TLS (WP, DLC); G. Fruth to WW, Sept. 19, 1914, TLS (WP, DLC); and J. C. Osgood and forty-seven others to WW, Sept. 23, 1914, TLS (WP, DLC).

## Draft of a Telegram to Raymond Poincaré[1]

[Washington] September 19, 1914.

I received Your Excellency's communication of September tenth in which you protest against the claim ⟨of the German Government⟩ that dum-dum bullets were made in a French Government shop and used by French soldiers, and in which you charge ⟨that German troops have, since the beginning of the war, used bullets of that sort and have committed other breaches of international law.⟩ *on your part, that such bullets have been used and other breaches of international law committed by your adversaries.* I assure your Excellency that I am not unmindful of the honor done to the United States by you in turning to it at this time of crisis as *to* a nation which abhors inhuman practices in the conduct of a war. In this your confidence in the people and government of the United States is not misplaced. The time will come when this great conflict is over and when the truth ⟨will be known and unquestioned⟩ *can be impartially determined.* When that time arrives those responsible for ⟨wanton⟩ violations of the rules of civilized warfare, *if such violations have occurred,* and for false charges against their adversaries, must *of course* bear the burden of the ⟨universal condemnation⟩ *judgment* of the world. ⟨In fixing the guilt of these criminals against humanity and of these traducers of an honorable foe the United States, as a signatory of the Hague Conventions, will perform its duty.⟩                [Woodrow Wilson]

T telegram (SDR, RG 59, 763.72116/31, DNA).

1 Words in angle brackets were in Lansing's draft and were stricken out by Wilson; italicized words were added by Wilson. The telegram was sent as revised by Wilson. It is printed in *FR-WWS 1914*, p. 798.

## To Edward Mandell House

The White House Sep 19th 14

Think there can be no harm in your going on

Woodrow Wilson

T telegram (E. M. House Papers, CtY).

## From Edward Mandell House

Dear Governor:          New York City. September 19th, 1914.

I am returning you Mr. George V. L. Meyer's letter.[1]

I do not think think well of letting him inject himself into the situation. You have ample machinery among your own immediate following to do all that is necessary.

From the beginning I have thought it was a mistake to push this peace movement too strongly at first. The publicity given to the Bernstorff-Straus conversations have not had a good effect.[2] It is an exceedingly delicate undertaking and any misstep may be fatal to your final influence.[3]

What I would advise, is to let me go along with the negociations, about which I wrote you last night, until we find we can go no further in that direction. Then I have something else to suggest to you.

I would discourage all outside efforts by the statement that you were doing all that was possible at this time, but without going into any detail.

I shall be in Washington next week.

Affectionately yours,   E. M. House

TLS (WP, DLC).

[1] This letter has not been found in either WP, DLC, or in SDR. However, it was G. v. L. Meyer to WJB, Sept. 11, 1914, expressing the opinion that, "at the psychological moment," Wilson and Bryan would "play a most important part in the bringing about of peace" and offering his services as an experienced diplomat whenever they might be needed. See Mark Antony DeWolfe Howe, *George von Lengerke Meyer: His Life and Public Services* (New York, 1920), pp. 510-511.

[2] They had been widely publicized in the press. See Link, *Struggle for Neutrality*, pp. 196-200.

[3] House also sent to Wilson about this time WHP to EMH, Sept. 10, 1914, TCL (WP, DLC), saying that the Germans had "roped in Oscar Straus" and were "fooling" Bryan. The Allies, Page went on, were determined to uproot German militarism, and the Germans wanted "to save their mutton." "And if we begin mediation talk now on that basis," he concluded, "we shall not be wanted when a real chance for mediation comes. . . . Put the President on his guard."

## From William Jennings Bryan

My Dear Mr. President:         Asheville, N. C. Sept. 19, 1914.

The European situation distresses me. The slaughter goes on, and each day makes it more apparent that it is to be a prolonged struggle.

All parties to the conflict declare that they did not *want* war, that they are not *responsible* for it and that they desire peace,— and to make their positions more nearly identical, they desire an enduring peace.

I cannot but feel that this nation, being the only great nation on friendly terms with all, should urge mediation, since none of the nations engaged are willing to take the initiative.

The responsibility for *continuing* the war is just as grave as the responsibility for *beginning* it, and this responsibility, if pressed upon the consideration of the belligerent nations, might lead them to consent to mediation,—no nation can afford to refuse. Of course, each one would like to have the war stop at such a time as to give it the prestige of having the advantage, but war necessarily has in it an element of uncertainty; successes may alternate, as for instance, when the Germans almost reached Paris and then were driven back. It is a gamble even when no natural cause intervenes—and natural causes have at times turned the tide of battle, as when the Spanish Armada was scattered and, if you will not consider it irreverent, the Lord never had a better opportunity, or reason than now, to show his power.

The world looks to us to lead the way and I know you deeply desire to render every possible assistance. Both sides seem to entertain the old idea that fear is the only basis upon which peace can rest. This idea was boldly stated by the Turkish Ambassador when opposing the sale of ships to Greece. He said the only way to insure peace in that part of Europe was for Turkey to dominate the situation. And, so, the Kaiser sees peace in a victory which will ensure the supremacy of Germany, while the allies see peace only in a success so signal as to crush the German war machine.

It is not likely that either side will win so complete a victory as to be able to dictate terms and if either side does win such a victory, it will probably mean preparation for another war. It would seem better to look for a more rational basis for peace. Your suggestion, namely, that the manufacture and sale of arms and ammunition shall be a government monopoly, is most excellent.[1]

It has also been suggested that armaments shall be diminished; that all armies shall be reduced in size with a view to reserving them for internal use in preserving order; that nations shall enter into an agreement to respect present boundaries, etc.

I believe that a compulsory investigation of disputes before hostilities begin, such as our treaties provide for, would go far toward preventing war, but the most potent of all influences for the promotion of peace is the substitution of friendship for hatred, and your plan of taking away the pecuniary interest which private corporations now have in war, will make it easier to cultivate friendship.

Mediation would give opportunity for the consideration of all plans and I see no other way in which these plans can be considered or even proposed, for complete success by either side would make that side feel that it is in a position to compel peace by the exercise of superior force.

Would it not be worth while for you to address a note to all the combatants reciting the awful horrors of the conflict and pointing out, First, that all deny responsibility for the war and that all express a desire for peace and, Second, that responsibility for continuance of such a war is as undesirable as responsibility for beginning it and that such responsibility attaches to this nation, as well as to the participants if, by mediation, we can assist in bringing it to a close. Earnestly appeal to them to meet together and exchange views as to the terms upon which permanent peace can be insured. They could be reminded that, while mediation cannot be asked or accepted without conditions, the parties are under no compulsion to accept unsatisfactory terms, also that while an armistice during mediation would, on general principles, be desirable, it might operate unequally upon the combatants and is not therefore, essential to mediation.

From the answers received there is reason to believe that such an offer would not be refused and if it succeeded, you would have the satisfaction of knowing that you had rendered an international service almost, if not quite, without a parallel.

I feel so deeply that this is worth trying that I desire to confer with you about it on my return, but I send this letter in advance that you may have time to consider the reasons herein advanced.

Even if it fails, and that cannot be known until the offer is made, you will have the consciousness of having made the attempt. With assurances of respect, I am, my dear Mr. President,

Very truly yours,   W. J. Bryan

HwLS (WP, DLC).
¹ Wilson must have made this suggestion to Bryan in conversation. He had not yet announced any such policy.

# From Sir Cecil Arthur Spring Rice, with Enclosure

PERSONAL AND CONFIDENTIAL.

Dear Mr. President,            Washington. September 19, 1914.

I venture to enclose for your information the paraphrase of a telegram which I received from Sir Edward Grey in answer to a telegram of mine reporting an accusation circulated in the press to the effect that England was opposed to peace and demanding exorbitant terms.

I enclose this telegram not of course with any idea of influencing your policy but merely as the statement of a point of view which I am sure you will be interested to know.

I have the honour to remain with profound respect, dear Mr President

Your most obedient humble servant    Cecil Spring Rice

TLS (WP, DLC).

## E N C L O S U R E

Paraphrase of a Telegram from Sir E. Grey to Sir C. Spring Rice.

I have received your telegram of yesterday reporting the German Ambassador's statement as circulated in the press that Germany was ready to make peace on moderate terms but that England was opposed to peace.

My view is as follows.

Germany planned this war, and chose her own time for forcing it on Europe. No one was in the same state of military preparation as Germany was when war began.

What we require for our future security is that we may be able to live free from a menace of this kind.

A series of able writers, instructors of Germany, from Treitschke downwards, have openly taught under the sanction of the Government that the main object of German policy must be to crush Great Britain and to destroy the British Empire. We want to be sure that this idea no longer inspires German policy.

A cruel wrong has been done to Belgium, wanton destruction has been inflicted on her and her resistance has been punished by wholesale acts of cruelty and vandalism. Is Germany prepared to make reparation for these acts?

If Germany really desires the mediation of the United States these facts must be considered in drawing up the conditions of peace. But we have no indication that Germany is prepared to consider them, and up to the present moment we have neither stated nor heard any conditions of peace. There is no evidence whatever that the suggestions which appear to emanate from the German Ambassador are authorised by his Government, or really meant.[1]

T MS (WP, DLC).
[1] This telegram was sent as E. Grey to C. A. Spring Rice, Sept. 18, 1914, T telegram (FO 371/2223, No. 50578, p. 73A, PRO).

## To Mary Allen Hulbert

Dearest friend,          The White House 20 September, 1914.

My little household is looking up a bit. Cousin Mary Smith, who was in the hospital here for seven weeks after an operation for appendicitis which proved very serious indeed, was well enough last week to travel and I took her up to Cornish, whither, two weeks eariler, I had taken my sister and her little family. I went with her so that we could have a special car and she be saved any change on the way. I stayed there from Saturday to Monday only. Now only Helen Bones is here (though Dr. Grayson is really of the household and my dear baby, Nellie, is in and out all the time, taking many of her meals here.) Helen, too, you know, has been seriously ill, her illness culminating about the time my darling left us desolate, and her recovery has been slow. She did not want to go to Cornish, and could be best taken care of here, where she seems happier than anywhere else; and she and I are for the time the whole family. It is very strange: I feel almost as if I had lost my sense of identity and were living in some new, unfamiliar world! But there are big, imperative things that have not changed: my duty and the big tasks that press, press, press the days through and forbid, prevent, my thinking of myself, thank God. I am trying not to dwell even for a moment at a time on what is going to happen to me personally: and I am happy to say that most of the time I succeed. You have noticed, I dare say, that the papers and the politicians have been talking lately about a second term for me in the presidency; but you will know that that has not been in *my* thoughts. For the moment I am approved of and trusted by the party and the country and am popular. But I am not deceived. I know by what tenure a man holds popularity. It is only a tenancy at will, and may be terminated without notice. Any day I may find it my duty to do something that will make me intensely unpopular, it may be, the object of fierce and passionate criticism. The place has brought me no personal blessing, but only irreparable loss and desperate suffering. I am not complaining; I am only stating the facts, and letting you see the very inside of my mind. I want you to know how I am faring, what I am thinking, and what I am not thinking. For I want you to know that I manage to live and to be stimulated by work and to love a task that makes me useful. My loss has made me humble. I know that there is nothing *for me* in what I am doing. And I hope that that will make me more serviceable. I have succeeded so far, I believe, only because I have not sought my own pleasure in the work or in the office, and have, more than my predecessors, devoted my entire time and energy, alike of body and of mind, to the work of administration and of leadership to be done from day to day. And now self is killed more pitilessly than ever,—there is *nothing but the work* for me. It is very sweet to me that the loving thoughts of dear friends follow me from day to day, and I think the country as a whole thinks of me more tenderly and more indulgently since the blow fell upon me; and I derive a great deal of comfort and deep pleasure in thinking of the friends who are dearest to me,—of their interests and fortunes rather than of my own. It pays to be wiped out on[e]self if only to be forced into another world of sympathy, where oneself is *not* the centre,—a bigger world in which there is little to fear and great gain of affection to be won and enjoyed. Please think of me as perfectly well, physically, perfectly calm most of time, and speaking of myself only when I think a friend will wish to know.

Please write me that you are well, that the long interval since you wrote is not due to anything untoward that has touched either you or any you love, and that you often think of

Your devoted friend,   Woodrow Wilson

WWTLS (WP, DLC).

## From Edward Mandell House

Dear Governor:        New York City. September 20th, 1914.

Spring-Rice took both breakfast and luncheon with me and has just left for Washington.

We had a thoroughly satisfactory talk and he has sent a cablegram to Sir Edward Grey, a copy of which I will bring with me to Washington.

After a perfectly frank discussion, we concluded that it was best not to have a conference with Bernstorff at present. I shall tell you why when I see you.

The surmise that all England wants is a permanent guaranty

of peace, by disarmament and other effective measures, and a proper indemnity for Belgium, is quite right.

Sir Cecil in his cablegram has suggested that Sir Edward obtain from Russia and France the conditions upon which they would be willing to consider peace proposals so that he might submit them to you.

He thought it important that you make no suggestions as to the character of such proposals, but continue to exercise the impartial position of being the medium of communication between the warring nations.

Sir Cecil expressed his indignation at the action of Sir Lionel Carden[1] and said he would cable his Government suggesting that he should not be sent to Brazil, or to any other place on the Western Hemisphere. He wanted me to write Tyrrell that it was my judgment this should be done. However, I do not think it wise for me to do this for it can be reached in other ways.

I explained to him the ship purchasing bill, and that it was the intention to make the purchase with Panama bonds instead of cash. He thought that this changed the entire aspect of that situation, and he expressed himself cordially in favor of it. He thought his Government would much prefer the United States to have the German ships than to have them as they are, provided the Germans got no cash or cash credit for them.

He has entirely overcome his prejudice against Villa, and thinks now he is perhaps the most satisfactory man in Mexico. He has sent word to Villa that if he continues to merit the good opinion of everyone as he has in the recent past, his Government will forget some things that have happened.

Your faithful and affectionate,   E. M. House

TLS (WP, DLC).

[1] Carden was interviewed by newspaper reporters on board ship in New York harbor just before sailing for England on September 16. He was alleged to have remarked that Mexico City had been in a state of anarchy when he departed thence three weeks before; and that it was "a desperate shame" for American troops to be withdrawn from Mexico, leaving "hundreds of Americans stranded and helpless in a lawless country." *New York Times*, Sept. 17, 1914. Spring Rice on his own initiative declared to Bryan in a telephone conversation that same evening that the interview was "unauthoritative," and he expressed regret for the incident to Lansing on the following day. *Ibid.*, Sept. 18, 1914. On September 18, the State Department sent a note to the British Foreign Office inquiring if the interview was authentic. Following his arrival in England, Carden admitted that he had given an interview, but denied criticizing the Wilson administration's Mexican policy. *Ibid.*, Sept. 19 and Oct. 16, 1914.

## Sir Cecil Arthur Spring Rice to Sir Edward Grey

Private.                                  Washington Sept: 20 [1914]

Following is message to you from a friend of President widely known who asked me to see him in New York to discuss situation.

"On my suggestion German Ambassador was willing to enter into communication with Sir C. Spring-Rice direct. The latter however answered that as the three Powers were bound to make peace simultaneously he could not receive a separate communication.

"I think that German Ambassador is not acting without instructions.

"Conversations here on the subject of eventual mediation would be attended with considerable difficulties. But the following considerations seemed to force themselves on attention. If the war continues either Germany or Russia becomes supreme in Europe. Both alternatives are fatal to balance of power. It would be better to begin negotiations before the balance is upset.

"From this point of view President may be anxious to facilitate negotiations now. The bases for these may be your two principles: 1. A final end to militarism and a durable peace. 2. Compensation to Belgium. If other Powers are willing to make suggestions in order to effect an agreement on basis of these two principles (which principles would at once command unanimous sympathy of the world) conversations could begin at once whether the war continues or not. If the Powers have other proposals to make it would be as well to make them known as soon as possible before Germany or Russia have obtained complete mastery. President would probably be willing to facilitate exchange of ideas as friendly intermediary and without expression of opinion.

"Germany is doing her best to put England in the wrong by creating the impression that England is rejecting Germany's friendly offer. England incurs the danger of losing sympathy here if she were to persist in a 'non possumus' attitude and although it is fully understood that she cannot enter into any negotiations without the knowledge and consent of her allies it would be to advantage of the latter if Germany were forced to show her hand."

Hw telegram (E. Grey Papers, FO 800 84/2, PRO).

Remarks at a Press Conference

September 21, 1914

I have read only one paper this morning, gentlemen, but that says that it is understood that the President intends to call a world congress and do a lot of very foolish things.[1] I want to know, who understood that, and from whom? I am not as big a fool as I look, and if you will just go on the assumption that I am not a fool, it would correct a good many news items.

I think, Mr. President, you can act on the assumption that we are wholly acting on that assumption.

But regarding items like that, elaborately set forth, a column long of it, "it is understood to be the purposes of the administration," coming from Washington, make an impression and will probably be transmitted to the other side, and other things that I am earnestly, let me say prayerfully, trying to do for the peace of the world may be blocked by all this talk of things that are impossible and unwise, and in themselves unworkable. That is what disturbs, gentlemen, but here we are, in the presence of a world crisis. This is no child's play. We may make it impossible for the United States to do the right thing by constantly saying that she thinks of silly things to do.

Let us at least propose things that grown up people would think of. I think that it is very important that we should be of age in our plans. Please, do your best not to let that happen again. I am not accusing or suspecting even anybody, but I know that by cooperation you can prevent that kind of thing happening. I saw it in a form that didn't look like special correspondence, and therefore I am afraid it has appeared in a number of papers.

Mr. President, the attitude of the press generally has been satisfactory, hasn't it?

Admirable. I haven't anything to complain of. And the attitude of the article is all right. I don't think the person who wrote it intended to do any mischief. But I just wanted, if I might, to point out to you how mischief may be done without intending it.

What paper was it in, Mr. President, do you recall?

Well, it may have appeared only in that paper. I don't want to pick out a particular paper. . . .

Mr. President, Mr. Fuller is back in this country. Do you expect to see him?

I expect to see him on Wednesday.

Mr. President, have you any new information you can give us about conditions in Mexico?

> No. There's a great deal of new information from El Paso, but none of any importance.

Is there any date set for removal of the troops, Mr. President?

> I am going to see the Secretary of War today. My instructions were simply to effect it as soon as it could be effected, taking care of everything that has to be taken care of in the process.

JRT transcript (WC, NjP) of CLSsh (C. L. Swem Coll., NjP).
1 The editors have been unable to find this news report.

## To Sir Cecil Arthur Spring Rice

[The White House]
My dear Mr. Ambassador:                    September 21, 1914

I thank you sincerely for your note of September nineteenth with its paraphrase of a dispatch from Sir Edward Grey. I want you to know how highly I value such frank confidence and how useful such information is to me.

Cordially and sincerely yours,    Woodrow Wilson

TLS (Letterpress Books, WP, DLC).

## To William Joel Stone

My dear Senator:            The White House September 21, 1914

It seems to me of such peculiar importance just at this moment that the treaties with England, France, and Japan should be ratified that I venture to write this note to ask if you will not make unusual efforts to have a quorum of the committee present on Wednesday next when Mr. Bryan is to present the treaties to them.[1]

It would dampen the whole feeling of the country, I think, at this particular time if these treaties were not acted upon promptly and with cordiality.

I know that you will appreciate the spirit in which I write and I am happy that we are such friends that I can write as I please.            Faithfully yours,    Woodrow Wilson

TLS (RG 46, Records of the U. S. Senate, Senate 63A-F9, DNA).
1 The Senate consented to the ratification of "cooling off" treaties with Great Britain, France, and Spain on September 25. No treaty had been negotiated with Japan. Wilson must have had in mind the treaty with China, which had been favorably reported by the Foreign Relations Committee but had not yet been approved by the Senate. *New York Times*, Sept. 26, 1914.

## To Henry Watterson

The White House

My dear Colonel Watterson:          September 21, 1914

I was very much touched by your beautiful editorial on the death of the dear lady who is gone away[1] and I cannot deny myself the privilege of thanking you for it most sincerely. It showed a knowledge of her quality and an appreciation of her wonderful gifts which make it different from most of the tributes which have so generously been paid her memory, and I shall keep it very carefully among the things I value.

Sincerely yours,   Woodrow Wilson

TLS (H. Watterson Papers, DLC).
  [1] Untitled editorial in the Louisville *Courier-Journal*, Aug. 7, 1914.

## From Paul Fuller, with Enclosures

My dear Mr President:          N. Y. 21 September 1914

I returned from your mission Saturday Evening & had expected to leave for Washington to-day but am advised that your appointment for me has been postponed until Wednesday at noon.

As the Vera Cruz incident is ripening rapidly I take the liberty of enclosing the draft of my report, (which there has not been time to copy) & hope you may be able to read it before I have the pleasure of making an oral report

I am Mr President with great regard

Very truly Yours   Paul Fuller

PS I also enclose Mr Carranza's letter & translation   P.F.

ALS (WP, DLC).

### E N C L O S U R E   I

*Memorandum for the President*

On board S.S. Mexico, 18 Sept 1914.

In compliance with the Presidents instructions I left Washington for Mexico City on the 26th of August and by devious ways, intended to be direct, reached Vera Cruz on the 3rd of September. I was met there by Mr John R. Silliman, who remained with me until I left Mexico City on the 11th of September affording me every assistance. His familiarity with the situation in Mexico and his acquaintance with Mr Carranza and his entourage did much to accelerate what might otherwise have been a tedious and dilatory task.

We started for Mexico City by the first available train, which left on Friday morning at 6 a m reaching Vera Cruz at about 1 a m on Saturday. Mr Fabela, Secretary for Foreign Affairs was on the train & Mr Silliman made an appointment with him which enabled me without delay to open up the object of my visit to Mexico and ascertain the point of view of the man who holds the leading post of international relations in Mr Carranza's counsels, as well as to arrange an interview with Mr Carranza on the very day of my arrival at Mexico City. I have thought best to make a chronological record of the conversations, with a brief resumé of the judgments formed, so that the President may, if he choose, save time by consulting the judgments, and later verifying their soundness by reference to the record on which they are based.

I will merely preface this record with the remark that among the Constitutionalists in Mexico City, I met some men of merit and yet of conservative & moderating tendencies, laboring to temper the virulence of those who now seem to be in favor. Robles Dominguez, Luis Cabrera and Diaz Lombardo are among these & I think I should add General Obregon. Genl Cabral until recently Post Commander I did not meet, but his general repute puts him in this class. Fabela I consider a retrograde influence. Carranza impressed me as a man of good intentions but without any sufficient force to dominate his petty surroundings, and greatly hampered by the fear of lowering his prestige which hinders him from adopting conciliating measures or correcting mistakes, and makes him adhere to mistaken courses, adopted under pressure.

With this preface I begin the relation of the interviews, the substance of some of which have already been communicated by cable.

*Friday 4 Sept 1914.* Introduced to Mr Fabela, Secretary for Foreign Affairs, by Mr Silliman, on train from Vera Cruz to Mexico City. Conversed abt the object of my visit, discussed the duration of the interim Revolutionary Gov't & the need for early elections & the carrying out of the object of the Revolution: the observance of constitutional restrictions. Fabela urged the need of the Revolutionary Gov't until other reforms within the Revolutionary programme were inaugurated & established, such as the agrarian reforms, changes in taxation &c. I answered that those were questions of far-reaching policies which should be disposed of by representatives of the people duly elected & not by a Revolutionary interim Government whose function should be confined to preserving the peace & to such measures as were indispensable to the orderly processes of government, while the representative Government contemplated in the Constitution was being reconstructed. His reply was that elections would take time, & that the Congress when elected would take perhaps years in idle discussion on the reforms while immediate action was needed, & might in fact defeat them; that either of these results, delay or defeat, would surely bring the people to renewed rebellion & plunge the country into anarchy. . . . He then urged the recognition of the Provisional Gov't as the measure best calculated to enhance its prestige and aid it in consummating its work. I told him he could scarcely expect the resumption of international relations with a military uprising which although it had expelled the previously existing government had not yet installed any Constitutional successor. On the subject of recognition, he added that he was expressing his personal views as to its opportuneness or utility; that I would find the First Chief not at all solicitous on the question & quite willing to abide by whatever occurred.

Fabela took up the subject of Vera Cruz & its continued occupation; enlarged upon its bad effect upon the public mind & stated that in the City the inhabitants were already manifesting irritation towards the soldiers; that the continued occupation was illogical and was unexpected; that Pres. Wilson had expressly stated that the action taken was against Huerta & not against the Mexican people & that the continued military occupation of territory of the Mexican people after Huerta had been overthrown & sent into exile was convincing the Mexican people that the actions were not against Huerta but against them. To all of this I made no answer. . . .

Saturday, 5 Sept, 1914   Called on Carranza at the Palace at about 12:30 by appt made through Fabela; conducted there by Col Bermudez Castro the formal introducer of foreigners. I presented President Wilson's letter of introduction & at the request of Mr Carranza translated it to him, he expressed his gratification & I then said to him that I wished to emphasize Mr Wilson's earnest desire to see a perfect union of all the elements of the Constitutionalist Party and the earliest possible realization of their declared purpose,—the installation of a permanent Constitutionalist government; that with such a purpose the people and the President of the U. S. were in hearty sympathy and would gladly see it effectively and promptly carried out. To this I added that I was gratified to see by the morning papers that the First Chief had issued a call for a convention of the Generals of the army and the Governors of the States to be held on the 1st of October, in accordance with the Plan of Guadalupe and the addendum of Torreon. Mr Carranza replied that it was his earnest desire to have a permanent government installed, that he realized the limitations of the Revolutionary interim which could not meet the many problems which a Government would have to solve, among them the financial problem. That nothing was farther from his intention than to prolong the interim or make it the occasion of dictatorial power; that his call had been issued at the earliest available moment for many things of immediate necessity had required attention. "I have been spoken of as arbitrary—but military government is necessarily arbitrary—& I am anxious to have Constitutional government reestablished. I want every element of the party to be convened & consulted so that none can complain & all will submit to the common will & none may be able to say that I exercised undue influence towards the result. In that way there will [be] a union & the expression of the will of the majority in the formative process towards the reestablishment of the government"

In the course of further conversation, I said to him and to Mr Fabela, his Secretary of Foreign Relations, who assisted at the conference throughout, that the call for the convention of leaders was the first ray of sunlight shed on the problem of the early formation of a Constitutional Government and that we trusted to see all doubts on that subject promptly dissipated. After a time as the conversation proceeded Mr Carranza said "I have been misrepresented in the United States and held up as opposed or inimical to the U. S. & to Mr Wilson. I have not seen fit to defend myself against these charges, but I welcome the opportunity which your friendly frankness offers me of speaking to you with equal frankness. These statements are absolutely without foundation. I have the friendliest feelings for your people & for your President & any contrary reports have been circulated with malicious intent." On the subject of Zapata, Mr Carranza said that so far he had proved intractable, had refused to facilitate in any way a conference between them & that if he persisted in his revolt against the Constitutionalists he would have to be subdued by arms. He then added "Your visit furnishes me the opportunity of saying what I have hesitated to say heretofore: that Zapata has been encouraged in his hostile attitude by Americans who have made him believe that he is sustained in it by the U. S. Government. Mr Jenkinson who visited Zapata under the cover of the Red Cross has had this pernicious influence on him & the Red Cross has been made the vehicle of political manoevers to such an extent that I shall have to exclude it. A like influence from American sources has been exercised on Villa" To this I answered that I was aware of his pride of nationality & did not wish to suggest that he needed outside aid, but as he had imputed Zapata's attitude to American influence, I would with his consent ask the President to notify Zapata that his uncompromising attitude and his unwillingness to confer with the First Chief at some appropriate place could have no support from the United States, which expected from him a patriotic effort at union. Mr Carranza hesitated, & said that he could not ask alien aid to restore internal order which it was his duty to bring about & I replied that I did not expect any request from him, but would make the appeal unless he objected & advised him of it so that at no time could he complain that it was an undue interference with his internal affairs. As he still hesitated Fabela said, "Do it" and I accordingly sent you the cable to that effect. As we parted, I told him I should remain two or three days in the Capital during which time I should hold myself at his disposition while I awaited the letter to the President which he had promised me. After some polite offers to visit Chapultepec &c., he said that in any event he would see me again before I left

Monday 7 Sept. 1914. I was called on by Angel Caso, a representative of Villa & he showed me the program agreed upon & signed by Obregon & Villa, the Commanders of the North East & Northern Divisions, & brought in last night by Genl Obregon[,] Diaz-Lombardo, and Dr Silva, the Commission charged with the arrangement of the matters in issue between the Division of the North & Gen'l Carranza. This programme is in substantial accord with that laid down by Genl Villa in Chihuahua on the 18 of August & which I delivered to Presdt Wilson on my return from the mission to Villa. . . .

At the suggestion of Dr Silva and Mr Diaz Lombardo, I had a brief interview with Genl Obregon on the following day—8th of September to guage how far his support of the programme would be carried. Obregon is a stern, soldierly man, who seems to enjoy the general esteem as a man of good purposes and resolute character. I told him I had been gratified at the programme agreed upon between himself & Gen Villa & hoped it would be carried out. He said he hoped it would, but was reticent as [to] any assured expectation of its acceptance saying that it had been laid before the First Chief & would be discussed with him very soon. There was nothing strained or unnatural about his reticence, which seemed to be quite justified by the soldierly discipline of a subordinate unwilling to intimate to a stranger that his Chief might be made to yield to pressure. Obregon has resumed the Military Command of the Federal District. He spoke of his mission to Sonora in company with Gen Villa & confirmed the report that Gen Villa had ordered one of the regiments to remove the hat-bands they wore with the inscription: "*Viva Villa*" He was earnest in support of the suggested provision that no military in active service should be a candidate for an elective office, not only because of the danger of dictatorial tendencies of such an incumbent but because one military candidacy would unquestionably bring forth others, each supported by a group of armed followers with the opportunity and the disposition to influence the election, imperilling its peacefulness and its freedom, with the further danger that the same elements would express their repudiation of the result in violence rendered easy by the ready resort to their armed following.

On the subject of Zapata, Obregon expressed the opinion that there would be no intrinsic difficulty with him, as soon as he was freed from the influence of some bad advisers (Palafox & Serratos) & he felt confident that this would be done

8th Sept 1914. . . . An appointment had been made for a farewell call upon the First Chief, at which it was my intention to report the Presidents telegram in reference to Zapata[1] & to commend the new Villa-Obregon programme for the immediate installation of a Provisional Civil Government, and the early organization of a permanent Government by elections upon a Constitutional basis. The conference was delayed awaiting the arrival of the Secretary Fabela & finally as he did not appear I was ushered in to the First Chief. I told him I was glad that we were alone for I felt more free to speak to him as friend to friend, without the danger of diplomatic offense which might result from the presence of a Secretary of Foreign Relations. I then told him of the restlessness produced by the many arrests and seizures of property, alarmingly increased by his revocation of the decree which had seemed to discountenance them & to offer some degree of security against irresponsible assaults upon person & property, and asked if he could give me some explanation of his revocation. To this he replied that the decree of Sept

---

[1] WJB to the Brazilian Minister, Mexico, Sept. 7, 1914, T telegram (SDR, RG 59, 812.00/13116, DNA). The message was for John R. Silliman: "Please say to Zapata that this government earnestly desires that he shall confer with the Constitutionalists and cooperate with them in securing the needed reforms. It is advisable that he should call on Carranza personally in the City of Mexico. A frank and friendly exchange of views would be helpful to both. Say to him that the President feels that a peaceful adjustment is both desirable and possible. You should take assurances of Carranza as to Zapata's safe conduct. If Zapata refuses to go to the City of Mexico, some intermediate place might be agreed upon."

1st by the Post Commander and the Governor of the District had been issued without being submitted to him and without his approval; that he alone had the right to issue such a decree and that he could not tolerate such action on the part of subordinates and for that reason he had revoked it; that moreover the existing laws provided sufficient safeguards, and that the police in every country had the right to make arrests without previous complaints and that the authorities should not be dependent upon the individual action of citizens in making complaints as a condition precedent to making arrests but should be able to initiate proceedings of their own motion. As there are at present no courts or judges to whom appeal for redress can be made I deemed it useless to pursue the subject and passed on to the Zapata incident informing him of the President's telegram advising Zapata to conciliation and recognition of the First Chief.

I then took up the plan of immediate government organization agreed upon by Villa and Obregon, communicated to me by Dr Silva & Diaz-Lombardo, they being aware of my visit to Gen Villa for the purpose of urging the necessity of united action to that end. I told him that the plan so agreed upon was in consonance with the views of the President and that its early realization would enlist the sympathy and approval of our people. . . .

The Chief then took up the question of Vera Cruz; he said he had hoped I would take up the question with him as it was a matter of international import; that the continued occupation was without any justification and intolerable. The occupation had been directed against the action of Huerta specifically, and Huerta was now expelled and no longer had any semblance of even usurped authority; that under these circumstances the continued occupation could only be construed as hostile to the Mexican People, and that moreover the occupation of the Port since last April was in itself a sufficient reparation for the grievance which occasioned it. That the presence of American troops in such close proximity to the Mexican soldiers, might at any moment, produce friction and lead to conflict beyond his control. That he had no answer to make to the inquiries as to the reason for the continued occupation & he hoped that the U. S. would accede to the wishes of the Mexican Government for the evacuation. I inquired to what organized Government we could make any transfer of so important a port, as there was not even a Provisional Government in existence, but only a Revolutionary body in military occupation of the capital and other sections of the country; that it seemed to me there should be at least some central and recognized governmental authority duly organized and competent to deal with & settle the questions connected with the occupation—competent in other words for the discussion and adjustment of international differences involved in the surrender. He answered that the present government was fully organized and in operation; it had the equivalent of all the officials usually representing organized government, although under other names and temporary in character. To this I replied that he was aware that my mission was circumscribed and limited to friendly counsel & admonition as to the necessity for complete union among the Constitutionalists and the earliest possible organization of Constitutional Government capable of furnishing the guarantees to person & property which such a Government imparts and restoring the international status without which the peace and prosperity of the country could not be assured, & that consequently I had no power to reach any solution on the subject of Vera Cruz. The Chief said he understood that my mission gave me no power to determine the question, but that I could communicate his wishes on the subject to the President which I promised to do at once upon reaching Washington. At this point Secretary Fabela joined us & inquired of the First Chief whether he had presented the subject upon which they had previously conferred. We both replied that the matter had been discussed and Fabela then stated that he had been advised by the editor of the paper "El Liberal" that he was in daily receipt of complaints against the inaction of the Government with reference to the continued occupation of Vera Cruz, disclosing a degree of exasperation which must culminate in revolt. Upon this I left, advising the First Chief that I would return to the U. S. as soon as he sent me my passports and his promised letter for the President. . . .

Wednesday 9th Sept. . . . In the evening of Wednesday 9 Sept. Mr Fabela called on me at the Hotel to bring me the First Chiefs letter to the President. He asked me to read it; it repeats the plea made orally by the First Chief for the evacuation of Vera Cruz & Mr Fabela repeated at great length all the reasons advanced in support of the suggestion, adding that the army officers were greatly irritated & that Genl Aguilar's forces were very close to the American Soldiers & that the continuance of this proximity of rival forces involved great danger. He insisted that the organization of the Government was complete, to the extent of a thorough Custom House administration at Orizaba which neutralized or supplanted the Custom House established at Vera

Cruz as all importations were subject to further inspection and
to the action of the Constitutionalist Government at Orizaba. I
made but little reply to these claims contenting myself generally
with repeating the promise I had made to the First Chief that
I would call the attention of the President to the subject & would
repeat to him the statements made to me. . . .

## Resumé

I    Dissensions between the North & the South—Villa & Carranza
While these seem on the way to adjustment, the critical situation can scarcely be amended unless an earnest effort is made
to learn the public will and to hasten its accomplishment by
the early organization of a truly representative Government.
I have no hesitation in saying that this can best be done by
adopting such a programme as has now been agreed upon by
Villa & Obregon, and curtailing in the meantime the exercise
of irresponsible military rule which is interfering ruthlessly
with individual liberty and with the rights of property, both
of which could be sufficiently restricted and restrained by the
orderly application of the civil laws under which Mexico has
hitherto been governed

II    Amnesty or proscription?
*Vae Victis* seems to be the dominant note of the Southern or
Mexico City faction, and the continuance of government by
military decrees affords every facility and every temptation
for carrying the vengeful rule to the extreme where revolt is
the only alternative. The milder views expressed in Chihuahua
should be encouraged and to this end the immediate supremacy of the civil laws made the condition of any aid sympathy
or recognition

III    The early establishment of civil government is covered by the
preceding

IV    Agrarian reforms & constitutional changes can safely be left
to the legislative bodies whose election can be hastened. A
platform or pledges of reform can be agreed upon whose
adoption by the candidates will be a *sine qua non*. The Villa-
Obregon plan embodies such pledges.

V    The church question, or more properly the just treatment of
all ecclesiastical bodies must in my opinion await the formation of a responsible government. The wanton spoliation of
church property and the persecution of priests is unquestioned, but those now in power are not in mental condition
to give the subject rational treatment & I believe that present
insistence upon any particular line of action would result in

turmoil and confusion. Many of the things charged against the clergy, such as the supposed loan of P20,000,000 to Huerta[2] can I am credibly informed be readily disproved when minds shall have cooled sufficiently to accept proof. Time, tact, patience and the ordinary constitutional guarantees of due process of law should suffice to bring justice into this distorted and angry controversy

VI Whatever the result of the revolt against Huerta and the policy of government which the manner of his advent and the processes of his short rule made manifest; even if the triumph of his adversaries should be spoiled by their own dissensions or by their excesses and recognized unfitness to establish the orderly and impartial government for the establishment of which the strife was undergone, and further strife be needed to purge away unworthy ambitions and bring to the front the saving remnant of fit and worthy men who may make a government of the people & for the people; this new sacrifice had better be borne than to permit a relapse into the system which for more than a hundred years has proved inadequate for the advancement of the masses, and has brought the country to its present condition of profound distress.                              Paul Fuller[3]

Hw memoranda (WP, DLC).
   [2] About this loan, see Michael C. Meyer, *Huerta: A Political Portrait* (Lincoln, Neb., 1972), p. 168.
   [3] There is a very corrupt T transcript of this report in WP, DLC.

## E N C L O S U R E    I I

# A Translation of a Letter from Venustiano Carranza[1]

Mr President:                            Mexico, September 7th 1914

It was a great pleasure to receive the visit of Mr Paul Fuller who personally delivered to me Your Excellency's autograph letter of the 26th of August ultimo

Having regard to Your Excellency's commendation of your esteemed and estimable friend Mr Fuller, I accorded him the reception which he deserved and gave him all my attention.

In the interview which it gave me pleasure to have with Mr Fuller he conveyed to me the friendly feelings and good wishes of Your Excellency towards Mexico—feelings and wishes which I greatly appreciate because I believe in their sincerity.

In my conversation with Mr Fuller we exchanged views concerning the present situation of my country, and the great task which the government entrusted to me must carry out in the United Mexican States.

I avail myself of the opportunity afforded by the courtesy of Your Excellency in sending Mr Fuller with your kind autograph letter, to advise you that Mr Fuller will convey to Your Excellency the ideas I have expressed to him touching the international question now pending between the United States and Mexico by reason of the occupation of Vera Cruz by the American forces; this without prejudice to a discussion of the same matter with Your Excellency by my confidential agent in Washington, Lic. Rafael Zubáran, who has already received instructions on the subject.

The matter is of such grave import that its continuance would place the Governments and people of both countries in a most delicate situation, a circumstance greatly to be regretted, when the relations between your country and this might be so cordial

With assurances of my most distinguished consideration, I remain

Sincerely your friend and obedient servant    V. Carranza

Hw MS (WP, DLC).
  [1] The ALS original of this letter is in WP, DLC.


# From James Berwick Forgan and Others

Chicago, Illinois, September 21, 1914.

We have just been advised that the conference committee to which the Clayton anti-trust bill has been referred intends to report tomorrow in favor of reinstating in the Clayton bill the provision relating to interlocking bank directors. That provision was stricken out in the Senate. The European war has seriously upset financial conditions. The banks of this country have without stint or hesitation made every possible sacrifice and have utilized all of their resources to restore confidence and to improve conditions. It is unwise and dangerous to now legislate upon a subject of such vital importance to the banking interests of this country. It is equally unfortunate to incorporate any banking legislation into the Clayton bill which has to do with the regulation of trusts and monopolies. The proposed provisions most unjustly discriminates against banks, doing business in cities having a population of more than one hundred thousand inhabitants. It is upon the banks of the larger cities that the tremendous burden rests to protect the country against the prevailing financial disorders. We earnestly urge that you use your influence against the restoration of the objectionable provision.[1] We are sending a copy of this message to Secretary of the Treasury McAdoo.

Clearing House Committee of the City of Chicago.

James B. Forgan, Chairman

Orson Smith

Ernest A. Hamill,

John J. Mitchell,

Geo. M. Reynolds.

T telegram (WP, DLC).

¹ The section of the bill prohibiting interlocking bank directorates was restored by the conference committee, but with modifications exempting banks with assets of less than $5,000,000 and allowing interlocking directorates in banks located in the same city or town if it had less than 200,000 inhabitants. See 63d Cong., 2d sess., Senate Doc. No. 584, pp. 10-11.

## From Edward Mandell House

Dear Governor:                    New York City. September 22nd, 1914.

Bernstorff came to see me again yesterday in order to hear the outcome of Spring-Rice's visit.¹

I told him that Sir Cecil hesitated to go into a conference without the consent of his Government and without the knowledge of their allies. Bernstorff thought this reasonable. He justified his own action by saying that he thought the instructions from his Government warranted him in taking up negociations of this sort.

I told him I had an impression that Spring-Rice would communicate with his Government telling them in substance of what had been proposed and I thought it likely, in a few days, we might hear something further from him.

I think you should know the text of Spring-Rice's cablegram to his Government and I am risking enclosing it in this letter.²

It is perhaps better for me to remain here a few days longer. Spring-Rice said he would return whenever it was thought advisable.

Bernstorff thought it was not too early to begin conversations for the reason that they could hardly bring results in any event for some months.

Sir Cecil and I agreed that the Kaiser would probably be willing to accept such terms as England would be glad to concede provided the German war party would permit him. The most serious difficulty that will be encountered during negociations is the deep-rooted distrust England has for German diplomacy and promises. Something of this is also felt by the Germans towards England.

Another difficulty was expressed by Bernstorff to the effect that neither side wished to be placed in the position of initiating peace proposals. This can be avoided however, in some such way as is being done now, for they will soon find themselves talking about it and will not be so sensitive.

I cannot close without expressing to you my profound admiration of your reply to the Kaiser's communication. It is the most diplomatic and impressive document of the kind that it has ever been my pleasure to read. Everyone is talking about it.

Your faithful and affectionate,   E. M. House

TLS (WP, DLC).
  1 C. A. Spring Rice to E. Grey, Sept. 22, 1914, TLS (E. Grey Papers, FO 800 84/2, PRO), is a long report of this conversation.
  2 The enclosure is a paraphrase of C. A. Spring Rice to E. Grey, Sept. 20, 1914.


# From John Davison Rockefeller, Jr.

New York, September 22, 1914.

Mr. Welborn has sent me a copy of the reply which he has made on behalf of the Colorado Fuel & Iron Company to your letter of September 5th. As this reply is made on behalf of that company alone I feel at liberty both as one of its directors and as representative [of] a substantial minority interest to take a more active part in the matter than I did when it was in the hands of a committee representing all of the operators. Will you permit me therefore to say that I am in hearty sympathy with the spirit of earnest desire to meet your wishes which Mr. Welborn's letter manifests. I sincerely hope that as a result of the interview you have granted Mr. Welborn some practical plan may be envolved [evolved] which will be adapted to the peculiar situation of our company and be acceptable to our employees. I beg further to say that my time is at your disposal and that I will support any constructive plan which conserves the interests of the stockholders, the employees and the public.

John D. Rockfeller, Jr.

T telegram (WP, DLC).


# From Franklin Knight Lane

My dear Mr. President:        Washington September 22, 1914.

There is in Montana a roving band of Indians known as the Rocky Boy band. Their Chief is Little Bear. I have been trying to secure some land for these poor chaps for some time, without success. In appreciation of my efforts, Chief Little Bear today informs me that during the present war in Europe he and his band will remain neutral.   Cordially yours,   Franklin K Lane

TLS (WP, DLC).

## From Jesse Floyd Welborn

My dear Mr. President:        Washington, D. C., Sept. 23, 1914.

I promised in my forwarding letter of September 18th to advise you as to the names of the Colorado coal operators who would be with me this morning.

When I left Denver Saturday night I fully expected to be joined here today by at least one and possibly others, but I have received telegrams since arriving to the effect that the other operators had, at a meeting Sunday, decided to present their position in writing.

I made it clear from the start that I could speak in this matter for the Colorado Fuel & Iron Company alone, but I regret not to be accompanied by representatives of some of the other companies.

I sincerely trust, however, that even as it is you will feel that the interview this morning will have been to good purpose.

I am, with respect,   Faithfully yours,   J F Welborn

TLS (WP, DLC).

## Remarks at a Press Conference

September 24, 1914.

Does the conference report remove your objections as to some of the definitions of the Clayton bill?

You will notice that in sections 2 and 3 of the conference report the definitions are relieved of rigidity by saying that whenever those practices substantially lessen competition or tend to create a monopoly, those conditions are left to the judgment, by a subsequent section, of the trade commission. That gives the elasticity desirable.

Do you still expect to sign the bills together?

I do not know. My time on the trade commission bill is Saturday and I do not want to miss the pleasure of signing it, but I do not know whether I shall have the Clayton bill so soon as that or not.

It has been stated that if you sign the trade commission bill before the other, all the definitions in the Clayton bill might be regarded by the courts as amending the previous legislation.

That must have been some person whose study was unprofitable; it is too ingenious.

At any rate, you are not going to let the bill go without your signature?

No, I do not want it to become a law without my signature.

T MS (C. L. Swem Coll., NjP).

## Remarks to a Delegation Representing the Cotton Interests[1]

September 24, 1914.

Of course, I need not say, gentlemen, that the gravity of the situation is very manifest; and I want you to know that I have been giving a great deal of attention to it with the earnest desire to see some way by which the difficulties could be solved without committing the government in principle to any action which would plague us in the future. Because the danger, gentlemen, of the present situation is that, under the pressure of what appears to be necessity, we should make some radical departure from sound economic practice which in the future years we would very much regret. We have got to make great sacrifices, not to make fundamental mistakes.

Now I am not thereby implying a judgment as to any specific proposition. But I feel bound myself to guard against impulses when impulses are so strong, just as I feel it so necessary for us in an international situation to guard every impulse and see that we do not make any mistake which future generations will have the just cause to blame us for. But I want you to know how sincerely I appreciate the gravity of the situation and how entirely willing I am to consider anything that is laid before me by way of a practicable suggestion.

T MS (WP, DLC).

[1] Representative Robert Lee Henry of Texas and a delegation of men in the cotton business met with Wilson from 12 to 12:15 P.M. on September 24.

## To Franklin Knight Lane

My dear Mr. Secretary:     [The White House] September 24, 1914

I have your note about the action of Chief Little Bear. There is something very touching about it and I hope that if you have the opportunity you will convey to him my appreciation of his attitude.

It is delightful to hear that you are back again in good shape.
Cordially and faithfully yours,   Woodrow Wilson

TLS (Letterpress Books, WP, DLC).


## To Herbert Clark Hoover and Lou Henry Hoover

                                        The White House
My dear Mr. and Mrs. Hoover:        September 24, 1914.

The American Ambassador at London has brought to my attention the excellent work which you have been doing for the relief of the many Americans in that city, and it affords me much gratification to say that the loyal support and hearty cooperation which have been so generously extended have impressed me deeply and have lightened the burdens of these troublous times.

I extend to you, my dear Mr. and Mrs. Hoover, sincere thanks in my own name and in the names of the many Americans who profited by your untiring labors in England.

Cordially yours,   Woodrow Wilson

TLS (H. Hoover Papers, CSt-H).


## To Charles Stedman Macfarland

                                        [The White House]
My dear Mr. Macfarland:             September 24, 1914

I received and have read with the greatest attention the letter of August 20, 1914, from the Federal Council of the Churches of Christ in America, signed by the President, the Chairman of the Administrative Committee, the Chairman of the Commission on Peace and Arbitration, yourself, the Associate Secretary, and Dr. Sidney L. Gulick, representing the Commission on Japan. I need not tell you how sincerely I appreciate the approval expressed in that letter of the efforts I have made to bring about mediation and peace, and I am happy to have anticipated the suggestion of the Council in the matter of urging a genuine attitude of neutrality upon the people of the United States, and also to have been able to meet the suggestion of the Council in the matter of appointing a day of prayer.

Very sincerely yours,   Woodrow Wilson

TLS (Letterpress Books, WP, DLC).

## To John Philip White

My dear Mr. White:        [The White House] September 24, 1914

Allow me to acknowledge your letter of September seventeenth apprising me of the acceptance by the Mine Workers of Colorado in convention assembled in the City of Trinidad on September sixteenth, of the proposition which I submitted for the settlement of the Colorado coal strike.

I am very much gratified by their action and believe that it will be warmly approved by public opinion.

Sincerely yours,   Woodrow Wilson

TLS (Letterpress Books, WP, DLC).

## From David Benton Jones

My dear Mr. President:        Chicago September 24, 1914.

I saw Mr. Ripley of the Santa Fe road today, and he stated that he had appeared before three presidents on railroad matters, and that you were the only one who understood what the railroad men were talking about: that the other two presidents seemed to know very little and cared less. He added that he was glad to have his judgment in bolting the Republican party confirmed by your record of the past year and a half and their interview with you.

Should Mr. Ripley again have occasion to appear before you you can be sure that he has no reservations or hidden purposes or motives back of his mind. I have known him for over twenty years, and he is one of the very few railroad men I know of whom this could be said.

I was naturally greatly pleased to have him make this statement of his own accord, and I am sending it to you simply as a satisfactory little incident in the general grind of work.

Very sincerely yours,   David B. Jones.

TLS (WP, DLC).

## From James Viscount Bryce

*Private*

Hindleap, Forest Row, Sussex.

My dear President                        Sept. 24th 1914

May I say to you that so far as I have been able to collect their opinion, the wisest friends of peace on this side the ocean think you were altogether right in not renewing at this moment your

offer of mediation in this war? There would have been little—
or no—chance that any of the contending parties would now
accept it; and the prospects of a successful issue to your intervention at a later moment might have been prejudiced

The general feeling is—and though one of those who worked
hard for peace up to the last—I share it, that any attempt to patch
up a peace now could lead only to a sort of truce rather than
peace, an uneasy respite during which preparations for renewing the struggle would go on, armaments growing larger and
engines of destruction still more deadly. In this country the
great desire is to get rid once for all of these huge fleets & armies

We do continue to hope that a time may arrive, though it
may be months distant—how many no one can conjecture—when
an offer of mediation from you as the greatest & most respected
neutral may be very helpful. Believe me

Yours very sincerely   James Bryce

ALS (WP, DLC).


## From John Pierpont Morgan, Jr.

My dear Mr. President,          New York. September 24th, 1914.

I have your very kind letter of September 17th, and regret
that I conveyed to you simply the impression that I was "blue"
about the outlook. What I intended to convey was that I do feel
that certain things are being done which are likely to make conditions that are already difficult somewhat more so. That it will
all come right in the end, I have every confidence, but I dislike
seeing that end moved farther away than it need be. You will
remember also that my letter was written before your communication to Mr. Trumbull on the railroad situation was published,
and I must say that that letter, as expressing the point of view
of the Administration on that very pressing matter, has given
me, and I am sure many others, very great encouragement, as
being a clear statement of an attitude of the Administration
which had not been generally realized before.

Your confidence in the result of the bills in Congress is a great
satisfaction to me, and, while I do not as yet fully share it and
think it very probable that the result, which we all wish to obtain,
Congressmen and business men alike, will have to be obtained
by certain modifications as the operation of the laws becomes
clear, nevertheless I realize that your belief is reached after adequate thought and comparison of many views, and is, therefore,
entitled to very great weight. Certainly the splendid co-operation

between the best of the Government and the best of business, which at present exists, is most cheering, and I know that it makes many able to face the very complicated problems of the immediate future (the worst of them caused by no fault of this country) with confidence and with enterprise. It is hardly necessary for me to say again that, if there is anything that I or any of us can do to help in any part of the situation, our services are entirely at your disposal at any time.

I very greatly appreciate the kindness and encouragement of your letter, and wish to offer you my most sincere thanks for it.

I am, dear Sir, with great esteem and respect,

Yours very sincerely,   J. P. Morgan

TLS (WP, DLC).


## From Henry Watterson

My dear Mr. President:          Louisville, Ky., Sept. 24, 1914.

The death of Mrs. Wilson was a grievous shock to Mrs. Watterson and myself. It may have been through Robert and Hattie, but, somehow we had come to identify you in your domestic life and married happiness with ourselves and thus to know and feel a personal sense of the awful wrench. "God knew where the weak spot was and smote him there."

As one who has in his life survived more than one appalling tragedy, I can offer you the single assurance that

"Pain and grief,
Are transitory things no less than joy,
And though they leave us not the men we were
Yet they do leave us."

I take the words from Henry Taylor's "Philip Van Artevelde." If you are not familiar with that great dramatic poem, get the book out of the library. It deals with high and mighty things, as well as tender, and will bring you comfort. You will as you read of the Lady Adriana see as in a vision your own dear wife.

I hope that hereafter you and I will better understand one another; in any event that the single disagreeable episode will vanish and never be thought of more. In Paris last winter I went over the whole matter with Mr. McCombs and we quite settled and blotted out our end of it. I very much regret the use of any rude word—too much the characteristic of our rough-and-tumble political combats—and can truly say that I have not only earnestly wished the success of your Administration but have sought to find points of agreement, not of disagreement.

I am writing as an old man—old enough to be your father—who has the claim upon your consideration that all his life he has pursued the ends you yourself have aimed at, if at times too zealously and exactingly, yet without self-seeking or rancor.

    With Great Respect   Your Friend   Henry Watterson

TLS (WP, DLC).


## To Robert Lansing

My dear Mr. Lansing:    [The White House] September 26, 1914

Thank you for consulting me about the case of the Belgian Minister.[1]

I think it would be hardly right to let him go on. It might lead to complications and he would then have a right to wonder why we did not call his attention to the matter sooner.

My own judgment is that it would be well to have an informal personal conversation with him and call his attention to the inconvenience and embarrassment that may be caused this government by what he is said to be doing, and intimate to him that it would be very much appreciated by this government if he would refrain and, so far as possible, correct what he had already done.

    Cordially and faithfully yours,   Woodrow Wilson

CCL (WP, DLC).
  [1] R. Lansing to WW, Sept. 25, 1914, TLS (WP, DLC), with enclosures, calling Wilson's attention to the fact that the Belgian Minister to the United States, Emmanuel Havenith, was organizing a committee to collect funds for the relief of destitute women and children in Belgium. Lansing declared that this meant that "an official representative of Belgium is in fact soliciting money in behalf of his people, which indirectly inures to the benefit of his Government." "The question is," he continued, "does the humanitarian purpose of the movement affect its character so as to remove the charge of unneutrality? Is it advisable to permit the Belgian Minister to proceed with this movement without calling his attention to the inadvisability of his action, which may form an excuse for collecting subscriptions by officers of other belligerents, which, in fact, are for less humane purposes?"


## From Robert Lansing, with Enclosure

Dear Mr. President:    [Washington] September 26, 1914.

I enclose herewith a copy of a letter which I received to-day from Dr. Ernst Richard.[1]

Do you think it would be advisable to informally and orally communicate the contents of this letter to the Belgian Minister?

    Very sincerely yours,   Robert Lansing

TCL (SDR, RG 59, 763.72116/71½, DNA).
   1 Ernst D. Richard, Ph.D., German-born, active in the world peace movement, and Lecturer on the History of German Civilization at Columbia University.

ENCLOSURE

## Ernst Richard to the Secretary of State

My dear Mr. Secretary:        New York, September 24th, 1914.

I wish to call your attention to a report in yesterday's news-papers that Dr. Frederic S. Mason of 12 Fifth Avenue, New York, intends to bring over two Belgian girls to furnish actual proof of German atrocities. Special care is taken of these cases, as he says for this reason (not for humanity's sake, therefore, but for exhibition purposes). I write to ask you whether you think it desirable that specimens of the victims from all countries be brought to this country. What if the germans bring over the women who, they claim have been dragged naked by their hair through the streets of Belgian cities even before the outbreak of hostilities, or the soldiers whose eyes are said to have been gouged out by Belgian women, or the women whose breasts were torn off by Russian soldiers? What vista of nastiness opens before our eyes?

An unofficial suggestion on your part would probably be sufficient. But I appeal to your sense of humanity and good taste as well as to your patriotism: Pray, do all in your power to save us from this dismal spectacle, from the contagion of hatred and atrocity of which this proposition would be the certain beginning.

        Yours very respectfully, (signed)   Ernst Richard.

TCL (SDR, RG 59, 763.72116/71½, DNA).


## From Robert Lansing

Dear Mr. President:        Washington September 27, 1914.

I am sorry to disturb you today, but I think it very desirable that the enclosed enstruction to Mr. Page at London,[1] if it meets with your approval, should go forward by tomorrow's pouch, which closes at 2 P.M.

The subject of the instruction, namely the proposal to make the Declaration of London the law of naval warfare for the present conflict as modified by a British Order in Council, required careful consideration and considerable research before we took a definite position. As a result delay in instructing Mr. Page was unavoidable, although every day's delay was to be regretted.

I hope, therefore, that you will find it possible to examine the papers enclosed so that, if you approve, the instruction may be sent in tomorrow's pouch. Otherwise it will postpone the transmittal four or five days.

I cannot but feel that the action of the British Government calls for unqualified refusal of this Government to acquiesce in its legality and that our objections should be clearly and firmly stated.

The British Order in Council will suggest to you, I think, the obnoxious Orders in Council of the Napoleonic Wars, and will, if its provisions are called to public attention in this country, cause severe criticism in the press.

I inclose in addition to the instruction copies of (A) Mr. Page's dispatch enclosing the Order in Council, and the memorandum of the Foreign Office,[2] (B) the Articles in the Declaration of London which are modified by the Order, and (C) a pamphlet containing the Declaration itself, and the Report of the Drafting Committee. In addition to these documents I also inclose (D) a memorandum by Professor Eugene Wambaugh, and (E) a memorandum by the Joint State and Navy Neutrality Board.[3]

If you think time would be saved by oral explanation of these papers, I can be summoned at any time by telephone as I will be either at the Department or at my residence.

Very sincerely yours,   Robert Lansing.

TLS (SDR, RG 59, 763.72112/126, DNA).
[1] It is printed in *FR-WWS 1914*, pp. 225-32.
[2] Printed in *ibid.*, pp. 218-20.
[3] The above enclosures, not printed, are in SDR, RG 59, 763.72112/126, DNA.

## From the Diary of Colonel House

Washington, D. C. September 27, 1914.

I took the 12.08 train to Washington and was met at the station by McAdoo and Eleanor. They went to the White House with me and took dinner with us. After dinner we talked for awhile until a large package of papers came from the State Department marked urgent. This was the signal for McAdoo and the family to leave, and the President and I immediately got down to work.

Lansing had written a long letter to Page concerning the Declaration of London and its effect upon neutral shipping. He enclosed the modification of the Declaration which the British Government had made, and which they purpose enforcing during the war. As is known, the Declaration of London was not accepted by Great Britain. She was never satisfied with it and the matter drifted until the war caught us in its grip.

Lansing's letter of instruction to Page was exceedingly undiplomatic and I urged the President not to permit it to be sent. I also urged him, in spite of Lansing's protest that the letter must go at once, not to send it until further thought and a better understanding could be had on the subject. I suggested that he call Lansing over the telephone and find out something further about it. He did this but did not get much satisfaction, and he directed Lansing to send Page a despatch and later, instructions. In other words, he was sparring for time.

I then suggested that he permit me to have a conference with Sir Cecil Spring-Rice and get at the bottom of the controversy. He expressed warm approval of this plan. After this we went to bed pretty tired and somewhat worried.

T MS (E. M. House Papers, CtY).

## Remarks at a Press Conference

Sept. 28, 1914

Mr. President, is the reply of the Colorado coal operators[1] final, or is it one to be considered further?

> I think it is one to be considered further. I have just arranged to consult the Secretary of Labor about it.[2] He is in touch with the whole situation.

Did Mr. Welborn make a reply?

> No, he really did not make any reply. He simply made a number of interesting representations as to the situation out there. I do not understand that his company has come to a conclusion. The conclusion of this group of operators is on the whole favorable.

Can you tell us what further steps you expect to take, Mr. President?

> No, I cannot now, because I am discussing it in my own mind.

Mr. President, with reference to the shipping bill, do you share the general feeling that the urgency is passed?

> No, not in the least. The urgency has increased.

Mr. President, Judge Alexander said Saturday that his advices were that the emergency for it was over; that there were plenty of ships for it.

> For the ordinary trade, yes, but that is not what it is for. It is chiefly for the development of American trade where it will be unprofitable for private capital to develop it and

where I know for a certainty that private capital will not develop it. It could not be expected to.

Mr. President, you told us last week that the opposition to the bill was rather negligible.

So I was then informed.

Don't you think that it has grown?

Apparently it has. I don't know whether it is apparent or real. You know a few persons can make a great deal of noise sometimes, particularly a few persons who are interested from an investment point of view.

Does that alter your views or position any?

No, sir, because the circumstances are not altered. Opposition does not alter me; circumstances, I hope, do.

Mr. President, isn't that opposition chiefly toward taking it up at the present time rather than toward the proposition?

That may be. I don't know. I am going to confer with some of the members of the House just as soon as I can find space on my calendar. I will find that out; that may be all there is in it.

Can you say anything of the visit of Mr. Alexander or Mr. Underwood today?

That was about that subject.

Your present judgment is, Mr. President, that it ought to pass at this session of Congress?

Unless I learn something that changes my judgment in the matter. I don't mean something about the opposition to it, but something about the urgency.

How is the Philippine bill, Mr. President?

I don't understand that there is any trouble about that passing the House of Representatives.

Mr. President, to go back to the shipping bill: The seamen's bill, in a good many minds, is somewhat of a first step toward any action upon the shipping bill; is there any proposition to pass the seamen's bill at this session?

I don't know. I have fallen out of the conference on that.

Mr. President, is there anything you can say on the Mexican situation?

No, nothing intelligible. I don't know just how it is developing.

Is the opposition to the conference report on the Clayton bill among Democrats in the Senate confined to Mr. Reed, do you know?

No, I don't know; but it is confined certainly to a very small group.[3]

The group is not large enough to endanger the adoption of the report?

Oh, no; not so far as I know.

Is adjournment in October likely?

I should say so, though I have now stopped committing myself, having proved a false prophet. Still, I think Europe is more responsible for the false prophecies than we are.

Mr. President, do you expect all of these measures to go through both the House and the Senate this session?

I don't expect the Philippine bill to go through the Senate.

Do you expect the shipping bill to go through?

Well, I am waiting for these conferences. I don't know just what can be done with that.

Mr. President, has your attention been drawn to the opposition of western bankers to that provision in the conference report about interlocking directorates?

Yes, but there is a clear judgment among us that that ought to be done, and it is clearly pledged in the platform of the party.

Is it your intention to send Mr. Fuller back to Mexico at this time?

No, sir.

T MS (C. L. Swem Coll., NjP).

1 J. C. Osgood *et al.* (thirty-seven presidents or general managers of Colorado coal companies) to WW, Sept. 23, 1914, printed in the *New York Times*, Sept. 28, 1914. These operators began by accusing the Secretary of Labor and Labor Department officials of partisanship toward the strikers. They reaffirmed their determination not to enter into any kind of agreement with the United Mine Workers and, indeed, accused the leaders of that organization of entire responsibility for the widespread violence in Colorado. The President's proposed plan would at best be a palliative measure. They were determined to protect the 9,500 miners now peaceably at work. Wherever the responsibility for the situation in Colorado lay, the operators went on, the President's plan involved "a bargain between government and law on the one side, and violators of the law on the other." The operators in particular rejected the plan's proposal for grievance committees in each mine, saying that this was a favorite method of the United Mine Workers to "foment trouble and provoke strife." The operators claimed that they had always observed the laws of Colorado and ended by saying that they would be glad to cooperate with President Wilson and the State of Colorado in seeing to it that law and order were observed in the coal mining areas.

2 WW to W. B. Wilson, Sept. 28, 1914, TLS (WP, DLC).

3 About these attacks in the Senate against the Clayton bill, see Arthur S. Link, *Wilson: The New Freedom* (Princeton, N. J., 1956), pp. 443-44.

## To Robert Lansing

My dear Mr. Lansing:     [The White House] September 28, 1914

I think you would be justified in bringing this letter which I return to you to the attention of the Belgian Minister in an informal and friendly way. It opens a vista of possibilities which are indeed shocking and which we ought to take every honorable means to prevent.

Cordially and sincerely yours,   Woodrow Wilson

TLS (Letterpress Books, WP, DLC).

## To Henry Watterson

                                                    The White House
My dear Colonel Watterson:        September 28, 1914

Your kind letter has gratified me very deeply. You may be sure that any feeling I may have had has long since disappeared and that I feel only gratified that you should again and again have come to my support in the columns of the Courier-Journal. The whole thing was a great misunderstanding.

Sincerely yours,   Woodrow Wilson

TLS (H. Watterson Papers, DLC).

## From Robert Lansing, with Enclosure

Dear Mr. President:        [Washington] September 28, 1914.

I enclose a draft of telegram to the American Ambassador at London, in accordance with your direction this morning.

I confess I am not satisfied with it, because there seems so much to say which is not said. I hope you will please indicate any suggestions you may have as to changes.

Very sincerely yours,   Robert Lansing

CCL (SDR, RG 59, 763.72112/359A, DNA).

ENCLOSURE[1]

*Proposed Telegram.*

American Ambassador, London.

Strictly Confidential. You will immediately see Sir Edward Grey and state to him informally *and confidentially* that this Government ⟨has given careful consideration to⟩ *is greatly disturbed by* the intention of the British Government to change the provisions of the Declaration of London by the Order in Council of the twentieth August and to adopt the Declaration thus changed as the code of naval warfare for the present war. This Government ⟨as the result of its examination,⟩ feels grave concern at all of the proposed changes, especially those in Articles three and five of the Order in Council, which so materially affect the rights of neutral commerce. If the proposed rules are *sought to be* put into force and the matter becomes the subject of public discussion in this country, as it undoubtedly will, it is to be ⟨feared⟩ *confidently expected* that it will arouse a spirit of resentment among the American people toward Great Britain⟨,⟩ which this Government would extremely regret but which it would be unable to prevent. You will also point out that the enforcement of these rules by the British Government would furnish to those inimicable to Great Britain an opportunity, which they would not be slow to seize, *and which they are already using in our press upon the mere publication of the Order.*

Paragraph. You will further say that the President *earnestly* desires⟨, if possible,⟩ to avoid a formal protest to the⟨se⟩ proposed rules and their enforcement and hopes that the British Government will ⟨carefully⟩ *be willing to* consider the advisability of modifying ⟨the objectionable⟩ *these* features of the Order in Council, which possess such latent possibilities. ⟨of disturbing the existing relations between the peoples of the two countries.⟩

You will impress upon Sir Edward Grey the *President's conviction of the* extreme gravity of the situation and ⟨the⟩ *his* earnest wish ⟨of the President⟩ to avoid *every* cause⟨s⟩ of irritation and controversy between this Government and the Government of his Majesty.

In presenting the substance of this instruction to Sir Edward Grey you will assure him ⟨that it is done in the most friendly spirit⟩ *of the earnest spirit of friendship in which it is sent. The President is anxious that he should realize that the terms of the Declaration of London represent the limit to which this Gov't could go with the approbation and support of its people.*

Telegraph result of interview as soon as possible.

Lansing    Acting Secretary of State

T telegram (SDR, RG 59, 763.72112/359A, DNA).
[1] Wilson's deletions in angle brackets, his additions in italics. The revised version was sent as No. 218 on September 28 and is printed in *FR-WWS 1914*, pp. 232-33.

## From the Diary of Colonel House

September 28, 1914.

The President, Dr. Axson and I breakfasted together. After breakfast I went to McAdoo's for a short conference with him.

I had Hoover arrange with Billy Phillips for the use of his home, and I asked Sir Cecil Spring-Rice over the telephoned to meet me there at ten o'clock. The conference was a most interesting one.

I showed the Ambassador the letter Lansing had prepared to send Page. He was thoroughly alarmed over some of the undiplomatic expressions. One paragraph in particular he thought amounted almost to a declaration of war.[1] He said if that paper should get into the hands of the press, the headlines would indicate that war with Great Britain was inevitable, and he believed one of the greatest panics the country ever saw would ensue, for it was as bad or worse than the Venezuela incident. He said he did not know what I had accomplished in my busy life, but he felt sure I had never done as important a piece of work as in this instance. He felt it was fortunate I happened to be in Washington at this time and had caught the matter before it had gone further.

We discussed the best ways and means of getting out of the difficulty, which he said would never have arisen if the State Department had talked the matter over with him frankly in the beginning. His Government's attitude had been known at the State Department for a month, and yet not a word of objection had been raised. If he had known what the feeling of this country was he would have taken it up with his Government, and their attitude would have been modified As it was, they had already published their intention of doing the things to which our Government objected, and it would be difficult to handle it now in a way to save the *amour propre* of his Government.

We outlined a despatch for this Government to send to Page, and then we outlined the despatch which we thought he should send Sir Edward Grey. We agreed to be absolutely frank with one another, letting each know just what was being done so there could be no subterfuge or misunderstanding.

[1] Spring Rice referred, undoubtedly, to the following final paragraphs in Lansing's first draft:

"*Confidential.* You will not fail to impress upon His Excellency the gravity of the issues which the enforcement of the Order in Council seems to presage, and say to him in substance as follows:

"It is a matter of grave concern to this Government that the particular conditions of this unfortunate war should be considered by His Britannic Majesty's Government to be such as to justify them in advancing doctrines and advocating practices which in the past aroused strong opposition on the part of the Government of the United States, and bitter feeling among the American people. This Government feels bound to express the fear, though it does so reluctantly, that the publicity, which must be given to the rules which His Majesty's Government announce that they intend to enforce, will awaken memories of controversies, which it is the earnest desire of the United States to forget or to pass over in silence. This Government in view of these considerations ventures to suggest in no unkindly spirit and with the sole purpose of preserving the mutual good will which now exists between the people of the United States and the people of Great Britain, that the British Government may find it possible to modify their intention before it has been put into practice, as its realization seems fraught with possible misunderstandings which the United States desires at all times to avoid, and especially at the present when the relations of the two countries are so cordial and when their friendship rests upon the secure foundation of the mutual esteem and common ideals of their respective peoples."

The Ambassador was surprised that Lansing would use such language, which he attributed to ignorance and not to design. It caused me some amusement in thinking about the kind of diplomacy in which I was indulging. It is certainly original as far as I know, but I thoroughly believe in it. If nations were as frank with one another as individuals who mean to be honest, I believe the largest part of the difficulties between them might be averted.

It was agreed that I should hereafter be known as "Beverly" and when I telephoned it was to be under that name, and we were to meet at Phillips' without designating the place, merely by stating the hour agreeable to both.

The President was to have a conference with Lansing at eleven o'clock and it was necessary for me to hurry back to give him the Page letter, and also give him the benefit of the interview I had had with Sir Cecil. I arranged with the doorkeeper at the office to hold Lansing in one of the anterooms while I saw the President. I gave him in a few words the substance of my interview with the British Ambassador, and I pointed out the objectionable passage which he had marked and which I asked the President to assumed the responsibility for marking out when he calls Lansing's attention to its undiplomatic phraseology. Lansing was not to know anything of my conference with Spring-Rice.

After leaving the White House I went to the Department of Justice to see Gregory and confer with him about various matters. At one o'clock I returned to lunch at the White House. After lunch, the President, McAdoo, Tumulty and I conferred upon the New York situation regarding the Chairmanship of the State Executive Committee. It seems that William Church Osborn has declined to serve longer and that McCombs wants that position as well as being National Chairman. . . .

We returned to the White House at five where I have an engagement with Senator Culberson. Culberson and I drove until seven, and then I took "supper" with him and his family, first leaving word at the White House that I would not be there for dinner but would return at eight o'clock.

Culberson and I had a thoroughly good time recalling old time political incidents and campaigns. I found him much improved in health and spirits. He asked me to warn the President to be careful in his appointments for the Trades Commission. The Senate is disposed to regard such nominations very critically and it would be well to select the best men to be found.

In telling the President of this he said he would certainly choose the best men that could be found for a salary of $10,000. Men who were doing big things commanded more than that sum and would not accept such positions, and men who had made a success in life and were willing to accept such places, the Senate would probably not confirm.

I returned to the White House shortly after eight. Dr. Axson and Miss Bones were with the President in his study. We talked of the war and its probable effect upon literature. We thought it would be stimulating. The President read poetry aloud for an hour or more. After that Dr. Axson and Miss Bones left for bed and the President and I discussed public affairs for awhile. He declared if he knew he would not have to stand for re-election two years from now, he would feel a great load had been lifted from him. I thought he need not accept the Presidency unless he wished to, even if the Democratic Party demanded it, though I could understand why he would feel it a duty to do so provided his health permitted. I could not see what else he could do in life that would be so interesting. He replied that the thing that frightened him was that it was impossible to make such an effort in the future as he had made in the past or to accomplish anything like what he had accomplished in a legislative way. He feared the country would expect him to continue as he had up to now, which would be impossible. I thought the country would neither expect it nor want it. There were other things he could do which would be far more delightful in accomplishment, and would add even more to his fame. I referred particularly to his foreign policy which if properly followed, would bring him world-wide recognition.

Neither of us could see exactly how he could inject himself into the foreign situation in regard to peace at this time. We thought if the war became a draw, it was possible the Peace Conference would come to Washington and he might take part in the proceedings, or it was possible it might be necessary yo [to] send a commission abroad, but neither of us could wuite [quite] figure out how this was to be brought about. It was tentatively agreed that I should keep the matter in my hands and advise him what was being done.

I thought the Germans were more likely to want peace first, for the reason that their purpose had already largely failed, and if they were driven back into Germany, the Allies would close in upon them, and the neutral nations would also begin to bare their teeth, because they would know the end was not far off.

I told of my conversation with Spring-Rice and of the evident desire of the Allies to postpone peace negotiations. I thought the time would come when it would be necessary for him to bring some pressure. I thought this could be done indirectly through me so as not to make it quite official.

I also related Bernstorff's conversation with Wallace in which he said that Germany was ready to discuss peace measures[,] suggesting the advisability of my going to London to see what could be done with the British Government. The President thought this would not be advisable at present, and Spring-Rice, when I mentioned it to him, als[o] thought it best for me not to go for the moment, but to be ready to go at an opportune time. I disagree with them both, but have not pressed the matter because it might seem as if I wished to inject myself too prominently into the situation.

The President thought I should write Sir Edward Grey and tell him of the danger of postponing peace negotiations. If Germany and Austria are entirely crushed, neither of us could see any way by which Russia could be restrained. He thought I should bring this strongly to Sir Edward's attention. I suggested writing Sir William Tyrrell and reach Sir Edward Grey in that way. He advised me to do what I considered best.

I find the President singularly lacking in appreciation of the importance of this European crisis. He seems more interested in domestic affairs, and I find it difficult to get his attention centered upon the one big question.

Congress will adjourn now within a few days, and when it is out of the way, it is my purpose to make a drive at the President and try to get him absorbed in the greatest problem of world-wide interest that has ever come, or may ever come, before a President of the United States.

During one of our talks I was interested in hearing him outline some such form of government as I gave in Philip Dru. Some day when he is my guest in New York, it is my purpose to read from Philip Dru the constitution I wrote both for the nation and the states and see how far we differ. I have a feeling that we largely agree, although when I wrote Philip Dru I had never met the President nor read any of his books. As far as I can see, his thoughts and mine have run parallel for a long while, almost from youth.

It is his purpose after he retires from office to write a book which, for lack of a better name, he now calls "Statesmanship." It will relate to the essence of government, showing that it is something human, in which the personal equation largely enters, and that it is not absolutely scientific and arbitrary.

We talked much of leadership and its importance in government. He has demonstrated this to an unus[u]al degree. He thinks our form of government can be changed by personal leadership, but I thought the Constitution should be altered, for no matter how great a leader a man was, I could see situations that would block him unless the Constitution was modified. He does not feel as strongly about this as I do.

## Four Telegrams from Sir Cecil Arthur Spring Rice to Sir Edward Grey

Washington r. 8.50 p.m. September 28th, 1914.
No. 65. Treaty. Urgent. Very Confidential.
Your despatch No. 33 Treaty.

I hear from a secret source that United States Government are preparing a note which in forcible language raises objections to modifications imposed in Order in Council of August 20th to provisions of Declaration of London. It says that United States Government would have been prepared to accept Declaration as a whole (as Germany has done) but cannot agree to modifications which revive doctrine of continuous voyage and practically impose a paper blockade. Particular objection is raised to clauses 3 and 5 which afford facilities to the Courts to declare practically all goods consigned to neutral ports such as Rotterdam or Gothenburg as liable to seizure on the ground that they are for a person under control of authorities of the enemy State.

There is every sign that there will be a violent agitation set on foot in this country where exporting interests are very deeply affected and Dernburg[1] is using every effort to fan flame.

No one in State Department has mentioned subject to me which is an ominous sign.

T telegram (FO 372/601, No. 53883, p. 77, PRO).
[1] Bernhard Dernburg, former German Colonial Secretary, who came to the United States in August 1914 as a representative of the German Red Cross. By this time he had organized the German Information Service, located in New York, the nucleus of the German propaganda organization in the United States.

Urgent. Private.          Washington September 28th, 1914.
My telegram Treaty No. 65.
Modifications of Declaration of London.

President's friend sent for me to-day and showed me despatch to United States Ambassador in London which was sent to President last night ready for signature in order to be despatched at once. Note contained one or two discourteous expressions which I pointed out. But what is ominous is that no word has been spoken either to President or to me and Press to-day shows signs of having been tuned.

President's personal message was as follows:

There is every sign that feeling of this nation may be changed in a moment if it is thought that England is reviving old claims hostile to trade between neutrals. Great interests are involved which will affect many sections of the country but what will arouse most sentiment would be the idea that England intends to cripple all trade except her own and to do so is going back on principles enunciated by herself and confirmed at London Conference 1909.

Secretary of State is away and note was, I believe, drafted by the legal advisers of State Department and Treasury. It is signed by Councillor of State Department whom I have seen every day but who has never mentioned the subject.

I urged that the President should send an explanatory Telegram to United States Ambassador in order to prepare the way but this may be opposed by State Department. I hear that Germans here expect a conflict between United States and Great Britain to arise out of this question.

The President is now in consultation with his friend and Councillor of State Department. A further communication is promised me.

I fear that the question may prove very serious and gravely affect relations between United States and Great Britain.

T telegram (E. Grey Papers, FO 800 84/2, PRO).


Washington September 28, 1914.

No. 66. Treaty.
### Modification of Declaration of London.

President sent Counsellor of State Department with a message to the effect that United States Ambassador has received confidential and unofficial instructions to bring matter of orders of August 20th to your serious attention.

There are indications that matter is arousing attention in the country and may lead to bitter feeling which will be utilized with great effect. It is also embarassing to the President not to be able to accept the Declaration of London as general rule for prize-courts of all nations.

Following suggestions are made confidentially by Counsellor.

1. Certain articles like petroleum, wire-fencing, motors which are shown by recent events exclusively used for military purpose may be added to list of absolute contraband under power given in Article 23.

2. Clause 3 and 5 of order could be easily evaded in Holland by consignment to a Dutch subject who could re-consign to a German. This as a fact is done. The only practical way of preventing this is by an agreement with Holland for an embargo. It has been a rule of British and American diplomacy and may be of priceless value to England that foodstuffs should be given generous treatment. Matter is of great sentimental importance here and at present moment of great practical importance. President is most anxious that this question should not be raised in the form of a change in Declaration. Suggestion therefore is that an arrangement be made with Holland with proviso that unless carried out more severe measures will be taken.

Interest here centres on foodstuffs and cotton. The latter is safe in any case. Generous treatment of the former is most desirable.

Clause 6 is not necessary because an instruction to Courts to use general report as indication of meaning of Declaration would be sufficient and arouses opposition of Senate who did not ratify it.

Some solution is urgently required as soon as possible before agitation has taken shape.

T telegram and Hw telegram (FO 372/601, No. 54116, pp. 92-93; FO 115/1770, pp. 12-13, PRO).


Washington September 28th.

Private. My telegram Treaty No. 66.

President's friend has arranged that the official be converted into unofficial despatch and United States Ambassador be instructed to confer with you privately.[1] I do not know if he has been instructed by telegraph, but it would be well, in any case, to take up matter with him at once and arrange settlement of main points which (sic) would be acceptance of Declaration of London and increase in list of unconditional contraband with Holland as to re-export of grain.

Orders of August 20th as it stands cannot be accepted here and would certainly lead to violent agitation.

T telegram (E. Grey Papers, FO 800 84/2, PRO).
[1] Lansing's note of September 26, 1914, was sent to Page for his information and background in talking with Grey.

## From John Philip White and Others

Dear Sir:                Indianapolis, Ind., September 29th, 1914.

We have learned through press reports and otherwise that the coal operators of Colorado have asked for certain modifications of the basis for a three-year-truce of the mining trouble in Colorado, recently proposed by you.

Our acceptance of your proposal was based upon the assumption that it would likewise be agreed to without change by the coal operators.

There are certain features of the proposition which we too would like to have modified or changed. We did not ask for this because we felt that the occasion required full compliance with your very earnest wish. Our position now remains the same as when we forwarded to you our letter of acceptance. We are willing to abide by the proposed basis of adjustment submitted by you.

If however, there are to be any modifications of any sections of the proposed basis in order to meet the requirements of the coal operators of Colorado, then we too ask the privilege of requesting a change in certain sections thereof. We ask in the event of any change that we be given the opportunity of presenting our objections to certain features contained therein with a view to having them changed or eliminated altogether.

We repeat our acceptance of your proposed basis of settlement without change, providing only that the same will be agreed to by the coal operators of Colorado in like manner.

Very sincerely yours,<br>
John P White    President,<br>
Frank. J. Hays    Vice-President,<br>
Wm. Green.    Secretary-Treasurer.

TLS (WP, DLC).

## Walter Hines Page to the Secretary of State

London, Sept. 29, 1914.

758 CONFIDENTIAL. I promptly took up your number 218, September 28 with Sir Edward Grey. He expresses the most earnest wish to avoid every action that will give offense to our Government or cause public criticism in the United States. But he pointed out first that the Declaration of London was never ratified by the British Government and secondly that the modifications of the Declaration of London which are criticised were promulgated

before his communication to me transmitted to you in my number 483 of the twenty-sixth August. The British purpose he went on to say was to prevent the enemy from receiving food and materials for military use and nothing more. I explained that the people of the United States had a trade with Holland apart from supplies and materials meant for Germany and that our Government could not be expected to see that sacrificed or interfered with. In addition to the intrinsic merits of the case I reminded him of the grave danger of American public criticism which I was sure he did not wish to provoke.

He proposed a discussion of the whole matter with a view to arriving at a satisfactory understanding. This discussion begins tomorrow between him and his attorney general on one side and Anderson and me on our side.

American Ambassador, London.

T telegram (WP, DLC).

## Sir Cecil Arthur Spring Rice to Sir Edward Grey

Private.                                    [Washington, Sept. 29, 1914]
Your private Telegram of Sept. 29th.[1]
President drafted telegram himself last night having refused to approve draft prepared by State Department. Press has been quieted for the present. I will give him your message. I strongly urged unfairness of raising question after this long silence without a word of warning and he understands. Secretary of State who has returned did not mention subject although question was raised in Senate today. Meanwhile Netherlands Minister[2] has officially informed me of embargo on export of foodstuffs from the Netherlands.

Hw telegram (E. Grey Papers, FO 800 84/2, PRO).
    [1] E. Grey to C. Spring Rice, Sept. 29, 1914, Hw telegram (E. Grey Papers, FO 800 84/2, PRO). Grey's entire telegram is paraphrased in the first four sentences of C. A. Spring Rice to WW, Sept. 30, 1914.
    [2] Chevalier Willem Louis Frederik Christiaan van Rappard.

## From the Diary of Colonel House

[Washington] September 29, 1914.
While in Washington, the President, McAdoo, Burleson, Tumulty and I had a conference regarding the Shipping Bill. We met to decide whether to push it at this session or let it go over. I was strongly in favor of letting it go over, for the reason that the President and the Congress are both exhausted and at the

breaking point. If the President should push this measure, it would take Congress well into November to finish it, and members failing of election, would hold him responsible for their defeat.

It was decided to let Congress adjourn as soon as possible, preferably by the 10th of October or before, and then reconvene them around the middle of November. Burleson and McAdoo are strongly in favor of the Shipping Bill, and so is Lane. Houston is against it. The President has not taken the matter up with the Cabinet for discussion which some of them resent, and I think they are justified in doing so.

The President discussed Mr. Bryan's attitude regarding a second term with me. He had heard nothing further from Mr. Bryan since my conversation with him. I found, however, from Burleson that Mr. Bryan now said he thought the President should and would be re-nominated. Mr. Bryan has not lost any of his objections to a second term, but he sees it is inevitable. The President said, "in the event the second term plank becomes an issue, I will be compelled to fight it, for I am strongly opposed to any limitation. If you could trust the American people in other matters, you could also trust them to choose their own leaders as long as they desired them."

## To William Bauchop Wilson

My dear Mr. Secretary:     The White House September 30, 1914

I learn from friends on the Pacific Coast who are as much interested in the matter as I am that the treatment of Chinese students coming to this country by our immigration officers is almost as unsatisfactory as ever, subjecting them to very serious mortification. I wish very much that it might be ordered that Certificate No. 6 properly filled should entitle them to entrance without further examination on this side of the water. Every item of this sort is of importance, particularly at this time when the feeling between nations is perhaps more important than anything else.

Having conferred with you previously about this matter, I know that I am speaking into a sympathetic ear.

Cordially and sincerely yours, Woodrow Wilson

TLS (received from Mary A. Strohecker).

## Two Letters from William Jennings Bryan

My dear Mr. President:        Washington September 30th, 1914.

The situation in Nicaragua is perilous. I have been trying to get a report on the Nicaragua Treaty but I have found it impossible to secure a quorum and they cannot make a report without a quorum.

I am satisfied that a majority would report favorably on the Treaty if a quorum could be secured but for one reason or another Senators are absent and week after week passes without action.

I therefore ask you to consider the advisability of bringing some pressure to bear upon the Senate. A message would, I think, be effective but you may regard that as an extreme measure. It seems to me that we owe it to Nicaragua to make every possible effort to secure the ratification of this treaty at once. If it goes over the session there is no telling what may happen. Please let me know what you think can be done. I have done all in my power but the Senators seem to be so tired and worn that they will not come together. We could not have secured a favorable report on the other treaties if there had been any objection.

With assurances of high respect I am, My dear Mr. President,
Very sincerely yours,   W. J. Bryan


My dear Mr. President:        Washington September 30th, 1914.

I enclose a memorandum which I have received today from Mr. Phillips regarding the situation in Liberia.[1] I also enclose a resolution that was presented by the Committee whose names are signed.[2]

We have not been able to do much for the colored man in the way of appointments to office, but that makes it the more necessary that we should meet such a condition as this seems to present.

Do you suppose an appropriation for the assistance of the people there would commend itself to congress? Even a small appropriation would, I think, have a good effect.

With assurances of high regard I am, my dear Mr. President,
Very sincerely yours,   W. J. Bryan

TLS (WP, DLC).
[1] Wilson returned the memorandum. It is W. Phillips to WJB, Sept. 30, 1914, TLS (SDR, RG 59, 882.48/12, DNA), calling Bryan's attention to "the need of some policy in regard to the Republic of Liberia, that is, a decision whether this Government will take steps to relieve the destitute condition of the people of that country."
[2] It is missing.

# From William Jennings Bryan, with Enclosure

My Dear Mr President                    [Washington, Sept. 30, 1914]

I enclose memorandum of conversation between Mr Lansing & the British Ambassador. I have gone over his opinion on the British additions to London Declarations and his position seems to me sound & I agree with him that Page & Anderson should have your views as soon as possible so as to avoid any possible misunderstanding. I also enclose Resolution introduced by Burgess.[1] Do you see any objection to it? I do not.  With assurances etc I am

Very truly yours   W. J. Bryan

ALS (WP, DLC).

[1] George Farmer Burgess, Democratic congressman from Texas. The enclosure is missing. However, the resolution (House Concurrent Resolution 48), introduced by Burgess on September 16 and referred to the Committee on Foreign Affairs, called "attention to the necessity for precaution and conscientiousness on the part of citizens and the press concerning neutrality." *Cong. Record*, 63d Cong., 2d sess., p. 15249. No action was taken on it.

E N C L O S U R E

DECLARATION OF LONDON                *Memorandum of conversation*
AND ORDER IN COUNCIL                 *with British Ambassador.*
OF AUGUST 20, 1914.                  September 29, 1914.

In compliance with a telegraphic request from the President I called last night at 9:30 on the British Ambassador after sending a telegraphic instruction to London directing the American Ambassador to take up informally and confidentially with Sir Edward Grey the subject of the Order in Council modifying the Declaration of London and its menace to the friendly feeling of the American people for Great Britain.

I asked the Ambassador if he had seen the editorial in the Washington Post of that morning relative to the Order in Council.[1] He said that he had and that he appreciated the effect of such criticism on public opinion. I then told him of the instruction sent to London and asked him if he wouod [would] not lend his aid to secure the cancellation or modification of the Order in Council, which I was sure would arouse a storm of protest when its provisions were understood and would be successfully used by the enemies of Great Britain in this country.

The Ambassador replied that he certainly would assist in any way that he could, that he fully appreciated the gravity of the situation, and that he had already telegraphed his Government several times in relation to the matter but would do so again immediately in view of the instruction sent to Ambassador Page.

A discussion of the provisions of the Order in Council followed in which, the Ambassador said that he agreed that the Order in Council practically made foodstuffs absolute contraband, which was contrary to the British traditional policy as well as to that of the United States. He said that the immediate cause had been the introduction through Rotterdam in first days of the war of large quantities of food supplies for the German army in Belgium, and that it seemed absolutely necessary to stop this traffic.

I replied that, while I appreciated that such reasons must weigh very heavily with those responsible for the successful conduct of the war, it seemed unfortunate that some other means could not have been found to accomplish the desired purpose, either by getting the Netherlands to place an embargo on foodstuffs and other conditional contraband or by agreeing not to re-export such articles. The Ambassador said that he agreed that would be much the better way, and that he believed it could be done.

He said that now the chief anxiety seemed to be in regard to shipments of copper and petroleum and also of Swedish iron, and that the British Government was stopping vessels with such cargoes and purchasing them. He suggested that possibly the difficulty created by the Order in Council could be removed by rescinding it and adding to the list of absolute contraband petroleum products, copper, barbed wire and other articles of like nature now used almost exclusively for war purposes.

I said that as to this suggestion I could not speak for the Government but that it seemed worthy of consideration as it might offer a means of getting rid of the Order in Council which certainly menaced the very friendly relations existing if it became the subject of discussion by the press. I told him that I did not think that the feeling, which the Order in Council would arouse when generally understood, would be among the shippers as much as among the American public at large; and that, even if no case arose under it, the fact that the British Government had issued a decree, which menaced the commercial rights of the United States as a neutral, in violation of the generally accepted rules of international law, would undoubtedly cause irritation, if not indignation, and might change the sentiment of the American people, of which Great Britain had no reason to complain at the present time.

The Ambassador said that he realized that, and that he would do everything in his power to remove any cause of complaint against his Government for threatened interruption of our commerce with a neutral country, and he appreciated the consideration shown by the President in taking up the matter informally and not lodging a formal protest against the Order in Council. He felt that the Foreign Office must see how expedient it was to change its action, which was entirely contrary to the attitude previously held by the British Government, and had been so frankly stated by Lord Granville in 1885. He hoped that it would turn out in the way we both wanted.

Robert Lansing

T MS (WP, DLC).
    [1] "A New and Dangerous Rule," *Washington Post*, Sept. 28, 1914, discussing the British Order in Council. The *Post* said that the Order in Council in effect gave the British navy authority to capture conditional contraband of war, even if bound to a neutral port. Such a procedure would be "a great blow" to American commerce. "Is England justified," the writer asked, "in making and enforcing such a sweeping order? Can she enforce it against American exports without involving herself in difficulties with the United States?" The United States had a "right" to carry on trade with neutral nations, and it could not afford "to relinquish that right, or permit it to be overridden by any nation under the pretext of military necessity."


## Walter Hines Page to William Jennings Bryan

763. CONFIDENTIAL                    London, September 30, 1914.

At conference today Grey showed me Spring-Rice's cable explaining the suggestion made by the Counselor of the State Department and took that as the basis of discussion. He agrees to two points: First, to make a new list of absolute contraband and Second to prepare a new order in council to replace all the orders which have been issued modifying the Declaration of London. In this new order he will endeavor to meet our wishes so far as that is possible. The new list of contraband and the draft of the new order he will discuss with me as soon as they are ready.

He further stated that the British Government have accepted an assurance from the Netherlands Government that the exportation of food stuffs from Holland will be prevented by the existing embargo against such exportation. This will open the way for American cargoes of food stuffs consigned to Holland to go there without interference and any cargoes of food stuffs now detained by Great Britain if any are now detained will be released. This last seems to me an important concession in our favor. I suggested to Grey that the publication of this fact might have a good effect and he consents for you to give this last fact to the press if you so desire.

This whole subject was discussed at a cabinet meeting this

morning and it was evident at our conference that the Government desire to meet our wishes so far as the most relentless war ever waged will permit them.

American Ambassador, London.

T telegram (WP, DLC).

## From Frank J. Hayes

Dear Mr. President:    Denver, Colo., Sept. 30, 1914.

Since our acceptance of your proposal to settle the Colorado coal strike the coal operators of this state have seen fit to issue misleading statements concerning the justice of our claims.

We have no desire to reply publicly to the operators letters, feeling that such action on our part might widen the breach between us, but it might not be amiss for us to inform you that they have endeavored to deceive you in regard to this strike.

To begin, permit me to say that their figures on production are not correct and that said figures have been padded in order to make a showing. For verification of my claim in this respect I would most respectfully refer you to the Chief Inspector of Mines of the state of Colorado.

I also wish to call your attention to the fact that there are approximately 20,000 men, women and children on strike; that we have had but very few desertions from our ranks since the strike began. We are paying the same amount of relief today ($37,-500.00 per week) that we paid to the strikers at the beginning of the struggle more than one year ago. For proof of this statement we will submit to you, if desired, our weekly relief list showing the names and number of people on strike; also cancelled checks from our International office. The strikers are residents of Colorado, and have worked in the mines of this state for a number of years.

It is true that the operators have imported a number of men into the coal fields from other states in violation of the labor laws of Colorado. These imported, inexperienced men, with very few exceptions, are neither a credit to the state nor to the operators, and are recruited largely from the slums of the large cities.

In regard to the criminal charges they have preferred against us, suffice it to say that since the strike began the hired gunmen of the coal companies have killed thirty-five of our people, a large number of them being women and children. For years the gunmen of the operators have ruled in Southern Colorado, and the state government has been unwilling or powerless to give the mine workers any protection.

Five of the demands of the strikers are based upon the laws of the state. If these laws had been enforced I feel confident that there would not have been a strike in the coal mines of Colorado. It is the only time in the history of coal mining in this country when the mine workers were forced to strike in order to secure law enforcement. As every student of this situation knows, this is not only a strike to secure a measure of industrial freedom but it is also a struggle to secure constitutional government for all the citizens in the Colorado coal fields.

More than one thousand men have been killed in Colorado's coal mines during the past decade, and, so far as I can learn, the courts in Colorado have not returned a single verdict against the coal companies for the slaughter of these miners. In all of the suits to recover damages the coal companies "fixed" the jury and controlled the trial judge. Hundreds of lives could have been saved if the laws of the state had been enforced.

Since the last great strike, which occurred in 1903, thousands of miners have been discharged for demanding rights given to them by the laws of this state and for expressing a desire to belong to the union of their craft.

The United Mine Workers of America did not seek this strike, and, personally, I did everything I could to prevent it. We tried for several months to secure a joint conference with the operators, hoping to adjust the grievances of the miners in the council hall of reason rather than on the industrial battlefield. The operators refused to hear the grievances of the miners and discharged a large number of men who were voicing their complaints. The Colorado mine workers, themselves, in convention assembled, when all peaceful efforts to secure justice had failed, declared this strike.

As proof of the justice of our claims permit me to say that the citizens of Colorado, almost to a man, have been with us in our struggle since it began and have expressed their sympathy and tendered their support on innumerable occasions.

There is a great deal more I could say concerning this unfortunate controversy, but I know that you are a busy man and I do not want to take up and [any] more of your time.

In conclusion, permit me to say that the miners of Colorado have every confidence in you and deeply appreciate the fair position you have taken in this industrial conflict, and while your proposal does not give us all we desire, inasmuch as we forfeit recognition of the union and an advance in wages, which thirty-four small independent companies have granted us since the strike began, we felt, in view of the long duration of this strike and the loss of life incident thereto, that it should be the patriotic duty of both sides to promptly accept your peace proposal and to work together for the common weal.

The position of the operators is indefensible and we sincerely trust that you will not permit them to delay action on your proposal for months to come, which now seems to be their accepted plan of procedure.

You will have our fullest co-operation at all times, and we sincerely trust that success will soon crown your efforts.

With assurance of my high personal regard, I am,

Very truly yours,    Frank J. Hayes

TLS (WP, DLC).

## William Phillips to Joseph Patrick Tumulty

Dear Mr. Tumulty:                      Washington. September 30, 1914.

I have received a letter from President Lowell of Harvard University quoting an extract from a letter which he has just received from Mr. Graham Wallas whom I feel sure the President knows all about. President Lowell asks me to send Mr. Wallas's suggestion to the President. It is as follows:

"We are all hoping that President Wilson will be patient and persistent in attempting mediation. The tangle of interests and passions is so great that negotiations can hardly be started except by a disinterested outside power. Do you think that President Wilson will be willing to strengthen his own hands by sending over a few personal representatives who know Europe and are known there, to be connected, more or less loosely, with the Embassies? They could at least make a beginning of collecting materials for future mediation. * * *

"Good-bye—remember that our hope for the return of sanity and order into the world depends mostly on the United States."

Sincerely yours,    William Phillips.

TLS (WP, DLC).

## From the Diary of Colonel House

[Washington] September 30, 1914.

The President and I had a final confidential talk after breakfast. It was arranged either for him to come to New York to see me or I am to return here to see him. . . .

The President told me while I was in Washington that almost

at the beginning of hostilities, he had received a letter from President Eliot of Harvard urging that the United States declare war against Germany.[1] The President was so impressed with it that he brought the letter to the attention of the Cabinet, although without any idea of acting upon it favorably. He looked for the letter to show me, but was unable to lay his hand on it while we were talking.

When we were discussing the seizure of vessels by Great Britain, he read a page from his History of the American People, telling how during Madison's Administration, the War of 1812 was started in exactly the same way as this controversy is opening up. The passage said that Madison was compelled to go to war despite the fact that he was a peace-loving man, and desired to do everything in his power to prevent it, but popular feeling made it impossible.

The President said: "Madison and I are the only two Princeton men that have become President. The circumstances of the war of 1812 and now run parallel. I sincerely hope they will not go further."

I told the British Ambassador about this conversation. He was greatly impressed, and said that in his cablegram to Sir Edward Grey he would call attention not only to the passage in the President's book, but to his comment to me upon it.

[1] C. W. Eliot to WW, Aug. 6, 1914, Vol. 30.

## From Sir Cecil Arthur Spring Rice, with Enclosure

*Personal*

Dear Mr President               Washington. September 30 1914

Sir Edward Grey begs me to assure you that he very much appreciates the way in which you have raised the question of the Order in Council and that he will do all in his power to meet your views.

He must consult the Cabinet and he hopes to be able to come to an arrangement through Mr Page with as little delay as possible. Had our government been warned sooner the question would have been discussed at an earlier stage. The very strong line taken by the State Department about the declaration of London and the Order in Council (which was dated August 20), suddenly and without warning after so long an interval, has come as a complete surprise. All I knew about it personally was that some objection would be taken to the British attitude but I was not told what the nature of the objection was. Nor I presume was Mr Page informed or he would certainly have spoken to Sir Edward.

I hear to day from Grey that he has had a long talk with Mr Page with whom as you know he has very pleasant and cordial relations and whom, if I may say so, he trusts entirely.

I enclose a short account of this interview as described to me by Grey. The allusion to the attitude of the two Governments in former years is to the well known cases which came before the Supreme Court of the United States of British blockade runners who made Nassau their head quarters.

I bear in mind Mr Madison.            Cecil Spring Rice.

I am making an arrangement with the Netherlands Minister for reassuring Chicago exporters. The Netherlands Government has placed an embargo on the export of certain articles to Germany, and takes the responsibility of purchasing on itself. He will inform me of this officially and I will inform our Consuls.

TLS (WP, DLC).


ENCLOSURE

Telegram from Sir E Grey                September 29 1914

I have just had a conversation with the United States Ambassador. I explained to him that the Declaration of London had not been ratified owing to the strong opposition which had developed in Parliament. Our position towards the treaty was therefore the same as that of the United States towards a treaty which the Senate had refused to consent to. The main point was the doctrine of Continuous voyage. This doctrine had been upheld in the United States Courts and it must remain as a part of the accepted doctrine of international law until abrogated by an agreement between the governments. The doctrine enunciated in the Order in Council of August 20 had been applied in previous wars and should be judged in the light of the rules of international law hitherto accepted and inforced.

With regard to the statement that all the powers had acted on the declaration of London Germany had treated pit props as contraband although consigned to private firms.

The objects aimed at in the proclamations had been to restrict the supplies for the German Army and also to restrict the supply to Germany of such materials as could be used in manufacturing war munitions.

We feel it essential to have a working agreement with the

United States Government in this matter although we cannot at once withdraw the Order in Council for reasons which will be obvious. But it can be stated at once that the United States has raised the question of the interference with neutral trade under the orders in Council and that the British Government has agreed to discuss these rules without delay. This discussion will in fact begin tomorrow with Mr Page and Mr Chandler Anderson.

It is most important to bear in mind that up to date the British Government has not confiscated a single cargo. Certain cargoes have been diverted but payment in full has been made and the exporter has suffered no loss. Pending an agreement and a change in the proclamations we will at once examine any case about which there is a complaint.

I cited the instance of a cargo of copper consigned direct to Krupp and the news that Krupp was making large orders of copper for the manufacture of projectiles. The Ambassador said that there was no desire to protect people who deliberately and directly traded with Germany to supply the government with war supplies but there was a strong feeling in favour of feee [free] trade with Holland. [1]

T MS (WP, DLC).
    [1] This copy was a paraphrase of E. Grey to C. A. Spring Rice, Sept. 29, 1914 (FO 372/601, No. 54705, pp. 98-99, PRO). Any significant differences between the texts of telegrams received by Spring Rice and the copies that he sent to Wilson will be noted.


## Remarks at a Press Conference

October 1, 1914

Mr. President, can you tell us anything about your hope for an adjournment of Congress or a recess?
    That is a subject upon which I have so often discoursed that I know nothing new to say. I think the leaders on the hill hope for an adjournment by the tenth of the month.
An adjournment or a recess?
    An adjournment.
Mr. President, have the circumstances changed your opinion as to the urgency of the ship purchasing bill?
    No, but I have assurances that that will be very promptly taken up.
Promptly taken up at the next session or this?
    At the next session.
You think, then, that when they do adjourn they will adjourn until December—or November 15th?
    Well, as I understand it, they will adjourn and then it will be

left for our counsel together when the next session should occur.

That is as to whether there will be an extra session?

Whether Congress should convene earlier than December or not. . . .

What is the last word from Mexico, Mr. President?

I have no information that I think you have not already. Apparently the prospects for an accommodation there are good.

Mr. President, have you any comment to make on the New York election at the primaries?

No, sir.

If there should be an adjournment on or about October tenth, do you still stand by your declaration in the Doremus letter[1] that you will not enter into any of the campaigns personally?

Oh, yes. What is keeping me here is not only, perhaps not chiefly, the business of Congress, but the whole situation of the world.

Even if Congress should adjourn, do you intend to remain here?

Yes.

Mr. President, with regard to those protests from the Catholics regarding the situation in Mexico,[2] have you taken any action on that?

There isn't any action to take. We have been doing everything that it was possible to do in that matter, and I am afraid that there isn't anything at present that can be done beyond what we have already attempted. Mr. Tumulty tells me that Mr. Bryan has taken it up.

Mr. President, about the Colorado situation, are you still working along the lines of that tentative basis of settlement, or is there something new?

I am working along those lines still.

Do you expect to see the Secretary of Labor about that situation soon?

As soon as he comes back. He is in Pennsylvania now.

Mr. President, do you contemplate doing anything soon about the withdrawing of federal troops?

Well, all that is part of the problem I am trying to solve. I am trying to bring about a settlement which will make the presence of the troops unnecessary. . . .

Can you say anything, Mr. President, as to just how far that discussion has gone between the State Department and Ambassador Spring Rice?

It hasn't gone as far as the newspapers report. As a matter of fact, I think it can be summed up in this way—that the

British government is most friendly in its attitude and most willing to discuss anything to which this government enters an objection, and I have no doubt that a satisfactory arrangement can be arrived at.

Have we had any communication, Mr. President, with the Holland government with reference to this issue?

None whatever. I am informed—I mean through the newspapers, not officially—that the government of Holland laid an embargo on certain shipments itself.

That is, across its frontier?

Across its frontier, yes.

The contention of Great Britain, as I understood it, was that anything sent to Holland would find its way across the frontier. That was its original objection.

I can't answer that specifically. I would say, just among ourselves here, for your information, that, as I understand it, they are not trying to interfere with trade that is as a matter of fact neutral, but that they are anxious to prevent such shipments through Holland as are in fact non-neutral. That is what it comes to. Of course, it is very difficult to state a rule that will cover that without the rule working as if it were a general interference with neutral trade. I think that is the difficulty they are trying to work out.

T MS (C. L. Swem Coll., NjP).
1 WW to F. E. Doremus, Sept. 4, 1914, Vol. 30.
2 About this matter, see Link, *Struggle for Neutrality*, p. 468.

# William Jennings Bryan to Walter Hines Page

Washington, October 1, 1914.

Your 758, September 29, 7 p.m.

*Confidential.* The Department's instruction of September twenty-sixth in re the Declaration of London and Order in Council, which has been mailed to you, you will not present to Sir Edward Grey until you are specifically instructed to do so by telegraph. You should use the instruction, however, for your own information in the informal discussions in which you are engaged as it defines the position of this Government as to the acceptance of the Declaration of London as a code of naval warfare for this war and states the objections of this Government to the Order in Council and the reasons for this Government's refusal to agree to any material modification of the Declaration, of which reasons not the least is the view which the German and Austrian Governments would undoubtedly hold of an acceptance of modifications of the Declaration which would be of special advantage to their enemies. Paragraph.

The press of this country are beginning to discuss the question and will undoubtedly do so more and more as complaints are being made of seizures of cargoes destined to Netherlands ports.

Bryan

T telegram (SDR, RG 59, 763.72112/360, DNA).

## Three Letters to William Jennings Bryan

My dear Mr. Secretary:          The White House October 1, 1914

I am returning herewith Mr. Phillips' memorandum concerning the situation in Liberia. I return it with an aching heart because it seems almost intolerable to turn away from these suffering people without giving them the sligh[t]est assistance, and yet I verily believe that it would be useless and only irritating to attempt to get an appropriation for them at this time. We would have neither the Houses nor public opinion back of us, because there is not time to make the whole necessity evident.

Cordially and faithfully yours,   Woodrow Wilson

My dear Mr. Secretary:          The White House October 1, 1914

I have your note about Nicaragua and have just written to Senator Stone to use what influence he can to obtain a quorum and a report. I am distressed that we should have failed in the matter.

In haste

Cordially and faithfully yours,   Woodrow Wilson

TLS (W. J. Bryan Papers, DNA).

My dear Mr. Secretary:          The White House October 1, 1914.

Thank you for having let me see the enclosed memorandum of the conversation between Mr. Lansing and the British Ambassador.          Faithfuly yours,   Woodrow Wilson

TLS (SDR, RG 59, 763.72112/12938½, DNA).

## To William Joel Stone

My dear Senator:              [The White House] October 1, 1914

The Secretary of State and I are agreed that the situation in Nicaragua is really perilous. If the Nicaragua Treaty is not reported out, there may be very serious complications there which we shall have to handle and another burden would be added to those which we are carrying. I venture, therefore, to write this note to ascertain if it will be possible within the next few days to get a quorum of the committee to act on that treaty. I would not trouble you in the matter if it were not so clear to me that it is my bounden duty to do so.[1]

Cordially and faithfully yours,   Woodrow Wilson

TLS (Letterpress Books, WP, DLC).
[1] Stone did not succeed in getting a report on the treaty at this time.


## To Sir Cecil Arthur Spring Rice

My dear Mr. Ambassador,    The White House 1 October, 1914.

I am greatly obliged to you for your kind note of yesterday and for the copy you enclosed of the despatch from Sir Edward Grey concerning the Orders in Council. It is a source of real comfort and reassurance to me that this serious matter is in the hands of real friends, on both sides. It is evident that the newspapers are going to make a solution of the difficulty as embarrassing as possible, and they will be encouraged to do so from many iyfluential quarters; but that need not daunt us, for we mean to do the right and wise thing.

With sincere regard,

Cordially Yours,   Woodrow Wilson

WWTLS (FO 115/1770, p. 27, PRO).


## From Sir Cecil Arthur Spring Rice, with Enclosure

Dear Mr President              Washington. October 1 1914

I have at once informed Sir E Grey of the terms of your letter in which I know he will most cordially agree. I enclose a telegram which I received last night.

With profound respect I have the honour to be

Your most obedient humble servant   Cecil Spring Rice

ALS (WP, DLC).

ENCLOSURE

Telegram from Sir E. Grey to Sir Cecil Spring Rice.

[London] 30 September 1914.

I have proposed to United States Ambassador that we should draw up a new proclamation of contraband to supercede previous ones in this respect: we should not mention Declaration of London as we do not think an unratified document to which great exception was taken in Parliament here should be constituted a new doctrine of international law.

But the proclamation would be on lines of suggestions conveyed in your telegram of September 28[1] and when the draft is ready we will communicate it to the United States Ambassador and discuss its provisions if necessary before finally settling it.

Meanwhile relying on embargo of Netherlands Government on export of foodstuffs any foodstuffs consigned to Holland and at present detained will be released and neutral ships will not be detained on ground of containing foodstuffs.

There remain certain cargoes of copper and petroleum, former I believe consigned direct to Germany and to Krupps which we are detaining.

Ambassador asked that to calm public opinion something should be made known by United States Governmand and I agreed to its being stated that it is understood that British Government intend to revise their proclamation with regard to contraband and meanwhile in neutral ships goods such as foodstuffs consigned to Holland in respect of which the Netherlands Government have placed an embargo on exportation will not be treated as contraband.[2]

TC telegram (WP, DLC).
[1] That is, Spring Rice's Treaty 66, printed at Sept. 28, 1914.
[2] This telegram was sent as E. Grey to C. A. Spring Rice, Sept. 30, 1914, T telegram (FO 115/1770, p. 25, PRO).

## From James Kerney

My dear Mr. President:   Trenton, New Jersey October 1st, 1914

I spent yesterday with some Democratic friends in New York and am convinced that their desire is to make the fight along lines that will harmonize with the high character of the National Administration. Any suggestion that may be made will be respected and it is desirable that such aid as is possible should be given in the fight.

There is just one disquieting element and that is the declaration of Stuart Gibboney (professing to be an Administration mouthpiece) that Hennessey is to make an independent run, ostensibly with Federal backing.[1] There is already an abundance of unnecessary bitterness to be ironed out; and some of the methods employed for Hennessey in the primary are apt to come up to plague us at critical times in other places. Particularly in the up-state districts tactics were resorted to that have no place in decent American politics, and the unfortunate part of it is going to be that we may have difficulty in proving that they were not countenanced by some of our friends. But that's a bridge we can cross when we come to it.

Just at this juncture, inasmuch as the New York Democrats have overwhelmingly selected men of good repute and ability, nothing should be done by pretended friends to jeopardize success, especially when men of other parties are ready to support the Administration as a matter of patriotic duty. It is unfair to burden you with this sort of thing, but a lot of these reformers don't appear to be very good sports.

Yours very sincerely,   James Kerney

TLS (WP, DLC).

[1]John A. Hennessy was soundly defeated by Martin H. Glynn for the Democratic nomination for governor in the primary election held on September 28. As it turned out, Hennessy did not run as an independent candidate, but he did support the Republican nominee, Charles Seymour Whitman.

## Sir Cecil Arthur Spring Rice to Sir Edward Grey

Dear Sir Edward                    Washington. October 1 1914

Your interposition in the matter of the declaration of London has been most fortunate. I had suspected for some time that something was up among the lawyers in the State Department especially one of them. But I could extract no hint of what was intended. The only indication was a rather unfriendly atmosphere. I received one day a sudden massage from a friend of yours here who said he wished to see me. He then told me that he happened to be sitting with the President when a large package was brought in from the State Department. The President was very tired and did not want to look at it. He was told it was to go off by mail the next morning. He read it and to his astonishment it was a sort of ultimatum couched in not too friendly terms,—the sort of document which would really have convulsed the world if it had got out as it certainly would if it had been despatched. The two men were astonished the more so as the

Secretary of State had been away for some time, tired with his exertions in procuring peace treaties, and was at that moment at a distant watering palce [place] with his wife. The President said that the document although signed could not go at once. I saw it and was really astonished at the tone in one or twwo of the sentences. I merely remarked that if it went off as it was there would be a big catastrophe equal or worse than that brought on by Cleveland's Venezuela despatch. It was arranged that instead of the despatch a telegram should be sent giving the general heads for a friendly discussion. This is now taking place.

The President is very much impressed by the gravity of the question because it touches the pockets and the prejudices of so many of the People. It happens to be just the sort of question which takes the popular fancy and also enlists the monied people as well. He has written a book on the history of the country and in this book there is a passage describing the appearance of a somewhat similar question before the war of 1812 and the unconscious way in which it was handled by Madison who seemed to have no idea to what a point the question would lead the country. He said 'I only hope I shall be wiser.' That night he ordered the man chiefly responsible to come to the Embassy and there we had a talk and drew up a scheme which seemed to offer some good hope of a solution. But I fear we are not out of the wood yet as there will continually arise new aspects of the question and there will be continual attempts to envenom the sore. In fact one very gross one occurred today which I attribute to influences in New York.[1] It is on the whole desirable that the final settlement should take place here as the people here are better able to guage public opinion which might repudiate a settlement arrived at by Americans in London

Yours very sincerely   Cecil Spring Rice

TLS (E. Grey Papers, FO 800/84/2, PRO).
    [1] On October 1, some morning newspapers (e.g., the New York *World*) reported that Spring Rice had informed the State Department on September 30 that his government intended to seize goods classed as conditional contraband of war destined for Germany or Austria, even when such goods were carried in American ships and consigned to neutral ports. That same afternoon, Lansing issued a statement denying that Spring Rice had made any such declaration; however, Lansing admitted that the general subject was under discussion. *New York Times*, Oct. 2, 1914.


## To Florence Stevens Hoyt

My dear Florence,          The White House 2 October, 1914.

Thank you with all my heart for your letter with the reports of conversations with Ellen. The whole thing touched me very deeply,—your thoughtfulness and the sweet flavour of my dear one which the quotations so unmistakably carry. How wonderful she was, in her thought, which went to the heart of things, no less than in the whole loveliness of her nature! Every day, it seems to me, I find something new by which to measure my loss, which is yet truly immeasurable, and yet can be in part understood by those who knew her as we did. How empty everything (everything personal to myself) seems without her. My hardest task is to keep my courage and my vigour and go through with the day's work. Please let me have anything else that comes back to you from time to time.

I hope that the summer refreshed you and that you are well, very well. You must come over and see us whenever you feel free. I expect the family back about the first of next month. Only Helen is here with me now. She had a hard time of it, dear little girl, but seems practically well now.

With love to all,

Affectionately yours, Woodrow Wilson

WWTLS (WP, DLC).

## From Robert Lee Henry

### MEMORANDUM FOR THE PRESIDENT.

*By R. L. Henry and the Committee.*[1]

Washington, D. C. [Oct. 2, 1914]

The Secretary of the Treasury could announce that within one week he will deposit in the national banks throughout the South several hundred million dollars and very largely dispel the gloom overhanging the Southern States on account of the prostrated and paralyzed cotton market. He has this indisputable right under Sec. 5153, Revised Statutes, which gives him plenary powers.

In March, 1913, a terrible storm-flood swept over the Ohio valley. In Mr. McAdoo's annual report of 1913, in the very front page, with apparent exultant pride, he recites: "The banks of that city were afraid to reopen their doors because of the temporary impairment of confidence." He further adds: "The Citizens Relief Committee asked that a representative of the Department be sent right away to see about financing our banking institutions. * * * A national bank examiner was immediately dispatched to Dayton, and within twenty-four hours after his arrival, the Department designated *every national bank in Dayton as a Government depositary*, and announced that it would deposit in said national banks $2,000,000 of *Government funds*, to be secured by State, municipal, or other local bonds acceptable to the Secretary of the Treasury. The effect of this action was to restore confidence *at once*. The banks reopened their doors, and instead of the anticipated need of $2,000,000, the Treasury was called on for only $182,000." If Mr. McAdoo would use this example of depositing millions in a small locality like Dayton and spread out public funds in the same proportion over the entire South, he could promptly save our people from the impending disaster now upon them. A simple announcement of his intention would preserve his native land from bankruptcy. He has unquestioned authority to say to every national bank in the South: "Take cotton as security at 8 cents per pound, require the farmer's note running for 12 months, bearing three per cent interest. Do this as the fiscal agent of the Government under Sec. 5153, Revised Statutes. The Government will at once place in your hands the public funds to finance these transactions." Thus, as he saved Dayton, Ohio, last year, he can rescue thirty millions of people in the South.

He can deposit the money, make terms with every national bank in the South as trustees, persuade them as fiscal agents to gather in warehouse receipts on cotton and utilize those receipts as security for the loan of Government funds at a very low rate of interest, as he did when he scattered his crop funds throughout the States in 1913. He justly glories in that on page 2 of his report and is proud that he *stretched the precedents*. He says: "The Secretary announced that as security for such deposits, '*high class commercial paper*' would be accepted at 65 per cent of its face value, etc." He adds: "This was an *unprecedented step*, because *commercial paper* had never before been accepted as security for Government deposits." And, "The moment it became known that the Government stood ready to assist, the tension was relieved, business resumed a normal aspect, and the fall movement of crops, trade and commerce proceeded upon an easier and safer basis [than] for many years past."

Let the Secretary shift the Government deposits, now about $74,000,000, to the South, sell two hundred millions of Panama Canal bonds to those getting up gold pools for Europe and on New York City loans and utilize our cotton as security for the Government loans, as he did "*commercial paper*" last year, and in one short week he can rescue the South from ruin and a wild orgy of bankruptcies soon to ensue.

If Mr. McAdoo needs a little more legal authority to do this, he can win the President in an instant to help him, and the message of both to Congress can strengthen and free their hands in an hour to do just as they please to find a way to save a billion dollar cotton crop. Aye, if they wish it, and will say the word, we can instantly add to those Government deposits and the proceeds from the Panama Canal bonds combined two hundred million dollars more *by the issuance of United States notes.*

It is with them. Congress can provide the additional funds when they say go forward, and we can authorize them in a few brief words to use our cotton this year as security instead of "bonds" and "commercial paper," as done last year, and the glorious deed is done. Will the Secretary rise to the occasion? He can. R. L. Henry

TS MS (WP, DLC).
[1] The executive appointment diary for October 2, 1914, says only: "11.30 to 12.30 Rep. Henry & Committee." However, this "committee" probably included some if not all of the members of the committee from the cotton and tobacco states formally organized in the House caucus room in the Capitol on October 7, about which see Link, *Struggle for Neutrality*, p. 96.

## From Louis de Sadeleer

Excellency, New York, Oct. 2nd 1914.

My Colleagues of the Royal Commission sailed for Europe last Wednesday. At the request of my many American friends my colleag[u]es have begged me to remain a few days longer in New York.

I have sent two private letters to the Honorable Secretary of State, Mr. Bryan, but the newspapers have announced that he is absent from Washington, and I therefore do not know if my messages have reached him.

Their object is of the most urgent nature, and for this reason I am taking the most respectful liberty of sending your Excellency a copy of them.[1]

I have the profound conviction that one word from the much respected and beloved President of the United States of America, spoken in the name of civilization and humanity, shall prevent new crimes from being committed by the soldiers of the German Army, and shall spare the lives of thousands of innocent people.

I am equally certain that your humane intervention, according to everything I have learned during my stay, will be applauded by all the citizens of your powerful country.

These barbaric acts which are putting civilization back many centuries, and are recalling the time of Attila, have provoked universal reprobation.

This is an unofficial message to you, fulfilling only what I consider as a duty of my conscience, dictated by the profound respect of the principles of justice which I have defended and honored all my life, and prompted by the desire to see observed the rules admitted by all international law imprinted in the hearts of humanity.

The most sympathetic and cordial reception that Your Excellency extended to the Special Mission of the King of the Belgians, and for which the Belgian Nation is most grateful, encourages me to take this initiative.

I beg Your Excellency to accept the renewed homage of my most respectful feelings and the expression of my highest consideration.

L. de Sadeleer    Minister of State of Belgium

TLS (WP, DLC).
    [1] L. de Sadeleer to WJB, Sept. 28, 1914, TCL (WP, DLC); L. de Sadeleer to WJB, Oct. 2, 1914, TCL (WP, DLC). Both letters argued that the United States Government, and especially President Wilson, should speak out against the alleged crimes and destructive acts of the German armed forces in Belgium.


## From the Diary of Colonel House

October 2, 1914.

Cleveland Dodge came by appointment early this morning. I wished to discuss with him the State Chairmanship, in reference to his brother-in-law, William Church Osborn. I also showed him Walter Pager's [Page's] recent letter giving a statement of his income and outgo for the past year, and asked him for a check in compliance with his understanding with the President. It was agreed that he should give me a check for $10,000. to start with made payable to Arthur W. Page, and that Arthur was to send London exchange to his father without any explanation as to where it came from.

Dudley Malone telephoned in reference to the State Democratic Ticket. He is to see me later in the day.

The other day in Washington when talking about the Clayton Bill and of Senator Reed's attack upon it, the President said that "Senator Reed is the most comprehensively ignorant man I have ever met," and added, "Culberson has made the bill so weak you cannot tell it from water."


## To William Cox Redfield

My dear Mr. Secretary:        [The White House] October 3, 1914

Thank you for your note about what it will be possible to do to call attention to the opportunity for trade with Spain.[1]

I notice that you presided yesterday over a meeting which discussed the shipping interests. I hope that you were able to guide them away from antagonism to the plans of the administration. I noted how the conference was made up and how the intrenched shipping interests predominated and it must have been a hard task if you were able to accomplish it.

I regard the shipping bill as of capital consequence to the administration and I hope that you were able to do something to determine their point of view.

Cordially and sincerely yours,   Woodrow Wilson

TLS (Letterpress Books, WP, DLC).
¹ W. C. Redfield to WW, Oct. 2, 1914, TLS (WP, DLC).


## To James Kerney

Personal and Private.

My dear Kerney:          [The White House] October 3, 1914

Thank you very warmly for your letter about the situation in New York. It is a great comfort to have an absolutely trustworthy friend who can guide us in this matter.

I note what you say about Stuart Gibboney and shall certainly see what I can do about it.

In haste, with warmest regard,

Faithfully yours, Woodrow Wilson

TLS (Letterpress Books, WP, DLC).


## To William Gibbs McAdoo

My dear Mac:          The White House October 3, 1914

Will you please note what is said in the second paragraph of this letter? I hear the same sort of thing from so many quarters that I am forced to believe that Gibboney is acting unwisely. It would be a very serious mistake for Hennessey to run after the primaries had turned so decisively against him and it would be the gravest sort of mistake for anyone professing to be our friend to support such a purpose.

Don't trouble to dictate an answer to this letter. We will speak of it when I see you next.

Affectionately yours,   Woodrow Wilson

TLS (W. G. McAdoo Papers, DLC).

## From William Cox Redfield

My dear Mr. President:        Washington October 3, 1914.
    Your favor of the 3d is received.

I regret that you have been misinformed. I presided yesterday over no meeting whatever of any kind, nor was the shipping interest the subject of the conference at which I was present for a short time. I did not attend the afternoon session and do not know what went on.

The subject of shipping came up incidentally for a very brief time, and so far as it went I agreed with what was said. I must frankly confess that I do not understand the purpose of the shipping bill. It did not come before me in its inception and a careful reading of the statements of the Secretary of the Treasury before the congressional committee does not enlighten me. I see points of view from which the action is desirable and of course am in no sense opposed, certainly not publicly. There are doubtless reasons other than those stated in the committee hearing which have led to the legislation. I assume them to be good without question, but I do not know what they are and shall be glad to be informed. Certain it is, however, that there is no present or seemingly no immediate future need for additional ships to go to South America, for those there are have not sufficient cargoes nor near prospect of any, and I had supposed, perhaps mistakenly for I do not assume to know the facts, that this was one of the purposes of the measure. I shall be glad to be advised at your convenience in the matter.

                    Yours very truly,    William C. Redfield

TLS (WP, DLC).


## To Frank J. Hayes

My dear Mr. Hayes:        [The White House] October 5, 1914
    I am sincerely obliged to you for your letter of September thirtieth. As a matter of fact, I have been paying very little attention to charges and counter-charges. I have been earnestly trying to ascertain for myself from disinterested quarters just what the facts were and, therefore, have felt that I was justified in pressing for the settlement suggested.

I believe I have already expressed my gratification that the mine workers should have accepted the suggestion. At present there seems to be a very considerable reluctance on the part of the mine operators to take the same action, but I am still hoping that they will see that it is right that they should do so.

Cordially and sincerely yours, Woodrow Wilson

TLS (Letterpress Books, WP, DLC).

## From Sir Cecil Arthur Spring Rice, with Enclosure

*Personal*

Dear Mr. President, Washington. October 5th 1914.

I telegraphed to Grey after receiving a visit from Lansing making certain suggestions with which you are familiar. I venture to enclose the telegram which I have received in reply. I trust that a satisfactory solution will now be found and I can only say that if this is the case it will be greatly due to the considerate attitude of this Government and especially, if I may say so, of yourself.

I fear that many difficulties may still be in store for us. The misery caused by the war is not confined only to belligerents. Neutrals too have their share. But I am sure that the American people will not forget that in 1861 and 1862 the whole labouring population of Lancashire was thrown out of work, but because they believed the struggle here to be one for liberty and justice, the very men on whom starvation fell were most steadfast in repudiating the demand that the British Government should intervene.

I have the honour to be with profound respect,
Your most obedient humble servant Cecil Spring Rice

TLS (WP, DLC).

### E N C L O S U R E

Telegram from Sir Edward Grey, Dated October 4, 1914.

I have informed United States Ambassador that we are drawing up a new Proclamation to repeal all previous provisions with regard to contraband. It will provide:

1. An enlarged list of absolute contraband. Foodstuffs will not be in this list but we want to put in petroleum, nickel, possibly copper, rubber and other things used mainly or exclusively in Germany for war and materials of war.

2. A list of conditional contraband with a statement that ar-

ticles in this list will not be interfered with when consigned to a neutral firm at a neutral port—in other words the doctrine of continuous voyage will not be applied.

3. A statement that where we have reason to believe a neutral country or port is being used as a base of supplies for the enemy's army or Government or for providing the enemy with materials for war, we shall endeavour to negotiate an arrangement with the neutral Government and if that is found impossible we reserve the right to take more effective steps with regard to conditional contraband.

I hope to give a draft copy of the proclamation to the United States Ambassador early next week.[1]

T MS (WP, DLC).
    [1] This was sent from London as E. Grey to C. A. Spring Rice, Oct. 4, 1914, Hw telegram (FO 372/601, No. 5553, p. 157, PRO).

## From Josephus Daniels, with Enclosure

Dear Mr. President:                    Washington. Oct. 6, 1914.

The conditions in the South have not been—they cannot be—exaggerated. I was in Raleigh on Saturday and had a talk with Mr. Poe, editor of the Progressive Farmer. It has a subscription list of 200,000. At my request Mr. Poe has written his views upon suggested remedies. I hope you can read it, though it is rather long.              Sincerely,   Josephus Daniels

ALS (WP, DLC).

### E N C L O S U R E

## Clarence Poe to Josephus Daniels

*Personal*

My dear Mr. Daniels:            Raleigh, N. C., Oct. 5, 1914.

Agreeable to our conversation Saturday, I write to set down the facts as to the cotton situation as I see them.

*Conditions*: Simply because of international complications over which we had no control, the South finds practically half the value of its greatest money-crop confiscated by war. Our people worked, planned and made the crop on the basis of fourteen cent prices. Instead of that we have seven cent prices. I don't need to tell you what this means to our poorer people, tenants and small farmers, and it is hitting the well-to-do almost as hard. Mrs. Aycock,[1] for example, told me night before last that her brother Lee,[2] whom you know, may have to sell his fine plantation, simply because of inability to collect from the people to whom he has sold goods—and of course a plantation might not bring much over half its value if forced on the market now.

*The Remedy*: But you know conditions. What you are concerned about is a remedy. I repeat that I do not believe our Southern farmers expect their Southern Congressmen to do the impossible. The vast majority will be content if provision is made so that they can carry the crop until conditions become normal again. Warehouse charges are high and if to these charges a high rate of interest must be added, the vast majority of cotton growers will insist on selling anyhow and by thus forcing a market already glutted to purchase several million more bales, there is no telling where prices may stop.

You know I am not radical. I do feel, however, that the Administration ought to furnish money so that farmers can borrow at reasonable rates enough to carry the crop, and that it is practically under pledge to do so.

*What Administration Leaders Have Said*: At the Southern Cotton Congress in August when I saw you, Senator Hoke Smith assured us that within thirty days $300,000,000 of emergency currency would be available for financing cotton—and we all felt satisfied. More than this, at the Cotton Conference called by him, Secretary McAdoo said:

> "I am convinced that there is *adequate power under existing law to issue through the National banks all the currency to meet any reasonable demand that may develop*, in any part of the country, and that it is not necessary to extend the note-issuing privilege to State banks. The Secretary of the Treasury already has the power to issue one billion dollars of additional National bank currency if it should be required, but I cannot imagine a condition when any such need will arise."

And again:

> "State banks are actually depositing their securities with the National banks, and the National banks are getting the issue against those securities and turning it over to the State banks. It is perfectly simple to get it. There is no difficulty about that."

Mr. McAdoo also declared that the money must be used *"for harvesting and carrying the crop until a reasonable market can be found* and for the needs of legitimate business."

All this was taken by the South to mean that the Administration would at least recognize the seriousness of the cotton crisis to the extent of furnishing money so that the farmers could carry the crop—and I am sure this is what Mr. McAdoo intended.

*But What Are the Facts?*: But the facts are that we have not been able to get from the banks the help indicated by the foregoing utterances. In fact, as he returned from the Washington meeting, where he heard Mr. McAdoo make the aforementioned statements, a leading North Carolina banker said to me: "I see mighty little help for the farmer in anything that has been adopted. Many of our banks owe New York larger amounts than we are getting in emergency currency, and we have got to take this currency and pay off these debts. We must save ourselves before we can save anybody else."

The State banks, furthermore, report that they can't get additional currency from their National banking correspondents. Even the offer to issue emergency currency to 75 per cent of the value of warehouse receipts was illusive. In the first place this did not insure any increase at all in the total volume of currency, but was to be part of the 125 per cent total issue (based on capital and surplus) previously allowed National banks. And warehouse facilities have been so poor in the South that Mr. A. W. McLean[3] tells me it is virtually impossible to get receipts which the North Carolina Currency Association will accept at all.

*More Direct Action Needed*: In a word, the banks have fallen down on their job—not voluntarily perhaps, but involuntarily. They have been framed for serving commercial interests, and they are afraid to risk making heavy loans to agricultural interests. For example, I deal with the Raleigh Banking and Trust Company here. I want to see them do all they can for the farmer, but I don't want to see them lend so heavily that they cannot take care of me in a pinch. And so it goes. Unless a fund is set apart to be used exclusively for the relief of cotton, I don't believe it will get to the man whose sweat made the crop.

It looks to me as if the plan for selling $200,000,000 worth of Panama Canal bonds and issuing treasury notes on the basis of the gold received, the money to be lent on cotton at 3 or 4 per cent interest, is probably the most feasible plan yet proposed.

*Something Must Be Done*: Southern cotton growers not only feel that the National Government ought to help in a great crisis like this, but that it has pledged itself to help. You will recall that only a few days ago Mr. Underwood speaking in the House, justified the levy of additional war taxes instead of withdrawing $75,000,000 of Government deposits from National banks, saying the Government should have gone "to the rescue of these institutions whose solvency was jeopardized, not by any fault of their own, but by the conditions coming from the war zone of Europe."

I realize, of course, the importance of preserving the integrity of our financial institutions, but should not a Government "concerned even more about human rights than about property rights," as President Wilson has expressed it, realize the no less imperative need for going to the rescue of men and women, boys and girls, whose humble hopes for proper food, clothing, housing and education have been "jeopardized not by any fault of their own" but by these same war conditions.

Unless the Government can provide $200,000,000 to $400,-000,000 for lending on cotton until conditions become normal, I believe it will fail in a duty; violate what the South regards as a pledge; fail to give agriculture the help which we believe would have been extended to finance or commerce under like conditions; and open the way for political disturbances that may imperil party supremacy in the South. I hope you will give us the aid of your powerful influence.

Cordially yours,    Clarence Poe

TLS (WP, DLC).
[1] Cora Lily Woodard Aycock, widow of Charles Brantley Aycock, Governor of North Carolina, 1901-1905.
[2] Leonidas Polk Woodard of Wilson, N. C.
[3] Angus Wilton McLean, lawyer and politician of Lumberton, N. C., later governor of the state.

## A News Report

[Oct. 7, 1914]

PRESIDENT OPPOSES VALORIZING COTTON

Washington, Oct. 7.—Administration indorsement of Representative Henry's plan to issue Federal notes to the extent of $500,000,000 to lend to the cotton planters of the South was definitely refused today. The President told a delegation from North Carolina, including the Senators and Representatives of that State, that there was now an ample volume of currency in the country to furnish the necessary relief and that further currency legislation by Congress was not needed.

The President said he would like to see the Federal Warehouse bill, known as the Lever bill, become a law at the present session, and he let it be known that the plan advocated by Festus J. Wade, a St. Louis banker, to create a cotton pool of $150,000,000 to buy up cotton at current prices had his entire approval.[1] . . .

The President's attitude on the Henry bill was a distinct blow to the Southern members of the House, who had been conducting a filibuster to force the cotton subject upon the consideration of Congress before the end of the present session. Mr. Henry, demonstrating that his interest in the proposal had not abated on account of the information from the White House, compelled the House to submit to five roll calls today during consideration of the Clayton Anti-Trust bill conference report. As a result, instead of concluding the allotted five hours of general discussion, only two hours were consumed, and it is doubtful, if Mr. Henry keeps up his tactics, if the remaining three hours of debate can be squeezed in tomorrow.

The President said to his North Carolina visitors that the cotton situation furnished a problem which must be solved, not with the heart, but with the head, and that in finding the solution the fabric of the country's currency system should not be disturbed. He pointed out that the basic trouble was the diminished demand abroad for cotton, caused by the war, and that, however much it was desired to do so, there seemed to be no immediate opportunity of bringing the war to a close or of restoring the demand for cotton through any arbitrary process.

Representative Small[2] of North Carolina, who was with the delegation at the White House, tonight summarized the President's position as follows:

"The President is profoundly interested, and within the limitations of economic law and safe finance he will do all in his power to help. It was evident that he was not in sympathy with any plan to valorize cotton, and regarded any such proposal as unwise and dangerous. He would like to see the Federal Warehouse bill[3] become a law before this session closes, but does not believe any further legislation necessary. He considers that the situation can be met, in so far as it can be met at all, by mobilizing our currency for making advances and handling the cotton crop, and that this must be done largely through the banks of the country. To that end, he says, the Secretary of the Treasury and the Federal Reserve Board will render all the assistance in their power."

The House Committee on Banking and Currency is scheduled to meet tomorrow afternoon, at which time the Henry bill will be considered. Mr. Henry will be present to urge a favorable report to the House. Chairman Glass of the committee, who is opposed to the legislation, was confident tonight that the bill would be refused support by the committee.

Printed in the *New York Times*, Oct. 8, 1914.

[1] About the cotton pool plan and its fate, regarding which there will be much discussion in subsequent documents, see Link, *Struggle for Neutrality*, pp. 99-101.

[2] John Humphrey Small.

[3] See n. 6 to remarks at a press conference, printed at Oct. 19, 1914.

## To Louis de Sadeleer

My dear Sir:                    [The White House] October 7, 1914

I am very much moved by your letter from New York bearing date the second of October and beg that you will believe that I refrain from any public expression of any judgment at all in the serious matter you have laid before me only because I think it my duty to withhold all judgment concerning it until everything is made clear with regard to the war and its many distressing incidents. When the time for summing up comes, I feel that we shall be in possession of so many more facts than we now have, and then we shall be upon very much firmer ground in coming to conclusions.

Cordially and sincerely yours,    [Woodrow Wilson]

TLS (Letterpress Books, WP, DLC).


## To Josephus Daniels

My dear Daniels:              The White House October 7, 1914

Thank you for sending me Clarence Poe's letter. I will read it at the earliest possible opportunity.

In haste        Affectionately yours,    Woodrow Wilson

TLS (J. Daniels Papers, DLC).


## From William Bauchop Wilson

My dear Mr. President:          Washington October 7, 1914.

The Clayton anti-trust bill will soon be placed in your hands for approval or disapproval. The bill has the hearty support of the trade unionists of the country. The feature of it drawing a distinct dividing line between labor and commodities is particularly gratifying to them. They look upon it as being a new Magna Charter for labor. For that reason, if you approve the measure, Mr. Gompers, President of the American Federation of Labor, is desirous of securing the pen with which the bill is approved.

If you can not comply with his desires otherwise I take the liberty of suggesting that you pursue the same policy as on some other occasions, and use more than one pen.

Faithfully yours,    W B Wilson

TLS (WP, DLC).

Remarks at a Press Conference

October 8, 1914

How is the cotton situation, Mr. President? Have you reached
any solution of the problem in your mind?

> No, sir, I wish I had. I have been trying to, very hard, but
> I haven't seen anything yet which seemed to be workable. Of
> course, as I said the other day, the cause of the problem is
> the European war, and we can't account for that. It's the
> large proportion of our cotton generally bought abroad and
> the fact that we depend for our gold balance for so large a
> part from the cash sale of cotton.

There is no chance of a corner—I don't mean corner exactly, but
suppose those men put up their hundred and fifty million, is there
no chance of their buying cotton enough to control cotton in any
dangerous way?

> I don't see it. Really, the cotton pool, so-called, this fund
> would be so generally subscribed for that there wouldn't be
> any one group or person who could cooperate and control
> it. . . .

Mr. President, will you see that committee from St. Louis tomorrow?

> I didn't know there will be a committee.

Yes, there will be a committee.

> I don't know, sir. I haven't, so far as I know, an appoint-
> ment with them.

They have an engagement with the Federal Reserve Board
at three o'clock. You haven't approved any of these various bills
that have been submitted to you?

> No, sir. I have simply taken them all under consideration,
> so far as I can, to determine the matter.

Have you expressed disapproval of any of them yet, Mr. President?

> Only in the sense that, as I have said, I didn't see anything
> yet proposed that would be feasible.
>
> I believe, for my own part, to use the phrase, what is upper-
> most in our minds, that at present the mobilization of the
> currency of the country, the treasure of the country, will
> suffice if that mobilization will be effected, and I don't see
> any reason to doubt that it can. It is not the lack of sufficient
> currency, because there is more currency in the country
> than there ever has been, but the lack of means, so far, of
> putting it at the disposal of the persons who most need it
> in this particular situation.

Mr. President, what is the grain situation? Grain is being exported in unprecedented amounts.

I don't know that there is any difference, any difference as to the export, except, of course, men miss the cotton and they can wear old clothes, even if they are rags. And the cotton situation is partly an anticipated situation. Only in Texas has the cotton been gathered, as I understand it, and it is yet to be gathered in most of the cotton belt.

Well, if the Federal Reserve Board assisted in the operation, wouldn't the situation be very much improved?

It would be very much improved, yes. And for that reason, the directors who are now chosen, so far as the southern region is concerned, are very active. You know, they have been consulting and were, within the last forty-eight hours, very active in trying to get the system under way.

Mr. President, are there any features of the tax bill as it now stands in the Senate that you can comment on?

To tell the truth, I don't know just how it does stand. I have had so many other things to occupy the foreground that I am not informed in detail at all. Of course, it will have to go through conference yet.

JRT transcript (WC, NjP) of CLSsh (C. L. Swem Coll., NjP).


## From Robert Lansing, with Enclosures

Dear Mr. President:                    Washington October 8th, 1914.

I am sending to you the papers showing the unofficial interchange of views between the British Ambassador and myself in regard to the Declaration of London of which I spoke to you this morning.

I hope you will pardon me if I call your attention to the confidential nature of these documents, and ask that they be returned to me after you have had opportunity to read them.

Very sincerely yours,   Robert Lansing.

TLS (WP, DLC).


### E N C L O S U R E   I

## Robert Lansing to Sir Cecil Arthur Spring Rice

*Personal* and *Confidential.*

My dear Mr. Ambassador:          [Washington] October 2, 1914.

The inquiry, made of the belligerents early in August in regard to the adoption of the Declaration of London, was in the hope that a code of naval warfare might be adopted by all the nations at war so that causes of controversy would be reduced as far as possible and neutrals, as well as belligerents, would not be in doubt as to the rules, which would be enforced during hostilities.

Germany and Austria agreed to the adoption of the Declaration conditioned upon adoption by their enemies. The Order in Council of August 20th prevented the object sought by our inquiry. As a result the Declaration is non-effective as a naval code.

I have examined the Declaration and Order in Council in view of our recent conferences on the subject, and I wish to make the following suggestions which seem to me to be worthy of consideration.

Under Articles 23 and 25, if the London Declaration is adopted, a belligerent has the right to add to the lists of absolute and conditional contraband given in Articles 22 and 24. This right appears to be arbitrary except that notification must be given, and except that in the case of absolute contraband the added articles must be those "exclusively used for war." This latter phrase may be open to more than one interpretation, but it is manifest that "exclusively" can not be literally interpreted; for example, a literal interpretation would exclude dynamite sticks used in mining from being declared to be absolute contraband as they do not seem to fall under the term "explosives specially prepared for use in war" (Article 22, section 3). Manifestly such an exclusion was not intended. My personal view is that in interpreting "exclusively used in war" there must be taken into consideration the methods of warfare, the locality to which articles are presumably destined, and the situation which exists at the time of declaration and notification of the articles added to the absolute contraband list. This seems to me the common sense point of view of Article 23.

If my view is the correct one then Article 1 of the Order in Council is not a modification of the Declaration but merely an act performed under its provisions.

Now the point I am driving at is just this. Do not the powers conferred upon a belligerent by Articles 23 and 25 furnish sufficient means to protect the interests of your Government without modifying the Declaration at all? If I understand your main object it is that you are seeking to apply the doctrine of "continuous voyage" to certain articles now listed as conditional contraband, but which you consider munitions of war. If such articles can be treated as absolute contraband upon notice, what is the use of modifying the articles of the Declaration?

As to the other provisions of the Order in Council, namely Articles 2, 4 and 6, are they of sufficient importance to interfere with the great advantage to all parties, both belligerents and neutrals, to be gained by a unanimous agreement to abide by the rules of the Declaration during the continuance of hostilities?

If in place of the Order in Council of August 20th and those supplemental to it, the British Government would issue an Order in Council, and obtain from their allies similar decrees, accepting the Declaration of London without change, the German and Austrian Governments would be bound to do so. Then your Government could act under Articles 23 and 25, which do not require assent either by an enemy or a neutral.

I offer the foregoing suggestions in an entirely unofficial and personal way for your own consideration, and I will be glad to talk them over whenever you wish.

I am, my dear Mr. Ambassador,

Very sincerely yours,    Robert Lansing

TCL (WP, DLC).

## E N C L O S U R E   I I

**DECLARATION OF LONDON**

*Informal Memorandum of Conference at British Embassy 9 p.m., October 2, 1914, with the British Ambassador.*

The suggestions in my "personal and confidential" letter of the 3rd [2nd] were discussed.

The Ambassador said that he personally considered the suggestions an excellent solution of the difficulties raised by the Order in Council of August 20th, and that he would present them to his Government by telegraph. He said that he did not think that the Foreign Office appreciated that Germany and Austria had agreed to abide by the Declaration of London if the allies also agreed; that he fully understood the great advantage it would be to have a uniform code of naval warfare; and that he realized the especial importance of it to the United States in order that Americans engaged in commerce with belligerents would know exactly what they might rely upon as a measure of their rights and duties as neutrals.

In view of the importance of submitting these considerations to the Foreign Office before any steps were taken in London to modify the Order in Council of August 20th, the Ambassador said that he would draft a telegram to Sir Edward Grey at once, and he asked me to remain until the telegram was drafted.

He then proceeded to draft a telegram along the lines of the suggestions in my letter to him. This we went over together and made certain changes, and the Ambassador added a statement of his own as to the satisfaction with which an unqualified acceptance of the Declaration by Great Britain and her allies would be received in this country.

The Ambassador said that he would send me a copy of the telegram as sent the next morning.          Robert Lansing.

TS memorandum (WP, DLC).


# E N C L O S U R E   I I I

## Sir Cecil Arthur Spring Rice to Sir Edward Grey

*Unofficial*                                [Washington] October 2, 1914.

Following is result of conversation with Counsellor of State Department: The enquiry made by the USG of the belligerents early in August in regard to adoption of declaration of London was made in hope of reducing causes of controversy in present war. Germany and Austria agreed on condition that the others did also. Consequently it is very important that allies should agree.

If GB after accepting declaration without change added under articles 23 and 25 to the list of absolute and conditional contraband, she would gain what appears to be her chief object while only using powers conferred in the declaration. It is true article 23 uses words "exclusively used for war" but this cannot be literally interpreted, e g case of dynamite sticks. In interpreting this expression there must be taken into consideration methods of warfare, destination and conditions existing at time of the additions.

Do not the powers under articles 23 and 25 furnish sufficient means to protect British interests without modifying declaration at all? Articles 2, 4 and 6 of the O in C seem hardly important enough to justify sacrifice of principle of unanimous agreement? For if GB and her allies issue order accepting declaration of London Germany and Austria are bound to do the same.

I presume embargo of the export of certain articles could be arranged separately with certain countries under a threat of taking other measures on the principle that e g Holland cannot allow her territory to become the base for military operations.

I have little doubt that the acceptance by GB of the declaration without modification for this war only for reasons stated in first para[graph] would be taken as satisfactory solution of the present difficulty and create wide-spread satisfaction.

[Foregoing has been read and approved by Counsellor, 3 first paras summary of his letter, last 2 added with his concurrence.][1]

TC telegram (WP, DLC).

1 Bracketed sentence in the telegram sent to London: C. A. Spring Rice to E. Grey, Oct. 2, 1914, T telegram (FO 115/1770, p. 41, PRO).

## From Edward Mandell House

Dear Governor:                    New York City. October 8th, 1914.

Sir Cecil Spring-Rice took breakfast with me this morning. He came unexpectedly and is here to meet Lady Spring-Rice who lands today.

He wanted my opinion as to whether I agreed with him as to the inadvisability of permitting Sir James Barrie and other propagandists to lecture in behalf of Great Britian and the Allies. I told him I thought you were becoming tired of the efforts made by both sides at war to stir up public feeling in this country, and that I thought he had given his Government good advice in asking them to do nothing in this direction.

I asked him if he saw any light in the direction of peace. He saw none. He expressed himself as being very glad that you were doing nothing. In his opinion, it would be a mistake for you to make any move just now for it would probably prejudice the cause later.

He asked me to read up on the diplomatic correspondence between England and this country during the years of '62 and '63 and note the reply which Lincoln's Government gave Great Britain when she proposed mediation. He said they went so far as to reply that any steps taken in this direction would be regarded as an unfriendly act. It is very clear therefore that what is best is to do nothing at present, but to keep in touch with the situation as you are doing and be ready when the hint is given. Sir Cecil thinks that this time will arrive, but just when, he is not now prepared to say.

He tells me that the peace compact between Russia and Japan was practically agreed upon between themselves before they came to America, and that conversations had been going on for several months prior to the close of the war.

He told me also that Austria had already made overtures to Russia, and that it was understood she was much more anxious than Germany to conclude peace.

He has promised to keep me informed concerning every phase of the situation so that I may in turn give it to you unofficially.

Affectionately yours,   E. M. House

TLS (WP, DLC).

## To Sir Cecil Arthur Spring Rice

My dear Mr. Ambassador,    The White House 9 October, 1914.

It was very kind of you to send me your note of October fifth enclosing Sir Edward Grey's despatch about contraband and an alteration of the O[r]der in Council.

I have been keeping in touch with Mr. Lansing, and want to tell you how warmly I appreciate the spirit in which you have been cooperating with him to bring this delicate matter to a satisfactory settlement.

With warm regard and appreciation,
Faithfully Yours,    Woodrow Wilson

WWTLS (FO 115/1770, p. 54, PRO).

## To James Viscount Bryce

My dear Lord Bryce:    The White House October 9, 1914

Thank you sincerely for your letter about mediation. My own judgment accords entirely with yours in the matter. I shall be very careful to suit my action to the developments.

I need not tell you how deeply concerned we constantly are about the great contest. Our thoughts are upon it constantly and upon our friends whose hearts must be so much distressed.

Cordially and sincerely yours,    Woodrow Wilson

TLS (J. Bryce Papers, Bodleian Library).

## From Joseph Patrick Tumulty

The White House.
Memorandum for the President:    October 9th [1914].

I have returned to you your letter to Secretary Wilson in which you state that you will be glad to let Mr. Gompers have the pen with which you intend to sign the Clayton bill.[1] The fiercest criticisms against the Clayton bill were those aimed at the exemption feature and the prominent part played by Mr. Gompers in this matter. Do you think it wise to aggravate the criticism by giving Mr. Gompers the pen?[2]

I had already told Congressman Carlin that I would consider his request that the pen be handed to him. Might not this be a diplomatic way of getting out of the difficulty?

The Secretary.

T MS (WP, DLC).
[1] WW to W. B. Wilson, Oct. 8, 1914, TL (WP, DLC).
[2] See S. Gompers to WW, Oct. 16, 1914.

# From Edward Mandell House

Dear Governor:                    New York City. October 9th, 1914.

I had an unhappy hour with McCombs yesterday. I will tell you of it when we meet. He knows all about our activities in keeping him out of the State Chairmanship.

I have done what I could to keep out of this New York situation, but it has been impossible and now I am trying to give it some direction.

Glynn's Secretary told me yesterday that if the Administration had backed the Governor cordially, he would have overthrown Murphy by now. He said at one time the Governor was on the eve of making a declaration against Murphy.

I think it worth while to try him out after the election and see if he can [be] brought to do this. I have arranged a conference here, at the apartment, for next Tuesday at 5.30 in which the Governor, the Mayor, Frank Polk and I will take part. Mitchel will then determine whether or not he will support Glynn and how cordially.

Let me suggest that you do not write any letter commending Glynn or Gerard[1] until after this conference occurs. I have told Glynn, through his Secretary, that it was your desire that all factions should present a united front and, if for any reason, the Mayor and his official family did not support him cordially, I did not know what effect it might have upon your enthusiasm.

I would also suggest that you do not make any New York appointments until after the election, particularly in regard to postmasters. This is important and I think you should let Burleson know.

I had a conference last night with Mr. Wiggins, President of the Clearing House Association[2] and a Mr. Frank Sales[3] whom, I understand, is a prominent and wealthy cotton manufacturer of New England. Sales suggested that the cotton manufacturers were adopting a short-sighted policy by not buying cotton at present prices, hoping to get it cheaper.

He thinks it would be better for everyone, including the manufacturers themselves, if cotton prices could be maintained upon a profitable basis to the growers and he also thought that the leash in which business is now held could not be fully loosened until the cotton situation was solved.

Wiggins agreed to undertake to form a committee of New York bankers consisting of himself, Vanderlip, Hepburn, Woodward[4] and perhaps one or two others to formulate a plan to work out this problem.

They are to meet with me Tuesday of next week and if they present some tangible plan, I shall ask you to let me bring them to Washington to confer with you and McAdoo. If this interferes with anything that is being done, or if you do not approve of it, please let me know.    Affectionately yours,    E. M. House

TLS (WP, DLC).
  1 Ambassador Gerard had defeated Franklin D. Roosevelt in the Democratic senatorial primary on September 28 and was now the Democratic candidate for the United States Senate.
  2 Albert Henry Wiggin, president of the Chase National Bank, New York.
  3 Frank Arthur Sayles, of Pawtucket, R. I.
  4 Frank Arthur Vanderlip, president of the National City Bank, New York; Alonzo Barton Hepburn, chairman of the board of directors of the Chase National Bank; and William Woodward, president of the Hanover National Bank, New York.


## To Edward Mandell House

My dear Friend:                The White House October 10, 1914
   Each one of your letters makes me value more highly your friendship and your discretion.
   This is just a line to let you know how much I appreciate them and that I have no comment except of commendation upon what you are doing. I will see McAdoo probably sometime today and let you know if there is anything in what you are purposing and doing in New York upon which he wishes to make any comment or suggestion.
   In haste      Affectionately yours,   Woodrow Wilson

TLS (E. M. House Papers, CtY).


## Sir Cecil Arthur Spring Rice to Sir Edward Grey

Private.        Washington (r. 9.10 a.m. October 10th. 1914)
   Straus spoke to me again about peace, assuring me that German Ambassador was anxious that the matter should not be dropped. I said that official German statement left no doubt as to Germany's rejection of all idea of peace negotiations and that we were bound to believe German Government rather than German Ambassador.
   Austrian Ambassador seems to have pressed Colonel H. in same sense.
   Secretary of State is willing and so is President but to a less degree. Colonel H. said he was holding latter back.
   I pointed out danger of acting before all parties were agreed in desiring mediation and referred to attitude of United States Government towards foreign intervention at time of Civil War

and War with Sapin [Spain]. H. agreed but repeated that "door was on latch."

In the course of conversation H. said that if Germany attacked undefended English towns with bombs it would be "inconsistent with pledges given here" from which I conclude President has had some communications with German Government on the subject.

T telegram (E. Grey Papers, FO 800/84, PRO).

## To Mary Allen Hulbert

Dearest Friend,                The White House 11 October, 1914.

I am afraid that I am a most unsatisfactory correspondent these days. The fact is, that I feel so dull and without spirits that I am ashamed to write. There is nothing in me that can give pleasure to those I deeply care for and wish to help. I fight to keep going: and succeed through a sort of routine. Here is a typical day's routine: Immediately after an eight o'clock breakfast Swem, my stenographer, comes over to the house and I dictate my letters and go over the papers on my desk which are waiting to be read. Then, about a quarter before ten, I go over to the office and until one receive visitors and delegations of all sorts. When lunch is over (and I am often late to it) I receive one or two more formal visits, such as from an ambassador; then I hurry into my playing clothes and go off to one or other of the golf courses and play golf till the sun goes down. By the time I get home and have a bath and dress there are only a few minutes, fifteen or twenty, before dinner in which to go over and sign the papers awaiting my action on the table in the office. After dinner, there are generally other consultations necessary on pending business or foreign affairs, or papers to prepare on questions which only I ought to formulate, since I am ultimately responsible; and I fall into bed so tired I cannot think. And it is best so. But all this makes Sunday, the only day I have for any letters I may write myself, a day when all my faculties seek rest and are in a sort of coma, and I am no good. I generally sleep (or at any rate stay in bed) until it is time to dress for church and ride all afternoon into the far country round about the city, dozing and silent. Dear little Helen goes with me, a perfect companion because glad to think of me and what is best for me and not anxious to talk and have her own way, bless her heart for the unselfishness! But I hate to think how dull it must be for her, and chide myself for accepting such sacrifices. In a few weeks now the dear little daughter at Cornish[1] will be back; and I see my darling Nell every day. She is here watching constantly over her indefatigable but constantly overworked husband, to whom the whole country turns daily in these troubled times for financial counsel and assistance. She sees almost as little of him as Helen sees of me. It may be better when Congress adjourns (or, rather, *if* Congress adjourns), but for the present it is a killing pace for all of us! All this, my dear friend, is not by way of excuse or apology, for I know that you wish neither and that, with you, neither is necessary. Your kindness and indulgence and your power to understand are without limit. But I am none the less ashamed of my letters, and wonder why you should wish for them. Your letters, on the other hand, grow more and more like your old self. It is wonderful that they should. I can imagine your loneliness and what it must mean to you, who were meant for anything but that. But it is so, none the less, and it makes me happy to witness it. I get the refreshment from your letters that those get who are with you, and to whom you give yourself in so extraordinary a degree. Indeed you seem to exhaust yourself for them and to give so much that reaction sets in afterwards, so that you feel their praise and appreciation to be a sort of unintentional mockery when the loneliness and the sadness descend on you again. Are you tired after the letters? They now give me again what I used to get from them before the blow fell upon you of your dear mother's going. I am so glad to have you tell me what others say to you and about you of a personal sort. It is the best interpretation to me of your health and spirits and, in general, of how you are faring. Please give me every scrap of the sort you happen to remember from time to time. And please do not forget to give me your Boston address. You have told me *how* you and Allen are to live this winter, but have not told me *where*.

I am quite well. I seem to be tough against all sorts of strain and all sorts of deep suffering. I have a vast deal to be thankful for; and shall, I hope, never yield to the weakness of being sorry for myself.     Your devoted friend,   Woodrow Wilson

WWTLS (WP, DLC).
¹ Margaret.


## Remarks at a Press Conference

October 12, 1914

Mr. President, is there anything about adjournment?

No, I haven't heard anything definite at all.

Anything further about the Colorado strike situation, Mr. President?

Nothing at all. I understand that Governor Ammons is re-organizing the militia of the state so as to relieve the federal troops of their duty, but just how far that has gone, I don't know. There is no change in the situation. . . .

At the risk of [breaking] over a straw, Mr. President, you have taken no action or steps with reference to European peace except as to that first note?

No. A good many are taken for me.

Have you heard anything from Mr. Carnegie, Mr. President?

No, not a word.

Anything from Mexico?

No. I saw some dispatches in this morning's papers which surprised me. I didn't know that there was any firing over the border. Apparently that is some local difficulty.

Have you received anything from that, Mr. President, as to the requests on the Veracruz situation—the protection of those merchants down there, those merchants who have had the municipal government?

Nothing definite has come about that.

Has any time been fixed for the definite withdrawal of our troops?

Well, we are anxious to get away immediately. We are simply waiting for the things that are necessary to arrange to have somebody to hand over the authority to. We can't simply drop the city and leave it to take care of itself.

Doesn't that hinge on that reply?

It hinges in part on that. Of course, we can't exact anything of the Mexican authorities with regard to their own citizens, but we have a right to expect, of course, that proper arrangements will be made to transfer authority.

Mr. President, do you expect to sign the Clayton bill today?

Yes.

There is some idea that you might not sign that bill and get out a statement?

No, sir. I don't want to have statements becoming chronic.

Mr. President, have you any choice between the House and Senate revenue bills?

To tell the truth, I haven't read the Senate revenue bill. Has it been reported out of the conference?

Yes.

I haven't read it yet. I shall begin to get deeply interested when it gets to me from the conference.

Mr. President, have you any information regarding business conditions throughout the country after the first flurry of the war?

I haven't any systematic information I can think of, no,

but from what I can learn, the great bulk of business is going very normally, as much as it is disturbed by the cotton situation; and the lack of adequate international exchange is of course disturbing. But I have every reason to hope that that will be facilitated and put on as good a footing as is possible in the circumstances.

Imports improving?

They are improving.

The war tax?

It hasn't shown any such marked increase as to affect that increase, unfortunately.

Have you received any intimation from the British government relative to the embargo on wool, except the telegram from Consul General Skinner?

No, sir, nothing at all.

Is that conditional contraband list righting itself?

I think it is righting itself. I get that impression. Of course, it hasn't come to any definite conclusion yet. Understand, of course, that under the practices of international law, nations at war have the right, within certain limits, to increase the lists of the things which are to be considered contraband or conditional contraband, as the case may be, because of the circumstances arising in the war itself, and the use that is being made of what is shipped. So it is bound to be a little bit fluid for a time.

The question of neutral ships and neutral ports, that has been eliminated?

That has been eliminated.

But the revamping of that list by the British government. They revised their list on certain foodstuffs, whether countries such as Holland could transport to neutral ports, and would that apply to all those nations—Turkey, Sweden? Isn't there a danger of merchants being a little overfearful? Take, for example, the sending of that ship in ballast to bring back the cargo and supplies. It is suggested to me from pretty high quarters that they haven't got the government back of it.

They have certainly got the government back of it to the limits of all our rights, of course; and I don't think our rights will be interfered with.

Has Great Britain called any attention to the export of grain to Sweden and Norway?

There are always exports to those countries.

It was particularly heavy.

That might be, because those countries always draw on the Russian grain fields.

Mr. President, have you received any note from Ambassador Jusserand about German atrocities?

> Yes, sir. The State Department sent me over a formal representation of the French government about it.

It will be handled the same way as the other?

> Yes.

Was that recently?

> Yes. Within five days. At a guess, some time last week.

You have merely filed them?

> Of course, we acknowledge them in the proper way, but we can't form any conclusions with regard to the matter.

There isn't anything the government can do at all with this matter?

> Except reserve judgment.

JRT transcript (WC, NjP) of CLSsh (C. L. Swem Coll., NjP).

## To John Worth Kern

My dear Senator:                [The White House] October 12, 1914

I know that I need not say to you or to any of my colleagues in the Senate that my letter to Mr. Underwood[1] was no less an expression of my feeling of the deep indebtedness of the party and of the country to the Democratic members of the Senate than of my appreciation of the work of the House. We are all, happily, a single team, moved by the same spirit.

But I want to give myself the personal satisfaction of sending you a line of warm congratulation and of deep personal appreciation. I am sure we shall all be able in the years to come to look back upon the special and the long session of the Sixty-third Congress with genuine gratitude that we should have been given the opportunity to serve the country in so many ways. Many problems, no doubt, still await us, but they will, I am sure, be met in the same spirit, and, I earnestly hope, with the same success.

> Cordially and sincerely yours,   Woodrow Wilson

TLS (Letterpress Books, WP, DLC).
1 It is printed at Oct. 17, 1914.

## From Sir Cecil Arthur Spring Rice, with Enclosure

*Private*

Dear Mr President                Washington. 12 October 1914

Sir Edward Grey informs me privately that Sir L Carden is at present on leave and that he will not again be sent to an American post.

I take this opportunity of enclosing Sir Edward Grey's telegram about the Declaration of London. It contains a statement which is misleading namely that any proposal was made by you, Sir, or your government on the subject of articles of unconditional contraband.

The articles quoted were mentioned by me in the course of a private and confidential conversation with the Counsellor of your State Department, Mr Lansing as instances of articles which experience had shown to be used exclusively for war at the present moment. Mr Lansing explained that he could not speak for the government but that some such suggestion seemed worthy of consideration as it might offer a means of getting rid of the British Order in Council and returning to the ground of the Declaration of London.

The misconception has been fully explained to Sir Edward Grey and I am sure that the situation will be now perfectly understood.

I have the honour to offer to you, Mr President, the assurance of my profound respect,          Cecil Spring Rice

ALS (WP, DLC).

ENCLOSURE

TELEGRAM FROM SIR E. GREY TO SIR C. SPRING RICE.

Foreign Office, October 9, 1914.

I had already had a single draft Order in Council prepared and printed to give to the United States Ambassador here before your telegram arrived.

It had always been my intention to show draft Order in Council to the United States Government before issuing it with the object of coming to an agreement before any Order was issued.

The United States Ambassador here will telegraph text of draft Order in Council to Washington.

I have given the United States Ambassador the following note of explanation:

Order in Council has been drafted in accordance with the communication made to the United States Ambassador on October 3. It provides an enlarged list of absolute contraband as there indicated.

Additions consist of:

A. Petroleum and motors *as suggested by the United States Government.*\*

B. Certain ores and metals which are largely used in the manufacture of munitions of war and for which the peace use must practically have entirely ceased during the present struggle, namely Haematite iron, Nickel, ferrochrome, copper and lead.

C. Motor tyres and rubber.

With regard to conditional contraband Article 35 of the Declaration of London is left standing and will therefore exclude as regards conditional contraband application of doctrine of continuous voyage in respect of goods consigned to a neutral port. The right to seize conditional contraband on a ship bound for neutral port is however maintained by Article 3 (2) b. in respect of cases where no consignment in neutral country is disclosed in the ship's papers. A great proportion of cargo shipped to Rotterdam is consigned merely "to order" and may be intended for transit to the enemy country. In such cases and where goods are carried with a through bill of lading to the enemy country Article 35 would not apply.

Article 4 of draft Order in Council is intended to cover cases where no satisfactory arrangement can be come to with a neutral Power to lay an embargo on export of goods required in the enemy country for use in war and there is reason to believe the country is being used by the enemy as a source of supplies for his armed forces.[1]

* This is misleading. No such proposal was made

C S R

TC telegram (WP, DLC).
[1] This telegram was sent as E. Grey to C. A. Spring Rice, Oct. 9, 1914, Hw and T telegram (FO 372/601, No. 57976, pp. 269-70, PRO).


# To Oliver Peck Newman[1]

[The White House]

My dear Mr. Commissioner:                    October 13, 1914

This is just a line to ask you if you do not think it would be just in making up your estimates to include an increase of twenty-five cents a day for the "White Wings" who work on the streets of the city. Their present wage seems a pitiful dole.[2]

Cordially and faithfully yours,    Woodrow Wilson

TLS (Letterpress Books, WP, DLC).
[1] A commissioner of the District of Columbia.
[2] This appeal was prompted by H. F. Hollis to WW, Oct. 12, 1914, TLS (WP, DLC), reporting that Washington streetcleaners earned an average net salary of $398 a year.

# From Edward Mandell House

Dear Governor:                    New York City. October 14th, 1914.

I brought Glynn and Mitchel together yesterday afternoon. They had an entirely satisfactory understanding. Mitchel will announce his cordial support today and I promised to ask you to also write the Governor a letter and give it to the press tomorrow.

This clears up all differences in New York for the moment and we now present a united front. They wish to publish a million copies of your letter so I hope you will make it as strong as you feel that you consistently can. I am enclosing some suggestions giving Glynn's record.[1]

I am more hopeful than ever that, with the warm endorsement of the Governor, we can induce him to have a final break with Murphy. What he said to Mitchel confirmed this belief.

The conference with the bankers last night concerning the cotton situation was satisfactory. I objected to the Wade plan because of the excessive interest. The local banks would be compelled to pay something over 8% and, heaven knows, what the money would cost the borrower.

Davison[2] proposed that the fund of $150,000,000. should be placed in the hands of the Federal Reserve Board for distribution at an interest charge of 6% upon a valuation of six cents per pound on the cotton. After much discussion, this was finally agreed to.

Mr. Wiggin is to confer with Mr. Wade this morning and try and get his cooperation on that basis.

I talked with McAdoo last night and he at first thought that the Federal Reserve Board would not undertake this, but, I am sure, with a little pressure from you and from him they will be willing to do so.

This is an emergency matter of the greatest importance and the ordinary technicalities and niceties should not be allowed to stand in the way. The South feels that a calamity has come upon them much as a flood, fire or any other such devastating element and they can never be made to believe that the Government should not in some way come to their relief. If this plan goes through, they will be satisfied that the Administration has met the emergency.

                    Affectionately yours,    E. M. House

I have just had a final talk with Wiggin and Wade and everything is satisfactory. McAdoo has agreed to take hold of it, and I have no doubt that a very difficult situation will soon be overcome.

TLS (WP, DLC).

<sup></sup>1 He enclosed two newspaper clippings and a draft by Glynn of a letter of commendation by Wilson.

2 That is, Henry Pomeroy Davison of J. P. Morgan & Co.

## Remarks at a Press Conference

October 15, 1914

Mr. President, you will sign the Clayton bill today, I understand? Are there any comments you care to make on it.

No, sir, I believe not. I am going to make some general comments on the session which will include that.

May that be taken to conclude the business legislation that is desired for some time to come?

Of course, there is still to be determined just what legislation will be enacted with regard to railroad securities. That is an unfinished question, but I believe it is a question which the committees in Congress are not ready to deal with yet.

The present situation doesn't require any legislation on that subject, does it?

I suppose not.

Mr. President, Mr. Walters[1] saw you today on the cotton situation?

Yes, one may say it was on the cotton situation. It was about the general effects of the cotton situation on the business situation. Mr. Walters wasn't by any means pessimistic about it.

Mr. President, you expect to have Congress take up the railroad securities bill at this next session, do you not?

I can't say that I have any definite opinion about it, because I haven't consulted with them about it for some months now.

Can it be considered as part of your program now?

Not part of the immediate program, no.

Mr. President, in view of the fact that the next session is a short session and will have to busy itself in large part with appropriation bills, is there any particular program, such, for instance, as the adoption of a budget system looking to greater economy in the public expenditures?

Well, I am afraid it is past hoping for that we can do anything so systematic as that at the short session, but I think that is in everybody's mind to accomplish as soon as possible.

Has there been any conference looking to the cutting down of estimates?

Well, so far as I am concerned there has been; that is to say, in cabinet we have gone over the matter repeatedly very carefully and with a view to studying every possible economy, and there are going to be reductions proposed. The trouble is that with each additional piece of legislation there is some additional function which necessarily involves the expenditure of more money. But, aside from new functions, it will be possible, I think, all along the line to keep the expenses down.

You think then that the appropriations of next year will be below those of this year?

I have every reason to think so, yes.

Mr. President, has any figure been set as a maximum over which they should not go at this short session?

You mean in the appropriations?

Yes.

That would be quite impossible until the whole thing is co-ordinated.

What is the news from Mexico today, Mr. President?

None today. The news of the last forty-eight hours is very encouraging indeed. I think Mr. Tumulty was discussing that with some of your number.

Are there any new developments in the Colorado strike situation?

None at all, sir.

Mr. President, is there anything new in the foreign trade situation?

No, except that there is a constant though slow improvement in everything except the movement of cotton, but even that cannot be considered as definitely bad, because the movement of cotton hasn't begun.

We are sending all the cotton they will take?

They have bought very little so far. One element of the situation, you see, is that a very large part of the crop is not picked yet, not ready for market, and the buying has not definitely begun. I have surmised, without knowing, that that was due to the fact that, with the cotton exchanges closed, it was very difficult for any systematic buying to occur, because they would not know at what price to buy it.

Mr. President, have you heard anything at all about any demand for American goods, any unusual demands, in countries that have been dependent on Europe heretofore?

I haven't had any official information to that effect. I have got it in letters and in conversations that the demand is considerably greater than it was.

Does that apply to South America?

That applies to South America. It applies to Spain. It applies,

I believe, to the Scandinavian countries, though I am speaking out of a recollection that would have to be verified.

Do you recall, Mr. President, what classes of goods were wanted? I know those countries you mention have taken a considerable part of the cotton that has been shipped out.

Well, it was chiefly in cotton fabrics, as this information reached me.

Had you heard anything from Japan on that question?

No.

Mr. President, is there anything you can tell us of the possibility of reopening the stock exchange?

No, I know nothing about that.

Mr. President, what have been your latest reports as to the ships coming in under the American registry?

Well, I haven't had any very lately—not within three weeks. At that time it was about one a day coming in, an average something like that.

Mr. President, in the development of a commerce with foreign countries, especially with South America, isn't the difficulty less an unwillingness to buy than an inability to pay?

That is one of the elements; not so much their inability to pay as their habit of having long credits extended to them. I believe in their trade with other countries they have had credits of from six months to a year. That was possible to manage because their banking connections were foreign connections and not American. So that our problem is to establish the machinery of credit at the same time that we are establishing the trade itself.

There are some steps being taken in that regard?

Yes, there are.

That is, they are being taken by private bankers?

By private banking institutions, yes, sir. Or, rather, by national banking institutions. Those that I happen to know were national banks.

Mr. President, can you tell us something about your engagements after Congress adjourns? I know you are going to Pittsburgh, at least I understood so.[2]

That is in fulfillment of an invitation made extending so long ago when I was less prudent than I am now. That is the only engagement ahead of me.

Have you made any response yet to the invitation of the City of New York to attend that celebration of the three-hundredth anniversary of—

No, that group of clergymen who were here the other day

pressed it upon me very cordially. I could not give them any definite answer.

You haven't made any political engagements?

No, none at all.

Mr. President, Congressman Gardner of Massachusetts has introduced a resolution calling for a special commission to inquire into the preparedness of the United States for war?[3] Would you care to express in advance an opinion on that?

No.

Mr. President, is it your desire or intention to make public the letter to Mr. Palmer in which you discussed the presidential term plank of the Democratic platform?[4]

You mean that old letter?

Yes.

No; I am not thinking about that just now.

Mr. President, you had quite a long talk with Mr. Stimson;[5] I was wondering whether you had any particular ideas in mind with regard to increasing our trade relations with Argentina.

So far as I recollect now, trade wasn't mentioned. We wanted to talk over our general policy with regard to establishing the real foundations of friendship between the United States and the Latin-American countries, in which he was very deeply interested.

Mr. President, the State Department made a statement as to commerce with belligerent nations.[6] Do you understand that loans to belligerents would be in the contraband category?

I would prefer that what I say now should not be quoted, because it is an off-hand opinion. My own information is that loans stand in the same case as anything else—loans from private individuals. You see how wrong it would be for me, so far as I can speak for the government, to have any attitude about it of any kind. All that we can do is what we did yesterday, namely, state what is international law.

Is the situation any different now than it was a few months ago at the time of the outbreak of the war?

The situation hasn't changed at all, so far as I know, but I don't want to express any opinion about it.

T MS (C. L. Swem Coll., NjP).

[1] Henry Walters of Baltimore and New York, chairman of the board of the Atlantic Coast Line Railroad Co.

[2] His speech to the Pittsburgh Y.M.C.A. is printed at Oct. 24, 1914.

[3] The reporter was referring to H.J.R. 372, which Augustus Peabody Gardner had introduced earlier that day, calling for a national security commission consisting of three senators, three representatives, and three presidential appointees. Gardner hoped the commission would throw "a public searchlight" on America's alleged unpreparedness for war. "In my opinion," Gardner said, "the effect of vast sums of money spent by Andrew Carnegie in his peace propaganda has

been to blind Americans to the fact that our national security from a military point of view is undermined." The country faced the German "menace to the principles of democracy," Gardner declared, and should begin at once to prepare if it expected "to be able to resist high-handedness when the day of necessity comes." *New York Times*, Oct. 16, 1914; *Cong. Record*, 63d Cong., 2d sess., p. 16694, pp. 16745-47.

4 Printed at Feb. 5, 1913, Vol. 27.

5 Wilson saw Frederic Jesup Stimson, newly appointed Ambassador to Argentina, at the White House on October 14.

6 A general statement, issued on October 15, concerning American trade with belligerents under the rules of international law. It is printed in *FR-WWS 1914*, pp. 573-74.

## A News Report

[*Oct. 15, 1914*]

### AMERICAN BANKERS MAY MAKE LOANS
### TO WAR NATIONS

Washington, Oct. 15.—American bankers, individually or collectively, may make loans, large or small, to the nations of Europe now at war. There is no law on the statute books which prohibits it, and there is no ruling of international law by which they can be prevented from doing so.

From the highest authority the correspondent of The World learned the foregoing, as well as the fact that when President Wilson stopped J. P. Morgan and a group of New York bankers, a few weeks after the outbreak of the war in Europe, from making a loan to France, he did so by dissuasion and not by reference to any power possessed by the Chief Executive to force them to refuse the loan.

The flat statement of the Administration yesterday, issued through the State Department, that contraband and conditional contraband, including guns and ammunition, could be sold by American citizens to citizens of the Governments at war or to the Governments themselves without violating the neutrality of the United States, led to inquiry to-day as to the making of loans, and the right of bankers and banks to do so.

The statement was based on an article of the second Hague convention of 1907, which said:

"A neutral power is not required to prevent the exportation or transit, for the account of either belligerent, of arms, munitions and, in general, of anything which may be useful to any army or fleet."

From the same sources it was ascertained that President Wilson will follow the same course in the future he pursued when Morgan & Co. approached the State Department on the subject. On the other hand, if bankers or banks make loans to any of the belligerent nations without consulting the President or any of his advisers, the President will not lift his hand to stay them. He will take no cognizance of their actions.

The right of bankers to negotiate foreign loans to belligerents has been upheld in American legal decisions, and during the Russo-Japanese war a loan for Japan was floated in the United States. . . .

Printed in the New York *World*, Oct. 16, 1914.

## To Robert Lansing, with Enclosure

Dear Mr. Lansing,          [The White House] 15 October, 1914

For fear this should not reach you promptly otherwise, I am sending it to you within a few minutes of its receipt here.

The tone of it is so candid and sincere, and so earnest that I am sure you will wish to send our reply at once.

Cordially   Woodrow Wilson

ALS (SDR, RG 59, 763.72111/505½, DNA).

### E N C L O S U R E

## From Sir Cecil Arthur Spring Rice

*Personal*

Dear Mr. President,          Washington. October 15th 1914.

I enclose decypher of a telegram which I have just received from Sir Edward Grey.

My Government is doing all in its power to avoid interference with neutral trade, especially with the trade of the United States; but in the life and death struggle in which we are now engaged it is essential to prevent war supplies reaching the German armies and factories.

When the United States was involved in a similar struggle a question arose, that of the trade with the Southern States, through British colonies, on which the British Government accepted the doctrine of continuous voyage, even though it entailed serious loss on their own people. It is this same doctrine which we are now ready to abandon if we can receive adequate security from neutral nations that they will not become the bases for supplies of the forces which are devastating Belgium and France.

My Government, in deference to your wishes, has withdrawn

the Order in Council, but until the new one is issued it is impossible to make the arrangements with neutral powers which are so essential for our safety.

If a British force were devastating Mexico I do not suppose that the United States would allow it to draw its supplies either directly or by transit through United States territory: and if any nation protested against an embargo I do not suppose that American public opinion would endorse that protest.

The export figures of American trade show the immense increase of exports of all sorts, so that even from the commercial point of view this country has already found its compensation, and it is now abundantly proved that early last summer Germany was laying in supplies with a view to a war and has stated officially that she has enough to last two years. All that we now aim at is that (having no neutral ports ourselves, through which we can import) Germany may not be allowed to avail herself of her usual ports of supply (for instance in Holland) in order to feed her army and supply her factories with war materials.

We do not for a moment ask that this country should depart from the principles of absolute neutrality but merely that she should acquiesce in the enforcement of a doctrine which she herself has always insisted on—namely that a belligerent has the right to take measures to prevent its enemy from using a neutral as a port of entry for belligerent purposes. All that we ask is that you do not now abandon in the interest of our enemy a doctrine which you have in past times successfully asserted against ourselves.

I have the honour to be    with profound respect
    Dear Mr President
        Your most obedient humble servant
                                        Cecil Spring Rice

Tel from Sir E Grey                              October 14 1914

It is essential that we should have United States observations as soon às possible in order that we may issue a list of contraband of war that will not meet with objections from the United States Government.

We do not object to the principle of the Declaration of London provided we can prevent German army and war factories such as Essen being supplied through neutral countries.

To effect this it is essential to depart from strict rules of Declaration of London as to list of absolute contraband and to apply stricter measures as to conditional contraband in cases where a neutral country is being used as a base of supplies for German army and materials for munitions of war.

Does State Department realise that under the Rhine Convention between Holland & Germany goods consigned to Rotterdam may on arrival there be declared in transit and pass on to Germany in spite of any embargo on export by Netherlands Government?

Till our new proclamation is issued we cannot make arrangements with neutral governments for insuring that goods consigned to them, however contraband, are not re-exported. We were hoping to make an arrangement with Netherlands Government: but even this is in suspense pending discussion of new proclamation with United States Government.

We are most anxious to come to an agreement with United States Government for otherwise we shall have to choose between a dispute with United States Government or giving up all attempts to prevent Germany from getting free supplies for her army and materials for all munitions of war; either alternative would or might be fatal to our chance of success and insure ultimate German victory and disappearance of Great Britain as a fully independent Power in Europe. I understand importance to the United States of seeing that there is as little interference as possible with trade. In this interest we have for present ceased to detain any foodstuffs for Rotterdam or to demand any guarantee from Netherlands Government about them and these are no doubt going up the Rhine which is direct route to Germany's army.

Petroleum, copper, rubber and everything else will follow suit unless we can speedily come to an arrangement about a new proclamation. Enormous quantities of petroleum are now being shipped to Holland and Scandinavian countries and are causing us much anxiety.[1]

TLS and T telegram (SDR, RG 59, 763.72111/505½, DNA).
[1] This telegram was sent as E. Grey to C. A. Spring Rice, Oct. 14, 1914, Hw telegram (FO 372/601, No. 58795, pp. 303-304, PRO).

## To Martin Henry Glynn

My dear Governor Glynn:   [The White House] October 15, 1914

I am very glad to hear of the hopeful prospects of the campaign in New York. I feel a most cordial interest in it, as I need hardly say, and want to give myself the pleasure of expressing to you personally my earnest hope that the voters of the state will return you to your post as Governor with an emphatic majority.

Your record is open and to be judged for itself. You have not kept anything back, but have acted with candor and directness. The Democratic voters of the state have given you their decisive approval at the primaries. I hope that every man who goes to the polls next month will look upon your candidacy as embodying the cause of progressive legislation and the advancement at every point of the interests of the people.

You have my cordial best wishes.

Sincerely yours,    Woodrow Wilson

TLS (Letterpress Books, WP, DLC).


## To Nancy Saunders Toy

Dear Friend,                The White House 15 October, 1914.

Your letter[1] was most welcome. You give me news of a world of thought with which I am not in touch and points of view which are novel to Washington; and the generous, affectionate friendship which shows itself so finely in every line you write cheers and sustains me more than you know. You see I am trying just now what I must believe to be the most difficult thing in the world: I am trying to live, and to live without loss of energy and zest for the daily task, on a broken heart. Voices like yours seem to me real. Friendship like yours gives me something to take hold of and take breath for my lungs from.

It is amazing how one can continue to function in all ordinary, and some extraordinary, matters with a broken heart. I would not have believed it. I deemed it impossible when I began the experiment. But it is possible; and I think the method is this: not to sit and look on,—especially not to sit and look on at oneself,—but to project oneself as far afield as possible, into fields where one's personal feelings count for nothing, or should count for nothing, except enhanced sympathy and quickened insight. Our own skies are so overcast by the influences of the storm raging in Europe that there is a vast deal to do to keep heart in others and that is the best way to keep our own hearts alive.

It actually looks as if it were possible that Congress would adjourn before the elictions. That will help a little to lighten the breaking weight of daily anxieties and plannings that must be watched all day and all night. The thing that is giving us the greatest concern just now is the situation of the South in view of the tremendous curtailment of the market for her one marketable crop, the cotton. For a little it looked like bankruptcy, and that is among the disturbing possibilities yet, but the first hysteria is past, bankers and others are getting their real thinking caps on, and it now seems likely that we shall be able to carry the unsaleable five million bales over till next season, induce the southern farmer to plant half a crop only next year, and come off with whole skins at least, though without much to clothe them with.

My little family (all except Helen Bones) are still at Cornish, but they will be coming back soon now and we shall, with sad hearts, but, I hope, with brave ones, effect our reorganization for the winter, with my fine Margaret as head of the household. It is splendid to see how she has risen to the task already, and how it has brought her sweet qualities out, and her strength. She grows with every responsibility put upon her. I am sure I am going to be proud of my little assistant.

I am well, and I am delighted to say that dear Helen is almost entirely herself again. The lines from Whittier helped![2] My warm regards to Mr. Toy.

Your affectionate friend,   Woodrow Wilson

WWTLS (WP, DLC).
[1] Nancy S. Toy to WW, Oct. 9, 1914, ALS (WP, DLC).
[2] The verse that she had enclosed is missing.

## From Robert Lansing

Dear Mr. President:                Washington October 15, 1914.

Referring to our conversation of last evening in regard to the negotiations relative to the Declaration of London I send you herewith the objections to the Draft Order in Council of the British Government,[1] which they propose as a substitute to the Order in Council of August 20th.

The sum total of the objections is that the Order in Council of August 20th is repealed in no particular, but on the contrary is reenacted with changes and additions which make its provisions even more objectionable.

If these objections seem to you to be sound, they should, I think, be telegraphed to Mr. Page in London as Sir Cecil Spring-Rice today showed me a telegram from Sir Edward Grey asking for our comments on the proposed Order in Council as soon as possible. It would seem best also to give a paraphrase of the telegram to Sir Cecil in order that he may be fully advised of this Government's views.

Even though the telegram is long, it seems to me advisable that Mr. Page should be supplied with the arguments which will be urged on the British Ambassador here.

I regret to have to trouble you with this matter but in view of Sir Edward Grey's urgent request for the views of this Government, which is not unreasonable in the circumstances, I felt this Memorandum should be in your hands tonight.

A copy of the Order in Council of August 20, 1914 and of the substitute Order in Council now proposed by the British Government are also inclosed.

Very sincerely yours,    Robert Lansing.

TLS (SDR, RG 59, 763.72112/157, DNA).
  1 The draft Order in Council is printed in *FR-WWS 1914*, pp. 244-46. Lansing's draft telegram is printed in *FR-LP*, I, 253-55. Lansing and Wilson used this draft in writing RL to WHP, Oct. 16, 1914, 3 P.M., printed at that date.

## Walter Hines Page to William Jennings Bryan

CONFIDENTIAL. FOR THE PRESIDENT: London, October 15 1914.

Present controversy about shipping. I cannot help fearing we are getting into deep water needlessly   The British Government has yielded without question to all our requests and has shown a sincere desire to meet all our wishes short of admitting war materials into Germany. That it will not yield. We would not yield it if we were in their place. Neither would the Germans. The English will risk a serious quarrel or even war with us rather than yield. This you may regard as final.

Since the last lists of contraband and conditional contraband were made such articles as rubber and copper and petrolium have come to play an entirely new part in war. They simply will not admit them. Nothing that can be used for war purposes in Germany now will be used for anything else. Representatives of Spain, Holland and all the Scandinavian States have conferred with me. They agree they can do nothing but acquiesce and file protrests and claims. They admit that England has the right to revise the list. This is not a war in the sense we have hitherto used the word. It is a world-clash of systems of government, a struggle to the extermination of English civilization or of Prussian military autocracy. Precedents have gone to the scrap heap. There is a new measure for military and diplomatic action. Suppose we press for a few shippers' theoretical rights. The American people as a whole gain nothing and the result is friction with Great Britain which is precisely what a very small minority of agitators would like. Great Britain can any day close the channel to all shipping or can drive Holland to the enemy and blockade her ports.

Look a little further ahead. If Germany win, it will make no matter what position Great Britain took on the Declaration of London. We shall see the Monroe Doctrine shot through. We shall have to have a great army and a great navy. If England win, and we have an ugly academic dispute with her because of this controversy, we shall be in a bad position for helping to compose the quarrel or for any other service.

The present controversy seems here, close to the struggle, academic and of the smallest practical consequence compared with the grave danger we incur of shutting ourselves off from a position to be of some service to civilization and to the peace of the world.

There is no practical need to consult other neutral governments. If we accept the proposed new Order in Council all the others will accept it and thank us after the event. Their representatives all come to me for advice and leadership here.

The question seems wholly different here from what it probably seems in Washington. There it is a more or less academic discussion. Here it is a matter of life and death for English speaking civilization. It is not a happy time to raise controversies that can be avoided or postponed. Nothing can be gained and every chance for useful cooperation for peace can easily be thrown away and is now in jeopardy. In jeopardy also are our friendly relations with Great Britain in the sorest time of need in her history. I know that this is the correct, larger view. I recommend most earnestly the substantial acceptance of the new Order in Council or our acquiescence with a reservation of whatever rights we may have; and I recommend prompt information to the British Government of such action. I should like so to inform Grey.

So far as our neutrality obligations are concerned I do not believe that they require us to demand that Great Britain should adopt for our benefit the Declaration of London which has never been ratified by Great Britain or any other nation except the United States[1] and the effect of which in its application to the situation presented by this war is altogether to the advantage of Germany.

I have delayed to send this perhaps too long for fear I might possibly seem influenced by sympathy with England and by the atmosphere here. But I write of course solely with reference to our own country's interest in its position after the reorganization of Europe. Anderson and Laughlin agree with me emphatically. Page

T telegram (SDR, RG 59, 763.72112/164, DNA).
[1] Page was mistaken. The United States had not ratified the Declaration of London on account of the failure of the British government to do so.

## From Edward Mandell House

Dear Governor:              New York City. October 15th, 1914.

I think your letter to Glynn is fine and I am calling his attention to the fact that you have made an exception of him in giving him an individual endorsement.

Hapgood and Crane lunched with me today and I made them understand why the Administration was taking the stand for Glynn and other regular primary nominees. Sometimes is [it] is difficult for an independent to see that a party leader has to act differently from an ordinary voter.

Affectionately yours,   E. M. House

TLS (WP, DLC).

## To Walter Hines Page[1]

Washington, October 16, 1914. 1 p.m.

323 STRICTLY CONFIDENTIAL AND PERSONAL. To be deciphered by the Ambassador himself. This telegram will be followed by another in reply to your telegram Number 806, October ninth stating the objections of this Government to the proposed Order in Council, which the Department's unnumbered instruction of September twenty-sixth will make clear.

The desire of this Government is to obtain from the British Government the issuance of an Order in Council adopting the Declaration without any amendment whatsoever and to obtain from France and Russia like decrees, which they will undoubtedly issue if Great Britain sets the example. Such an adoption by the allied Governments will put in force the acceptance of the Declaration of London by Germany and Austria, which will thus become for all the belligerent powers the code of naval warfare during the present conflict. This is the aim of the United States.

It cannot be accomplished if the Declaration is changed in any way as Germany and Austria would not give their consent to a change.

In the frequent informal and confidential conversations which have taken place here and in the admirable frankness with which Sir Edward Grey has stated the reasons for the action which Great Britain has deemed it necessary to take in regard to the Declaration, this Government feels that it fully understands and appreciates the British position, and is not disposed to place obstacles in the way of the accomplishment of the purposes which the British representatives have so frankly stated.

The confidence thus reposed in this Government makes it appreciate more than ever the staunch friendship of Great Britain for the United States, which it hopes always to deserve.

This Government would not feel warranted in offering any suggestion to the British Government as to a course which would meet the wishes of this Government and at the same time accomplish the ends which Great Britain seeks, but you might in the strictest confidence intimate to Sir Edward Grey the following plan, at the same time stating very explicitly that it is your personal suggestion and not one for which your Government is responsible.

Let the British Government issue an Order in Council accepting the Declaration of London without change or addition, and repealing all previous conflicting Orders in Council.

Let this Order in Council be followed by a Proclamation adding articles to the lists of absolute and conditional contraband by virtue of the authority conferred by Articles 23 and 25 of the Declaration.

Let the Proclamation be followed by another Order in Council, of which the United States need not be previously advised, declaring that, when one of His Majesty's Principal Secretaries of State is convinced that a port or the territory of a neutral country is being used as a base for the transit of supplies for an enemy government a Proclamation shall issue declaring that such port or territory has acquired enemy character insofar as trade in contraband is concerned and that vessels trading therewith shall be thereafter subject to the rules of the Declaration governing trade to enemy's territory.

It is true that the latter Order in Council would be based on a new principle. The excuse would be that the Declaration of London failing to provide for such an exceptional condition as exists a belligerent has a right to give a reasonable interpretation to the rules of the Declaration so that they will not leave him helpless to prevent an enemy from obtaining supplies for his military forces although the belligerent may possess the power and would have the right to do so if the port or territory was occupied by the enemy.

When the last mentioned Order in Council is issued, I am convinced that a full explanation of its nature and necessity would meet with liberal consideration by this Government and not be the subject of serious objection.

I repeat that any suggestion, which you may make to Sir Edward Grey, must be done in an entirely personal way, and with the distinct understanding that this Government is in no way responsible for what you may say.

Lansing   Acting Secretary of State

T telegram (SDR, RG 59, 763.72112/164, DNA).
 [1] Earlier drafts of the following telegram have not survived. It was probably drafted by Lansing, and was certainly edited by Wilson. It is printed in part in *FR-WWS 1914*, pp. 249-50.

## To Walter Hines Page[1]

Washington, October 16, 1914 3 p.m.

324 Your telegram No. 806, October 9th.

*You may say to Sir Edward Grey that it is the earnest desire of this Government to reach an agreement as to the Declaration of London which will be mutually satisfactory, and that it is a matter of sincere gratification that the British Government have shown equal anxiety to meet the wishes of this Government in revising the Order in Council which seemed objectionable to this Government.*

*Nevertheless the United States is bound to recognize the rights of neutrals and to avoid accepting rules which it considers will place undue restrictions upon their exercise, not only because by accepting them undesirable precedents may be created for the future but also because acceptance by this Government might be construed by the enemies of Great Britain to be contrary to that strict neutrality which it is the earnest wish of the President to preserve throughout the present war.*

*It is, therefore, in no unfriendly spirit but in the hope and confident expectation that some more acceptable way may be found to accomplish the ends sought by the British Government that this Government offers the following objections to the Order in Council which has been proposed as a substitute for the Order in Council of August twentieth.*

First. The proposed Order in Council does not accept the Declaration of London without change, hence this Government is convinced that such modified acceptance would not be satisfactory to other belligerents, who have accepted the Declaration ⟨conditionally upon its acceptance⟩ *upon the condition that it is accepted* by all the belligerent powers.

⟨*Second.* If all or a part of the belligerents accepted the Declaration of London the proposed modifications and additions to the Declaration, by increasing the restrictions on neutral commerce beyond those imposed by the Declaration or by international law, would not be acceptable to neutral nations including the United States.

⟨The foregoing objections to the proposed Order in Council are general in nature, depending upon the fact that the proposed modifications and additions make unanimous acceptance of the Declaration of London as a code of naval warfare impossible.⟩

As to the provisions of the proposed Order in Council ⟨considered in detail⟩ this Government ⟨makes the following⟩ *as a neutral and in the interest of neutral commerce is constrained to make the following* objections:

Second. The proposed Order in Council leaves unrepealed Articles 2, 3, 4 and 6 of the Order in Council of August 20th. Of these Articles Numbers 3 and 6 are especially objectionable to this Government *for reasons which have already been stated.* ⟨Articles 2 and 4, while less objectionable, are amendments to the Declaration and so prevent its unqualified acceptance.⟩

Third. The proposed Order in Council, while it purports to repeal Article One of the Order in Council of August twentieth, in fact reenacts that Article and extends the lists of contraband set forth by many additions. These additions could have been made under Articles twenty-three and twenty-five of the Declaration if it had been adopted without change, hence it was needless to modify the Declaration itself. This same objection was made to Article One of the Order in Council of August twentieth, and applies equally to its reenactment in an amended form.

Fourth. The substitution of Sub-Article B of Article two of Section three of the proposed Order in Council for Article five of the Order in Council of August twentieth ⟨is, from the standpoint⟩ *seems to be more restrictive* of neutral ⟨interests, more objectionable⟩ *rights* than the repealed Article five. ⟨That⟩ Article *five* was intended to preserve the doctrine of "continuous voyage" in relation to conditional contraband. ⟨While purporting to abandon the doctrine Sub-Article B not only reenacts it but goes⟩ *Although Sub-Article B purports to do away with this doctrine, it in fact appears to go* even further than Article five in applying it. If "continuous voyage" is eliminated, no ship carrying articles listed as conditional contraband is liable to capture when its cargo is to be discharged in a neutral port even if the ultimate destination of the cargo is the enemy government. By Article five of the Order in Council of August twentieth a ship destined to a neutral port is liable to seizure if the consignee of ⟨the cargo of⟩ conditional contraband *on board* is an enemy government, its agent or a person under its control. By Sub-Article B, in the proposed Order in Council a ship and cargo are liable to capture, if the goods carried are ⟨listed as⟩ *in the list of* conditional contraband, even though *they are* to be discharged at a neutral port, provided Quote no consignee in that country of the goods alleged to be conditional contraband is disclosed in the ship's papers. Unquote. In fact the terms of the Sub-Article permit capture of a ship bound for the port of one neutral country, if the cargo is consigned to a person resident in another ⟨neutral country. The substitute is manifestly far more obnoxious *harsh and objectionable* than the original Article 5.⟩ *country not at war.*

Fifth. Section four of the proposed Order in Council introduces a new ⟨principle into international law, which⟩ *doctrine into naval warfare and* imposes upon neutral commerce a restriction, which appears to be without precedent ⟨in modern times⟩. An analysis of the provisions of this section shows that, in the discretion of one of His Majesty's Principal Secretaries of State, a neutral country may be clothed with enemy character and that the legitimate trade of another neutral with such country may be subjected to the rules which are applied to contraband trade with enemy territory ⟨as such rules are laid down in Article 3 of the Order in Council of August 20th⟩. In brief this section ⟨means⟩ *appears to declare* that articles, listed as conditional contraband, shipped in a neutral vessel to a neutral country makes the vessel and its cargo liable to seizure if ⟨the British authorities⟩ *certain members of the British Government* are satisfied that supplies or munitions of war are entering enemy territory from the neutral country to ⟨a port of⟩ which the vessel is bound even though the consignee is within the neutral country. The ⟨purpose⟩ *effect* of this provision ⟨seems⟩ *would seem* to be ⟨to gain all the rights of⟩ *that* a belligerent *would gain all the rights* over neutral commerce with enemy territory without declaring war against the neutral country which is claimed to be a base of supply for the military forces of an enemy. ⟨If the British Government seek belligerent rights they must *ought to* bear the burden of belligerency. They cannot *should not* declare a nation⟩ *It seems inconsistent to declare a nation* to be neutral and treat it as an enemy; and ⟨expect⟩, *if it does so*, other neutral nations ⟨to submit to having⟩ *can hardly be expected to permit* their commerce *to be* subject⟨ed⟩ to rules which only apply to commerce with a belligerent. ⟨If a neutral nation's trade with a neighboring belligerent constitutes an unneutral act, the remedy is an ultimatum, not a restriction of the trade of an innocent neutral nation with the nation whose acts are complained of.⟩

*You may also say to Sir Edward Grey that the President is convinced that, if the same ⟨patience⟩ forbearance and cordiality*

*continue, which each Government has shown up to this time in*
*the discussion of this question, a solution will speedily be reached*
*which will be acceptable to both.*

Robert Lansing.

T telegram (SDR, RG 59, 763.72112/157, DNA).
1 The following telegram was based on Lansing's memorandum or draft telegram cited in RL to WW, Oct. 15, 1914, n. 1. Wilson and Lansing composed the telegram printed below in conference, probably on October 16. The draft of the revised telegram is missing. In the telegram printed below, Wilson's additions, some of which are in Lansing's handwriting, are printed in italics; his deletions in angle brackets. This telegram is printed in *FR-WWS 1914*, pp. 250-252.

## To Walter Hines Page[1]

Washington, October 16, 1914 6 pm

Strictly confidential, to be deciphered by the Ambassador only. Yours October 15th, 11, p.m.

Beg that you will not regard the position of this Government as merely academic. Contact with opinion on this side the water would materially alter your view. Lansing has pointed out to you in personal confidential despatch of this date how completely all the British Government seeks can be accomplished without the least friction with this Government and without touching opinion on this side the water on an exceedingly tender spot. I must urge you to realize this aspect of the matter and to use your utmost persuasive efforts to effect an understanding, which we earnestly desire, by the method we have gone out of our way to suggest, which will put the whole case in unimpeachable form.

This is private and for your guidance. Woodrow Wilson.

Lansing   Acting Secretary of State.

T telegram (SDR, RG 59, 763.72112/164, DNA).
1 There is a WWhw draft of this telegram with SDR, RG 59, 763.72112/164, DNA. This telegram is printed in *FR-WWS 1914*, pp. 252-53.

## To Sir Cecil Arthur Spring Rice

Personal and private.

My dear Mr. Ambassador,      The White House 16 October, 1914.

Each time I get one of your notes with an important enclosure I feel afresh the generous spirit of friendship in which you are acting and find myself given fresh heart in handling a perplexing and delicate matter.

I have made some suggestions to Mr. Lansing which he will convey to you. I am anxious not to take a merely negative position, but to affirmatively assist, so far as it is proper and possible for me to do so, in the solution of the questions of neutrality we have been discussing; and I hope we have found a way.

Cordially and sincerely Yours, Woodrow Wilson

WWTLS (FO 115/1770, p. 102, PRO).

## To Edward Mandell House

My dear Friend: Washington October 16, 1914.

I have no doubt McAdoo will see you in New York and tell you about the cotton fund. The plans suggested did not turn out to be feasible, but there are other plans which will work if the bankers in New York will accept McAdoo's suggestions. This whole thing throws additional work on McAdoo, I am sorry to say, who is overworked, and very much overworked, already, but apparently there is no escape from that. I am sometimes quite anxious about him.

I yesterday wrote and gave out, as you have seen by this time, a letter to Governor Glynn. I am going to write one to Ambassador Gerard today.

You are certainly helping in a wonderful way and we are all your debtor.

In haste Affectionately yours, Woodrow Wilson

TLS (E. M. House Papers, CtY).

## To James Watson Gerard

My dear Mr. Gerard: [The White House] October 16, 1914

I have been torn by conflicting desires in the matter of your candidacy for the United States Senate. I have so deeply regretted that the Government should lose your services at Berlin, where you have distinguished yourself, and yet, of course, I shall look forward with the greatest satisfaction to seeing you in the Senate. This is just a line to congratulate you on the judgment of the primaries and to express my warmest good wishes for the campaign and my pleasure that the prospects should be so bright.

Cordially and sincerely yours, Woodrow Wilson

TLS (Letterpress Books, WP, DLC).

## From Sir Cecil Arthur Spring Rice

Personal and private

Dear Mr President          Washington. 16 October 1914

I cannot refrain from thanking you from my heart for your most kind letter.

I spoke to Mr Lansing today who told me of the measures taken under your orders for safeguarding the just rights of neutrals while respecting those exigencies of war in which, unfortunately, all countries, even the most peaceable may be involved.

May I add that the spirit shown by your government in these most difficult and dangerous negotiations will I am sure be fully appreciated by my government. In the strain and stress of these terrible times it is indeed a consolation to find at least one quarter where there is a firm and constant desire for a just and friendly settlement.

I have the honour to remain    with profound respect
your most obedient humble servant    Cecil Spring Rice

ALS (WP, DLC).


## From Samuel Gompers

My dear Mr. President        Washington, D. C., October 16, 1914.

I deeply appreciate your thoughtfulness and courtesy in sending me one of the pens with which you signed the Clayton bill. It will be added to my collection of historic pens, among them being the pen with which President Cleveland signed the bill making Labor Day a legal holiday.

Permit me at the same time to take this opportunity of expressing to you my great appreciation of your approval of the Clayton Bill, the labor provisions of which are indeed a magnificent piece of legislation, according to the working people of our country the rational, constitutional and inherent rights of which they have too long been denied.

Very sincerely yours,    Saml. Gompers.

TLS (WP, DLC).


## To Oscar Wilder Underwood

My dear Mr. Underwood:    The White House October 17, 1914

I cannot let this session of Congress close without expressing my warm admiration for the fidelity and intelligence with which the programme outlined in April and December of last year has been carried out, and my feeling that the people of the country have been served by the members of this Congress as they have seldom, if ever, been served before. The programme was a great one and it is a matter of deep satisfaction to think of the way in which it has been handled.

It had several distinct parts and many items, but, after all, a single purpose, namely, to destroy private control and set business free. That purpose was manifest enough in the case of the tariff and in the legislation affecting trusts; but, though perhaps less evident upon the surface there, it lay at the very heart of the currency bill, too. May I not add, even though it lies outside the field of legislation, that that, and that chiefly, has been the object of the foreign policy of the Government during the last eighteen months?

Private control had shown its sinister face on every hand in America, had shown it for a long time, and sometimes very brazenly, in the trusts and in a virtual domination of credit by small groups of men. The safest hiding place and covert of such control was in the tariff. There it for a long time hid very shrewdly. The tariff was a very complicated matter; none but experts thoroughly understood its schedules. Many of the schedules were framed to afford particular advantages to special groups of manufacturers and investors. That was the soil in which trade combinations and combinations of manufacturers most readily grew, and most rankly. High prices did not spring directly out of the tariff. They sprang out of the suppression of domestic, no less than of foreign, competition by means of combinations and trade agreements which could be much more easily contrived and maintained under the protection of a high tariff than without it. The European war came before the withdrawal of this much coveted opportunity for monopoly could show its full effects and active competition bring prices to their normal level again; but it is clear enough already that the reduction of the tariff, the simplification of its schedules so as to cut away the jungle in which secret agencies had so long lurked, the correction of its inequalities, and its thorough recasting with the single honest object of revenue, were an indispensable first step to reestablishing competition.

The present Congress has taken that step with courage, sincerity, and effectiveness. The lobby by which some of the worst features of the old tariff had been maintained was driven away by the mere pitiless turning on of the light. The principle was adopted that each duty levied was to be tested by the inquiry whether it was put at such a figure and levied in such a manner as to provoke competition. The soil in which combinations had grown was removed lest some of the seeds of monopoly might be found to remain in it. The thing had needed to be done for a long time but nobody had ventured before to undertake it in systematic fashion.

The panic that the friends of privilege had predicted did not follow. Business has already adjusted itself to the new conditions with singular ease and elasticity, because the new conditions are in fact more normal than the old. The revenue lost by the import duties was replaced by an income tax which in part shifted the burden of taxation from the shoulders of every consumer in the country, great or small, to shoulders more certainly able to bear it.

We had time to learn from the actual administration of the law that the revenues resulting from the double change would have been abundant had it not been for the breaking out of the present war in Europe, which affects almost every route of trade and every market in the world outside of the United States. Until the war ends and until its effects upon manufacture and commerce have been corrected we shall have to impose additional taxes to make up for the loss of such part of our import duties as the war cuts off by cutting off the imports themselves,—a veritable war tax though we are not at war; for war, and only war, is the cause of it.

It is fortunate that the reduction of the duties came first. The import duties collected under the old tariff constituted a much larger proportion of the whole revenue of the Government than do the duties under the new. A still larger proportion of the revenue would have been cut off by the war had the old taxes stood and a larger war tax would have been necessary as a consequence. No miscalculation, no lack of foresight, has created the necessity for the taxes but only a great catastrophe world-wide in its operation and effects.

With similar purpose and in a like temper the Congress has sought in the Trade Commission bill and in the Clayton bill to make men in a small way of business as free to succeed as men in a big way, and to kill monopoly in the seed. Before these bills were passed the law was already clear enough that monopolies once formed were illegal and could be dissolved by direct process of law and those who had created them punished as for crime. But there was no law to check the process by which monopoly was built up until the tree was full grown and its fruit developed, or, at any rate, until the full opportunity for monopoly had been created. With this new legislation there is clear and sufficient law to check and destroy the noxious growth in its infancy. Monopolies are built up by unfair methods of competition, and the new Trade Commission has power to forbid and prevent unfair competition, whether upon a big scale or upon a little, whether just begun or grown old and formidable. Monopoly is created also by putting the same men in charge of a variety of business enterprises, whether apparently related or unrelated to one another, by means of interlocking directorates. That the Clayton bill now in large measure prevents. Each enterprise must depend upon its own initiative and effectiveness for success and upon the intelligence and business energy of the men who officer it. And so all along the line: monopoly is to be cut off at the roots.

Incidentally, justice has been done the laborer. His labor is no longer to be treated as if it were merely an inanimate object of commerce disconnected from the fortunes and happiness of a living human being, to be dealt with as an object of sale and barter. But that, great as it is, is hardly more than the natural and inevitable corollary of a law whose object is individual freedom and initiative as against any kind of private domination.

The accomplishment of this legislation seems to me a singularly significant thing. If our party were to be called upon to name the particular point of principle in which it differs from its opponents most sharply and in which it feels itself most definitely sustained by experience, we should no doubt say that it was this: that we would have no dealings with monopoly, but reject it altogether, while our opponents were ready to adopt it into the realm of law and seek merely to regulate it and moderate it in its operation. It is our purpose to destroy monopoly and maintain competition as the only effectual instrument of business liberty.

We have seen the nature and the power of monopoly exhibited. We know that it is more apt to control government than to be controlled by it: for we have seen it control government, dictate legislation, and dominate executives and courts. We feel that our people are safe only in the fields of free individual endeavor where American genius and initiative are not guided by a few men as in recent years, but made rich by the activities of a multitude, as in days now almost forgotten. We will not consent that an ungovernable giant should be reared to full stature in the very household of the government itself.

In like manner by the currency bill we have created a democracy of credit such as has never existed in this country before. For a generation or more we have known and admitted that we had the worst banking and currency system in the world, because the volume of our currency was wholly inelastic: that is, because there was more than enough at certain seasons to meet the demands of commerce and credit and at other times far too little: that we could not lessen the volume when we needed less nor increase it when we needed more. Everybody talked about the absurd system and its quite unnecessary embarrassments, sure to produce periodic panics; and everybody said that it ought to be changed and changed very radically; but nobody took effective steps to change it until the present Congress addressed itself to the task with genuine resolution and an intelligence which expressed itself in definite action. And now the thing is done.

Let bankers explain the technical features of the new system. Suffice it here to say that it provides a currency which expands as it is needed and contracts when it is not needed: a currency which comes into existence in response to the call of every man who can show a going business and a concrete basis for extending credit to him, however obscure or prominent he may be, however big or little his business transactions.

More than that, the power to direct this system of credits is put into the hands of a public board of disinterested officers of the Government itself who can make no money out of anything they do in connection with it. No group of bankers anywhere can get control; no one part of the country can concentrate the advantages and conveniences of the system upon itself for its own selfish advantage. The board can oblige the banks of one region to go to the assistance of the banks of another. The whole resources of the country are mobilized, to be employed where they are most needed. I think we are justified in speaking of this as a democracy of credit. Credit is at the disposal of every man who can show energy and assets. Each region of the country is set to study its own needs and opportunities and the whole country stands by to assist. It is self-government as well as democracy.

I understand why it was not possible at this session to mature legislation intended specially for the development of a system for handling rural or, rather, agricultural credits; but the Federal Reserve Act itself facilitates and enlarges agricultural credit in an extraordinary degree. The farmer is as much a partner in the new democracy of credit as the merchant or manufacturer. Indeed, special and very liberal provision is made for his need, as will speedily appear when the system has been a little while in operation. His assets are as available as any other man's, and for credits of a longer term.

There have been many other measures passed of extraordinary importance, for the seeion [session] has been singularly rich in thoughtful and constructive legislation; but I have mentioned the chief acts for which this Congress will be remembered as very notable indeed. I did not mean when I began to write to make this letter so long, and even to mention the other legislation that is worthy of high praise would extend it to an inordinate length. My purpose in writing was merely to express my own great admiration for the industry and the leadership, as well as the wisdom and constructive skill, which has accomplished all these things.

I wish I could speak by name of the many men who have so honorably shared in these distinguished labors. I doubt if there has ever been a finer exhibition of team work or of unhesitating devotion to the fulfillment of party pledges,—and yet the best of it is that the great measures passed have shown, I venture to say, no partisan bias, but only a spirit of serious statesmanship. I am proud to have been associated with such men, working in such a spirit through so many months of unremitted labor at trying tasks of counsel. It has been a privilege to have a share in such labors. I wish I could express to every one of the members who have thus cooperated together my personal appreciation of what he has helped to do. This letter may, I hope, serve in some sort as a substitute for that.

I look forward with confidence to the elections. The voters of the United States have never failed to reward real service. They have never failed to sustain a Congress and administration that were seeking, as this Congress and, I believe, this administration have sought, to render them a permanent and disinterested benefit in the shape of reformed and rectified laws. They know that, extraordinary as the record is which I have recited, our task is not done; that a great work of constructive development remains to be accomplished, in building up our merchant marine, for instance, and in the completion of a great programme for the conservation of our natural resources and the development of the water power of the country,—a programme which has at this session already been carried several steps toward consummation. They know, too, that without a Congress in close sympathy with the administration a whole scheme of peace and honor and disinterested service to the world of which they have approved cannot be brought to its full realization. I would like to go into the district of every member of Congress who has sustained and advanced the plans of the party and speak out my advocacy of his claims for reelection; but, of course, I cannot do that; and with so clear a record no member of Congress needs a spokesman. What he has done speaks for itself. If it be a mere question of political fortunes, I believe the immediate future of the party to be as certain as the past is secure.

The Democratic party is now in fact the only instrument ready to the country's hand by which anything can be accomplished. It is united, as the Republican party is not; it is strong and full of the zest of sober achievement, and has been rendered confident by carrying out a great constructive programme such as no other party has attempted; it is absolutely free from the entangling alliances which made the Republican party, even before its rupture, utterly unserviceable as an instrument of reform; its thought, its ambition, its plans are of the vital present and the hopeful future. A practical nation is not likely to reject such a team, full of the spirit of public service, and substitute, in the midst of great tasks, either a party upon which a deep demoralization has fallen or a party which has not grown to the stature that would warrant its assuming the responsible burdens of state. Every thoughtful man sees that a change of parties made just now would set the clock back, not forward. I have a very complete and very confident belief in the practical sagacity of the American people.

With sincere regard and admiration,

Faithfully yours,   Woodrow Wilson[1]

TLS (O. W. Underwood Papers A-Ar).

[1] Wilson dictated an incomplete draft of this letter to Swem and then edited it. This copy is in the C. L. Swem Coll., NjP. Wilson gave Tumulty a copy of this draft. Tumulty started to edit and expand it, and then instead wrote Wilson a memorandum suggesting extensive changes and additions ("Memorandum for the President," n.d., WP, DLC). Following Tumulty's suggestions, Wilson wrote a new and much longer draft in shorthand, which conforms very closely to the final version. The undated WWsh draft is in *ibid.* Wilson dictated the final draft to Swem, reading from his shorthand draft.

The letter to Underwood was published widely as a campaign document.

## To Mary Allen Hulbert

Dearest Friend,                    The White House 18 October, 1914.

I am tired and infinitely dull to-night, not fit to write a letter to a lady of wit and understanding; but I must send you a line or two to greet and welcome you at your new quarters, No. 49 Gloucester street, Boston. I shall await with the keenest interest your impressions of the new partner who is to be associated with you and Allen in the house-keeping venture: a vast deal will depend on him. Not that you cannot captivate and get along with anyone you have a mind to; but it will be a bore if he is not such a fellow as it [is] easy to like and establish easy terms with. I shall await particulars, therefore, with anxious curiosity.

It was fine to see the good spirits of your last note from Nantucket. Boston, I hope and believe, will rest you, by force of a new interest. You seem to *belong* anywhere, either in a desert, a lonely garden, a city, a ball room, a salon,—anywhere. I think you are most content when out in the free out-of-doors, with the Nature which seems so to stimulate and revivify you; but the city is your domain, too, for no one understands or enjoys "folks" more than you do, whatever their kind or degree; and you do the folks as much good as they do you. Tell me all about Boston,— your part of it and from your point of view. I am sure it will be the most interesting Boston I have ever heard of. And I need to be interested. I seem to be doing my present tasks automatically, pretty much, and sadly need to have my thoughts guided a bit.

I am well; deeply glad that my little notes help; touched every day by the sweet services of dear Helen, now quite well again (with care) and at my side the moment I need her, bless her heart!

My warmest regards to Allen.

Your devoted friend,    Woodrow Wilson

WWTLS (WP, DLC).

## To Annie Josephine Wilson Howe

Dearest Sister,                    The White House 18 October, 1914.

Thank you with all my heart for your sweet letter.[1] It gave me genuine pleasure and comfort. Better than that, it seemed to me to show you in a happier frame of mind. I think that that was the source of the deepest pleasure it gave me. I have you on my thoughts a great deal. Your happiness is very much at my heart,— and everything that concerns you; and I hope and believe that days of less anxiety are ahead of us.

I hope that you are to have time to see us here before you settle down in New York. Can you come,—for a few days, at any rate, —without interfering with the essential plans about Annie and her studies?

I hear that you have already hit upon appartments in New York. I hope that you will like them and find them convenient and comfortable. Where are they to be?

Dear Helen is a great comfort to me. She is well again,—entirely well, I believe, and is constantly with me when I am free from the office,—even goes out and goes around the golf courses with me, taking her exerci[s]es that way and giving me pleasure into the bargain. She is a dear!

I keep well. I cannot say that I have recovered my spirits. I find it hard to care about anything, and perform my duties rather in order to forget than with the zest of earnest work; but they do keep me busy; I do not allow myself to mope; and the day's work is done, I hope without any difference being evident between the way I do it now and the way I used to do it.

Dearest love to all. What a sweet picture that was you drew of Josephine at her birthday party! Bless her dear little heart.

Your loving brother, Woodrow Wilson

WWTLS (WC, NjP).

[1] Annie W. Howe to WW, Oct. 11, 1914, ALS (WP, DLC).

## Remarks at a Press Conference

October 19, 1914

Mr. President, are you still adhering to your plan of not appointing a Federal Trade Commission until the December session?

> Yes, sir, chiefly because I haven't time to make a careful selection before that time.

On Saturday, Mr. President, Senator Stone said something in the Senate.[1] Had he discussed that with you before he said it?

> No, sir.

There is nothing you could add to it?

> Oh, no.

Mr. President, in that connection, one of the British vessels outside of New York, Tuesday—I think it was—seized the tank steamer *Brindilla*, formerly a German vessel but now owned by the Standard Oil Company.

> So I saw by the papers this morning.

Under the general rule of international law, isn't it true that a vessel, even carrying contraband from one neutral point to another neutral point, is exempt from seizure?

> That is the general rule. So far I know nothing of the official circumstances of this seizure. Indeed, the only thing I do know about is what I saw in the papers this morning.

[1] Senator Stone, on October 19, denounced the search of the United Fruit Company's *Metapan* by officers from the French cruiser, *Condé*. The ship was under American registry and flying the American flag when it was boarded and searched. Five Germans were segregated from the other passengers and forced to sign a statement binding them not to engage in war against France. Senator Stone, warning the warring powers that the neutral rights of the United States must be respected, said: "I think it is an opportune time to say that belligerent powers, if they care for the regard and friendship of this republic to themselves, recognize and strictly observe the rights and privileges of a neutral power. . . . It is well for other nations to know that we will not look with indifference upon a violation of the rights of our Government or our own people." *New York Times*, Oct. 18, 1914; *Cong. Record*, 63d Cong., 2d sess., pp. 16765, 16769.

Mr. President, we haven't taken any official cognizance of the nearness of foreign warships to our ports either at New York or elsewhere?

We have no right to do that.

In the Franco-Prussian war we took it seriously. The French government withdrew their ships.

I don't know anything about that. Any ship has the right to come no closer than the three-mile limit.

Mr. President, have you an engagement to meet Sir George Paish?[2]

No, sir. I understood that he was in town. I would like very much to see him. I had it in mind to send word that I would like to see him, but I haven't done so yet.

Can you give us an idea, Mr. President, of what matters are going to be taken up by Sir George Paish and the Secretary of the Treasury?

No, I cannot, because I don't know fully the circumstances that brought him over here. I judge from what I have heard unofficially that it is to ease the methods of exchange between the two countries.

Mr. McAdoo told us that he discussed the cotton situation.

Yes, sir.

Mr. President, you said at the last conference that you heard that some national banks in this country were trying to establish a basis of credits with South America. Has that gotten any further?

What I meant was that one or two banks were establishing branches in South America. I haven't heard anything about that recently.

Have you been advised of any move by the German government to have Mr. Whitlock removed from his official position and retained as a private citizen?

No, sir, I haven't heard that.

Mr. President, there were some reports last week that the government had now changed its attitude on the matter of foreign loans by private individuals; is there any foundation for that?

None whatever.

Is it opposed to neutrality to loan to foreign nations?

I won't discuss it. I will just say that the government has not changed its attitude.

2 Joint editor of *The Statist*, 1900-1916; at this time adviser to the British Treasury. Paish came to confer with McAdoo, members of the Federal Reserve Board, and prominent New York bankers about adjustment of credits between the United States and England, and then to investigate and report to his office about industrial and economic conditions in the United States. Wilson did see Paish.

Do you know, Mr. President, what are the chances of getting the seamen's bill into conference?

> No, I do not. Amidst the many other things that we have been handling, I haven't been asking about that recently.

Are there any new developments in the Colorado situation, Mr. President?

> None at all that I am informed of.

Are negotiations still going on with the operators?

> No, not strictly speaking. They have declined to accept the plan that I suggested to them, except with modifications that would take all the essential features out of it.

Mr. President, from something you said last week, I was in doubt whether you intended to include the Adamson bill and the water power bill in your conservation program?

> I think I said that it was not, properly speaking, part of the conservation program. That is a sort of what one might call an historical accident. By conservation, we mean the handling of the public domain, really, and its resources. The Adamson bill referred to the navigable waters in those portions of the United States not owned by the government. That is the reason that, technically speaking, it is not part of conservation at all, though in the broader sense it is a very important part of conservation.

The Adamson bill is regarded as a very important point?

> Yes, because of its whole collateral effect on the whole conservation policy.

Do you favor the bill in its present form?

> It was pulled about a good deal in the House, and I haven't read its present form; but so far as I know it is satisfactory.

It is satisfactory to conservationists?

> I am a conservationist. It ought to be satisfactory to me.

Is there anything you can tell us on the Mexican situation, Mr. President?

> No, sir, except that I hear a good many things being told that are not so. Apparently somebody is still interested in having things occur down there that do not occur.

There was a report a few days ago that Mr. Silliman arranged with General Aguilar those details about Veracruz. Has that been finally decided?

> No. I received a dispatch to that effect, that he had a conference.

That must be, of course. Whatever Aguilar might—

> Yes, of course. The authorities in Mexico City are in a fluid condition just now.

Has there been any reply to Carranza as to his attitude on several points this government wanted to know about?

> No direct reply. I understand that—this was indirectly, and I will just have to give it as rumor—that he referred to those matters about what I take leave to call the "Hot Springs" conference.[3]

Mr. President, this morning's papers say there is a schism in the administration on the armament question. Is that true?

> I can answer that, gentlemen. There is no schism in the administration over armaments or anything else.

About armaments in Europe or here.

> I didn't know we had any, in the European sense.

The leading article in one of our morning papers sets forth that there is a decided division of opinion in the administration over the question whether we should or should not increase our armaments.[4]

> I say there has been no discussion of the subject, and there hasn't been a chance to be a schism.

Mr. President, did you notice the propaganda that Mr. Gardner of Massachusetts has stirred with reference to that? Have you ever expressed yourself at all in regard to the army and the navy —a proper army and navy, or anything of that sort?

> No, not at all.

And that hasn't been put down as one of the arguments in your next year's program?

> Not so far.

Would you care to say anything about it?

> No; it is something that has been discussed a long time. I remember it just the way it has been discussed just now ever since I was ten years old. I remember that far back, so I am quite familiar with it as a subject.

Do you intend, Mr. President, to recommend to Congress that an appropriation be made for a larger number of auxiliary vessels?

> I have no such present purpose. As I say, we have not discussed the matter, much less formed any policy.

Mr. President, do you think it is a good thing to discuss those things right now?

> As a mental exercise, I don't think it does any harm. Have to be joshing some in this regard.

---

[3] A conference of revolutionary leaders, meeting at Aguascalientes, for the purpose of establishing a new government. It had been in formal session since October 10, but most activity was suspended while awaiting arrival of the *Zapatista* delegates.

[4] The Editors have been unable to identify this article.

Does the same hold true with regard to the cotton bill—the cotton bond bill?

>You mean the one in the House?

Yes.

>Yes, I don't see any harm in discussing that. I think every possible thing that can be done to relieve the situation in the South ought to be thoroughly discussed. . . .

Mr. President, going back to cotton a moment. You saw Colonel Ewing[5] this past week, I believe. This morning he has got a suggestion in the papers about restricting the acreage of cotton next season to 50 per cent of the present crop. I was wondering whether he discussed that with you.

>We did not discuss cotton at all. We discussed the management, the carrying out of the protection against floods in the lower Mississippi entirely—carrying out a thoroughgoing policy about that. Of course, the suggestion about a limitation of the acreage of planted cotton is being discussed everywhere.

That would be a state question?

>I don't see how it would be anything else.

(A question was asked about warehouses which the stenographer did not hear distinctly)

>Answer: I have been very much in hopes that the House would pass the so-called Lever bill.[6] The Senate has already passed it.

That is almost necessary?

>I think so, yes. You see, we want to help by means of warehouse certificates, and if there are no warehouses there cannot be warehouse certificates, of course. There are warehouses, but I mean not enough.

Will the element of federal supervision satisfy the government as to the conditions, et cetera, of the securities, involving their soundness?

>Yes, oh yes.

JRT transcript (WC, NjP) of CLSsh (C. L. Swem Coll., NjP).

[5] Robert Ewing of New Orleans. He visited the White House on October 14.

[6] The Lever-Smith warehouse bill, S. 6266 and H.R. 18359, which established federal inspection and licensing of warehouses for cotton, tobacco, grain, and other agricultural products. Its purpose was to facilitate borrowing by farmers against warehouse receipts. The bill passed the Senate but failed in the House. *Cong. Record*, 63d Cong., 2d sess., pp. 16189-90; Link, *Struggle for Neutrality*, pp. 98-99.

## To James Watson Gerard

[Washington, Oct. 19, 1914]

PRIVATE and confidential, to be deciphered only by the Ambassador himself.

I venture with not a little hesitation to make this suggestion to you in confidence, that you see some member of the government upon whom you are likely to make the deepest impression in such a matter and whose influence you can count upon as great and say that nothing is making so unfavourable, not to say fatal, an impression in this country as the dropping of bombs from airships upon cities elsewhere than upon fortifications, with no result except terror and the destruction of innocent lives. I am deeply interested in maintaining a real neutrality of public opinion here and a scrupulous fairness of judgment but my efforts are being wholly nullified, I fear, by these occur[r]ences and will be so long as the present use of bombs where they can be of no possible military service continues. I have ventured therefore upon the very unusual course of making this suggestion, a suggestion of sincere friendship. This should be done, of course, as upon your own initiative and entirely unofficially, merely as a voluntary act of personal good will and friendship.[1]

WWT telegram (SDR, RG 59, 763.72116/336a, DNA).
[1] Gerard must have conveyed this message as Wilson suggested. There is no reference to it in the German Foreign Office Archives.

## From Brand Whitlock

London, October 19, 1914.

Repeated under request: quote: In two weeks the civil population of Belgium, already in misery, will face starvation. In view of this fact and at the request of the relief committee I venture to call your attention to my telegram to the Department dated October nineteenth, 10 a.m., in the conviction that your great heart will find some way by which America may help to provide food for these hungry ones in the dark days of the terrible winter that is coming on. Whitlock. Unquote.

Page

T telegram (WP, DLC).

## From Robert Lansing, with Enclosure

Dear Mr. President:        Washington October 19, 1914.

The enclosed telegram from Petrograd (No. 67, October 16, 6 P.M.) is of so much importance that I would like your approval of the draft telegram in reply before sending it.

It would be most gratifying if a treaty such as is proposed could be negotiated, but even to accomplish this, which would certainly bring much credit to your Administration, as it would be accomplishing the seemingly impossible, it seems to me that we should in no way intimate that a Russian credit loan would be favorably received. I have avoided the subject in the proposed reply.[1] Does it seem to you that it could be possibly construed as an admission that Count Witte's[2] mission would be looked upon with favor by this Government?

Very sincerely yours,    Robert Lansing.

TLS (WP, DLC).
[1] See the Enclosure printed with WW to RL, Oct. 20, 1914.
[2] Sergei Witte, Minister of Finance, 1892-1903, a major promoter of Russian modernization. He was made a count for his work as head of the Russian delegation to the Portsmouth Peace Conference of 1905.

### E N C L O S U R E

## Charles Stetson Wilson[1] to the Secretary of State

Petrograd, October 16, 1914.

Count Witte called on me and told me in strict confidence that Russian Government had suggested to him to go to America to raise loan as he is well known there besides being President of Russian financial commission. On account of age and health would prefer not to accept but has told Government he will do so in case decision is made, on two conditions only. First, Russia must make commercial treaty with the United States whereby all American citizens, Jews, Christians, naturalized or native, furnished with American passport shall have equal treatment in Russia.

Second, He must be assured that Russian Government will pass legislation improving social and economic conditions of working classes, as without these two conditions considers chance of securing loan impossible. I pointed out difficulty of loan from the point of view of American neutrality. Witte replied that Russia's proposal unlike those of France and Germany. No funds would leave the United States but whole loan would be spent there in purchasing from American manufacturers goods needed in Russia. Transaction therefore very advantageous to the United States.                                                      Wilson

T telegram (WP, DLC).
¹ First Secretary of the American Embassy in Petrograd.

## From Joseph I. Essig and Others

Dear Sir,                                    Washington D C. Oct. 19, 1914.

We the undersigned employees of the "Public Buildings & Grounds," hasten to thank you for the kind words spoken on our behalf. After years of effort to obtain a living or minimum wage—$2 per day without avail, we now see success in sight, as you have taken up our case, for which we are sincerely grateful. We cannot close without offering a word of thanks to your secretary the Hon Jos. Tumulty[.] In him we recognize a true friend to the workingman.

In the meantime Mr President we ask you if something could be done to induce the chief of our department to give us temporary raise in wages to tide us over this winter until Congress acts in our case.                         Very sincerely yours
                                             Jos. I Essig,
                                             Hershall Reese
                                             Thaddues E McGowan

ALS (WP, DLC).

## Robert Lansing to Walter Hines Page

                              Washington, October 19, 1914. 5 pm

Unnumbered
STRICTLY CONFIDENTIAL AND PERSONAL. The confidential and personal telegrams to you from the President and myself dated October sixteenth, together with this telegram, must not be placed on files of Embassy but be held by you personally in greatest secrecy.            Lansing   Acting Secretary of State

T telegram (SDR, RG 59, 763.72112/164, DNA).

## An Outline of Welcoming Remarks

                    Greeting to American Bar Association,
                              20 Oct., 1914.

Appreciation of Introduction and greeting.
It is in times of stress like this that a nation, like an individual, proves its temper and quality.

The law of nations and neutrality: a law sustained only by moral forces, only by principle and the spiritual obligation,—the spirit of right and fairness.

May I not suggest that there is some danger that the law which is sustained by the force of a nation is a little too apt to depend upon the mere force of an organized community rather than upon the rational and moral sanction which is its real justification and support? Can the law grow and express changing life only by statutory amendment? Are we not, as lawyers, custodians of a *spirit*, of a principle, not so much of command as of justice?

The mistress of the modern world is opinion: the standard of opinion is the moral judgment of mankind. The last and abiding verdict is the verdict of history, which speaks the mind of mankind. At the bar of that tribunal we sit all of us. The life of the law is in our *moral perceptions*.

W.W.   10/19/14

WWT MS (WP, DLC).

## Remarks to the American Bar Association[1]

[[Oct. 20, 1914]]

Mr. President,[2] gentlemen of the American Bar Association:

I am very deeply gratified by the greeting that your president has given me and by your response to it. My only strength lies in your confidence.

We stand now in a peculiar case. Our first thought, I suppose, as lawyers, is of international law, of those bonds of right and principle which draw the nations together and hold the community of the world to some standards of action. We know that we see in international law, as it were, the moral processes by which law itself came into existence. I know that, as a lawyer, I have myself at times felt that there was no real comparison between the law of a nation and the law of nations, because the latter lacked the sanction that gave the former strength and validity. And yet, if you look into the matter more closely, you will find that the two have the same foundations, and that those foundations are more evident and conspicuous in our day than they have ever been before.

The opinion of the world is the mistress of the world; and the processes of international law are the slow processes by which opinion works its will. What impresses me is the constant thought that that is the tribunal at the bar of which we all sit. I would call your attention, incidentally, to the circumstance that it does not observe the ordinary rules of evidence; which has sometimes suggested to me that the ordinary rules of evidence had shown some signs of growing antique. Everything, rumor included, is heard in this court, and the standard of judgment is not so much the character of the testimony as the character of the witness. The motives are disclosed, the purposes are conjectured, and that opinion is finally accepted which seems to be, not the best founded in law, perhaps, but the best founded in integrity of character and of morals. That is the process which is slowly working its will upon the world; and what we should be watchful of is not so much jealous interests as sound principles of action. The disinterested course is always the biggest course to pursue not only, but it is in the long run the most profitable course to pursue. If you can establish your character, you can establish your credit.

What I wanted to suggest to this association, in bidding them very hearty welcome to Washington, is whether we sufficiently apply these same ideas to the body of municipal law which we seek to administer. Citations seem to play so much larger a rôle now than principles. There was a time when the thoughtful eye of the judge rested upon the changes of social circumstances and almost palpably saw the law arise out of human life. Have we got to a time when the only way to change law is by statute? The changing of law by statute seems to me like mending a garment with a patch; whereas law should grow by the life that is in it, not by the life that is outside of it.

I once said to a lawyer, with whom I was discussing some question of precedent, and in whose presence I was venturing to doubt the rational validity, at any rate, of the particular precedents he cited, "After all, isn't our object justice?" And he said, "God forbid! We should be very much confused if we made that our standard. Our standard is to find out what the rule has been and how the rule that has been applies to the case that is." I should hate to think that the law was based entirely upon "has beens." I should hate to think that the law did not derive its impulse from looking forward, rather than from looking backward, or, rather, that it did not derive its instruction from looking about and seeing what the circumstances of man actually are, and what the impulses of justice necessarily are.

Understand me, gentlemen, I am not venturing in this presence to impeach the law. For the present, by the force of circumstances, I am in part the embodiment of the law, and it would be very awkward to disavow myself. But I do wish to make this intimation, that in this time of world change, in this time when we are going to find out just how, in what particulars, and to what extent the real facts of human life and the real moral judgments of mankind prevail, it is worthwhile looking inside of our municipal law and seeing whether the judgments of the law are made square with the moral judgments of mankind. For I believe that we are custodians, not of commands, but of a spirit. We are custodians of the spirit of righteousness, of the spirit of equal-handed justice, of the spirit of hope which believes in the perfectibility of the law with the perfectibility of human life itself.

Public life, like private life, would be very dull and dry if it were not for this belief in the essential beauty of the human spirit, and the belief that the human spirit could be translated into action and into ordinance. Not entirely. You cannot go any faster than you can advance the average moral judgments of the mass, but you can go at least as fast as that, and you can see to it that you do not lag behind the average moral judgments of the mass. I have in my life dealt with all sorts and conditions of men, and I have found that the flame of moral judgment burned just as bright in the man of humble life and limited experience as in the scholar and the man of affairs. And I would like his voice always to be heard, not as a witness, not as speaking in his own case, but as if it were the voice of men in general, in our courts of justice, as well as the voice of the lawyers, remembering what the law has been. My hope is that, being stirred to the depths by the extraordinary circumstances of the time in which we live, we may recover from those depths something of a renewal of that vision of the law with which men may be supposed to have started out in the old days of the oracles, who communed with the intimations of divinity.

Printed in *Address Delivered before the American Bar Association* . . . (Washington, 1914), with additions and corrections from the full text in *Report of the Thirty-Seventh Annual Meeting of the American Bar Association* . . . (Baltimore, 1914), pp. 6-9.

[1] An address of welcome to the thirty-seventh annual meeting of the American Bar Association. The audience, assembled for the occasion in the Memorial Continental Hall of the Daughters of the American Revolution in Washington, included the Chief Justice and the Associate Justices of the Supreme Court of the United States, members of the diplomatic corps, members of the cabinet, justices of the supreme court of many states, and a large number of well-known lawyers.

[2] William Howard Taft.

## To Robert Lansing, with Enclosure

My dear Mr. Lansing:        The White House October 20, 1914

I return the enclosed papers with the amendment I suggested last evening over the telephone.

Cordially and sincerely yours,    Woodrow Wilson

TLS (SDR, RG 59, 861.51/78½, DNA).

### ENCLOSURE[1]

October 19, 1914.

*Confidential.* Your No. 67, October 16th, 6 P.M. This Government would view with much satisfaction the negotiation of a commercial treaty with Russia along the lines indicated in the first of the two conditions upon which Count Witte makes his acceptance of a mission to the United States depend. Do I understand that it is Count Witte's desire to come as a special envoy to negotiate such a treaty or that he desires the treaty to be signed before he visits this country?

Please advise the Department promptly as to any further developments in regard to the subject. *It would be manifestly improper for this government to take any part in facilitating a loan to one of the belligerent governments. It would not be frank to lead Count Witte, whose stipulations as you report them do him so much honour, to expect this.*[2]

T telegram (SDR, RG 59, 861.51/78½, DNA).
  [1] Sentences in italics WWhw.
  [2] This telegram was sent as RL to the American Ambassador, Petrograd, Oct. 20, 1914, T telegram (SDR, RG 59, 861.51/78½, DNA).

## To Powell Evans[1]

My dear Mr. Evans:        [The White House] October 20, 1914

My friend, Roland S. Morris, has shown me your letter to him of October ninth and his reply. The correspondence interests me so much that I am going to take the liberty,—I hope that neither you nor he will think it an unwarrantable liberty,—of adding a word or two of my own to what he has written.

The situation is just this: the reconstructive legislation which for the last two decades the opinion of the country has demanded and which political parties have vied with each other in promising in one form or another has now been enacted. That programme is practically completed. Until the present European war is over and normal conditions have been restored it will not be possible to determine how readily or how completely the business of the country has adjusted itself to the new conditions. When that is clear instrumentalities already created will be ready and in operation which will show just where the laws are working in harmony with the facts and where they are not.

Meanwhile, and for a long time to come, legislative questions will be questions of progress, of suiting means to new ends, of facilitating business and using to the utmost the resources of the country in the vast development of our business and our enterprise, which, I think, has but just begun. In such circumstances, what sort of man do you wish to have represent you in the United States Senate? A man who wishes to hark back to the old conditions but cannot? A man who can, possibly, obstruct but who can do nothing more? Or a man with the zest and vision of a new age, a man full of the spirit of Pennsylvania as she is going to be? Is it not a matter of principle and of quality? Should you not have a man of high principle not only, but a man with his face toward the future, ready to help make things and not merely trying blindly to prevent things which cannot be prevented. If Pennsylvania wishes to be adequately represented in the great enterprises of the new age of free endeavor, Pennsylvanians can hardly, I should think, hesitate in making their choice of a Senator.

I have seen Mr. Palmer tested. I know his quality. Pennsylvania ought to accept and trust him and through him play her proper part in the constructive policies of a new generation. They will stumble if they walk forever with their heads over their shoulders. Men of your sort will, I am sure, be the last to do that.

Cordially and sincerely yours,   Woodrow Wilson[2]

TLS (Letterpress Books, WP, DLC).
[1] President of the Merchant and Evans Co., tin plate manufacturers of Philadelphia. He was a Republican supporter of Wilson.
[2] There is a WWsh draft of this letter in WP, DLC. Wilson's letter was published in support of A. Mitchell Palmer's candidacy.


## From Robert Lansing, with Enclosures

Dear Mr. President:          Washington October 20, 1914.

I enclose you a paraphrase of a telegram to-day from Mr. Page and also copies of two telegrams handed to me by the British Ambassador, all relative to the Declaration of London.

It seems to me that in view of the rigid attitude of the British

Government further attempts to obtain an agreement on the Declaration of London would be useless. We must, therefore, stand on the rules of international law which have been generally accepted without regard to the Declaration. In the matter of the transfer of vessels this will be a decided advantage. The great loss is the failure to have a definite code, which will undoubtedly be the source of numerous controversies.

It is to be regretted that in spite of all that has been done, the purpose of the negotiation has failed.

Probably it would be well to await the new proclamation before acting, although a protest might be entered against certain articles which the British Government on September 21st declared contraband.

Very sincerely yours,   Robert Lansing

TLS (WP, DLC).

ENCLOSURE   I

London, October 19, 1914.

864, CONFIDENTIAL. Your 323, October 16. Your instructions have been followed literally. The Declaration of London will not be accepted by Sir Edward Grey without amendment: First, for the same reason that the report of the drafting committee would not be accepted, namely, that because Parliament declined to ratify it; and, second, for the reason that the Declaration of London itself forbids additions to contraband list of such articles as rubber and iron ore which now seem to be necessary for the manufacture of war materials. Sir Edward Grey could not accept proposition No. 2 in your telegram for the reason that to accept the London Declaration as a whole and then to issue a proclamation in contravention of part of it would not of course be possible.

All hope of his acceptance of the Declaration of London as a whole therefore is finally ended. Sir Edward is appreciative, courteous, and willing to go to any length that he can to meet our wishes. But for the reasons given he will not accept the Declaration.

Your objections to the new Order in Council have been presented.

Up to this point the situation stood thus: Sir Edward had refused to accept American proposal of the Declaration as a whole and you had refused to accept his proposal for the approval of the new Order in Council. This left us just where we were before the controversy began, with all the proposals which had been made wiped off the slate.

Sir Edward then began anew in the best temper and spirit. He remarked that his object was to meet our desires and to disturb and derange the commerce of neutrals as little as possible in the necessary conduct of the war. He recalled that the British Government had confiscated no American cargo. Sir Edward started out anew by suggesting the following: British Government would accept the Declaration of London with two amendments: First amendment, addition to the conditional contraband and absolute contraband lists of the articles named in the draft of the new Order in Council, which articles I telegraphed to you and to which you have made no objection. Sir Edward states that these articles can not be added if the Declaration is accepted as a whole. See Section 28. Second amendment, the British Government reserve the right to stop contraband and conditional contraband cargoes which are consigned in blank to a neutral country and which are destined obviously for the enemy country. Sir Edward expects to consummate arrangements with Holland and the Scandinavian states whereby they will guarantee not to export supplies of military material to a country of the enemy.

Sir Edward proposes to have a proclamation issued to the foregoing effect, repealing all previous proclamations. And Sir Edward does not request the acceptance by the United States of this proclamation, but he hopes that the United States will make no protest against it but that the United States will be satisfied by declaring a reservation of all rights under international law and usage, if any harm shall be done to our commerce by the execution of the proclamation, and that the United States will take up any cases of damage as they arise and if any occur. Sir Edward remarked that this procedure would be the same under any arrangements that could be made and that he was convinced that cases of actual damage would not occur after the British Government had put into effect the proposed proclamation. Spring-Rice has been informed of this plan by telegraph. An explanation by the United States that it reserves all her rights under international law and usage will, Sir Edward hopes, allay and prevent criticism of the Government at home. We will throw the responsibility upon the British Government if our assent to the proclamation is withheld.

American Ambassador, London.[1]

---

[1] A slightly different version of this telegram is printed in FR-WWS 1914, pp. 253-54.

E N C L O S U R E   I I[1]

Sir E. Grey Oct. 17

A simple acceptance of the Declaration of London would in effect bind us to carry out every detail of an instrument which we have never ratified and to which objection has been taken in Parliament.

Experience of war has shown that free list of Declaration of London contains some articles that are now used in Germany exclusively or mainly for purposes of war.

We also want to reserve right to apply doctrine of continuous voyage where we can get no satisfactory agreement with a neutral country that will prevent it becoming base of supplies for enemy government or army.

We cannot accept all definitions in Monsieur Renault's report:[2] I believe this has not been accepted in United States.

I see difficulty of United States Government binding itself beforehand to accept text of our Order in Council: on the other hand we do not wish to issue an Order that will lead to a protest from United States Government.

Order does in effect accept Declaration of London departing substantially only from specific lists of contraband and non-contraband and reserving right under certain conditions to apply doctrine of continuous voyage, which I believe up to and even during discussion on Declaration of London every authority in United States upheld.

I think simplest course would be for us to issue new Proclamation and for United States Government not to enter any protest on understanding that it will not in practice be used to prevent bona fide trade with neutral countries. United States Government would not then be bound by a partisan[3] acceptance of our Proclamation and would reserve right to deal with application of it on merits of particular cases: but we should not be confronted with an objection in principle that could only be met by withdrawal of Proclamation.

I am informed that Paragraph 3 of proposed Proclamation could not be made a matter of interpretation by Courts as suggested by State Department.[4]

---

[1] This and the following Enclosure were telegrams from Grey to Spring Rice, who gave copies of them to Lansing.

[2] He referred to Louis Renault, *La Conférence navale de Londres* (Paris, 1909).

[3] Grey wrote "definite," and Spring Rice's decode is incorrect.

[4] This telegram was sent as E. Grey to C. A. Spring Rice, Oct. 17, 1914, Hw telegram (FO 372/601, No. 60037, pp. 329-30, PRO).

E N C L O S U R E    I I I

Sir E. Grey Oct. 19/14

Result of discussion with United States Ambassador and Mr. Anderson is that to proceed on lines of my telegram No. 116 Treaty[1] seems the most practicable course.

Our new list of contraband conflicts with Article 28 of the Declaration of London and therefore prevents an unqualified acceptance of the Declaration.

We proposed however to draw up a more general[2] proclamation repealing all Royal Proclamations, accepting the Declaration of London in general terms but making the exceptions contained in draft proclamation already submitted.

We should be willing to make it clear to the United States Government that our object was solely to prevent contraband goods from reaching an enemy and not to interfere with bona fide commerce with any neutral State.

We should not ask United States Government to accept Proclamation but should like it to be understood that while reserving all rights under international law as regards treatment of any particular cargo, they would not enter any protest against the Proclamation itself or the list of contraband as being invalid.

You should explain this and my telegram No. 116 to State Department: United States Ambassador is also telegraphing.

TC telegrams (WP, DLC).
  [1] Just printed.
  [2] Grey wrote "simple." E. Grey to C. A. Spring Rice, Oct. 19, 1914, T telegram (FO 372/602, No. 63214, p. 66, PRO).

## From Robert Heberton Terrell

Dear Sir:                    Washington, D. C. October 20, 1914.

I write to thank you for your letter to the Commissioners of the District of Columbia endorsing the movement started by the Brightwood Citizens' Association and Mr. Wm. McK. Clayton to increase the wages of those laborers in our Street Cleaning department known as the "White Wings." Nearly all of this class of employers [employees] are colored men. I have had occasion to talk with many of them since your letter appeared in the public press and they have given expression to their deep appreciation of your interest in their behalf. I am quite sure that many of them will find a way to thank you in a more direct manner themselves.          Very respectfully,   Robert H. Terrell
                              Municipal Court, D. C.

TLS (WP, DLC).

## Two Letters from Robert Lansing

Dear Mr. President:                Washington October 20, 1914.

The capture by a British cruiser of the Standard Oil tank steamer BRINDILLA, which has arrived at Halifax under a prize crew, brings up for immediate decision one phase of the question, concerning which I addressed you yesterday in submitting a letter from Mr. Peters, Assistant Secretary of the Treasury.[1]

The vessel at the outbreak of hostilities was the GEORGE WASHINGTON, a steamer of German register owned by a German corporation, a subsidiary company of the Standard Oil Company. She was transferred to the Standard Oil Company, the purchase money being paid, was renamed the BRINDILLA and obtained an American register. On a full statement of the facts of the transfer the Bureau of War Risk Insurance issued a policy on the hull of the vessel for a voyage to Alexandria, Egypt, with the privilege of coaling at Sicily or the Azores. The cargo of the vessel consists of illuminating oil.

This case is, therefore, a transfer of flag rather than a transfer of ownership, but, if the British Government intend to deny the right of transfer of flag during hostilities, as this seizure would indicate, it is evident that transfer of ownership will be treated as invalid and vessels purchased from enemies of Great Britain will be seized as prize.

It seems to me that the only course is to make an immediate and vigorous protest against the action of the British authorities in seizing an American vessel bound to a neutral port.

Very sincerely yours,   Robert Lansing

[1] Andrew James Peters, former Democratic congressman from Boston.

Dear Mr. President:                Washington October 20, 1914.

I enclose a telegram which, if it meets with your approval, I will send to the American Ambassador at London, relative to the seizure of the tank steamer JOHN D. ROCKEFELLER.[1] This case does not raise the issue of transfer of flag or ownership, but the seizure is based I assume on the undoubted purpose of Great Britain to interrupt all traffic in petroleum to neutral ports near Germany.

If you approve the telegram, will you please return it to me?

Very sincerely yours,   Robert Lansing

TLS (WP, DLC).
[1] It is printed in *FR-WWS 1914*, p. 325.

# From Sir Cecil Arthur Spring Rice

*Personal*

Dear Mr. President,                    Washington. October 20, 1914.

I saw Mr. Lansing today and told him that I was without any news as to the seizures of American oilships. I remarked that the immense supplies of oil received by neutrals after the withdrawal of our proclamation, which was made in deference to your wishes, had been nothing less than alarming. The evidence was convincing that an attack by submarines and Zeppelins was contemplated and supplies of oil were absolutely essential to Germany. The measure taken, even if irregular, as to which I expressed no opinion, was a measure of obvious self-defence and was imperatively demanded by popular opinion.

If we are in the wrong, we must of course pay the penalty and see that the United States are not losers by wrongful action.

I am sure, Mr. President, that your people will understand our motives just as well as we shall understand your protest. We each wish to defend our rights. But I am sure you will remember that the rights we are defending are our existence.

I enclose copies of two telegrams which I have received from Sir Edward Grey.[1] The first I kept back with Sir Edward's consent until he had had time to see Mr. Page.

The general situation is this. We are trying to conclude agreements with the neutrals in order to prevent them from becoming the base of supplies for the enemy and in order to enable them to supply themselves. We have nearly concluded these agreements. I am at the present moment instructing the Consuls to attest the signatures of neutral consuls here on documents showing that articles exported from this country are subject to an embargo in the country of their destination, and are not therefore liable to seizure. But these agreements must have a sanction and unless we are able to threaten neutral governments that we shall resume our liberty of action unless they keep their agreements, those agreements have no sanction. We must therefore have a clause which gives us this power. If the United States protest, we shall either have to issue the Proclamation in spite of the protest or abandon all hope of carrying out measures which are absolutely essential to our very existence.

What Sir E. Grey asks is that the United States should reserve its right to protect its interests in each case as it arises but that they should not enter a protest against the Proclamation itself *before* it is enforced.

May I add that experience during the Russo-Japanese war

shewed us that it was possible to settle each question as it arose between us and Russia, and the questions were many and difficult.

I must apologise for taking so much of your time but I have been emboldened by your invariable courtesy to trespass on it once more.

I have the honour to remain with profound respect, dear Mr President,

Your obedient humble servant   Cecil Spring Rice.

TLS (WP, DLC).
[1] E. Grey to C. A. Spring Rice, Oct. 17 and 19, 1914, printed as Enclosures with R. Lansing to WW, Oct. 20, 1914.

## Walter Hines Page to the Secretary of State

London, October 20, 11 p.m. 1914.

Your 323 continuing confidential to be deciphered Lansing only and shown to the President. I hope we can find Sir Edward Grey's proposal acceptable as an emergency working plan. Our Government in dealing with our shippers can throw the whole responsibility Great Britain. I believe that the practical working of the plan will develop few grievances and interruptions.

There are certain large facts to remember. Every other belligerent government than Great Britain is now wholly military. Their foreign secretaries have ceased to act independently. Many departments of this Government also have been taken under the control of the War Department and the Foreign Office would no doubt have before now been so controlled but for the strong personality of Sir Edward Grey. If the War Department should control the Foreign Office, as it may in case of military or naval disaster, negotiations such as these would be practically suspended and it would probably be impossible to make any satisfactory diplomatic arrangement. It is no time for arguing a case for general conduct but only for the best action possible in a great emergency. We have practically no direct commerce with Germany; and we have commerce with neutral countries on the North Sea only because Great Britain has been unwilling to have that sea mined and because Sir Edward Grey has held his Department as no other belligerent Foreign Secretary has. If we have a quarrel now the new peace treaty will require its submission to a commission and we can recover only the same damages which we may recover under Grey's proposal without a quarrel. Our own Government upheld the doctrine of continuous voyage during the Civil War which Grey now, in a similar necessity, wishes us to let pass without formal protest.

Anderson was with me at yesterday's conference and concurs in this telegram and at my request is sending one of his own.

If you cannot accept Grey's proposal please ask President to send House here for a conference before further action is taken. Grey will go to the furthest length under these unprecedented conditions to respect our rights and wishes but he will not consent to admit war materials to Germany. It seems to me that it would be the greatest misfortune in the world to permit a serious difference now between these two Governments. Under Grey's plan we can throw full responsibility on British Government and we will suffer the least possible delay or damage or indignity. But if we assume that we are working under normal conditions and proceed with elaborate arguments on that assumption, we shall have a break, gain no substantial advantage, and alienate the two governments and peoples for a generation. The hope of every patriotic man on either side of the ocean will be disappointed and such good will as is now left in the world will be gone.                    American Ambassador London.[1]

T telegram (SDR, RG 59, 763.72112/193, DNA).
[1] This telegram is printed in *FR-WWS 1914*, pp. 255-56.


# Remarks Upon the Inauguration of the Federal Reserve System[1]

Mr. Hamlin, and Gentlemen:                    October 21, 1914.

I am genuinely glad to have this opportunity to look you in the face and to say how glad we are to have this new system inaugurated and under such auspices, because I have kept in touch with the processes so far as I could, and it cheers me very much to know with what easy cooperation you are going about your business.

I believe, gentlemen, that we shall look back upon the beginning of this system with genuine satisfaction, and that it will give the country more and more satisfaction as it is developed in operation. For my own part, I believe that the best thing that can be done for the country is to open the banks at the earliest possible date; otherwise we should seem to doubt their efficacy. Otherwise we should seem to discredit in part the very thing that we are undertaking.

For my feeling about the present situation is this, gentlemen: the only thing lacking is confidence. The circumstances of the world are extraordinary, but we ought not to allow our mental attitude to be extraordinary. We are more nervous than there is cause for, and if we go about business as if nothing were happening, business will take care of us as we take care of it. That is my conviction. I will not again use the word "psychology," but there is a psychological element, there is a state of mind involved in this thing which it would be very useful if we were to correct, and the way to correct it, with others, perhaps, is to correct it in ourselves—to feel that there is nothing to wait for in putting business upon the footing upon which it is to remain, I hope, for a great many years to come.

But when I started out, I did not expect to say these things; I merely expected to tell you how sincerely gratified I am to have the opportunity of meeting you and of telling you how I congratulate the country upon being in the hands in the matter of banking of such a body of men.

T MS (WP, DLC).
[1] The directors of the Federal Reserve banks met in Washington on October 20, 21, and 22 to determine a date for the opening of the Federal Reserve System and to consider a report by the secretary of the Federal Reserve Board, Henry Parker Willis. The directors and others called at the White House to pay their respects.

## To William Phillips

My dear Mr. Phillips:        [The White House] October 21, 1914

Thank you for your note to Tumulty apprising me of the correspondence with the Legation at Brussels in regard to the relief of famine in Belgium. It seems to me the Department has taken just the right course.[1]

Cordially and sincerely yours, Woodrow Wilson

TLS (Letterpress Books, WP, DLC).
[1] B. Whitlock to WJB, Oct. 16, 1914, T telegram (WP, DLC); W. Phillips to JPT, Oct., 19, 1914, TLS (WP, DLC); R. Lansing to B. Whitlock, Oct. 19, 1914, TS telegram (WP, DLC). A Belgian committee had been formed at Brussels, under the patronage of the American and Spanish ministers, for the purpose of importing foodstuffs for starving Belgian civilians. The State Department had informed the British government that relief shipments would receive an American diplomatic guarantee and had asked the German government for a guarantee of immunity against seizure of such shipments. Both governments had responded positively.

## From Robert Lansing

Dear Mr. President:        Washington October 21, 1914.

I enclose herewith a telegram which I have drafted in accordance with our conversation this morning relative to the Declaration of London.

If it meets with your approval, will you kindly return it so that it may be sent at once to Ambassador Page?

Very sincerely yours,    Robert Lansing

TLS (WP, DLC).

## To Robert Lansing, with Enclosure

[The White House, Oct. 21, 1914]

Approved as altered    W.W.

Would it not be well to show this to S.-R. before you send it,—for any comment or suggestion he might have to make? W.W.

ALI (SDR, RG 59, 763.72112/189, DNA).

### E N C L O S U R E[1]

Washington, October 21, 1914.

373. Your number 864, October nineteenth, Declaration of London.

Inasmuch as the British Government consider that the conditions of the present European conflict make it impossible for them to accept without modification the Declaration of London you are requested to inform His Majesty's Government that in the circumstances the Government of the United States feels ⟨compelled⟩ *obliged* to withdraw its suggestion that the Declaration of London be adopted as a temporary code of naval warfare to be observed by belligerents and neutrals during the present war; that therefore, this Government ⟨must⟩ *will* insist that the rights and duties of the United States and its citizens in the present war be defined by the existing rules of international law and the treaties of the United States irrespective of the provisions of the Declaration of London; and that this Government reserves to itself the right to enter a protest or demand in each case in which those rights and duties so defined are violated or their free exercise interfered with by the authorities of His Britannic Majesty's Government.

Lansing.    Acting Secretary of State[2]

T telegram (SDR, RG 59, 763.72112/189, DNA).

[1] Words in angle brackets deleted by Wilson; words in italics are Wilson's.

[2] This telegram was sent on October 22 and is printed in *FR-WWS 1914*, pp. 257-58.

## From Walter Hines Page, with Enclosure

Dear Mr. President:                             London. Oct. 21, 1914.

I have been and am puzzled by Mr. Lansing's dispatch (no. 323, Oct. 16) and your confidence in the plan that he proposed. I enclose a copy of the essential parts of the dispatch. It contains 2 propositions—(1) that G't Britain accept the Declaration of London without any change or addition whatever, and (2) that the British Gov't then issue a proclamation, setting forth that, since the Declaration is conflicting and does not provide for emergencies, G't Britain interprets it to mean what she requires it to mean—the U. S. not being privy to this, *altho' it is the U. S. that suggests it.* Now the Declaration itself distinctly forbids the addition of copper & iron ore and rubber and hides to the contraband list. England could not add these to its list and accept the foregoing plan—in good faith and with truth; and these have become, since the Declaration was drawn up, among the most important articles of warfare. I have surely misunderstood, or Mr. Lansing failed to see where his proposal w'd lead. I am aware, of course, of his over-work (as we are all over-worked), and I am not writing in a critical spirit but in a spirit of mere inquiry to get my own bearings and of helpful suggestion (if it be helpful) to work out a satisfactory result. Of course I know that Mr. Lansing did not mean that I shd. make a dishonourable proposal. But I cannot see how he could think that Sir Edw. Grey cd. accept this proposal, which, as we see it here, surely is not frank.

When I telegraphed you that the discussion is "academic," I did not mean that the subject itself is academic but that our excessively argumentative treatment of it seemed academic to me— *e.g.* our continued insistence on the Declaration of London after England's positive declination three times to accept it *in toto.* England never accepted it, in peace. Parliament declined to accept it—in effect rejected it. This Government, then, could hardly be expected to accept it in a time of war, in the face of its own Parliamentary objection. Yet we continue to make its acceptance the first condition of our now reaching an agreement. That is what I meant to call "academic." It surely isn't practical or effective.

Still I tried for the fourth time to persuade Sir Edw. to accept it *in toto*—such were my instructions—and then to issue another Proclamation, as explained in Mr. Lansing's dispatch. "Do you mean that we should accept it," he askd., "and then issue a proclamation to get around it?"—with some approach to irritation. And the interview ended with a feeling on my part that I had lost ground and really been put on the defensive by my insistence on his acceptance of the Declaration for the fourth time—coupled now with a proposal that could not be made to appear wholly frank and friendly.

I will not say that such instructions are not agreeable—that's not important nor to the point—but I will say that they are not effective in the dealings of two great, friendly, frank, and truthful nations.

It is one thing and an easy thing to present a question informally (wh. doesn't bind anybody); but it's a different thing to say that the idea is wholly my own and not my Government's, when it isn't. I did not tell him who's idea it is, but only that I was discussing the subject informally. I must be spared from saying that anything is my *"personal suggestion and not one for which my Gov't is responsible"* when this is not true.

Of course the matter of this controversy is very real and serious, a tender spot, as you call it. But it has arisen in all naval wars—long before the Declaration was prepared. England makes her contraband list; she will prevent contraband from reaching the enemy if she can; if she seize cargoes she must prove they are contraband or suffer heavy damages and heavier criticism and ill will; and if she detain neutral ships or cargoes not contraband she suffers the same penalty in even heavier degree. She's got to give assurance to neutrals what she will do and what they may expect. *She's* got to take the responsibility for every act—under the usage of international law. By becoming *a party to her Proclamations beforehand we run a certain risk of agreeing beforehand to her procedure*, thus embarrassing ourselves when definite cases come up. We must take no responsibility, but reserve all our rights under international law and usage and so inform our merchants and shippers. Then the responsibility is shifted from us to England—responsibility for her general plan or code of procedure. We are then free to make the most of every case of indignity or deflection or confiscation.

This, England is perfectly willing to agree to; and, in her naval conduct, she is going to give *us* as little offence as possible, if we act frankly, in good faith, and trust to her good faith and cease to irritate her & to cause delay by long argumentative general objections to her plan of procedure.

At any rate, looked at as a practical matter and not as a case in court, this is all that we can do—or we can fight. Of course that's absurd—I mean talk of war is absurd and criminal. If we come to an open quarrel, we've still got to take this course, for our new peace treaty forbids us to fight till a commission shall report on the quarrel. We can claim damages for any harm we may suffer without a quarrel; or we may quarrel and then claim the same identical damages. The difference will be only this— that in one case the two greatest nations in the world and the two friendliest peoples & the two great governments that are the only hope of human freedom & human progress will be at ill will (the last good will now existing anywhere in this insane world gone); or these two great nations can remain the only friendly great powers on earth. I think the stake is too big to risk for the satisfaction of arguing to the finish about proposi- tions of general procedure *before the event* or about the accept- ance of a Declaration that was rejected in time of peace.

All other neutral governments (so I understand) have accepted this plan.

The Admiralty are making almost open complaint that Sir Edw. Grey in his consideration for the rights of neutrals is "badly in the way" of their preventing war materials from reaching the enemy. I think we can trust something to such a man. Or—what is the alternative? I once heard you say that it took you 20 years to recover from your legal training—from the habit of mind that is bent on making out a case rather than on seeing the large facts of a situation in their proper proportion. Remember that all this discussion has so far been on a general code or plan of action, to wh., if our suggestions are accepted, we in effect make ourselves a party, whereas more important than any code or plan is the spirit in which it is carried out. All our preliminary argu- ment implies a distrust of the British Government in the way they will carry it out.

Sir Edw Grey and I have been over the whole ground, back- ward and forward, helped by Mr. Anderson and his (Grey's) legal advisers, time and again. I have told him that we want only—

(1) a clear preservation of our neutrality;
(2) no tampering with our commerce with neutral nations;
(3) no tampering with our commerce with *any* nation except in contraband;
(4) a strict respect for all our rights under international law & usage.

He wants only to prevent war-materials from reaching Ger- many—nothing more. He does not wish to hinder our commerce nor to irritate us. He will do every thing he can to prevent it. The peculiar complication is, of course, the reaching of Germany with war-materials through Holland, Denmark, Sweden, and

Italy. He will do his best to avoid trouble. He will make those Gov't's help him so far as they can, by friendly persuasion, not by declaring them "enemy territory" as regards trade. And if we suffer injury he is willing to make reparation, case by case.

If we can trust him (as we must, since there's nobody else to trust in the matter) and cease long arguments about general plans and codes & put the whole responsibility on him and take up case by case—there will still be some chance for a little faith and good will in the world.

Yours faithfully   Walter H. Page

ALS (WP, DLC).

E N C L O S U R E

The Essential Parts of Mr. Lansing's<br>Confidential Dispatch, no. 323, of Oct. 16.

"The desire of this Government is to obtain from the British Gov't the issuance of an Order in Council adopting the Declaration of London without any amendment whatsoever."

*This is not true.*

"You might in the strictest confidence intimate to Sir E. Grey the Department's plan as follows stating very explicitly *that it is your personal suggestion & not one for wh. your Gov't is responsible.*

"Let the British Gov't issue an order in Council accepting the Declaration of London without change or addition * * *.

*Hardly frank.*

"Let this Proclamation be followed by another Order in Council, *of wh. the U. S. need not be previously advised*, declaring that when (the British Gov't) is convinced that a port or a territory of a neutral country is being used as a base for the transit of

*In the delicate and danger-
ous temper of the present,
this w'd have a strong tendency to drive Italy, Holland,
Denmark, & Sweden to war
against England.*

supplies for an enemy Gov't, a
Proclamation shall issue declaring that *such port or territory
has acquired enemy character
in so far as trade in contraband
is concerned and that vessels
trading therewith shall be subject to the rules of the Declaration governing trade to enemy's
territory.*

*I can hardly believe that
such a subterfuge or mis-
representation of the real
facts is necessary between
what I hope I may call
large-minded and perfectly
frank and truthful repre-
sentatives of two great
friendly nations. My relations with Sir Edw. have
not been built up on this
basis and could not survive
this method of dealing—
long.*

"I repeat that any suggestion
which you may make to Sir Edw.
Grey must be done in an entirely
personal way and with the distinct understanding that this
Gov't is in no way responsible
for what you may say."

We have a great and embarrassing emergency. We can reach
a good working basis by frankly trusting to one another's good
will and good intentions and good faith. This Gov't, you may be
sure, doesn't wish to offend *us*. But Mr. Lansing's attitude is
argumentative, critical of every clause and proposal (a lawyer
pushing his case) with a tone of distrust of every statement of
his opponent, and with proposals that are not frank—he wd. put
them forward as mine, not his, he disclaiming all responsibility.
This, Mr. President, is not effective. A different manner w'd
accomplish more—all we want, in fact.               W.H.P.

P.S. I have been in some doubt about sending this letter lest it
may seem to you a criticism of Mr. Lansing. I do not so mean
it in the least—only a criticism of his method of approach to the
subject. G't Britain is our friend. As a friend we can do with her
all we wish. This state of mind we show in this controversy regards her as an opponent in court, whom we are fighting & propose to fight. Again, this tone & temper seem to me to have regard
only to this controversy & to the present moment. Wise diplo-

macy regards the next decade—the next 25 years. What will our relations be then? And how will our conduct of this controversy affect them? That's what I mean, & I do not mean the slightest personal criticism of Mr. Lansing or of anybody else. I am the last man who can for one moment afford to sit in judgment on any other man for what I regard as mistakes. I need too much charity myself.                                                     W.H.P.

Hw MSI (WP, DLC).


## From Edward Mandell House

Dear Governor:                    New York City. October 21st, 1914.

I have received the following cablegram from Page today through his son Arthur.

"God deliver us or can you from library lawyers. They often lose chestnuts while they argue about burns. See our friend and come here immediately if case is not already settled. Of utmost importance."

He sent two messages, one to Arthur direct saying:

"Please deliver second message to the Thirty-fifth Street house."

I hardly know to what he refers, but perhaps you do. It may be the Declaration of London matter.

I notice that Northcliffe[1] in his papers and the London Post are demanding that the Government seize neutral vessels carrying reservists or contraband cargoes.

If you think I can be of any service, please wire me and I will come to Washington immediately. Page is evidently disturbed.

Affectionately yours,   E. M. House

TLS (WP, DLC).
[1] Alfred Charles William Harmsworth, 1st Baron Northcliffe, founder and publisher of the London *Daily Mail* and, since 1908, the proprietor of *The Times*.


## From Cleveland Hoadley Dodge

My dear President:                    New York October 21, 1914.

I know you will think it very wicked in me to chuckle over the misfortunes of old time friends, but perhaps when I tell you my particular sin, you may forgive me and possibly sympathize with me.

I have just been lunching with Cyrus McCormick and Jacobus, and most of our talk consisted in expressions of gratitude for the wonderful way in which you are handling the present situation. They were on their way to the Trustees' meeting tomorrow, and told me that Sheldon had been the last two years insisting upon getting a definite statement regarding the celebrated Wyman bequest of $3,000,000 (?). Cyrus said Sheldon would probably make a report tomorrow giving the definite ascertained facts that the income received from the Wyman bequest has, so far, amounted to only $2500 a year and probably would not amount to more than this sum for a good many years to come. As we knew before, the bequest consisted largely in unimproved property near Salem, and the value of that seems to dwindle every year, and most of the equity is being eaten up in taxes and expense. It is possible that sometime in the long future the College may receive half a million to three-quarters million dollars from this property,[1] but meanwhile there is no income from it. They also told me that Hibben seems to have aged ten years since he became President, and is terribly depressed at the lack of support which his friends have given him. I must confess that, horrible as it seems, I came away from the luncheon with quite cheerful spirits. Of course this information is confidential, but I thought you would like to hear it.

Sincerely hoping that your health is standing this terrible strain, and that you are getting a little golf occasionally, believe me          Very affectionately yours,   C. H. Dodge

The Wyman Bequest served one great purpose, namely to give you to the World in this awful crisis. West's Deanery[2] must look "pretty good" to him.

TLS (WP, DLC).
  [1] Dodge was substantially correct. See J. M. Raymond and A. F. West to WW, May 22, 1910, n. 3, Vol. 20.
  [2] Wyman House, the residence of the Dean of the Graduate School.


## To Robert Lee Henry

My dear Mr. Henry:          [The White House] October 22, 1914

The passage of the cotton warehouse bill seems to me an essential measure for the relief, or the partial relief, of the South. It is one of the concrete things that we can do and should do. May I not urge that you use every endeavor to promote its immediate passage?     Sincerely yours,   Woodrow Wilson

TLS (Letterpress Books, WP, DLC).

## Remarks at a Press Conference

October 22, 1914

Mr. President, can you tell us something in regard to the seizure of the *John D. Rockefeller*?

> Nothing that is at all authoritative or conclusive about it. We have asked for an explanation and particulars, but they haven't reached us yet, so far as we know.

Have you got a report yet, a report that was asked for in regard to the facts concerning the capture of the *Brindilla*?

> No, sir. That's not the same case.

Can you say anything generally, Mr. President, in regard to the whole question?

> No, sir. . . .

Have you heard anything from Mexico today or yesterday? . . . Is it true, Mr. President, that Villa has some forces at Aguascalientes?

> So far as I know he does not, unless there were forces that were already there when the convention assembled.

What is the status of the administrative questions relative to the withdrawal of troops?

> I understood that Carranza had left it to the convention, but I have lost sight of it in the last day or two.

Mr. President, do you know any of the details in regard to the arrangement in London for the American committee to take charge of the relief of the Belgians?[1]

> No. I heard something through London from Belgium to the effect that a committee of that sort had been formed, but I thought in Belgium.

Mr. Hoover, who has been head of the American Relief Committee in London, seems to have charge of it.

> I simply learned that there was no opposition by any government to the attempt to relieve those who were in danger of starving there. Mr. Tumulty just told me that the British Ambassador has just telephoned that the *John D. Rockefeller* has been released.

That Belgian matter, Mr. President, that is purely a private matter, not governmental?

> Not governmental at all. We did receive some inquiries as to whether there was any opposition to our consular officers acting to transmit the supplies, but if they did it would be merely as individuals and not as representatives of the government.

Mr. President, there have been some statements from abroad

with regard to the status of Mr. Whitlock, the American Minister to Belgium, as to whether he still held the office of American Minister while the Germans control the capital and most of the country. Could you tell us something about that?

> Well, if Mr. Whitlock should come to Washington, he would still be Minister to Belgium.

Is he performing any functions at all?

> Well, of course he can't perform the ordinary functions of communicating with the Belgian government, because it isn't there to communicate with.

Mr. President, did Mr. Tumulty say whether the crew had been released as well as the *John D. Rockefeller*?

> The objection had been, it seems, that it was a cargo ordinarily not assigned to a particular assignment, so that if it is released, this means that the crew are released also. I assume so. That is only a conclusion. . . .

Mr. President, have you furthered your plans at all about spending the interim between congressional sessions—

> No.

Your idea is to stay here?

> Yes. I am tied by the leg. I can't get away. I saw Mr. Burgess, I think from Texas, this morning, and he said he was going to make an address in Texas, and he would show me how, if I went, by starting from New York, to Galveston, I would have four free days. I explained to him that I didn't dare have four free days.

Mr. President, did you know about the informal conversations between Mr. McAdoo and the Reserve Board and Sir George Paish—they come from him—as to the definite proposition of settling the government's notes and exchange?

> No, I did not know. I have generally kept informed, but Mr. McAdoo has been in bed, and I have lost track there a bit. . . .

They are also perfectly willing to stimulate cotton exports to England.

> Yes. Sir George Paish intimated as much as that to me.

Because, you see, their factories presently will be standing still unless the cotton begins to be shipped.

I know it has also been suggested, Mr. President, that the British factories would pay a very large amount on American cotton immediately, and store it, in order to reduce the balance of trade. Have you heard anything of that sort?

> No, I haven't. I only heard somebody—I have forgotten who it was now—say that of course if the price of cotton was

very low, they would naturally buy as much as possible at a low price and store it against the operations of another season.

Have they some cotton on hand?

> I don't know. Of course they have a little. I don't know how much.

The trouble about buying cotton, I understand, on the other hand, is that nobody knows what its bedrock price is, because it may go still lower.

> Yes, that's the trouble with everybody. I really don't see why that should hold anybody back, because no matter what price they buy at now, they are going to get high prices for their goods, so that even the man that bought it at a relatively high price would certainly cover his operations, though he would not make as large a margin of profit as the man who bought at the low price.

Mr. President, after the cotton shipments, of course, that will consume a large part of this debt that the United States owes England. It won't balance it. And there is some intimation that England would be willing to take some short term securities for the balance. Can you give us any idea of the nature of those securities?

> No, sir.

Mr. President, I understand that a letter was read on the floor of the House this morning, from you, asking that the warehouse bill be passed before the adjournment. I was wondering whether the same thing would apply to that last amendment of the currency act?[2]

> I ought to have included that in the letter. In hurriedly writing it, I omitted it. I do stand for that. It would certainly facilitate other things we are trying to do to help the cotton situation in the South.

JRT transcript (WC, NjP) of CLSsh (C. L. Swem Coll., NjP).

[1] About the organization and work of the Belgian Relief Commission, see Herbert Hoover, *An American Epic* (4 vols., Chicago, 1959-64), I, *Introduction, The Relief of Belgium and Northern France, 1914-1930*, pp. 1-18, 55-61, 87-90, and *passim*; and Frank M. Surface and Raymond L. Bland, *American Food in the World War and Reconstruction Period* (Stanford, Cal., 1931), pp. 12-14.

[2] S. 6505, a bill to amend Sections 16 and 19 of the Federal Reserve Act. S. 6505 made rediscount facilities immediately available to the regional reserve banks that they would have been able to acquire only after three years under the Federal Reserve Act. Proponents argued that it would strengthen the five reserve banks serving the cotton- and tobacco-growing states and tremendously expand credit facilities in the South. *Cong. Record*, 63d Cong., 2d sess., pp. 16945-53. The bill died in the House. *Ibid.*, 63d Cong., 3d sess., pp. 31-33.

## To Robert Lansing

My dear Mr. Lansing:  [The White House] October 22, 1914

I quite agree with you that the only course to take in the matter of the tank steamer Brindilla and in other similar cases is to make an immediate and vigorous protest against the action of the British authorities in seizing an American vessel bound to a neutral port.

In haste

Cordially and faithfully yours,  Woodrow Wilson

TLS (Letterpress Books, WP, DLC).


## To Robert Marion La Follette

My dear Senator:  [The White House] October 22, 1914

I have heard with sincere sympathy and concern of your illness. I hope that it will be of brief duration, and I am writing this line merely to express my sympathy and the hope for your speedy recovery.

Cordially and sincerely yours,  Woodrow Wilson

TLS (Letterpress Books, WP, DLC).


## From Sir Cecil Arthur Spring Rice

*Personal*

Dear Mr President  Washington. October 22 1914

I telephoned to Mr Tumulty that the Rockefeller had been released and that the cause of her detention had been that the oil (declared to be conditional contraband in August) was consigned "to order" and not to the Danish Company.

The detention of the "Brindilla" is owing to a suspicion as to her real destination which combined with the change of flag justified, in the eyes of the British authorities, her detention for enquiry. Every effort will be made to expedite the hearing of the case. It is unfortunate that an attempt was made by the German part of her crew to scuttle the ship.

I hasten to communicate the above which I submit with all respect and have the honour to remain your most obedient humble servant  Cecil Spring Rice

P.S. I should add that the Admiral in charge reports that he was unable to give his official permission to the U S Consul to communicate with the ship because when the application was made the ship had already been handed over to the judicial authorities: but that he had recommended the Consul to apply to them. The question was settled. I regret the delay and the misunderstanding and hope that no great inconvenience resulted.    C S R.

ALS (WP, DLC).


## From Lindley Miller Garrison

My dear Mr. President:        Washington. October 22, 1914.

What I am about to write is entirely outside of my own Department, and my only excuse must be found in the importance of the subject matter, its urgency, and the intense interest which I have, along with all of us, to do whatever can be done under the circumstances.

It looks now as if, with respect to the cotton situation, there will be no formulated and regulated solution. Undirected and unregulated laws of supply and demand are the only things left to deal with the situation. In view of the unprecedented character of the emergency, it would seem as if this were a most unfortunate result. There does not seem to be any way in which the States individually can successfully handle the matter. There does not appear to be any way at all in which the national Government, through Congressional action, can handle it. If, by using agencies of the national Government in a way which does not at all complicate or embarrass us; and if, without laws of doubtful, if not absolutely unconstitutional character, we can yet render service, I feel that that would be the most desirable, if not imperative, way of handling the matter.

It has seemed to me that, with all these considerations in mind, you might summon to Washington those who represent the purchasers of cotton (that is, the manufacturers), and those who represent the sellers of cotton (that is, the growers); in addition, summon the gentlemen interested in the Wade fund, and representatives of the bankers who would be naturally involved in this matter. Let the Secretary of Commerce, for instance, formulate and place before them the proposition. By way of inducement, he would set forth that if the situation is left to take care of itself, it undoubtedly will spell disaster of large proportions, and that this disaster should be averted if possible, and that it can be averted if all those in interest will act fairly, patriotically, and with large rather than narrow personal vision. That if left to settle itself, the attitude of the purchaser will be to wait to the point of exhaustion on behalf of the seller and then purchase at the very lowest possible price which such exhaustion would compel. On behalf of the seller, there would be the desperate effort to hold on for the highest price that could possibly be obtained under the adverse conditions. In this latter effort the banking facilities of the Nation would be strained to a very undesirable limit. It cannot be to the real interests of the purchasers (that is, the manufacturers) to force the sale of this cotton to themselves at such a low price as to practically put the cotton-growers out of business. While such a course would be immediately profitable to the manufacturer, it would in the end be a very costly thing for him to do, because he would thus so abnormally reduce the coming crops as to result in very high prices being then demanded for what little cotton would be raised. If the buyer does not give the seller a fair proportion at least of what it has cost the seller to raise the cotton, the chances are that the seller will not be in a position to go on raising cotton, and this in the end would be detrimental, if not disastrous, to the manufacturer (that is, the purchaser). On the other hand, the natural desire of the seller (that is, the grower) to get a very large price for his cotton under the circumstances, would be unjustified in view of the abnormal conditions existing. He must be satisfied if he gets what, under all conditions, is fair. Unless there is some mediation, there does not appear to me to be any way to obtain a reasonable solution. The bankers, who presumably stand ready to advance money to a very large extent, cannot, of course, do anything until they know how much cotton will be taken, at what price, how much will be left, what that can fairly be said to be worth for the purpose of making loans thereon, together with such light as they can get on the probable size of next year's crop,—which, of course, would be a very large factor in determining what that left over from this year is worth.

As things are now, as I understand it, there is simply a going around in a circle, no one being able to make a move in a straight line, because he does not know what the other parties are going to do. This will continue, as I said above, as I see it, to the point of exhaustion and disaster.

Now, if what I have just set forth, is a correct portrayal of the situation, then it is to the ultimate advantage of everybody to get together with a view of having the manufacturers (that is, the purchasers) consider how much, under all the circumstances, they can use, and what, under all the circumstances, is a proper and fair price for them to pay; then have the sellers (that is, the growers) consider whether, under all the circumstances, that is not a proper price at which they should sell, and have them agree to sell. Thereupon it would be known definitely just how much cotton is to be taken out of the market and at what price. We would then know how much would have to be carried over to next year, and could determine what proper restriction should be put upon the crop of next year. Thereupon the various growers could, by common consent, agree to reduce, each in the same percentage, their next year's crop so as to produce only the agreed amount. The Department of Agriculture incidentally could give them information as to what could be substituted by way of crop for the percentage of their land which would not then be used for cotton. Of course the whole matter would have to be done upon the basis of wise, honest, unselfish, patriotic action. It would not be regulated by any laws, and would have to be put upon the highest basis of fair dealing as between man and man.

It is possible that any agreement reached would be in contravention of the Sherman and other anti-trust laws, and it is possible, therefore, that there might have to be some State legislation which compelled them to do certain things, rather than their agreeing to do them. I am persuaded, however, that as a result of such a meeting, a practicable, comprehensive plan could be devised, which could then be carried out with whatever other legislation or action might be required.

In conclusion, this plan, if it could be carried out, would settle our present debt in England; because, if the Manchester purchasers would take their normal amount of cotton, or anything like it, the gold which we otherwise will either have to pay or arrange with respect thereto, will not have to be sent there. If we can pay in cotton, we do not have to pay in gold, and I think their attitude is such that they will be very glad indeed to avoid calling on us for the gold.

Sincerely yours,   Lindley M. Garrison

TLS (WP, DLC).

## From Henry Lee Higginson

Dear Mr. President:                    Boston. October 22, 1914.

Now that Congress has gone home, will you allow me to congratulate you on the work which has been done by that body with your guidance and help? The banking bill is going to work well, and I wish with you, that it should be put to work at once. If it had been in use in June, it would have saved us much trouble and money. Such times as the present wear men out physically and mentally; indeed, every panic kills many good men, and always the best, for their consciences are livelier than those of others.

The tariff bill will work out well. I am afraid that Congress has interfered too much with business, and am sure of one thing: that it has made the positions of directors so sour that it will be difficult to get good men to take them. Many men are leaving those positions, and only a high sense of duty would induce me now to take any directorship. However, we shall see how the new laws work. Nobody can truly prophesy.

I have always felt uneasy about the very large corporations, and yet believe that, if well conducted, with due regard to the public and to the stockholders, they will be a real benefit. It seems to me that the Interstate Commerce Commission, which is now trying the railroad rates again, is not of the requisite high quality, for its duties are of very great importance and should command men of high grade, large knowledge and excellent judgment. The tone of these men in conducting their examinations is not judicial but that of an advocate. This I know: that it is difficult to sell railroad bonds and more difficult to induce people to buy railroad shares. I know also, from our large European correspondence, that the Europeans are asking for higher rates for our railroads and, not getting them, will sell more of their holdings, which are still very large. In our office we cannot advise people to buy railroad shares, and only the best railroad bonds. I note that on various Roads the rolling stock is running down for lack of money. In every business it is a little more and a good profit, a little less and no profit at all or a loss,—and it is so with the railroads.

But what I particularly like is your belief that, with the new banking system in order and Congress at home, we shall move on; that people are more frightened than hurt, and that the nation ought to have a good business. Often fright comes from a wish to meet every obligation promptly, and the best people are the most timid, for men fear far more to hurt their credit than they do to hurt their purses.

For some weeks I have been telling people that, with our good crops and with the demand for food supplies, clothing, blankets, horses, shoes and the like, we ought to have a good business. The cotton men can stand low prices perfectly well, and any sensible man will tell you that men do not need to make money every year.

It has been a very trying time in which you have been in the

White House, and I agree with President Taft that you are entitled to our best support,—and you shall have it.

With kindest wishes, I am

Respectfully yours,   Henry L. Higginson

TLS (WP, DLC).

## To Sir Cecil Arthur Spring Rice

My dear Mr. Ambassador:    The White House October 23, 1914

Thank you sincerely for your note of yesterday. I was very much relieved to hear of the release of the Rockefeller and have no doubt that the case of the Brindilla will be handled with the same candor and promptness.

I hope that you think the last message to Page about the Declaration of London, etc., is a satisfactory one.

In haste, with warm regard,

Cordially and sincerely yours,   Woodrow Wilson

TLS (FO 115/1770, p. 170, PRO).

## To Edward Mandell House

My dear Friend:            The White House October 23, 1914

Thank you for your letter of the twenty-first. I am a little disturbed by the messages Walter Page is sending recently. It is very necessary that he should see the difficult matters now under discussion between us and the British Government in the light in which they are seen on this side of the water, and I am sorry that he should think the argument of them from our point of view the work of mere "library lawyers." We are very much helped by his advice, but I hope that he will not get into an unsympathetic attitude. We are handling matters of the greatest difficulty, because they must be handled under the influence of opinion, and it would be very unfortunate if he were to become unsympathetic or were to forget the temper of folks at home, who are exceedingly sensitive about every kind of right.

I am just off tonight for a visit of questionable usefulness to Pittsburgh.

The attempt of Congress to adjourn yesterday was a failure and it may be that if they do not succeed today, I shall be prevented from going, after all. Privately, I should not be sorry.

In haste      Affectionately yours,   Woodrow Wilson

TLS (E. M. House Papers, CtY).

## To Henry Lee Higginson

My dear Major: [The White House] October 23, 1914

That was a very kind letter you wrote me yesterday. You must have known that I was feeling a little blue by reaction and strain and needed cheering, and you have cheered me very much.

I believe with you that the main work of the session is going to work out into things which, when we have tried them, we shall approve, and I believe that all that is needed now is confidence on the part of the business men of the country to embrace great opportunities and achieve great results.

As I have said always, I am not afraid of big corporations merely because of their size, and I believe that properly managed they can be of great service to the business of the country, but I am afraid of businesses of different sorts interlocked with one another and organizations within the same field of business nominally independent but really under a single direction.

These things we shall work out with moderation and, I hope, with wisdom, and I am sure that men like yourself will give the heartiest cooperation and the fairest judgment of the result.

Cordially and sincerely yours, Woodrow Wilson

TLS (Letterpress Books, WP, DLC).

## To Frank J. Hayes

My dear Mr. Hayes: [The White House] October 23, 1914

Upon receipt of your letter of October seventeenth[1] with its enclosure, which I herewith return with appreciation of the privilege of being allowed to see it, I at once instituted an inquiry, of which this is the result:

Upon communicating with the Governor of Colorado I find that what has seemed to be the gathering of the state militia recently was not made with the least intention of displacing, or even supplementing, the forces of the United States, but took place because of a rifle competition on October 14-18 at Golden, Colorado, a competition authorized by the War Department. The militia of the state are being recruited, as of course you know, but there is nothing in that to which the War Department could possibly object.

We learned upon inquiry, also, that the men being recruited into the National Guard of the state were being recruited from the several neighborhoods of the state with which the several companies of the militia would naturally be connected, and that men were not being brought for that service from outside Colorado.

We cannot upon inquiry verify the impression that men are being introduced into the mines as workmen from outside the state. I know that there is a widespread impression that this is being done, but after an inquiry very carefully made we can find no evidence of it.

Cordially and sincerely yours,   Woodrow Wilson

TLS (Letterpress Books, WP, DLC).
¹ F. J. Hayes to WW, Oct. 17, 1914, TLS (WP, DLC).


## To Cleveland Hoadley Dodge

My dear Cleve:          The White House October 23, 1914

I must say I was malicious enough to chuckle over the contents of your letter with a very deep content. I comfort myself and justify you in a like feeling by the knowledge that what we strove for at Princeton was a very great and noble principle and that it is only in the interest of what is right that those who opposed and who have conducted their opposition in a way that was, to say the least, not honorable should be discomfited.

It was a genuine delight to hear from you as it always is.

Affectionately yours,   Woodrow Wilson

TLS (WC, NjP).


## From Robert Lansing

Dear Mr. President:          Washington October 23, 1914.

In view of the fact that we have notified Great Britain that our suggestion as to the adoption of the Declaration of London is withdrawn and that this Government will stand upon its rights as defined by the existing rules of International Law, should we not give a similar notice to the other belligerent governments stating as a reason for the withdrawal of the suggestion the unwillingness of some [of] the belligerents to accept the Declaration without modification?

Very sincerely yours,   Robert Lansing.

Yes; by all means. W.W.¹

TLS (SDR, RG 59, 72112/242½A, DNA).
¹ This was done in a circular telegram on October 24. It is printed in *FR-WWS 1914*, p. 259.

# From Robert Lansing, with Enclosure

Dear Mr. President:          Washington October 23, 1914.

I spoke to you the other day about a conversation I had with a representative of certain banking interests in New York regarding the use of Treasury notes of the French Republic in this country in payment for purchases by that Government. Since then I have had conversations with representatives of other banking interests in New York, which relate to a similar type of loan to Russia as well as to France. You will also recall that this same subject was dealt with in a memorandum handed me by the Russian Ambassador a few days ago, which you returned with an oral explanation as to the attitude of this Government.

I have gone over the matter pretty carefully with these gentlemen and without comment submit in a memorandum, for your consideration, what I consider to be their views in regard to the situation. I have told them that I could make no statement until I had laid the matter before you. They naturally are anxious to know as soon as possible what your views are.

I should hesitate to ask your direction in this matter, were it not for the fact that there is evidence of a desire on the part of these institutions to do nothing which would in any way embarrass the Government or go contrary to your wishes, even if the law permitted them to do so.

Very sincerely yours,   Robert Lansing.

TLS (WP, DLC).

# ENCLOSURE

## Summary of Information
### in regard to credits of Foreign
### Governments in this country
### and the relation to trade.

The outbreak of the European war came at a time when this country owed a large amount to Europe, particularly to England in the form of short time drafts, maturing between the outbreak of the war and the end of the year. The amount, while large, was not abnormal, considering the volume of our trade relations and was directly due to the anticipated shipment of cotton during the autumn.

War conditions have made cotton bills unavailable for the settlement of this balance against us and it can only be wiped out by the shipment of the goods, in lieu of the cotton, that are now needed and desired by the various European countries. This is true, regardless of any temporary bridging over of the situation, and it has been the policy of the financial institutions in New York, as far as possible and proper, to stimulate the unprecedented and unusual buying by foreign governments and their nationals that is now going on in this country. Since the beginning of the war I am informed that one bank alone has received cabled instructions for the payment of more than $50,000,000 for American goods and that the volume of this business is increasing. Owing to war conditions, this buying is necessarily for cash and it is of such magnitude that the cash credits of the European governments are being fast depleted. Lately it has been urged by certain manufacturers and by representatives of some of the foreign governments, that the banks should provide temporary credits for these purchases. Recently the Norwegian Government arranged an advance of some three million dollars, practically all of which is to be expended for cereals in this country. Very recently the Russian Government, it is stated, has placed directly, and through agents, large orders with American manufacturers—orders so large that their cash credit has been absorbed and they have sought to obtain overdrafts, secured by gold deposited in their state bank, of some five million dollars.

Some of the manufacturers have been asked to take short time Treasury warrants of the French Government in payment for goods and have, in turn, asked the banks if they could discount them or could purchase warrants direct from the French Government for the purpose of replenishing their cash balances. The same question has been asked as to English Consols and Treasury securities, while some of the banks have been approached by German correspondents with the suggestion that, without naming a particular security, the banks sell securities to increase their cash account in America.

The representatives of the banks state that they feel the necessity of aiding the situation by temporary credits of this sort, otherwise the buying power of these foreign purchasers will dry up and the business will go to Australia, Canada, Argentine and elsewhere. They say that it may in the end come back to the United States but that, in their opinion, the critical time for American finance in our International relations is during the next three or four months and, if we allow these purchases to go elsewhere, we will have neglected our foreign trade at the time of our greatest need and greatest opportunity.

It seems to be the desire of the banks to be absolutely in accord with the policies of this Government, both in its legal position and in the spirit of its operations and, while very anxious to stimulate our foreign trade, they do not wish to, in any respect, act otherwise than in complete accord with the policy of the Government.

For the purpose of enabling European Governments to make cash payments for American goods, it is suggested to grant to them short time banking credits, to both belligerent and neutral governments, and where necessary or desirable replenish their cash balances on this side by the purchase of short time Treasury warrants. Such purchases would necessarily be limited to the legal capacity of the particular bank and, as these warrants are bearer warrants without interest, they could not and would not be made the subject of a public issue. These securities could be sold abroad or be readily available as collateral in foreign loans and would be paid at maturity in dollars or equivalent in foreign exchange.                                   Robert Lansing.

TS memorandum (WP, DLC).

## A Memorandum by Robert Lansing

[Washington] 9:30 p.m. October 23, 1914.
*Memorandum of a Conversation with
the President at 8:30 this evening
relative to loans and bank credits
to belligerent governments.*

From my conversation with the President I gathered the following impressions as to his views concerning bank credits of belligerent governments in contradistinction to a public loan floated in this country.

There is a decided difference between an issue of government bonds, which are sold in open market to investors, and an arrangement for easy exchange in meeting debts incurred in trade between a government and American merchants.

The sale of bonds draws gold from the American people. The purchasers of bonds are loaning their savings to the belligerent government, and are, in fact, financing the war.

The acceptance of Treasury notes or other evidences of debt in payment for articles purchased in this country is merely a means of facilitating trade by a system of credits which will avoid the clumsy and impractical method of cash payments. As trade with belligerents is legitimate and proper it is desirable that obstacles, such an [as] interference with an arrangement of credits or easy method of exchange, should be removed.

The question of an arrangement of this sort ought not to be submitted to this Government for its opinion, since it has given its views on loans in general, although an arrangement as to credits has to do with a commercial debt rather than with a loan of money.

The above are my individual impressions of the conversation with the President, who authorized me to give them to such persons as were entitled to hear them, upon the express understanding that they were my own impressions and that I had no authority to speak for the President or the Government.

Robert Lansing.

Substance of above conveyed to Willard Straight[1] at Metropolitan Club, 8:30 p.m. October 24, 1914.　RL.

Substance of above conveyed to R. L. Farnham[2] at the Department, 10:30 a.m., October 26, 1914.　RL.

TS memorandum (SDR, RG 59, 763.72111/630½, DNA).
[1] A partner in J. P. Morgan & Co.
[2] Roger Leslie Farnham of the National City Bank of New York.

## An Address to the Pittsburgh Y.M.C.A.[1]

[[Oct. 24, 1914]]

Mr. President,[2] Mr. Porter,[3] ladies and gentlemen:

I feel almost as if I were a truant, being away from Washington today, but I thought that perhaps if I were absent the Congress would have the more leisure to adjourn. I do not ordinarily open my office at Washington on Saturday. Being a schoolmaster, I am accustomed to a Saturday holiday, and I thought I could not better spend a holiday than by showing at least something of the true direction of my affections; for, by long association with the men who have worked for this organization, I can say that it has enlisted my deep affection.

I am interested in it for various reasons. First of all, because it is an association of young men. I have had a good deal to do with young men in my time, and I have formed an impression of them which I believe to be contrary to the general impression.

[1] Delivered in Exposition Music Hall on the occasion of the seventieth anniversary of the Pittsburgh Y.M.C.A.

[2] Ralph Warner Harbison, Princeton 1898, associated with the Harbison-Walker Refactories Co., manufacturers of fire bricks; father of Elmore Harris Harbison, Princeton 1928, and Frederick Harris Harbison, Princeton 1934, longtime, distinguished professors of history and economics, respectively, at Princeton, both now deceased.

[3] Henry Kirke Porter, president of H. K. Porter Co., manufacturers of light locomotives; Republican congressman from Pittsburgh, 1903-1905.

They are generally thought to be arch radicals. As a matter of fact, they are the most conservative people I have ever dealt with. Go to a college community and try to change the least custom of that little world, and find how the conservatives will rush at you. Moreover, young men are embarrassed by having inherited their fathers' opinions. I have often said that the use of the university is to make young gentlemen as unlike their fathers as possible. I do not say that with the least disrespect for the fathers; but every man who is old enough to have a son in college is old enough to have become very seriously immersed in some particular business and is almost certain to have caught the point of view of that particular business. And it is very useful to his son to be taken out of that narrow circle, conducted to some high place where he may see the general map of the world and of the interests of mankind, and there be shown how big the world is and how much of it his father may happen to have forgotten. It would be worthwhile for men, middle-aged and old, to detach themselves more frequently from the things that command their daily attention and to think of the sweeping tides of humanity.

Therefore, I am interested in this association, because it is intended to bring young men together before any crust has formed over them, before they have been hardened to any particular occupation, before they have caught an inveterate point of view; while they still have a searchlight that they can swing and see what it reveals of all the circumstances of the hidden world.

I am the more interested in it because it is an association of young men who are Christians. I wonder if we attach sufficient importance to Christianity as a mere instrumentality in the life of mankind. For one, I am not fond of thinking of Christianity as the means of saving individual souls. I have always been very impatient of processes and institutions which said that their purpose was to put every man in the way of developing his character. My advice is: Don't think about your character. If you will think about what you ought to do for other people, your character will take care of itself. Character is a by-product, and any man who devotes himself to its cultivation in his own case will become a selfish prig. The only way your powers can become great is by exerting them outside the circle of your own narrow, special, selfish interests. And that is the lesson of Christianity. Christ came into the world to save others, not to save himself; and no man is a true Christian who does not think constantly of how he can lift his brother, how he can assist his friend, how he can enlighten mankind, how he can make virtue the rule of conduct in the circle in which he lives. An association of young men might be an association that merely had its energies directed in every direction, but an association of Christian young men is an association meant to put its shoulders under the world and lift it, so that other men should feel that they have comrades in bearing the weight and heat of the day; that other men would know that there were those who cared for them, who would go into places of difficulty and danger to rescue them, who regarded themselves as their brother's keeper.

And, then, I am glad, too, that it is an association. Every word of its title means an element of strength. Young men are strong. Christian young men are the strongest kind of young men, and when they associate themselves together they have the incomparable strength of organization. The Young Men's Christian Association once excited, perhaps it is not too much to say, the hostility of the organized churches of the Christian world, because the movement looked as if it were so nonsectarian, as if it were so outside the ecclesiastical field, that perhaps it was an effort to draw young men away from the churches and to substitute this organization for the great bodies of Christian people who associated themselves in the Christian denominations. But after a while it appeared that it was a great instrumentality that belonged to all the churches; that it was a common instrument for sending the light of Christianity out into the world in its most practical form, drawing young men who were strangers into places where they could have companionship that stimulated them and suggestions that kept them straight and occupations that amused them without vicious practices; and then, by surrounding themselves with the atmosphere of purity and simplicity of life, catch something of a glimpse of the great ideal which Christ lifted when He was elevated upon the cross.

I remember hearing a very wise man[4] say once, a man grown old in the service of a great church, that he had never taught his son religion dogmatically at any time; that he and the boy's mother had agreed that, if the atmosphere of that home did not make a Christian of the boy, nothing that they could say would make a Christian of him. They knew that Christianity was catching, and if they did not have it, it would not penetrate. If they did have it, it would penetrate while the boy slept, almost; while he was unconscious of the sweet influences that were about him, while he reckoned nothing of instruction, but merely breathed into his lungs the wholesome air of a Christian home. That is the principle of the Young Men's Christian Association—to make a place where the atmosphere makes great ideals contagious. That

---

[4] His father.

is the reason that I said, though I had forgotten that I said it,[5] what is quoted on the outer page of the program—that you can test a modern community by the degree of its interest in its Young Men's Christian Association. You can test whether it knows what road it wants to travel or not. You can test whether it is deeply interested in the spiritual and essential prosperity of its rising generation. I don't know of any test that can be more conclusively put to a community than that.

Now, I want to suggest to the young men of this association that it is the duty of young men, not only to combine for the things that are good, but to combine in a militant spirit. There is a fine passage in one of Milton's prose writings, which I am sorry to say I cannot quote, but the meaning of which I can give you, and it is worth hearing. He says that he has no patience with a cloistered virtue that does not go out and seek its adversary. Ah, how tired I am of the men who are merely on the defensive, who hedge themselves in, who perhaps enlarge the hedge enough to include their little family circle and ward off all the evil influences of the world from that loved and hallowed group. How tired I am of the men whose virtue is selfish because it is merely self-protective! And how much I wish that men by the hundred thousand might volunteer to go out and seek the adversary and subdue him!

I have had the fortune to take part in affairs of a considerable variety of sorts, and I have tried to hate as few persons as possible. But there is an exquisite combination of contempt and hate that I have for a particular kind of person, and that is the moral coward. I wish we could give all our cowards a perpetual vacation. Let them go off and sit on the sidelines and see us play the game; and put them off the field if they interfere with the game. They do nothing but harm, and they do it by that most subtle and fatal thing of all, that of taking the momentum and the spirit and the forward dash out of things. A man who is virtuous and a coward has no marketable virtue about him. The virtue, I repeat, which is merely self-defensive, is not serviceable even, I suspect, to himself. For how a man can swallow and not taste bad when he is a coward and thinking only of himself, I can not imagine.

So that I say, be militant! Be an organization that is going to do things! If you can find older men who will give you countenance and acceptable leadership, follow them; but if you cannot, organize separately and dispense with them. There are only two sorts of men worth associating with when something is to be done. These are young men and the men who never grow old.

5 In the address printed at Feb. 24, 1912, Vol. 24.

Now, if you find men who have grown old, about whom the crust has hardened, whose hinges are stiff, whose minds always have their eye over the shoulder, thinking of things as they were done, don't have anything to do with them. It would not be Christian to exclude them from your organization, but merely use them to pad the roll. If you can find older men who will lead you acceptably and keep you in countenance, I am bound as an older man to advise you to follow them. But suit yourselves. Do not follow people that stand still. Just remind them that this is not a statical proposition; it is a movement, and if they can't get a move on them they are not serviceable.

Because life, gentlemen—the life of society, the life of the world—has constantly to be fed from the bottom. It has to be fed by those great sources of strength which are constantly rising in new generations. Red blood has to be pumped into it. New fiber has to be supplied. That is the reason I have always said that I believed in popular institutions. If you can guess beforehand who your rulers are going to be, you can guess with a very great certainty that most of them won't be fit to rule. The beauty of popular institutions is that you don't know where the man is going to come from, and you don't care so he is the right man. You don't know whether he will come from the avenue or the alley. You don't know whether he will come from the city or from the farm. You don't know whether you will ever have heard that name before or not. And therefore you do not limit at any point your supply of new strength. You do not say it has got to come through the blood of a particular family or through the process of a particular training, or by anything except the native impulse and genius of the man himself. Therefore the humblest hovel may produce you your greatest man. A very humble hovel did produce you one of your greatest men. And so that is the process of life—this constant surging up of new strength of unnamed, unrecognized, uncatalogued men who are just getting into the running, who are just coming up from the masses of the unrecognized multitude. You don't know when you will see upon the level of the masses of the crowd some great stature lifted head and shoulders above the rest, shouldering its way, not violently, but gently, to the front and saying, "Here am I; follow me." And his voice will be your voice, his thought will be your thought, and you will follow him as if you were following the best things in yourselves.

And so, when I think of an association of Christian young men, I wonder that it has not already turned the world upside down. I wonder, not that it has done so much, for it has done a great deal, but that it has done so little; and I can only conjecture that it does not realize its own strength. I can only imagine that it has not yet got its pace. I wish I could believe, and I do believe, that at seventy it has just reached its majority, and that from this time on a dream greater even than George Williams[6] ever dreamed will be realized in the great accumulating momentum of Christian young men throughout the world. For, gentlemen, this is an age in which the principles of men who utter public opinion dominate the world. It makes no difference what is done for the time being. After the struggle is over, the jury will sit, and nobody can corrupt that jury.

At one time I tried to write history. I didn't know enough to write it, but I knew from experience how hard it was to find an historian out, and I trusted I would not be found out. I used to have this comfortable thought as I saw men struggling in the public arena. I used to think to myself, "This is all very well and very interesting. You probably assess yourself in such and such a way. Those who are your partisans assess you thus and so. Those who are your opponents urge a different verdict. But it does not make very much difference, because, after you are dead and gone, some quiet historian will sit in a secluded room and tell mankind for the rest of time just what to think about you. And his verdict, not the verdict of your partisans, and not the verdict of your opponents, will be the verdict of posterity." I say that I used to say that to myself. It very largely was not so. And yet it was true in this sense: If the historian really speaks the judgment of the succeeding generation, then he really speaks the judgment also of the generations that succeed him, and his assessment, made without the passion of the times, made without partisan feeling, made in other circumstances, made when the air is cool, is the judgment of mankind upon your actions.

Now, is it not very important that we who shall constitute a portion of the jury should get our best judgments to work and base them upon Christian forbearance and Christian principles, upon the idea that it is impossible by sophistication to establish that a thing that is wrong is right? And yet, while we are going to judge with the absolute standard of rightness, we are going to judge with Christian feeling, being men of a like sort ourselves, suffering the same temptations, having the same weaknesses, knowing the same passions; and, while we don't condemn, we are going to seek to say and to live the truth. So that what I am hoping for is that these seventy years have just been a running start, and that now there will be a great rush of Christian principles

6 Sir George Williams, founder of the Y.M.C.A.

upon the strongholds of evil and of wrong in the world. Those strongholds are not as strong as they look. Almost every vicious man is afraid of society, and if you once open the door where he is, he will run. So that all you have to do is to fight, not with cannon, but with light.

May I illustrate it in this way? The Government of the United States has just succeeded in concluding a large number of treaties with the leading nations of the world, the sum and substance of which is this—that, whenever any trouble arises, the light shall shine on it for a year before you do anything. And my prediction is that, if the light has shone on it for a year, it won't be necessary to do anything; that after we know what happened, then we will know who was right and who was wrong. Because I believe that light is the greatest sanitary influence in the world. That, I suppose, is a scientific commonplace, because, if you want to make a place wholesome, the best instrument you can use is the sun—to let his rays in, let him scorch out all the miasma that may lurk there. So with moral light: It is the most wholesome, rectifying, and most revealing thing in the world, provided it be genuine moral light; not the light of inquisitiveness, not the light of the man who likes to turn up ugly things, not the light of the man who disturbs what is corrupt for the mere sake of the sensation that he creates by disturbing it, but the moral light, the light of the man who discloses it in order that all the sweet influences of the world may go in and make it better.

That, in my judgment, is what the Young Men's Christian Association can do. It can point out to its members the things that are wrong. It can guide the feet of those who are going astray; and when its members have realized the power of the Christian principles, then they will not be men if they do not unite to see that the rest of the world experiences the same emancipation and reaches the same happiness of release.

I believe in the Young Men's Christian Association because I believe in the progress of moral ideas in the world; and I don't know that I am sure of anything else. When you are after something, and have formulated it, and have done the very best thinking you know how to do, you have got to be sure for the time being that that is the thing to do. But you are a fool if in the back of your head you don't know that it is possible you are mistaken. All that you can claim is that that is the thing as you see it now, and that you cannot stand still; that you must push forward the things that are right. It may turn out that you made mistakes, but what you do know is your direction, and you are sure you are moving in that way. I was once a college reformer, until discouraged, and I remember a classmate of mine saying, "Why, man, can't you let anything alone?" I said, "I let everything alone that you can show me is not itself moving in the wrong direction, but I am not going to let those things alone that I see are going downhill"; and I borrowed this illustration from an ingenious writer who says, "If you have a post that is painted white and want to keep it white, you can't let it alone; and if anybody says to you, 'Why don't you let that post alone,' you will say, 'Because I want it to stay white, and, therefore, I have got to paint it at least every second year.'" There isn't anything in this world that won't change if you absolutely let it alone, and therefore you have constantly to be attending to it to see that it is being taken care of in the right way and that, if it is part of the motive forces of the world, it is moving in the right direction.

That means that eternal vigilance is the price, not only of liberty, but of a great many other things. It is the price of everything that is good. It is the price of one's own soul. It is the price of the souls of the people you love; and, when it comes down to the final reckoning, you have a standard that is immutable. What shall a man give in exchange for his own soul? Will he sell that? Will he consent to see another man sell his soul? Will he consent to see the conditions of his community such that men's souls are debauched and trodden underfoot in the mire? What shall he give in exchange for his own soul, or any other man's soul? And since the world—the world of affairs, the world of society—is nothing less and nothing more than all of us put together, it is a great enterprise for the salvation of the soul in this world as well as in the next. There is a text in Scripture that has always interested me profoundly. It says godliness is profitable in this life as well as in the life that is to come; and if you don't start it in this life, it won't reach the life that is to come. Your measurements, your directions, your whole momentum, have to be established before you reach the next world. And this world is intended as the place in which we shall show that we know how to grow in the stature of manliness and of righteousness.

And so I have come here to bid Godspeed to the good work of the Young Men's Christian Association. I love to think of the gathering forces of such things as this in the generations to come. If a man had to measure the accomplishments of society, the progress of reform, the speed of the world's betterment, by the few little things that happened in his own life, by the trifling things that he can contribute to accomplishments, he would indeed feel that the cost was much greater than the result. But no man can look at the past, of the history of this world, without seeing a vision of the future of this world; and when you think of the accumulated moral forces that have made one age better than another age in the progress of mankind, then you can open your eyes to the vision. You can see that age by age, though it is a bitter struggle in the dust of the road, though often mistaking the path and losing its way in the mire, mankind is yet—sometimes with bloody hands and battered knees—nevertheless struggling step after step up the slow stages to the day when each shall live in the full light which shines upon the uplands, where all the light that illumines mankind shines direct from the face of God.[7]

Printed in *Address of President Wilson at Y.M.C.A. Celebration* . . . (Washington, 1914), with editorial corrections from the CLSsh (C. L. Swem Coll., NjP) and many corrections from the complete text in the *Pittsburgh Post*, Oct. 25, 1914.

[7] There is a WWT outline of this address, dated Oct. 22, 1914, in WP, DLC.

## From Edward Mandell House

Dear Governor:                    New York City. October 24th, 1914.

After I had sent that cablegram of Page's I regretted it for the reason that he seemed unduly disturbed.

It is difficult to get a proper viewpoint when so far away and when listening to only one side of the case.

This country is now so strongly anti-German that you would be upheld in things which ordinarily would raise a storm. But, even so, England should be held to the letter and spirit of the law if we are to maintain our attitude of strict neutrality.

Affectionately yours,   E. M. House

I hope it will soon be possible for you to come over for a few days. The change of scene will do you good.

TLS (WP, DLC).

## From Sir Cecil Arthur Spring Rice, with Enclosures

*Personal*

Dear Mr President                    Washington. 24 October 1914

I venture to transmit with this letter two telegrams: one from the Governor General of Canada and the other from Sir Edward Grey.

I have the honour to be with profound respect

Your most obedient humble servant   Cecil Spring Rice

ALS (WP, DLC).

ENCLOSURE I

Telegram from His Royal Highness the Duke of Connaught
   to Sir Cecil Spring Rice.          Dated October 23, 1914.
Steamship "Brindilla."

My Ministers state that Canadian Government know nothing of refusal to allow American Consul at Halifax to communicate with Captain and no such refusal has been authorised by them. They see no objection whatever to permitting Consul to communicate with Captain and they have so advised their officials at Halifax.

ENCLOSURE II

Telegram from Sir E. Grey to Sir C. Spring Rice,
   dated October 24, 1914.

*Personal*

I am very glad that the United States Government no longer insist upon the Declaration of London in its entirety: this decision will smooth the path very much. I am very sensible of the friendly spirit shown by the President and my Conversations with Mr. Page have been most pleasant.

It is absolutely necessary for us in the present circumstances to detain ships carrying oil and copper till we make sure that their cargoes are really going to be landed and consumed in a neutral country; it must not however be assumed that when a ship is detained her cargo is going to be captured or confiscated. In the meanwhile I am doing my best to secure arrangements with neutral countries of such a nature as will avoid delay to neutral shipping while giving us adequate security.[1]

TC telegrams (WP, DLC).
  1 This was Spring Rice's somewhat expanded version of E. Grey to C. A. Spring Rice, Oct. 24, 1914, T telegram (FO 115/1770, p. 178, PRO).

## From Sir Cecil Arthur Spring Rice, with Enclosure

*Personal*

Dear Mr President            Washington. 24 October 1914

I beg to enclose copy of a telegram received from Sir Edward Grey. There was reason to suspect the Brindilla of intending to supply one of the German cruisers. This information however did not come from any source that I know of nor did it pass through my hands. It should be easy to prove or disprove.

Sir George Paish tells me that the negotiations about exchange are going on well but that it will be a week before anything is decided. He thinks the question of the purchase of cotton depends on whether or no there is reason to believe that bottom prices have been reached. I have received a report from Newport News informing me that cotton shipments were impossible owing to the difficulty of getting payments effected.

I have telegraphed to London that a statement as to the attitude of the British Government as to shipments of cotton to belligerents is expected.

I have the honour to remain with profound respect
Your most obedient humble servant    Cecil Spring Rice

I have explained to Sir Edward Grey the great importance of the cotton question as it now presents itself.

ALS (WP, DLC).


ENCLOSURE

Telegram from Sir E. Grey to Sir C. Spring Rice.    Oct. 24, 1914.

United States Ambassador has informed me that the United States Government abandon the Declaration of London and reserve their rights and obligations according to Treaties and International Law.

We had drawn up a new Proclamation adapted as far as possible to the views expressed by the Ambassador and Mr. Anderson previously adopting the Declaration of London but making some modifications. It does not differ substantially from Proclamation already submitted to the United States Government but I have given a copy confidentially to the Ambassador.

I understand that the United States Government will not protest against the Proclamation when issued but will deal with cases as they arise on their merits.[1]

Instructions are being sent that information now received appears to show that the voyage of the "Brindilla" was bona fide and that unless there is reason to suppose she was intending not to go to Alexandria but to supply the enemy, she should be released. We do not wish to raise question of transfer of flag in this case.

TC telegram (WP, DLC).
[1] What Grey actually wrote to this point follows: "The American Ambassador informed me to-day that his Government abandoned the Declaration of London,

not having realised all the difficulties there were in applying it; but they reserved the rights and duties of the United States Government and citizens, under international laws, irrespective of the Declaration of London, to enter a protest when these were violated or their free exercise interfered with. The Ambassador said that it was not explicitly stated, but he understood this to mean that the United States Government would not make any protest against the issue of our Proclamation. He assured me again that it had not been, and was not, their intention to give us trouble." E. Grey to C. A. Spring Rice, Oct. 23, 1914, T telegram (F.O. 372/602, No. 63204, p. 63, PRO). Copies of this telegram were sent to the King and cabinet.

## From Sir Cecil Arthur Spring Rice, with Enclosure

Personal

Dear Mr President                    Washington. 25 Oct 1914

I have the honour to enclose a telegram just received from Sir Edward Grey. It is in answer to the request for information as to our attitude which was made by the State Department after receiving representations from the New York Chamber of Commerce.

I have the honour to be with the most profound respect
        Your obedient humble servant    Cecil Spring Rice

ALS (WP, DLC).

E N C L O S U R E

Copy of telegram from Sir Edward Grey

Dated October 25, 1914.

You can give assurance that cotton will not be seized. It has not been put in any of our lists of contraband and as State Department must know from draft Proclamation in their possession it is not proposed to include it in our new list of contraband. It is therefore as far as we are concerned in the free list and will remain there. But we do not in our new Proclamation accept free list of the Declaration of London as regards some articles other than cotton.

Does the State Department realise that though we detain cargoes of contraband to make sure that they are really intended for neutral countries and have retained some cargoes such as copper destined for Krupp, we have not yet taken a single cargo without paying for it and have let all proceed that were really destined for neutral countries?[1]

TC telegram (WP, DLC).
    [1] This telegram was sent as E. Grey to C. A. Spring Rice, Oct. 25, 1914, Hw telegram (FO 372/602, No. 63127, p. 56, PRO).

# Henry Thomas Rainey[1] to Joseph Patrick Tumulty

My dear Mr. Tumulty:          Washington, D. C. October 25, 1914.

I will leave for the Illinois Campaign today.

I am very sorry indeed that we have been unable to obtain for Mr. Sullivan and our Illinois Ticket the endorsement of the President.

I thank you sincerely for your efforts.[2]

According to all the rules which govern these matters I cannot avoid the opinion that we ought to have had it and that we were entitled at least to an expression from the President to the effect that the candidates selected in our Primary ought to receive the endorsement of the Democrats.

I think we ought to have had an endorsement from him saying that he did not approve of the fight being made in his name in Illinois against Mr. Sullivan.

Our failure to receive the endorsement of the President will, of course, cost us many thousand of votes in Illinois. We will, however, carry on the fight and do the very best we can to win without it.

Thinking that perhaps the President may relent later in the week, I will instruct the Chairman of our Central Committee to open any letters that may be addressed to me in his care, and to make public any endorsement of Mr. Sullivan and the Congressional and State Tickets in Illinois, the President may send us.

I leave at 6:15 today on the Pennsylvania, and will speak in Chicago tomorrow night. It was at this meeting that we had hoped to be able to read a letter from the President.

I can be reached at any time this week, C/o Hon. Arthur Charles, Chairman Democratic State Committee, Sherman House, Chicago, Illinois.

Very truly yours,    Henry T Rainey

TLS (WP, DLC).

[1] Democratic congressman from Illinois.

[2] Some progressive Democrats, led by Senator Robert L. Owen, formed the Wilson-Bryan Democratic League and opposed Roger C. Sullivan in the Illinois Democratic senatorial primary. Sullivan was supported by Tumulty, Rainey, and many regular Democrats. Owen, appealing to Wilson to stand with the progressives, denounced Sullivan as a reactionary and dishonest political boss. R. L. Owen to WW, June 5, 1914, TLS (WP), enclosing a T memorandum "submitted *at request of President*" (WP, DLC). Wilson remained neutral. Sullivan won the nomination in the primary in September by a plurality of 31,000 votes. Tumulty and Rainey then put heavy pressure on Wilson to write a letter endorsing Sullivan. Wilson did compose a lukewarm letter to Rainey, but then decided that he simply could not support Sullivan and never signed the letter. There are several versions of this letter: an undated WWsh draft in the C. L. Swem Coll., NjP; a TLS with WWhw emendations and Hw emendations by an unknown person, dated Oct. 12, 1914 in WP, DLC; a TCL with emendations by the same unknown person, dated Oct. 12, 1914, in WP, DLC; and an undated TL in WP, DLC—the final version.

Many Democrats voted for the Progressive candidate, Raymond Robins, enabling the incumbent, Republican Senator Lawrence Y. Sherman, to win re-election.


## Remarks at a Press Conference

October 26, 1914

Mr. President, do you think that the various developments of recent days have to some extent cleared up the cotton situation so as to obviate the necessity of emergency legislation?

> Yes, I do. I thought all along it was likely to clear it up. Not, of course, completely. The only way to restore the cotton situation is to stop the war; but the most that could be done financially to help the situation was in course of being done, and every day makes me more certain that that is true.

Have we now virtually a clear market in Europe? There is a story this morning about the willingness of Great Britain to let cotton go into Germany.

> I had not heard of that feature of it. You see, it is an absolutely necessary thing, and, as it happens, it heads the list of the things that are not contraband, and there is every reason why all the ports possible should be opened to it, and I think they will be.

With Great Britain not interfering with the shipment of cotton and the possibility of getting cotton into Germany, wouldn't that furnish a very marked measure of relief?

> I should think so, though I am not informed as to the mills in Germany—as to just how far they are being operated—but I should assume that that would make a great deal of difference.

As a matter of fact, the cotton exports are already increasing, are they not?

> Yes, but increasing by a very small figure.

Mr. President, can you give us any clear insight into the Mexican situation today other than the newspaper accounts furnish?

> I haven't seen the morning papers; being away on Saturday, I have been clearing my desk at the house. What is the latest news?

The newspaper accounts this morning indicate further disturbances between Carranza and Villa?

> I am sorry to say I haven't any light to throw on it at present.

Is there anything you can tell us about the Colorado situation, Mr. President?

> There is no new development there that I know of.

Are there any plans about removing the federal troops?

> Not at present; no, sir. . . .

Mr. President, is there anything new you can tell us about the tank steamer *Brindilla* belonging to the Standard Oil Company?

> No, except that that matter is being handled in a very friendly way, and that it will come out all right.

Is there any information to show that the change of registry question is being considered in connection with the release of the *Brindilla*?

> No, I think not.

So far as you know, it is not being considered in this case?

> I think not. That is my information, but I am not perfectly clear on that.

Mr. President, have you any plans for getting early consideration of some of the left-over legislation, like the immigration bill and the seamen's bill?

> I am going to discuss, after the election, of course, when I can get hold of them, with the leaders of the Senate what program will be possible. Of course, we don't want to attempt an impossible number of bills at the short session, because the Senate will have only the time before it receives the appropriation bills from the House. I should say, at a guess, that would be until about the first of February, perhaps.

Can you say as to whether the bills which have passed either one or both of the Houses will have precedence over the bills which have not been taken up at all; take, for instance, the seamen's bill?

> We will have to consider what their order of importance is. You see, there is a very important general leasing bill, the general dam bill, and a number of large measures of that sort of general policy, and the Philippine bill, which would naturally occupy the foreground.

You feel fairly certain that they will get away on the fourth of March next?

> They have got to. There is a constitutional limitation. They cannot sit longer than noon on the fourth of March.

Mr. President, have you any information from the South to the effect that they share the hopeful feeling with regard to the cotton situation that you just expressed?

> I haven't any information at all one way or the other from them, but I have received a variety of impressions. I haven't found businessmen from the South very deeply apprehensive about the situation. It may be that those that were ap-

prehensive did not come to me, but those that did not, and a good many people who were apprehensive, did come to me, were not businessmen, strangely enough.

There is cash available to cover all safe loans in the South, isn't there?

Oh, yes. The trouble is not the amount of money available, but the basis on which it is to be loaned. Of course, you have to ascertain a probable price for cotton before you can establish a basis for credit.

What is the status in your mind of the ship purchase proposition?

Why, it hasn't any different status in my mind from that in your mind. It hasn't been brought up yet.

Is it going ahead?

I expect it to, unless there is something else of greater importance. As I just said, in a short session precedence is given to those things that are of the greatest consequence.

T MS (C. L. Swem Coll., NjP).

## To Sir Cecil Arthur Spring Rice

My dear Mr. Ambassador,   The White House 26 October, 1914.

I am sincerely obliged to you for your note of Saturday, with its enclosures.

Thanks to your own fine spirit in these trying days, and the fine spirit of Sir Edward Grey, I hope and believe that all matters of delicacy between our two governments will be handled without serious difficulty or embarrassment.

I am cheered to hear that Sir George Paish thinks the prospects good for satisfactory commercial arrangements.

Cordially and sincerely Yours,   Woodrow Wilson

WWTLS (FO 115/1770, p. 204, PRO).

## From Robert Lansing, with Enclosure

Dear Mr. President:                Washington October 26, 1914.

I am sending you a letter of October 24th from Mr. Charles K. McIntosh, Vice President of The Bank of California, relating to the renewal of the Japanese Land Controversy. The letter, I think, presents the matter very clearly and is worthy of consideration.

The Japanese Ambassador has just called in regard to the same subject and I told him that it was doubtless a campaign agitation, as to the seriousness of which we would be better able to judge after election.

Under instructions from his Government he has asked for an appointment with you, which has been arranged for twelve o'clock tomorrow. He will present the same subject to you.

Very sincerely yours,   Robert Lansing.

TLS (WP, DLC).


ENCLOSURE

## Charles Kenneth McIntosh to Robert Lansing

Dear Mr. Lansing:                    New York October 24, 1914

In the necessarily brief talk I had with you in Washington a day or two ago, I may not have made myself quite clear as to the situation which is giving some of us on the Pacific Coast no little concern.

With the Act passed at the last session of the Legislature of California, concerning the onwership of lands in California by aliens, you are of course familiar. I would only remind you that it contains a clause permitting aliens to lease for a period agricultural lands in that state.

A campaign is now on in the State and on November 3rd, many legislative officers will be chosen. The leaders of organized labor in California have selected this time to renew the agitation in regard to the land law and are evidently preparing to present to the Legislature—when next convened—an amendment to the Alien Land Bill—which will eliminate the leasing clause therefrom.

A series of questions directed to all candidates of all parties for legislative offices, issued by "The Legislative Conference representing the California State Federation of Labor, The State Building Trades Council, The Affiliated Central Councils and local unions throughout California," contains the following:

"Do you favor amending the Alien Land Law by
eliminating the leasing clause?"

No publicity beyond the issuance of the circular referred to has yet been given to the matter, but it is believed that without doubt organized labor contemplates a vigorous attempt to totally bar Orientals from our lands. The probable effect upon the people of Japan of a reopening of that question would, in our judgment, cause the Administration and the Nation serious embarrassment, and possibly grave concern, particularly so at this time, when Japan is at war and every effort is being made to maintain our absolute neutrality and when she—Japan—is at present engaged in policing the Pacific and keeping open the trade routes over which our commerce is being carried.

It was our thought, therefore, that the situation should be made known to your Department and through to the President, in order that if possible steps be taken to at least postpone any discussion of the subject until the war has been ended and the public mind of each nation is in a state permitting a calmer consideration than we believe to be likely now.

We feel that a suggestion made at this time by the President to the governing authorities of the American Federation of Labor at Washington, reminding them of their patriotic duty, would offer the greatest hope of accomplishing the desired result.

May I ask that you give your earnest consideration to the subject, and if your views as to its best solution coincide with ours, that you take such steps as seem proper to bring about the desired result.

I would appreciate your informing me of your views at your convenience, and I will communicate them to our friends at home.

I am,          Very truly yours,   C K McIntosh

TLS (WP, DLC).


## From David Ignatius Walsh

Dear President Wilson:         Boston, October 26 1914.

A delegation of colored people representing the International Independent Political Equal Rights League has just called upon me and requested that I give my assistance in two matters.

First: They wish me to arrange for an interview with you for the Rev. Byron Gunner,[1] who has been selected as the spokesman of their organization which is composed of colored people throughout the country and who is desirous of presenting their views in the matter of race segregation in the departments of government.

Second: They desire me to express to you my own personal views upon race segregation. As I said in a previous letter,[2] I am decidedly opposed to any condition existing in Washington or elsewhere that could be interpreted as discriminating against our colored population. There are in Massachusetts some 50,000 law-abiding, patriotic colored people and I respectfully urge that any conditions which exist tending to humiliate this race be eliminated.

I think that it cannot be too often emphasized that our government should be very careful to avoid discrimination against color or race and every effort should be made to have all our people fully realize that they enjoy equal rights and equal privileges.                    Yours very truly,   David I. Walsh

TLS (WP, DLC).
  [1] Pastor of Brook Chapel (Presbyterian) in Hillburn, N. Y., since 1907.
  [2] D. I. Walsh to W. M. Trotter, Oct. 11, 1913, TCL (WP, DLC).

## From Henry Lee Higginson

Dear Mr. President:                    Boston. October 26, 1914.

Thank you for your very kind letter of October 23d, and I am glad that anything of mine has given you pleasure. This letter will not be so pleasant, as it is about the railroads.

We have a house in London, the senior partner of which is a very intelligent Englishman. He has no interest in railroad stocks nor have we in this office unless in a very limited way, and it will be a long time before we ask people to buy railroad stocks. We do like to sell railroad bonds if they are good and people want them, but, like any other shop-keeper, we deal in what people want: and I always advise people to buy what they want. A letter has just come from this partner in reply to my inquiry as to future business. He speaks of the very great demand for money to pay insurance life losses, and reminds me that we have to compete with the whole world, for South America also is calling on England for a good deal of money, and as she has very large investments there, she must support South American enterprises. I asked him whether the English would sell American securities, and he said: "I believe that nobody will sell more than they can help, provided their confidence in American securities is not shaken. Most people are prepared to see dividends cut on common stock, but as long as there is no default on interest on bonds which have been sold to the public here as investment securities, I believe that confidence will continue. One thing I think would help confidence in future sales of American securities more than anything else, and that is that the railroads be granted a readjustment of freight rates. There is some talk of the issuing houses in London writing a simultaneous letter on this subject to their corresponding houses. The question is in the air yet, and I may refer to it in a later letter."

Again and again he has spoken of the same thing but not so emphatically, and he says much more on the subject. Now pray notice that he is free from personal investments in railroad shares, and as we deal a good deal in industrial enterprises and public service corporations, we are not dependent on railroad bonds; but the *country* is dependent on the good standing of railroad bonds bought here and abroad.

You and Mr. McAdoo have been doing your best to readjust the finances of this country, have been helping in the matter of exchanges between here and Europe, and have been willing to part with gold in order that we should pay our debts on the other side. We have a very close money-market which will be relieved presently. We have closed our stock exchanges to prevent a shower of securities from the other side. We need the European capital if we can keep it, and we also need to get more presently. Some of the Europeans are still buying good industrial and public service corporation securities as we know from our own sheets, and they are inclined to buy more. We can shock them or satisfy them just as we please. If the Interstate Commerce Commission, instead of attacking the railroads, were to listen to the men who understand the business, and not listen to Mr. Brandeis, who is not a judge of their affairs and who is saying things which are injurious to our railroads and, therefore, to our national credit, we should go on well. Because some railroads have been badly managed is no reason for thinking that all our railroads are guilty in any way. The Commission is willing that the railroads should suspend their dividends if necessary rather than raise their rates, or at any rate Mr. Brandeis is. It is to be borne in mind that railroads can sell their bonds much better if they pay fair dividends. In some states like our own a railroad cannot sell any bonds to the savings banks, which are very large investors, unless the railroads pay dividends, and it is a pall over all New England this day that the banks will very possibly throw out a great many securities, because the railroads are not paying dividends. Naturally a man puts his money into a corporation where there is a good margin, and the dividends are the margins.

When I think how much pains you, your Cabinet and Congress have taken to make credits easier, to give us an excellent bank act, to put the financial questions of our country into a comfortable condition, and then think that you are missing the very important point of satisfying our large customers in Europe, I sit and wonder.

May I repeat that I do not care about the value of railroad shares, except in so far as it affects our great public and the credit of the railroad corporations? We are, as I said to you the other day, ready to move on, but our largest industry—the railroads—is not in good condition, and will not be so until properly paid for its work. The sum in addition seems plain: The railroads pay more for everything, more especially for labor, and they get nothing more for their service. Of course they will not satisfy the public with limited service, and yet they can give no more.

Whether you can say anything to the Interstate Commerce Commission, whether you choose to do so lies with you, and of course I cannot know; but I do give you the opinion of this excellent man, my London partner.

There seems to me no danger of the railroads earning too much for a long time to come. Talking with one of the great New York men the other day, he said to me: "I sold all my railroad shares some years ago because the railroads were not having fair treatment and because I wished to advocate their cause. I have saved a lot of money by it and should not think of buying any of them back." This is a man whom you know well, who is out of business, is simply an investor, and spends his time doing excellent public work—an impartial, clear-sighted, able citizen.

In the last clause of your letter to me you say that you are not afraid of the big corporations, but are afraid of the interlocking of one with another, and you add: "These things will work out with moderation and I hope with wisdom, and I am sure that the men like yourself will give the heartiest coöperation and fairest judgment of the result." I certainly shall try to do so, but I am sure of what I have written to you.

I repeat that we should not think of advising anybody to buy railroad shares, and we should be very chary of advising them to buy railroad bonds. If we feel that way, we cannot advise our European friends to buy railroad bonds unless of the very best, and we know that people in our line of business feel just as we do.

The business world, which includes all the investors of the country—and it is they who hold the capital of the country—would be very glad to see an able, well-informed, judicial Board which would manage the business of the Interstate Commerce Commission. It is a tremendous charge on their shoulders, and yet they are not equal to it, and they employ as counsel a man who has sworn to attack the railroads in every way. It is not as men say in the world a "fair and square deal,"—and if there is anything that you have tried for, it is that—a fair and square deal.

I am, with great respect.

Very truly yours,    H. L. Higginson

TLS (WP, DLC).

## A Thanksgiving Proclamation

[Oct. 28, 1914]

It has long been the honoured custom of our people to turn in the fruitful autumn of the year in praise and thanksgiving to Almighty God for his many blessings and mercies to us as a nation. The year that is now drawing to a close since we last observed our day of national thanksgiving has been, while a year of discipline because of the mighty forces of war and of change which have disturbed the world, also a year of special blessing for us.

It has been vouchsafed to us to remain at peace, with honour, and in some part to succour the suffering and supply the needs of those who are in want. We have been privileged by our own peace and self-control in some degree to steady the counsels and shape the hopes and purposes of a day of fear and distress. Our people have looked upon their own life as a nation with a deeper comprehension, a fuller realization of their responsibilities as well as of their blessings, and a keener sense of the moral and practical significance of what their part among the nations of the world may come to be.

The hurtful effects of foreign war in their own industrial and commercial affairs have made them feel the more fully and see the more clearly their mutual interdependence upon one another and has stirred them to a helpful cooperation such as they have seldom practiced before. They have been quickened by a great moral stimulation. Their unmistakable ardour for peace, their earnest pity and disinterested sympathy for those who are suffering, their readiness to help and to think of the needs of others, has revealed them to themselves as well as to the world.

Our crops will feed all who need food; the self-possession of our people amidst the most serious anxieties and difficulties and the steadiness and resourcefulness of our business men will serve other nations as well as our own.

The business of the country has been supplied with new instrumentalities and the commerce of the world with new channels of trade and intercourse. The Panama Canal has been opened to the commerce of the nations. The two continents of

America have been bound in closer ties of friendship. New instrumentalities of international trade have been created which will be also new instrumentalities of acquaintance, intercourse, and mutual service. Never before have the people of the United States been so situated for their own advantage or the advantage of their neighbours or so equipped to serve themselves and mankind.

NOW, THEREFORE, I, WOODROW WILSON, President of the United States of America, do hereby designate Thursday the twenty-eighth of November next as a day of thanksgiving and prayer, and invite the people throughout the land to cease from their wonted occupations and in their several homes and places of worship render thanks to Almighty God.[1]

IN WITNESS WHEREOF I have hereunto set my hand and caused the seal of the United States to be affixed.

DONE at the City of Washington this twenty-eighth day of October in the year of our Lord one thousand nine [SEAL.] hundred and fourteen and of the independence of the United States of America the one hundred and thirty-ninth.

By the President:

ROBERT LANSING,
*Acting Secretary of State.*

Printed copy (WP, DLC).
[1] There is a WWsh draft of this proclamation in WP, DLC.

## To Walter Hines Page

My dear Page: The White House October 28, 1914

I was just reading carefully last night your last letter dated the fifteenth of October,[1] written in a way to give me a wonderful impression of the state of mind that prevails among the most thoughtful men connected with the government over there.

The whole thing is very vivid in my mind, painfully vivid, and has been almost ever since the struggle began. I think my thought and imagination contain the picture and perceive its significance from every point of view. I have to force myself not to dwell upon it to avoid the sort of numbness that comes from deep apprehension and dwelling upon elements too vast to be yet comprehended or in any way controlled by counsel. You need not doubt, my dear friend, that we comprehend and look into the murky darkness of the whole thing with the same thoughts that you have, though, of course, on this side of the water our own life is, at any rate, still free, and I fancy we can manage a little more perspective than it is conceivable should be obtainable from any point of view on your side the water.

I have been distressed to have to maintain our recent debate with Sir Edward Grey, but it was absolutely necessary that we should discuss the matters Mr. Lansing presented, because not the least part of the difficulty of this war is going to be the satisfaction of opinion in America and the full performance of our utmost duty as the only powerful neutral. More and more, from day to day, the elements (I mean the several racial elements) of our population seem to grow restless and catch more and more the fever of the contest. We are trying to keep all possible spaces cool, and the only means by which we can do so is to make it demonstrably clear that we are doing everything that it is possible to do to define and defend neutral rights. This is in the interest of all the belligerents no less than in our own interest. I mean that if we are to remain neutral and to afford Europe the legitimate assistance possible in such circumstances, the course we have been pursuing is the absolutely necessary course. Please do not suppose that we are not able to see the thing from the point of view of others, but always remember that it is as necessary for them as it is for us that we should present and emphasize our neutral point of view.

But these things must be obvious to you. This letter is not a sermon, it is a message of friendship and sympathy and of sincere appreciation for the letters by which you enable me to see what is going on about you as you, yourself, see it.

Faithfully yours,   Woodrow Wilson

TLS (W. H. Page Papers, MH).
[1] W. H. Page to WW, Oct. 15, 1914, ALS (WP, DLC).

## To Sir Cecil Arthur Spring Rice

My dear Mr. Ambassador,   The White House 28 October, 1914.

Again let me thank you warmly for the despatches you have let me see from Sir Edward Grey. The situation seems to be clearing up very happily,—as well as it can in extraordinary circumstances such as the present. I am particularly gratified that the way is opened so far as possible for the shipment of our cotton. That is quite in the spirit of sound international law.

With warm regard,

Cordially and sincerely Yours,   Woodrow Wilson

WWTLS (FO 115/1770, p. 203, PRO).

## From William Gibbs McAdoo

Dear Mr. President:                    Washington October 28, 1914.

For sometime I have felt that it might be of great value if this Department, through the medium of the State Department, could extend an invitation to each one of the Central and South American Governments to send its Finance Minister or some responsible and duly accredited financier to have a conference with the Secretary of the Treasury, looking to an improvement in the financial relationships between the United States and the Central and South American countries. These Governments might also be asked to send three representatives of the banking interests of each country to join in the conference. If this should be done, it would be my idea to have the Secretary of the Treasury invite representative American bankers to join in the conference. If the shipping bill shall be passed and we shall succeed in establishing reliable steamship lines to these countries, the next important step is to establish more intimate and more effective financial relations with these countries. Such a conference would, in my judgment, be productive of excellent results. The date should be about the 1st of February next. If you approve of this suggestion, I shall be very happy to take it up with the State Department and work out the necessary details.

Faithfully yours,    W G McAdoo

TLS (WP, DLC).

## From Walter Hines Page

Dear Mr. President:                         London. 28. Oct. '14

In 48 hours after we withdrew the demand for the British acceptance of the Declaration of London without change, every detained American ship and cargo was released but one, and I have no doubt that that one will be released in another 48 hours. I do not mean to imply in the least that these ships and cargoes were held, so to speak, as hostages: I do not believe that that idea entered anybody's mind. But so long as we held up their general policy, it was impossible—or surely the more difficult—to get at these concrete cases. They couldn't issue their revised list of contraband which shippers all over the neutral world were waiting for, and the ships of other neutral nations were detained as ours were. Now, I think, we are going to have the minimum of trouble.

As soon as the insistence on the Declaration was withdrawn,

I was in a position to talk to Sir Edw. Grey with the old-time frankness about the whole subject, wh. had become impossible so long as I had to lecture him on the necessity of accepting a general code that his Parliament and every other European Government had rejected in peace, when they considered it on its merits. I told him again of the universal, especially the American, sensitiveness about any interference with commerce; I hoped that he wd. impress on his Admiralty the need of the greatest caution; I told him that the stopping of ships just outside New York produced a worse effect than stopping the same ships on this side;* I suggested and urged that in every case he shd. at once have a full report made to us, as soon as a ship was stopped, why it was stopped—a full report of all facts and suspicions—and not to wait till the ship's captain reported to the American owners of the ship or of her cargo, and the owners reported to our Government & our Government made demands of his Government —all that loses time and causes additional irritation; and that he might be sure that our Government will take up every single case of detention with vigour. I suggested that each Government might, in my opinion, permit the utmost and the promptest publicity of the facts in every case. If, for instance, the facts had been published that the ship wh. was detained (with a cotton cargo) at Stornaway, Scotland, was detained by the Scotch owners and not by the British Admiralty—there cd. have been no irritation about that.

I can now push every case vigorously; and I am sure he will do his best to induce his naval officers to be careful. *There's* the difficulty: naval men don't have to settle the trouble that they cause. I am hopeful that we may now get through without serious trouble. Sir Edward and I had a little tilt at compliments to-day. I have to see him every day now. "I don't like to make myself a nuisance," I said; "but your navy must think we are fond of controversies about ships; and we must, of course, take every case up promptly." "You must really believe me," said he, "when I say that I am glad to see you; for I will say, though you push hard, you play fair." "You can stop the pushing, Sir Edw.," I said, "when your naval men learn to resist the impulse to stop every ship that comes along: don't you suppose they enjoy it?" "*I* don't enjoy it." Then, after a sad sort of smile—"More oil ships? —if only that be no going to the Germans, it's all right: I'll do what you like and beg your pardon. But it musn't get through, you know." . . .

* He has since told me the British cruisers stay over there for fear the interned German boats might put to sea.

Now we can go on without being a party to any general programme, but keep our independent position wherein we can vigorously stand up for every right and privilege in every case. . . .

Again, the report seems to have gone far and wide on your side that this Gov't was going to put cotton on the contraband list. There was never the slightest notion of doing this. Weeks ago, I askd. the question of my own accord; and four times now I have had Sir Edw. Grey say that his Government never contemplated such a thing. Who set *us* looking for that mare's nest? These odd things look as if somebody were making a business of putting up jobs of controversy or suspicion for us about things that are not true—merely manufactured, by whom & for what purpose? Another similar story was about this Government's improperly influencing insurance rates. I looked everywhere for evidence of that, finding not the slightest. Somebody seems bent on making each Government believe something untrue about the other.

But these mare's nests have no eggs and are, perhaps, not troublesome more than the useless labour they put us to.

Yours heartily—[(]for Mr. Wilmeth can take this, if I stop here),                                        Walter H. Page

ALS (WP, DLC).


## To Edward Mandell House

My dear Friend:                    The White House October 29, 1914

You need not fear that you made a mistake in sending me Page's telegram. His official telegrams and his letters to me disclose his state of mind very fully and, while I do not feel that it would be just to critcise him in the least, I fear that there is a slight danger in the intense feeling he has for the English case. I do not mean the danger of his neglecting to carry out our instructions very loyally, but the danger of his putting himself out of touch with American feeling altogether.

I wish with all my heart I could get away, but getting away means to[1] many things to regret when I get back that I have learned the lesson.

Now that the weather is fair and cool here, we shall be expecting you just as soon as you can get here after election, when I hope with all my heart that you can bring Mrs. House with you.                    Affectionately yours,   Woodrow Wilson

TLS (E. M. House Papers, CtY).
[1] Wilson dictated "so."

## To Winthrop More Daniels

Personal.

My dear Daniels:          The White House October 29, 1914

I know how you feel and I am sure you know how I feel, but I am awaiting the decision of the Commission in the newly opened rate case with deep and serious anxiety. I believe that a concession to the railroads is absolutely necessary to steady and relieve the present extraordinary difficulties of the financial situation.

It is for that reason that I am taking the liberty of sending you this letter of Major Higginson's, which I think in the main is true. I wonder if it would make any impression on any of your colleagues to see it.

With the warmest regard, always

Faithfully yours,   Woodrow Wilson

TLS (Wilson-Daniels Corr., CtY).

## To Henry Lee Higginson

Personal and Confidential.

My dear Major:          [The White House] October 29, 1914

I have your letter of October twenty-sixth and agree with its main conclusions almost entirely. I would if I thought it justified make some very plain recommendations to the Interstate Commerce Commission, but they are as jealous of executive suggestion as the Supreme Court would be, and I dare say with justification. I can only hope and believe that they will see the rate case in a new light in the new circumstances.

Cordially and sincerely yours,   Woodrow Wilson

TLS (Letterpress Books, WP, DLC).

## A Translation of a Letter from Raymond Poincaré

Mr. President and Illustrious Colleague: Paris, October 29, 1914.

Mr. Butler[1] was so kind, some months ago, as to invite me to the formal session of the American Academy of Arts and Letters. However strong my desire was to seize this happy occasion of meeting Your Excellency, I had expressed the fear that the duties of my office would not permit me to accept this gracious invitation. Events which have taken place in Europe, since that time, and which have a vital importance for the liberty of peoples, naturally prevent me today from leaving France. I do not wish, however, to let Mr. Brieux[2] leave without begging him to transmit to you the renewed assurances of my fraternal sentiments and of my friendship. The French Academy, the faithful guardian of the literary traditions of my country, has charged Mr. Brieux to convey to the brilliant American civilization the greeting of the ancient and immortal Mediterranean civilization.

Permit me to join to this collective homage the personal assurance of my lively admiration for the great Republic over whose destinies you so nobly preside. Let me add also to it the expression of the steadfast sympathy which the free democracy, of which I have the honor to be the representative, feels for your glorious nation.

Be pleased to accept, Mr. President and dear Colleague, the assurances of my most devoted consideration.

R. Poincaré.[3]

T MS (WP, DLC).
[1] Nicholas Murray Butler.
[2] Eugène Brieux, French dramatist, who was coming to the United States to represent the French Academy at a meeting of the American Academy of Arts and Letters.
[3] The ALS of this letter is in WP, DLC.

## From Morris Sheppard, with Enclosure

My dear Mr. President:    [Washington] October 29, 1914.

At the request of Mr. J. R. Heyler of Texarkana, Ark., I beg to send you herewith for your consideration a letter which he has written me regarding the cotton situation in Texas.

Yours very sincerely,    Morris Sheppard

P.S. This is a simple but pathetic echo of the ruin now running riot in the South. May God in his infinite wisdom point us some path to safety. M.S.

TLS (WP, DLC).

### ENCLOSURE

## J. L. Hegler to Morris Sheppard

Dear Senator:    Texarkana Ark. Oct 24, 1914

I never had the exalted pleasure of addressing a U. S. Senator before. I am going to give you a short history of the conditions as they exist in East Texas today: to say they are deplorable puts it mild.

There are people in your home town Texarkana who does not have the actual necessaries of life. We have the nations chief crop (Cotton) which is practicaly a worthless commodity. people whom I know to have worked in the burning sun winters cold and rain and not the necessaries of life looks bad does'nt it?

Of course I know Senator that America had nothing to do with bring on that war but Senator dont you think that if the good old U. S. A. was to stop feeding them that the [war] would stop. It occurs to me that encourages the warring nations to fight. If it did not involve the Labor and Money of the South I would say fight it out. Mr Shepherd you know I believe that it will ruin the Democratic party. Now I am not so assumptious as to believe that that [sic] the party has a thing to do with the prices of commodities but you know there is. Know men who have always voted the Democratic Ticket and to[o] by the hundreds who will either vote a Republican or Socialist Ticket if things dont change by Nov 3rd. . . .

Now Senator I have told you what the conditions are not as I am in any perticular tight place myself, but hundreds of my fellow men are is what promped me to address you   is there no known remedy. We have the goods but no demand for them: please try my Senatorial friend and give us some help some way   people cannot get a Dollar for nuthing, and no security will not reach it.

I believe in you   I believe in his Excelency Hon Woodrow Wilson and believe also in God that there is a way to be devised whereby this crop will do what it should do: pay the debts, and have money for the poor farmer to live on. its ours and we should have it. Can you help and will you help.

I would have writen to the President had I known he would have gotten it. Will you please hand this missive to his Excelency. May I have the pleasure of having an answer from you. I'll expect it. from one who has and is your political friend

J. L. Hegler.

ALS (WP, DLC).


## Two Letters from William Gibbs McAdoo

Dear Mr. President:                    Washington October 29, 1914.

I return herewith the Secretary of War's letter addressed to you under date of October 22d, which you sent to me with the request that I give you my opinion "as to whether there is in it the germ of anything that we could do with profit and good results."

I regret to say that there is not.

The Secretary states some obvious difficulties in the cotton situation and suggests as a remedy that the cotton manufacturers and cotton producers or growers be assembled in Washington for a conference for the purpose of agreeing upon a price for cotton and upon the amount of cotton that should be definitely taken out of the market at the agreed price. "Thereupon," as he says, "the various growers could by common consent agree to reduce, each in the same percentage, their next year's crop so as to produce only the agreed amount."

It is utterly impracticable to assemble the vast number of cotton growers in the South, and even the manufacturers in the United States, in a convention or conference, and if it could be done it would be utterly impossible to reach an agreement between the manufacturers and the cotton producers as to a proper price for cotton, even if such an agreement would not be in plain violation of the Sherman Anti-Trust Law. Moreover, the cotton problem is international and any effective agreement affecting absorption of the supply would require as parties to it the foreign spinners as well as the domestic spinners. It is utterly impossible to effect any effective agreement of this character about cotton, whether lawful or unlawful.

As you are aware, the Treasury Department took hold of the cotton problem actively on the 7th of August last. A conference was first held here between the banking interests and the shipping interests, with a view to reestablishing the foreign exchange market, which is of essential importance to the cotton movement, and the restoration of shipping facilities between various American ports and foreign countries which had been disturbed by the sudden withdrawal of the great German mercantile fleets.

Following this conference, which resulted in much good—among other things the establishment of the War Risk Insurance Division of the Treasury for the purpose of protecting our commerce by adequate war risk insurance—a conference was held under the auspices of the Treasury on the 24th and 25th of August, in which leading cotton manufacturers from all parts of the country, as well as leading bankers, cotton producers, warehouse-men, and others, participated. As a result of that conference a strong committee was appointed, which recommended to the banks, to the manufacturers, and to the growers of cotton that transactions on the basis of cotton (as security even for loans) at 8 cents per pound, were reasonable and that cotton transactions ought to be made upon such a basis.

In addition to this the Treasury Department announced that it would accept notes secured by cotton warehouse certificates at 75% of their face value as a basis for issuance of national bank currency. This left the banks free to lend at as high a value on cotton as they chose to put upon it, with the certainty that they could convert 75% of the loans so made into national bank notes. In addition to that large amounts of government funds were deposited in the Southern banks for the purpose of enlarging their credit facilities.

These practical measures have been most effective in the cotton situation, but they have not, of course, been sufficient to restore the normal demand for cotton at the prices which prevailed prior to the outbreak of the European War. The real difficulty in the cotton situation is an economic one, namely, the sudden destruction of a large part of the demand, leaving the market surfeited with an excessive supply with a consequent decline in price.

The only practical way to help the cotton situation is, in my judgment, the formation of a cotton loan fund, such as that upon which this Department has been working in conjunction with the Federal Reserve Board and the banking interests of the country for some time. We are now hopeful that a fund aggregating $135,000,000 may be provided shortly for this purpose. It is proposed to loan this fund on cotton at the rate of 6 cents per pound for a period of 12 months, and with the privilege of a six months' extension. If the entire fund should be loaned on this basis it would take off the market four and one-half million bales of cotton for a period of one year, certainly, and for a period of 18 months possibly. It is hoped that the effect of such action will be to stimulate the demand and to enhance the price of the cotton remaining on the market, but this in turn is going to be affected by the probabilities of the size of next year's cotton crop.

Every effort is going to be made through the banks and merchants to discourage the planting of the usual crop of cotton next year and to encourage the Southern farmer to diversify his crop, planting say one-half cotton and the remainder in food products. Undoubtedly a large effect can be produced through this method, but the extent to which this may be secured is by no means certain or calculable. Of course, the only effective agency through which a restriction of cotton acreage might be enforced next year is the Legislatures in the different cotton States. These have, up to the present time, resolutely refused to favor any legislation of this character, and I feel quite sure that it will be impossible to secure it. . . .

In addition to the efforts I have just described, Sir George Paish and Mr. Basil B. Blackett were, upon my invitation, sent by the British Government to confer with me and American bankers, with a view to still further improving the conditions of foreign exchange and of helping the cotton situation. Their visit has been fruitful of good results already. Growing out of these discussions and as a result of the negotiations of the State Department with the British Government, assurances have been received from that Government that cotton is on the free list and will remain so, and that shipments of cotton, even to the ports of belligerent powers, under neutral flags will be respected.

I hope that I have been able to make measurably clear the work that is being done in the cotton situation, and that the things that are being done may not only be productive of real beneficial results but that they may be of such character as to command your approval.

Faithfully yours,   W G McAdoo

PERSONAL. *Confidential*

Dear "Governor":                    Washington October 29, 1914.

I must apologize for not having replied sooner to your letter of the 3rd of October, but I am sure you know how pressed I have been and that the neglect has not been wanton.

You enclosed a letter from Mr. Kerney, in which he says "There is just one disquieting element, and that is the declaration of Stuart Gibboney (professing to be an Administration mouthpiece) that Hennessey is to make an independent run, etc."

I am surprised that Mr. Kerney should assert that Mr. Gibboney has made any such "declaration," because he has never done anything of the kind. On the 30th of September, the day before Mr. Kerney's letter was written, the Brooklyn Eagle published a statement over Mr. Gibboney's signature, explicitly denying that there was any purpose to run Mr. Hennessey as an independent candidate for Governor. In this connection I enclose a letter from Colonel House dated October 7th, also a letter from Mr. Gibboney, addressed to Colonel House, on the same day.[1] I hope that you may find time to read them.

In this connection I wish also to hand you for your confidential information, a letter from Mr. Rush, the new Surveyor of the Port of New York,[2] with a statement of a conversation he had had recently with Mr. Saxe, Counsel to Governor Glynn, and a certain Mr. Beers, of New York,[3] a well-known lobbyist whose connections and affiliations with the interests who have always been opposed to you and with the "machine," similarly always opposed to you, are notorious among those who have knowledge of the interests and the New York "machine."

The New York "situation" has been rendered extremely difficult ever since your election by the interference of men outside the state professing to enjoy your confidence and to be speaking, more or less, with your sanction, and who have been in too close touch with the New York "machine" and the very interests which you have always opposed. To those of us in New York who know only too well the meaning and the effect of the activities of the Murphyized New York "machine" and its affiliated selfish interests, and who, before the Convention and since have been your strongest friends and supporters in the face of every kind of difficulty, it has been discouraging that a consistent policy in opposition to the "machine" in New York has not been pursued from the beginning of your administration. My own efforts, my dear Governor, have been constantly back-capped and thwarted. I feel that I ought to tell you this because I have felt keenly the mistakes that were being made in New York. As a result, the nominees of the party on the state ticket whom we are obliged to support, and whom I am supporting with all my might and main, have decided elements of weakness, which all of us in New York have known from the beginning might prove fatal to Democratic success. If the administration's policy since March 1913 had been one of consistent opposition to the "machine," unmistakably manifested through its appointments to office, and in other ways, I am sure that the nominees of the party today would be of such a character that Democratic success in the state would not be the least in doubt.

In spite of all that I have said, Mr. Gibboney and your loyal friends in New York undertook to make the best fight possible to preserve and hold intact the best element of the party in the state, in order that it might have some semblance of organization for use in your behalf in the contest that must come in the future. When that contest comes your only dependable reliance in New York will be this decent and independent element. Without money and without organization, your friends succeeded in electing about one-third of the State Democratic Committee, and carried, as I am told, for County Chairman, thirty-three out of sixty-two counties of the state. This gives the independent democrats an effective representation in the state organization, and if they are properly supported in the future, it may enable them to destroy Murphyism and to regenerate the New York democracy.

You must forgive me for writing at such length, but I have felt obliged to say this much in justice to Mr. Gibboney and to your other loyal friends in New York, who have unselfishly and with extraordinary devotion, stood by you from the beginning. I am not willing to have them maneuvered into a position where you can be made to believe that they and not the "machine" is deserving of criticism or condemnation.

Faithfully yours,   W G McAdoo

As I read this letter, it might seem that I was criticising your course, but of course I am not. I mean only to criticise those who have favored a course which I believe has been most unfortunate.

TLS (WP, DLC).
  [1] E. M. House to W. G. McAdoo, Oct. 7, 1914, TLS (WP, DLC); S. G. Gibboney to E. M. House, Oct. 7, 1914, TLS (WP, DLC).
  [2] The letter from Thomas E. Rush is missing, but the typed statement of the conversation is in WP, DLC.
  [3] William C. Beer, lobbyist and agent for certain New York banking interests.

## Viscount Sutemi Chinda to Baron Takaaki Katō

2066　暗　華盛頓発　本　省　着　大正3年10月29日　后9・00

加藤外務大臣

珍　田　大　使

第381号

往電第371号（排日案防止）ニ関シ本件ハ国務長官ノ帰華ヲ待チ第一次ニ於テ同官ニ開談スルヲ以テ適当ノ順序トナスヘキモ閣下宛沼野領事往電第314号（「マツキントツシ」代リテ出発）ノ件モアリ又此頃 Gulick 博士カ大統領ニ面謁ノ上本邦ヨリノ通信ニ基キ本邦人民ノ米国ニ対スル反感ヲ述ヘ可成速カニ日米問題ヲ解決スルノ必要ヲ説キタル事実アリ旁々此ノ際本件ニ付キ大統領ノ注意ヲ求ムルコト利益ナリト思考シタルニ付10月26日国務長官代理ヲ訪ヒ本件ノ事実ヲ詳述シテ大統領ノ引見ヲ請ヒタルニ同代理ハ加州労働派

ノ運動ニハ毎度選挙ニ伴フ政事上ノ駈引モ多少之レ有ルヘ
キモ之レニ対シナルヘク予防ノ手段ヲ講スヘキハ無論ナル
ヲ以テ委曲大統領ニ具申ノ上速カニ引見ノ手続ヲ執ルヘキ
旨答ヘタル結果本使ハ翌27日大統領ニ面謁ヲ遂ケ御訓令ノ
趣意ヲ敷衍シ加州労働派ノ活動ノ実況ヲ語リ並ニ往電第24
号 (1月25日国務長官ト会見) 中「帝国政府参同ハ排日気勢
ヲ緩和スルノ効アルヘシ云々」国務長官ノ談話ヲモ引援シ
テ帝国政府カ飽迄博覧会参同ヲ実行スルノ決心ヲ執ルニ至
リタルハ畢竟排日気勢緩和ノタメ出来得ル限リノ手段ヲ尽
サントスル精神ニ出タルモノナル事由ヲ説明シタルニ大統
領ハ右ニ対シ加州労働派ノ活動ハ実ニ遺憾ニ堪ヘサル所ナ
ルカ右ニ関スル日本国政府ノ憂慮ハ至極尤モナル次第ニシ
テ米国側ニ於テモ之ニ対シ予防ノ方法ヲ講スヘキハ勿論ナ
ルモ其ノ実行手段トシテハ加州ニ対シ直接際立タル運動ヲ
試ムルカ如キハ啻ニ憲法上不可能ナルノミナラス実際ニ於
テ地方人ノ反抗心ヲ挑発シ却テ目的ニ背馳スル結果ヲ見ル
ノ虞アルヲ以テ飽迄間接ノ方法ニ依ルノ外ナシ排日運動ノ
中心ハ労働派ニアルカ故ニ自分ハ既ニ同派ノ某有力者ニ会
談シ加州ニ於ケル形勢ニ付其ノ注意ヲ促スト同時ニ難局予
防方ニ付同氏ノ尽力ヲ求メ置キタリ尤モ右会話ハ24時間以
内ノ出来事ナレハ其ノ効果如何ハ只今之ヲ知ルニ由ナキモ
相当実効ヲ上クルニ至ルヘシト信ス尚向後モ同一ノ目的ヲ
以テ右以外ニ適当ノ手段ヲ執リ出来得ル限リ防禦方法ヲ講
スヘシト述ヘラレタリ右談話ヨリ察スルニ大統領ハ国務長
官代理ノ具報ニ接セルヤ否直ニ Gomper 氏ト会談ヲ遂ケ其
ノ尽力ヲ求メタルモノノ如ク其ノ語気態度ヨリ見ルモ大統
領ニ於テハ大ニ本件ヲ重要視シ居ルモノト認メタリ

Hw telegram (MT 3.8.2.274-7, pp. 94-99, JFO-Ar).

TRANSLATION

Washington, D. C., received October 29, 1914, 9:00 P.M.

No. 381 In reference to outgoing telegram No. 371, it would have been the appropriate procedure to have waited for the return to Washington, D. C., of the Secretary of State and to discuss the matter first with him. However, because of the outgoing telegram No. 314 from Consul Numano[1] to you and because of the fact that Dr. Gulick[2] met the President to talk about the antipathy of our people to the United States and the urgent necessity of solving the Japanese-American problems as soon as possible, I thought that it would be in our interest to call the President's attention to this matter at that time. Therefore, on October 26 I visited the Acting Secretary of State, explained the facts of the matter to him in detail, and requested an interview with the President. The Acting Secretary of State replied that he would inform the President of the matter and take steps to get me an interview immediately, since he thought that, as a matter of course, preventive measures should be taken, even if the actions of the California's labor faction have partially arisen in response to the political bargain in the coming election. As a result, on the next day, the 27th, I met the President. I conveyed the messages in your instructions to him and talked to him about the present state of the activities of the California labor faction. At the same time, citing the statement of the Secretary of State conveyed in the outgoing telegram No. 24, "The participation of the Imperial government would be effective in mitigating the anti-Japanese sentiments* * *," I explained to him that it was because the Imperial government would be willing to take every possible means to mitigate the anti-Japanese sentiments that we have decided to participate in the exposition in any circumstances. In response to this the President deeply regretted the activities of the California labor group and thought that the United States should also take preventive measures against it, since he entirely agreed with the concerns of the Japanese government about the matter. He said, however, that they could not take direct and conspicuous measures vis-à-vis the State of California, because it not only would be impossible from the point of view of the Constitution, but also might antagonize the local populace, and in the end such measures would result in adverse effects. Therefore, they would take all possible indirect measures. Since the source of the anti-Japanese sentiment is the labor faction, he said, he had already conferred with a certain influential member of the group[3] and warned him about the situation in California and asked him to cooperate in taking preventive measures. Since this conference took place in the past *twenty-four* hours, the President said, he was yet unable to observe the effect, but he had good reason to expect a fairly positive impact. He also told me that he would also take other appropriate steps and try all possible preventive means. Judging from the above interview, it seems to me that the President had already talked with Mr. Gompers[4] as soon as he had been informed of the situation and my request by the Acting Secretary of State. Judging from his attitude and expression, I believe that the President does regard the whole matter with the utmost seriousness.[5]

[1] Yasutaro Numano, acting Consul-General of Japan in San Francisco.

[2] Sidney Lewis Gulick had conferred with Wilson about "America's Japanese problem" on February 2, 1914 (see S. L. Gulick to WW, Feb. 9, 1914, Vol. 29). If there was a later conference, the newspapers, White House appointment diaries, and correspondence in the Wilson Papers do not reveal its date.

[3] Probably Anthony Caminetti, the Commissioner General of Immigration, who had previously served as Wilson's liaison with California labor groups in regard to Japanese questions. Here again the White House appointment diaries show no recent meeting with him or anyone else connected with California politics, but the "conference" may well have been by telephone, or perhaps Wilson saw Caminetti unknown to the head usher in the White House.

[4] The appointment diaries do not contain any reference to a recent talk with Samuel Gompers, but this, too, may have occurred by telephone.

[5] A bill to prohibit the leasing of land by aliens ineligible to citizenship was introduced in the California Assembly on January 22. On the following day, Governor Hiram W. Johnson put a quietus on the measure by announcing that he would veto it if the legislature passed it, adding that there was no valid reason for amending the alien land act of 1913. *New York Times*, Jan. 24, 1915. There is no evidence of written communication between Wilson and Bryan and Johnson about this measure. However, Bryan told Ambassador Spring Rice that he had "induced Governor of California to prevent further anti-Japanese legislation, and is most anxious that nothing should occur to inflame public opinion." C. A. Spring Rice to E. Grey, Feb. 4, 1915, printed telegram (FO 371/2322, No. 13504, p. 73, PRO). Bryan, and perhaps Wilson also, must have worked discreetly through intermediaries in Washington and California to put pressure on Governor Johnson.

## To Mary Allen Hulbert

Dearest Friend,                    The White House 30 October, 1914.

How deeply, how completely I sympathize with you in your anxiety and sorrow about your son, words cannot say.[1] This is just a line of affectionate friendship upon receipt of the news. Since I have received no telegram, I am hoping with all my heart that the crisis is over and that your hope grows into reassurance.

Your devoted friend.   Woodrow Wilson

WWTLS (WP, DLC).

[1] He was in Boston and "lay at the point of death." Mary Allen Hulbert, *The Story of Mrs. Peck* (New York, 1933), pp. 244-45.

## To Edward Mandell House

The White House Nov 2, 1914.

Shall expect Mrs House and you on Wednesday with the deepest pleasure.                    Woodrow Wilson.

T telegram (E. M. House Papers, CtY).

## To Charles Francis Adams

Confidential.

My dear Mr. Adams:        [The White House] November 2, 1914

I have read your letter of October twenty-ninth[1] with a great deal of interest. I think you know already how strong I feel the case of the railroads to be before the Interstate Commerce Commission.

The question that I have been debating with myself is this: How far am I at liberty, if at all, to express to that commission my opinion, or, rather, my convictions, in this matter, and if I should think it wise or permissible to act, what form should my action take?

I see no reason to hope that the attitude of the commission will be changed; it was so fixed and showed itself so inveterate in the former decision.

Cordially and sincerely yours,   Woodrow Wilson

TLS (Letterpress Books, WP, DLC).
[1] C. F. Adams to WW, Oct. 29, 1914, TLS (WP, DLC).

## To William Gibbs McAdoo

My dear Mac:        [The White House] November 3, 1914

I have your memorandum of October twenty-eighth and think that it would be a splendid idea to have a conference with representatives of the Central and South American governments about business matters. I wish very much that you would take the matter up with the State Department and I will cooperate in every way that you desire.[1]

Affectionately yours,   Woodrow Wilson

TLS (Letterpress Books, WP, DLC).
[1] McAdoo did call a Pan-American Financial Conference, which met in Washington on May 24, 1915.

## To Anna Orme Crawford[1]

My dear Mrs. Crawford:     [The White House] November 3, 1914

Dr. Homer McMillan[2] has suggested that I write you a few lines about the memorial fund to Mrs. Wilson which the ladies assembled last summer at Montreat so graciously suggested,[3] and I comply with his request with the greatest pleasure.

Mrs. Wilson had often conferred with me on the subject of how best to aid in the great cause of the education of the young people of the Southern mountains and I know, therefore, very clearly what her own wise judgment in the matter was. She felt very strongly that the further multiplication of independent schools was a mistake, and not only that, but that the imperative need of the situation was that the various schools devoted to the education of the mountain youth should be drawn into definite cooperation; that no line should be drawn between church schools and those which were independent of church control; that a common cause should be made of the whole matter and that without rivalry or jealousy of any sort all interested in this great enterprise should act as nearly as possible as a common organization.

I know that nothing would have pleased her or touched her enthusiasm more than a fund devoted to this purpose and administered in this way. I need not tell you that she was a devoted and loyal adherent of the church and faith of her fathers, and yet I think she would have deplored a denominational fund administered with denominational restrictions. As I understand the purposes of the ladies who met at Montreat, their wish was that, while the fund they were contemplating should be administered by the Board of Home Missions of the Southern Presbyterian Church, it should be devoted not merely to the Presbyterian schools, but to all schools that could be benefited through it or assisted by it. She was deeply interested, for example, in Miss Berry's school at Rome, Georgia, the home of her youth, and would have desired, I have no doubt, that that school should be included in any benefits the fund might confer. I cite this merely as an example.

I feel, therefore, that in commending this generous enterprise, conceived and to be administered in this way, I am only saying what she herself would have said. Personally, I have been very deeply touched by this evidence of the full comprehension by the ladies of the church of the real character and purpose of the splendid lady who is gone, and I am very much gratified to learn that you have undertaken to play an active part in the creation of the fund.

Cordially and sincerely yours,    Woodrow Wilson

TLS (Letterpress Books, WP, DLC).
    [1] Anna Orme (Mrs. C. P.) Crawford of Milledgeville, Ga., organizer of the Women of the Synod of Georgia and first president of the Georgia Synodical, 1910-1912; Atlanta area chairman of the Ellen Wilson Memorial Fund.
    [2] The Rev. Dr. Homer McMillan, secretary of the executive committee of the Board of Home Missions of the Presbyterian Church, U.S., since 1906.
    [3] About this meeting, see WW to Sally C. Hughes, Aug. 25, 1914, Vol. 30.

## To Cleveland Hoadley Dodge

My dear Cleve:              The White House November 3, 1914

You are quite right about the matter of the memorial fund to be raised in memory of Mrs. Wilson for the education of the mountain youth, and yet I have not known how to control it. Some very splendid women, all Presbyterians, started the idea this summer and did it in such a beautiful spirit that, of course, it was impossible for me to throw cold water on it. Being Presbyterians, they put the matter in the hands of the Presbyterian Board of Home Missions. The same man who came to see you came to see me about it (the Rev. Homer McMillan) and I tried to impress him, as I am going to try again, with the necessity that the fund should be administered in a non-sectarian spirit and with the broadest sort of purpose. I have a letter from him now,[1] which I am about to answer,[2] telling me of the persons he is asking to serve as a committee, and this will give me another opportunity to expound to him Mrs. Wilson's views, which you know so well and which were so very definite and, it seems to me, so very wise.

I will let you know what progress is made in the matter of turning the thing in the right direction. I have had my fears that this association that has its headquarters here, and with whom Mrs. Wilson cooperated, is apt to go a little wild without Mrs. Wilson's guidance and I, alas, have not time to play an active part in it.

Your letter to Margaret[3] was full of good sense as usual, and I am answering it for her because of my deep interest in the whole matter.

With deep affection,

Faithfully yours,    Woodrow Wilson

TLS (WC, NjP).
    [1] H. McMillan to WW, Oct. 31, 1914, TLS (WP, DLC).
    [2] WW to H. McMillan, Nov. 3, 1914, TLS (Letterpress Books, WP, DLC).
    [3] C. H. Dodge to Margaret Wilson, Oct. 19, 1914, TLS (WP, DLC).

# From Hollis Burke Frissell

Sir:                              Hampton, Virginia November 3, 1914.

I have long wanted to write to you and express the gratitude that many of us feel for the admirable work you have accomplished in saving this country from war with Mexico, and bringing the representatives from South America into cooperation with yourself in this great movement. I believe that what you have done will be of tremendous importance in working out the race problem throughout the world.

Heretofore I have felt that important as the race problem in this country is, your time and thought are so engrossed with other questions of most serious consequence, that you ought not to be disturbed even with so vital a subject as bringing into cooperation for mutual improvement, the white and black races of the country. Mr. John R. Mott said not long ago at Atlanta, that the race problems of the world were to be solved here where there are more Christian blacks and whites than in any other country. After a trip around the world I am convinced that he is right, and that you are to have an important part in working out the solution.

You are acquainted with Major Moton, our school Commandant.[1] He has started what is known as the Negro Organization Society, through which he has brought together nearly all of the negro societies in Virginia and concentrated their thoughts and efforts upon the improvement of their health conditions, their farms, their schools, and especially their homes. Last year they held a meeting in Richmond at which 5000 blacks and 1000 whites were present, and where Governor Mann, Mrs. B. B. Munford,[2] Dr. S. C. Mitchell, and Major Moton spoke. On the "Clean up Day" through the efforts of this Organization over 135,-000 aegroes [negroes] at least were induced to clean up their yards and houses. In all this the Southern white people of Virginia have been most sympathetic and helpful.

The part which your lamented wife had in the improvement of the negro homes in Washington in the cleaning up of the alleys there, makes me sure of your own interest in this most important movement.

On the twelfth of this month the Negro Organization Society is to hold a meeting in Armory Hall, the largest hall in Norfolk, at which Major Moton will preside, and Booker Washington will speak. This gathering has the backing of the Chamber of Commerce and the Board of Trade, the former having given up a meeting of its own in order to make the Organization Society's meeting possible, in Armory Hall.

It is probable that a delegation from the Board of Trade of Norfolk, of which I may also be a member, will wait upon you on Thursday, to see if you will speak at that meeting. You will understand, I am sure, that this Society has nothing whatever to do with politics or social equality, or any like movement. Major Moton has shown remarkable wisdom and it seems possible that under his direction this movement may extend throughout the South and make it possible for the negroes to cooperate with the whites in bringing about better conditions.

I trust that if this delegation goes to Washington you will find it possible to give it an opportunity of presenting a plea for your help.[3]    Respectfully yours,   H. B. Frissell   Principal.

TLS (WP, DLC).
  [1] Robert Russa Moton, commandant of the Hampton Normal and Agricultural Institute since 1890.
  [2] Mary Cooke Branch (Mrs. Beverly Bland) Munford of Richmond, educational reformer, president of the Co-operative Education Association of Virginia (1910-1925). At this time she was actively engaged in attempts to establish a college for women at the University of Virginia and was assisting in founding the Virginia Industrial School for Colored Girls.
  [3] They met with Wilson on November 5.


# From Walter Hines Page

Dear Mr. President:                      [London] 4 Nov. 1914

There are certain personal things that I've been trying for some time to say—all kept in silence so far by the pressure of public subjects.

My most appreciative thanks for the handsome cheque sent me by House, from some mysterious source that (since I'd trust my immortal soul to you and him) I do not even care to know. Of course I shd. stay here now if it cost the last cent I have; but this cheque makes it financially easy to stay. More thanks than I know how to express.

Then, to put small things next big ones—my daughter[1] got a scolding when she came back and told me that she left Washington before your kind invitation to call reached her. She told me she wrote her explanation and excuses. She was rushing to get back before all the ship-routes became mine-strewn; and this is now fast coming to pass.

And most important of all. House informs me that you are in good physical trim. That's cheerful as well as most important. I am frequently askd. about your health—not because the questioner supposes that you are ill, but because he means that the world can't afford now to have any uncertainty on that score.

The darkest days, I fear, are not yet come here. When more British ships are blown up & more & more of the sea is German mined & when more and more neutral ships are sunk (pray Heaven, not an American one!) and when it is discovered how many Englishmen are among the innumerable dead in France, a shudder of horror will seize all England. It is most solemn now: the men who think look back over their history & see no time so murderous & perhaps none so dangerous & uncertain. All that holds the world together is the friendship and kinship of our country & this I never forget for one moment—this fact that just now is the most important fact in the world; and I do thank God it is *you* that are where you are, so that this will not be forgotten on our side in any small controversy that may come. That Lincoln-like man, Sir. Edw. Grey, never forgets it. He is, so far, the strong, pathetic figure of the time.

"Steady, steady"—I say to myself every day, "& look a long way ahead. It's the big, lasting, profound things that count now, not the little tasks of the passing day or of the changing humour"; and I try to keep the rudder true.

Always heartily yours,   Walter H. Page

ALS (WP, DLC).
1 Katharine Alice Page.


## From the Diary of Colonel House

Washington, November 4, 1914.

Loulie and I took the 12.08 for Washington. . . .

We arrived at the White House in time to dress for seven o'clock dinner. Secretary and Mrs. McAdoo and the two Misses Smith of New Orleans were the only other guests.

After dinner the President immediately took me into his study. I was fearful that McAdoo would not like this, but he seemed not to mind and soon left for home.

We first discussed McAdoo and the Metropolitan Life offer.[1] I started the discussion by saying that McAdoo felt that his health would give way if he continued to work as hard as he had during the past year, and I felt sure he thought, in the event he stayed on, there would be no possible chance for his higher ambition to become President, although McAdoo, perhaps, did not realize

1 McAdoo had been offered the presidency of the Metropolitan Life Insurance Co. at a salary of $85,000. See House Diary, Oct. 20, 1914, T MS (E. M. House Papers, CtY).

himself that he had this ambition or that it was guiding his intentions.

The President was surprised when I mentioned the advisability, from McAdoo's viewpoint, of severing his connection with the Administration, and he argued the question with me. However, I soon convinced him that it would be a political impossibility for McAdoo to be a successful candidate from within the Cabinet because of his relationship to the President.

He thought McAdoo's connection with a large financial institution like the Metropolitan Life would absolutely destroy any chance he might have. We allowed the matter to stand there for the moment and began discussing McCombs.

I advised him of the book McCombs was writing[2] and of the falsehoods he was telling about us both, at the same time, I thought it wrong for Tumulty to get information from McCombs' former secretary in the way he had. I understood Maurice Lyons was giving him copies of McCombs' confidential letters. The President agreed that this was wrong, but said he did not see how it could reflect upon him, Wilson. I answered by saying that Tumulty had induced McAdoo, his son-in-law, to give Lyons an office and it would look like they were all in collusion to bribe Lyons to betray McCombs. The President was distressed and asked me to talk to Tumulty.

He asked what I thought of his making a speech to the business men of the country regarding the result of the elections, since Tumulty thought the republicans would claim that their victories[3] would bring about prosperity and people would accept that as the reason for better times. He was disinclined to make the speech and considered it would do more harm than good, for he could not conceive the American people stupid enough to let the republicans get away with such nonsense. I advised that the speech would do no harm, perhaps would do good, but to make it or not as he felt inclined.

In talking of McAdoo leaving the Cabinet, I thought Carter Glass might be thought of as a successor. He had confidence in Glass, both in his ability and integrity, but he knew nothing of finance and he thought John Skelton Williams would be a better man. The trouble with Williams is that the bankers of the country and many of the business men in the East dislike him. I think

2 It was published posthumously as William F. McCombs, *Making Woodrow Wilson President* (New York, 1921).

3 The returns of the elections on November 3 showed a Republican gain in the House of Representatives and Republican victories in the state elections in New York, Pennsylvania, Ohio, Illinois, Wisconsin, and Kansas. In New York State, Republicans made a clean sweep of both houses of the legislature and won the gubernatorial and United States senatorial contests.

it is without cause, but nevertheless, I question the advisability of his selection. This, however, is something that can be taken up later.

He spoke of the result of the recent elections, and was distressed because it seemed hardly worth while to work as hard as he had worked during the past two years and to have it so stantly [scantily] appreciated. I tried to console him by stating that he was not running and they were voting for others and not for him. He replied "People are not so stupid not to know that to vote against a democratic ticket is to vote indirectly against me."

He spoke of the loss of prestige he would have not only in Congress but in Europe. He said their first impression over there would be that he had been defeated, and although the later returns would indicate otherwise, in the general disturbed conditions they would have time only to get a first impression. He seemed thoroughly weary and heartsick, and it took my best endeavors to put him in a better frame of mind. I told him I was much comforted in the returns; the West had supported him beyond our expectations, and for the first time we had run up against a practically solid republican party.

We then took up the Belgian relief plan. I read him a cablegram from Page which was address[ed] to "The Secretary of State and Colonel House." He authorized me to carry out the suggestions made by Page.

We passed then to the question of a reserve army. He baulked somewhat at first and said he thought the labor people would object because they felt that a large army was against their interests. He did not believe there was any necessity for immediate action, he was afraid it would shock the country. He made the statement that no matter how the great war ended, there would be complete exhaustion, and, even if Germany won, she would not be in a condition to seriously menace our country for many years to come. I combatted this idea, stating that Germany would have a large military force ready to act in furthering the designs which the military party evidently have in mind. He said she would not have the men. I replied that she could not win unless she had at least two or three million men under arms at the end. He evidently thought the available men would be completely wiped out.

I insisted it was time to do a great constructive work for the army and one which would make the country too powerful for any nations to think of attacking us. He told me there was reason to suspect that the Germans had laid throughout the country concrete foundations for great guns similar to those they laid in Belgium and France. He almost feared to express this knowledge aloud, for if the rumor got abroad, it would inflame our people to such an extent that he would be afraid of the consequences. General Wood has the matter under investigation, and he asked me to caution Wood to be very discreet.

I spoke of General Wood's desire to be sent abroad and asked him to let him go in order that we might have at least one man in our army with some experience. He said they would not accept him. I replied that Wood thought otherwise and it was something for him to work out in his own way.

He also had reason to believe the Germans had constructed wireless stations in the Maine Woods and in the mountains of California, probably in the tops of trees, and were communicating in that way. The secret service men are to try and discover the whereabouts of such plants.

In speaking of the building up of our army, I thought if the Allies were successful there would be no need for haste, but if the Germans were successful and we then began our preparations, it would almost be equivalent to a declaration of war, for they would know we were directing our preparations against them. I therefore urged that we start without delay so that we might be ready and avoid being placed in such a position. The President does not seem to fully grasp the importance of such matters.

We went to bed at ten o'clock.


## From Cleveland Hoadley Dodge

My dear Mr. President:          New York November 5, 1914.

It was very kind in you to write so fully in reply to the letter which I wrote to Margaret regarding the memorial fund in memory of Mrs. Wilson. I am very glad that you do not think I "butted in" unnecessarily, and I sincerely trust that the effort to enlarge the scope of the memorial may be successful. If there is any further aid which I could give, pray command me.

Now that election is over, allow me to tender my congratulations, that in spite of the hard times and the almost complete annihilation of the Progressive Party, the Democratic party has gained a majority in the Senate, and has secured a small majority in the House. The fact that the majority is no larger emphasizes your great political wisdom in putting through during the first session, most of the important legislation which the Party platform demanded, and it is certainly better that the reaction should come now rather than two years from now, when I sincerely trust the times may be better and the wisdom of your legislative measures may be better demonstrated. I do not think that any of us feel particularly badly about the result in New York State. It was difficult to get up very much enthusiasm for either Glynn or Gerard. Mr. Whitman is evidently pluming himself for the Republican nomination for the Presidency in 1916, and if, as is very likely, he should succeed in being nominated, I do not think that we would ask for anything much easier.

I sincerely hope that you are getting a little rest during the recess, and with best wishes believe me,

Affectionately yours,   C H Dodge

It was awfully nice to see the McAdoos last Sunday & to find Nellie so well & happy.

TLS (WP, DLC).

## From Charles Francis Adams

South Lincoln, Mass.,
My dear Mr. President:                    November 5, 1914.

I have to acknowledge the receipt of yours of the 2d instant, in which you acknowledge my letter of October 29th.

You are correct in your supposition that I understood your attitude as respects our transportation system. It was, indeed, a knowledge of this fact which induced me to write as I did, my desire being, in so far as lay in my power, to strengthen your hands.

In the letter before me, you suggest a difficult query,—"How far am I at liberty, if at all, to express to that commission my opinion, or, rather, my convictions, in this matter, and if I should think it wise or permissible to act, what form should my action take?"

So far as my own communication, to which you refer, is concerned, the course proper to be pursued is sufficiently obvious. You could refer it, for such consideration as it might deserve, to the Commission. Taken for what it was worth, it would then go into the grand result.

So far as other action on your part, calculated to affect the conclusions of the commission, is concerned, the question does not seem to me to present serious difficulty.

The Railroad Commission is not a judicial tribunal. It is a part of the administrative organization; and, in my belief, it is the duty of the Chief Executive to treat it as such. He is the responsible head of the administrative machine; and in that machine no factor, with the exception of the banking interests, plays a more important part than the transportation agencies. This, as we are at present organized.

Under these circumstances, it is, in my judgment, not only a right, but the duty, of the Supreme Executive, to have his position clearly set forth and fully understood. The single essential thing is that any action taken or influence exerted should be of record, so that, if not immediately made public, its publicity may be anticipated as probable.

The distinction, however, between an administrative commission and a judicial tribunal should be always in mind. Between the two there is no similarity; and the attitude of the Chief Executive towards one has no bearing whatever on his attitude towards the other.

This, however, is rather a large subject to dispose of in a casual letter. It is one which, had you leisure, it would afford me much satisfaction to discuss with you. I shall be at my Winter home in Washington on and after Saturday of this week, and wholly at your service.

I write with interest on this topic,—one which, with long intermissions of time, has been revolving in my mind now for over forty years. I feel decidedly as respects the administrative function, in so far as the Executive is concerned. It is the province of the Executive, and cannot be abdicated.

Very respectfully, etc.,   Charles Francis Adams

TLS (WP, DLC).


## From the Diary of Colonel House

[Washington] November 5, 1914.

The President and I talked last night about the cotton pool plan. He was afraid Gregory would not give an opinion favorable to the legality of it and asked if I would not talk with him. I did this and found that while he thought the practice of giving an opinion in advance inadvisable, yet he felt sure the cotton pool did not violate the Sherman Act. However, before giving an opinion, he wanted the President to carefully consider whether it was of sufficient value to warrant the Department in departing from its rule. He cited the Tennessee Coal and Iron case during Roosevelt's Administration. An opinion was handed down then by the Department of Justice, stating that there was no violation of the Sherman Act in the Steel Company's acquisition of that property, and now the Government was suing the Steel Corporation, largely on the basis of their assumption of that property.

He called attention to the fact that the Attorney General's Department under Roosevelt declared there was no ground for suit against the New Haven Directors for what they were doing, but many of the Directors who were now indicted had assumed office after that opinion was given, and it was not impossible this question was raised for the purpose of its bearing upon the New Haven indictments.

I saw Harding,[1] who is chairman of the cotton pool committee, and discussed the dat[a] which he is getting up regarding it for the benefit of the Attorney General, before an opinion can be written.

There were no visitors at luncheon. After lunch we went out to the golf course which took practically all the afternoon. After dinner we immediately went to the study and took up the personel of the Trades Commission. Much to my delight, we had no difficulty in agreeing upon the membership and within the hour. I warned him as to the composition of this commission and to guard against putting anyone on it even indirectly connected with a corporation coming under its purview.

He then spoke of his recent appointment, Hall, (on the Commerce Commission)[2] as unsatisfactory. He was given an unexpired term, and he comes up for reappointment next month. The President does not wish to reappoint him because his friend Daniels, whom he appointed from New Jersey, tells him Hall is unfit. Hall, however, voted against the increase of rates, and the President was indiscreet enough to say to Senator Thomas of Colorado, from which State Mr. Hall hails, that he hoped Hall would vote for the increase. Now the President believes if he dismisses Hall there will be good reason to believe he has done so because of his vote.

I asked the President to remember one thing and that was never to look at political expediency, but to do the big thing and the right thing, and, in the long run, that would be not only the best for the people, but best for him individually. This stirred him to some enthusiasm and he declared he shared my feeling in the matter and he intended doing what was best at all costs.

We went to bed at ten o'clock, tired and contented.

[1] William P. G. Harding.
[2] Henry Clay Hall.

## To Josephus Daniels

My dear Daniels:        The White House November 6, 1914

I am so afraid of getting the delicate and difficult questions arising in connection with our neutrality confused or mishandled in any way that I am going to ask if you will not have a conference with Mr. Lansing and with Secretary McAdoo to effect very definite arrangements for cooperation between the three departments in these matters. I think we cannot be too careful in these things and I believe that these three departments ought to keep in systematic touch with one another.

I know that you will be willing to do this for me.

Faithfully yours,   Woodrow Wilson[1]

TLS (J. Daniels Papers, DLC).
    [1] Wilson sent the same letter, *mutatis mutandis*, to Lansing and McAdoo on November 6.

## To Robert Russa Moton

My dear Major Moton:    [The White House] November 6, 1914

I have been very much interested in the accounts I have heard of the work you are attempting to do through the instrumentality of the Negro Organization Society and feel that you are to be especially congratulated on the deep interest which has been manifested by the white people of Virginia and the South in the plans now maturing for the betterment of conditions among the negro people. I think one of the happiest circumstances of recent times is this cooperation between the white people and the negroes in the South in intelligent efforts to advance the economic success and comfort of the negroes and put them in a position where they can work out their own fortunes with success and self-respect. I wish I might attend the meeting at Norfolk in person, in order to express my interest and sympathy, but I cannot and I hope that you will feel at liberty to read this letter to the meeting.        Sincerely yours,   Woodrow Wilson

TLS (Letterpress Books, WP, DLC).

## To Thomas Jones Pence

Dear Tom:        The White House 6th November 1914.

I am greatly distressed to hear that you are not well. I hope that it will turn out to be nothing worse than a chance to get some real rest and at the same time feel that you *can* lie up for a little.

And certainly no man ever deserved a rest more entirely than you do. I have watched your work in the campaign with gratitude and deep admiration. You have been the motive force of the whole thing, and I thank you with all my heart. The results are, in my view, wonderful and full of deep encouragement. We now have a majority party and can set to work to increase and strengthen it throughout the nation.

This is not a dictated note: this little typewriter is my pen.

With warm regard,

Faithfully Yours,   Woodrow Wilson.

TCL (R. M. Simms Papers, NcD).


# Two Letters from William Gibbs McAdoo

Dear Mr. President:            Washington November 6, 1914.

As you are aware, I have, ever since the outbreak of the European war, been making every possible effort to help the cotton situation in the South, a distressing situation which has been created by that war. Among the many things that have been considered, the organization of a group of banks and bankers to subscribe a fund of $100,000,000 to $135,000,000 to be known as a "cotton-loan fund," seems to be the only way of extending a large amount of practical relief. This plan has been evolved after many conferences of leading bankers of the country, the Federal Reserve Board, and myself. I enclose a memorandum entitled, "Outline of Plan," together with a letter addressed to me by Hon. W. P. G. Harding, a member of the Federal Reserve Board, dated November 5th, giving some facts in relation to the cotton situation, and which is necessary to a fuller understanding of the plan.[1]

A number of the bankers have raised the question as to whether or not this plan violates in any way the Sherman anti-trust law, the recently enacted trades commission bill and the so-called Clayton bill. The only way they can be satisfied is by an opinion from the Attorney General. If the Attorney General should render an opinion that the plan does not violate the laws to which I have referred, I am satisfied that the fund can be promptly raised.

You will, of course, understand that the agency of the Secretary of the Treasury and of the Federal Reserve Board, as provided for in the plan, is wholly outside of our official duties; we shall act purely as a voluntary organization for the purpose of extending relief to a most important industry affecting a large part of our population and a large section of our country, and from purely patriotic motives. It will impose upon myself and my associates on the Federal Reserve Board important duties and responsibilities of an extremely onerous character, but we are willing to assume them in order to meet a critical situation.

The opinion we seek from the Attorney General will not deal with a question of law arising in the administration of this Department, but will be an opinion as to whether or not the doing of certain acts would constitute a violation of penal laws of the United States. The rule and practice of the Department of Justice prevents it from giving an opinion in these circumstances unless requested by the President.

In view of the extraordinary situation in the South and the necessity for immediate and effective action, it seems to me that you would be justified in asking the Attorney General to render an opinion in this matter. May I respectfully ask that you do so?　　　　　　　Faithfully yours,　W G McAdoo

TLS (WP, DLC).
[1] These enclosures not printed.


PERSONAL.

Dear "Governor":　　　　　　Washington November 6, 1914.

Up to this evening we have succeeded in getting subscriptions to $80,000,000 out of the $100,000,000 alloted to the non-cotton states. With a favorable opinion from the Attorney General I believe that we can get the remainder quickly—at least, I hope so.

Somebody or some interest is exceedingly active in trying to defeat the plan. This comes perhaps from two sources; a certain element of selfish spinners and a certain element of hostile and unprincipled politicians. I think we shall beat them.

　　　　　　Affectionately yours,　W G McAdoo
TLS (WP, DLC).


# From Elias Milton Ammons

Sir:　　　　　　Denver November Six Nineteen Fourteen.

Supplementary to my letter of sometime ago in relation to the withdrawal of Federal Troops from Colorado[1] I deem it important that you should know what I find the condition to be after election.

Many of the strikers in the southern district particularly are in a very rebellious mood and threaten as soon as Federal Troops are withdrawn to destroy some of the mines and the non-union men employed. This sentiment seems to exist especially among some of the foreigners who have been led to believe that they are martyrs to a principle and would go to any length to keep the fire burning. I believe this condition is brought about very largely by the organizers in charge of the striking colonies.

The election here must not be taken as an expression of disapproval of your administration but as an endorsement of a law enforcement policy.[2] I believe this is the general understanding over the state. Its effect will probably influence the strike situation after a little while. The danger as I see it lies in the bitter disappointment of some of the strike leaders over the election and might occasion outbreaks if a sudden change were made from the Federal Troops to the state authorities. I am thoroughly convinced that if the change would not be made for a little while yet and then be made gradually there would be no further danger. I have tried to get the best information possible and I really think the safest course would be to let the matter rest just a little longer. I do not believe that one quarter of the threats would even be attempted of fulfillment but the danger lies in the fact that the threats are made by leaders and might be carried out in a very serious degree by some of those in the ranks.

Our falls are generally characterized until along in December by pleasant weather and there is little danger of severe weather until towards Christmas time, so that a week or two longer stay here would make little difference so far as weather conditions are concerned.

I shall be in a position to take charge of the situation if you wish it at the time mentioned in my former letter but give you this view of the situation believing it would be better to allow at least a little further time to elapse after election and believing also that the troops should be removed gradually.

I would appreciate it if you would have me fully advised of the time and plan of withdrawal of troops for the reason that some of the inside talk among the strikers is that all they want is a couple of hours' time between the leaving of the Federal Troops and the arrival of the state in order to reap vengeance on some particular properties and people.

Again thanking you for the effective assistance given us in the time of great need and assuring you that our best thinking people fully appreciate it, I am

Yours very truly,   E M Ammons

TLS (WP, DLC).

1 E. M. Ammons to WW, Sept. 28, 1914, printed as an addendum in this volume.

2 Ammons's assessment of the election results in Colorado was accurate. The Republican gubernatorial candidate, George Alfred Carlson, who had campaigned for law and order and was backed by the coal operators, easily defeated his Democratic opponent. The only prominent Democrat to win re-election was Attorney General Fred Farrar, who also had the support of the coal operators for his efforts to secure indictments against the strike leaders. See George S. McGovern and Leonard F. Guttridge, *The Great Coalfield War* (Boston, 1972), pp. 307-309.

## From the Diary of Colonel House

[Washington] November 6, 1914.

Another matter the President and I discussed was the question of always telling the truth. He contended again that when newspaper men asked questions involving his foreign policy, he felt entirely justified in lying to them, and he said Mr. Bryan told him he felt the same way. I remained silent and the President knew that I did not agree with him, for we have discussed this many times. . . .

We dined at the White House and afterward went promptly to the study. Soon after we sat down, a telegram came from Randolph announcing the coming of a baby boy[1] to Mona. I took the telegram to Loulie, and the President congratulated us both warmly.

The President and I talked of the trouble brewing between McAdoo and Tumulty. McAdoo believes that despatches being sent out from Washington unfriendly to him certainly emanate from Tumulty. One has just appeared in the New York World laying the result of the New York defeat to McAdoo's "amateur" activities. I told him that McAdoo thought Tumulty too near the interests. One of his closest friends was Otto Carmicheal [Carmichael], who is Dan Reid's secretary.[2] The President did not know who Reid was. He said a Mr. Reid had come to see him and he wondered if he was the man.

In talking of this the President became flushed and excited and wanted to know if McAdoo had gone crazy. That kind of talk sounded to him more like McCombs than McAdoo. His face became grey and he looked positively sick. I was unable to lift him out of this depression before bedtime. He said he was broken in spirit by Mrs. Wilson's death, and was not fit to be President because he did not think straight any longer, and had no heart in the things he was doing. He asked if I had noticed it. I said I had not. He hoped I would talk to both McAdoo and Burleson and straighten out New York appointments and not let them worry him about them. I promised to do the best I could, but I advised appointing the cleanest, ablest, most progressive men he could find and not let anyone influence him in making machine appointments for the purpose of getting any further measures through Congress.

Since Burleson and McAdoo have the responsibility of getting administration measures through Congress, they naturally wish such help as they can get from the President through appointments. I am worried for the reason that he shows reluctance in going to the bottom of situations of this sort. He should get the truth and have it over with.

Before I went to bed I tried to brace him up by telling him what great work he had to do in foreign affairs, but it was useless.

[1] Randolph Foster Tucker, Jr., son of Randolph Foster Tucker and Mona House Tucker.
[2] Daniel Gray Reid, New York financier, a founder of the United States Steel Corp. and president or chairman of the board of several large business concerns.

## To Thomas Watt Gregory

[The White House]
My dear Mr. Attorney General: November 7, 1914

I am sending the enclosed papers, submitted to me by the Secretary of the Treasury,[1] in order to ascertain whether in your opinion the proposed "cotton loan fund" may be lawfully formed. I know that it is contrary to the practice of the department to give opinions beforehand as to contemplated transactions, and I think that such opinions ought never in ordinary circumstances to be given, but the circumstances with regard to the handling of the great cotton crop which have been created by the European war are most extraordinary and seem to justify extraordinary action. It is for that reason that I venture to ask you to depart in this case from the usual practice of your department.

It occurs to me that the "fund" contemplated stands in a class by itself. It is hardly conceivable that such arrangements should become settled practices or furnish precedents which would be followed in the regular course of business or under ordinary conditions. They are as exceptional in their nature as the circumstances they are meant to deal with and can hardly be looked upon as, by possibility even, dangerous precedents. It is for this reason that I feel the more justified in asking for your opinion in the premises.

Cordially and sincerely yours, Woodrow Wilson[2]

TLS (Letterpress Books, WP, DLC).
[1] That is, WGM to WW, Nov. 6, 1914, with its enclosures.
[2] There is an undated WWsh draft of this letter in WP, DLC.

## From Josephus Daniels

Dear Mr. President:                    Washington. Nov. 7, 1914.

A conference has been arranged for this morning and the State, Treasury and Navy will co-operate to the end that our combined judgment will be employed in the line of your letter of yesterday.[1]          Sincerely,   Josephus Daniels

ALS (WP, DLC).
[1] The three departments collaborated informally.

## From William Gibbs McAdoo

Dear Mr. President:              Washington November 7, 1914.

I enclose a telegram from the Traders National Bank of Fort Worth, Texas,[1] from which you will see that one of our difficulties now in shipping cotton is the inability to secure insurance on ships sailing under neutral flags other than the American. This simply emphasizes the importance of passing the shipping bill. What we need is more ships under the American flag, and I know of no other way in which to get them quickly. I bring this to your attention merely as a concrete example of the serious difficulties that confront us.

Faithfully yours,   W G McAdoo

TLS (WP, DLC).
[1] This telegram is missing.

## From Hugo Münsterberg[1]

Cambridge, Massachusetts,
Dear Mr. President:                    November 7, 1914.

After some thorough discussions in the last few days with leading men in various parts of the country—Anglo-Americans, Irish-Americans and German-Americans—I consider it my duty to present to you one aspect of the present political situation of which, by chance, I probably have more inside knowledge than anyone else in the country. My articles and my recent book on the war,[2] my personal connections and even the sensational attacks on my Harvard position have worked together. More than ever before the Germans in the whole country and no less the sympathizers with the German cause have turned to me with their advice and suggestions and with the request to organize the widespread dissatisfaction. Hence I have been in oral or written contact with thousands. Knowing in this way what a certain large part of the population really thinks I should feel it a wrong not to put my information at the disposal of the President.

I regret even that I did not do it a few weeks ago. I am fully convinced, yes, I know it as a fact, that the strongest factor in the surprises of last Tuesday's elections was the firm will of the friends of Germany to demonstrate against what they call the submission of the administration to England's wishes. This was intentionally not brought into the public dispute, as at the present stage of passionate unfairness of the newspapers it was to be feared that a political party discussion about the war would make the situation worse. I am not in party politics, and yet I am so fully convinced that your intention, as expressed in your neutrality declaration, is the ideal one that I regret indeed not to have put a word of warning at your disposal. Some few acts and words from the White House two or three weeks ago could have relieved the tension and would have saved at least four states more for the administration party.

But now is the time to think not of what might have been done, but of what can be done. I trace three great possibilities. One large part of my informants insist on a rush of the German, Swedish, Jewish and Irish vote into the Republican camp as an act of rebellion against the present administration which yields, as it seems to them, to every anti-German wish and which "has not done anything to secure fairness for Germany" in the public opinion of the country. This very large and influential group sees in the recent election only the beginning of the movement. It urges all sympathizers to begin now after the elections with a regular systematic campaign and to take care that the Democratic party becomes tabooed as the one which has made America practically an ally of England. They do not join the Republican party from any party interest, but simply because it is the only party besides the Democrats which can exert power.

The second very substantial group differs on this point. They claim that the Republicans as such will remain just as unwilling to stem the hostility which the press has stirred up. They consider, therefore, the need of a new political party with the one warcry "Independence from England." They are embittered against English newspaper influence, English trade influence and English influence on American foreign policies, and they consider Roosevelt as the one man who could give to such a party a tremendous strength. From long letters which I have received from Roosevelt in recent weeks, I know well that this is not exactly his attitude.[3] Yet there is no doubt that he understands the German position very fully and that this moment of the shipwreck of the Progressive party may make him willing to identify himself with this issue, as he would have immediately more than a third of the population behind him.

Nevertheless there remains a large number, and my own sympathies are with them, who are convinced that the country would be best served if the party in power would still be able to cluster the German, Irish, Jewish voters and all the German sympathizers with its traditional Democratic friends. It is not yet too late. I am doing my very best to shape and push matters in this direction. Nobody wants onesided support of Germany by America; everyone stands on the basis of your declaration. Looking backward, they do not want to attack any nation, but take the ground which I have marked out in my little book, when I emphasized again and again that no nation is to be blamed and that every one did the righteous thing. But they are much more interested in the present and in the future development. They do not want Germany to suffer by interpretations and decisions which help the allies only, and they do not want public opinion to become poisoned by hatred to such a degree that even after the war decades may have to pass before the racial antipathies on American soil can fade away. I know that fundamental decisions as to party politics will be made in the next few months, and if they are once made they will hold over for the next two years, however the war may go on.

I confess, beyond mere party politics, I like so many others indulged in the hope that Washington would become the place where the peace could be made and where your powerful influence might lead to better days. It is perfectly clear that that is absolutely impossible as long as in the feelings of the German sympathizers the United States appear simply as an emotional province of Great Britain. The hopes for the Democratic party hardly ever have been more identical with the hopes of the whole country than in this hour. If your administration succeeds in winning this third of the nation which will make its vote dependent upon your attitude toward Germany it will give to the United States the unparalleled honor of making peace in this war of wars.

Very respectfully yours,   Hugo Münsterberg.

TLS (WP, DLC).

[1] Professor of Psychology at Harvard University since 1892, prolific author of both scholarly and popular books on psychology, very active in the German propaganda campaign in the United States since the outbreak of the war.

[2] Münsterberg's articles appeared in newspapers: for example, "Fair Play!" *Boston Herald*, Aug. 5, 1914. His book was *The War and America* (New York and London, 1914).

[3] See T. Roosevelt to H. Münsterberg, Oct. 3 and Nov. 2, 1914, in Elting E. Morison and John M. Blum (eds.), *The Letters of Theodore Roosevelt* (8 vols., Cambridge, Mass., 1951-54), VIII, 822-27.

# From the Diary of Colonel House

[Washington] November 7, 1914.

The President arose early and played golf with Dr. Grayson before breakfast. He returned at 9.30 for his regular breakfast. Grayson told me, and so did the President, that he had passed a wretched night. Of course I understood the reason whh [why]. I spoke to McAdoo of my conversation with the President and he also was greatly disturbed. . . .

There was no one outside the family at luncheon. The President asked me to take a long automobile ride with him, but I was too busy and the weather is too cold for me to enjoy a ride in the open car. He then offered to take a closed car, but I would not permit this. . . .

There were no outside visitors for dinner, but the President artfully evaded getting alone with me in his study. He was afraid I would renew the McAdoo-Tumulty controversy. However, he need not have worried. We had a delightful evening. He began by talking about German political philosophy and how wrong their conclusions usually were. He spoke of himself as a disciple of Burke and Bagehot. This is literally true, for he is always quoting from one or the other, mostly from Bagehot.

He began to speak of a flexible or fluid constitu[t]ion in contradistinction to a rigid one. He thought that constitutions changed without the text being altered, and cited our own as an example. At the beginning, he thought, there was no doubt but there was no difference of opinion as to the rights of the states to secede. This practically unanimous opinion probably prevailed down to Jackson's time. Then there began, after the War of 1812, a large sentiment for union which finally culminated in our Civil War, and a complete change of the Constitution without its text being altered.

Just then the ladies came in the sitting room where we were, and I got him to read some poems, something he very much likes to do. He read William Watson's "Wordsworth's Grave" and afterward, at my request, "Gray's Elegy." He also amused himself with any number of limericks. We did not go to bed until around 10.30.

# To William Gibbs McAdoo

My dear Mac:                The White House November 8, 1914

What you say in connection with this telegram is quite true, and yet I foresee that if we bought what are probably the only ships we could buy for the service you have in mind in connection with the shipping bill, some very serious and difficult questions would arise. The French Government in particular has taken an inflexible position about the transfer of flags in such circumstances, and its position is giving me and the State Department the greatest concern.

Affectionately yours,    Woodrow Wilson

TLS (W. G. McAdoo Papers, DLC).


## To Mary Allen Hulbert

Dearest Friend,              The White House 8 November, 1914.

I am sure that if Allen had taken a serious turn for the worse I should have had some message from you about it. As the days have gone by, therefore, and brought no word of his condition I have let myself feel more and more reassured, and happy with the confidence that the danger had passed and the terrible germ been conquered. For of course I felt the full tragedy of the fear you were suffering. I know how much of life is wrapped up for you in your son. I know how you cling to those you love and live in them. And so I was deeply anxious; and am correspondingly relieved,—I hope with cause!

There is much less of the strain of daily work and the struggle to get things done upon me now, and I am finding time to get a little rest; but I am not sure that I am the better for that. Time to rest means time to think about myself, and that is bitterness indeed. It were much better that I should be in the grip of something imperious in its claim upon my attention every moment I can keep awake. I keep a steady front to the world, but my heart is in a whirl day and night. My own individual life has gone utterly to pieces. I do not care a fig for anything that affects me. I could laugh aloud to see the papers, and those for whom they write, assuming every day that a second term in 1916 is in my thoughts and that I want it! If they only knew my supreme indifference to that and to everything else that affects me personally, they would devote their foolish and futile brains to some other topic that they do not understand!

I am well. My chief real interest is GOLF; because that is the only thing that really diverts me and gets me "out of myself." What a true and striking phrase that is: and how blessed a thing it is to get out of myself into the joy of breathing the pure air of out-of-doors and taking zest in what is merely a matter of physical skill! It seems to put oxigen into my heart and give it the power to breathe as well as into my lungs and refresh them.

How jolly, how wonderful it would be if, instead of having this single diversion, the friends I love best were within call and I could go to them and sit for long familiar talks and the interchanges of sympathy that are better than oxigen and are fit to keep alive on! Washington is a hideously empty place, a desolately lonely place. There is no human intercourse in it,—at any rate for the President, God pity him!

It does not relieve things much, delightful as it is, to invite such friends into one's thought, for that is a make-believe intercourse, after all, and often only emphasizes the loneliness. I am glad I can write and get answers to my letters. And I hope that what I write does not seem wholly selfish and self-centred, and gives a little pleasure to those to whom my thought goes out with such deep and grateful affection.

Your devoted friend,   Woodrow Wilson

WWTLS (WP, DLC).

## From the Diary of Colonel House

[Washington] November 8, 1914.

The President desired me to go to church with him but I compromised by having Loulie go. Mr. Bryan had just arrived from the West and I felt it necessary to see him. I wanted to find what his views were regarding the army. I found him in violent opposition to any kind of increase by the reserve plan. He did not believe there was the slightest danger to this country from foreign invasion, even if the Germans were successful. He thought *after war was declared* there would be plenty of time to make any preparations necessary. He talked as innocently as my little grandchild, Jane Tucker. He spoke with great feeling and I fear he may give trouble.

I asked what legislation he thought should be enacted during the next two years. He mentioned a national primary law, and a law prohibiting a second term. I was in hopes he had forgotten that. He was also full of his plan of "stabilizing" as he terms it, the prices of railroad securities, both stocks and bonds.

When I mentioned these things to the President he said we could reach the army increase in a way probably that would not excite criticism, and that Mr. Bryan was unreasonable in his views in regard thereto. He thought Mr. Bryan had mentioned the second term matter for his benefit, knowing I would repeat it, but he expressed the opinion that he, Bryan, would not mention the subject directly to him. As to a primary law, the President and I discussed that thoroughly. We agreed that it was a most difficult thing to satisfactorily bring about.

I gave him my experience in Texas. How little the campaigns cost under the old law, and how much they had increased under the primary system, so that no one excepting a rich man or one backed by riches, could afford to run for Governor. Culberson's campaign which I managed, cost only $1400.00 while the aggregate campaigns of all the candidates in Texas under the primary system would perhaps be well over $100,000.

I advised the President to let Bryan direct and take charge of the primary bill. I thought he would get as tangled in it as a fly in molasses. I told him not to help him out, but to encourage him to go on, and I gave it as my opinion that the very fact that Bryan was the Administration's sponsor for the measure, would certainly kill it. I think he liked this advice and no doubt will accept it.

As to the railroad stabilizing plan, he thought it was quite like Bryan's impracticability.

He read me a letter from Walter Page in which Page gave an account of an interview Colonel Squiers, our Military Attaché, had with Lord Kitchener.[1] Kitchener sent for him, and it was intimated that he should come in full dress, as the Earl would be dressed in that way. The President said, "Is that not like British directness?" I shall not try to repeat what Kitchener said, but the most interesting part was that he thought the war would probably be over in two years. He also thought when the winter rains set in and the ground became soft, the Germans would not be able to handle their big guns. He told Squiers of a plan they had of ripping open the German Zeppelins, if they should make a raid up on England. They attach long wires to aeroplanes with a sharp hook at the end, and it is their purpose to fly with great rapidity over the Zeppelins, and let the hooks rip the gas bags. This does not strike me as being feasible.

I thought when the Germans were driven back within their own borders, it would be advisable for me to go there and urge the Kaiser to ask him, the President, to mediate.

The President did not express an opinion one way or the other as to the advisability of this, excepting he thought the Kaiser would hesitate to admit defeat, which that would practically be doing.

He insisted upon our remaining longer, and asked me to come as often as I could. He was exceedingly solicitous and affectionate, and promised to come over to me at this week end if it was at all possible.

I was afraid I had given him a wrong impression concerning McAdoo and some of the members of the Cabinet when I was talking to him the other night. I did not believe any of them excepting Mr. Bryan were consciously candidates for the Presidency, and that I had spoken perhaps with some exaggeration. He replied, "We know one another so well that even if something is said in the course of a conversation we did not quite mean, we each of us would understand it."

He expressed regret that the war had not been postponed for a little while because he thought we might have prevented it.

We discussed the propriety of bringing Ambassador Herrick home. I advised being careful and not to make him a martyr. He promised to avoid this, but thought the situation was in such shape that it was necessary to have Sharp assume his duties, since he was now the regularly constituted Ambassador. He will notify the French Government of his purpose to recall Herrick and then see what happens.

We left on the four o'clock train for New York.

1 WHP to WW, Oct. 22, 1914, TLS (WP, DLC), enclosing G. O. Squire to WHP, Oct. 17, 1914, TC memorandum of interview with Lord Kitchener (WP, DLC).

## To William Gibbs McAdoo, with Enclosures

My dear Mac.,          The White House 9 November 1914.

When you get time, will you do me the favour to look over the enclosed papers?[1] They are from Paul Reinsch, o[u]r Minister to China and concern matters of the deepest interest and the largest importance, which I should like to talk over with you when we get an opportunity for a confab of some deliberateness and length.     Affectionately Yours,   Woodrow Wilson

WWTLS (W. G. McAdoo Papers, DLC).
1 Those not printed are P. S. Reinsch to WJB, July 3, 1914, TC telegrams, Nos. 293 and 294 (WP, DLC). No. 293 repeated the argument in Reinsch's long letter to Wilson. In addition, it discussed the problem of emigration from Asiatic nations to the United States, declaring that there would be increasing friction with both China and Japan unless some "equitable" solution could be found. No. 294 discussed the need for private banking and trade associations, as well as improved diplomatic and consular services, to promote commerce with China.

ENCLOSURE I

## From Paul Samuel Reinsch

Dear Mr. President:                               Peking Oct 5 '14

I deeply regretted not to be able to see you during my short
stay in Washington, although I was glad to know that you had
been prevailed upon to take a much needed rest in the mountains of New England. In the great bereavement that has come
to you, depriving you of the loving companionship and wise helpfulness of your dearest friend, I have thought of you always
with the deepest sympathy but also with the feeling that the
faith in God which has been your support in bearing your great
public responsibilities would also sustain you now through a
sense of continuing communion of soul with your dear departed.

I am enclosing with this letter one relating to important matters connected with China.

With sincere regard and the most earnest good wishes for
your continued well-being, I am, dear Mr. President,

                    Faithfully yours   Paul S. Reinsch.

ALS (WP, DLC).


ENCLOSURE II

## From Paul Samuel Reinsch

PERSONAL

Dear Mr. President:                          Peking, October 5, 1914.

In accordance with my promise to lay before you any matters
of supreme importance which might arise in connection with
my mission to China, I desire to invite your personal attention
to certain phases in the present situation which I have also reported to the Secretary of State.

Through the earnest efforts of two generations of Americans,
our country has been able to achieve an enviable position of good
will, trust and confidence among the Chinese people: Americans
being widely active in educational, religious and benevolent work
have impressed the Chinese with our feeling of friendliness. The
same spirit has animated the American merchants active here:
their spirit of fairness corresponds to that policy of justice to
the Chinese which is the tradition of our diplomacy. The Chinese
have a highly developed sense of justice, and they have therefore appreciated most highly the attitude towards them taken

by our Government. The Chinese feel that the American people take real satisfaction in the development of China towards a more complete, independent and strong national life.

America may be said to have achieved the real position of leadership, based upon justice, good will, fair dealing and helpfulness. It is a position which other nations have envied because they believe that it was acquired in a selfish spirit and designed to lead to material benefit. They are therefore trying to weaken and discredit the influence of the United States. Now, it happens that the Chinese Government and people are beset by the greatest difficulties and dangers: they are attempting to reform their political methods and institutions largely in the direction of the experience and example of the United States, to which they look up to as a model to be imitated; and this great change in national methods and practices naturally encounters enormous difficulties, which are aggravated by the intrigues of foreign countries to which such a development of the Chinese nation would not be welcome.

In order to carry out administrative reforms, to organize credit and economic life upon a national basis, and to support its authority as against local movements and disaffection, the Chinese Government has needed the financial help of the outside world. The sources from which this has so far been forthcoming are not favorable to the independent development of Chinese life: every new money advance is used further to circumscribe China's freedom.

Considering the position of leadership which the United States and its ideals have held, the Chinese Government has, during the past year, appealed again and again most earnestly for American financial support. The Chinese have come to realize that America's action can not take the form of political assistance, but they hope that the good will of the United States may take the form of cooperating with China in the upbuilding of her economic and financial activities, upon which national strength is ultimately based. The Chinese are constantly being told by persons ill-disposed towards us that the United States will do nothing for them; that our action here is based upon empty talk, and that when it comes to real helpfulness the Chinese must rely on the other nations.

It would not be necessary for the United States to undertake the financing of China: the situation is such that if the United States would only do its share China would receive that margin of support which would keep her from falling under the complete dominance of forces not favorable to her national development. So it comes about that through a comparatively limited investment, and without in any sense taking control of China's financial affairs, the United States will be able to do a very great service. This would have the moral effect of freeing China from the pressure of those who maintain that she cannot get support elsewhere: while just at the point where the foreign financial influence would threaten to crush China's independence, even a small amount of support from another source would offer safety. The influence of American financial support in liberating the credit of China would, therefore, be entirely out of proportion to the actual amount invested.

If the Chinese Government could get such financial support in the United States, it would have the following results: The argument that American helpfulness is a matter merely of words could not longer be made; and the organization of China's economic life and credit could proceed, free from constant subordination to the political desires and demands of outside nations. The Chinese, freed from this unfavorable political pressure, would be able to follow their own desires in political matters: i.e., they would be free to develop republican institutions. It is not too much to say that the further development of republicanism in China depends upon how far China can be made independent of outside political pressure, exercised through financial means.

That Americans should take their share in the financing required in China is also highly desirable from the point of view of those activities in which we are interested in the Far East. If, in the matters upon which the life of the Chinese nation depends, America becomes a negligible quantity, the moral influence of the agents of our civilization and culture at work in China will inevitably be weakened. Should China's national independence be over-ridden, the cultural work of missionaries, teachers, and doctors would be seriously threatened.

The improvement of the Huai River region, which is now being planned with American support and under American auspices, would constitute a memorable instance of what such financial assistance would mean to China at the present time. It is not only that the livelihood and existence of over 20,000,000 human beings would be secured and that nearly 5,000,000 acres of the finest agricultural soil would be added to the active resources of China, but the significance of this work would be still more far-reaching. It would be an object lesson, teaching China that through scientific work and technical efficiency the very underlying conditions of national life can be modified in a direction of improvement; it would show them the assured possibility of bettering their life through improved methods and would thus react on all branches of public and private activity in China; and it would be a calamity both to China and to the United States if this great work should not be carried out promptly. Incidentally, I am happy to stated that the report of Colonel Sibert's Commission proves this enterprise to be even more promising of good results than we had anticipated. Unfortunately, I am informed that this year the conditions within this region are worse than they have been during the last decade, so that again millions of people will during this winter suffer extremely. This is an added reason for the rapid execution of this great work.

The Huai River improvement will be a memorable enterprise and of great benefit to the Chinese nation. But the Chinese are now in such acute need of financial support that in addition to the above it is highly desirable that American financial support should be available. It is not a large amount that is needed: G$50,000,000. would go far to render the effective organization of China's administration and financial reform possible. If wisely employed, it would serve to liberate and organize the vast forces of economic activity and of credit which the Chinese nation contains. The difficulty of the Chinese Government does not lie in the absence of abundant resources, but in the fact that international and internal difficulties have combined in retarding the organization of these resources. Relatively, the financial burden of the Chinese State is the smallest in the world. A great opportunity awaits men who will, without political afterthought, assist China in organizing these activities. For financial strength, considering the habits of its people, China should ultimately become a second France.

The Chinese Government is extremely desirous to have the financial assistance of Americans in the organization of its economic life, because they know that Americans will be just and will not come with political motives. They have therefore approached American interests for the above purpose: in May they gave Mr. G. N. Guest, of New York, a commission to secure a loan of G$25,000,000. for the purpose of more completely organizing the Bank of China, and its branches. In making a concession of oil lands to the Standard Oil Company of New York, they secured the incidental promise that the Standard Oil Company would use its good offices in helping China to secure on the American money market a loan for organization purposes. The Chinese Government has now commissioned Mr. Roy S. Anderson, of that Company, to negotiate for a loan of this nature. I may say incidentally, that this agent, the son of an American missionary and teacher in China, knows the Chinese thoroughly both as a nation and in their leading personalities. He is thoroughly in touch with the progressive movement in China and is one of the men who has been foremost in representing American political experience and ideals among them. He left China before my return, but should he call upon you I desire to commend him to your courtesy and attention and I am sure that you will find his account of the Chinese situation highly interesting.

I have ventured to call your personal attention to the financial situation in China, because it is felt, by the Chinese high officials and by Americans here and at home, that if you could give your personal interest and support to measures of cooperation of Americans in the upbuilding of China's economic and financial organization, all the activities in which Americans are interested in China would benefit through the realization of a direct helpfulness in giving effective aid to China's independence and national development. Should Americans not participate in a helpful way at this critical juncture in the development of China, it is to be feared that very bad results would follow, threatening disorganization and the impairment of all opportunities to be of assistance to the Chinese people in other matters as well. I cannot fully express to you the seriousness of the situation. China is at the parting of the ways. Whether her destiny is to be one of peaceful and orderly development along the lines of constitutional freedom and self-government, or whether she is torn asunder in civil conflict and international intrigue: this depends in no small measure upon whether active assistance can be given to the Chinese at the present time in effectually organizing the activities of their national life. Should those Americans who are disposed to assist the Chinese at this juncture have the assurance of the good will of the American Government, their efforts and their work would have the promise of success.

I have enclosed for your reference two despatches to the Department of State which deal more fully with the situation.

With the renewed expression of the highest respect and with sincere wishes for your continued well-being, I am, dear Mr. President,          Faithfully yours,   Paul S. Reinsch

TLS (W. G. McAdoo Papers, DLC).

## To Paul Samuel Reinsch

My dear Mr. Minister,          The White House 9 November, 1914.

This is just a line to express my sincere regret that I did not have the opportunity to see you and have a talk with you while you were in Washington, and also my deep appreciation of your kind letter of the fifth.

The matters you write me of I recognize as of capital and immediate importance. I am planning to take them up with several of my colleagues here who may prove good counsellors in devising ways by which we may effectually act upon your interesting suggestions, and I hope that something concrete and lasting will come out of our conferences.

Let me congratulate you on the way in which your work is developing and on the manner in which you are handling it.

With much regard,

Cordially Yours,   Woodrow Wilson

WWTLS (P. S. Reinsch Papers, WHi).

## To Nancy Saunders Toy

Dear Friend,          The White House 9 November, 1914.

I am sure you will not guage the welcome your letters[1] command by the length of time it takes me to sit down for an answer. Somehow the day's work seems absolutely to exhaust my initi[a]tive. Almost every day there is some interval when I *could* sit down before this little machine and write. If I were to do so as often as the thought comes and as often as I feel the warmth about my heart that comes whenever I recall the generous messages of dear friends, I would be at its keys many times a day. But with the accomplishment of the tasks of duty each day my energies seem to lag; I want to rest even from thinking; I especially shrink from dwelling upon anything personal to myself. My instinct is to seek some occupation that will take my thoughts far afield where there is nothing that can concern me, as to the reading of some far-away, improbable tale that does not seem to be of this world at all, or of any other unintelligible world. In short I want to run away, to escape something. It is selfish; it is puerile; it is, I trust, short-lived; but it is often my master these barren days! After all, the hardest enterprise in the world is to rule one's own spirit! After that to rule a city were pastime! And the worst of it is, that elections bring on self-examination in a flood: a cross-questioning of all one's enterprises, a re-examination of all the means available for carrying them out. The grounds for reassurance enumerated by Dr. Rhodes while you rode with him in the motor are all very good and very valid and (e[x]cept the possibility of a second term, which I pray I may be spared) sufficiently comforting to keep discouragement at arm's length; but, after all is said that can be said, there was the very strong reaction, at least in the East, and good reason furnished for raising the question abroad (where alone I care for personal prestige just now) whether I could really be accepted as the spokesman of the United States. What I get solid satisfaction out of is the support the West gave us, the real heart of America, which has hitherto really never manifested its confidence in the Democratic party by *majorities*. That gives me vital comfort and a very lively hope. We have had a change of venue. A different part of America now decides, not the part which has usually arrogated to itself a selfish leadership and patronage of the rest. For the first time it turns to the Democratic party. A few years ago there were only two lone Democrats in the Senate from any part of the country west of Kansas City (always excepting Texas), but now there are to be seventeen. A party that has been called sectional is becoming unmistakably national. The sweep of its influence and power is immensely broadened. *That* puts tonic in my lungs. I love to breathe an air that blows out of the heart of the mighty continent. Even if there be no happiness in any thought of my personal fortunes, there is deep cause for gratitude and thankfulness that we are trusted to serve a great people. Personal happiness is a small matter by comparison! If one could only keep that thought burning and vital all the time how much easier life would be. Is it not strange, does it not bespeak our essential individual littleness, that personal happiness should dwell in the little things (little by comparison with the fate and progress of peoples) and in the things that touch us intimately and privately, and not in the big circumstances of our lives? And yet it is so. The love that embraces mankind does not make us happy, but only the love that gives us the intimacy of a dear one who is in fact part of our very selves. We are sustained by the daily touch, the constant sympathy and union in little things, the little things that make up the life that the world knows nothing about. It is a cold, barren region where these things are not. There is no getting any companionship out of the policies of a state or the furtunes [fortunes] of a nation! We are sunk far, far below the likeness in which we were made: we got the likeness but not the substance and character, God forgive us! All of this discourse means only that your letters are a delight!

Your affectionate friend,    Woodrow Wilson

WWTLS (WP, DLC).
1 The letter from Mrs. Toy to which this is a reply is missing.

## From Edward Mandell House

Dear Governor:            New York City. November 9th, 1914.

Charles R. Crane, Norman Hapgood and a progressive from Illinois by the name of Walter S. Rogers[1] called this morning to tell me that there had been a constant pilgrimage to Oyster Bay since the elections and that Roosevelt had turned his followers loose[,] advising them to use their own inclinations as to future party affiliations.

They think he intends getting out of the country again for a good long period. The purpose of their visit was that we might take some means to gather in our share of his following.

Rogers told me that he knew E. W. Scripps[2] quite well and he felt sure, with some encouragement, we could get his entire string of twenty odd newspapers for you. I promised to keep in touch with him and to bring this result about if possible.

The Belgian Minister, Bertron, Robert de Forrest and Green of the Rockefeller Foundation[3] are to come at five this afternoon in order to see if some arrangement can be made to coordinate the different relief committees into one, as suggested by Walter Page. I will report to you upon this tomorrow.

I wish you could know what a happy time I had with you during the past few days. Please come on Friday and let us have the next Saturday and Sunday here. I am sure the change will do you good.            Affectionately yours,    E. M. House

Gen. Wood lunched with me. He says the man (Dwight Braman)[4] who thinks that concrete foundations are being laid, is quite crazy on that subject, and for me to say to you there is absolutely nothing in it.

TLS (WP, DLC).
1 Walter Stowell Rogers, assistant to Crane in the Crane Co. of Chicago.
2 Edward Wyllis Scripps, owner of a chain of newspapers in the Midwest and Far West, founder of the United Press and the Newspaper Enterprise Association.
3 Jerome Davis Greene, at this time secretary and trustee of the Rockefeller Foundation.
4 Dwight Braman, head of the banking and brokerage firm of Dwight Braman & Co. of New York.

## Sir Cecil Arthur Spring Rice to Sir Edward Grey

Private                                            Washn 9 Nov 1914

Your friend[1] gave me a satisfactory message from the President. Some serious protests will have to be made as to action supposed to be injurious to American interests but general sentiment inside & outside the administration was sympathetic and was gradually realising the true nature of the struggle and that it affected this country most nearly. But he hoped nothing would be said about the 'destruction' of Germany as the object was not destruction of any one power but the preservation of all.

I understand from a confl adviser of this administration that if German ships in N Y were converted into armed cruisers and preyed on American commerce a very serious view of the matter would be taken here.

The elections are a defeat for the President but not so great a defeat as was expected after the tariff bill. The contraband matter did not play a part thanks to your prompt action. But Congress will be troublesome.

Hw telegram (FO 115/1776, p. 35, PRO).
  [1] Colonel House.


## Remarks at a Press Conference

November 10, 1914

Mr. President, have you any personal comment to make on the elections?

> No, sir. It is very evident that the Democrats are gaining control of the government.

As the head of the party, Mr. President, wouldn't you like to make some more extensive comments than that?

> No, sir. My comment will, I hope, be the action of the next two years. I am very much more interested in doing things than talking about them.

Can you explain the embargo situation to us, Mr. President?

> Which embargo?

With reference to the British embargo on exports from her colonies. There is a very strong effort to get wool shipments to the United States.

> No. I can't explain that any further than it has been in the public prints, because, of course, that is domestic policy which there is no reason why she should explain to us.

There are very strong efforts made to get the State Department to take some action, such action as it could. It is a question as to whether anything could be done.

It would naturally be. Of course, if anything were done, it would be only by influence. We have no rights in the matter. Mr. President, have you given any thought to the trade commission appointments?

Yes, sir, I have given a great deal. I haven't made any selections yet.

There is a report in the morning papers that Mr. Redfield is to be one.

If you have had the experience I have, you won't believe what you see in the papers. I mean about matters of that sort. Of course, there will be speculation of all sorts, but I have made no selection. . . .

Mr. President, when do you hope to send those names to the Senate?

Just as soon after the convening of Congress as possible. Mr. President, Mr. Gardner this morning—yesterday—in discussing his resolution, said that there would be a number of civilians who would testify at the hearing on the resolution, and that there would be many army and navy officers, provided their departments let them. Can you say anything?

I can't say anything. Hypothetical questions I can't answer.

JRT transcript (WC, NjP) of CLSsh (C. L. Swem Coll., NjP).

## To Hugo Münsterberg

The White House

My dear Professor Munsterberg:       November 10, 1914

I have received and read with a great deal of surprise your letter of November seventh. Certainly no administration ever tried more diligently or watchfully to preserve an attitude and pursue a line of conduct absolutely neutral. I would consider it a favor if you would point out to me what are considered the unneutral acts of which this administration is thought to have been guilty. If we have done anything contrary to our professions, I should certainly wish to correct the mistake if it were possible to do so. We have acted in strict accordance with international law, so far as we know.

Very sincerely yours,    Woodrow Wilson

TLS (H. Münsterberg Papers, MB).

## To Walter Hines Page

My dear Page:          The White House November 10, 1914

You may be perfectly sure that you do not weary me with your letters. They give me an intimate view of men and things which I could not obtain without them and are invaluable to me. I cannot have too many.

I only wish that I could return the service in kind by going into the detail of our action and our difficulties and our personalities here. That, unhappily, is out of the question; for one thing, because I have not your gift of presenting these things vividly, but chiefly, because the pressure of a multitude of things throughout the day seems to deprive me of the kind of initiative necessary for writing good letters.

I am glad that the situation has been as much simplified as possible by our no longer insisting on the Declaration of London. Any mistakes that were made then can now easily be forgotten.

I am particularly interested in what you tell me of your conversation with General French's two friends.[1] My only comment at present is that what they suggested seems to me a programme which needs as its premise the practically complete defeat of Germany and not merely a stand-off fight, because it involves to a very considerable degree a dismemberment of the German Empire. But, after all, it is not the details that interest me in these suggestions, but the general judgment as to the prospects of the war and the general principle involved in the outlined settlement. It gives me much to think about. It would indeed be a very great privilege if I could play any part in bringing settled peace to Europe.

Cordially and faithfully yours,    Woodrow Wilson

TLS (W. H. Page Papers, MH).

[1] WHP to WW, Oct. 29, 1914, ALS (WP, DLC). Page reported on a luncheon conversation with two unnamed associates of Field Marshal Sir John Denton Pinkstone French, commander in chief of the British Expeditionary Force. These men predicted that the war would reach a stalemate by the summer or autumn of 1915 and that Wilson woud then be asked to mediate. The "broad principles" of a settlement would be "such as these":

"Every country must maintain its nationality—Belgium must be Belgium, of course; Alsace-Lorraine must be French, if they are French & so wish to be; Schleswig-Holstein Danish, if they are Danish and wish to be; Poland, the same principle; the South-German States go with Austria, if they so wish, the Slav. states now Austrian become Russian, etc. etc. The German colonies are left as pawns to trade with in working out the details of the bargain."

The reduction of armies and navies would be more difficult: they should "be discouraged by treaties." A large German indemnity to Belgium would also be difficult to secure, but the Allies would probably insist upon it.

Page believed that this discussion represented a personal message to him from French, though the General obviously could not send it openly.

## From Edward Mandell House

Dear Governor:          New York City.   November 10th, 1914.

In my conference yesterday with the Belgian Minister, de Forrest and others, de Forrest told me that Senator Root had just told him that he might tell me in confidence that, in his opinion, it would not be wise for you to appoint a general committee, for the reason that it would be considered a breach of neutrality.

I called up Wallace and asked him to see Bernstorff and find whether he was willing for such a committee to be named by you.

Wallace has just telephoned that Bernstorff was glad to do anything in the matter that was desired. He is now arranging, I think, a meeting between Bryan and Bernstorff for tomorrow.

This will cover any possible complication. The reason I wanted Wallace to see Bernstorff first was in order to advise him as a friend to make no objection.

Affectionately yours,   E. M. House

TLS (WP, DLC).


## To Ralph Pulitzer

Personal.

My dear Mr. Pulitzer:     [The White House] November 11, 1914

I have more than once felt constrained to thank you for the wonderfully and generous and very thoughtful support which the World has given me editorially, but I particularly want to thank you for the editorials which have followed the election. The one immediately following election served to put heart in me in an extraordinary degree.[1]

I hope that you and those associated with you in the editorial office of the World realize how much these things mean to me and how deeply appreciative I am of such support.

Cordially and sincerely yours,   Woodrow Wilson

TLS (Letterpress Books, WP, DLC).
[1] He referred to "Wilson's Triumph," New York World, Nov. 6, 1914, which repudiated Republican claims that the election was a severe defeat for Wilson and his party and pointed out that the President would continue to have Democratic majorities in both houses of Congress despite the efforts of an essentially re-united Republican party.

## From Edward Mandell House

Dear Governor:          New York City. November 11th, 1914.

Dumba called this afternoon. He told me he had communicated with his Government the substance of our last conversation and in reply they had instructed him to say: First, to ascertain whether the German Government was willing to enter into any conversations. If not, then he was to refrain, himself, from any further discussion, excepting to say that the Austrian Government received with sympathy the ideas which I conveyed to him, and are, on principle, not opposed to any mediation which might secure honorable terms for Austria-Hungary, as well as for Germany.

He was to lay particular stress upon the fact that he could not enter into a discussion of peace terms excepting jointly with Germany. Second: If Germany was ready to discuss peace, he was to tell me the points which his Government had selected from my suggestions as being worthy of discussion. He was not to say this to me, however, unless Germany acquiesced, but he was willing to transgress his authority and inform me what his real instructions were.

His Government thought that the realization of a guaranty for peace by lightening the burden of armaments seemed difficult, although they would be glad to begin a more detailed discussion if Germany consents.

The above, Dumba dictated and I wrote down verbatim. He talked very freely of conditions and was afraid that peace negociations could not be begun because there seemed no probability that the Germans would be driven back within their borders for the present, and he understood from me that it was very improbable that the Allies would consent to such a discussion until this happened.

He also thought there would be much difficulty with Russia because of her determination to take over, in one way or another a large part of Austrian territory. He admitted that they were surprised at the efficient manner in which the Russians were conducting their campaign.

It was understood that no one was to have the substance of this conversation excepting you and Count Bernstorff.

Dumba returns to Washington next week and desires to present his compliments to you. I hope you will receive him and will think it wise to keep in friendly touch with the representatives of the warring countries.

I spoke to him about the Belgian Relief Committee. He said

there would be no objection on the part of his Government to your appointing any committee you desired and that both his Government and the German Government would welcome any aid that this country might give that unhappy people.

Affectionately yours,   E. M. House

TLS (WP, DLC).

## From James Ambrose Gallivan

Your Excellency:                    Washington, D. C. Nov. 11, 1914.

I have just learned that on Thursday at 11 A.M., a delegation of colored citizens are to be given an audience with Your Excellency. I understand that they desire to protest against segregation based on race prejudice. I have been asked by a representative body of colored men in Boston to say to you that they are anxious that if said segregation exists in the departments of the Government that if [it] be abolished. I join with them in this request in order that the reputation for justice and equality of our National Democratic party may be maintained. I agree with Governor Walsh of our state that if there is any condition existing in Washington or elsewhere that could be interpreted as discriminating against our colored population, it should be ended and with him I agree that "every effort should be made by our government to have all our people fully realize that they enjoy equal rights and equal privileges."

Yours very truly,   James A. Gallivan<br>12th Massachusetts.

TLS (WP, DLC).

## Sir Edward Grey to Sir Cecil Arthur Spring Rice

[London] Nov. 11: 1914

According to information which has reached this Department from trustworthy sources the German liners in American ports are now ready to sail at any moment.

The British Government has the strongest reason for suspecting that a plan has been formed and now may be carried into execution very soon for the participation of many of these fast ships in belligerent operations which have been pre-arranged under instructions from Berlin with the German cruisers which at the present moment are in the Pacific.

If possible obtain an audience with the President and speak

most urgently to him as to the extremely serious consequences which such a contingency would entail. You should leave no doubt in his mind that if these German liners are eventually found to engage in belligerent action against us after the many warnings which we have addressed to the United States Government public opinion in England would hold us bound to hold the United States Government responsible for the consequences, which might possibly include very serious losses to the shipping and trade of Great Britain and her Allies.

TC telegram (WP, DLC).

## Sir Cecil Arthur Spring Rice to Sir Edward Grey

Private.                              Washington November 11th 1914

President is much incensed with Germans here who are threatening to found a new political party directed against him and who are spending very large sums on press. He hints feeling here is becoming almost warlike and that he was reluctant to raise questions likely to embitter public opinion. He is aware that if German ships do get out and prey on commerce public opinion will be much stirred up especially if we have shown our wish to help commercial situation by accepting exchange proposal and your conciliatory attitude with regard to contraband.

T telegram (E. Grey Papers, FO 800/84, PRO).

## An Address to the President by William Monroe Trotter

[[Nov. 12, 1914]]

One year ago we presented a national petition, signed by Afro-Americans in thirty-eight states, protesting against the segregation of employes of the national government whose ancestry could be traced in whole or in part to Africa, as instituted under your administration in the treasury and postoffice departments.[1] We then appealed to you to undo this race segregation in accord with your duty as president and with your pre-election pledges. We stated that there could be no freedom, no respect from others, and no equality of citizenship under segregation for races, especially when applied to but one of the many racial elements in the government employ. For such placement of employes means a charge by the government of physical indecency or infection, or of being a lower order of beings, or a subjection to the

Wilson and Tumulty in the Oval Office

Wilson and House at Cornish, September 1914

The President and the Secretary of State

Sir Edward Grey

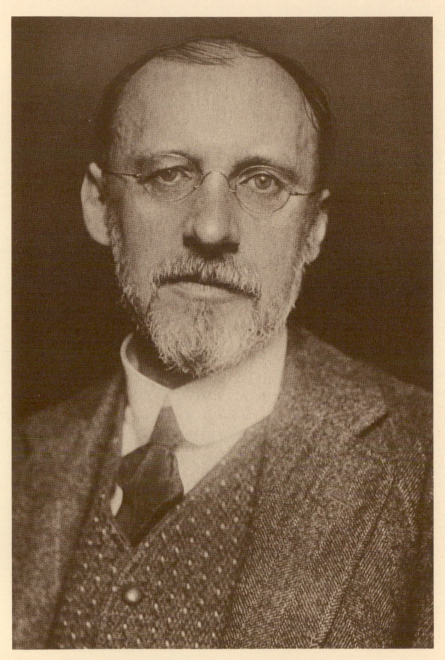

Sir Cecil Arthur Spring Rice

Francisco Villa

Venustiano Carranza

William Monroe Trotter

prejudices of other citizens, which constitutes inferiority of status. We protested such segregation as to working positions, eating tables, dressing rooms, rest rooms, lockers and especially public toilets in government buildings. We stated that such segregation was a public humiliation and degradation, entirely unmerited and far-reaching in its injurious effects, a gratuitous blow against ever-loyal citizens and against those many of whom aided and supported your elevation to the presidency of our common country.

At that time you stated you would investigate conditions for yourself. Now, after the lapse of a year, we have come back, having found that all the forms of segregation of government employes of African extraction are still practiced in the treasury and postoffice department buildings, and to a certain extent have spread into other government buildings.

Under the treasury department, in the bureau of engraving and printing, there is segregation not only in dressing rooms, but in working positions, Afro-American employes being herded at separate tables, in eating, and in toilets. In the navy department there is herding at desks and separation in lavatories; in the post-office department there is separation in work for Afro-American women in the alcove on the eighth floor, of Afro-American men in rooms on the seventh floor, with forbidding even of entrance into an adjoining room occupied by white clerks on the seventh floor, and of Afro-American men in separate rooms just instituted on the sixth floor, with separate lavatories for Afro-American men on the eighth floor; in the main treasury building in separate lavatories in the basement; in the interior department separate lavatories, which were specifically pointed out to you at our first hearing; in the state and other departments in separate lavatories; in marine hospital service building in separate lavatories, though there is but one Afro-American clerk to use it; in the war department in separate lavatories; in the postoffice department building separate lavatories; in the sewing and bindery divisions of the government printing office on the fifth floor there is herding at working positions of Afro-American women and separation in lavatories, and new segregation instituted by the division chief since our first audience with you. This lavatory segregation is the most degrading, most insulting of all. Afro-American employes who use the regular public lavatories on the floors where they work are cautioned and are then warned by superior officers against insubordination.

We have come by vote of this league to set before you this definite continuance of race segregation and to renew the protest and to ask you to abolish segregation of Afro-American employes in the executive department.

Because we cannot believe you capable of any disregard of your pledges we have been sent by the alarmed Americans citizens of color. They realize that if they can be segregated and thus humiliated by the national government at the national capital the beginning is made for the spread of that persecution and prosecution which makes property and life itself insecure in the South, the foundation of the whole fabric of their citizenship is unsettled.

They have made plain enough to you their opposition to segregation last year by a national anti-segregation petition, this year by a protest registered at the polls, voting against every Democratic candidate save those outspoken against segregation. The only Democrat elected governor in the eastern states was Governor Walsh of Massachusetts, who appealed to you by letter to stop segregation. Thus have the Afro-Americans shown how they detest segregation.

In fact, so intense is their resentment that the movement to divide this solid race vote and make peace with the national Democracy, so auspiciously revived when you ran for the presidency, and which some of our families for two generations have been risking all to promote, bids fair to be undone.

Only two years ago you were heralded as perhaps the second Lincoln, and now the Afro-American leaders who supported you are hounded as false leaders and traitors to their race. What a change segregation has wrought!

You said that your "Colored fellow citizens could depend upon you for everything which would assist in advancing the interest of their race in the United States." Consider that pledge in the face of the continued color segregation! Fellow citizenship means congregation. Segregation destroys fellowship and citizenship. Consider that any passerby on the streets of the national capital, whether he be black or white, can enter and use the public lavatories in government buildings, while citizens of color who do the work of the government are excluded.

As equal citizens and by virtue of your public promises we are entitled at your hands to freedom from discrimination, restriction, imputation and insult in government employ. Have you a "new freedom" for white Americans and a new slavery for your "Afro-American fellow citizens"? God forbid!

We have been delegated to ask you to issue an executive order against any and all segregation of government employes because of race and color, and to ask whether you will do so. We await your reply, that we may give it to the waiting citizens of the United States of African extraction.

Printed in the *Chicago Defender*, Nov. 21, 1914.
¹ See W. M. Trotter's address to the President and Wilson's reply and a dialogue, all printed at Nov. 6, 1913, Vol. 28.

## Remarks by Wilson and a Dialogue

November 12, 1914

[Wilson] Now let me see—because, in the first place, let us leave politics out of it. If the colored people made a mistake in voting for me, they ought to correct it and vote against me if they think so. I don't want politics brought into it at all, because I think that lowers the whole level of the thing. I am not seeking office. God knows that any man that would seek the presidency of the United States is a fool for his pains. The burden is all but intolerable, and the things that I have to do are just as much as a human spirit can carry. So that I don't care the least in the world for the political considerations involved. I want you to understand that. But we are dealing with a human problem, not a political problem. It's a human problem.

Now, I think that I am perfectly safe in stating that the American people, as a whole, sincerely desire and wish to support, in every way they can, the advancement of the Negro race in America. They rejoice in the evidences of the really extraordinary advances that the race has made—in its self-support, in its capacity for independent endeavor, in its adaptation for organization, and everything of that sort. All of that is admirable and has the sympathy of the whole country.

But we are all practical men. We know that there is a point at which there is apt to be friction, and that is in the intercourse between the two races. Because, gentlemen, we must strip this thing of sentiment and look at the facts, because the facts will get the better of us whether we wish them to or not.

Now, in my view the best way to help the Negro in America is to help him with his independence—to relieve him of his dependence upon the white element of our population, as he is relieving himself in splendid fashion. And the problem, as I have discussed it with my colleagues in the departments, is this, for I had taken it very seriously after my last interview with a committee of this organization. If you will leave with me all the instances you have just cited, I will look into them again. But the point that was put to me, in essence, was that they were seeking, not to put the Negro employees at a disadvantage, but they were seeking to make arrangements which would prevent any kind of friction between the white employees and the Negro employees.

Now, they may have been mistaken in judgment. But their objective was not to do what you gentlemen seem to assume—to put the Negro employees at an uncomfortable disadvantage—but to relieve the situation that does arise. We can't blink the fact, gentlemen, that it does arise when the two races are mixed.

Now, of course color outside is a perfectly artificial test. It is a race question. And color, so far as the proposition itself, is merely an evidence of the development from a particular continent; that is to say, from the African continent.

Now, it takes the world generations to outlive all its prejudices. Of course they are prejudices. They are prejudices which are embarrassing the Government of the United States just as much with other races, that is, some other races, as they are embarrassing us about the race that is derived from African descent. And so we must treat this thing with a recognition of its difficulties.

Now, I am perfectly willing to do anything that is just. I am not willing to do what may turn out to be unwise. Now, it is the unwise part that is debatable—whether we have acted in a wise way or not. If my colleagues have dealt with me candidly—and I think they have—they have not intended to do an injustice. They have intended to remedy what they regarded as creating the possibility of friction, which they did not want ever to exist. They did not want any white man made uncomfortable by anything that any colored man did, or a colored man made uncomfortable by anything that a white man did in the offices of the government. That, in itself, is essentially how they feel—that a man of either race should not make the other uncomfortable. It works both ways. A white man can make a colored man uncomfortable, as a colored man can make a white man uncomfortable if there is a prejudice existing between them. And it shouldn't be allowed on either end.

Now, what makes it look like discrimination is that the colored people are in a minority as compared with the white employees. Any minority looks as if it were discriminated against. But suppose that the Negroes were in the majority in the departments in the clerkships and this segregation occurred? Then it would look like discrimination against the whites, because it is always the minority that looks discriminated against, whereas the discrimination may not be intended against anybody, but for the benefit of both.

I am not deciding this question, you understand. I am only saying that everything that has been done is just. I have not inquired into it recently enough to be sure of that. But I want to get you gentlemen to understand this thing from the point of view of those who are trying to handle it. It is a very difficult question. Nobody can be cocksure about what should be done. I am not cocksure about what should be done. I am certain that I have been dependent upon the advice of the men who were in immediate contact with the problem in the several departments. They have assured me that they have not put Negro employees at a disadvantage in regard to rooms and lighting that was inconvenient. I have put that up to them again. I haven't had time to look at the conditions myself, but I have again and again said that the thing that would distress me most would be that they should select the colored people of the departments to be given bad light or bad ventilation yet worse than the others, and inferior positions, physically considered.

Now, they have not intended to do that, I am quite sure, from the assurances of many of the cabinet. It may be that some have been taking information from their subordinates without going to look at what was actually done. But, at any rate, that is the spirit of the heads of the departments, for I consulted with them very gravely about this, and I think their spirit is mine in the matter.

I want to help the colored people in every way I can, but there are some ways, some things that I could do myself that would hurt them more than it would help them.

Now, you may differ with me in judgment. It is going to take generations to work this thing out. And mark these pages, it will come quickest if these questions aren't raised. It will come quickest if you men go about the work of your race, if you will go about it and see that the race makes good and nobody can say that there is any kind of work that they can't do as well as anybody else.

That is the way to solve this thing. It is not a question of intrinsic equality, because we all have human souls. We are absolutely equal in that respect. It is just at the present a question of economic equality—whether the Negro can do the same things with equal efficiency. Now, I think they are proving that they can. After they have proved it, a lot of things are going to solve themselves.

Now, that is the whole thing. We must not misunderstand one another in these things. We must not allow feelings to get the upper hands of our judgments. We must try to do what judgment demands now, as has been said to Mr. Trotter. I think you have the memoranda, and I will look into it again. I will look into it, and I accept the assurances that were given me, and I have repeated them to you. That is all I can do.

[Trotter] May I ask one question, Mr. President? What do you think about the result of this present condition in the departments, where it has already operated to the detriment of so many of the employees, where some of them have been placed in a position where they are now humiliated and indisposed as a result of this humiliating condition: having to go so far from their work to the toilet rooms, and then the condition also where employees in the government have not only been reduced from clerkships to laborers, but have next been forced right out of the departments entirely.

[Wilson] I haven't known of such incidents. My question would be this: If you think that you gentlemen, as an organization, and all other Negro citizens of the country, that you are being humiliated, you will believe it. If you take it as a humiliation, which it is not intended as, and sow the seed of that impression all over the country, why the consequences will be very serious. But if you should take it in the spirit in which I have presented it to you, it wouldn't have serious consequences. Now, that is what I think about it. It is the misunderstanding, as I honestly believe it to be, that is going to be serious, much more serious than the facts justify.

Now, as for demotions and things of that sort, I haven't taken them up. I didn't know about that.

[An unknown person] Mr. President, these colored clerks, and clerks of other nationalities, have been working together, side by side, in peace and harmony and friendship for fifty years without distinction and separation based upon their race. Mr. President, it is entirely untenable to say that race feeling or race friction necessitates any of this separation of Afro-American clerks. It is absolutely contrary to the facts of the case. Mr. Trotter has told you that, even under a Democratic administration, it was not found to be necessary to separate clerks.

[Trotter] We are not here as wards. We are not here as dependents. We are not here looking for charity or help. We are here as full-fledged American citizens, vouchsafed equality of citizenship by the federal Constitution. Separation and distinction marking, because of a certain kind of blood in our veins, when it is not made against other different races, is something that must be a humiliation. It creates in the minds of others that there is something the matter with us—that we are not their equals, that we are not their brothers, that we are so different that we cannot work at a desk beside them, that we cannot eat at a table beside them, that we cannot go into the dressing room where they go, that we cannot use a locker beside them, that we cannot even go into a public toilet with them.

Think of it, Mr. President, that any pedestrian walking the streets of the national capital, whether he be white or black, can enter and use any of these public toilets in the government buildings, and that Americans of color who are doing the work of the government cannot do so.

Now, Mr. President, there cannot be any friction with regard to going into a public toilet. They have been going into the public toilets for fifty years. They were going into the public toilets when your administration came in. When your administration came in, under Mr. John Skelton Williams, a drastic segregation was put into effect almost at once.

Mr. President, we insist that the facts in the case bear us out in truth—that this segregation is not due to any friction between the races, but is due to race prejudice on the part of the official who puts it into operation.

Mr. President, citizens, as they are picked out, especially in a country where there are many races and many nationalities—and everyone is picked out to be subjected to a prejudice of theirs —they are going to be subjected to all kinds of mistreatment and persecution everywhere throughout the country. They are necessarily objects of contempt and scorn, because segregation is not only a natural order of things, but it is the way of progression and more segregation. The very fact of any racial element of government employees being by themselves is an invitation in the public mind. That fact cannot be denied nor disputed.

Now, Mr. President, this is a very serious thing with us. We are sorely disappointed that you take the position that the separation itself is not wrong, is not injurious, is not rightly offensive to you. You hold us responsible for the feeling that the colored people of the country have—that it is an insult and an injustice; but that is not in accord with the facts, Mr. President. We, if anything, lag behind. Why, Mr. President, two years ago among our people, and last year, you were thought to be perhaps the second Abraham Lincoln.

[Wilson] Please leave me out. Let me say this, if you will, that if this organization wishes to approach me again, it must choose another spokesman. I have enjoyed listening to these other gentlemen. They have shown a spirit in the matter that I have appreciated, but your tone, sir, offends me. You are an American citizen, as fully an American citizen as I am, but you

are the only American citizen that has ever come into this office
who has talked to me with a tone with a background of passion that was evident. Now, I want to say that if this association
comes again, it must have another spokesman. You wouldn't do
me, then, a possible injustice.

[Trotter] I am from a part of the people, Mr. President.

[Wilson] You have spoiled the whole cause for which you
came.

[Trotter] Mr. President, I am sorry for that. Mr. President, America that professes to be Christian cannot condemn
that which [blank]

[Wilson] I expect those who profess to be Christians to come
to me in a Christian spirit.

[Trotter] Mr. President, I have—now, don't misunderstand me,
I have not condemned the Christian spirit. I am pleading for
simple justice. Mr. President, I am from a part of the people who
will take me at my word. I am from a part of the people. If my
tone has seemed so contentious, why my tone has been misunderstood. I am from a part of the people, and I would like to be able
to say, and do so, [that you are] without prejudice.

[Wilson] Please leave me out and argue the case.

[Trotter] I was simply trying to show how my people feel,
Mr. President, because it is the truth that we who led in this
movement are today, among our people, branded as traitors to
our race on segregation.

[Wilson] As traitors to your race?

[Trotter] As traitors to our race, because we advised the colored
people to support the ticket. That is the reason we do it. I am
sincere in this feeling. I want to show, Mr. President, their feeling in the matter, not my feeling. I am telling you the truth. We
ought to be truthful, Mr. President. We ought to be frank and
truthful. I hope you want to be frank and true and not be false
to your faith. Now, Mr. President, you know it would be an un-
manly thing to appear to be false.

[Wilson] These other gentlemen are not—

[Trotter] Believe me because I have been in the midst, and I
work in this cause. And we have tried to get the colored people
to reason in this matter. Their feeling is more [intense on this
matter] than on others. Any portrayal, we found, led them to
resent this thing. No, Mr. President, that is God's earnest truth,
that we are as we seem to be, Mr. President—that we cannot be
respected by our fellow citizens if we are to be segregated by the
federal government. Our plea to you, Mr. President, from the

bottom of my heart, is not to have the federal government make concessions to the prejudices of anybody.

We grew up in this country, and we know these various racial elements—the Latin, the Slavic, the Oriental, the differences, the conglomeration of races. And when they look around, they find we are treated differently from the way they are treated. I have given my life to this work of trying to relieve [the lot of] our people. God knows I want to relieve it, but I am trying to find the right way.

Mr. President, my whole desire is to let you know the truth we know. We see how it is impossible to make you feel what this thing is like, which injures. And they feel alienated by bringing any kind of separation in the public service. Because, Mr. President, it has been taken as an example in our every turn of our daily lives, in every turn of it. The government employees, if it were possible to have a separation without humiliation—if that position is adopted outside these limits—then for us, you know, this, if that is the position that is adopted, it is going to be inconceivable for colored clerks to concur with that separation.

There are great dangers, Mr. President, far more than there are advantages. We of course—of course, we do feel that there is a political aspect of the case, because, you know, we felt that there might be a question about this thing, and you know that we went on your declaration and things that you said. And, as I say, we are simply asking that conditions obtain that have obtained before. We would be false, Mr. President, false to ourselves and false to you, if we went out and led you to believe that we could convince the colored people that there was anything but degradation.

[Wilson] I don't think it's degradation. That is your interpretation of it.

[Trotter] Mr. President, as for your expression about having the two races work together without the dissatisfaction of either party, I want just to ask this question: If I am appointed to a government position, and a white man is in the same office, and either one becomes dissatisfied with the other, without any reason for it, should either be considered? Should it not be ignored simply as a dispute? Unless all those things occur in the abstract.

[Wilson] That is, if you do the work being done. If you harm the one, you are doing an injury to the other. It seems to me that is the situation.

Well, I am very much obliged to you. I will look into it again.

[Trotter] Mr. President, I hope that you don't feel toward me as you did a little while ago. I think you made a mistake. I assume great responsibility in the whole matter.

[Wilson] But that part we must leave out. Politics must be left out, because, don't you see, to put it plainly, that is a form of blackmail. I am only saying that you are conscious of that, or that you would tell me contrary to that. But you must reflect that, when you call upon an officer and say you can't get certain votes if you don't do certain things, that is the kind of course which ought never to be attempted. I would resent it from one set of men as from another. You can vote as you please, provided I am perfectly sure that I am doing the right thing at the right time.

[Trotter] Just one word, Mr. President. We were trying to bring about racial harmony throughout the country.

JRT transcript (WC, NjP) of CLSsh (C. L. Swem Coll., NjP).

## A News Report

[*Nov. 12, 1914*]

### PRESIDENT RESENTS NEGRO'S CRITICISM

Washington, Nov. 12.—Segregation of white and negro civil service employes in Government departments, a system inaugurated during the present Administration, is to be continued. President Wilson made clear his views on the subject today when he received a delegation representing the National Independence Equal Rights League. The President resented the attitude of the spokesman, William Monroe Trotter, of Boston, who was quoted as having attempted to cross-examine Mr. Wilson, when the President explained that the question was not a political one, and that he would not be influenced in his decision by the threats of the league to oppose the Democratic Party. . . .

Trotter then led the way from the President's office. Once outside Trotter said:

"What the President told us was entirely disappointing. His statement that segregation was intended to prevent racial friction is not supported by facts. For fifty years negro and white employes have worked together in the Government departments in Washington. It was not until the present Administration came in that segregation was drastically introduced, and only because of the racial prejudices of John Skelton Williams, Secretary McAdoo and Postmaster General Burleson."

Others in the delegation included the Rev. Byron Gunner, of Hillburn, N. Y., President of the league; Thomas Walker, Chairman of the Washington branch of the league; M. W. Spencer, of Wilmington, Del., the Rev. E. E. Ricks, and F. Morris Murray, of Virginia.[1]

As the delegation was leaving the White House, Trotter announced that a mass meeting would be held next Sunday at the Asbury Methodist Episcopal Church in Washington to protest against the attitude of the Administration.[2]

Printed in the *New York Times*, Nov. 13, 1914.

[1] The Rev. Edgar Ethelred Ricks was pastor of the First Baptist Church (colored) of Washington. Maurice W. Spencer and Freeman H. M. Murray were also associated with Trotter and the National Independent Equal Rights League.

[2] Josephus Daniels later recalled Wilson's comment on the affair. "Daniels," said Wilson, "never raise an incident into an issue. When the negro delegate threatened me, I was damn fool enough to lose my temper and to point them to the door. What I ought to have done would have been to have listened, restrained my resentment, and, when they had finished, to have said to them that, of course, their petition would receive consideration. They would then have withdrawn quietly and no more would have been heard about the matter. But I lost my temper and played the fool. I raised that incident into an issue that will be hard to down." J. Daniels to F. D. Roosevelt, June 10, 1933, TLS (F. D. Roosevelt Papers, Official File 237, NHpR).

## To Elias Milton Ammons

[The White House]
My dear Governor Ammons:                November 12, 1914

Immediately upon the receipt of your letter of the sixth, I got into consultation with the Secretary of War. Together we have gone very carefully over the question raised by your letter. It is our judgment that it would probably be a serious mistake for the troops of the United States to be withdrawn piecemeal and the forces of the State slowly substituted for them. We fear that this would give rise to a divided authority and a divided responsibility, which would be fair neither to the State nor to the Government of the United States. We are, of course, desirous of doing everything that we possibly can do to facilitate the restoration of normal conditions and it is my own very earnest hope that the State may be able to take over the control of the whole matter at a very early date.

I know your own disposition in the matter and would appreciate it very much if upon your return from Wisconsin you would consider the matter in the light I here put it and let me know when you think the final arrangements could be made.

With warm regard,

Cordially and sincerely yours,   Woodrow Wilson

TLS (Letterpress Books, WP, DLC).

## From William Jennings Bryan

My dear Mr. President:          Washington November 12, 1914.

I enclose an opinion in regard to the sale of Submarines.[1] I fear that we would be "skating on thin ice" if we adopted the rule suggested.

It may be within the rules of neutrality but I am afraid we could not convince the average citizen there is any difference between allowing a vessel to be completed here and allowing the parts to be made so that a complete vessel could be shipped and the parts assembled in another port.

If you are in doubt about the matter I would like to talk with you before the matter is finally settled, as I think there is danger in this proposition.

With assurances of high respect I am, my dear Mr. President
Yours very sincerely,   W. J. Bryan

TLS (WP, DLC).

[1] The question involved the legality under international law of the sale of unassembled submarines to the British government by the Fore River Shipbuilding Co. and the Bethlehem Steel Corp. The enclosure, RL to WJB, Nov. 12, 1914, TLS (WP, DLC), asserted that the sale of parts of warships was not unneutral. About this affair, see Link, *Struggle for Neutrality*, pp. 61-62, and Gaddis Smith, *Britain's Clandestine Submarines, 1914-1915* (New Haven, Conn., 1964).

## From Joseph Patrick Tumulty

The White House,
Memorandum for the President:          November 12, 1914

The Secretary of Labor asks if the President will make an appointment to see John D. White, president of the United Mine Workers' Association; William Greene, a member of the Ohio Legislature, who is secretary of the Association; and F. J. Hayes, the vice president of the Association.

They would like to see the President next week if possible, and the Secretary presumes that they wish to discuss the Colorado strike situation. He would like to have 3 or 4 days' notice, so that he may wire them.

Thursday, the 19th an hour.   W.W.

TL (WP, DLC).

## From Paul Wilkinson Pope[1]

My dear Woodrow,          Phila. Pa. Nov 12th, 1914

My wife has been desperately ill for the past month, and now the doctor says in order to save her an operation is necessary which will cost, with hospital expenses, the sum of $150.00; but being a stranger here and the cost of living so high, I need $50.00 more than I have or have any way of raising. Will you lend me the $50.00 until Dec 1/14. I hope you will pardon me for the liberty I take in asking this favor of you; but you are the only person in this northern country I know to whom I can appeal. The doctor says my wife must be operated on in the early part of next week          Sincerely yours   P. W. Pope

ALS (WP, DLC).
¹ Wilson's classmate at Princeton, who held a minor federal office in Philadelphia.

## A News Report

[Nov. 13, 1914]

### RAISE SEGREGATION ISSUE

#### Politicians Said to Have
#### Taken up Trotter Case.

Washington, November 13.—William Monroe Trotter, the negro editor, of Boston, whose remarks to President Wilson on the question of race segregation in the executive departments of the Government, during the course of an interview yesterday, debars him from further appearances at the White House, has brought the segregation issue squarely to a head, in the opinion of well-informed persons in Washington. While the President declined specifically to treat the issue from a political point of view, it was evident to-day that the opponents of the Administration intend to make a political issue out of the incident, notwithstanding the fact that no one could be found to defend the methods employed by Mr. Trotter in stating his case to the President yesterday.

White House officials to-day remained firm in their determination not to make public any portion of the interview between the President and the committee of the National Independent Equal Rights League, of which Trotter was the head.

Ever since the Wilson Administration came into office the leaders of the colored race have complained of discriminations in various executive departments of the Government. The separation of the races in various offices was, in fact, undertaken in some instances before arrangements could be made to prevent some inconveniences in working conditions.

President Wilson took this matter in hand more than a year ago, and the statement is now vouched for officially in all the departments, according to the information received by the President, that there are no further discriminations anywhere. The issue at the present time, according to officials of the Administration is squarely one of segregation *per se*.

Whatever of race segregation has been attempted at Washington has been wholly the action of individual executives. A limited form of segregation has been in vogue in the Post Office Department, and also in the Treasury Department. In the latter Department, John Skelton Williams, the present Controller, a Virginian, is known to hold pronounced views on the subject, and it is doing him no injustice to say that these views were undoubtedly in mind when separate toilet facilities were provided for the colored employees in the Department, and when separate tables were set aside for the colored employees of the Bureau of Engraving and Printing. In none of the Departments presided over by Northern men, so far as known, has segregation been attempted even in a mild form.

The truth of the situation, as it affects the President, seems to be that while he has had nothing to do officially or otherwise with the issuance of any order relative to segregation, he has deemed it good administration to permit his Cabinet officers to readjust their working forces as they pleased. The segregation line, as drawn, seems to have a sectional aspect, but the fact remains that in no instance, so far as known, has there been any intent, in applying it, to discriminate between the races as to working conditions.

Personally, President Wilson has treated the negro clerks well. At the instance of the Secretary of the Treasury, he recently promoted Richard Green, a negro messenger of long and faithful service, to a clerkship, and at the suggestion of Secretary Bryan he similarly promoted Edward Savoy, the Secretary's personal messenger. Both of these promotions required Executive orders.

He also nominated a negro to be Registrar of the Treasury, but the nomination stirred up so much hostility among the Southern Senators that the candidate withdrew, and an Indian, Gabe E. Parker, finally was appointed and confirmed. While the White House is somewhat disturbed over the incident, there is no reason to believe that the President will take any action as a result of the protest except to investigate allegations of individual discrimination. In fact, the President told Trotter yesterday that he had "spoiled his case."

Trotter always has been a representative of an element in his race which has sharply criticised much that has been done in the interest of the colored people by such leaders as Booker T. Washington, whose programme of industrial education for the

negro as a solution of the race problem has never had his unqualified support. He has been an equal rights advocate and has
fought stubbornly against even the slightest discrimination
against his people because of their color.

To-day the White House made public a letter from Wade H.
Carter, a negro employee of the Land Office at Oakland, Cal., who
wrote:

"We wish to state that it is the opinion of a large number
of colored Government employees with whom we have discussed
the question that the colored men and women have fared equally
well, if not better, under your Administration as they have under
any previous one. We have been in the service only a short time
and found conditions better than we supposed. We do not think
that Mr. Trotter and his organization represent the most thoughtful members of his race."

Printed in the New York *Evening Post*, Nov. 13, 1914.

## To William Jennings Bryan, with Enclosure

Dear Mr. Bryan,          [The White House] 13 November, 1914.

Will you not see to it, please, that this statement is sent by
wire to-night to someone who can show it to-morrow to Carranza and to someone also who can show it at the same time
to Guiterez,[1] for their information.

In haste,          Faithfully Yours,   Woodrow Wilson

WWTLS (SDR, RG 59, 812.00/13766a, DNA).
[1] See n. 1 to remarks at a press conference printed at Nov. 17, 1914.

### E N C L O S U R E

Both General Carranza and the Convention at Aguascalientes
having given the assurances and guarantees we requested, it
is the purpose of the Administration to withdraw the troops of
the United States from Vera Cruz on Monday, the twenty-third of
November.

All the persons there for whose personal safety this Government had made itself responsible have now left the city. The
priests and nuns who had taken refuge there and for whose safety
fears were entertained are on their way to this country.[1]

WWT telegram (SDR, RG 59, 812.00/13766a, DNA).
[1] This message was sent to the Brazilian Minister in Mexico City, to Carothers,
and to others on November 13.

## To Paul Wilkinson Pope

My dear Pope:            [The White House] November 13, 1914

I am sincerely sorry to hear of your wife's illness. Enclosed you will find my check for $50.00. I am glad to make the loan in the circumstances.

In haste            Sincerely yours,    Woodrow Wilson

TLS (Letterpress Books, WP, DLC).


## From Ralph Pulitzer

Dear Mr. President:            New York. November 13, 1914.

Many thanks for your very kind words of appreciation of The World's editorials on the election results! I, myself, think that we pretty thoroughly punctured the balloon which the Republicans were being permitted to inflate to really plausible proportions.

I believe that the recent elections occurred at a time psychologically very opportune from our point of view. The people who would have registered a hard-times vote against the Administration in any event had the opportunity to get this vote "off their chests" when the time of depression had reached the ebb, and now, having registered their protest, they will be open-minded towards the steady improvement in conditions which I believe will set in.

With warm congratulations on the vote of confidence which the recent elections constituted, believe me

Faithfully yours,    Ralph Pulitzer.

TLS (WP, DLC).


## From Julius Rosenwald[1]

Dear Mr. President:            Chicago November 13, 1914.

I have read with sympathetic interest the accounts in the Chicago newspapers of your experience yesterday at the White House with William M. Trotter. Perhaps, in view of this, you would be interested in an experience I had with the same man last summer. In July I received an unpleasant letter from him. He up[b]raided me severely for my "inducement for segregation" in Y.M.C.A.'s, because I am trying to encourage the erection of Y.M.C.A. buildings for Colored men and boys in certain American cities. Undoubtedly Mr. Trotter is a notoriety seeker, whose methods are dismaying to the conservative members of his race.

With kind regards, I am,

Sincerely yours,     Julius Rosenwald

TLS (WP, DLC).
1 President of Sears, Roebuck & Co., 1910-1925, civic leader and philanthropist, with special interests in Jewish charitable and educational organizations and in the advancement of blacks and white Southerners.


## Sir Cecil Arthur Spring Rice to Sir Edward Grey

Dear Sir Edward,                    Washington. 13 November 1914.

I saw your portrait last night at a lecture on the war. It was loudly applauded and I regret to say that the Emperor William was hissed. The audience was a large one and sympathies were not divided. This is characteristic. The President told me that ninety per cent of the American people are very strongly in favour of the Allies. On the other hand the German-American is very often, although not always, a very strong and violent advocate of German kultur. The President seemed to fear that the methods of the Germans here were having an extremely exasperating effect upon American public opinion and that this Government was in some danger of having to face a violent racial division which has hitherto been avoided on this Continent. Once racial animosity breaks out the position of the government here will be one of great difficulty. The President said that his main and paramount duty was to preserve peace at home and abroad and he seemed to be afraid lest the task might become almost impossible. There seems to be no doubt whatever that the Germans took a very strong part, both in votes and money, in the last elections and this part was one hostile to this Administration. What the opposition is grounded upon it is hard to see but it certainly exists. For this reason the United States Government will no doubt have to make rather a a strong ex-parte statement as to their action in the matter of contraband. . . . The Jews show a strong preference for the Emperor and there must be some bargain. Since Morgan's death the Jewish banks are supreme and they have captured the Treasury Department by the simple expedient of financing the bills of the Secretary of the Treasury and forcing upon him the appointment of the German Warburg on the Federal Reserve Board which he dominates. Paish and Blackett were obliged to negotiate with Warburg and this results in a good deal of discontent among Christian banks of New York who think that the Administration is freezing them out. The Government itself is rather uneasy and the President quoted to me the text "he that keepeth Israel shall neither slumber nor sleep." One by one the Jews are capturing the principal newspapers and are bringing them over as much as they dare to the German side. . . .

Please excuse this long letter but all these questions are so intimately related that I feel it better to put all the figures in one picture.　　　　　　Yours sincerely　Cecil Spring Rice

TLS (E. Grey Papers, FO 800/84, PRO).

## From William Warner Bishop[1]

Sir:　　　　　　　　　　　　　　　Washington Nov. 14 1914

Unless our records are in error, the books listed below* have been in your possession for more than one month. If you have concluded your use of them, we shall be glad to have our messenger call for them—or such volumes as you may designate—on receipt of notification either by mail or telephone that they are ready.

　　Very respectfully　Herbert Putnam
　　　　　　　　　　　Librarian of Congress
　　　　　　by W W Bishop
　　　　　　　Superintendent of Reading Room

| *Jul. | 3 | 1914. | Stretton. | Queen of Country. N. Y., 1883.[2] |
|---|---|---|---|---|
| " | 8 | " | Williams. | Thomas Jefferson. N. Y. 1903. |
| " | " | " | Hamilton. | Intimate Life. N. Y. 1910. |
| Jul. | 15 | " | Hannay. | Bad Times. |
| " | 21 | " | Mill. | Principal of Pol. Economy. v. 1-2, 1904. |
| " | " | " | Cudworth. | Intellectual system of Universe. v. 1-2, 1837. |
| " | 25 | " | Vaughn. | 700 Limericks Lyrics. 1906. |
| " | " | " | Rice. | Little book of Limericks. Chicago. 1910. |
| " | 29 | " | Rosebery. | Napoleon. N. Y. 1903. |
| " | 30 | " | Lippmann. | Preface to politics. |
| Aug. | 5 | " | Shaw. | Fanny's first play. London. 1914. |
| " | 10 | " | Lynde. | Hon. Sen. Sage-Brush. |
| " | " | " | Luther. | Woman of It. |
| " | " | " | Rosen Krantz. | Magistrates own case. 1908. |
| " | 17 | " | Silberrad. | Good Comrade. |
| " | 18 | " | Andrews. | Perfect Tribute. N. Y. 1908. |

| " | 19 | " | Whitehead. | Conventions auction Bridge. N. Y. 1914. |
| " | 26 | " | Wallas. | Human nature in politics. London. 1908. |
| " | 28 | " | Harris. | Uncle Remus. |
| Sep. | 2 | " | Singleton. | Paris. 1900. |
| " | 4 | " | Barclay. | Mistress of Shenstone. |
| " | " | " | Deland. | Partners. |
| " | 23 | " | Burnett. | T. Tembaron. |
| Oct. | 1 | " | Haggard. | Wander's Necklace. |
| " | " | " | McCutcheon. | Black is White.—Retd 10/20 |

TLS (WP, DLC).

¹ Bishop had been chief cataloguer (1902-1906) and reference librarian (1906-1907) at Princeton University before moving to the Library of Congress.

² The full citations follow: Julia Cecilia Collinson Stretton, *Queen of the County* (New York, 1883); John Sharp Williams, *Thomas Jefferson: His Permanent Influence on American Institutions* (New York, 1913); Allan McLane Hamilton, *The Intimate Life of Alexander Hamilton . . .* (New York, 1910); George A. Birmingham [James Owen Hannay], *The Bad Times* (London and New York, n.d.); John Stuart Mill, *Principles of Political Economy* (2 vols., New York, 1904); Ralph Cudworth, *The True Intellectual System of the Universe . . .* (2 vols., New York, 1837-38); Stanton Vaughn, comp., *Limerick Lyrics* (New York, 1906); Wallace and Frances Rice, comp. and eds., *The Little Book of Limericks* (Chicago, 1910); Archibald Philip Primrose, 5th Earl of Rosebery, *Napoleon: The Last Phase* (New York and London, 1902); Walter Lippmann, *A Preface to Politics* (New York and London, 1913); George Bernard Shaw, *Fanny's First Play . . .* (London, 1914); Francis Lynde, *The Honorable Senator Sage-brush* (New York, 1913); Mark Lee Luther, *The Woman of It* (New York and London, 1912); Palle Adam Vilhelm, Baron Rosenkrantz, *The Magistrate's Own Case* (New York, 1908); Una Lucy Silberrad, *The Good Comrade* (New York, 1907); Mary Raymond Shipman Andrews, *The Perfect Tribute* (New York, 1908); Wilbur Cherrier Whitehead, *Whitehead's Conventions of Auction Bridge . . .* (New York, 1914); Graham Wallas, *Human Nature in Politics* (London, 1908); Joel Chandler Harris, *Uncle Remus, His Songs and His Sayings* (New York, 1881, many later edns.); Esther Singleton, ed. and tr., *Paris as Seen and Described by Famous Writers* (New York, 1900); Florence Louisa Barclay, *The Mistress of Shenstone* (New York and London, 1910); Margaret Wade Deland, *Partners* (New York and London, 1913); Frances Hodgson Burnett, *T. Tembarom* (New York, 1913); Henry Rider Haggard, *The Wanderer's Necklace* (London and New York, 1914); George Barr McCutcheon, *Black Is White* (New York, 1914). The Editors have cited the edition or printing referred to by Bishop when he does so, unless it is incorrect; otherwise, they have cited the first edition.

# From the Diary of Colonel House

November 14, 1914.

Last Night Loulie and I went to dinner and theater with the Bertrons. He had the Belgian Minister and Mme. Havenath. The play was "The Only Girl" which I found amusing. Upon my return to the apartment I found a call from the White House. In answering it they told me the President would arrive at six o'clock this morning and would expect me to breakfast at six thirty. This changed my plans, and I had to notify the Police Commissioner and several others so it was well after midnight before I went to bed, and I arose at half past five.

The matter of entertaining a President within such confined quarters as our little apartment is not an easy undertaking, especially since I have no clerical force, excepting my one secretary.

With the President was Margaret Wilson and Dr. Grayson. We had our breakfast and then motored from the station to our apartment and from there to the Pipping Rock Club. The President played golf with Grayson and Gordon.[1] I remained at the Club. until their return. We had lunch quite promptly at one o'clock and afterward motored back to town, arriving at four.

The President and I did some work before we dressed for dinner. The main thing was to settle the Belgian Relief matter, which we did in a very few minutes. We also talked of the composition of the Trades Commission; and I had some letters to show him, two of them being from Col. Watterson concerning his Mexican policy, which the Colonel believes is likely to get him into difficulties.

People tried to get us over the telephone, and telegrams, special delivery letters and letters by messengers came in reckless profusion, until I told the maids to bring no more and to tell everyone we were out. I like the President to be quiet when he is with me and not to be disturbed by the importunities of friends and selfseekers.

We had a quiet dinner alone and then talked until nine o'clock upon many different subjects, largely however, upon psychical phenomena and the all absorbing question of a conscious personality after death. The President is very interested in these matters and takes a sane view of them. He does not lose his judgment in contemplating them, and yet he is broad enough to believe that it is well worth while to have them properly investigated by persons competent to do so.

I told him the progressives in Illinois had complained to me through Chas. R. Crane and Norman Hapgood, that in the early spring when Roger Sullivan's candidacy for the Senate was first mentioned, they had written to him, the President, concerning the matter. After waiting they received a letter from Tumulty saying he would call the matter to his attention. Not hearing from him, they wrote again in about a month, and received the same reply. After they considered enough time had passed they wrote again, and then Tumulty promised to bring the accumulated correspondence to the President's attention.

[1] Gordon Auchincloss, his son-in-law.

They claim that Tumulty failed to do this and that his purpose was to aid Sullivan who is a Catholic, and that there was a general conspiracy among the Catholics, aided by Tumulty, to keep information from the President.

The President said it was true Tumulty did not show him the correspondence, but he undoubtedly did it to save him from an embarrassing situation. If he had seen the correspondence, he would have been compelled to answer it. Not having seen it, he was enabled to get over a difficult situation. His reasoning is not altogether good, for the position Tumulty placed him in by withholding such correspondence is worse than any position that might be created by his having seen and met it. It shows Tumulty has a strong hold on him. It also shows that when he once gives his confidence it is hard to shake it. This I admire very much. The President is a peculiar man, in as much as he does not care for many people. He never seems to want to discuss things with anyone, as far as I know, excepting me. Even his Cabinet bore him with their importunities, and he often complains of them. It is really a defect in his usefulness as an Executive, for the reason that he does not get many side lights on questions. He seldom reads the newspapers and gains his knowledge of public affairs largely from the matters brought to his attention, and his general information is gotten from a cursory glance at the Weekly Press.

However, he is efficient in his manner of working. For instance, when we were discussing his message to the people concerning the Belgian Relief funds he said: "Now let us decide what points are best to cover." He took a telegraph blank having lines on it, and began to take down in shorthand the different points, he making some suggestions and I making others. There were about five points to be covered and he asked me to think if that were all. When we concluded there was nothing more, he called his stenographer and dictated the message in full.[2]

He has one of the best ordered minds I have ever come in contact with, although he is always complaining of forgetfulness. He said last night that he did not see how anyone could write an autobiography from memory. As a matter of fact, they cannot, unless a diary is kept.

At nine o'clock we took a walk from Fifty-third Street to Seventh Avenue and down Seventh to Broadway. We stopped at several places where crowds were collected to hear harangues, and as soon as he was discovered, we would pass along. By the time we reached Herald Square a great throng was following us, consequently we went in the 34th Street door of the Waldorf,

2 It is printed as an addendum in this volume.

went up in the elevator, crossed to the 33rd Street side and went out there, continuing our walk down Fifth Avenue to 26th Street where we took a motor bus back to Fifty-third Street.

The President seemed to enjoy himself thoroughly and said he would give anything if he could get out and be lost in the crowd. I suggested the next time he came I would have some whiskers for him. He thought that a great idea, but later said it would cause a terrible scandal if it were found out. He left me in doubt as to whether he wanted the whiskers or not.

When we reached home he began to tell me how lonely and sad his life was since Mrs. Wilson's death, and he could not help wishing when we were out tonight that someone would kill him. He has told me this before. His eyes were moist when he spoke of not wanting to live longer, and of not being fit to do the work he had in hand. He said he had himself so disciplined that he knew perfectly well that unless someone killed him, he would go on to the end doing the best he could.

He went to bed about half past ten but I remained up until nearly twelve, assorting my correspondence so that I might bring anything of importance to his attention in the morning.

November 15, 1914.

We took breakfast at 9.45, although I had been up long before. After breakfast we discussed public matters for awhile and then went to hear Dr. Jowett[1] at the Fifth Avenue Presbyterian Church. There was a large congregation although it was pouring rain. Dr. Jowett did not preach as well as usual, because he was probably trying too hard to do his best.

After church we motored to Riverdale to lunch with Mr. and Mrs. Cleveland H. Dodge. We left there shortly before four o'clock and motored to the Pennsylvania Station. The President looked well when he left, and seemed to have thoroughly enjoyed his two days diversion.

[1] The Rev. Dr. John Henry Jowett, pastor of the Fifth Avenue Presbyterian Church since 1911.

## To Henry Lee Higginson

My dear Major:     [The White House] November 16, 1914

Your letter of November tenth[1] gave me a good deal of comfort amidst great anxiety. I am heartily glad that you and your partner feel that we down here have been of real assistance in stiffening the courage and backing the efforts of our business men, and if this cotton loan fund can be put through, I shall feel that we are on the high road to a real recovery and regeneration of our business. I feel that it is absolutely necessary to complete that fund and I was greatly pleased the other day when Mr. McAdoo told me you had promised to lend your influential aid.

What you say about aid to the Belgians has a great deal of point in it. I have been trying to find some right way to act in that matter. The real difficulty is the super-sensitiveness of everybody on the other side involved in this calamitous war.

With warm regard,
Cordially and sincerely yours,   Woodrow Wilson

TLS (Letterpress Books, WP, DLC).
  1 H. L. Higginson, Nov. 10, 1914 (two letters), TLS (WP, DLC).

## From William Gibbs McAdoo

Dear Mr. President:          Washington November 16, 1914.

I have the honor to inform you that the twelve Federal Reserve Banks authorized by the Federal Reserve Act approved December 23, 1913, were formally opened for business today. May I take advantage of the opportunity to felicitate you, as well as congratulate you, upon the actual establishment of these banks, which are the result of the great piece of financial legislation with which your name is imperishably associated, and which promises, in my judgment, immeasurable benefits to the American people?
Faithfully yours,   W G McAdoo

TLS (WP, DLC).

## From Robert Russa Moton

My dear Mr. President:        Hampton, Virginia Nov. 16, 1914.

I wish most heartily and sincerely to thank you for your very kind and encouraging letter of November 6th, which was read at our meeting last Thursday night to an audience of between five and six thousand people of whom between a thousand and fifteen hundred were white. Negroes came from all parts of Virginia representing all kinds of organizations among Negroes and, of course, we had the leading white people of Norfolk present, men and women.

I doubt if you realize, Mr. President, how much encouragement and hope your letter gave my people. It undoubtedly encouraged our white friends also in the splendid service they are rendering along the lines of rational co-operation with black people for the highest development of all the people in this State and the South.

Your letter has been copied in several editorials within the past few days, to show your kindly feeling toward Negroes, as contrasted with the very unfortunate incident of Mr. Trotter, and I want to say that the Negroes, generally, do not in any way approve of Mr. Trotter's conduct at the White House. You perhaps don't know that Mr. Trotter was made to serve a jail sentence in Boston some years ago for breaking up a meeting[1] in which Dr. Booker T. Washington was speaking in the interest of race co-operation and encouraging his race, as he has always done, along lines of practical education, and I think the people who selected Mr. Trotter to head a committee to wait on the Chief Executive of the Nation were short-sighted, to say the least.

Again thanking you for your kindness and expressing my own regrets and the regrets of ninety-nine percent of the thoughtful Negroes of this land at Mr. Trotter's attitude and words, I beg to remain, Sir,                    Yours sincerely,   R. R. Moton

TLS (WP, DLC).

[1] About this incident, which took place in 1903, see Stephen R. Fox, *The Guardian of Boston* (New York, 1971), pp. 49-58.


## Remarks at a Press Conference

November 17, 1914

What are the facts in Mexico, Mr. President?

I don't know anything more than I take it for granted you already know. We have understood that General Carranza is willing to retire on the terms named, but we haven't heard directly from him, of course, and are merely receiving the reports that are got in the northern part of Mexico.

Do you prefer to hear from him directly?

I don't expect to hear from him directly.

Is there any intimation, Mr. President, with regard to the information on Villa?

None that hasn't come direct to you.

So that, so far as you know, there hasn't been any agreement between Carranza and Villa, though the dispatches would seem to indicate that there had been, not between them but each of them communicating with the new provisional president[1]—whatever his name is, I can't pronounce it. Has the new provisional president asked this government to recognize him? Do you so regard that letter, that telegram?

No. There's no suggestion of that in that message.

Well then, Mr. President, under the circumstances, it is not quite clear, is it, as to whom we will turn over the city of Veracruz?

No. But of course that is one situation not our responsibility, now that we have the promises that nobody will be molested and shouldn't be.

You don't look for a condition of anarchy, then, even though—

No. No, sir. You see, as a matter of fact, as we understand it, the men who were formerly in civil office are still there. They can merely resume their functions.

The customs which we have collected will remain in our custody?

Until there is some authority to turn them over to.

There is one story that they would be shipped to France?

No. They will be shipped to the Mexican government, when there is one. You see, one of the things we wanted assurance about was that the customs which we have collected wouldn't be collected all over again.

That assurance has been given?

Yes, that assurance has been given.

Mr. President, have you replied to the telegram of the new provisional president?

No. That was, as a matter of fact, addressed to the Secretary of State, conveying these assurances to the— . . .

Mr. President, have you taken up yet the question of appointing a committee to have charge of arranging Belgian relief?

I am taking it up before rejecting it. I have been urged to name some person through whom they might communicate with one another, or something of that sort. I haven't entirely rejected that idea. You see, there are a good many groups, and so forth, and it may be necessary to do something to facilitate our common action, but what that is hasn't yet been known. . . .

Mr. President, has Japan expressed any uneasiness on account of the election of legislators in San Francisco, California, who are reputed to be hostile to their aspirations here?

No. Some apprehension was expressed during the campaign because of the apparent effort to revive the land issue out there, but I could not follow the thing very carefully in any one place, but it seems that it has subsided. That attempt to revive that agitation subsided. . . .

Mr. President, has the cotton situation improved in recent weeks?
    I was reading in this morning's papers that conditions in
    the cotton exchanges, which opened yesterday, were very
    encouraging; some seven and three quarters and some
    figures still over that. Eight and a fraction. The paper stated
    that that was quite as good as had often happened in normal
    times. I mean, it was no wise—it had often happened in
    normal times.
Well, do you receive any direct reports from the situation, as to
whether the situation has improved?
    I haven't received anything one way or the other.
You don't know whether Mr. Henry, or those who are as in-
terested, I should say, as he is, intends to renew the agitation?
    I don't know anything about that.
There is an intimation that they might insist upon the preferen-
tial position for their bill, thereby threatening some of the appro-
priation measures?
    That is not in their hands. That is in the hands of the House
    of Representatives itself.
Yes, but they are part of the House.
    We will have to find out how big a part.
Is there anything new on the Colorado situation?
    No, nothing at all.

JRT transcript (CLSsh, C. L. Swem Coll., NjP).
    [1] Eulalio Gutiérrez, elected Provisional President by the Aguascalientes Con-
vention on November 1. After he had announced his assumption of power on
November 13, Bryan had sent warm congratulations, adding: "This Government . . . hopes that he will do everything in his power to bring about lasting
peace in Mexico." WJB to L. J. Canova, Nov. 16, 1914, *FR 1914*, p. 622. Gutiérrez's telegram of November 13 is printed in *ibid.*, pp. 620-21.


## To William Gibbs McAdoo[1]

My dear Mr. Secretary:    The White House November 17, 1914

    I warmly appreciate your letter of yesterday, for I share your
feeling entirely about the significance of the opening of the Federal Reserve Banks for business.
    I do not know that any special credit belongs to me for the
part I was privileged to play in the establishment of this new
system of which we confidently hope so much; in it the labor and

    [1] In drafting this letter, which was widely circulated as a campaign docu-
ment, Wilson relied heavily upon the outline suggested by Tumulty in a long
memorandum, "Message of the President" (T memorandum, C. L. Swem Coll.,
NjP).
    Wilson wrote a handwritten and shorthand outline and then a draft in his
own shorthand (both documents are in WP, DLC). He then dictated his shorthand draft to Swem. Swem's transcript is in the C. L. Swem Coll., NjP.

knowledge and forethought and practical experience and sagacity of many men are embodied who have cooperated with unusual wisdom and admirable public spirit. None of them, I am sure, will be jealous of the distribution of the praise for the great piece of legislation upon which the new system rests; they will only rejoice unselfishly to see the thing accomplished upon which they had set their hearts.

It has been accomplished and its accomplishment is of the deepest significance, both because of the things it has done away with and because of the things it has supplied that the country lacked and had long needed. It has done away with agitation and suspicion, because it has done away with certain fundamental wrongs. It has supplied means of accommodation in the business world and an instrumentality by which the interests of all, without regard to class, may readily be served.

We have only to look back ten years or so to realize the deep perplexities and dangerous ill-humors out of which we have now at last issued, as if from a bewildering fog, a noxious miasma. Ten or twelve years ago the country was torn and excited by an agitation which shook the very foundations of her political life, brought her business ideals into question, condemned her social standards, denied the honesty of her men of affairs, the integrity of her economic processes, the morality and good faith of many of the things which her law sustained. Those who had power, whether in business or in politics, were almost universally looked upon with suspicion and little attempt was made to distinguish the just from the unjust. They in their turn seemed to distrust the people and to wish to limit their control. There was an ominous antagonism between classes. Capital and labor were in sharp conflict without prospect of accommodation between them. Interests harshly clashed which should have cooperated.

This was not merely the work of irresponsible agitators. There were real wrongs which cried out to be righted, and fearless men had called attention to them, demanding that they be dealt with by law. We were living under a tariff which had been purposely contrived to confer private favors upon those who were cooperating to keep the party that originated it in power; and in that all too fertile soil all the bad, interlaced growth and jungle of monopoly had sprung up. Credit, the very life of trade, the very air men must breathe if they would meet their opportunities, was too largely in the control of the same small groups who had planted and cultivated monopoly. The control of all big business, and by consequence of all little business, too, was for the most part potentially, if not actually, in their hands.

And the thing stood so until the Democratic party came into power last year. The legislation of the past year and a half has in very large measure done away with these things. With their correction, suspicion and ill-will will pass away. For not only have these things been righted, but new things have been put into action which are sure to prove the instruments of a new life, in which the mists and distempers which have so embarrassed us will be cleared away; the wrongs and misunderstandings corrected which have brought distrust upon so many honest men unjustly. That is the main ground of my own satisfaction.

The tariff has been recast with a view to supporting the government rather than supporting the favored beneficiaries of the government. A system of banking and currency issues has been created which puts credit within the reach of every man who can show a going business; and the supervision and control of the system is in the hands of a responsible agency of the government itself. A trade tribunal has been created in which those who attempt unjust and oppressive practices in business can be brought to book. Labor has been made something else in the view of the law than a mere mercantile commodity, something human and linked with the privileges of life itself. The soil has everywhere been laid bare out of which monopoly is slowly to be eradicated. And undoubtedly the means by which credit has been set free is at the heart of all these things, is the keypiece of the whole structure.

This is the more significant because of its opportuneness. It is brought to its final accomplishment just as it is most imperatively needed. The war which has involved the whole of the heart of Europe has made it necessary that the United States should mobilize its resources in the most effective way possible and make her credit and her usefulness good for the service of the whole world. It has created, too, special difficulties, peculiar situations, to be dealt with, like the great embarrassment in selling our immense cotton crop, which all the world needs but against which, for the time being, the markets of the world are in danger of being artificially shut. That situation the bankers of the country are meeting so far as possible in a business-like fashion and in the spirit of the new time which is opening before us. The railroads of the country are almost as much affected, not so much because their business is curtailed as because their credit is called in question by doubt as to their earning capacity.[2]

[2] Here Wilson deleted the following in his dictated draft: "Foreign holders of their securities ⟨will⟩ may wish to sell what they hold at once, especially in these new and pressing circumstances, if it cannot be made clear to them that the earnings of the railroads will be adequate; and means ⟨must⟩ should be found to take care of that."

There is no other interest so central to the business welfare of the country as this. No doubt in the light of the new day, with its new understandings, the problems of the railroads will also be met and dealt with in a spirit of candor and justice.[3]

For the future is clear and bright with promise of the best things. While there was agitation and suspicion and distrust and bitter complaint of wrong, groups and classes were at war with one another, did not see that their interests were common and suffered only when separated and brought into conflict. Fundamental wrongs once righted, as they may now easily and quickly be, all difference will clear away. We are all in the same boat, though apparently we had forgotten it. We now know the port for which we are bound. We have, and shall have more and more as our new understandings ripen, a common discipline of patriotic purpose. We shall advance, and advance together, with a new spirit, a new enthusiasm, a new cordiality of spirited co-operation. It is an inspiring prospect. Our task is henceforth to work, not for any single interest, but for all the interests of the country as a united whole.

The future will be very different from the past, which we shall presently look back upon, I venture to say, as if upon a bad dream. The future will be different in action and different in spirit, a time of healing because a time of just dealing and co-operation between men made equal before the law in fact as well as in name. I am speaking of this because the new banking system seems to me to symbolize all of it. The opening of the Federal Reserve Banks seems to me to be the principal agency we have created for the emancipation we seek. The sixteenth of November, 1914, will be notable as marking the time when we were best able to realize just what had happened.

In the anxious times through which we have been passing you have, my dear Mr. Secretary, been able to do many noteworthy things to strengthen and facilitate the business operations of the country. Henceforth you have a new instrument at hand which will render many parts of your task easy. I heartily congratulate you upon the part you yourself have played in its conception and creation, and upon the successful completion of the difficult work of organization. A new day has dawned for the beloved country whose lasting prosperity and happiness we so earnestly desire.

Cordially and faithfully yours,    Woodrow Wilson

TLS (W. G. McAdoo Papers, DLC).
[3] Wilson wrote this sentence in his shorthand and dictated drafts as follows: "No doubt in the light of the new day, with its new understandings and new processes, public officials and men of business alike will see to it that the foundations are made secure here as elsewhere."

# From William Gibbs McAdoo

PERSONAL.

Dear "Governor":          Washington November 17, 1914.

Just a line to tell you that the cotton loan plan was consummated successfully this afternoon. I am making a public statement about it for tomorrow morning's papers.

Affectionately yours,   W G McAdoo

TLS (WP, DLC).

# Oswald Garrison Villard to Joseph Patrick Tumulty

Dear Mr. Tumulty:          New York November 17, 1914.

I hope you and the President will not overlook the enclosed editorials.[1] I cannot tell you what a pity it seems to me that an Administration so noble in its feeling for the under-dog and in every other respect, cannot do simple justice when it comes to the color line. May I not ask that you will at least submit our[2] and The World's[3] editorial to the President?

Sincerely yours,   Oswald Garrison Villard.

P.S. I enclose a paragraph in today's *Evening Post*[4] and want to congratulate you on the admirable way the army promotions are being made. You will recall our conversation, perhaps, early in the Adminstration; nothing can be better, I think, than what has already been done.   O.G.V.

TLS (WP, DLC).
    [1] Some of them are missing.
    [2] "The President and Segregation," New York *Evening Post*, Nov. 13, 1914. While not condoning William Monroe Trotter's "bad manners" during his interview with Wilson, the editorial declared that the President should make allowances for Trotter because of the "genuine wrongs" of which he complained. The Wilson administration had not merely tolerated but had drawn the color line where it had not previously existed. The basic problem, it continued, was Wilson's inability to put himself in the other fellow's place. Wilson's vision and imagination left him when it came to "the disfranchisement of women and to permitting his subordinates to inflict indignities upon American citizens in the immediate vicinity of the White House." As for Wilson's complaint that Trotter was indulging in "political blackmail" by threatening that blacks would henceforth vote Republican, the editorial said that this was "the time-honored American way of showing disapproval of an elective official's conduct." It was impossible to keep the problem out of politics. Blacks and whites had worked side by side in federal offices without friction for fifty years. "The Wilson Administration," the editorial concluded, "went out of its way to create the issue it now deplores, and cannot see its way clear to admitting its mistake and reverting to the only defensible position of absolute equality in the Government Service."
    [3] "No Jim-Crow Government," New York *World*, Nov. 13, 1914. "No President ever suffered more from the foolish indiscretions of members of his Cabinet than has Mr. Wilson," the editorial began. The "unfortunate interview" with Trotter was a prime example of this. "The President," it continued, "should

have foreseen this unfortunate issue when Mr. McAdoo and Mr. Burleson were carrying their color-line theories into democratic government." About Wilson's argument that segregation had been instituted to avoid friction between the races, the editorial commented that the President had failed to explain "why no such rule had been considered necessary until Mr. Burleson and Mr. McAdoo got into the Cabinet." Abandoning sarcasm, the editorial then went on:

"The President thinks that this is not a political question, but he is wrong. Anything that is unjust, discriminating and un-American in government is certain to be a political question. Servants of the United States Government are servants of the United States Government, regardless of race or color. . . . Whether the President thinks so or not, the segregation rule was promulgated as a deliberate discrimination against negro employees. Worse still, it is a small, mean, petty discrimination, and Mr. Wilson ought to have set his heel upon this presumptuous Jim-Crow government the moment it was established. He ought to set his heel upon it now. It is a reproach to his Administration and to the great political principles which he represents."

4 This brief, untitled editorial praised Wilson and Secretary of War Garrison for their "excellent" policy of promoting army officers by merit, citing a number of recently announced promotions as examples.


## To Robert Russa Moton

My dear Major Moton:    [The White House] November 18, 1914

Your letter of November sixteenth has gratified me very much indeed. The admirable spirit it breathes and the good judgment it so clearly indicates with regard to the best lines of development for our negro fellow-citizens excites my sincere admiration and approval. It is particularly delightful to me that my real temper and disposition in matters of this sort should be understood by those who themselves have the interests of the negro people most at heart, and I shall be happy at any time to render such assistance as I can in furthering the development to which you are devoting yourself.

Sincerely yours,    Woodrow Wilson

TLS (Letterpress Books, WP, DLC).


## To Mary M. Childs[1]

Personal.

My dear Miss Childs:    [The White House] November 18, 1914

I have received your letter of November thirteenth[2] and read it with genuine appreciation. I thank you sincerely for all that it contains that concerns myself.

You may be sure that I am deeply impressed with the movement for woman suffrage, but I have thought with you that it could best be worked out, and most solidly and conclusively, if developed from state to state, under the national constitution as it now stands, rather than by attempting a sweeping change in the fundamental law of the nation itself. I think such a change would be running too far and too fast ahead of the general public opinion of the country.

          Cordially and sincerely yours,   Woodrow Wilson

TLS (Letterpress Books, WP, DLC).
  1 Clerk in the Forest Service, Department of Agriculture.
  2 Mary M. Childs to WW, Nov. 13, 1914, TLS (WP, DLC).

## To Mary Eloise Hoyt

Dear Cousin,         The White House 18 November, 1914.

    Thank you with all my heart for your letter of the sixth.[1] You may be sure it was as great a pleasure to me to catch that little glimpse of you all as it was to you to see us.[2] And I would not take anything for the little pictures you give me of my dear one in the little memories that come back to you of times when you were with her. That picture of her on her knees at Assisi will live in my memory always!

    I have been thinking a great deal about your suggestion of taking some poor Belgian refugee to live with you. So far as the passage money is concerned, I would be happy to supply that, and think it a privilege to do so; but I am not sure of yourselves. The house is very small; the association would be very close and intimate; it would be all but impossible to make sure beforehand what sort of a person you were getting; and yet the arrangement once made would be practically irrevocable. Please think it over in very cold blood, and then count on me to help if you decide to make the venture. After all, if the experiment failed because of the character of the refugee, it would be as bad for her as for you, and as irremediable. One has to be wise as well as kind,—cannot be kind unless also wise.

    I cannot write letters. I can only send messages long enough to show with what affection I am thinking of you all, and how grateful I am for your letters.

          Affectionately Yours,   Woodrow Wilson

WWT fragment (received from W. D. Hoyt, Jr.); TCL (RSB Coll., DLC).
  1 Mary E. Hoyt to WW, Nov. 6, 1914, ALS (WP, DLC).
  2 Wilson had visited Mary and Florence Hoyt in Baltimore on November 1.

## From Samuel Gompers

Sir:         Philadelphia, Pa. Nov. 18, 1914.

    At the Thirty-fourth annual convention of the American Federation of Labor, held in the city of Philadelphia, Pa., beginning November 9, a resolution was introduced by the representatives of the coal and metalliferous miners of America, which was referred to the Committee on Executive Council's report, and which committee gave the subject matter recited and declared in the preambles and resolution the most thorough investigation and study during the past eight days, and at this day's session of the convention of the American Federation of Labor the committee recommended the adoption of the preambles and resolution above referred to.

After a thorough discussion of the entire subject matter in all its phases, the preambles and resolution and the committee's comment thereon were adopted by a unanimous vote. Copy of the preambles and resolution, as well as the committee's comment as adopted by the convention, is herein enclosed.[1]

It is the earnest hope of the American Federation of Labor that the subjects matter herein transmitted to you may receive your early, serious and sympathetic consideration and action.

We have the honor, Sir, to remain,

Yours very truly,

Saml. Gompers.

President. American Federation of Labor.

Attest:

Frank Morrison

Secretary.

American Federation of Labor.

TLS (WP, DLC).

[1] The resolutions (T MS, WP, DLC) reviewed the bitter coal strike in Colorado and Wilson's futile efforts for a settlement. They concluded by urging the President to seize the coal mines and operate them "in the interest of the people" until such time as the "civil and political rights of the people" were established, if the operators continued their unlawful refusal to accept the Wilson Plan.

## From Franklin Knight Lane, with Enclosure

Dear Mr. President:                Washington November 18, 1914.

Here are some facts regarding Mr. Hoover which I have gained from Judge Curtis H. Lindley,[1] whom you know.

Cordially yours,    Franklin K Lane

TLS (WP, DLC).

[1] Curtis Holbrook Lindley, lawyer of San Francisco, noted authority on mining law, and a close friend of Herbert Hoover.

E  N  C  L  O  S  U  R  E

### HERBERT C. HOOVER.

About 38 years of age.

Native of the State of Iowa (I think). Went to California when quite young. Entered Stanford University, worked his way through and graduated as Mining Engineer. Married Miss Lon [Lou] Henry of Monterey, California, who also graduated from Stanford as a Mining Engineer, with her prospective husband.

Mr. Hoover has been engaged in the practice of his profession in almost every section of the world. He had charge of the Imperial Mines of China, and with his wife was in Tien Tsin at the time of the Boxer Rebellion. There is probably not a mining engineer in the world with larger experience and higher connections. He is the managing director of the largest group of mines in the world—Russia—and identified with some of the greatest operations in the mining fields.

He and Mrs. Hoover have published a translation of Agricola's famous De Re Nutallica,[1] a magnificent contribution to mining and metallurgical literature, and for which the American Society of Mining and Metallurgy presented a medal to the translators at a public gathering in the City of New York.

Mr. Hoover is now the head of the American Belgian Relief Committee in London. He was also the leading spirit and organizer of relief for American refugees in London and on the continent at the outbreak of the war.

Mrs. Hoover recently visited California and through her instrumentality and initiative has aroused the public sympathy to such a degree that California's citizens have provided a shipload of provisions, chartered the American ship "Cameno" which sails for Rotterdam December 1, to relieve the starving non-combatants in Belgium.

Mrs. Hoover has also organized the California branch of a National Committee of Mercy, of which branch she is the honorary chairman and Mrs. Henry Payot is acting president. This committee has secured and is securing monthly contributions to last during the period of the war, and is for distribution to the suffering of all the belligerents, regardless of nationality.

Mr. Hoover was last year elected Trustee of the Stanford University. There is no American sojourning abroad who has a higher financial, mining or social status than Mr. Herbert C. Hoover.

He is wealthy.

T MS (WP, DLC).
[1] Georgius Agricola [Georg Bauer (1494-1555)], *De re metallica*, trans. Herbert Clark Hoover and Lou Henry Hoover (London, 1912).

## From Dudley Field Malone

Personal and Confidential.

Dear Mr. President:            New York November 19, 1914.

After discussing for five hours last night with some of your friends at the Catholic University in Washington the matters which we discussed yesterday morning,[1] I respectfully suggest that you give no further consideration to the idea of writing the letter which we spoke about.

I know this entire situation can be straightened out and, of course, when the truth is known the circumstances will redound to your lasting reputation and the honor of this administration. I have never asked before that you leave any matter exclusively in my charge, but I do most sincerely ask you to let me handle this entire situation quietly and privately, and with the right to consult with you briefly at such times as may be necessary to get your aid and to keep you informed.

You looked so tired yesterday, I do hope you will make it a rule for at least the next few weeks to get away for three days at the end of each week for a real rest.

Yours most faithfully,    Dudley Field Malone

TLS (WP, DLC).
[1] Criticism by American Roman Catholic leaders of the administration's Mexican policy.


## From Jacob Henry Schiff

Dear Mr. President:            New York, Nov. 19, 1914.

Will you permit me to write you on a matter which has recently considerably occupied my mind.

It is generally known—and has, no doubt, also come to your attention—that large quantities of ammunition are being purchased in this country by the belligerents in the European war and shipped abroad. This can, no doubt, not be prevented under the law, but nevertheless I am quite convinced that the furnishing of the weapons with which this terrible slaughter now going on in Europe is being carried on, by America, is immoral and obnoxious to a large majority of our people.

Shortly after the outbreak of the war, you made it known that your administration is opposed to the furnishing of funds, for war purposes, to the belligerents, though there is nothing against this in our laws. This was right and proper, and your action was widely acclaimed and willingly followed by private bankers and banks, except in one noted instance.

Is it not right that the furnishing of the weapons with which many thousands engaged in this terrible and awful conflict are killed and maimed, is perhaps more obnoxious and more immoral than if any financing were done in the United States for these nations, to which, quite correctly, objection has already been made?

I am very certain that this has likely already occurred to you, and will you not allow me to respectfully suggest that you make a public utterance—either by proclamation, if in your own wisdom you should feel this justified, or in any other manner which may commend itself to you—calling upon manufacturers of weapons and ammunition to stop selling their wares to the European belligerents or to their agents. I am sure, if this could be brought about, it would not only be an act of humanity, but it would, to some extent at least, shorten the conflict, the end of which can not now be foreseen.

It is true, we give freely to the Red Cross and other relief funds, but at the same time we furnish the means through which the terrible wounds, which we seek to help to heal, become inflicted.

Believe me, Mr. President, with assurances of high esteem,
Yours most faithfully,   Jacob H. Schiff

TLS (WP, DLC).


## From Elias Milton Ammons

Sir:          Denver   November Nineteen Nineteen Fourteen.

I found your letter upon my return from Madison.

I am convinced that my suggestion as to the manner of removal of the federal troops was not made clear to you. I send you, under separate cover, a map marked with blue and red lines showing the situation of the federal troops in Colorado. You will note that they are strung out at intervals for a distance of more than four hundred miles. The Routt County situation at Oak Creek is in no way connected physically with any of the others and the same is true of the field just north of Denver in the Boulder district. While the Fremont County district is close to the others, we found as a practical matter, that it is disconnected from the two southern counties, Los Animas and Huerfano, which are largely one so far as this strike is concerned.

You will see, therefore, there need be no conflict of authority in the removal of these troops in the manner suggested. If those in Oak Creek are withdrawn it will affect no other district. The same thing is true of the field north of Denver, and I am quite confident a similar condition exists as to Fremont County.

One special reason for suggesting the troops be taken out in the order mentioned is that there would be less danger of a general outbreak and greater safety in handling the situation than if they were withdrawn from all places simultaneously. I might refer to the fact that the relationship between the federal and state troops, at the time of the arrival of the federal troops, was much closer and without any divided authority or difficulty of dual jurisdiction, than that which I am suggesting at the present time.

I have taken up this matter with Adjutant General Chase, Senator Thomas and Attorney General Farrar and they agree with me fully in this conclusion. I assure you there will be no embarrassment if the Federal Troops are withdrawn as I have indicated.

If the plan proposed by us is accepted the withdrawal of the federal troops can begin at any time, provided I have reasonable notice in order that I may be prepared as the necessities of each district require. I suggest that all the troops can be safely withdrawn by the first to the tenth of December. I feel certain from past experience that many of the threats made of destroying the mines and their employes in case the federal troops are removed are idle. In this connection I may say that my reports show less drilling than before the election, which very pronouncedly declared against further lawlessness.

One problem to which I wish to call your attention is the condition where the mine owners and their guards have been disarmed, whereas the strikers still retain their guns, hidden handy enough to be available at any time. I would appreciate it if you would indicate to me what policy would be pursued in relation to retaining or returning the arms taken from the management of the mines if the complete disarmament of strikers is not to be effected.

It is becoming generally understood that my successor will follow the same general policy of law enforcement pursued by me. He was not only elected on public declarations of this kind made by himself during the campaign but has, since the election, announced that course.

Yours sincerely,   E M Ammons

TLS (WP, DLC).

# From Hugo Münsterberg

Cambridge, Massachusetts,
Dear Mr. President: November 19, 1914.

A few days ago I wrote to you from New York[1] in reply to your very kind letter of November 10th that I begged to postpone my reply until I reached my desk in Cambridge. Now after my return I indeed ask your permission to enter into some detail with regard to the neutrality question. But let me assure you beforehand that I interpret your inquiry as referring exclusively to the views which are expressed to me by American citizens who sympathize with the German cause or who are disturbed by the vehement hostility to Germany on the part of the American press.

My remarks refer in no way to the views of official Germany. Throughout my correspondence with officials in Berlin and in my conversations with men like Bernstorff, Hatzfeld,[2] Dernburg and so on, the neutrality question has seldom been touched, as from the day of your declaration they were fully convinced of your firm intention to resist any official violation. I never heard a word of complaint from an official source. But as I said in my recent letter the views of the American voters are entirely different. I myself abstain from any judgment, but can say that the points which I want to bring before you are selected because they are the ones which are repeated continually in the circles of German sympathizers. They have most deeply influenced the masses of voters and have led them to the belief that the State Department subordinates its decisions to the wishes of England. Hence the political upheaval, and the firm decision of the hyphenated vote to turn away from an administration to which it would otherwise be bound by many ties. Each matter in itself seems not momentous; yet it is the summation of minor complaints which has often a psychologically stronger effect than one great cause of suffering.

Let me emphasize three points to which my correspondents refer most frequently. First, all cables sent by and received by wire pass uncensored, while all wireless news is censored. This reacts against Germany, because England sends all her news by cable, whereas Germany alone uses the wireless. The matter is of grave importance. Second, the policy of the administration with regard to the holding up, detaining and searching of Germans and Austrians from neutral and American vessels is a

---

[1] H. Münsterberg to WW, Nov. 13, 1914, TLS (WP, DLC).
[2] Hermann, Prince von Hatzfeldt-Trachenberg, second counselor of the German Embassy in Washington.

reversal of the American policy established in 1812. It has excited no end of bitterness. Third, the United States permitted the violation by England of the Hague Convention and international law in connection with conditional and unconditional contraband. The United States, for instance, has not protested against the transference of copper from the conditional to the absolute list, although on former occasions the United States has taken a spirited stand against onesided interpretations of international agreements. In 1812, in the Russian Japanese War, and in the Boer War the United States insisted that a neutral nation has the right to send conditional as well as unconditional contraband to neutral nations without permitting an inquiry into its ultimate destination. She insisted that the consignee must be accepted in good faith. The United States, moreover, insisted that conditional contraband can be sent in neutral or in American bottoms even to belligerent nations, provided it was not consigned to the government, the military or naval authorities or to any contractors known to represent the belligerent government. By permitting this new interpretation the United States practically supports the starving out policy of the Allies. The nation by reversing its own policy thus seriously handicaps Germany and Austria in their fight for existence.

As I said, I emphasize these three points, because they return most frequently, but numberless similar matters contribute to the general impression. I think that the feeling of the Germans and Irish is correctly expressed in the following remarks of the editor of the "Fatherland."[3] He writes:

"We permit English warships to nose about in our harbors; we permit them to search our ships. In 1812 we went to war for smaller reasons. We raise no protest when England contemptuously disregards our citizenship papers. We even permit her to seize our cargoes of copper in her hope of monopolizing eventually our entire copper trade. She permits us to export dynamite, but she does not permit us to export oil, even to neutral nations. In other words England, while fighting Germany on the field of battle, is waging war on the United States commercially. She makes it impossible for us to profit by the war for she strangles our trade, except for such contraband as she and her allies need. It is time to reassert our declaration of independence. German-American citizens feel, rightly or wrongly, that the administration is hostile to them, because

[3] George Sylvester Viereck, German-born journalist and author of New York, another key figure in the German propaganda effort.

its interpretation of neutrality has been at all points disadvantageous to Germany."[4]

Many of the complaints refer more to the unfriendly spirit
than to the actual violation of the law. Here above all belongs
the unlimited sale of ammunition to the belligerents. The
administration originally advised Mr. Morgan that the making
of loans to the nations at war would not be looked upon with
favor by the President, and Mr. Morgan cancelled the plans. This
attitude has been given up; the State Department has emphasized
that money and arms may be sold to the belligerents, while
evidently the friends of peace had firmly hoped that the President would denounce the sale of ammunition or any other sale
which would be likely to prolong the war. Indeed our friends
of peace must regret this encouraging attitude with reference
to the sale of agencies of destruction, but the friends of Germany cannot forget that this sympathetic attitude of the State
Department under the conditions which objectively exist is not
only helpful to the prolongation of the war, but helpful exclusively to the Allies against Central Europe. The favorite interpretation of the Germans is even that the government makes itself
a party to the violation of neutrality by giving clearance papers
to vessels loaded with war material for England and France. They
say, moreover, that the President as Commander-in-Chief of the
Army and Navy could and did restrain the shipment of war
material into Mexico. Hence he has the same power to restrain
the shipment of such material to Europe.

Let me quote this also from a letter:

"As I read President Madison's message to congress of
January 1st, 1812, I find that the Wilson administration has
practically subscribed to conditions which in that early stage
of our history were considered an intolerable insult to our
existence as an independent nation. The blood of every man
of German descent must boil with indignation and resentment
on reading how even Americanborn citizens are arrested
aboard neutral vessels and in British ports, their passports
ignored, confined in jails and basely humiliated because they
bear German names or have German physical characteristics.
Read the private letter of Mr. J. O. Bennett to the Managing
Editor of the Chicago Tribune, which introduces a symposium
of proGerman essays by native American scholars in the new
pamphlet 'Germany's Just Cause.' Read the despatch of James
T. Archibald to the New York World of October 15th, in

---

[4] "The Judgment of the People in the Congressional Elections," *The Fatherland*, I (Nov. 18, 1914), 8.

which he says: 'Americans are imprisoned, although carrying passports and neutral ships captured.' Similar despatches have been sent to the Associated Press, and similar cases are reported in private letters finding their way into print. The mail of American citizens doing business in London has been rifled by Scotland Yard detectives, according to Mr. Bennett and his wife, and American correspondents threatened with arrest and worse for sending news favorable to Germany to American papers.

The State Department has demanded to know of the Turkish government whether it sanctions Turkish threats to Englishmen and Frenchmen, but it is manifesting a supreme indifference to the thousands of noncombatants of German and Austrian connection languishing in English and French concentration camps who are being judicially murdered, despite the fact that the interests of these nations are in the hands of the United States. I refer you to a remarkable article of Herbert Corey in the New York Globe for a graphic description of the barbarous hardships imposed on noncombatants confined in one English concentration camp. We protested against these conditions when they obtained in Cuba under Weyler, and we are preparing to protest to Turkey before anyone has been hurt, but we tolerate this barbarism when its victims are Germans and Austrians.

It seems so obvious that the administration is closing its eyes to all manner of expedients evasive of the laws of nations and of strict neutrality as they affect the Allies that the German-American element is rapidly conceiving an ineradicable spite against the administration. This element is usually submissive, but it is thoroughly aroused now and does not intend to be treated as a negligible factor in American political life."

From many sides very naturally much complaint is raised against the treatment of American mail on Dutch and other neutral steamers. Since the German government has published the official reply which it received from the Dutch government saying that England has indeed repeatedly destroyed the mail on board of Dutch steamers this case too is removed from mere newspaper gossip. I myself, like hundreds of thousands of others, have not sent a single letter to Germany in the last three months otherwise than by sending it under cover to friends in Holland, Norway or Italy. This situation is acknowledged as contrary to international law; and yet again America is evidently submitting to the whims of England.

Other letters complain much of the in itself small point that

Great Britain ships her own war material and soldiers across the territory of the United States, for the Canadian Pacific, upon which troops and ammunition were shipped to Halifax, passes through the state of Maine. Many are indignant about the Honolulu incident.[5] Others protest against America's serving the interests of England by interfering with possible wireless stations in Mexico and South America. In the last few days the new arrangement as to the coaling of warships in the Panama Zone is the centre of attack, as it is evident that England and France are favored by it, as they have colonies in the neighborhood, while Germany is again put at a disadvantage. I could go on with such details without end. They all contribute to the one general impression that the administration favors the Allies, partly by positive acts of interpretation, decision and interference, partly by submitting silently to English acts hostile to the anti-English belligerents.

Finally I beg for permission to send you as material which may not have reached your office as yet an English translation of an article in the semi-official "North German Gazette" in Berlin, which appeared on October 25th, 1914.[6] It stands, of course, only indirectly in relation to the content of my letter, as this is a complaint of official Germany against England. But since probably in a few days this complaint will become known through the German-American newspapers and since it will strongly reenforce the feeling that England's arbitrary actions on the ocean ought to awake a protest from America in the interest of international commerce, the content of this Berlin article will surely soon be added to the list of German-American complaints. It therefore seems perhaps not unfit to enclose here the translation.

Very respectfully yours,   Hugo Münsterberg

TLS (WP, DLC).
  [5] See "Note No. 7. The Honolulu Incident," in Robert Lansing's memorandum on Münsterberg's letter, printed as an Enclosure with RL to WW, Dec. 9, 1914.
  [6] This enclosure not printed.


## To Samuel Gompers

[The White House]

My dear Mr. Gompers:                 November 20, 1914

I have your letter of the eighteenth and have read its contents and enclosures with a great deal of interest.

I do not wonder that the Federation should have discussed so carefully the perplexing and distressing situation in Colorado or that it should have suggested unusual means of settling the difficulties there. But I have had the law very carefully looked into and am entirely without authority to do what the resolutions suggest. I have discussed the matter very thoroughly with the Secretary of Labor.

We are still not without hope that we may find a way to relieve the situation in some degree.

Sincerely yours,   Woodrow Wilson

TLS (Letterpress Books, WP, DLC).

## To Franklin Knight Lane

My dear Lane:              [The White House] November 20, 1914

Thank you sincerely for what you sent me about Mr. Hoover. It is certainly most interesting and satisfactory.

Faithfully yours,   Woodrow Wilson

TLS (Letterpress Books, WP, DLC).

## From Jessie Woodrow Wilson Sayre

[Williamstown, Mass.]

Dearest, sweetest Father,              November 20th, 1914

The Springfield Republican, a paper *you* recommend, says today that you are coming here for Thanksgiving. Of course we don't believe *any* paper, but it gives me an excuse for asking you again. Oh if you only could, it would be such a blessing on us and on our home! And if you could get here for Wednesday evening, our first wedding anniversary, our joy would be complete, as complete as possible with one so necessary for our happiness not with us in person. We know she is with us in spirit and you would be, too, father darling, even if you stay in Washington but to have you under our roof and at our board would make us so wonderfully thankful that we must beg you to come. But, darling father, you know we wouldn't ask you to do one little thing that means extra fatigue or strain, and so we will understand perfectly whatever you decide to do. We only want you to know how we *want* you.

The Garfields are more than anxious to stow away all extra people so you and Cousin Helen, Margaret and Uncle Stock and the Doctor all will be welcome and find room in plenty.

If you can't come Wednesday, too, we will be more than grateful for Thanksgiving Day and after.

With a whole overflowing heartful of love

from your adoring daughter   Jessie

I am sure people would let you be quiet here. They have been thoughtful to me in many ways.

ALS (WP, DLC).


## To Martha Berry

My dear Miss Berry:          [The White House] November 21, 1914

Thank you sincerely for your kindness in sending me the pictures of the young ladies who carried the beautiful flowers to Mrs. Wilson's grave. Will you not let me express at the same time my very deep interest in the school and in all that concerns it? Mrs. Wilson had its welfare very much at heart and, therefore, it touches me very deeply that the children of the school should think of her as of a true friend who is gone.

I am glad to find the fame of the school spreading rapidly in this part of the country and hope that as it is better known it will be more and more generously supported.

Cordially and sincerely yours,   Woodrow Wilson

TLS (Letterpress Books, WP, DLC).


## To Araminta Arabella Cooper Kern[1]

My dear Mrs. Kern:          [The White House] November 21, 1914

Thank you very warmly indeed for your letter.[2] I was earnestly hoping for news of John Junior and am delighted that the news is so reassuring. Please give him my love and tell him that I think of him very often and am so glad that the operation is over and everything has gone so well.

Cordially and sincerely yours,   Woodrow Wilson

TLS (Letterpress Books, WP, DLC).
  [1] Wife of Senator John Worth Kern of Indiana.
  [2] It is missing.


## From Frederic Clemson Howe

Ellis Island, New York Harbor, N. Y.
My dear Mr. President:                    November 21, 1914.

I feel that the Democratic party should fall heir to the group of socially minded men and women who have been the heart and brain of the Progressive party. That, however, is really secondary to the need of a comprehensive social and industrial programme both national and local, such as Germany and Great Britain have developed in recent years. This programme might include:

1. Extension of social insurance, for accident, sickness, old age, and out of work.

2. Nation wide employment agencies or labor exchanges, clearing from a central office.

3. Wandering artisans' homes or lodging houses which might be identified with the immigration stations.

4. An insurance and pension scheme for Federal employees.

5. Land credit banks, measures for which are now pending in Congress.

6. Ruralization of the urban population and incoming aliens through a central Federal office in touch with the public domain and private owners willing to dispose of their holdings under contracts approved by the Government.

7. The extension of the Immigration Service so as to make it an agency of service to the alien after he has been admitted, such service to include education, naturalization training, employment, etc.

Possibly a voluntary commission like the Country Life Commission might be appointed to work out in detail such a problem[1] for legislative consideration at the regular session of the next Congress.

I remain,      Very sincerely yours,    Frederic C. Howe
                                        Commissioner.

TLS (WP, DLC).
[1] Howe undoubtedly said "program," and his stenographer misread his notes.


## To Mary Allen Hulbert

Dearest Friend,          The White House 22 November, 1914.

I confess to a feeling of apprehension tonight because I have heard nothing further of Allen and yourself since you merely thought him out of danger. And yet I know that if things had gone wrong you would have let me hear of it; and so I pluck up heart and reassure myself. But I do most earnestly desire to hear, —and to hear that all is well, or in a fair way to be! It would help my spirits greatly, which are heavy and uncertain these days, in which there seems to be nothing but burdens and anxieties! Life is hard to *lighten* and make go with painless ease!

It seems, indeed, as if my *individual* life were blotted out, or, rather, swallowed up, and consisted only of news upon which action must be taken; troubles of trades or regions or communities that one must lend the influence of the government to lesson [lessen] or relieve; problems of trade that must be worked out in spite of the war; credits that must be strengthened and put upon their feet again; alarms that must be quieted; errors that must be corrected; plans that must be made upon a great scale out of uncertain elements; controversies that must have the sting and danger taken out of them; businesses that must be encouraged or got out of a tangle. Government is become a sort of special providence, and we dare not stop and think how unfit or inapt we are to be Providence at all. How can one live an individual life in the midst of all this? What difference does it make what happens to him, or whether he can find happiness or not? The day's work must be done, and he must play his full part in doing it. It matters little how much life is left in him when the day is over. He is entitled to no margin of it for his own use. I play golf every day, but only to keep alive and spend and be spent! I write this not to make complaint,—that were silly and wicked besides; but only to record a singular thing: how one in such circumstances seems to realize his submergence and to be made to feel that his individual life is suspended and cast out of the reckoning,—even in his own consciousness. He knows that his own happiness and enjoyment are neither here nor there in the place in which he is put, the task which a ruling of Providence has assigned him. He must wait for that until the task is finished and it is lawful and right again for him to think of himself. I do not kick against the pricks. Rebellion would be as petty and contemptible as it would be futile,—a thing for the gods to laugh at. It is not a little strange to be made thus impersonal. It almost imperils one's sense of identity. I suppose that it is by being put in such a position and kept there too long that a man, if he be a fool, comes to think of himself as different from his fellows, born to rule their destinies, not to share them, and responsible only to God, not to any mere men who have no high place or supreme vision. I suppose some men like it. I do not. I long for the time when I may be released and allowed an individual life and daily fortune again. But here I must stay for a little while; and the less I analyze my feelings the better. They are wholly irrelevant, and only mess and belittle matters when they intrude. Woodrow Wilson does not matter; but the United States does and all that it may accomplish for its own people and the people of the world outside of it. It is a mighty fine thing to be part of a great endeavour, whether I personally enjoy it or not. Personal enjoyment is neither here nor there, anyway. Those who seek it do not get it; those who forget about it in something bigger and finer often run upon it unawares; and it is best that they should be shut off from the conscious quest by imperative circumstance with which it were absurd to quarrel. With which sententious remark, I change the subject and say that I am perfectly well; that I hope that you are, and hope it with all my heart; and that few things which affect me personally would do me so much good as to hear that your heart is relieved about your son.

Your devoted friend,   Woodrow Wilson

WWTLS (WP, DLC).

## To Dudley Field Malone

Personal.

My dear Dudley:          [The White House] November 23, 1914

Thank you for your letter of the nineteenth. Of course I will act upon your advice not to write the letter you suggested. I had my serious doubts, anyway, as to the wisdom of that course and am glad to get your counsel to the contrary.

In haste

Faithfully and affectionately yours,   Woodrow Wilson

TLS (Letterpress Books, WP, DLC).

## To Robert Lansing

Personal and Private.

My dear Mr. Lansing:     [The White House] November 23, 1914

I am preparing my annual message to Congress. One of the bills I want to urge upon the attention of the Houses is the shipping bill, which would involve, as you know, in all likelihood, the purchase of a number of ships that have been owned hitherto by subjects of one or other of the belligerents. You will remember that a little while ago the attitude of the English Government in this matter of the transfer of flag during hostilities seemed to be very different from the attitude of the French Government. I would like very much before writing my message to know just what you think the attitude of those two governments would be towards the purchase by a corporation in which the United States Government was interested of such ships as those now belonging to the North German Lloyd and the Hamburg-American Companies, and which are interned in our waters.

I know that you have had conversations with M. Jusserand and

Sir Cecil Spring-Rice that would throw some light upon this question, and I would like to know your full impressions before going further with my message.

Cordially and sincerely yours,    Woodrow Wilson

TLS (Letterpress Books, WP, DLC).

## To Lucius William Nieman[1]

My dear Mr. Nieman:    [The White House] November 23, 1914

Now that the battle is over and the smoke has cleared away, a number of things appear very clear and they are things which are calculated to give us the deepest encouragement. One of these things is the success of Mr. Husting in Wisconsin.[2] I know how important a part your editorial support played in the election of Mr. Husting. I want to give myself the pleasure, therefore, of expressing my admiration for your course and my deep appreciation that the party as represented by Mr. Husting in this contest should have had such ungrudging and generous support from you.

With much regard,

Sincerely yours,    Woodrow Wilson

TLS (Letterpress Books, WP, DLC).
 [1] Editor and publisher of the *Milwaukee Journal.*
 [2] Paul Oscar Husting, Democrat, had just been elected to the United States Senate.

## To Mary Allen Hulbert

Dearest Friend,        The White House 23 November, 1914.

This morning comes your welcome letter of Thursday last (I wonder where it has been in the meantime?) with the reassurance about Allen I was hoping for. I cut one of my fingers badly with my razor this morning and it is hard for me to write on this machine and avoid striking the suffering member; but I can at least send you a line to say how glad I am that you have him at home again. What a terrible time you have had! And how like your delightful, whimsical, complicated self this letter is that has just come. You will pull out of anything! And you will give always more than you get; and yet be vitally alive and eager in all your dealings with the world about you.

No, I am not to be in Boston on the 9th. I do not know how that bit of invention originated. I never gave any, even a provisional, promise that it could rest on. I wish it *were* true, if only I might have a glimpse of you. But nothing is true that I want to be true, so far as I am personally concerned. I must doggedly tred the way pointed out without my choice.

I am afraid there is nothing I dare venture to do by way of carrying out your friend's request. The German authorities are exceedingly jealous of the transmission of private mail, whatever its character, through official channels; and there are no others at my disposal. I wish that there were some way to aid. What will come of all this nightmare who can say, and who will venture, or care, to guess?

With sincerest congratulations to you both, and affectionate messages from us all,

Your devoted friend,   Woodrow Wilson

WWTLS (WP, DLC).

## From Robert Lansing

*Personal and Private.*

My dear Mr. President:        Washington November 23, 1914.

I fear that I cannot give a very satisfactory answer to your letter of to-day as to the probable attitude of the French and British Governments in the matter of the transfer of ships of belligerent nationality during hostilities, and particularly of transfers to a corporation in which the United State Government is interested.

In the first place I think that a distinction should be made between the transfer of flag and the transfer of ownership. In the case of the transfer of flag there have been numerous cases of ships of foreign register owned by Americans or by companies subsidiary to American companies which have been transferred to American register without opposition by either the British Government or the French Government. A vessel of this sort was the tank steamer BRINDILLA. It was seized and taken to Halifax, but was later released, the British Government stating that it did so without passing upon the legality of the transfer. In spite of this reservation I think that the British Government will recognize such transfers, and in view of the silence of the French Government it is fair to assume that no objection will be made by them.

The transfer of ownership as well as of flag, which is the type of transfer to which your letter refers, is a different matter.

I have not discussed the subject for some time with M. Jusserand, but the last time we did so he was most emphatic in his opposition. There is no question but that the French Government in their official utterances have denied the validity of the sale of a merchant vessel by a belligerent to a neutral on the ground that it is always done for the purpose of avoiding the consequences of belligerency. While this has been their consistent attitude for the past one hundred and forty years I am, nevertheless, unable to find a single case in which a French prize court has condemned a vessel so transferred on account of the illegality of the transfer.

While M. Jusserand referred to the French practice in regard to such transfers, he spoke more feelingly upon a consequence of such sales rather than upon the legal right. He asserted that for Americans to purchase German steamships interned in our ports would release a large amount of German capital and relieve the companies of the constant expense of caring for the vessels and of maintaining their crews. The moneys thus made available, he asserted, would be employed to carry on the war against France, so that it would amount to giving aid to the enemy.

Applying this idea to purchases by this Government the Ambassador said that, if the purchases were made, the action would menace the unbroken friendship of France for this country, for whose liberty Frenchmen had shed their blood and contributed their wealth, etc., etc.

Stripped of its sentimentality the argument came to this, that the purchase of interned German ships by this Government would be of material aid to Germany and that to give such aid would be an unneutral and unfriendly act, which the French Government would resent; and that, being contrary to the French theory of legality of transfer, the purchases would be considered invalid and the vessels liable to condemnation as prize.

I should also call your attention to the fact that at the time the shipping bills were being publicly discussed Ambassador Herrick reported that the French Government were bitterly hostile to the idea, raising objections similar to those urged by M. Jusserand.

The British Ambassador in the conversations, which I have had with him on this subject, has been far less definite than his colleague in expression of his views. I think that this is due to the fact that he is unwilling to differ with the French attitude and yet he cannot agree with it as it would be entirely contrary to the position which the British Government has invariably taken in regard to transfers of belligerent-owned vessels.

He has spoken of the release of German capital, which would result, but I was not impressed with the sincerity with which he advanced it as an argument. Recently, in discussing the withdrawal of the suggestion of this Government as to the Declaration of London and the assertion that our rights and duties would be determined by the existing rules of international law, I made the comment that at least the ambiguity of the article of the Declaration relative to the transfer of belligerent merchant ships would no longer vex us, as the right to make such transfers was well established so far as the practice of the United States and Great Britain was concerned. He admitted that this was probably so, but added that it seemed to him to be unneutral to give assistance to a belligerent, thus falling back on the French argument.

To sum up my impressions from the conversations I have had with the two Ambassadors:

I believe that the French Government will vigorously oppose the purchase of German vessels by this Government on the ground that the purchase is invalid, and also on the ground that this Government by making the purchase would violate its neutrality and would act in an unfriendly manner toward France.

I believe that the British Government, while giving a measure of support to their ally on the second ground mentioned, would not, in view of the long established British doctrine as to the right to make such purchases, seriously oppose the validity of the transfers, though I have no doubt their validity would be subjected to prize-court proceedings.

I regret that I cannot give you a more definite impression as to the probable position of the British Government, but the announced position of the French Government, so adverse to the British doctrine, prevents, I think, a free expression of opinion by Sir Cecil.

Very sincerely yours,   Robert Lansing.

TLS (WP, DLC).

## From Edward Mandell House

Dear Governor:          New York City. November 23rd, 1914.

Since you were here I have been seeing everyone whom it was thought could give some intelligent advice regarding the New York situation.

When I see you I will give you a summary of what was learned. In the meantime, will you not read what ex-Congressman Magner has to say about Brooklyn.[1] He is one of the most intelligent with whom I have talked, and I asked him to submit his views in writing.

I am also enclosing what seems to me an accurate and encouraging description of affairs in the City of Mexico which you may or may not care to read.[2]

There are one or two things I wish you would let me discuss with you in regard to your message, when you are ready to get at it.

If you go to Williamstown it would make me very happy if you could stop with us either going or coming.

Affectionately yours,   E. M. House

TLS (WP, DLC).

[1] [Thomas Francis Magner], T memorandum (WP, DLC), saying in effect that the only hope for the Democratic party in New York and the nation was the destruction of the Tammany organization.

[2] [W. A. McLaren], T memorandum, Nov. 3, 1914 (WP, DLC).

## Remarks at a Press Conference

November 24, 1914

I see that somebody has been unfailing in finding interesting things for me to do. I don't think of half the things to do that other people think of. I understand that I am going to visit the Senate in secret session, and introduce the members of the cabinet in the House, and a wealth of interesting things I had not thought of, I suppose, in addition to the conference of neutrals.

Now that they have been suggested to you, how do they appeal to you?

I am like the Scotch caddie. You remember the old caddie who was caddying for a very poor player; at least he was playing very badly that day. And he nodded in confidence, and he said, "I dare say you have seen a worse player on this course?" The old fellow didn't say anything, so he thought. He said, "I dare say you have seen a worse player on this course?" The old caddie said, "I heard you the first time. I was thinking!"

Somebody in this morning's paper recalled the fact that in one of your early books, Mr. President, you favored the budget system, and suggested that the Secretary of the Treasury should be in the House, at least to explain the appropriations.

Well, as a matter of fact, that is an old story. Though very few people seem to remember, committees of the Senate themselves have, I believe, three times—twice certainly—reported in favor of that, that is, in favor of high cabinet officers being given seats—the right to be present in the houses and take part in the debate, answering questions, though of course not to vote. Nobody but the Constitution can give them that.

It has not been voted on in the Senate?

I believe one of the reports that I recall was made by a committee of which, I believe, Senator Pendleton[1] was chairman, so it is not a new matter. It is a matter which has been talked about intermittently for thirty years, to my certain recollection.

Senator Stone, in the *Star* yesterday, suggested in an interview, after it had been printed elsewhere, he said he thought it would be a good idea for the President to come into the Senate to explain international diplomatic subjects; other than that, he did not think it was good.

The question really had not been raised. As a matter of fact, it is not going to be, so far as I know.

Isn't it a fact, Mr. President, that President Washington went to an executive session?

Oh, yes. He went to several.

Have you anything from Mexico this morning?

Yes, I have just read several telegrams, all of which are reassuring. I mean, as to the preservation of order and the control of any forces that might give foreigners trouble.

Mr. President, what, in your opinion, has been the big thing achieved by the taking and the evacuation of Veracruz?

Well, now, do you mean my own? If I speak to you, not for publication, that is the only way I can speak about it, because in the first place we are in there because of the action of a naval officer. Understand that we didn't go in on the choice of the administration, strictly speaking; but a situation arose that made it necessary for the maintenance of the dignity of the United States that we should take some decisive step; and the main thing to accomplish was a vital thing. We got Huerta. That was the end of Huerta. That was what I had in mind. It could not be done without taking Veracruz. It could not be done without some decisive step— to show the Mexican people that he was all bluff, that he was just composed of bluff and showed that; and that is all they ever got. That part is not for publication. I am sure I can trust you. But it is important that it should guide your own thought in the matter, because apparently we are in there for nothing in particular, and came in for nothing in

[1] Senator George Hunt Pendleton of Ohio. About the Pendleton bill, see Arthur S. Link, *Wilson: The Road to the White House* (Princeton, N. J., 1947), pp. 18-19.

particular, and I don't wonder that people who don't look beneath the surface couldn't see that the objective was to finish Huerta, and that was accomplished. The very important thing—the thing I have got at heart now—is to leave those people free to settle their own concerns, under the principle that it's nobody else's business. Now, Huerta was not the Mexican people. He did not represent any part of them. He did not represent any part. He was nothing but a "plug ugly," working for himself. And the reason that the troops did not withdraw immediately after he was got rid of was that things were hanging at such an uneven balance that nobody had taken charge; that is, nobody was ready to take charge of things at Mexico City. I have said all along that I have reason to feel confident, as I do feel confident, that nothing will go seriously wrong with Mexico City, so far as the interests we are surely responsible for are concerned. Of course, we can't protect Mexican citizens. That is another matter. That is the whole thing. I am very glad, in confidence, to let you know just what is in it.

Mr. President, upon what basis do these foreign nations from time to time ask us to look out for their interests there? I mean, for instance, yesterday the French and British ambassadors made inquiries; and several days ago the Spanish ambassador asked us about protection of Spanish citizens, and we gave them some reassuring information. Are we assuming that task?

Not exactly. No. I think that it is simply a recognition on the part of some countries, without any suggestion from us, that we are Mexico's nearest friend, that we are the neighbors who can—the only powerful neighbor who can be looked to—to exercise influence in such matters. I think that is the whole of the truth. They are a long way off. They would find us, in most instances, doing what we could, and perhaps easily doing it. At any rate, more easily doing it— that is all there is to it.

All they ask is just to use our good offices, not to attempt to dictate in any way to Mexico how she should go?

I think what they really expect is this: That any representations we make to Mexico, she will naturally feel are the most important that could be made to her. I think that is all.

Mr. President, have you considered the proposal, and its feasibility, of the American Federation of Labor, to place the coal mines under federal receivership?

That suggestion was made to me; and Mr. Wilson, the Secretary of Labor, asked, I believe, the solicitor of the department about it. There is no precedent in law for any such act. So, without any, I didn't look it up.

Do you mean by that, that it is not being seriously considered at this time?

Oh, it couldn't be if it weren't legal.

You didn't say it was not.

I should say that there is no legal warrant for it in the precedents and in the decisions of the courts.

There was a report from [Denver] several days ago that Governor Ammons was considering sending you word asking you to remove the troops. Has that been received yet?

No. . . .

Mr. President, the Department of Commerce officials seem to think that the new registry law has resulted very satisfactorily in bringing in a large number of vessels under the American flag. Will that have any effect on your wishes regarding the purchase of a number of ships?

That will depend. I haven't seen the results yet. I haven't seen the statistics. There are so many channels of trade in which we are needing ships that we need a very great number. But I haven't received any recent inquiries. For example, the last I heard—about five or six days ago—was that there were plenty of orders for cotton but no ships to send it in from the southern ports—for example, Galveston. They may be over it now, but when I last heard, that was the trouble.

JRT transcript (WC, NjP) of CLSsh (C. L. Swem Coll., NjP).

## From Edward Mandell House

Dear Governor:     New York City. November 24th, 1914.

There has been another suggestion made for the Trades Commission which I want to bring to your attention.

Such progressives as Frank P. Walsh and, I am told, Colonel Roosevelt and Colonel Nelson, would very much like to see Judge Albert D. Nortoni[1] of Saint Louis appointed.

If Nortoni is fit for the place the appointment would have many advantages at this time.

I am sending you a letter which gives some information concerning him.[2] You will see what Walsh[3] has to say about Nelson and I have similar information concerning Mr. Roosevelt.

If you advise I will write to Roosevelt and Nelson asking them to give me their direct estimate.

Affectionately yours,   E. M. House

TLS (WP, DLC).

¹ Albert Dexter Nortoni, judge of the Missouri Court of Appeals, St. Louis; Progressive candidate for Governor of Missouri in 1912.

² S. H. West to EMH, Nov. 21, 1914, TLS (WP, DLC). West's biographical sketch of Nortoni was based on his own close friendship with the Judge. It stressed the fact that Nortoni was not "of Italian blood" but "of the Puritan and oldest American stock." West also took care to note that Nortoni was a "Bull Moose" in politics: "I happen to know that he and Roosevelt are warm friends, and have been for many years, and I also know that Roosevelt would be 'Delighted' to see Judge Nortoni appointed on the Commission."

³ F. P. Walsh to N. Hapgood, Nov. 20, 1914, TLS (WP, DLC), stating that William Rockhill Nelson had a "very high opinion" of Nortoni, and suggesting that Hapgood write Nelson to secure a written endorsement of Nortoni.

# From the Diary of Colonel House

November 25, 1914.

There has been much going on but of little interest, until last night. Dr. Grayson called up while we were dining at the Ritz, and said the President wished me to breakfast with him this morning at six o'clock as he passed through New York on his way to Williamstown. The outgoing train did not leave until 8.52 so we had nearly three hours together.

The President was up and dressed when the train arrived at six o'clock, which I thought exceedingly considerate, for I did not expect to see him until around seven.

We talked of many matters. He does not expect to get through at this short Session of Congress more than the Conservation Bill and the Philippines Bill, and he is doubtful whether it will be wise to attempt to get the Shipping Bill going. I thought unless it was put through at this Congress it would be useless to attempt to in the next when out [our] majority would be narrow, and that its usefulness to meet immediate needs would be lost. I advised him to pay less attention to his domestic policy and greater attention to the welding together of the two Western Continent[s]. I thought the Federal Reserve Act was his greatest constructive work, and was the thing that would stand out and make his administration notable. Now I would like for him to place beside that great measure a a [sic] constructive international policy, which he had already started by getting the A.B.C. nations to act as arbitrators at Niagara. I thought the time had arrived to show the world that friendship, justice and kindliness were more potent than the mailed fist.

He listened attentively to what I had to say and asserted that he would do it, and would use his speech at San Francisco when he opened the Exposition to outline this policy.

I went further in my explanation of this international policy in relation to the Americas by showing how futile the policy of this Government had been in the past. In wielding the "big stick" and dominating the two Continents, we had lost the friendship and commerce of South and Central America and the European countries had profited by it.

We spoke of the ever present topic of the war. I have gotten in [it] from good authority that Italy would now be with the Allies if she had been prepared. She found her equipment was not sufficient to be effective, but she is putting herself in shape to get into the war just as soon as she is ready and can make her forces worth while. I thought Roumania would also join the Allies. He expressed pleasure at this, and hoped these two countries would not delay too long.

I again insisted that Germany would never forgive us for the attitude we have taken in the war, and if she is successful, she will hold us to account. I told him that I had it on fairly good authority that the Kaiser had it in mind to suggest to us that the Monroe Doctrine should extend only to the Equator, which would leave Germany free to exploit Brazil and the other South America countries. Brazil seems to be the main object of Germany's desires. He replied that the war was perhaps a Godsend to us, for if it had not come we might have been embroiled in war ourselves.

I spoke again of our unpreparedness and how impractical Mr. Bryan was. I urged the need of our having a large reserve force and he replied "Yes, but not a large army," an amendment which I accepted. I particularly emphasized the necessity for greater artillery plants and more artillery.

He said Jacob Shiff had written him suggesting that since he had urged our bankers not to lend money to belligerants, he thought that he should also urge our people not to seel [sell] arms and ammunition to them. The President did not say what he replied to Shiff, but he said that his policy would be a foolish one as it would restrict our plants and, in a way, make us less prepared than now.

He mentioned Bryan's desire to have our national prohitition [prohibition] made a party measure, and of his counter position which is for local option. I thought it sad that reformers of the Bryan type retarded rather than accelerated the things they most desired, that prohibition was coming as rapidly as was needful, and it was coming sanely and permanently, and there was no need to do something which might give it a setback.

He said Bryan had some personal feeling in the matter since the saloon men had always opposed him, and that back of his policies there was oftentimes personal resentment which should be absent. I reminded him how useful Bryan had been and declared that everything that was unpopular was laid to Bryan. The President had just told me about the Belgian Relief Committee and why he had not made the appointment. He asked, "did you wonder why I did not make it?" I did not because I laid it to Mr. Bryan. He said, "there it is again, poor Bryan, it is unfair that he should be made the target for everything, and most of the time unjustly so."

I was amused to hear the President say a little later that he intended to put Mr. Bryan in touch with the Chairman of the House Committee on Elections in regard to the primamry [primary] matter. He never referred to it as being a suggestion of mine, and he perhaps by now believes he thought of it himself, for we are all prone to forget where we get our ideas, and he not more so than I and others.

We talked of the Colorado strike situation. The miners are at the end of their tether financially and they desire the President to appoint the Mediation Committee in order that they may accept it and end the strike, thus saving their faces. They believe that public opinion will later force the operators to arbitrate through the Mediation Board, differences that come up between them. This news is of the most confidential character because the miners do not wish it known that they are at the end of their resources.

On the other hand, Houston has been in touch with the Rockefellers and they are as eager for the settlement as the miners, and they told Houston, in the event the strike was called off, they were willing to accept most of the demands of the men. I thought it a pity Houston could not get this in writing, but the next best thing was for him to tell the Rockefellers that he had informed the President what they had said, and the President had acted upon this. He thought this a good suggestion.

We touched lightly upon the Catholic question. I told him it was something we would have to go into sometime more fully, for it presented many phases of trouble.

I asked what he had determined to do about reappointing Hall on the Interstate Commerce Commission, and advised him to tread lightly there, for there were many lurking dangers in dismissing him. He admitted this, but thought he could get a much better man for the place.

We spoke of the Bull Moosers, and how entirely unpractical and theoretical most of them were. It was seldom you could get one of them who was a good tool to use for the public service. I called his attention to Judge Nortoni of St. Louis, which my letter to him of yesterday explains. He said that George L. Record of New Jersey was a Bull Mooser, and it would not do to appoint another of that political faith. I had forgotten this for the moment.

After breakfast we walked for a lone [long] while up and down the station platform, enjoying the keen air. The President does not particularly like cold weather, though, and said he preferred it warmer.

## To Mary Celestine Mitchell Brown[1]

My dear Friend:      Williamstown, Mass., November 26, 1914

Nothing could have been more generous upon your part or could have touched me more than that in the midst of your own grief in the loss of your dear father your thought should have turned to me and should have been, not of yourself, but of my loneliness.[2] What you say of it is only too true, and I find greater drains made every day upon my power of self-control. I tell you this in order that you may realize how deeply and intensely grateful I am for the hand you reach out to me, and how I shall cherish the thought that that hand is always ready to clasp mine in sympathy and helpfulness.

We have thought of you again and again, and again, during the last the last [sic] few days. I am sure you know how much and with what deep affection we sympathize with you, because I know in some degree how you were bound to the dear father who is gone.

I am having a little cheer here in the sight of dear Jessie, but will be back in Washington by Saturday morning.

Your sincere and grateful friend,    [Woodrow Wilson]

CCL (WP, DLC).
[1] Wife of Edward T. Brown.
[2] Mary C. M. Brown to WW [c. Nov. 23, 1914], ALS (WP, DLC). Her father, Henry Sparrow Mitchell, had died on Nov. 10, 1914.

## To Augustus Peabody Gardner

My dear Mr. Gardner:      Williamstown, Mass., November 26, 1914

I have your letter of November twenty-third,[1] for which I thank you.

You may be sure that I do not have an attitude of indifference to the great subject which you broach, but I should like very much to have a conference with you before the resolution you have in mind is offered, in order to present my views to you more fully than it is possible to do in a letter.

Sincerely yours,   Woodrow Wilson

TLS (Letterpress Books, WP, DLC).
¹ It is missing.

## From John R. Mott

Mr President,                              New York November 26th, 1914

I have just returned from Europe. It has been a never-to-be-forgotten experience to be in Britain, Germany and France at this possibly the most fateful moment in their life. It has been a solemn privilege to look into the very soul of these nations under circumstances when both their best and their worst are revealed as by fire. You will understand when I add that I have tried to enter into fellowship with the sufferings of great peoples. I trust that I have been enabled to accomplish even more than was anticipated. I owe more to you personally than I can express.

Mr Dodge, with whom I spent a long evening the day I landed, expressed the hope that I might tell you much that I reported to him. I told him that it was my intention to write you at once. Should it be entirely convenient for you, I shall esteem it an honor to place as much time at your disposal as you may desire. Matters have come up in the pathway of my mission which you may wish to have me report to you with more or less fulness. I could go to you at any time in the period December 4 to 13 inclusive or on any day after Christmas. Should you decidedly prefer, I could arrange to meet an appointment on December 1 or 2.¹

With renewed expression of deepest gratitude for all that your personal interest and cooperation have meant to me on my recent journey, and with sincere thankfulness to God for the wonderful and absolutely unique relation you sustain to the present world situation,                              Faithfully yours   John R. Mott

ALS (WP, DLC).
¹ Wilson saw Mott on January 6, 1915. About their meeting, see C. R. Crane to WW, Jan. 10, 1915, n.1.

## To Lindley Miller Garrison

My dear Mr. Secretary:   [The White House] November 28, 1914

I do not know whether a man always wishes to be congratulated on reaching his fiftieth birthday, but I am going to take the liberty of sending you a message of sincere congratulation because I want you to know how much I enjoy my association with you and how highly I appreciate the services you are rendering the country in your present post. I hope that you will have a great many more birthdays and that upon each one of them there will be the same occasion for gratification at the thought of the high work you are privileged to do.

Cordially and sincerely yours,   Woodrow Wilson

TLS (Letterpress Books, WP, DLC).

## From Robert Lansing

Dear Mr. President:          Washington November 28, 1914.

In view of information reaching the Department in regard to the possible construction of submarines by American manufacturers for belligerent governments, I discussed the matter with Secretary Bryan on November 12th and later on the same day put my opinion in the form of a letter to him, which, I think, he called to your attention.

As my opinion did not, as Mr. Bryan informed me, coincide with the views of neutrality held by you or by him, I submitted the question to the Joint State and Navy Neutrality Board in a letter dated November 17th, in order that the legal aspect of the subject might receive critical consideration. The Board has sent me its report, and, as it is in my opinion correct from the standpoint of international and municipal law, I have approved it.

I am sending you a copy of the report[1] together with a copy of my letter of the 12th with no intention of obtaining a modification of your views as to the propriety of sales of this sort, which is essentially a matter of policy; but I think it my duty to lay before you the fact that in the opinion of the Neutrality Board, which I think is sound, there is no *legal* obstacle to such sales, and no authority conferred by law upon this Government to prevent sales or to punish American manufacturers who make them.

In order to carry out your wish, made to me over the telephone a few days ago, that submarines in sections should not be sold here, I think that it would be well for the Department to be advised as soon as possible of the action which it should take in this matter, either formally or informally, since it is possible that the manufacturers may proceed without asking the Department's views if they have been advised by counsel that the sales are not illegal.          Very sincerely yours,   Robert Lansing.

TLS (WP, DLC).
[1] James Brown Scott *et al.* to RL, TC memorandum, Nov. 25, 1914 (WP, DLC).

# From William Gibbs McAdoo

*Personal*

Dear "Governor":                    Brunswick, Georgia Nov. 28, 1914

I enclose a clipping from the N. Y. Herald, Nov. 24,[1] containing excerpts from a speech by Ambassador Naon in Philadelphia a few days ago in relation to South American trade.

You will observe that he speaks of the necessity for sufficient vessels as the *first* consideration, if we are to enlarge our South American markets.

I dont know what you have decided about the Shipping Bill and I dont want to press my views against your better judgment but I feel that I ought to say that I think it will be a great mistake not to push the shipping bill through the next Session. I know, of course, the difficulties, but if we are convinced that the measure itself is wise, we ought not to hesitate because the fight will be hard or even if there is a chance of defeat. I believe that we can win the fight if you undertake it with your usual vigor and determination.

It is certain that conventions of South American financiers and trade conferences and other things will have little effect unless we establish steamship lines, competitive in quality, speed and reliable sailings, and with *reasonable* rates, with those of European countries. We must have a merchant marine under our flag if we are going to get anywhere in our efforts to build up our export trade and make our tariff policy successful. The only way to get it is to put the Government behind it at the beginning. That alone will give that confidence to the American business man, in the permanency and reliability of the lines, that will justify and encourage him in making the necessary efforts to win foreign markets.

Moreover the European War is likely to last some time. Our shippers get inadequate protection under foreign flags—even of neutrals. They get inadequate insurance and none at all to some ports. Our War Risk insurance Bureau can insure ships under our flag only.

Our changed registry laws will not give us enough ships. We cannot reform our navigation laws in time, if ever. The opportunity is here *now* to create a merchant marine and capture a large part of the worlds markets but we must take it *now*. We may not, I believe *will not*, have the opportunity a year hence.

We need this merchant marine to carry out the large policies you have already so successfully inaugurated.

The thing is worth fighting for and I believe we can win.

On the financial side—the next requisite to shipping is finance. We can do a great deal through the Federal Reserve System—but we can do a great deal more through some amendments I have in mind. These wont be worth much without the necessary marine lines.

This is a beautiful place and we are having a wonderfully restful time except for the "mail" which pursues us. Nell is as well as can be. She grows more lovely each day. I am more tired than I thought I was but am taking on new energy every day.

We both send best love to you all. We expect to return about the 8th December.  Affectionately yours  W G McAdoo

P.S. I wrote Cobb about the negro question[2] and asked him to Washington after I return. I told him I knew you would be pleased to see him. I think it would be very politic if you would send him a line and ask him to lunch with you if he comes down. You ought to talk to him anyway on general matters.[3]

ALS (WP, DLC).
  [1] "Trade Advice by Ambassador Naon," *New York Herald*, Nov. 24, 1914.
  [2] W. G. McAdoo to F. I. Cobb, Nov. 26, 1914, HwCLS (W. G. McAdoo Papers, DLC). The full text of the letter follows:
"Dear Mr Cobb,                                    Brunswick, Georgia, Nov. 26, 1914
  "I am taking advantage of the first opportunity I have had to write you in relation to the Worlds recent editorial on 'Jim Crow Government' which it is needless for me to say distressed all of us in Washington the President included. We all value the splendid work the World has done for the Cause and for the Administration and it is because we are jealous of its good opinion and do not want to lose its support, unless deserved, that I venture to write this letter.
  "I am ignorant of the assumptions upon which the Worlds editorial were based. I wish I knew them as I could write more satisfactorily. It seems certain, at any rate, that you have assumed the truth of the charge that there is complete segregation of the races in the Treasury Department. If you have, I am not surprised because so much falsehood has been disseminated that it begins to gain verity from mere reiteration. The charge is *untrue* as to the Treasury Department, except to this extent: *Separate toilets* have been assigned to whites and blacks in the Treasury building and in the office of the Auditor of the Interior Department. The toilets assigned to the blacks are just as good as those assigned to the whites. There is no discrimination in quality. I do not know that this can properly be called segregation.
  "The matter came up this way: Last year Asst. Secy. Williams gave directions for separate toilets in the Treasury building. Mr. Woo[l]lley, Auditor for the Interior Dept, issued a written order to the same effect for the Auditors office. This order, by the way, concluded with the usual formula 'By direction of the Secretary of the Treasury.' As a matter of fact I did not know of these orders until some time after they had gone into effect. They relate to details of administration with which it is impossible for the Secretary to keep fully informed. His time is necessarily absorbed in the larger problems which are constantly pressing upon him in this great department. I do not say this to escape responsibility. On the con[trary] I assume it all because after the matter was brought to my attention I felt that the orders should stand. Had I revoked them after the issue had been raised even greater dissatisfaction would have arisen among the whites.
  "I am not going to argue the justification of the separate toilets orders, beyond saying that it is difficult to disregard certain feelings and sentiments of white people in a matter of this sort. The whites constitute the great majority of the employees and are entitled to just consideration, especially when such consideration does not involve the deprivation of the negro of any essential and inherent right—any more, for instance, than the provision of separate toilets

for the higher officials of [the] department would be a denial of the rights of the ordinary employees. These separate toilets orders have been the chief cause of all the campaign that has been waged against the Treasury Department. For obvious reasons the matter could not be freely discussed in the press. Our enemies, therefore, had to seek other grounds for their campaign and resort to falsehood and misrepresentation was therefore necessary.

"I will instance a few of these misrepresentations. It has been repeatedly charged that there is segregation in the Auditor's Office for the Post-Office Department and that I am responsible for it. If there is segregation there, it occurred under Mr Tafts administration. I have absolutely not changed conditions there since I took office. I have even retained the Republican Auditor, Mr [Charles A.] Kram, who will testify to the facts I have stated. I have kept Kram, in spite of strong democratic pressure and to the disappointment of many of my political friends, because he has made a fine record in establishing a new system of auditing the Post Office accounts with great saving of money to the Government. Mr. Villard, in his speeches and in his paper, has attacked me for conditions created by the Republican Administration of Mr Taft and in spite of the fact that I have invited him to go through the Treasury Department and see for himself how untrue are the things he has been saying. He has never accepted the invitation.

"Again we have been attacked for certain conditions that existed in the old building of the Bureau of Printing & Engraving. These conditions were created under Republican Administrations and I had nothing to do with them. Here again I have retained the Republican Superintendent of the Bureau. He is a very efficient man and I have put the interest of the service above political considerations.

"Last March we moved the Bureau of Ptg & Eng. to the new building and the conditions which gave rise to complaint have been completely removed.

"Again it has been charged that I have discriminated against the negro in the matter of promotions and appointments in the Dept.

"Here is the complete refutation:

"In the last 2 years of Mr. Taft's adm. the total number of negroes promoted was 263.

"In the past 1 yr & 8 mos. of Democratic adm. the total number of negroes promoted was 294—increase 31.

"In the last 2 yrs of Mr. Taft's Adm. the total number of negroes appointed was 145.

"In the past 1 yr & 8 mos. of Democratic Adm. the total number of negroes appointed was 398—increase 253.

"I am speaking only of the Treasury Department appointments in Washington D. C. Now it is better for me not to publish these facts in the form of a defense because it only causes more trouble with the Extremists both in the North and in the South. These Extremists in the North claim that we are doing too little for the Negro while the Extremists in the South claim that we are doing too much. So it has seemed better from the standpoint of public service, for me to remain silent under constant misrepresentation & I have, therefore, done so.

"The truth is that all this outcry against the administration is grounded primarily in partisanship & hypocrisy. For instance: the most conspicuous case of segregation in Washington is the separate public schools for whites & blacks. The Republican party is, I understand, responsible for that and yet we hear nothing of it. I am sure that everybody in Washington regards these separate schools not only as wise but as essential. No complaint is made about it and no essential or other right of the negro is denied because of it—nor is any injustice done to him.

"This whole campaign is merely an attempt to injure the President and the Administration. It had its inception, I am told, in the discontent of a few republican negroes in the Department who try to pass as *Whites* (they are very light mulattoes) and who have been assiduous in trying to make trouble. Joined with them are a few disgruntled negro democrats—so-called—who have been expecting and demanding recognition of a kind that it is difficult to give—as a reward for their alleged support of the President in the last election. These people have succeeded in arousing Mr Villard, Mr Storey and other well-meaning men who are peculiarly susceptible to any cry of negro discrimination and are almost fanatical on this subject when an official of Southern origin is charged with responsibility for it. Of course the Republicans have eagerly seized the opportunity to make trouble for the administration and are fanning the flame of racial hatred all they can. Anything with them to injure and destroy the administration! Naturally every good and orthodox representative of the selfish interests joins in the cry and lends a helping hand.

"The negro has been treated justly and fairly in the Treasury Department. I am just as earnest in the desire that he have justice as anyone but the agitators want more than justice, they want enforced social equality, which of course, cannot be brought about by law or otherwise.

"It is because we do not want you to be misled that I have ventured to write you this long and, I fear, tedious letter. The cause for which the World and the President are fighting is too vital to the people of this Country to permit it to be hurt by misunderstandings among its friends and supporters.

"Now, I want to make a suggestion. Wont you run down to Washington some day after I return (about Dec. 6th) and let me show you through the department or have you shown through the department? The latter would be better. You can see for yourself how fairly the negro is being treated.

"Moreover, we can, I think, make your visit a very pleasant and perhaps, informing one. I know the President will be delighted to see you.

"I am very tired out and am trying to get a little rest here before Congress meets.                                    Sincerely Yours W G McAdoo"

[P.S. omitted]

3 Insofar as is known, Wilson did not write to Cobb. There is no evidence that Cobb visited the White House at any time through December 31.


## Two Letters from Edward Mandell House

Dear Governor:              New York City. November 28th, 1914.

I saw Mr. Low last night and obtained his consent to act in the Colorado mining strike matter.

I told him you would communicate with him direct. He has a great deal upon his shoulders and it is fine of him to take on this additional burden. I would suggest that you write him of your appreciation.

He thought it inadvisable for the Industrial Relations Committee to continue their hearings there, and he hoped you would find some way to discontinue their activities.

Affectionately yours,   E. M. House


Dear Governor:              New York City. November 28th, 1914.

During my conversation with Mr. Low last night he thought it would be a graceful and popular thing for you to invite Roosevelt and Taft to take part in the Panama Canal opening. He thought if you went upon the first battleship you could place the second at the disposal of Roosevelt and the third at Taft's disposal. He thought they would appreciate it beyond measure and the country would approve, because each of them had taken a conspicuous part in the building of the Canal.

I told Mr. Low I would write you of his suggestion.

Affectionately yours,   E. M. House

TLS (WP, DLC).

## Paul Samuel Reinsch to William Jennings Bryan

No. 460. STRICTLY CONFIDENTIAL

Sir:                                         Peking, November 28, 1914.

I have the honor to report on the effect of the Japanese action in Shantung upon the state of public feeling in China.

While in itself the Japanese attack upon Tsingtau was extremely unwelcome to the Chinese and filled their minds with grave forebodings, it was the subsequent action of Japan in extending her occupation along the entire railway to Tsinanfu and including therein the mining properties of the Germans that caused for a time a dangerous condition of public feeling among the Chinese, as it seemed to indicate that the occupation of the military base of Tsingtau was to be merely an incident and to serve as excuse for extending Japanese political influence throughout the Province of Shantung. The Chinese Government vigorously, though vainly, protested against the disregard of neutrality which was involved. I have the honor to enclose copies of the protests, which were furnished the Legation by the Foreign Office.[1] It is probable that no action of any foreign power has come so closely home to the Chinese and has demonstrated to them so forcibly the dangers to which national weakness exposes them as have these last inroads of the Japanese in Shantung. It was only with difficulty that the Central Government could restrain an anti-Japanese movement, both among the military and among the population in general. The old fighter, Chang Hsun, whose troops are stationed in southern Shantung telegraphed the Government his readiness to oppose the Japanese. He was, however, promptly called to Peking for a conference and impressed with the supreme need of preserving the peace.

The reports which came from Japan of discussions there on the political future of China, had a further disquieting effect. Count Okuma's[2] declaration that a large increase in the military forces of Japan was necessary in order to preserve the peace of the Far East was interpreted as meaning that Japan was ready to take advantage of the present opportunity for making good her actual domination throughout eastern Asia. The Chinese felt that any alliance or cooperation with Japan would inevitably take the form of the total subjection of China to the political dominance

[1] Chinese Foreign Office to the Japanese Minister, Sept. 27, 1914, TC memorandum; Chinese Foreign Office to the Japanese Minister, Sept. 27, 1914, TCL; and Chinese Foreign Office to the Japanese Minister, Sept. 30, 1914, TCL, all in SDR, RG 59, 793.94/205, DNA.

[2] Marquis Shigenobu Okuma, Prime Minister of Japan.

of her neighbor. They extremely distrust all professions of friendship and all declarations of policy on the part of Japan. . . .

To sum up, the Chinese think that they have every reason to believe that at the present time, in order that advantage may be taken of the unusual opportunity created through the European War,—an opportunity which may never occur again,—the Japanese are trying, with or without the formal participation of their Government, to create a situation in China which, through unrest, insecurity, and general demoralization, will seem to justify intervention on the part of Japan. If such a situation cannot be brought about, the Chinese suspect the Japanese of endeavoring to disseminate reports unfavorable to China to the effect that revolution is rife, that there is danger of an anti-foreign movement, and in general that the situation in China is unstable and threatening. . . .

The British in China have looked upon the new adventure of Japan with a great lack of enthusiasm; though they of course welcome the losses inflicted upon their enemy in war, they are evidently apprehensive of the results which may flow from the occupation of Shantung by Japan. The British Legation itself was not informed of the impending move at Tsingtau until the ultimatum had been issued. Should Japan actually decide to turn Shantgung into a Japanese sphere of influence, it would seem inevitable to me that serious conflict would sooner or later arise between British and Japanese interests in China. As such a step on the part of Japan would be interpreted as tending to the division of China, it would further strengthen the sphere of influence policy on the part of Great Britain, France and Russia; but as Japan, which now maintains a garrison at Hankow and which is already developing important interests in the Yangtze Valley, would feel the establishment of a British control in the Yangtze Valley as unfavorable to herself, friction is unavoidable unless Japan should limit her action in Shantung to economic enterprise on a basis of equality with other nations.

While the present relations between Japan and Russia are most friendly, it is plain that the Russians, too, are fully aware of the dangers imported into the Chinese situation through the action in Shantung. Taken together with recent Japanese advances in Inner Mongolia, a situation may be created in Northern China which would probably be regarded as dangerous by the Russians. When recently discussing the reports of unrest in China, the Russian Minister said to me in significant terms that "the situation itself does not impress me as serious; the only thing about it that is serious is that the Japanese say it is serious."

As to Japan herself, there is a distinction between the action so far taken in China and the conclusions drawn from the supposed probabilities of the situation and from discussions in Japan of general policies with respect to China. A great deal of the suspicion of Japanese policy is undoubtedly due to the fact that a situation is known to exist in China which would make it easier than ever before for Japan to follow out a policy of political advance: so it is presumed that Japan will desire to take advantage of this opportunity to the fullest extent.

It is, however, evident that the Japanese are at present put before the decision as to what their continental policy is to be in general purpose and in detail. The unusual opportunity which has presented itself in the train of the European War, the elimination of Germany for the time being as a factor in the Far East, the fact that the other great European powers are the allies of Japan and are entirely preoccupied with the war in Europe, would seem to give to Japan an opportunity for exercising an influence in China the like of which could not have been hoped for even by the greatest optimists. Whether this opportunity is now to be exploited in order to extend political predominance over a part or all of China, or whether the advantageous situation is to be utilized merely to create a favorable basis for Japanese economic enterprise on the mainland: that is a decision which now has to be made. There can be no doubt that Japan has ambitions to play the part of leadership on the Continent; the only question is what character will that leadership assume. From the public discussion which is going on in Japan, both on the part of responsible statesmen such as Count Okuma and on the part of the press, it is plain that the Japanese nation is fully aware of the extent of the opportunity and of the momentousness of the decision. . . .

The position of American influence and enterprise in China, as that of the other leading nations, will be deeply affected by the policy of Japan. As the American attitude of good will towards China has in the past been understood by the Chinese to imply a readiness to give them a certain amount of support in times of need, large hopes were entertained as to what the United States—rich and powerful beyond measure, in the minds of the Chinese—would do to help China to maintain her integrity, independence and sovereignty. Other nations, not a little jealous of the good will which the Chinese have so generously given us in the past, were not slow to point out to them that American friendship was a bubble, which vanished before any concrete facts, such as the violation of China's neutrality. But the Chinese, after all, did not fail to realize that it did not lie within the proper sphere of political action for the United States to come to the rescue with political and military support. As, however, in the past the Chinese have encouraged the development of American activities in China, looking upon them as a safeguard to their own national life, since they are conducted in a fair spirit and without political afterthought, China now hopes and expects as a minimum that Americans will stand by their guns and will not allow themselves to be excluded by political intrigue or by force from their share in the development and activities of China. . . .

From every point of view the policy of steadfastly holding and protecting our own and maintaining our right to share in the future development of this country, which will be of every growing importance to our people, would seem to be worthy of the strongest support. . . .

There is nothing in all this which would be incompatible with a policy of the frankest understanding with Japan. The Japanese are prone to believe that American action in China has an eye on them; that it is the purpose of American diplomacy in China to block the plans of Japan. As a matter of fact, each American enterprise in China is treated on its own merits as to its usefulness and prospects here without any attention to any possible effect it might have upon Japan. During my first interview with the present Japanese Minister, Mr. Hioki,[3] he stated plainly that as the United States was preventing the settlement of Japanese in America, we could not in fairness object if Japan tried to develop her activities and influence on the Continent of Asia. However, while American good will goes out in the fullest measure to any legitimate development of Japanese strength and prosperity, the American nation also has duties towards China and towards its own citizens, and only as the recognized rights of these are respected and safeguarded may Japanese activities in the Far East expect American approval.

I have the honor to be, Sir,

Your obedient servant,   Paul S. Reinsch

TCL (WP, DLC).
3 Eki Hioki.

## A Statement on the Colorado Coal Strike

[Nov. 29, 1914]

The strike of the miners in Colorado which has now lasted for twelve months has attracted the attention of the whole country and has been accompanied by many distressing and tragical circumstances. The mediation of the Government of the United States was offered early in the struggle, but the operators of the mines were unwilling to avail themselves of it or to act upon the suggestions made in the interest of peace by representatives of the Department of Labor authorized by statute to serve in such cases. It became necessary to send federal troops to the district affected by the strike in order to preserve the peace; but their presence could of itself accomplish nothing affirmative.

After long waiting, therefore, and the disappointment of many hopes of accommodation, I ventured, after taking counsel with representatives of the Government who had been on the field and made themselves thoroughly familiar with all the circumstances of the case, to propose a plan of temporary settlement, to be put into operation for a period of three years and to afford means of amicable consultation and adjustment between the mine operators and their employees, pending agreement upon such terms and arrangements as might be made the basis for permanently satisfactory relations between them.

The plan seemed to me obviously fair and sensible. The striking miners promptly accepted it; but the mine operators rejected it, saying in response to my earnest appeal that they objected to its most essential features: namely, the proposed arrangements by which the miners might state their grievances through a committee, and by which differences might be settled by reference to a commission appointed by the President of the United States.

I think the country regretted their decision and was disappointed that they should have taken so uncompromising a position. I have waited and hoped for a change in their attitude, but now fear that there will be none. And yet I do not feel that I am at liberty to do nothing in the presence of circumstances so serious and distressing. Merely to withdraw the federal troops and leave the situation to clear and settle itself would seem to me to be doing something less than my duty after all that has occurred.

I have, therefore, determined to appoint the commission contemplated in the plan of temporary settlement, notwithstanding the rejection of that plan by the mine operators, and thus at least to create the instrumentality by which like troubles and disputes may be amicably and honourably settled in the future, in the hope, the very earnest and sincere hope, that both parties may see it to be not merely to their own best interest but also a duty which they owe to the communities they serve and to the nation itself to make use of this instrumentality of peace and render strife of the kind which has threatened the order and prosperity of the great State of Colorado a thing of the past, impossible of repetition so long as everything that is done is done in good temper and with the genuine purpose to do justice and observe every public as well as every private obligation.

The Honourable Seth Low, of New York, Mr. Charles W. Mills, of Philadelphia,[1] and Mr. Patrick Gilday of Clearfield, Pa.[2] have most generously and unselfishly consented, at my request, to serve as members of the commission. I owe to these gentlemen my own warm thanks not only, but also, I believe, the thanks of their fellow-citizens throughout the country. They will place themselves at the service alike of the miners and the operators of the mines in Colorado in case controversy between them should in the future develop circumstances which would render mediation the obvious way of peace and just settlement.[3]

T MS (WP, DLC).
    [1] Proprietor of a Pennsylvania coal mining company, with extensive experience as a labor-management conciliator.
    [2] President of the Second District of the United Mine Workers of America.
    [3] There is a WWsh draft of this statement dated "Nov. 1914" in WP, DLC.

## To Robert Lansing

My dear Mr. Lansing:          The White House November 30, 1914

As I intimated to you, I gave the matter very serious thought when the question of the submarines was brought up. I feel that it is really our duty (in the *spirit*, at any rate, of the Alabama decision) to prevent submarines being shipped from this country even in parts, and I hope that you will find a way of checking and preventing this if it is contemplated.

    Always
          Cordially and faithfully yours,    Woodrow Wilson

TLS (SDR, RG 59, 763.72111/1073½, DNA).

## From Edward Mandell House

Dear Governor:          New York City. November 30th, 1914.

I am enclosing a clipping from the Springfield Republican,[1] in which I concur.

As I said to you when you were here, I feel that the wise thing for you to do is to make your foreign policy the feature of your Administration during the next two years.

The opportunity to weld North and South America together in closer union, is at your hand, and, do you not think you should take some initiative in this direction before your speech at the Panama Exposition? You might take that occasion to amplify it, but in the meantime, there are many things that might be done to give it further acceleration.

I believe too, that an opportunity will present itself, or can be made for you to do world-wide service in bringing about an adjustment of international relations before or soon after this war is ended.

The history of this war must necessarily be largely the history of today, and no President has ever been given so splendid a chance to serve humanity as a whole.

Will you not get the Atlantic Monthly for November and read Ferrero's "The European Tragedy."[2] It bears out my feeling that the Kaiser was forced into this situation.

Affectionately yours,   E. M. House

TLS (WP, DLC).
   [1] An undated clipping of an editorial.
   [2] Guglielmo Ferrero, "The European Tragedy," *Atlantic Monthly*, cxiv (Nov. 1914), 681-88, which said that the principal cause of the war was "the prestige and the power of the military caste in Germany." Even William II, the "only . . . pacifist in Germany," had been unable to prevail against the military branch in the crisis of July and August 1914.


## From Walter Hines Page

Dear Mr. President,                    London. Nov. 30. 1914.

   . . . In matters of more importance, we are more fortunate. I feel a lessening uneasiness about our shipping troubles with Great Britain, in spite of the increasing volume of the troubles and in spite of the definite efforts (two of which have pretty clearly come to view here) of Germans to make trouble—in spite, too, of the untruthfulness of merchants on each side of the ocean. They misinform this Government and they misinform our Government—of course not always, but just often enough to produce a skeptical feeling till the facts have been independently found out. My lessening uneasiness comes not so much of my management of these cases (tho' I do try to do my full duty with all promptness and vigour) as of the almost pathetic eagerness of this Government to avoid even the slightest difficulty with us. They wouldn't quarrel if we tried to make them quarrel— unless the controversy were about some capital subject. Certainly they will not quarrel about any cargo. They are more careful in dealing with us than they are in dealing with their allies. For example—the French Government made a desperate effort to induce the English to put cotton on the contraband list. The English and the French could, of course, have got all the cotton they want as easily as they get it now. But they wouldn't, for the very good reason of their fear of offending us. I happened to hear about this, first from the French lawyer who came over here from the French Foreign Office to get cotton made contraband, and afterwards Sir Edward Grey told me. Up to this time not an American contraband cargo has been stopped but the British Government has bought it—not one confiscated, so far as I am informed. They let food and cotton and general cargoes thro' (*which they don't want to do*) *because we send them*; and they buy copper and petroleum etc. to make the difficulty with us as little as possible. The system works itself down to this. They do not interfere with our non-contraband trade. I think that contraband has been on every ship detained and an unsatisfactory assurance that its destination is a neutral country. But, if we suffer damage, we must claim damage—I see no other way. If we suffer insult or indignity—that's another matter; and they are very careful about that.

Yet there are some very unsatisfactory features of this business. The delay and the increasing danger of shipping because of mines and naval operations and the closing of the North Sea. The danger and the delay increase—partly surely because of naval activity, but whether wholly for this reason, I don't know. At least one ship a day is blown up. The British navy bombard the Germans on the Belgian co[a]st. German cruisers come far down towards the Channel and sink British merchantmen, and mines and submarines are apparently everywhere. Many shippers have in mind and in fear the general naval engagement which everybody expects at some time and which may endanger the sea anywhere and everywhere—possibly German cruisers at large so that only American & Dutch & other neutral ships may go at all.

Another unsatisfactory fact is the delay in getting answers and information from the Government about shipping questions. The Admiralty does the detaining. The Admiralty is in command. The Admiralty is infinitely busy. The Admiralty doesn't have to settle the controversies that its own actions give rise to. Although Sir Edward Grey is the most powerful member of the Government under normal conditions, these days he constantly apologizes to me about delays. I send our secretaries to the secretaries of the War Office and I make unofficial complaints myself as I meet War Office men outside. But it isn't often that I can hurry them or the Admiralty. A merchant ship or its cargo is an incident to them—a negligible incident.

Nor is *all* the delay on their side. Anderson and a Foreign-Office lawyer were given the task weeks ago by Sir Edward Grey and me to draw up an exact statement whereby we hope (if the two Governments agree) to get the embargo lifted on hides, raw rubber, manganese &c. Well, they sit and sit and sit—these two lawyers. Certainly they don't move. They impress importers and exporters and our commercial attaché and consul-general, & sit & sit & sit. Meantime the man in Cleveland, O., who wants his wool may die of old age. I swear I believe I could draw up this thing in one uninterrupted day, if I had such a thing. Anderson has been and is very helpful, but he has the lawyer's way. I've often wondered if the risk of going wrong were not less than the danger of their inevitable delays.

Anderson, by the way, is going home to attend to some private affairs; but I wish him to return. His faults are only the faults of the craft in general. At any time he may be of the greatest service, as he was during those weeks of the Declaration of London *redivivus.*

The Germans are indescribably angry with the British. They question and criticize everything. At bottom they hate and distrust us also. The English are slow beyond any decent patience. The Austrians mechanically follow the Germans in their restrictions. The Turks ask twice a day about their consuls. Untruthful merchants in the U. S. misinform our Government. The British Admiralty and War Office cause interminable delay. I never know what a day will bring. Depression hangs over everybody as a London fog. But all these are incidental—are as nothing, if we keep fair & considerate dealing—these two Governments with one another; for upon this hangs the destiny of the world. The Prime Minister and Sir Edward Grey never forget this and I use their appreciation of our friendship as far as it is manly to use it. And their attitude will enable us to pull through. As I say, all else is of minor consequence. Ours, of course, is the future of the world. When the world recovers its senses, its first remark will be, "Thank God for the United States." And so say I now.                 Heartily Yours,   Walter H. Page

ALS (WP, DLC); P.S. omitted.

## From Sun Yat-sen

Tokyo, Nov. 30, 1914.

Appeal you for humanity sake prevent Morgan company contracting loan for Yuenskikai.[1] Money cannot restore peace in China. Only maintain Chinese Huerta longer. Make peoples suf-

fering more. Yuenshikai turns republic despotat. People determine overthrow him. Struggle already began Kwangtung
Kwangsi. Other provinces soon follow. Hopking strict neutrality
from America.                                    Sunyatsen.[2]

T telegram (WP, DLC).
    [1] That is, Yuan Shih-k'ai, president-dictator of China.
    [2] "Please refer this telegram to the State Department and ask their comment
on it. The President." T memorandum (WP, DLC).


## Remarks at a Press Conference
December 1, 1914

Mr. President, have you got any word from Mr. Low and those
other gentlemen, when they expect to come to Washington?

> No. There is no immediate occasion for them to come to
> Washington.

It was stated in one of the New York papers that they would be
here.

> That may be an arrangement they have made with the De-
> partment of Labor. There is no special occasion for their
> organizing immediately. Our appointment, you understand,
> had nothing to do with the present strike, but with future
> difficulties.

Mr. President, could you explain what is to be done out there
in Colorado, pending any action by this commission?

> There is nothing to be done. Of course, I am waiting for an
> official announcement from the governor of the state that
> he is ready to take over any guarding, any means there, to
> keep the peace that it is necessary to maintain.

As soon as he announces that, you will withdraw the federal
troops?

> I expect to.

What is the status of Congressman Gardner and his resolution?
He is excited.

> I don't determine his status. That is a matter for Congress,
> of course.

Do you expect to have a talk with him?

> I hope I shall.

Are you in general sympathy or unsympathetic with his resolution?

> I won't discuss that now. . . .

Mr. President, do you desire action on the Burnett bill this session?

> You mean the immigration bill?

Yes.

I have no desire one way or the other about that.

Mr. President, are you giving any encouragement to the proposed amendment of the Sherman law which will enable exporters to cooperate to meet the competition of foreign—

That has a number of times been brought to my attention— I mean, that subject. I must say that my mind is swaying on the subject. I haven't yet satisfied myself with a judgment about it. There are two very good sides to the argument.

Reports were published recently[1] that you had made some informal, unofficial protests regarding the dropping of bombs in Europe. Could you tell us exactly what you did?

Well, if your information is correct, perhaps the best thing to do would be not to discuss it.

I had no information on the subject.

I mean, the information that is current in the newspapers. I didn't mean you.

Mr. President, could you give us any of the high spots of your coming message to Congress?

No. I am afraid the light might fade from them if I test them beforehand.

Will it be a long message?

No, I hope not. I am trying to be moderate.

Anything from Mexico, Mr. President?

No. Mr. Tumulty says that there are dispatches he just referred to the State Department which are quite hopeful in character, so far as he finds they show complete order in every place where foreigners might be concerned—in Veracruz and Mexico City.

Have you had any communication from Gutiérrez?

None whatever. Of course, you understand that it is better to be on your guard about reports from Mexico. There are a very large number of our fellow citizens determined to have trouble down there, whether it exists or not, and the safe thing is not to believe anything you hear—from anybody. . . .

Mr. President, do you favor the rivers and harbors bill at this coming session?

Well, there will be one, I suppose, whether I favor it or not. I thought the rivers and harbors bill was like a law of nature—it is an annual event.

You are to see Mr. Sparkman[2] today?

I am to see him today. I don't know just what the scope

of the discussion will be. He said he wanted to see me before
Congress convenes.

Mr. President, there is a great deal of talk now on this question
of a larger army and navy, in connection with this Gardner
resolution. Otherwise I notice this morning there are some
mysterious high officials near the White House [who] are quoted
as being opposed to it.

> So I saw. That interested me very much. I don't know
> anything about it. It is astonishing how much is going on
> inside the government that I learn from the newspapers.

Mr. President, are you able at this time to tell us something
about your visit with Mr. van Dyke?

> That I think has no special purpose. Dr. van Dyke and I are
> old friends and colleagues, and he has come down to take
> lunch with me and report on things before lunch.

Have you any information that he bears a special message?

> I have no information that he does. I think not.

Mr. President, is there still any time for this ship purchase bill?

> Oh, yes.

You have recently given that further thought, have you?

> It is a case of not again, but still. I have been thinking
> about it all the time.

The last time we talked with you about it, you said that you had
no late information as to the number of ships.

> That is true, but I am getting more and more information.

Do you expect to pass the Philippines bill at this session?

> I certainly hope so.

Mr. President, have you taken up with the senators the question
of ratifying the Safety-at-Sea Convention?

> Not recently, no.

JRT transcript (WC, NjP) of CLSsh (C. L. Swem Coll., NjP).
  ¹ New York *World*, Nov. 27, 1914; New York *Evening Post*, Nov. 27, 1914;
*Washington Post*, Nov. 28, 1914.
  ² Stephen Milancthon Sparkman, Democratic congressman from Florida, chairman of the Committee on Rivers and Harbors.

## To Lindley Miller Garrison

My dear Mr. Secretary:          The White House December 1, 1914

May I not ask you to express to General Funston and the
officers under him at Vera Cruz, and through them to the troops
who served there, my warm approbation and admiration of the
way in which a difficult and delicate situation was handled?
I believe from what we have learned that the effect of the oc-

cupation was to give our friends the Mexicans a very different impression of the United States Army and the spirit of the United States Government from that which they entertained before General Funston took his troops there. I am sure that I speak the feeling of the whole country when I commend the efficiency, the courage, and the discretion with which the expedition and occupation were carried out.

Cordially and sincerely yours,    Woodrow Wilson

TLS (WDR, RG 94, AGO Doc. File, File 2149991, DNA).


## To Robert Lansing

My dear Mr. Lansing:        The White House December 1, 1914

I would be very much obliged if you would read the enclosed letter from Professor Munsterberg[1] and send me a memorandum, if you would be so kind, of the answers and comments that might be made upon his statements. Here at last is a very definite summing up of the matters upon which German anti-administration feeling in this country is being built up, and perhaps it would be wise to take very serious notice of it. The case they make out is *prima facie* very plausible indeed.

Cordially and sincerely yours,    Woodrow Wilson

TLS (SDR, RG 59, 763.72111/1074½, DNA).
[1] That is, H. Münsterberg to WW, Nov. 19, 1914.


## To Seth Low

My dear Mr. Low:        The White House December 1, 1914

I want you to know how deeply I appreciated your generous and patriotic action in accepting the appointment I took the liberty of urging upon you through the Secretary of Labor and my friend, Mr. House. I know at what sacrifice of personal convenience you do this and I the more deeply appreciate it. It is characteristic of the public spirit you have always shown.

Cordially and sincerely yours,    Woodrow Wilson[1]

TLS (S. Low Papers, NNC).
[1] Similar letters were WW to C. W. Mills, Dec. 1, 1914, TLS (Letterpress Books, WP, DLC), and WW to P. Gilday, Dec. 1, 1914, TLS (Letterpress Books, WP, DLC).

## To Edward Mandell House

My dear Friend: The White House December 1, 1914

Thank you with all my heart for your letters. They guide me in many matters in the most serviceable way.

I have written to Mr. Low, and I have also taken steps to convey the intimation you suggested to the Industrial Relations Committee. It is certainly a most inopportune time to start an investigation out there.

Thank you warmly for letting me see Mr. Hugh Wallace's letter.[1] Your own explanation of the matter entirely satisfies me, but my present judgment is that we had better let the Belgian relief alone and see if it is not possible to give it informal guidance.

I am working on my message. You intimate in one of your letters there is something you would like to suggest. Was it the Army matter?

In haste Affectionately yours, Woodrow Wilson

TLS (E. M. House Papers, CtY).
[1] H. C. Wallace to E. M. House [Nov. 28, 1914], TCL (WP, DLC).

## To Sadie Cooper Hoyt

My dear Aunt Sadie: [The White House] December 1, 1914

I need not tell you how the suggestion of your letter of November twenty-eighth[1] appealed to me. I have thought many times of Cousin Robert and wondered what it was possible for me to do for him, but each time I have realized that it would be a great mistake to appoint any relative of mine to office. It would put him in a false position and it would put me on the defensive for the rest of my term, for the public regards such things very critically indeed.

If you hear of any way in which I can assist Cousin Robert to a business or other preferment of any kind, I would be sincerely obliged if you would give me the information promptly.

It was a pleasure to hear from you and I wish that the news might have been better of the dear people for whom I have so deep and genuine an affection.

With love to all,

Cordially and sincerely yours, Woodrow Wilson

TLS (Letterpress Books, WP, DLC).
[1] It is missing.

## From William Jennings Bryan

My dear Mr. President:          Washington December 1, 1914.

I beg to submit for your consideration the following:

Our interests justify us in suggesting mediation to the belligerent nations.

(a) The war is throwing a heavy burden upon the United States and deranging business. The cotton growers have suffered a loss of not less than $100,0000,000 by the restriction of their market; several other lines of industry have suffered severely; the loss to business generally, due to a suspension of credits, has amounted to many hundreds of millions. The Government has been compelled to resort to new forms of taxation to make good the decrease in import duties.

(b) Transportation is interrupted both on land and sea and the railroad situation is likely to become embarassing.

(c) Delicate questions are constantly arising in connection with our efforts to maintain neutrality. These may not only affect our relations with the belligerents but they disturb political conditions in this country and threaten to turn attention from our economic problems.

2nd. We owe it to other neutral nations to do everything in our power to bring the war to a close. They are suffering relatively more than we and are less able than we to endure the hardships which, without their fault, have been thrown upon them. Complaint has already been made against some of the neutral nations that they have not enforced neutrality; other neutral nations are complaining of the acts of belligerents in interfering with neutral commerce—the friction and irritation are increasing. These neutral nations look to us to represent the third party—"the bystanders" who, though innocent, suffer while the combatants fight.

3d. We owe it to the belligerent nations, as a friend to all of them, to earnestly advise them to consider the peaceful settlement of their differences. Their feelings are so deeply stirred that they take counsel of their anger rather than of their sober judgment; they cannot consider the question with calmness and their pride will not allow them to ask mediation—the offer must come from us.

Four months have elapsed and each of the nations at war has witnessed a failure of its plans and calculations—the uncertainty of the result must now be apparent to all. The chance is decreasing that either side can win such a decisive victory as to enable it to dictate terms, and even if either side should win such a victory the peace that would follow would be built upon fear, and history proves that permanent peace can not be built upon such a foundation.

Mediation does not mean that any of the combattants shall accept terms that are unsatisfactory, but that they shall propose terms, and surely these Christian nations ought to be willing to state to the world the terms upon the acceptance of which they are willing to cease hostilities, leaving responsibility for a continuance of the war to rest upon those who propose unreasonable terms or reject reasonable terms. All disclaim responsibility for the beginning of the war and there is no tribunal to fix the blame, but responsibility can be fixed for a continuation of the war if any nation is unwilling to state its terms or if, in stating its terms, it makes demands which are not just and fair.

When, at the beginning of the war, you proposed mediation, none of the nations expressed a willingness to consider a conference, but now, after appalling losses on both sides; now when all must confess failure to accomplish what they expected; now when the cup of sorrow is overflowing and when new horrors are being added daily, it would seem to be this nation's duty, as the leading exponent of Christianity and as the foremost advocate of world-wide peace, to approach the warring nations again and earnestly urge them to consent to a conference with a view to coming to an understanding which will enable them to lay down their arms and begin the work of reconstructing a permanent peace on the basis of justice and friendship.

With assurances of high respect I am, my dear Mr. President,
Very truly yours,   W. J. Bryan

TLS (WP, DLC).

## To Edward Mandell House

My dear Friend:          The White House December 2, 1914
The Springfield Republican is right; the questions of the immediate future are no doubt to be foreign questions, and I am not at all sure that I have the wisdom to meet and solve them, but with the help of counsellors like yourself I hope that it will be possible to guide the old ship in a way that will bring her credit and make her serviceable to the world. These things give me, you may be sure, deep concert and solicitude. I am right now making plans to do what I hope will be wise things in regard to our relations with the other American States.
Affectionately yours,   Woodrow Wilson

TLS (E. M. House Papers, CtY).

## To Walter Hines Page

My dear Page:                    [The White House] December 2, 1914

I have allowed my absorption in tremendous public questions to make me guilty of a very serious breach of courtesy. I have never sent a letter of thanks to the American Luncheon Club, of which I believe you are President, for the gift of the golf bag and sticks which they were so generous and thoughtful to have made for me by Mr. Braid and sent to me by my cousin, John Wilson. I have not only appreciated the gift most sincerely, but I have played with the clubs almost every day and have had many occasions to thank my thoughtful friends of the Luncheon Club in my heart, if I have not with my lips. So much have I thought about it indeed that I discovered with a shock today that I had not sent this acknowledgment.

Will you not make my humble apologies to them and beg them in the circumstances to forgive me and to believe that it has not been due to any fault of my heart.

Always            Faithfully yours,   Woodrow Wilson

TLS (Letterpress Books, WP, DLC).

## From William Jennings Bryan

My dear Mr. President:            Washington December 2, 1914.

The situation seems to be clearing up in Mexico. Villa and Zapata are working in harmony and Gutierrez seems to be about to assume authority over most of the country. The occupation of Carranza is not likely to last long.

In view of the fact that Gutierrez will probably be the head of the Government would it not be well to send him a strongly worded representation—similar to that sent sometime ago to Villa and Carranza—emphasizing the necessity of protecting religious worship and religious property, also those devoted to religious work, and reiterating our statements in regard to the protection of the rights of foreigners and the importance of granting amnesty to those guilty of offenses purely political.

With assurances of high respect I am, my dear Mr. President,
                    Yours very truly,   W. J. Bryan

TLS (WP, DLC).

# William Jennings Bryan to Joseph Patrick Tumulty

Dear Mr. Tumulty:          Washington December 2, 1914.

In the opinion of this Department the telegram from Dr. Sun Yat-sen does not merit attention.

The Department of State has no knowledge of any negotiation with Messrs. J. P. Morgan and Company for a loan to China.

Two Chinese officials of subordinate rank arrived in the United States a few weeks ago. One is connected with the Ministry of Finance and reported that he came to study banking methods. The other is connected with the Ministry of Communications and is said to be investigating railway management.

A few days since the Department learned from a reliable source, but neither from the bankers nor the officials concerned, that the Chinese officers mentioned above had visited the National City Bank of New York and solicited a loan.

In the view of this Department the making of such a loan to China by an American bank on fair terms would be advantageous not only to China but to the United States.

It does not seem probable, however, that China will be able to obtain any loan in the United States under present conditions.

The information in possession of the Department does not confirm Dr. Sun's statements that the people are determined to overthrow President Yuan[,] neither is there any evidence that a struggle to this end has already begun in Kwantung or anywhere else save in the plotting of Dr. Sun in Japan and General Huang Hsing in the United States. There is, therefore, no occasion for the observance of neutrality.

That these two men and their followers are endeavoring to create a rebellion is quite true and recent newspapers from China intimate a fear that uprisings may be attempted.

But unless these revolutionists are able to obtain financial and moral support from some other country than their own, their efforts seemed doomed to failure. The information in the possession of the Department tends to show that the substantial people of China, south as well as north and even in Dr. Sun's own province, are standing by President Yuan.

That the methods of the latter savor of the dictator rather than the President may be true; but one can scarcely pass judgment upon the matter without knowing all the circumstances. It is understood that Professor Goodnow, who was President Yuan's adviser,[1] sustains his action.

It is true beyond all question that conditions in China have very much improved within the past year, that the brigandage

which disturbed four of the central provinces has been suppressed, that order is being restored generally throughout the
country and that the revenues which up to a year ago were
nearly all consumed locally are now contributing to the support
of the central government.

Financial conditions are undoubtedly bad enough, even now,
but if Dr. Sun's plans were carried through, I fear the situation
would become so much worse that foreign intervention would
be almost unavoidable.

Yours very sincerely,   W. J. Bryan

TLS (WP, DLC).
1 Frank Johnson Goodnow, President of The Johns Hopkins University, had
served as legal advisor to Yuan Shih-k'ai, 1913-14.


## To William Jennings Bryan

My dear Mr. Secretary:    The White House December 3, 1914

I have your letter of yesterday about the advisability of sending a note to Gutierrez about protecting religious worship and
religious property, etc.

I think that such a message is highly desirable if it can be sent
through some person known to be *persona grata* to those now
in charge of affairs at Mexico City and who can convey it confidentially and unofficially.

I feel that there is a very considerable embarrassment involved
in sending what might seem to be official communications to the
new government before it has got a little more firmly in the sad-
dle.

I am heartily glad to see things clearing up, as they seem to
be, in Mexico. I pray most earnestly it may be indeed the beginning of the end.

Always       Faithfully yours,   Woodrow Wilson

TLS (W. J. Bryan Papers, DNA).


## From William Jennings Bryan, with Enclosure

My dear Mr. President:      Washington December 3, 1914.

I am sending you a telegram to our Legation in Santo
Domingo. Immediate action is necessary and I will ask you to
please make such correction as is necessary to bring the instructions in conformity to your wishes, and then send it to the State
Department telegraph office to be sent.

If there are any changes important enough to make you desire to confer with me before sending the telegram you can so inform me.

With assurances of high respect I am, my dear Mr. President,
Yours very truly,   W. J. Bryan

TLS (WP, DLC).


E N C L O S U R E[1]

Washington, December 3, 1914.

Your Tuesday one p.m.,[2] and previous relevant correspondence. The opposition by absenting itself for the purpose of preventing a constitutional quorum has manifested its purpose to obstruct the will of the majority expressed at a free and fair election. This being the case the provisional president, in the exercise of his constitutional powers, should issue a decree declaring that a majority of the national assembly is a quorum, to enable the oath of office to be administered at once. If provisional president is unwilling to assume this responsibility, you will confer with the provisional president and president-elect, Jimenez, and if they *jointly* approve, you may fix a day and hour in the near future when the new president will be recognized by this Government and full authority turned over to him, with the understanding that he will *before that* at once take the oath of office in the presence of the national assembly, provided a majority of both houses is present. Notify the leaders of the opposition that while their co-operation is desirable and should be given, from patriotic motives, still, if they withhold their co-operation this Government will give all necessary support to Jimenez and his government with the view to the establishment of order and the promotion of peace and prosperity. It is hoped that the minority will appreciate this opportunity of giving hearty support to the new government. Insurrection and revolutionary opposition will not be tolerated and if any such obstruction is attempted the leaders will be held personally responsible. Commander Willard of the HANCOCK will be instructed in the same sense.

Five thousand dollars per day will be allowed for the present, but inform Jimenez that as soon as order is restored and the government fully established it is expected that the expenses of the army will be largely reduced, so that education and public works may receive their just proportion of public revenues. Report attitude of the provisional president and president-elect Jimenez.

Bryan

T telegram (SDR, RG 59, 839.00/1631, DNA).
  ¹ Words in italics added by Wilson.
  ² Chargé [John Campbell] White to the Secretary of State, Dec. 1, 1914, FR 1914, p. 257: "Provisional President expresses unwillingness to issue decree declaring majority of National Assembly a quorum, on grounds of unconstitutionality, contravention of Wilson plan, and existence of bi-cameral legislature which relieves him of his legislative power. He prefers that solution of crisis shall come from Washington. Respectfully suggest that Department name date on which it will recognize Jiménez as President, turning over funds to him. Consider any further delay conducive to disorders."

## From the Diary of Colonel House

Washington, D. C. December 3, 1914.

This has been a remarkable day with the telephone constantly ringing. The President telephoned from Washington and asked me to come down immediately so that we might be together in the evening and go over his message.

I took the 12.08 train. In the meantime, there was a constant rush of callers and telephone calls. I never wanted to go less, for Gordon teleph[o]ned that Janet was reaching a crisis.¹ However, I felt it my duty to go.

I arrived at 5.40 and was met by a White House automobile. The President had inquired for me and had left word that he was over at his office, where I found him signing his mail. A little later Burleson came to discuss postoffices with him. I left them before they were through in order to dress for dinner.

No one was at dinner excepting Dr. Grayson and the conversation was casual. After dinner the President recited several new limericks, and read a whimsical poem or two, and then we settled down to work.

We went over his message carefully, but there were only a few suggestions which I made and which largely had reference to foreign conditions. I knew fairly well, of course, what the message was to be from recent conversations with him, and I was glad he had not inserted any new matter regarding domestic legislation.

He said he had read my letter and the clippings from the Springfield Republican with considerable interest, and thought we were right in our conclusions that he would be judged from now almost wholly by the way our foreign affairs were conducted. He spoke with extreme regret of Mr. Bryan's unsuitability for

¹ She was about to have a baby.

the office of Secretary of State, but did not know what could be done. He intimated that it might be well to let him leave the Cabinet in the event he desired to do so because of some policy with which he might disagree. We both thought he had served his usefulness as Secretary of State, and that it would be a good thing for the administration and for the country if he would pleasantly take himself out of the Cabinet.

The President read a memorandum which Mr. Bryan had given him which he said he had saved to read with me. It was an earnest argument for the President to again offer his services as mediator. I was certain it would be entirely footless to do this, for the Allies would consider it an unfriendly act, and further it was not good for the United States to have peace brought about until Germany was sufficiently beaten to cause her to consent to a fundamental change in her military policy. I reminded him that from my conversation with Dumba, Austria was willing to negotiate for peace upon a reasonable basis of reduced armaments, but that Germany had declined to do so. When Germany was pushed back within her own borders I thought it would be advisable for me to go there and see the Kaiser and endeavor to get his consent to two conditions. One being the indemnity of Belgium, and the other such a reduction of armaments as would insure lasting peace in Europe. With that as a basis, I could go to England with some hope of success.

He agreed to this, but thought it would be exceedingly difficult for the Kaiser to consent to such conditions because of his entourage who would advise against it. I was hopeful that both the Kaiser and his advisers by that time would see it was either peace upon the terms mentioned, or something very much worse.

Going back to Mr. Bryan, the President said that he, Mr. Bryan, did not know that he, The President, was working for peace wholly through me, and he was afraid to mention this fact to him for fear it would offend him. He said Mr. Bryan might accept it gracefully, but not being certain, he hesitated to tell him. I advised not telling him for the moment.

The President had a feeling that I could do more to initiate peace unofficially than anyone could do in an official capacity, for the reason I could talk and be talked to without it being binding upon anyone, and we might in this way arrive at conditions. He has placed this problem squarely up to me. I am glad of it, provided he will give a little more time to the discussion of it, and provided he does not allow others to inject themselves into it.

Lanier Winslow, Gerard's secretary, is leaving for Berlin on

Saturday, and I asked the President if he had any messages to send the Ambassador by word of mouth. He said he had some letters from Germany written by Americans married to Germans, stating that Gerard and some of his Embassy staff were anti-German, and were too free in expressing their opinions. He asked me to caution Gerard about this, and intimated if the matter became serious, he would recall Gerard.

He asl [also] asked me to caution Walter Page about being pro-British. Page is writing letters to the State Department which excite attention, and both Mr. Bryan and Mr. Lansing have spoken to him about it. I promised to attend to both matters. See my letters of today to both Page and Gerard.

I gave him Ferrero's article in the November Atlantic Monthly to read, because it seemed to me to be about as sane an exposition of the situation as I had seen.

I also gave him Warburg's brief on the Federal Reserve Board,[2] a copy of which Warburg had already sent McAdoo. The President's took McAdoo's view, which to me, is the wrong one, although I did not seriously argue the point with him. If the Federal Reserve Board is to perform its functions properly, it will not do to make it an adjunct of the Treasury Department to be absolutely dominated by the Secretary.

The President is sometimes inconsistent in these matters, for the very thing is happening now that he so earnestly deprecated when McAdoo was trying to have a board appointed which would be wholly subordinated to his wishes.

I advised the President to start the practice of giving to the public, State papers similar to the "White, Yellow" and other papers given out by every civilized nation excepting outs [ours]. I thought it would have to come sometime, and I would like his administration to receive the credit of it. He admitted this, but did not like to begin it under fire. I replied there had not been enough demand for it or criticism because of not having it, for anyone to make the charge that he was giving way under pressure or criticism. He then said he did not see how he could do it with Mr. Bryan as Secretary of State, and if he got someone in the State Department to aid Mr. Bryan, it would probably be a man of Mr. Bryan's choosing, and as unfit as Osborn or some of the others of his selection.

I asked if it was not possible to bring about a greater degree

---

[2] Paul M. Warburg's memorandum is missing in both the Wilson and House Papers. From what House writes below, it is obvious that Warburg argued strongly for establishing the independence of the Federal Reserve Board vis-à-vis the Treasury Department.

of civic service reform during his administration. I spoke of the evils of the spoils system and how it debauched our political life. He agreed to this, but did not believe it would be possible to get any law through Congress, and he recalled Mr. Bryan's feelings upon the subject as being typical. However, if I were in the President's place, I would make an effort and leave the responsibility of failure upon Congress.

In speaking of Germany, I asked if he recalled how the Kaiser drew around him only the rich of every nation. The Morgans and their counterparts were the ones he saw from the United States. It was the same with Great Britain. He[3] seems possessed with the power of wealth, and his whole economic scheme seemed to me wrong and wholly material. France, England and the United States do things for humanity to a certain extent, but Germany is evidently actuated by a selfishness which knows no bounds and which has led her, as it does individuals, to wreck.

While we were talking and almost at the same hour that the announcement came of the birth of Randolph Tucker Jr.[4] the announcement came that Louise Auchincloss was born to Janet. It was a curious coincidence and the President and I both remarked upon it. We were in the same room, in the same chairs, in the same positions, and it was the same time of day and we were discussing questions of world-wide importance each time.

We were busy until nearly eleven o'clock, and seeing how tired the President looked, I suggested that he go to bed and let me change my clothes and go to my train. I felt I must return to New York because of my precious Janet. Grayson took me to the station and talked until nearly midnight before leaving me.

[3] The Kaiser.
[4] See n. 1 to the extract from the House diary printed at Nov. 6, 1914.

## Edward Mandell House to James Watson Gerard

Dear Judge:                    New York City. December 4th, 1914.

I was with the President yesterday and he asked me to say to you to please be extremely careful not to permit anyone connected with the Embassy to express any sentiment whatsoever that is not strictly neutral.

Complaints have come to him from Americans married to Germans that indiscreet remarks have been made. He feels very strongly upon this subject and I am not only sending you a message through Lanier, but think it best to write directly.

And this reminds me to ask whether you received my letter

of August 17th enclosing you a copy of one which I wrote to the Kaiser last June.[1] I have never heard from you upon the subject.

With warm regards for both Mrs. Gerard[2] and yourself, I am

Faithfully yours,   [E. M. House]

CCL (E. M. House Papers, CtY).
    [1] House's letter to the Kaiser is printed as an Enclosure with EMH to WW, July 9, 1914, Vol. 30.
    [2] Mary Daly Gerard.


## Edward Mandell House to Walter Hines Page

Dear Page:                    New York City. December 4th, 1914.

I have just returned from Washington. The President was interested in the letter you enclosed to me under cover of yours of November 9th.[1] I am wondering if you know just how reliable the person is who wrote the letter.

The President wished me to ask you please to be careful not to express any un-neutral feeling either by word of mouth, or by letter, and not even to the State Department. He told me that both Mr. Bryan and Mr. Lansing had remarked upon your leaning in that direction, and he thought it would materially lessen your influence.

The President feels very strongly about this and I am sending the same message to Gerard.

Faithfully yours,   E. M. House[2]

TLS (E. M. House Papers, CtY).
    [1] Page enclosed this letter in WHP to EMH, Nov. 9, 1914, ALS (WP, DLC). From Page's ambiguous description of the enclosure, it seems to have been a letter written by a German lady who said that her country had to keep up the war effort "so long as it has food & powder & men."
    [2] Page returned this letter to House.


## From Joseph Patrick Tumulty

The White House

Dear Governor:          Friday evening, December 4, 1914.

This evening when discussing your Message, I felt that I was burdening you after a hard day and so I could not impress upon you the importance of the thing I had been urging for some days; namely, making some mention of business in your Message. I had so much respect for Colonel House's judgment that I hated to be found disagreeing with him. But unfortunately from what you told me, his judgment was based on the attitude of the New York business man toward everything you had said with reference to business. Of course, the New York business man will never give us full credit for anything we have done; but I am thinking of the ordinary business man throughout the country.

It seems to me that your failure to mention business legislation and the completion of our programme regarding it, will lead to further suspicion and doubt. What you said regarding business some months ago was taken with a grain of salt because at that time business legislation of a radical character was pending. Now that that is out of the way, it has seemed to me that this time—the opening of Congress—was the dramatic moment to re-state your position with clearness and certainty. The business situation throughout the country is most critical and the people are looking at this time for something more than statistics; they are looking for encouragement from the head of the Nation.

You will find in the newspapers on Wednesday,[1] all over the country, comment on the fact that you were silent on the matter of business and from this silence will be drawn the inference that further legislation with reference to business is being considered, with the consequent agitation and uncertainty.

Respectfully,   Tumulty

TLS (WP, DLC).
[1] The day following that on which Wilson was to deliver his Annual Message.

## Two Letters from Seth Low

Dear Mr. President:          New York December 4th, 1914.

I thank you sincerely for your very kind letter of December 1st. It will be a pleasure to me if I can be of service in helping to bring about better conditions in Colorado, and it adds to my pleasure to know that in trying to do so I am holding up your hands. You have given us all so fine an illustration of devotion to the public duty that he would be a poor American who should fail to respond in kind.

I am, dear Mr. President,

Faithfully yours,   Seth Low.

Dear Mr. President:          New York December 4th, 1914.

My experience leads me to think that it is very desirable that both I and my Colleagues should have from you, in writing, some authority to act upon the Commission the appointment of which you have publicly announced. It is desirable, also, that it should be known among ourselves, and also publicly when action be-comes necessary, whether you wish me to act as Chairman of a

Commission of Three, or to be the umpire contemplated in the plan for a three-year truce originally suggested by you.

If we are to act under your earlier plan, the question of expenses becomes an important one, because that plan contemplated that the expenses would be met equally by the operators and the miners. Inasmuch as many, if not all, of the operators have declined to accept the plan, it should be made clear to us, I think, before we incur expense how the expenses are to be met.

If you have any general instructions to give for our guidance, I need not assure you that we shall be glad to receive them. Possibly the time has not yet come when you care to do this; but perhaps later you may think it desirable.

My Associates and I are to hold a conference at the Department of Labor on Saturday, December 12th, at 9:30 A.M. Any communication sent to me in care of the Department of Labor will reach me. I expect to reach Washington on Tuesday evening and to remain until Saturday afternoon.

Very respectfully, yours,   Seth Low

TLS (WP, DLC).


## An Interview

[Dec. 5, 1914]

A TALK WITH THE PRESIDENT

By Samuel G. Blythe

"The first time I knew I had made an appreciable impression in politics, the first time I felt even passably sure I was getting on, was when I was running for governor and was touring the northern part of New Jersey.

"We say, over there, that New Jersey is a bag, tied round by a string in the middle, the northern half and the southern half rather dissimilar in many characteristics, and the Pennsylvania Railroad representing the string. I was on my tour, making my speeches and meeting the voters. At one town, after I had spoken and was greeting my audience, a big, beefy, hearty fellow came up to me, gave me a tremendous thump on the back and roared:

" 'Doc, you're all right!' "

The President swung his right arm through the air to illustrate the blow, and gave a fine, robust imitation of the voice of his energetic supporter. Then he laughed, and I laughed, and the President said: "At that moment I felt sure I had arrived."

We were sitting in his private study on the second floor of the White House at eight of an evening in early December. He had just completed his address to Congress and had sent it to the printer, and his desk was still littered with scraps of paper on which there were notes in his minute handwriting, with books and documents and all the paraphernalia for address making.

The President had taken the chair he uses for his work at the desk. He had pulled it round and had asked me to take a seat near by. He slid easily into a most comfortable attitude, with one hand in a trousers pocket and the elbow of his other arm resting on the arm of the chair. He leaned back in the chair, crossed his legs, made a sort of circle of the thumb and first finger of the hand not pocketed, and peered at me through the circle. There was a twinkle in his eye.

"Now," he said, "what shall we talk about?"

"Well," I suggested tentatively, "the world is full of a number of things."

"It is," he replied, "but a good many of them are not talkable subjects at the present time."

So we took preparedness for war, and business and currency, and trusts, and Mexico, and the shipping problem, and rural credits, and the European war, especially the European war, and set them up on the mantelpiece—squat, grouchy little manikins of pressing problems that had been and are pressing—and left them, in a scowling, uneasy row, to jostle one another and growl over the lack of appreciation of their importance, and went gayly to our talk, regardless of the mutterings of the grouchy pressing-problem manikins and their efforts to edge themselves into the conversation.

That was last night. And this morning, as I am writing, I have taken some more things and put them alongside the others. I have set up there what was said about the philosophy and psychology of politics; of the vitality and adaptability of the Constitution; of motives of various persons; of the maneuvering of various intrigants; of numerous abstract considerations and corollaries—because I want to write a human document about one of the most human men I ever met or knew.

There is a general disposition to regard the President as a thinking machine, as a large and brilliant but gelid intellect, incased in a nonresponsive and highly insulated covering. He is thought of and talked of as mostly brains—and cold, analytical, logical brains at that; and there can be no denying that he has those commodities in full supply. The other side of him is not so generally known, principally because his rise in public life has been so rapid and his transfer from academy to arena occurred so few years ago.

Wherefore, it seems about the proper time to set down the fact here that Woodrow Wilson, President of the United States, is one of the most kindly, courteous, considerate, genial and companionable of men; that, so far from being aloof from the people, his passion is the people, the real people, and his sole desire is to serve them so long as his term of office shall continue, and afterward in such measure as he may. He holds his position to be that of a man connected with his fellow men by a peculiar relationship of responsibility, and the vivid sense of that responsibility is doubtless accountable for the impression of aloofness. However, that is not what I started out to say. The point that presses at this time is that the President of the United States weighs one hundred and seventy-six pounds, and that those one hundred and seventy-six pounds are mostly bone and muscle. There is not an ounce of excess baggage in the way of flesh about him. He lives out-of-doors as much as he can. His face is tanned and so are his sinewy hands. His eye is bright and clear. His laugh is hearty and unaffected. His spirit is good. He is buoyantly healthy. He sleeps well, eats well, works hard, and plays whenever he has a chance.

His principal recreation is golf. He plays every day, usually with Doctor Grayson, and goes to most of the links about Washington.

"I suppose," I said, "you are a good golf player?"

"Why do you say that?" he asked.

So I told him of a great millionaire I had seen playing golf once, playing with a personal attendant. The great millionaire would take his stance, waggle his club, contort himself in the most approved style, and make his wallop at the ball. It would dribble along a few yards or slice into the rough; and the personal attendant would assume an attitude of intense admiration and exclaim:

"Well played, sir; a marvelous shot!"

"I reckon," I said, "the President of the United States cannot fail publicly to be a good golfer."

"No," he replied; "I suppose not. I remember that, not long ago, when I played at Piping Rock, the papers said I went round in a highly sensational eighty. The fact was, that day was one of the worst golf days I have had since I began, and it took me one hundred and forty-six strokes to make the round.

"Golf," he continued, "is my physical and mental barometer. I know how I feel when I begin to play. For example, last night I worked until midnight on my address to Congress. There was a certain portion of it that I wanted to get into a satisfying shape, and I found it difficult to express my ideas. I toiled over it; and when I went to bed I suppose the wheels of my mind kept whirring, for I was not particularly refreshed this morning. I did not notice it when I got up; but when I went to the first tee I soon found I was not in form, and it was not until I had foozled over three holes that I got back, forgot everything and began to enjoy the game.

"Before I took up golf I used to ride my bicycle a great deal. I said then that I knew the state of my nerves by the condition of my legs as soon as I mounted my wheel. If I started off jauntily I was all right; but if I found it an effort there was something wrong. I enjoyed riding a bicycle," he said. "To my mind there is nothing more pleasant than to ride through an agreeable countryside, not hampered by any set itinerary or forced to go anywhere you do not want to go. It was always my plan to go where I wanted to, and to make no provision for the morrow. When I got up I would select some place and make that journey in an entirely hit-or-miss spirit of vagabondia.

"I rode my bicycle in Europe several times, and reached many places rarely seen by the tourists—little out-of-the-way corners; and the experiences were delightful. I liked to meet and talk and perhaps journey with the other vagabonds on the road, who, free from all sense of responsibility, went where they liked and when they liked, and were always prepared for whatever adventure might ensue.

"I like to be with people, to rub elbows with them. It must be a very ordinary crowd not to interest me. Nothing bores me so much as a conventional assemblage, and nothing interests me so much as a crowd of people on a street, any street, who are just human beings, filled with human passions and joys and sorrows, and not trying to be what they are not.

"When I was at Johns Hopkins I walked a great deal. My companions were always surprised because I did not prefer to go into the country, to walk with them out in the open. Instead, I always insisted on plunging down to where there were the most people, to mingle with them and talk with them, and observe them, and have a good time with them. When you walk in the country the stillness and the aloneness of it press back on you, push you back into yourself; but in the crowd on the city street you can get out of yourself, and can perhaps get into the spirit of the people, who are the Nation."

He stopped and looked out the window at the full moon, which was aiding the searchlight to make the Washington Monument a massive shaft of silver.

After a moment I elucidated one of my pet theories of golf, to the effect that no person of great imagination can be a crack golfer; because, instead of keeping his mind on the ball and his eye on it, and attending strictly to the business of hitting the ball, the imaginative person fails to think of what he should do to the ball, but makes a mental picture of what he shall do to it; fancies it flying straight and true for two hundred yards. Whereas the golfer with no imagination thinks only of the business at hand, which is hitting the ball.

The President laughed.

"I must have a highly gifted imagination then," he said. "But isn't it a satisfying game? There is nothing I know of that gives a man more pride of accomplishment than a good drive or a good approach, or a shot well played."

"Lately I have been trying to master the brassy; and on one links I made a wonderful shot one day. Every time I walk over that spot I have a thrill of pleasure, of pride of accomplishment. Only to-day I waited, at the club where I was playing, for a four-some to get away. One of the men made a remarkable drive. It was a beauty—two hundred and twenty-five yards I am sure, and straight down the middle. I fancy it was not a customary sort of drive for him, but, whether it was or not, you could see the pride in that man's legs as he walked away. His legs radiated pride, and so did his back. He had accomplished something.

"My chief golf fault is that I raise my eyes just before I finish my stroke. You see, when I began to play it was difficult to get caddies and I was forced to caddie for myself. Inasmuch as I had ample use for all my funds, the question of lost balls was of moment; so I grew into the habit of raising my eyes to watch the course of the ball, for if I didn't I knew I should lose ball after ball. That fault is pretty firmly implanted in me and it interferes with my progress."

I told him of a certain distinguished member of the Supreme Court of the United States who took up golf. In discussing his progress the eminent jurist said: "I have taken many lessons from the professional. He assures me that my form is perfect; but," he added ruefully, "I cannot hit the ball."

"There's a commentary on Washington!" said the President. "There are so many men about here whose form is perfect, but who cannot hit the ball. That's all this amounts to—hitting the ball—hitting the ball. And that reminds me," he continued, lean- ing forward in his chair and laughing—"that reminds me of a man I knew, a relative of Mrs. Wilson's whom we called the Colonel, who wanted to learn golf. He was at one of the clubs in the South; and he went to the grounds keeper and told him he desired the poorest caddie of the lot.

" 'I don't want one of those wise ones,' he said. 'You give me the worst one you have, and I'll teach him to caddie my way; and he can give me such information as I need.'

"So they gave him a short, squat negro they called Elephant, a big hulk of a boy with not a gleam of sense apparently. The Colonel started off. He made a sort of drive and proceeded to where the ball lay, tagged by Elephant. He found the ball in a depression. Elephant handed him an iron. The Colonel looked at the iron and looked at Elephant. He surveyed the ball. Then he turned to Elephant and shouted:

" 'What'll I do, boy? What'll I do?'

" 'Hit the ball, suh!' said Elephant. 'Hit the ball!'

"That's the philosophy of politics—of everything!" And the President sat back in his chair. "Hit the ball; hit it as well as you can—but hit it!"

Since I had been in that room before, they had hung a fine, big American flag on the wall—a flag about six feet long. I asked about it.

"They gave me that flag at the unveiling of the Kearny Statue,"[1] the President said; "and I hung it there on the wall."

The conversation drifted along, touching on some things naturally connected with topics then pressing, and not unconnected, in a way, with the flag. And just here I want to say that President Wilson is the most conscientiously neutral man of all neutral men concerning the war in Europe. I talked with him intimately for more than two hours, and there was not a syllable from him about the great war; not an intimation that he knew there was a war; not an opinion or a comment, though he has forty war problems before him every day.

And, of course, the talk came to politics. I said that, in my opinion, and from my experience, the actuating motives in politics are vanity and jealousy.

"Yes," the President replied; "that is true—or egotism, rather, which amounts to the same thing. My father was a Presbyterian minister and all that implies in the very highest sense. On Sunday afternoons, after his sermon in the morning, he used to lie down on the couch by the fire. I would sit on the rug beside him and we would have wonderful talks. He told me once, I remem-

[1] Wilson's speech at the unveiling of the statue of General Philip Kearny is printed as an addendum in this volume.

ber, when discussing this subject, that the old casuists had resolved all sins into the one great sin of egotism, because that consists in putting oneself before God."

He made a wry face.

"I don't suppose," he said, "that any man has greater opportunity than I to discover that the predominant trait in humans and in politics is vanity—egotism—the exaltation of self. This recalls a visit I had recently from a most able man, a man I have known for years, who is genuinely talented, highly cultured, affable and conscientious, and honest and correct in his usual relations with men. Still, when anything comes that bears any relation to himself—to his exalted ego—he forgets every principle he has, and forestalls all his culture and all his kindness to get for himself what he deems he deserves, because of his intense egotism.

"I found this out long before I went into public life. I discovered it soon after I became the head of Princeton, and it has been impressed on me more and more in my service as Governor of New Jersey and in my service here. The truly great politician —the statesman—you know, is the man who can take an impersonal view of politics—the impersonal view."

"But," I interrupted, "you do not find many of that kind, do you?"

"I think," the President replied, "that every really great man in politics, either in this country or abroad, was impersonal in his relations to his politics and his place. Take Lincoln, for example. You remember the stories of his troubles with Stanton, his Secretary of War? One of them is that once, when Lincoln sent an order to Stanton, Stanton tore up the order, refused to obey it, and said to the messenger:

" 'You go back and tell Lincoln he is a damned fool!'

"The man went back and told Mr. Lincoln.

" 'Did Stanton say I am a damned fool?' the President asked.

" 'He did.'

" 'Well,' said Lincoln, 'Stanton generally knows what he is talking about.'

"That's what I mean," continued the President earnestly, "the power to substract one's personality from the subject at hand. It is more necessary here than elsewhere. One cannot consider these problems as an individual. One must consider them impersonally, as an executive, appointed for a certain time to administer the office he holds, with due regard to the requirements of the people, and not in any sense with regard to his own predilections or prejudices or passions. I am responsible for running the Government as best I know how; but I am not the Government. The people are the Government."

"I heard Premier Asquith say practically the same thing," I said.

"Yes," continued the President; "but we have the better of Asquith in a way. Asquith is more vitally the government of England, with his Cabinet, than we are the Government over here, for Asquith and his ministers sit in the Commons; they are there to be questioned, and to direct, and to demand support, and to meet opposition. If they are defeated they can go directly to the country for support or rejection. They have to take part. Whereas, over here, if the Congress requires anything of a member of the Cabinet, say, and he does not see fit to answer that requirement, he can say an answer is not compatible with the public welfare, and let it go at that. We have greater power and less direct responsibility."

"Well, Mister President," I said, "you are on the inside in this place, looking out, and the rest of the world is on the outside, looking in. What is the most interesting thing about the presidency from your viewpoint?"

"The power of decision," he replied. "The knowledge that I, by virtue of the position I hold, can decide matters that are of moment to our people and to the rest of the world. With that, of course, comes the tremendous sense of responsibility; but that is the most interesting thing—painfully interesting at times —painfully!

"And," he went on animatedly, "I discover that I am not relying entirely on any present situation when I am called on to make these important decisions. By that I mean the influence which directs me isn't entirely the present influence, the influence exerted by the particular set of circumstances at hand, but is a culminative influence predicated on information I have secured in former times, of former circumstances, and of former procedure.

"That is to say, I have stored away in my mind, to be drawn on, a certain amount of information that comes to be of the greatest use in such contingencies. When a phase of a question comes up before me I not only consider that phase or that question in view of the present circumstances but in view of past circumstances. I suppose I am helped in this because I once wrote a history of the United States.

"Let me tell you why I wrote that history. I had no particular intention of being a historian. That was not in my mind. What was in my mind was to write a book on the development and philosophy of American politics. I wanted to do that. But when I came to do it I soon found I did not know enough to write such a book. I had not the information. So, in order to learn the history I needed, I wrote a history. Some time before I wrote that history I had written an essay telling how history should be written.[2]

"When I wrote that essay I had no idea I should become a historian; and when I wrote my history I discovered that my performance did not measure up at all to the critical requirements I had laid down in the essay I had written, discussing the proper manner in which history should be written. My mistake was in laying down rules before I began the practice. Probably if I should write such an essay now, it would conform more closely to my performance than to my propaganda.

"Then I came into public life; and the book about politics is yet to be written."

"But you will write it," I said.

"Yes; I shall write it," he answered—"provided there is anything left of me when I get through with this job."

"The thing that has most impressed me about the presidency since I began to know about Presidents is the incredible loneliness of the man in it," I said.

"Yes," the President replied; "it is a lonely place. It is necessarily solitary. Human nature is so constituted that a position of advantage invariably is utilized by the person occupying it. A President can have no intimates; because, no matter how unselfish those intimates may be at the beginning, inevitably they will seek to take advantage of that intimacy before the end. A President has so much to give, you know; and good resolutions of unselfish behavior cannot withstand the pressure of the temptation to ask for something on an opportunity provided by that intimacy.

"It is a lonely place; but that very loneliness has its compensations, and those compensations are great. Standing alone here I feel and know that I am in closer conscious touch with the people. I can hear them better; sense their wants and their dues better; come closer to them than I could if I were surrounded by a group, either large or small, who were constantly dinning into my ears their own thoughts, ideas, desires and opinions. I am in closer conscious touch with the outside. There are no walls of selfish humans between me and the country. There is no babble of near-by voices to deafen my ears to the real demands from the great outside."

[2] "On the Writing of History," printed at June 17, 1895, Vol. 9.

The President rose, walked to the window, and motioned for me to come and stand beside him. He pulled back the curtain and pointed out over the great sweep of the White House lawn, where the spray of the fountain glittered in the moonlight; where the shadows of the naked trees were sharply silhouetted on the turf; where, beyond, the Monument stood silvery in the light, and where the dome of the Capitol rose majestically in the far distance.

"Often," he said, "I stand here and look out over this picture; and I say to myself; 'This isn't Washington, with its petty politics and its little strifes, and its concentration of interests, and its puny ambitions and jealousies and egotisms and vanities and intrigues. This is the wide country—the busy East; the sweep of the prairies of the West; the breath of the forests; the grandeur of the mountains.' I am not shut up here. I am in conscious relation with all the people, and that, my dear friend, is the compensating advantage for the loneliness of my place."

"I love my fellow man. No person takes keener delight in his society than I do. I have my friends and I love them; but I realize that the circumscriptions of my position are not an unmixed evil. I may be lonely because of the necessities of my place; but my vision is clearer than it would be were I surrounded by a group—any group—of well-meaning and zealous friends with interests of their own.

"Do not misunderstand me, I beg of you. Do not think or say that I take no delight in the society of my fellows. No man is more gregarious than I. As Lincoln said: 'I reckon no man likes his fellow men better than I do, and no man sees less of them socially.' It goes with the place, and, as I have explained, it is not altogether undesirable."

We stood there for a minute silently. Then he put his hand on my shoulder and we walked back to our chairs.

"What," I asked, "is the most disagreeable feature of the presidency?"

"Patronage," he replied without a moment's hesitation—"patronage, and the genuine astonishment and resentment of personal friends that I cannot take care of them merely because they are personal friends. Politics, you know, as it is widely considered, consists in taking care of one's personal friends. Now I should like to do that, love to do it; but I cannot. And I am constantly perplexed at the genuine aggrievement of those friends because I cannot and do not.

"I would willingly take the coat off my back and give it to a friend who needed it. My friends can have anything I have that is mine; but I cannot give them what is not mine. These offices are not mine. They belong to the people. They are the nation's. Merely because a man is a personal friend of mine, or has been something or other that makes him think he is, is not a valid reason for bestowing on him an office that does not belong to me, but is mine only to administer through the proper person selected as the active agent. The obligation incumbent on me, as the distributor for the moment of these offices, is to find efficient men to hold them, not personal friends to hold them and get the emoluments.

"I do not think my generosity or my sense of deep and lasting friendship for my real friends can be questioned; but there is a higher obligation than any personal obligation: that is my obligation to the people of this country, who have put me in this place temporarily to administer their governmental affairs for them and who demand of me that I shall administer them for the people and not for the individual, even though that individual be myself or some one close to me.

"Moreover," he went on, his voice vibrant with earnestness and sincerity, "it is my firm impression that patronage ruins more potentially great men than any other one political influence. By that I mean that many a man who comes into public life hampers his true development by his devotion to patronage hunting, and his limitations thereby, more than in any other way. They spend their time running to get a job here and a job there.

"Of course there is a reason for it, because most of them owe their positions in public life to the work of the men back home, and they feel they must do what can be done for those men, and for their own men—the organization—in order that they may have future and continued success at the polls. But, as my observation goes, many a man in public life has not developed to half of his true capacity because of this ceaseless devotion to the harassing details of patronage. Some of them, to be sure, wouldn't develop very much if there were no patronage; but it is my firm opinion that if patronage could be eliminated we should have a bigger, broader, more patriotic and more useful body of legislators than we now have.

"I am not insensible to the demands made on public men who, in their turn, make those demands on me; but I deprecate them. I see fierce contests over Federal offices; consume hour after hour listening to the claims of one set of men or another; and I am convinced that, except for mere organization purposes, the people, as a mass, are not interested and do not pretend to be.

"Take the postmastership of any of our large cities, for example. When one of those contests for appointment is on you would think, to hear the proponents and opponents of the candidates tell it, that the very foundations of the Republic will rock if one man is not appointed or if another man is. And yet, I venture to say, the only concern of the great mass of the people over the postmastership of one city is that they get their mail promptly and that the office is administered honestly and efficiently. Let me repeat: If patronage could be eliminated we should have a much broader, more patriotic, more capable and more useful set of legislators."

"Is patronage the chief of your troubles?" I asked.

The President turned and looked at me with a sort of quizzical smile on his face.

"Troubles!" he exclaimed. "Troubles! Why, my dear sir, the White House is the clearing house for trouble!"

He stopped and laughed—laughed with his head thrown back and his shoulders shaking.

"After I was elected," he said, "and before I came to Washington, many advisers sought me to advise. Most of them told me, with solemn portent, that the thing I must guard against most was flattery. " 'Beware,' they exhorted, 'of the fawning sycophant! Steel yourself against the insidious flatterer. Do not be misled by the words of the honeyed tongue.' "

He laughed again.

"It's a joke," he said—"a joke. I haven't been bothered with flatterers. Of course there are some few obvious gladhanders who can be set down instantly where they belong; but, you may believe me, there has been no excess of flattery since I have been here. No person comes to you when things are going right. That is expected. Every person comes to you when things are going wrong. That is what I meet with day after day—trouble—complaint—things that have gone wrong—things that have bogged down. They want me to straighten them out. They want help. They want to tell me their troubles—and they do; you may be quite sure they do.

"The White House is the clearing house for trouble—not only Washington troubles, departmental troubles, governmental troubles, but hundreds and hundreds of the people write here to tell their private grievances and to ask for redress or for my aid. When things are going right we hear little about them; but when things go wrong we hear all about them—and there is no flattery about it, either. Flattery hasn't bothered me in the least. I don't have to fend off flatterers. My defensive tactics are employed against kickers.

"There's another thing that goes with the job which I do not like, and that is the eternal ko[w]towing to the President. Every time I go anywhere it is an event. If I want to go on the May-flower I can't go as Woodrow Wilson, seeking a little recreation; but I must go as the President and be piped over the side and have the officers standing stiffly round, and all that.

"And it is so everywhere. Some day I hope to get a chance to visit some of the interesting places in this town and see the sights. I can't do it now, because the minute I stick my head into a public building they turn out the guard and I can't see anything for the crowd of officials surrounding me. It's maddening!

"They have recently adopted some rather complicated regula-tions about automobile lights here in the District of Columbia. They are hard to understand, and we have put in a good deal of time trying to comply with them. We have been stopped by policemen two or three times because we have not had our lights right. Each time, as soon as the policeman discovered he had stopped me, he ran madly away—not walked, but ran. I have called after them in a vain endeavor to stop them and ask what is wrong, in order that the fault may be corrected; but each time the policeman has galloped down the street and away from me.

"I hate that. I despise any person who takes advantage of his position to evade any responsibility. I remember, when I was president of Princeton University, being out on the campus one night when the Seniors were to have some rites particularly sacred to them. They had a space railed off on the lawn. I was with some friends, and we started to go within the inclosure. A man stopped me. He said I wasn't a Senior and had no right with-in that select inclosure. I turned away.

" 'Why,' said one of my friends, 'you are president of this university and can go anywhere you like!'

" 'No,' I said; 'the mere fact that I am president gives me no right to go where I am not invited or where custom operates against me.' "

"And it is so with the presidency and with any other position. I despise a person who will use his position to gain an advantage for himself, or to evade any responsibility, or to avoid any obliga-tion."

"Still," I commented, "there are some few of that class in Washington—as you have observed, no doubt."

The President shot a quick glance at me.

"Some few!" he said dryly.

We talked of many other things, discussing various statesmen and the correctness of certain policies. He showed me why a writer was wrong who said he could not be a progressive Democrat if he admired Edmund Burke, and explained his liking for Burke and quoted much from Burke's orations.

The President said he intends to make some speeches on his return from the San Francisco Exposition next spring—"because," he remarked, "I shall have something to say to the people then. I have felt that it was not for me to appear in the rôle of a prophet before the people; but when this Congress is over we shall have a substantial record of things achieved, and I want to talk to the people about what we have done—not about what we intend to do."

He commented on the recent elections, expressing his satisfaction over the fact that, as he views it, the Democratic party is now a majority party and has great hopes for the future.

"I remember you said once that you read detective stories," I remarked. "Do you still read them?"

"I devour them," he replied. "I mean, of course, the better class of detective stories.

"I like the theater, too, and especially a good vaudeville show when I am seeking perfect relaxation; for a vaudeville show is different from a play, though I am intensely interested in the drama in all its phases. Still, if there is a bad act at a vaudeville show you can rest reasonably secure that the next one may not be so bad; but from a bad play there is no escape. Of course"— and he turned his face away—"I cannot go to the theater now."

He walked over to the window.

"Good night, Mister President," I said.

"Good night, Blythe," he answered, and as I turned at the door he was still standing by the window, looking, with misty eyes, at the great Monument, towering silvery in the cold moonlight.

Printed in the *Saturday Evening Post*, CLXXXVI (Jan. 9, 1915), 3-4, 37-38.

## From Edward Mandell House

Dear Governor:                    New York City. December 5th, 1914.

Earl Harding[1] rang me up a few minutes ago and said that Vick was in a highly nervous condition, having heard that you had accused him of drunkenness while in Santo Domingo, and having said he would have been dismissed if he had not resigned.

Harding desired to know whether I knew if you had made such a statement. I told him I was sure you had not. I also told him that you were having the Santo Domingo matter investigated, and asked him if it would not be possible to keep the World from publishing anything in regard thereto until after this investigation had been made.

His reply was that he did not think this could be done, for the reason that the Herald and Tribune were also contemplating making the matter public, and he thought it would be best for all concerned to have the World do it first.

I hate to write you of such disagreeable things and do so only with the thought that something may yet be done from Washington to prevent its publication.[2]

Affectionately yours,    E. M. House

TLS (WP, DLC).
 [1] Reporter for the New York *World*.
 [2] The New York *World* on December 7 began publication of a series of articles exposing the scandal surrounding the appointment of James Mark Sullivan as Minister to the Dominican Republic and his conduct in that post. The series continued in the issues of December 8, 9, 10, 11, and 13, 1914. See Link, *The New Freedom*, pp. 107-10.


## From Henry White

*Confidential*

Dear Mr President,                    Washington. Dec. 5th, 1914

I was only able to see Bernstorff yesterday upon his return from a visit to New York.

He has heard nothing on the subject about which I promised you to speak to him—"officially" from his Foreign Office—; but one of its important officials, whom I know personally, has written him, in a private letter, that the sentiments of our Ambassador are generally believed to be as described in the letter from Berlin which you have seen.

Bernstorff went on to say that, as I had spoken to him on the subject and we are old friends & colleagues, he would add confidentially that his wife, who is home at Munich but of course in frequent communication with Berlin, had mentioned the subject in several of her letters to him. He is therefore afraid that there can be no doubt about the prevailing impression, which I fear has been increased by indiscretions on the part of several of the subordinates at the Embassy—*not* Grew the 1st Secretary,[1] whose demeanor has I understand been irreproachable and even sympathetic.

I said suggestively in the course of conversation: "But I dont think there is anything to be done about it here, do you?" to which B. replied "Certainly not, but it is nevertheless unfortunate," as of course it is under existing circumstances.

On the other hand, to be perfectly fair, I ought to say that Spring-Rice who has just been to see me—also an old friend—in talking over confidentially matters international, in connection with the war, happened to say: "By the bye Gerard rather put his foot into it not long ago in a speech at Leipzig when he said that all America is pro-German in this war"—a speech of which I had not heard.

There is no doubt that Gerard's manners are unsympathetic, to use no stronger term. I know of two American-born ladies whom he has reproached for having married Germans instead of Americans, one of them being particularly offended because his remarks were made to her at a time of great anxiety for the safety of her husband, who is at the front. I dare say he only meant to be jocose!

I venture to suggest, Mr. President, that the situation would be very materially improved, if you could see your way to writing our Ambassador a private letter, telling him in general terms & without mentioning names that you have heard from various sources that an impression exists in Germany that his sympathies are anti-German. If you say that you do so as an act of friendship and to put him on his guard, without any intimation that you believe these rumors to be true, he could not be otherwise than appreciative of your kindness. I am quite sure that were I in his place, I should have been profoundly grateful to you for such a proof of your confidence and consideration, and it will certainly make him more careful in the future.[2]

The circumstances in which he finds himself are very exceptional and particularly difficult for one who has not been trained to diplomacy, especially if he be tactless by nature, not blessed with good manners, and have been a political partisan at home. In one of the letters mentioned by Bernstorff, it was suggested that Gerard, being rather vain, does not consider that the Emperor has treated him with sufficient intimacy and is therefore anti-German; as to the truth of which I have no knowledge and I only mention it, as showing that people are evidently "talking."

I must not omit however to say that everyone in Berlin appears to find Mrs. Gerard charming and most sympathetic which of course helps the situation.

If I can be of any further use to you, dear Mr President, in this or any other matter, pray consider me entirely at your disposal as an old public servant.

Yours Very Sincerely   Henry White

I think I mentioned to you the other day[3] that there is no doubt about the zeal with which Gerard worked for our compatriots when I was in Berlin; often till past midnight. And he must have advanced a large amount of money out of his own pocket; much of it given away, I imagine.

ALS (WP, DLC).
  1 Joseph Clark Grew.
  2 Wilson may have written such a private letter. However, it is not extant in the collection of Gerard Papers at the University of Montana.
  3 White conferred with Wilson at the White House on December 2.

## From Lucius William Nieman

The President,                          Milwaukee, Wis., Dec. 5, 1914.

Permit me to thank you for your cordial note of Nov. 23. I appreciate what you say regarding our work for a senator who could be depended upon to support the cause which found expression in your election, and has been advanced by your administration. I believe Mr. Husting, as a senator, will be an object lesson to not a few so-called Democrats now in the senate. Mr. Husting is a man of independent thought, but his independence has not shown itself by playing into the hands of the enemies of his party and of its principles.

As for The Journal, I have felt that the best way it could serve the country was by supporting men who could be trusted to help to free government from the influences which have controlled it for the benefit of the few. Convinced of the great necessity of strengthening the cause in the senate, and certain that our state was with us, we went to great lengths in this case, even taking a hand in selecting a candidate whose trustworthiness could not be doubted and whose election was more probable than that of any of the other Democrats who were available.

That in doing this we have given support to you is, I need not say, a cause of great personal gratification.

                          Very sincerely yours,   L. W. Nieman.
TLS (WP, DLC).

## From Charles W. Mills

My dear Mr. President:          Philadelphia December 5, 1914.

I find your very gracious letter of December 1st on my return from the mines this morning, and I sincerely appreciate your very kind expressions.

Since the announcement of the appointment of the Commission I have received a great many letters, some from Colorado, three from New York, and two from Boston. The general sentiment in Colorado from the letters which I have received, is very antagonistic, and if the statement made before the Federal Industrial Relations Commission at its meeting in Denver yesterday to the effect that "since the Government troops have been in Colorado some 400 mine guards have been recruited into the State Militia" is true and if the further statement in today's Public Ledger that "preparatory to the State Militia taking control of the strike zone, a car of equipment has been shipped to Walsenburg and unloaded for the State troops. Included in the shipment were two 3″ field pieces with shrapnel, target-practice, shell and such calibre ammunition. These cannons have a maximum range of 9000 yards," is also true, such statements do not make for peace and it is very unfortunate that they should be given such publicity at this time.

I would appreciate the honor very highly if you can see your way clear to give me fifteen minutes on Friday of next week before our conference, which Secretary Wilson advises me will be held in his office on Saturday morning.

Again thanking you for the very generous consideration given me and hoping that I may be worthy of the confidence bestowed, and our efforts be productive of the good results which we all hope for.     Yours very respectfully,   Chas. W. Mills

TLS (WP, DLC).


## To Mary Allen Hulbert

Dearest Friend,               The White House 6 December, 1914.

I fear that I write very, very dull letters; but the sad truth is, that I am a very dull fellow. I don't know but that I always was; but in the old days there did sometimes seem to be spirit in me and a sort of vivacity that served instead of some other and better things that go to make a fellow a good comrade and companion. Now that is gone. The days sap me,—sap me easily and quickly,—and I am left cold and heavy, and therefore with nothing to give. I know exactly the sort of letter I ought to write you, and would give more than I can say to be able to write. You are lonely, and are not used to being lonely. You are without intimate and interesting friends, there in Boston, and are accustomed to being surrounded by them. You are anxious, about many of the essential things of your own and of your son's life. My letters ought to dispel the loneliness, take the place of the friends, and make the anxieties seem easy to bear, or, at least, take the pain out of the wounds they make. For that I would

need to speak out of a mind fresh for your use; full of a rich
store of all sorts of things, intimate and strange as well, that
would take your thoughts off of yourself and off of everything
that might suggest fatigue and discouragement; and with the
sort of magic of insight which knows the thoughts it is going to
meet and the particular mood it will have to deal with. But, before I can turn to personal letters I must do the duties of the
day, and they take every energy I have in me and exhaust it;
must think the problems of my own personal life out, and that
leaves me with a heavy heart, fit company for nobody! How
happy it would make me, whatever it might cost me, if I could
send you cheer, and nothing but cheer, and reassurance and
thoughts that seem somehow to be compounded out of the heart
rather than out of the mind, so that you could live on them and
feel refreshed and made over! I know that you will understand
and pardon. But that does not help. That only means that you
will have an additional burden put upon you, the additional burden of having to think of a friend in distress and having to give
deep sympathy out of a weary heart, already carrying all it can
carry. I want to help, not to demand help. How it would refresh
and help me to give, give, give without stint or limit. Oddly and
paradoxically enough, that seems to be the only way to fill an
empty heart: to give out of it,—to give what it itself needs. The
most I can do, being dull and sodden with the drain that goes
on all day, is to think of you with a keen, deep comprehension
of what you need and I should like to give, even though I cannot
supply it. If I could see you your own irrepressible vivacity would,
I think, draw something out of me. As it is, I can only think what
glimpses the butcher and the green grocer and the fruit stall
man and the postman and the little people of every sort who live
near Gloucester Street get of a bigger, brighter more interesting
world from the beautiful lady who lingers to chat with them for
a moment as she goes her rounds marketing, and what conjec-
tures they may form of what she is, what she could tell them
if she would, what it might means to stand, as she does, where
they might "catch glimpses that would make them less forlorn:
    Have sight of Proteus rising from the sea,
    Or hear old Triton blow his wrethed horn"
You do not know how it pleases my thought to follow you on
those rounds. For I have seen you with simple folk. I know how
you rouse them out of their dullness and seem to make them for
the nonce brighter than they were. I know how they respond to
your touch, and how they adore you for bringing them to themselves, their best selves. It's the magic of sympathy. If I had it,

I could give you what you give them. Having it not, I can only tell you what I would give my head to be able to do. That is little; but it at least may serve as an index to my heart, even if it does show a stupid head. It costs to be used by the American people as a means of guiding their affairs! Their affairs are so vast and so complicated! it exhausts a chap utterly to keep up with them. I[t] prevents his being an interesting friend, but it does not prevent his being

                    Your devoted friend,   Woodrow Wilson

WWTLS (WP, DLC).


## A News Report and a Statement

                                                    [*Dec. 7, 1914*]

### WILSON AGAINST
### DEFENSE INQUIRY

Washington, Dec. 7.—At the very outset of the Congressional session it was made apparent that the recent discussion of the condition of the national defenses and the ability of the United States to engage in war would be one of the main topics of discussion in the Senate and the House for the three months of the session. In the Senate two resolutions and a bill dealing with the matter were presented, and it was noted that two of these three measures came from Democrats who are firm friends of the Wilson Administration. In the House a Republican Representative introduced two bills appropriating money to provide more adequate means of defense.

Cold water was dashed on the defense agitation by President Wilson today. He came out flatly, in a conversation with Representative Gardner, against the latter's proposal that there should be an investigation by a committee of Congress into the whole question of national military preparedness.

After Mr. Gardner left the White House, the President authorized the following formal statement:

"The President told Representative Gardner that he was opposed to the method of inquiry proposed by Mr. Gardner, because he thought it was an unwise way of handling a question which might create very unfavorable international impressions. He stated to Mr. Gardner that he was entirely in favor of the fullest inquiry by the committees of Congress, and that there were no facts in the possession of the Executive Departments which were not at the disposal of these committees."

Printed in the *New York Times*, Dec. 8, 1914.

## To Edward Mandell House

My dear Friend:          The White House December 7, 1914

I am sorry that Vick is having illusions, as some other people have had. Of course, I have never spoken of him except in the most friendly and considerate way. I never said that he had been drunk while on duty in San Domingo, or that he would have been dismissed if he had not resigned. Somebody is evidently trying to make trouble by lying to him.

I think that, so far as I can see, there is no way at all in which the papers can be kept from discussing this set of charges and countercharges, and I don't know that it will do any great harm. Of course, we want the facts known, but it is going to be a very difficult matter to find out exactly what they are.

It was a great pleasure to have you down here even for the few hours you could stay, and I sincerely hope that the young mother and her baby are prospering.

In haste       Affectionately yours,   Woodrow Wilson

TLS (E. M. House Papers, CtY).

## To Raymond Poincaré

My dear Mr. President:   [The White House] December 7, 1914

I feel honored to address you also as my colleague in letters and wish to thank you most sincerely for the kind message you were gracious enough to send through Monsieur Brieux.

I, of course, fully understand the circumstances which have made it impossible for you to visit the United States, but I wish, nevertheless, to express my sincere regret that it is not possible for you to do so, and I desire to take advantage of this occasion not only to express my warm personal respect and admiration, but also to assure you of the warm feeling of men of letters and of thought throughout the United States for the distinguished President of France.

The relations between our two peoples have always been relations of such genuine and cordial friendship that it gives me peculiar pleasure as the official representative of the people of the United States to send through you, the distinguished spokesman of France, my warmest greetings to the people of the great French Republic.

Be pleased to accept, my dear Mr. President and my admired colleague, the warm assurances of my sincere consideration.

Woodrow Wilson

TLS (Letterpress Books, WP, DLC).

## To Walker Whiting Vick

Personal.

My dear Mr. Vick:  [The White House] December 7, 1914

Please do not credit rumors that you hear, and do not believe that I have said anything at any time detrimental to you, for I have not. Please, when you want to know what I have said, ask me.

I have your letter of December first,[1] have read it with the greatest care, and am going to take steps to have a thorough inquiry made.

In haste  Sincerely yours,  Woodrow Wilson

TLS (Letterpress Books, WP, DLC).
[1] W. W. Vick to WW, Dec. 1, 1914, TLS (WP, DLC).

## From William Jennings Bryan

My Dear Mr. President:  Washington December 7, 1914.

I enclose herewith an Associated Press Dispatch[1] which you may not have seen. It is encouraging. Zapata and Villa seem to be acting together and they are certainly surprising the people who thought their entrance into the City of Mexico would be followed by massacre and robbery. Zapata was in control for a few days and order was preserved. Now Villa is there and the outlook seems to be good for the restoration of peace in distracted Mexico.[2]

With assurances of high respect, I am, my dear Mr. President,
Very truly yours,  W. J. Bryan

TLS (WP, DLC).
[1] This enclosure is missing.
[2] Gutiérrez had moved into the National Palace on December 3. Three days later Villa and Zapata entered Mexico City with their troops and were received by Gutiérrez and the diplomatic corps.

## From Josephus Daniels

Dear Mr. President:  Washington. Dec. 7. 1914

Yesterday I had a talk with Burleson about the Gardner resolution in pursuance to his suggestion. This morning I had a talk with Garrison. Am to see Henry to-morrow. After conversation with Garrison, we both thought it would be well if we could both talk to you about the matter. If convenient, we can call this afternoon or any time that suits you.

Sincerely  Josephus Daniels

ALS (WP, DLC).

# From Knox Taylor[1]

Dear Mr. President:

High Bridge New Jersey
7th December, 1914.

### PRINCETON FOOTBALL.

Remembering your able service on the Graduate Advisory Committee, and your interest in this matter before and since then, I know that, if you can spare the time, you will be able to give us some very valuable ideas that will help us in working out what I hope will be a new era in Princeton's football history.

Having served on the football committee for both 1911 and the past season, and having resigned from the Graduate Council in order to serve on the Board of Athletic Control and now having been asked to act as Chairman of the Board of Athletic Control during Dean McClenahan's absence abroad, I find myself saddled with what seems to be the leading part in the present football readjustment.[2]

I am endeavoring to approach the subject from both the viewpoint of men whose association with it has been such as yours, as well as from the viewpoint of coach and player, and there is no one in the first class whose opinion I would value more highly than yours.

If you have something special in mind, I should hear from you or see you soon; if you have not, I would be glad to see you later, as soon as some tentative plan is worked out and before it is finally approved.

Mrs. Taylor[3] and I will be in Baltimore and Washington anyhow from the 24th to the 29th of December inclusive, or I would, of course, be very glad to keep any appointment at any other time that you might care to give me.

While we have good material for the coming year and a most promising Captain in Frank Glick,[4] we want to work out a general coaching arrangement with a view to permanency rather than for just the one year.

Yours sincerely,   Knox Taylor

TLS (WP, DLC).

[1] Princeton 1895, president of the Taylor-Wharton Iron & Steel Co., High Bridge, N. J.

[2] The "readjustment" was necessitated by three straight Princeton football losses to Harvard, 1912-14, a loss to Yale in 1914, and ties with Yale in 1912 and 1913.

[3] Lucy Janney Miller Taylor.

[4] Frank Glick, a member of the junior class at Princeton.

## Remarks at a Press Conference[1]

December 8, 1914

Mr. President, Colonel Roosevelt, in his article on Mexico,[2] presented the testimony of certain individuals with regard to conditions that existed or are supposed to have existed there. Could you tell us, please, whether or not these persons made any private effort to submit this information to you?

> I can't say, because I didn't read the article. I don't know whom it refers to.

Then you don't know as to whether or not it agrees, of course, with the reports that you have?

> No. I didn't read it at all.

Mr. President, does your correspondence manifest any opposition to the military propaganda?

> I should say it would.

We find some evidence in the office of the *Star*. The letters we are getting there regarding Veracruz show something of that sort. I don't know if you—

> It indicates it very clearly. Mr. Tumulty suggests that one of the indications is that article in last evening's New York *Evening Post* from Mr. Nicholas Murray Butler, President of Columbia.[3] . . .

Is the suggestion of the Civic Federation for the creation of a national council of defense rather in line with Mr. Gardner's idea?

> I don't think it is in line with Mr. Gardner's idea. It is an idea not at all new. Of course, the whole question just at present is the proper method of action, and everybody wants the facts known very clearly and the policy discussed with the greatest frankness. But I think, for myself, there is a right way and a wrong way to go about it.

Do you regard the agitation as one part of the political campaign? Do you think it is a partisan matter?

> Well, I wouldn't like to say. I wouldn't like to say, for this reason, gentlemen. Whenever the foreign relations of the country are concerned, I think party should be left out of the question. Even in comment. At any rate, by anybody who represents the government.

Mr. President, do you think many evidences of outside influences are being used in favor of the increase of armaments?

> Well, no more evidences than words. I think you see, then, don't you, in short, what I am to say: I don't know any more about it than would be known to anybody. I have no special knowledge of it.

I meant, as taking the form of a lobby here?

That is what this article I referred to charges. As I say, I have no special information whatsoever.

Mr. President, I understand that Mr. Sullivan has made a request for an investigation on his behalf. Are you taking any steps?

Yes, I have taken steps.

Will you make any comment, Mr. President, regarding the bill, I think, of Senator Hitchcock, prohibiting the selling of munitions of war to foreign governments?

I haven't heard of it.

I think the bill was introduced yesterday.

I had just begun to look over the *Record*.

Mr. President, could you tell us what steps you are taking to investigate the Sullivan charges?

Well, I can't take the steps. I have instructed the department to take them.[4]

JRT transcript (WC, NjP) of CLSsh (C. L. Swem Coll., NjP).

[1] Wilson held this press conference at 10 A.M. He delivered his Annual Message to Congress (the following document) at 12:30.

[2] "Our Responsibility in Mexico," *New York Times*, Dec. 6, 1914, Sect. VI, p. 1.

[3] "War Preparedness," New York *Evening Post*, Dec. 7, 1914. Butler stated that the European war proved that the old argument that armaments insured peace was gone forever, and that the agitation in the United States for preparedness was dangerous to the country. "For the United States to be swept from her moorings now on the foolish supposition of an attack by Germany, or Japan, or England, or anybody else would be not only an act of folly, but national suicide. We would destroy at once our opportunity for the moral and political leadership which the whole world is looking to us to take . . . if we were to start a new armament race."

[4] WW to L. M. Garrison, Dec. 8, 1914, CCL (WP, DLC), requesting an investigation. See also WW to WJB, Dec. 10, 1914.


# An Annual Message to Congress[1]

Gentlemen of the Congress:                                    [Dec. 8, 1914]

The session upon which you are now entering will be the closing session of the Sixty-third Congress, a Congress, I venture to say, which will long be remembered for the great body of thoughtful and constructive work which it has done, in loyal response to the thought and needs of the country. I should like in this address to review the notable record and try to make adequate

[1] Wilson completed a shorthand draft of the following message and a transcript on his own typewriter probably on December 3, as we have learned from the House diary. Tumulty's letter of December 4 suggests that Wilson read the message to him on that day. Then, between December 5 and December 7, Wilson added certain sections to his shorthand and WWT drafts. The additions will be noted. The shorthand draft survives in WP, DLC. The WWT draft is missing, probably because Wilson sent it to the Public Printer for the reading copy. Wilson did not dictate a draft of this message to Swem, nor is any Swem copy of the WWT draft extant.

assessment of it; but no doubt we stand too near the work that has been done and are ourselves too much part of it to play the part of historians toward it.

Our program of legislation with regard to the regulation of business is now virtually complete. It has been put forth, as we intended, as a whole, and leaves no conjecture as to what is to follow. The road at last lies clear and firm before business. It is a road which it can travel without fear or embarrassment. It is the road to ungrudged, unclouded success. In it every honest man, every man who believes that the public interest is part of his own interest, may walk with perfect confidence.[2]

Moreover, our thoughts are now more of the future than of the past. While we have worked at our tasks of peace the circumstances of the whole age have been altered by war. What we have done for our own land and our own people we did with the best that was in us, whether of character or of intelligence, with sober enthusiasm and a confidence in the principles upon which we were acting which sustained us at every step of the difficult undertaking; but it is done. It has passed from our hands. It is now an established part of the legislation of the country. Its usefulness, its effects will disclose themselves in experience. What chiefly strikes us now, as we look about us during these closing days of a year which will be forever memorable in the history of the world, is that we face new tasks, have been facing them these six months, must face them in the months to come,—face them without partisan feeling, like men who have forgotten everything but a common duty and the fact that we are representatives of a great people whose thought is not of us but of what America owes to herself and to all mankind in such circumstances as these upon which we look amazed and anxious.

War has interrupted the means of trade not only but also the processes of production. In Europe it is destroying men and resources wholesale and upon a scale unprecedented and appalling. There is reason to fear that the time is near, if it be not already at hand, when several of the countries of Europe will find it difficult to do for their people what they have hitherto been always easily able to do,—many essential and fundamental things. At any rate, they will need our help and our manifold services as they have never needed them before; and we should be ready, more fit and ready than we have ever been.

It is of equal consequence that the nations whom Europe has usually supplied with innumerable articles of manufacture and

2 Wilson added this paragraph to his shorthand draft in response to Tumulty's letter of December 4.

commerce of which they are in constant need and without which their economic development halts and stands still can now get only a small part of what they formerly imported and eagerly look to us to supply their all but empty markets. This is particularly true of our own neighbors, the States, great and small, of Central and South America. Their lines of trade have hitherto run chiefly athwart the seas, not to our ports but to the ports of Great Britain and of the older continent of Europe. I do not stop to inquire why, or to make any comment on probable causes. What interests us just now is not the explanation but the fact, and our duty and opportunity in the presence of it. Here are markets which we must supply, and we must find the means of action. The United States, this great people for whom we speak and act, should be ready, as never before, to serve itself and to serve mankind; ready with its resources, its energies, its forces of production, and its means of distribution.

It is a very practical matter, a matter of ways and means. We have the resources, but are we fully ready to use them? And, if we can make ready what we have, have we the means at hand to distribute it? We are not fully ready; neither have we the means of distribution. We are willing, but we are not fully able. We have the wish to serve and to serve greatly, generously; but we are not prepared as we should be. We are not ready to mobilize our resources at once. We are not prepared to use them immediately and at their best, without delay and without waste.

To speak plainly, we have grossly erred in the way in which we have stunted and hindered the development of our merchant marine. And now, when we need ships, we have not got them. We have year after year debated, without end or conclusion, the best policy to pursue with regard to the use of the ores and forests and water powers of our national domain in the rich States of the West, when we should have acted; and they are still locked up. The key is still turned upon them, the door shut fast at which thousands of vigorous men, full of initiative, knock clamorously for admittance. The water power of our navigable streams outside the national domain also, even in the eastern States, where we have worked and planned for generations, is still not used as it might be, because we will and we won't; because the laws we have made do not intelligently balance encouragement against restraint. We withhold by regulation.

I have come to ask you to remedy and correct these mistakes and omissions, even at this short session of a Congress which would certainly seem to have done all the work that could reasonably be expected of it. The time and the circumstances are extraordinary, and so must our efforts be also.

Fortunately, two great measures, finely conceived, the one to unlock, with proper safeguards, the resources of the national domain, the other to encourage the use of the navigable waters outside that domain for the generation of power, have already passed the House of Representatives and are ready for immediate consideration and action by the Senate. With the deepest earnestness I urge their prompt passage. In them both we turn our backs upon hesitation and makeshift and formulate a genuine policy of use and conservation, in the best sense of those words. We owe the one measure not only to the people of that great western country for whose free and systematic development, as it seems to me, our legislation has done so little, but also to the people of the Nation as a whole; and we as clearly owe the other in fulfillment of our repeated promises that the water power of the country should in fact as well as in name be put at the disposal of great industries which can make economical and profitable use of it, the rights of the public being adequately guarded the while, and monopoly in the use prevented. To have begun such measures and not completed them would indeed mar the record of this great Congress very seriously. I hope and confidently believe that they will be completed.

And there is another great piece of legislation which awaits and should receive the sanction of the Senate: I mean the bill which gives a larger measure of self-government to the people of the Philippines. How better, in this time of anxious questioning and perplexed policy, could we show our confidence in the principles of liberty, as the source as well as the expression of life, how better could we demonstrate our own self-possession and steadfastness in the courses of justice and disinterestedness than by thus going calmly forward to fulfill our promises to a dependent people, who will now look more anxiously than ever to see whether we have indeed the liberality, the unselfishness, the courage, the faith we have boasted and professed. I can not believe that the Senate will let this great measure of constructive justice await the action of another Congress. Its passage would nobly crown the record of these two years of memorable labor.

But I think that you will agree with me that this does not complete the toll of our duty. How are we to carry our goods to the empty markets of which I have spoken if we have not the ships? How are we to build up a great trade if we have not the certain and constant means of transportation upon which all profitable and useful commerce depends? And how are we to get the ships if we wait for the trade to develop without them? To correct the many mistakes by which we have discouraged and all but destroyed the merchant marine of the country, to retrace the steps by which we have, it seems almost deliberately, withdrawn our flag from the seas, except where, here and there, a ship of war is bidden carry it or some wandering yacht displays it, would take a long time and involve many detailed items of legislation, and the trade which we ought immediately to handle would disappear or find other channels while we debated the items.

The case is not unlike that which confronted us when our own continent was to be opened up to settlement and industry, and we needed long lines of railway, extended means of transportation prepared beforehand, if development was not to lag intolerably and wait interminably. We lavishly subsidized the building of transcontinental railroads. We look back upon that with regret now, because the subsidies led to many scandals of which we are ashamed; but we know that the railroads had to be built, and if we had it to do over again we should of course build them, but in another way. Therefore I propose another way of providing the means of transportation, which must precede, not tardily follow, the development of our trade with our neighbor states of America. It may seem a reversal of the natural order of things, but it is true, that the routes of trade must be actually opened—by many ships and regular sailings and moderate charges—before streams of merchandise will flow freely and profitably through them.

Hence the pending shipping bill, discussed at the last session but as yet passed by neither House. In my judgment such legislation is imperatively needed and can not wisely be postponed. The Government must open these gates of trade, and open them wide; open them before it is altogether profitable to open them, or altogether reasonable to ask private capital to open them at a venture. It is not a question of the Government monopolizing the field. It should take action to make it certain that transportation at reasonable rates will be promptly provided, even where the carriage is not at first profitable; and then, when the carriage has become sufficiently profitable to attract and engage private capital, and engage it in abundance, the Government ought to withdraw. I very earnestly hope that the Congress will be of this opinion, and that both Houses will adopt this exceedingly important bill.

The great subject of rural credits[3] still remains to be dealt
with, and it is a matter of deep regret that the difficulties of the
subject have seemed to render it impossible to complete a bill
for passage at this session. But it can not be perfected yet, and
therefore there are no other constructive measures the necessity
for which I will at this time call your attention to; but I would
be negligent of a very manifest duty were I not to call the attention of the Senate to the fact that the proposed convention for
safety at sea awaits its confirmation and that the limit fixed in
the convention itself for its acceptance is the last day of the
present month. The conference in which this convention originated was called by the United States; the representatives of the
United States played a very influential part indeed in framing
the provisions of the proposed convention; and those provisions
are in themselves for the most part admirable. It would hardly
be consistent with the part we have played in the whole matter
to let it drop and go by the board as if forgotten and neglected.
It was ratified in May last by the German Government and in
August by the Parliament of Great Britain. It marks a most hopeful and decided advance in international civilization. We should
show our earnest good faith in a great matter by adding our
own acceptance of it.

There is another matter of which I must make special mention,
if I am to discharge my conscience, lest it should escape your
attention. It may seem a very small thing. It affects only a single
item of appropriation. But many human lives and many great
enterprises hang upon it. It is the matter of making adequate
provision for the survey and charting of our coasts. It is immediately pressing and exigent in connection with the immense
coast line of Alaska, a coast line greater than that of the United
States themselves, though it is also very important indeed with
regard to the older coasts of the continent. We can not use our
great Alaskan domain, ships will not ply thither, if those coasts
and their many hidden dangers are not thoroughly surveyed and
charted. The work is incomplete at almost every point. Ships
and lives have been lost in threading what were supposed to be
well-known main channels. We have not provided adequate vessels or adequate machinery for the survey and charting. We have
used old vessels that were not big enough or strong enough and
which were so nearly unseaworthy that our inspectors would
not have allowed private owners to send them to sea. This is a
matter which, as I have said, seems small, but is in reality very

[3] Wilson added these sentences about rural credits to his shorthand draft.

great. Its importance has only to be looked into to be appreciated.

Before I close may I say a few words upon two topics, much discussed out of doors, upon which it is highly important that our judgments should be clear, definite, and steadfast?

One of these is economy in government expenditures. The duty of economy is not debatable. It is manifest and imperative. In the appropriations we pass we are spending the money of the great people whose servants we are,—not our own. We are trustees and responsible stewards in the spending. The only thing debatable and upon which we should be careful to make our thought and purpose clear is the kind of economy demanded of us. I assert with the greatest confidence that the people of the United States are not jealous of the amount their Government costs if they are sure that they get what they need and desire for the outlay, that the money is being spent for objects of which they approve, and that it is being applied with good business sense and management.

Governments grow, piecemeal, both in their tasks and in the means[4] by which those tasks are to be performed, and very few Governments are organized, I venture to say, as wise and experienced business men would organize them if they had a clean sheet of paper to write upon. Certainly the Government of the United States is not. I think that it is generally agreed that there should be a systematic reorganization and reassembling of its parts so as to secure greater efficiency and effect considerable savings in expense. But the amount of money saved in that way would, I believe, though no doubt considerable in itself, running, it may be, into the millions, be relatively small,—small, I mean, in proportion to the total necessary outlays of the Government. It would be thoroughly worth effecting, as every saving would, great or small. Our duty is not altered by the scale of the saving. But my point is that the people of the United States do not wish to curtail the activities of this Government; they wish, rather, to enlarge them; and with every enlargement, with the mere growth, indeed, of the country itself, there must come, of course, the inevitable increase of expense. The sort of economy we ought to practice may be effected, and ought to be effected, by a careful study and assessment of the tasks to be performed; and the money spent ought to be made to yield the best possible returns in efficiency and achievement. And, like good stewards, we should so account for every dollar of our appropriations as to make it

[4] In the shorthand draft, this sentence reads: "Governments grow, piecemeal, both in their arrogance and in their functions. . . ."

perfectly evident what it was spent for and in what way it was spent.

It is not expenditure but extravagance that we should fear being criticized for; not paying for the legitimate enterprises and undertakings of a great Government whose people command what it should do, but adding what will benefit only a few or pouring money out for what need not have been undertaken at all or might have been postponed or better and more economically conceived and carried out. The Nation is not niggardly; it is very generous. It will chide us only if we forget for whom we pay money out and whose money it is we pay. These are large and general standards, but they are not very difficult of application to particular cases.

The other topic I shall take leave to mention goes deeper into the principles of our national life and policy. It is the subject of national defense.[5]

It can not be discussed without first answering some very searching questions. It is said in some quarters that we are not prepared for war. What is meant by being prepared? Is it meant that we are not ready upon brief notice to put a nation in the field, a nation of men trained to arms? Of course we are not ready to do that; and we shall never be in time of peace so long as we retain our present political principles and institutions. And what is it that it is suggested we should be prepared to do? To defend ourselves against attack? We have always found means to do that, and shall find them whenever it is necessary without calling our people away from their necessary tasks to render compulsory military service in times of peace.

Allow me to speak with great plainness and directness upon this great matter and to avow my convictions with deep earnestness. I have tried to know what America is, what her people think, what they are, what they most cherish and hold dear. I hope that some of their finer passions are in my own heart,—some of the great conceptions and desires which gave birth to this Government and which have made the voice of this people a voice of peace and hope and liberty among the peoples of the world, and that, speaking my own thoughts, I shall, at least in part, speak theirs also, however faintly and inadequately, upon this vital matter.

We are at peace with all the world. No one who speaks counsel based on fact or drawn from a just and candid interpretation

5 Wilson inserted the following paragraphs on national defense after he had completed his shorthand draft.

of realities can say that there is reason to fear that from any quarter our independence or the integrity of our territory is threatened. Dread of the power of any other nation we are incapable of. We are not jealous of rivalry in the fields of commerce or of any other peaceful achievement. We mean to live our own lives as we will; but we mean also to let live. We are, indeed, a true friend to all the nations of the world, because we threaten none, covet the possessions of none, desire the overthrow of none. Our friendship can be accepted and is accepted without reservation, because it is offered in a spirit and for a purpose which no one need ever question or suspect. Therein lies our greatness. We are the champions of peace and of concord. And we should be very jealous of this distinction which we have sought to earn. Just now we should be particularly jealous of it, because it is our dearest present hope that this character and reputation may presently, in God's providence, bring us an opportunity such as has seldom been vouchsafed any nation, the opportunity to counsel and obtain peace in the world and reconciliation and a healing settlement of many a matter that has cooled and interrupted the friendship of nations. This is the time above all others when we should wish and resolve to keep our strength by self-possession, our influence by preserving our ancient principles of action.

From the first we have had a clear and settled policy with regard to military establishments. We never have had, and while we retain our present principles and ideals we never shall have, a large standing army. If asked, Are you ready to defend yourselves? we reply, Most assuredly, to the utmost; and yet we shall not turn America into a military camp. We will not ask our young men to spend the best years of their lives making soldiers of themselves. There is another sort of energy in us. It will know how to declare itself and make itself effective should occasion arise. And especially when half the world is on fire we shall be careful to make our moral insurance against the spread of the conflagration very definite and certain and adequate indeed.

Let us remind ourselves, therefore, of the only thing we can do or will do. We must depend in every time of national peril, in the future as in the past, not upon a standing army, nor yet upon a reserve army, but upon a citizenry trained and accustomed to arms. It will be right enough, right American policy, based upon our accustomed principles and practices, to provide a system by which every citizen who will volunteer for the training may be made familiar with the use of modern arms, the rudiments of drill and maneuver, and the maintenance and sanitation of camps. We should encourage such training and make it a means of discipline which our young men will learn to value. It is right that we should provide it not only, but that we should make it as attractive as possible, and so induce our young men to undergo it at such times as they can command a little freedom and can seek the physical development they need, for mere health's sake, if for nothing more. Every means by which such things can be stimulated is legitimate, and such a method smacks of true American ideas. It is right, too, that the National Guard of the States should be developed and strengthened by every means which is not inconsistent with our obligations to our own people or with the established policy of our Government. And this, also, not because the time or occasion specially calls for such measures, but because it should be our constant policy to make these provisions for our national peace and safety.

More than this carries with it a reversal of the whole history and character of our polity. More than this, proposed at this time, permit me to say, would mean merely that we had lost our self-possession, that we had been thrown off our balance by a war with which we have nothing to do, whose causes can not touch us, whose very existence affords us opportunities of friendship and disinterested service which should make us ashamed of any thought of hostility or fearful preparation for trouble. This is assuredly the opportunity for which a people and a government like ours were raised up, the opportunity not only to speak but actually to embody and exemplify the counsels of peace and amity and the lasting concord which is based on justice and fair and generous dealing.

A powerful navy we have always regarded as our proper and natural means of defense; and it has always been of defense that we have thought, never of aggression or of conquest. But who shall tell us now what sort of navy to build? We shall take leave to be strong upon the seas, in the future as in the past; and there will be no thought of offense or of provocation in that. Our ships are our natural bulwarks. When will the experts tell us just what kind we should construct—and when will they be right for ten years together, if the relative efficiency of craft of different kinds and uses continues to change as we have seen it change under our very eyes in these last few months?

But I turn away from the subject. It is not new. There is no new need to discuss it. We shall not alter our attitude toward it because some amongst us are nervous and excited.[6] We shall

---

[6] Wilson looked Representative Gardner straight in the eye as he said this. G. J. Karger to W. H. Taft, July 27, 1915, TLS (W. H. Taft Papers, DLC).

easily and sensibly agree upon a policy of defense. The question has not changed its aspects because the times are not normal. Our policy will not be for an occasion. It will be conceived as a permanent and settled thing, which we will pursue at all seasons, without haste and after a fashion perfectly consistent with the peace of the world, the abiding friendship of states, and the unhampered freedom of all with whom we deal. Let there be no misconception. The country has been misinformed. We have not been negligent of national defense. We are not unmindful of the great responsibility resting upon us. We shall learn and profit by the lesson of every experience and every new circumstance; and what is needed will be adequately done.

I close, as I began, by reminding you of the great tasks and duties of peace which challenge our best powers and invite us to build what will last, the tasks to which we can address ourselves now and at all times with free-hearted zest and with all the finest gifts of constructive wisdom we possess. To develop our life and our resources; to supply our own people, and the people of the world as their need arises, from the abundant plenty of our fields and our marts of trade; to enrich the commerce of our own States and of the world with the products of our mines, our farms, and our factories, with the creations of our thought and the fruits of our character,—this is what will hold our attention and our enthusiasm steadily, now and in the years to come, as we strive to show in our life as a nation what liberty and the inspirations of an emancipated spirit may do for men and for societies, for individuals, for states, and for mankind.

Printed reading copy (WP, DLC).

## To Joseph Patrick Tumulty

[The White House, Dec. 8, 1914]

Mr. Mills, Mr. Seth Low, and Mr. Gilday are going to be in Washington for a conference at the Department of Labor on Saturday and I feel that I ought to see them. At the same time, I do not know how it is going to be worked out. If you would be kind enough to get at them through the Secretary of Labor, I would like to make an arrangement to see them at half-past two on Friday afternoon.          The President.

TL (WP, DLC).

## To Jacob Henry Schiff

Personal and Private.

My dear Mr. Schiff:          [The White House] December 8, 1914

I fear you must have thought me guilty of a discourtesy in not replying sooner to your letter of November nineteenth, but the fact is I wanted to think out very carefully the matter about which you wrote.

Not that it was the first time that I had tried to think it out, for it is one of the most perplexing things I have had to decide. The law standing as it does, the most I can do is to exercise influence, and in the case of the lending of money I was directly applied to for advice and approval. There my duty was clear. It was my duty to discourage the loans to belligerents. In the matter of sales of goods of all kinds, however, the precedents of international law are so clear, the sales proceed from so many sources, and my lack of power is so evident, that I have felt that I could do nothing else than leave the matter to settle itself. In a single recent case I saw my way clear to act. When it came to the manufacture of constituent parts of submarines and their shipment abroad, complete, to be put together elsewhere, it seemed to me clearly my privilege, acting in the spirit of the Alabama case, to say that the Government could not allow that, and the Fore River Ship Building Company which is said to have undertaken the contracts has canceled them.[1]

I am sure that you realize the very great delicacy and difficulty of my task in matters of this sort, and I wanted to make a very frank statement of them to you.

Cordially and sincerely yours,   Woodrow Wilson

TLS (Letterpress Books, WP, DLC).
[1] Wilson was correct in stating that the original contracts were canceled. However, Charles Michael Schwab, president of the Bethlehem Steel Co. and the prime mover in the submarine affair, found a way of circumventing Wilson's decision by shipping partially fabricated parts to Canada, where they were finished and assembled into completed submarines at the Canadian Vickers, Ltd., shipyard in Montreal. Ten submarines had been completed and sent to sea by mid-1915. See Smith, *Britain's Clandestine Submarines*, pp. 78-110, 122-32.

## To Henry White

My dear Mr. White:          [The White House] December 8, 1914

Just a line to thank you most cordially for your generous letter of December fifth. I valued very highly your kind service in the matter.                    Faithfully yours,   Woodrow Wilson

TLS (Letterpress Books, WP, DLC).

## From Paul Fuller and Others

New York, December 8, 1914.

Congressional action altering the rules of neutrality during warfare is contrary to accepted international law[;] aiding the inefficiency of one belligerent to protect its purchases of arms by forbidding all exportation of arms to the other belligerent is an absolute violation of neutrality. The bills proposed by Representatives Vollmer and Bartholdt[1] and by Senator Hitchcock, would, if enacted, put the United States surely on record as against the Allies.

Paul Fuller, Benj. F. Tracy; Frederic R. Coudert.[2]

T telegram (WP, DLC).

[1] Henry Vollmer, Democrat of Davenport, Ia., and Richard Bartholdt, Republican of St. Louis, Mo. Bartholdt was born in Germany; both men represented German-American districts.

[2] Benjamin Franklin Tracy, Secretary of the Navy, 1889-93; Frederic René Coudert, director of the Committee France Amérique and of the French Alliance in the United States. All the signers were members of the New York legal firm of Coudert Brothers.

## From James Watson Gerard

My dear Mr. President:                    [Berlin] Dec. 8th [1914]

Thank you for your very kind letter of Nov. 10th.[1]

Perhaps it is as well that I was not elected. There is work and to spare in Germany.

If I had known the exact situation at home I doubt if I should have "started," but we are so cut off here that it was a difficult question to decide.

Immediately on receiving your private cipher cable *re* German aeroplanes dropping bombs on Paris I took the matter up quietly in a certain quarter and since have not heard that Paris has suffered from bomb throwers.

The Germans are now quite bitter against the United States, both because of the general attitude of our people and Press, and because of the sale by Americans of munitions of war to France and England. Dancing on eggs is nothing to my present difficulties. The Germans also think that our Ambassadors and Ministers are not aggressive enough in looking out for German prisoners civil and military, in countries where the Germans are in our charge. This is a difficult question. I have suffered from German (popular not governmental) criticism here for insisting on good food, etc for the English prisoners. Herr Von Jagow suggested to me the advisibility of an International Commission. There are no fixed international rules as to *just what* treatment, clothes, food, covering & housing prisoners shall receive. Germans do not furnish clothes, English do.

The Chancellor sent for me today and I talked with him for an hour. He is here from the front for a few days. The Emperor takes the Chancellor & all Ministers with him. The Chancellor said he saw no prospect of peace. He spoke of the American sale of munitions & treatment of prisoners in England, France & Russia & seemed anxious to know whether Japan would send troops to Europe. Like all Germans of all classes he has no fear of the outcome. I have been working to get cotton in and dyestuffs and cyanide *out*—two articles on which our spinning and mining industry depend absolutely. The Germans know this but only allow a little out at a time & keep this as a club over us.

The hate against England is marvellous. France & Russia are passed by, but songs are made, poems composed & recited made up of the expression of an undying hate for the British.

The Germans are absolutely united, and ready for all sacrifices, and to me it seems impossible that such spirit and organization can lose. Thank you for what you say about Tom McCarthy.[2] I am proud to have such a friend and cannot see what I have done to inspire such devotion. Please give my kindest regards to Secretary McAdoo.

Very respectfully    James W. Gerard.

ALS (WP, DLC).

[1] It is missing in WP, DLC, and the Gerard Papers, University of Montana Library.

[2] Thomas D. McCarthy, former personal secretary to Gerard, had been in charge of Gerard's senatorial campaign headquarters in New York.

## To Edward Mandell House

My dear Friend:          The White House December 9, 1914

Well, the broadside has been fired off and I hope sincerely that it will have the desired effect in quieting those who are seriously in danger of making trouble for the country. You will see that I added one or two little passages after reading the message to you.

I am returning the article you were kind enough to let me see which Judge McAdoo wrote.[1] I am very glad to have had what was in his mind so clearly set forth.

We all join in warmest and most affectionate regards and hope that the young mother and baby are getting on finely.

Affectionately your friend,    Woodrow Wilson

TLS (E. M. House Papers, CtY).

[1] The Editors have been unable to locate this article by William McAdoo, Chief City Magistrate of New York.

## To Henry Morgenthau

Personal and Private.

My dear Morgenthau:    The White House December 9, 1914

Your letter of November tenth[1] has just been placed before me and is in every way most welcome. I have read it with the deepest interest and am not a little impressed by what you say as to the expectations entertained with regard to the possibilities of insisting on peace. You say you do not want to write me any detailed suggestions that have been made as no doubt I have them from various sources, but, as a matter of fact, none but the most general suggestions have been made and I would be very much obliged to you indeed if you would let me know your full thought and information on this great matter in which I should be so deeply interested to move when and as it is possible.

I deeply appreciate all the personal part of your letter, you may be sure, and want to say what genuine happiness I have had in learning of your success and of the admirable impression you have made in every way. It is evident from your own letter that you have gained in an unusual degree the confidence of the representatives of the other governments. This in itself is a great source of strength and opportunity for useful influence.

Please give my warmest regards to Mrs. Morgenthau and your son,[2] who I believe is with you, and believe me, with the warmest regard,          Your sincere friend,    Woodrow Wilson

TLS (WP, DLC).
    [1] H. Morgenthau to WW, Nov. 10, 1914, ALS (WP, DLC), reporting that, from his post in Constantinople, he had been able to study the real point of view of the governments of England, Germany, and Russia, as reflected by their ambassadorial representatives in Turkey. He concluded that all looked to Wilson as the "Peacemaker," that most of them admitted the folly of continuing the war, and that none of them wanted to be "the first to shout 'enough.' "
    [2] Josephine Sykes Morgenthau and Henry Morgenthau, Jr.


## To Dudley Field Malone

Personal and Private.

My dear Dudley:          [The White House] December 9, 1914

I am deeply distressed to hear of your neuritis and to know that the doctor thinks your condition in any sense or degree serious.[1] Be sure, my dear fellow, to take the very best care of yourself. I should be distressed beyond measure to have you suffer physically from any load you have been carrying.

And please don't give yourself any distress or concern about what Mr. Roosevelt is saying. The very extravagance and unrestrained ill feeling of what he is now writing serve to nullify any influence that his utterances could have. He cannot possibly in his present situation or temper cause any embarrassment which need give us a second thought. I am sincerely sorry that he should have so forgotten the dignity and responsibility of a man placed as he is who might exercise so great an influence for good if he only saw and chose the way.

We all join in sending you the most affectionate messages and the most solicitous wishes for your recovery. Don't let yourself be too much alarmed. I have myself gone through a very severe attack of neuritis in my time which, though very, very hard to bear and a great drain on my vitality, did not result in any permanent bad effects, notwithstanding that I went straight along with my work as you are doing.

Affectionately yours,  Woodrow Wilson

TLS (Letterpress Books, WP, DLC).
¹ D. F. Malone to WW, Dec. 7, 1914, TLS (WP, DLC).

## To Knox Taylor

My dear Taylor:        [The White House] December 9, 1914

I have your letter of December seventh. In reply to it, I must frankly say that I have no judgment to offer with regard to this year's football, because I have not been able to follow it with any attention; but for many years I have had the conviction, based upon observation at close range, that the real trouble with our teams is that they are coached too much, that the initiative of the captain and the players is entirely suppressed and they are made pawns merely in the hands of the coaches. I do not really think that it will make much difference whether there is one coach or a board of coaches. The thing will lack originality and go and conquering spirit just so long as the coaches play the game and not the members of the team. No doubt the youngsters ought to have graduate advice and criticism when and just so far as they wish it, but they ought to run the game themselves and in my opinion they are quite capable of doing it brilliantly. I think you would find that if the players were not constantly nervous lest they should be criticised and censured by the coaches for not doing exactly what they were told, they would play with a new dash and vigor that would surprise everybody.

If at any time I can be of any service to you in this or any other matter, I shall be very glad indeed.

Cordially and sincerely yours,  Woodrow Wilson

TLS (Letterpress Books, WP, DLC).

## Remarks to the American Red Cross Society[1]

[Dec. 9, 1914]

My duty this afternoon, ladies and gentlemen, is a very simple and agreeable one to me and does not involve, I believe, the responsibility of making an address of any kind.

I need not tell you that I am here chiefly for the purpose of showing my very deep personal interest in the work of this society and of expressing, if in no other way than by my presence, my desire actively to cooperate with the society in every way that it is possible for me to cooperate with it. I think that the society is just now charged with a peculiarly responsible duty. It is really the medium of the whole world, that part of it, at any rate, which is disengaged from the terrible present conflict in Europe, in ministering to those who need the ministrations of comfort and relief in these distressing circumstances. All eyes are centered upon this society, all efforts at relief come sooner or later into the counsels of this society. It is the more necessary, therefore, that we should cooperate with that spirit, which I believe we all think to be characteristic of America, the spirit of absolute disinterestedness: not thinking of ourselves, but thinking of the results we wish to achieve.

And those results are spiritual as well as material. You cannot administer material relief without administering it in a spirit which is evident in the ministrations themselves, and that spirit will be the spirit of America which has sought at all times to hold out a hand to those who are suffering, to those who have no other friends. Therefore, it is to my mind a very happy circumstance that this society should have some almost official relation with the Government of the United States, that there should be, at any rate, a formal connection between it and a government which has nothing to seek except the liberty and the safety and the progress of mankind.

I feel honored, therefore, and privileged to show my interest in the society by being here and serving as presiding officer for a few minutes.

T MS (WP, DLC).
[1] At its annual meeting at the Shoreham Hotel in Washington.

# From William Jennings Bryan, with Enclosure

My dear Mr. President:        Washington December 9, 1914.

I am sending you copy of a telegram[1] drawn in accordance with your instructions of yesterday. Will you please make such corrections as you may deem best and return so that I may be able to forward them at once.

I could not attend to the matter yesterday afternoon because of the meeting of the Pan-American Union.

With assurances of high respect I am, my dear Mr. President,
Yours very truly,   W. J. Bryan

TLS (WP, DLC).
[1] To Canada in Veracruz.


## E N C L O S U R E

Washington, December 9, 1914.

Please call upon Gen Carranza and say to him that the condition along the border at Naco is becoming very serious. A Considerable number of Americans have been wounded by shots fired across the line and several have died from wounds thus received. The Commanders of both factions of the Mexicans either cannot or will not control the forces under them. You are earnestly urged to send instructions to those who acknowledge alliegence to you, warning them against allowing any further violations of the rights of American citizens. Unless those in authority can prevent the firing of shots across the border it will become the duty of this government, much to its regret, to take such steps as may be necessary to protect American lives thus menaced by the employment of such force as may be required. Such force to be employed not for aggression but purely for defense and with no intention of invading the territory of Mexico or in any way interfering with its sovereignty or the right of its people to settle their disputes among themselves.

Repeat foregoing to Silliman substituting Gutierrez for Carranza.                        W. J. Bryan

T telegram (SDR, RG 59, 812.00/13984a, DNA).


# From Champ Clark

Dear Mr. President:        Washington, D. C. December 9, 1914.

It was kind and gracious to send me the box of roses—for which I am truly grateful.

I repeat what I said to you yesterday, that your address to Congress was a masterful, great speech. The demand for tickets of admission was greater than on any of your previous appearances before Congress, which, I take it, is a straw indicating the direction of the political wind.

Shortly after you were inaugurated, I told you that when you thought I could help along with things I was at your service and I still am.

Wishing you all good things,

I am          Sincerely Your Friend,   Champ Clark

ALS (WP, DLC).

## From Robert Lansing, with Enclosure

*Confidential.*

Dear Mr. President:          Washington December 9, 1914.

I have, in compliance with the request in your letter of the 1st instant, prepared and enclose herewith a memorandum on a letter of Professor Münsterberg, dated November 19th.

I regret that the memorandum is so long, but to controvert charges such as these requires argument based on a statement of facts. They cannot be met by denials alone. The memorandum is also unsatisfactory to me because I have been compelled to work on it at odd moments and have not had time to give it uninterrupted consideration.

It seems to me that the falsity of these charges, which are being so widely published and are arousing so much criticism of the Administration among the German element in this country, should certainly be exposed, but I am not convinced that the wisest way to do this is by an answer to Professor Münsterberg's letter. As I point out in the first comment in the memorandum, he is a German subject, in fact an agent of the German Government. I cannot feel that our foreign policy or its political effect upon the American people is a proper subject of discussion with a foreigner, who has not even the excuse of being accredited to this government as a diplomatic representative.

I appreciate that my opinion was not asked as to this matter and I have offered it on that account with some hesitation; but, without considering the proprieties, I think that the activities of these foreigners in our political affairs ought to be brought to the attention of the American people, and that would be difficult to do in a private letter to one of them.

It would seem as if some other channel of publicity could be found which would be more effective, less objectionable and give opportunity to discuss alien interference in the party politics of the United States.

I herewith return Professor Münsterberg's letter.

Very sincerely yours, Robert Lansing.

TLS (WP, DLC).

E N C L O S U R E

CONFIDENTIAL FOR THE PRESIDENT.

*Memorandum on*
*Professor Hugo Münsterberg's letter*
*to the President, dated November 19, 1914.*

PRELIMINARY COMMENTS.

I. *Interference of Aliens of Belligerent Nationality in the Political Affairs of the United States.*

Regard for the following facts are essential in dealing with a communication of this sort:

Professor Hugo Münsterberg is a German subject. Dr. Bernhard Dernburg is not only a German subject, but is probably (though the evidence at hand is not conclusive) a paid agent of the German Government sent to the United States to create sentiment in favor of Germany. These two are the principal leaders in arousing antagonism in this country to the policy of the Administration in its relations to the belligerent nations.

These two foreign writers have severely criticised this Government's conduct of its foreign affairs, have made charges unfounded in fact or in law, have distorted the truth, and have bitterly assailed the President and the Department of State for alleged injustice to Germany and undue friendliness for the cause of the Allies. In pursuing this campaign of misrepresentation and vilification they have done so by means of addresses and publications which have been widely circulated throughout the country relying upon the freedom of speech and of the press guaranteed to the people by the Constitution. If such criticisms and attacks by aliens had been made in Germany upon the German Government even in time of peace, they would undoubtedly have been summarily suppressed. The impropriety of such attempts by foreigners to influence citizens of the United States in their attitude toward the established Government is manifest.

Open participation in the discussion of our domestic politics and of our foreign policies by agents of a European monarchy, whether they are official or self-appointed, cannot but arouse antagonism to a power who will permit its subjects to forget their obligations as alien visitors owing a temporary allegiance to the United States and to seek openly to create political opposition to the Government.

The American people never have and never will brook foreign interference in their public affairs. They resent, and properly resent, foreign support or opposition when a policy of this Government is at issue. The people of this country are capable of managing their own affairs without the advice of aliens, who are seeking the interests of their own government and not the interests of the United States.

The object of Professor Münsterberg and Dr. Dernburg and other German subjects, engaged in the present pro-German propaganda in this country, appears to be two-fold.

Primarily it is to separate American citizens of German nativity or descent from the general body of the American people, to impress upon them that they are a distinct group of society, which on account of their blood are viewed with suspicion, if not with dislike, by their fellow countrymen, and to make them feel that they are first of all Germans.

Secondly their object is by means of this aroused spirit of racial allegiance to use this great body of citizens of German origin as a political machine, with which to threaten the Administration into showing special favors to Germany and Austria in the performance of the neutral duties of this Government. The menace of political opposition, if the present policy of the Government is continued, is openly proclaimed by aliens, who are devoting themselves to this propaganda and who by education and birth are out of all sympathy with American institutions, interests and ideals.

If the American people as a whole realize that these foreigners are attempting to direct our domestic affairs and are seeking to influence political action in this country to obtain special privileges for their own government, the propaganda, which is being carried on under the leadership of Professor Münsterberg and Dr. Dernburg, will awaken a resentment which will more than counteract the activities of these men and their followers.

II. *The Policy of the Government of the United States in its Relations with the Belligerents.*

There are two general reasons controlling the policy of the Government of the United States in relation to the observance of neutrality during the present war:

*First,* the duty which the United States as a neutral nation owes to all the belligerents, based upon the legal obligation which is imposed by international law and treaty stipulations.

*Second*, the desirability to avoid exciting bitter feeling between groups of the American people, whose sympathies are divided because of the composite character of our citizenship. This reason is a matter of domestic policy and expediency.

In addition to these two political reasons is the humanitarian one of preserving impartial friendship toward all the belligerent powers in order that this Government at the proper time may exercise its influence for the restoration of peace.

Neutral duty, which is defined by the established rules of international usage, by conventional agreements and by municipal statutes, is enforceable by the Executive operating under enacted law and the treaties in force. Beyond such legal authority the Executive possesses no power to compel obedience. Law is the sole measure of neutrality and of the government's duty to preserve it.

The second reason, based on expediency, has no legal authority to support it. No power is conferred upon the Executive to compel submission to the policy adopted, but the Government may by the exercise of its influence induce popular acceptance of such policy.

This Government may justly be held responsible for failure to enforce the legal rules of neutrality, but it is not bound to impose restrictions greater than those included in such rules. If the Government, as a matter of policy, advocates a neutrality beyond the legal requirements, it cannot rightfully be called to account for infractions of these extra-legal restrictions, since it has no power to prevent or to punish their violation.

III. *Presumptive Equality of Belligerents Essential to Strict Neutrality.*

In the enforcement of the laws of neutrality and in advocating an extension of neutral obligations, which domestic interests make expedient, this Government cannot take into account the advantage or disadvantage which may result to any of the belligerents through the enforcement of neutral duties. If one belligerent has by good fortune a superiority in the matter of geographical location or of military or naval power, the rules of neutral conduct cannot be varied so as to favor the less fortunate combatant. To change such rules because of the relative strength of the belligerents and in order to equalize their opportunities would be in itself an unneutral act, of which the stronger might justly complain.

This Government, in the enforcement of the laws of neutrality and in exercising its influence over the people as to their conduct toward the belligerents, must consider the hostile nations to be upon equal footing and to possess equal opportunities in the conduct of the war. Any other course would make the rules of neutrality a fluctuating standard which would result in constant confusion and in innumerable charges of partiality. Whether one belligerent or the other is successful, is not a matter of concern to a neutral government, and it cannot vary its rules or change its policy because of a particular triumph or defeat by either during the progress of the war. It must hold strictly to its obligations and to its general policy, however they may benefit one belligerent or injure another.

*Note 1. The Three Principal Complaints.* (Münsterberg letter, pages 2-3)

"First, all cables sent by and received by wire pass uncensored, while all wireless news is censored. This reacts against Germany, because England sends all her news by cable, whereas Germany alone uses the wireless. The matter is of grave importance."

The reason that wireless messages and cable messages require different treatment by a neutral government is as follows:

Communications by wireless cannot be interrupted by a belligerent. No physical power to interrupt exists except at the wireless stations. If one station is in neutral territory and another beyond danger in an enemy's country, a belligerent, however superior on the sea, cannot benefit by his superiority, but is powerless to prevent messages from passing unmolested, even though they convey information which materially affects his naval operations. Manifestly a neutral has no right to deprive a belligerent of one of the principal benefits of supremacy on the high seas. With a submarine cable it is otherwise. The possibility of cutting the cable exists, and if a belligerent possesses naval superiority, the cable is cut, as was the German cable near the Azores by one of Germany's enemies, and as was the British cable near Fanning Island by a German naval force. Since a cable is subject to hostile attack, the responsibility falls upon the belligerent and not upon the neutral to prevent cable communication.

A more important reason however, at least from the point of view of a neutral government, is that messages sent out from a wireless station in neutral territory may be received by belligerent warships on the high seas. If these messages, whether plain or in cipher, direct the movements of warships or convey to them information as to the location of any enemy's public or private vessels, the neutral territory becomes a base of naval operations, to permit which would be essentially unneutral.

As a wireless message can be received by all stations and vessels within a given radius, every message in cipher, whatever its intended destination, must be censored; otherwise military information may be sent to warships off the coast of a neutral. It is manifest that a submarine cable is incapable of becoming a means of direct communication with a warship on the high seas; hence its use cannot make neutral territory a base for the direction of naval operations.

"Second, the policy of the administration with regard to the holding up, detaining and searching of Germans and Austrians from neutral and American vessels is a reversal of the American policy established in 1812. It has excited no end of bitterness."

So far as this Government has been advised, no Germans or Austrians on an American vessel on the high seas, with two exceptions, have been detained or searched by belligerent warships. One of the exceptions to which reference is made is now the subject of a rigid investigation, and if the facts as alleged are established, vigorous representations will be made to the offending government. The other exception where certain German passengers were made to sign a promise not to take part in the war, has been brought to the attention of the offending government with a declaration that such procedure, if true, is an unwarranted exercise of jurisdiction over American vessels in which this Government will not acquiesce.

An American private vessel entering voluntarily the territorial waters of a belligerent becomes subject to its municipal laws, as do the persons on board the vessel.

There has been no reversal of the century-old American policy, which related to the removal of alleged American citizens and their impressment by Great Britain. It is in no way involved in the present case.

"Third, the United States permitted the violations by England of the Hague Convention and international law in connection with conditional and unconditional contraband. The United States, for instance, has not protested against the transference of copper from the conditional to the absolute list, although on former occasions the United States has taken a spirited stand against onesided interpretations of international agreements. In 1812, in the Russian Japanese War, and in the Boer War the United States insisted that a neutral nation has the right to send conditional as well as unconditional contraband to neutral nations without permitting an inquiry into its ultimate destination. She insisted that the consignee must be accepted in good faith. The United States, moreover, insisted that conditional contraband can be sent in neutral or in American bottoms even to belligerent nations, provided it was not consigned to the government, the military or naval authorities or to any contractors known to represent the belligerent government. By permitting this new interpretation the United States practically supports the starving out policy of the Allies. The nation by reversing its own policy thus seriously handicaps Germany and Austria in their fight for existence."

There is no Hague Convention which deals with absolute or conditional contraband, and, as the Declaration of London is not in force, the rules of international law only apply. As to the articles to be regarded as contraband there is no general agreement. It is the practice for a country, either in time of peace or upon the outbreak of war, to declare what articles it will consider as absolute or conditional contraband. It is true that a neutral government is seriously affected by this declaration, as the rights of its subjects or citizens are impaired. The right of the neutral, however, seems to be that of protest.

The record of the United States in the past is not free from criticism. When neutrals, we have stood for the most restricted lists of absolute and conditional contraband. As a belligerent, we have extended the lists of both according to our conception of the necessities of the case.

The United States has now under consideration the question of the right of a belligerent to include "copper unwrought" in its list of absolute contraband instead of in its list of conditional contraband. As the Government of the United States has in the past placed "all articles from which ammunition is manufactured" in its contraband list, and has declared copper to be among such materials, it necessarily finds some embarrassment in dealing with the subject. The doctrine of "ultimate destination" and of "continuous voyage" to which reference is made in the foregoing complaint but which is not specifically stated, is an *American doctrine* supported by the decisions of the United States Supreme Court. Against the rule of "continuous voyage" this Government has never in the past protested, nor can it consistently do so now, in view of the fact that, when it was a belligerent, it not only asserted but extended the rule and enforced it in its tribunals.

As no American vessel so far as known has attempted to carry conditional contraband to Germany or Austria, no ground of complaint has arisen out of the seizure or condemnation by Great Britain of an American vessel with a belligerent destination. Until a case arises and the Government has taken action upon it, criticism is premature and unwarranted.

The United States has made earnest representations to Great Britain in regard to the seizure and detention by the British authorities of all American ships or cargoes destined to neutral ports, on the ground that such seizures and detentions were contrary to the existing rules of international law, but our American doctrines have been such that we are seriously handicapped in urging our protests.

We have not accepted the principle that delivery to specific consigness in a neutral port settled the question of ultimate destination. We have claimed and exercised the right to determine from the circumstances whether the ostensible was the real destination. We have also held that the shipment of articles of contraband to a neutral port "to order," from which, as a matter of fact, cargoes had been transhipped to the enemy, is corroborative evidence that the cargo is really destined to the enemy, instead of to the neutral port of delivery. We have also held that a cargo of contraband shipped from one neutral port to another will be presumed to be meant for the enemy if destined to a port contiguous to enemy territory. It is thus seen that the doctrines which appear to bear harshly upon neutrals at the present time are analagous to or outgrowths from policies adopted by the United States when it was a belligerent.

*Note 2. The "Fatherland's["] Complaints.* (Pages 3-4 of Munsterberg's letter)

"We permit English warships to nose about in our harbors; we permit them to search our ships. In 1812 we went to war for smaller reasons."

The complaint is unjustified from the fact that representations were made to the British Government that the presence of war vessels in the vicinity of New York Harbor was offensive to this Government and a similar complaint was made to the Japanese Government as to one of its cruisers in the vicinity of the port of Honolulu. In both cases the warships were withdrawn.

It will be recalled that in 1863 the Department took the position that captures made by its vessels after hovering about neutral ports would not be regarded as valid. In the Franco-Prussian war President Grant issued a proclamation warning belligerent warships against hovering in the vicinity of American ports for purposes of observation or hostile acts. The same policy has been maintained in the present war, and in all of the recent proclamations of neutrality the President states that such practice by belligerent warships is "unfriendly and offensive."

"We raise no protest when England contemptuously disregards our citizenship papers."

American citizenship papers have been disregarded in a comparatively few instances by Great Britain, but the same is true of Germany. Bearers of American passports have been arrested in both countries. In all such cases the United States Government has entered vigorous protests with request for release. The Department does not know of any cases, except one or two which are still under investigation, in which naturalized Germans have not been released upon representations by this Government. There have, however, come to the Department's notice authentic cases in which American passports have been fraudulently obtained by certain German subjects. Such fraudulent use of passports by Germans themselves can have no other effect than to cast suspicion upon American passports in general.

"We even permit her to seize our cargoes of copper in her hope of monopolizing eventually our entire copper trade."

There is no question of the United States *"permitting"* Great Britain to seize copper shipments. In every case in which it has been done vigorous representations have been made to the British Government and our representatives have pressed for the release of the shipments.

"She permits us to export dynamite, but she does not permit us to export oil, even to neutral nations."

Petrol and other petroleum products have been proclaimed by Great Britain as contraband of war. In view of the absolute necessity of such products to the use of submarines, aeroplames and motors, the United States Government has not yet reached the conclusion that they are improperly included in a list of contraband. Military operations to-day are largely a question of motive power through mechanical devices. It is therefore difficult to argue successfully against the inclusion of petroleum among the articles of contraband. As to the detention of cargoes of petroleum oil to neutral countries, this Government has, thus far successfully, obtained the release in every case of detention or seizure which has been brought to its attention.

"In other words England, while fighting Germany on the field of battle, is waging war on the United States commercially. She makes it impossible for us to profit by the war for she strangles our trade, except for such contraband as she and her allies need. It is time to reassert our declaration of independence."

The fact that the commerce of the United States is interrupted by Great Britain is consequent upon the superiority of her navy on the high seas. If Germany possessed that superiority, it may be confidently assumed that our trade with Great Britain and France would be interrupted and that no articles useful to those countries in the prosecution of the war would reach their ports from this country.

The above quotation should be read with that in Note 3 below. The one complains of the loss of profit in trade which must mean trade in contraband with Germany and the other demands the prohibition of trade in contraband which of course refers to trade with the Allies. The inconsistency is obvious.

"German-American citizens feel, rightly or wrongly, that the administration is hostile to them, because its interpretation of neutrality has been at all points disadvantageous to Germany."

It is not unnatural that American citizens who are partisans of Germany should feel that the Administration is hostile not "to them" but to Germany. This feeling results from the fact that the German naval power is inferior to the British. It is the duty of a belligerent to prevent contraband from reaching an enemy. It is not the duty of a neutral. The partisans of Germany in this country appear to assume that some obligation rests upon this Government in the performance of its neutral duty to prevent all trade in contraband. No such obligation exists, and it would be an unneutral act of partiality on its part to take such action.

*Note 3. Trade in Contraband and War Loans.* (Letter page 4)
"Many of the complaints refer more to the unfriendly spirit than to the actual violation of the law. Here above all belongs the unlimited sale of ammunition to the belligerents. The administration originally advised Mr. Morgan that the making of loans to the nations at war would not be looked upon with favor by the President, and Mr. Morgan cancelled the plans. This attitude has been given up; the State Department has emphasized that money and arms may be sold to the belligerents, while evidently the friends of peace had firmly hoped that the President would denounce the sale of ammunition or any other sale which would be likely to prolong the war."

There is no power in the Executive to prevent the sale of ammunition to the belligerents.

Trade in munitions of war has never been restricted by international law or by municipal statute. It has never been the policy of this Government to prevent the shipment of arms or ammunition into belligerent territory, except in the case of neighboring

American republics, and then only when civil strife prevailed. Even to this extent the European governments have never so far as I know limited the sale of munitions of war. It is only necessary to point to the enormous quantities of arms and ammunition furnished by German manufacturers to the belligerents in the Russo-Japanese war and in the recent Balkan wars. No country has been able to compete with Germany in the manufacture and sale of arms and ammunition.

Furthermore, one of the compensations for the disorganization of neutral commerce and the restriction of markets has been the sale of contraband to the warring nations. Such trade has been recognized as a proper substitute for the loss sustained by neutrals as a direct result of war. The lack of profit from trade is complained of in Professor Munsterberg's letter.

The reason why the influence of the Government is not exerted to prevent the sale of contraband to belligerents while such influence has been exerted in preventing the flotation of war loans in this country is this: a war loan, if offered for popular subscription in the United States, would be taken up by those who are in sympathy with the belligerent seeking the loan. The result would be that great numbers of our people would become more earnest partisans, having material interest in the success of the belligerent, whose bonds they hold. This would not be confined to a few, but would spread generally throughout our country, so that our people would be divided into groups of partisans, which would be, in the views of the Government, most unfortunate and might cause a serious condition of affairs. On the other hand, contracts for and sales of contraband are mere matters of trade. The manufacturer, unless peculiarly sentimental, would sell to one belligerent as readily as he would to another. No general spirit of partisanship would be aroused—no sympathies excited. The whole transaction would be merely a matter of business.

This Government has not been advised that any general loans have been made by foreign governments in this country since the President expressed his wish that loans of this character should not be made.

*Note No. 4. Complaints in private letter quoted on pages 5 and 6 of Munsterberg's letter.*

It is unnecessary to quote the language of the writer of the letter which Professor Munsterberg furnishes. It is manifestly difficult to answer charges of so general a nature as the writer makes. The general charge as to the arrest of American-born citizens on board neutral vessels and in British ports, the ignoring of their passports, and their confinement in jails, requires evidence to support it. That there have been cases of injustice of this sort is unquestionably true, but Americans in Germany have suffered in this way as Americans have in Great Britain. This Government has considered that the majority of these cases resulted from over-zealousness on the part of subordinate officials. Every case which has been brought to the attention of the Department of State has been promptly investigated, and, if the facts warranted, a demand for release has been made.

As to the censorship of mails, Germany as well as Great Britain has pursued this course in regard to private letters falling into their hands. The unquestioned right to adopt a measure of this sort makes objection to it inadvisable. As to the detention of non-combatants confined in concentration camps, all the belligerents, with perhaps the exception of Servia and Russia, have made similar complaints and those for whom this Government is acting have asked investigations, which representatives of this Government have made impartially. Their reports have shown that the treatment of prisoners is generally as good as possible under the conditions in all countries, and that there is no more reason to say they are "languishing" in one country than in another country or that this country has manifested a "supreme indifference" in the matter. As Department's efforts at investigations seemed to develop bitterness between the countries, the Department on November 20 sent a circular instruction to its representatives not to undertake further investigations of concentration camps.

The representations to the Turkish Government relative to its threatening attitude toward the English, Russians and French and their consular officers were made upon the request of the Governments interested and pressed upon their suggestion.

*Note No. 5. Complaint as to destruction of American mail.* (Letter page 6)

No evidence has been filed with this Government, and no representations have been made that American mail on board of Dutch steamers has been "repeatedly destroyed." Until such a case is presented in concrete form, this Government would not be justified in presenting the matter to the offending belligerent. Complaints have come to the Department that mail on board neutral steamers has been opened and detained but there seem to be but few cases where the mail from neutral countries has not been finally delivered. When mail is sent to belligerent countries open and is of neutral and private character it has not been molested.

*Note 6. Transshipment of troops and war material across American territory.* (Letter page 7)

The Department has had no specific case of the shipment of convoys of troops across American territory brought to its notice. There have been reports to this effect but no actual facts have been presented. The transshipment of reservists of all belligerents including *Austria*, who have requested the privilege, has been permitted on condition that they travel as individuals and not as organized, uniformed or armed bodies. The German Embassy has advised the Department that it would not be likely to avail itself of the privilege.

Only two cases of the transit of war material across United States territory have come to Department's notice. One case was a request for shipment of Government arms and equipment across Alaska which was refused. Another was in regard to shipment of horses and mules on the Canadian Pacific Railway, to which Department replied that a commercial shipment not in the nature of a convoy of the Government such as is prohibited under Article 2 of Hague Convention No. 5, 1907, was allowable.

As this Government is not now interested in the adoption of the Declaration of London by the belligerents, the modifications of the belligerents in that code of naval warfare are of no concern to it except in so far as they affect its rights and those of its citizens under international law. In so far as these rights have been affected the Department has made every effort to obtain redress for violations suffered.

*Note No. 7. The Honolulu Incident.* (Letter page 7)

It is assumed that reference is made to the internment of H.M.S. GEIER and the German steamer LOCKSUN. The GEIER entered Honolulu on October 15th in an unseaworthy condition. The Captain reported the necessity of extensive repairs which would require an indefinite period for completion. The vessel was allowed the generous period of three weeks to November 7th to make repairs and leave the port or be interned; but a longer period was concluded to be out of the question, as a vessel could not claim time in which to repair a generally run down condition due to long sea service. A Japanese cruiser soon appeared off the port of Honolulu and the GEIER chose internment rather than departure from the harbor. On October 30th the Depart-

ment advised the German Ambassador of the proposed internment.

The arrival of the GEIER was followed soon after by that of
the steamer LOCKSUN which, it was found had delivered coal to
the GEIER en route and accompanied her toward Honolulu. As
she had thus constituted herself a tender to the GEIER she was
accorded the same treatment and interned on November 7th.

*Note No. 8. Coaling of warships in Panama Canal Zone.* (Letter page 7)

By Proclamation of November 13, 1914, certain special
instructions were placed on the coaling of warships or their
tenders or colliers in the Canal Zone. These regulations were
framed through the collaboration of the State, Navy and War
Departments and without the slightest reference to favoritism
to the belligerents. Before these regulations were proclaimed war
vessels could procure coal of the Panama Railway in the Zone
ports but no belligerent vessels are known to have done so. Under the Proclamation fuel may be taken on by belligerent warships only with the consent of the Canal authorities, and in
such amounts as will enable them to reach the nearest acces-
sible neutral port; and the amount so taken on shall be deducted
from the amount procurable in United States ports within three
months thereafter. Now it is charged the United States has
shown partiality, because Great Britain and not Germany happens to have colonies in the near vicinity where British ships
may coal while Germany has no such coaling facilities. Again
it is intimated the United States should balance the inequalities
of geographical position by refusal to allow any warships of
belligerents to coal in the Canal until the war is over.

*Note No. 9. German complaint against British changes in
Declaration of London.* (Letter page 7)

October 10 the German Foreign Office presented to the
diplomats in Berlin a memorandum, calling attention to violations of, and changes in, the Declaration of London by the British
Government and inquiring as to the attitude of the United States
toward such action on the part of the Allies. The substance of the
memorandum was telegraphed to the Department October 22,
and was replied to shortly thereafter to the effect that the United
States had withdrawn its suggestion made early in the war, for
the adoption, for the sake of uniformity, of the Declaration of
London as a temporary code of naval warfare during the present
war, owing to the unwillingness of some of the belligerents to

accept the Declaration without changes and modifications, and that thenceforth the United States would insist that the rights of the United States and its citizens in the war should be governed by the existing rules of international law.

Robert Lansing.[1]

TS memorandum (WP, DLC).
[1] Wilson sent a digest of this memorandum to Münsterberg by special messenger.


## From Frank J. Hayes

Denver, Colo., Dec. 9, 1914.

Convention of Colorado Mine Workers last night accepted the good offices of the commission you recently appointed and terminated the strike on that basis. Sincerely hope this commission will materially assist in promoting industrial justice in Colorado.

Frank J. Hayes, chairman,
Policy Committee, Colorado Mine Workers.

T telegram (WP, DLC).


## Remarks to the Ohio Valley Improvement Association[1]

[Dec. 10, 1914]

I am very much obliged to you ladies and gentlemen. I feel that I ought to say this to you: I think it is increasingly hazardous to treat individual projects by themselves. I think what the whole country expects of us, and has a right to ask of us, is that we should make a complete study of the Mississippi Valley and the tributary valleys, see what we are going to do about the whole question, and then proceed to do it in the sequence of projects that experienced engineers show us to be the right sequence. What we have been doing up to this time was to prevent damage, or prevent the consummation of damage, which need not have occurred at all if we had controlled the upper waters of the flood areas. We have not co-ordinated yet the different questions as to control of floods, and there is the use of the waters for commercial and navigation purposes. All those things are perfectly consistent with one another. You can control the floods best by controlling the waters in such a way that you can use them for navigation and power purposes. We ought to do these things co-ordinately, not separately. I say that because I want you to understand why I cannot recommend to Congress a separate project, a particular project, in the same breath in which I am recommending to them that we have a competent study made of the whole problem and then proceed to address ourselves to it after that study had been made. I thought I owed you that explanation. It will also show you my genuine interest in the whole question.

T MS (WP, DLC).
  [1] Some fifty members of the Ohio Valley Improvement Association and related organizations, in Washington to attend the National Rivers and Harbors Congress, were brought to the White House by Congressman Alfred Gaither Allen. Several of the visitors spoke briefly on the need for further improvements in the Ohio River Valley. *Cincinnati Enquirer*, Dec. 12, 1914.

## To Robert Lansing

My dear Mr. Lansing:    The White House December 10, 1914

Here is a telegram I have just received[1] upon which I would value your comment. Are these gentlemen right in the position they take, do you think?

I did not mean to have you take Münsterburg's letter quite so seriously as you did. I fear that I put a great burden of unnecessary work on you, but I am heartily obliged to you for the results which reached me last evening.

Cordially and faithfully yours,    Woodrow Wilson

TLS (SDR, RG 59, 763.72111/1332½, DNA).
  [1] Paul Fuller *et al.* to WW, Dec. 8, 1914.

## To William Jennings Bryan

My dear Mr. Secretary:    The White House December 10, 1914

As I admitted at Cabinet meeting in our conversation, I evidently made a mistake in sending Vick's allegations to the Secretary of War. I should have sent them to you.

In order to correct my mistake, I now send them to you and beg that you will take steps to institute a thorough investigation.

May I make the following suggestions:

Mr. Vick evidently feels, at any rate he asserts, that the State Department has taken and will take his charges very lightly. He is violently prejudiced and, therefore, I suggest that you arrange to have this matter put in the hands of someone who heretofore has not been in touch with it at all and who will be so evidently removed from intimate relationship either with yourself or with me as to be clearly a detached and impartial judge,

—I mean clearly to the public, upon whom Vick is trying to make an impression.

It may be that it will be well to choose some person entirely disconnected officially with the Government, some person of equal standing with Mr. Paul Fuller, for example, and equally disengaged from any interest of any official sort in this matter, and send him down there to San Domingo itself.

In the meantime, would it not be well to write to Mr. Vick, tell him that these things are going to be sifted to the bottom, and ask him to submit his proofs as he offers to do in the letter which I enclose?

Cordially and faithfully yours,   Woodrow Wilson

TLS (SDR, RG 59, 123 Su 51/63, DNA).

## To Champ Clark

My dear Mr. Speaker:    [The White House] December 10, 1914

Thank you warmly for your note of yesterday. Your notes always give me a great deal of pleasure, for they are always very generous.

Referring to your kindness in saying again how ready you are to help along with things, may I not express to you my very deep interest in the shipping bill? Each day additional evidence comes in of one kind or another of the great need for immediate action in this matter. For example, the ocean freight rates have increased, I am told, three fold, and some such action as is proposed by the bill would undoubtedly tend to remove that great impediment to the shipment of our goods. I think you would be interested if you had time some day to have a talk with Secretary McAdoo about the matter. He is full of the most interesting and important information concerning it.

Always

Cordially and faithfully yours,   Woodrow Wilson

TLS (Letterpress Books, WP, DLC).

## To Henry De La Warr Flood

My dear Mr. Flood:    [The White House] December 10, 1914

I am very deeply interested in the passage of the bill for the improvement of the diplomatic and consular service.[1] At the present time when so many responsibilities are thrown upon our Foreign Service, not only in caring for the interests of many other governments, but also in seeking new ways in which to enlarge our own commerce, it seems to me that nothing should be allowed to stand in the way of making both the diplomatic and consular services thoroughly adaptable to the new and changed conditions. The present inelastic system has outgrown its usefulness, and is utterly inadequate for existing requirements.

I hope, therefore, that Congress may find it feasible to pass the measure to which I refer so that it may become effective not later than January first.

With many thanks for your assistance in this matter, I am, my dear Mr. Flood,

Cordially and faithfully yours, Woodrow Wilson

TLS (Letterpress Books, WP, DLC).
¹ S. 5612, introduced by Senator William J. Stone on May 20, 1914. Designed to increase the flexibility of the diplomatic and consular services, the bill provided that henceforth all presidential appointments of secretaries in the diplomatic service and of consuls general and consuls would be to these offices in general rather than to a specific location as heretofore and authorized the President to assign or transfer them at will, as the best interests of the country might require. It also provided for some salary increases in the various grades, as well as additional pay for special duties. After passage by the Senate, the bill had been stalled in the House since October. Flood had the bill brought up and secured its passage on January 18, 1915. Wilson signed it on February 5. *Cong. Record*, 63d Cong., 2d sess., pp. 8872, 16830-832; *ibid.*, 3d sess., pp. 1777, 1779-86, 1841, 3230; 38 U. S. *Statutes at Large* 805 (1915).


## To Elias Milton Ammons

[The White House] December 10, 1914

Is it safe for me to assume that in view of the strike having been called off there is no longer any occasion for keeping the troops of the United States in Colorado? I sincerely hope that I may. It occurs to me that any formal substitution of the armed forces of the State for those of the United States would seem to discount the action of the strikers. Woodrow Wilson

T telegram (Letterpress Books, WP, DLC).


## To Frank J. Hayes

My dear Mr. Hayes: [The White House] December 10, 1914

May I not express my great pleasure at the result of the Convention of Colorado Mine Workers and my appreciation of the spirit in which the action seems to have been taken? I think that it should lead to happy, peaceful results.

Cordially and sincerely yours, Woodrow Wilson

TLS (Letterpress Books, WP, DLC).

## To John Worth Kern

My dear Senator:  [The White House] December 10, 1914

I write to ask if the steering committee would not be willing to take some action that would secure for the Water Power Bill and the General Leasing Bill an early consideration. I fear with regard to all the bills in which I am deeply interested that delays in beginning their consideration might be fatal to their passage.

I know that you will indulge me in making this suggestion.

Cordially and faithfully yours,  Woodrow Wilson

TLS (Letterpress Books, WP, DLC).

## From Robert Lansing

My dear Mr. President:  Washington December 10, 1914.

I am in receipt of your letter of to-day asking me to comment upon a telegram, dated the 8th, from Paul Fuller, Benjamin F. Tracy and Frederic R. Coudert, in which they assert that Congressional alteration of the rules of neutrality during warfare is contrary to accepted international law and is an absolute violation of neutrality.

I think these gentlemen are entirely right in the general principle asserted. Any change in our statutes by amendment or repeal would undoubtedly benefit one or the other of the belligerents. Whatever the purpose of a change the belligerent, whose interests were unfavorably affected, would be justified in protesting on the ground that the legislation was for the advantage of its enemy, and, therefore, unneutral. I have in a general way referred to this in Comment III of the Memorandum on the Münsterberg letter (page 6).

Some days ago I spoke to Secretary Bryan about this matter in anticipation of the introduction of bills in Congress for amendment of our neutrality statutes, and expressed an opinion substantially the same as that asserted by Messrs. Fuller, Tracy and Coudert.

At that time I called his attention to another application of the same principle which would come up at the meeting of the Governing Board of the Pan American Union. Briefly the point was this: If this principle was applied to the various schemes of neutralization of certain sea areas and of changing the general rules as to the treatment of belligerent warships, which had been suggested by certain South American republics, such changes would necessarily be unneutral because they would unequally affect the interests of the belligerents; and, unless the belligerents unanimously consented to them, their adoption would be a justifiable ground for complaint. The conclusion was that, as it was manifestly impossible to obtain unanimous consent, no modification of existing rules should be adopted during the present wars, though neutral rights and duties might be profitably considered informally by a Commission looking to future action after the wars were over.

I also discussed the subject in a confidential way with the Argentine Ambassador, who agreed entirely in the opinion that any present change in the rules would be unneutral and impracticable, and who suggested that a Commission be named for an informal exchange of views upon the subject. This was adopted by the Board at its meeting.

There is, however, another type of legislation in relation to the enforcement of neutral duties, which I do not think can be construed into an unneutral act and which it may be advisable, if not necessary, to enact. There are certain obligations as to neutral conduct imposed by treaties, which have never been incorporated in our laws so that the Executive possesses no power to prevent and the courts no power to penalize violations. The result is that, in attempting to enforce these obligations, we are skating on pretty thin ice, and if the authority of the officials should be questioned I am afraid of the result.

Furthermore, some of the penalties imposed by our present statutes are so inadequate that an offender would willingly suffer the penalty for the privilege of violation.

As legislation of this sort, affecting treaty provisions and statutes, would in no way change the rules of neutral conduct but would only confer powers for the proper enforcement of existing rules, there would be no element of unneutrality in its enactment.

I have taken up this matter with Mr. Warren, the Assistant Attorney General having charge of neutrality cases,[1] with the object of curing in some way this embarrassing state of the law which materially affects the proper enforcement of neutrality.

The telegram is herewith returned.

Very sincerely yours,   Robert Lansing.

TLS (WP, DLC).
[1] Charles Warren, distinguished lawyer and legal scholar of Boston.

## From Elias Milton Ammons

Denver, Colorado, December 10, 1914.

Think calling off strike should avoid necessity for state troops, if federal troops are kept in most dangerous districts for short time until matters can have time to adjust themselves. The mines being already filled with men sufficient to supply all demands for coal there may be but few places at first for strikers who have been led to believe through press and other reports there is plenty of room for them also. I believe operators will strain point to give work to as many men as possible. There is some danger of disappointment and there might be trouble. I am confident strike leaders will do their best to avoid disturbance but calling off of strike after men have been led to believe they are sure to win may loosen the hold of the leaders on them. We still have condition where one side is disarmed and the other not. I believe it would be entirely safe to remove troops after situation has quieted down under new conditions without necessity of replacing with state troops especially if the men scatter out and get work and the tent colonies are abandoned. There are among strikers many men who are not former employes and who have nothing to gain by calling off of strike. I still believe troops should be taken out in order suggested in my letter of November nin[e]teenth and therefore removed from Oak Creek and northern field before withdrawn from southern field. Believe it would be much better to have federal troops remain little longer than incur danger of being compelled to replace by state troops. Expect to be in Washington next week and would be glad to go over situation with you fully if you so desire. Please advise if you desire further particulars.                E. W. Ammons.

T telegram (WP, DLC).

## From Edward Mandell House

Dear Governor:            New York City. December 11th, 1914.

I have taken the trouble to get what I consider the normal public estimate of your message in regard to armaments, and I am satisfied that you have followed the course that will please our people as a whole.

You go far enough to satisfy any reasonable man and your reasons for not going further are, I think, conclusive. It must be patent to all that our protection lies in the Navy and must always largely be so.

I have a feeling that when this war is over, the whole world will have a different outlook in regard to militarism, and that public opinion in this country will applaud you for not being carried away by the excitement of the moment.

I am leaving for Boston in a few minutes to remain over Sunday. Janet and the baby girl are doing famously, and we are going to Chestnut Hill to see the new grandson there.

Affectionately yours,   E. M. House

TLS (WP, DLC).


## From Walker Whiting Vick

*Personal.*

Rutherford, New Jersey.

My Dear Mr. President:    December Eleventh Nineteenfourteen.

I am gratified to know by your letter of the Seventh that you will cause a thorough inquiry into the Dominican situation, which I barely outlined in my letter of December first.

May I be permitted to express the hope that the inquiry will be an independent one, free from the prejudices and pre-judgments which have characterized the attitude of Mr. Bryan? The unfitness of his various appointments to Santo Domingo is sufficient to justify public suspicion of the thoroughness and fairness of any investigation which he personally may direct.

I have always disbelieved that you had said anything derogatory of me, notwithstanding I was told positively that the statements came direct from the White House. The lies that have been told are only indicative of the ramifications of the Dominican conspiracy, the extent of which certain persons would keep from you at any cost.

The guarding of my reputation against secret and malicious misrepresentation, and determination to do my full duty toward you are my only objectives.

With deep appreciation, I am,

Faithfully yours,   Walker W. Vick

TLS (WP, DLC).


## To Lucy Marshall Smith

Dear Cousin Lucy,          The White House 12 December, 1914.

I was so much obliged to you for your letter.[1] I cannot tell you how much and how constantly we miss you both or how often our thoughts turn lovingly to you; and we are all the time hungry for news of you, great or small. No letters are pounced upon so promptly or so eagerly as yours and Cousin Mary's. Surely you know that you have a place in our hearts now that makes it a trial to be separated from you.

We are all perfectly well, except that Helen looks darker under the eyes than I like. Her chief care just now is "Hamish" the shapeless English sheep dog puppy Mrs. Davis[2] sent her. She takes care of him herself. While it is a care, I think it is also a diversion and a real pleasure to her.

We have just had the pleasure of having Cleve. Dodge with us and that admirable daughter of his, Elizabeth,[3] with a friend of hers, a Miss Appleton[4] from New York, of the family of well known publishers, a very interesting young woman, though so slender and fragile looking that I was afraid to breathe hard in her direction. Mrs. Sheridan's[5] daughter, Lillian Crompton,[6] is here, on a vacation from her husband and baby, and is a very sweet companion. She is to be sent to the dancing class to-night, after a horse-back ride this afternoon which will make dancing doubly interesting, since she has not been on a horse for years.

It seems like old times to have Congress here again, and the old hectic days of work have come back; but nothing seems to me in fact like the old times. I live in a different world and shall have to school my spirits to it. I have, I fear, made little progress yet in schooling them; but I tell myself that it is too soon to be discouraged. It may take a long while to learn how to live with a broken heart, and yet not slacken any energy that is needed for one's work!

All join me in dearest love to you both.

Your loving friend,   Woodrow Wilson

WWTLS (photostat in RSB Coll., DLC).
  [1] It is missing.
  [2] Probably Ellen-Duane Gillespie (Mrs. Edward Parker) Davis.
  [3] Elizabeth Wainwright Dodge.
  [4] Either Margarett S. Appleton or Mary W. Appleton, daughters of William Worthen Appleton.
  [5] Sarah MacDonald Sheridan of New York, one of Margaret Wilson's singing teachers.
  [6] Lillian Sheridan (Mrs. David Henry) Crompton of New York.

## To Nancy Saunders Toy

Dearest Friend,          The White House 12 December, 1914.

Your letters[1] have the rare quality of making me feel, after reading them, as if I had really seen you and had a talk with you of many things. I wish that I could return the visit by writing a like vivid epistle, with the person in it who wrote it! I seem to have fallen singularly dull. All the elasticity has gone out of me.

I have not yet learned how to throw off the incubus of my grief and live as I used to live, in thought and spirit, in spite of it. Even books have grown meaningless to me. I read detective stories to forget, as a man would get drunk! I am deeply grateful to you for the glimpses you give me of your dear mother and of my own lost sweetheart from the old letters you have been reading and from your diary. You know the kind of ministrations I need! And the politics! You are mistaken in only one thing. Men like Lodge and Gardiner do not annoy me. Partisan tactics, as such, only excite my contempt, and not a lively enough contempt to make me unhappy. Many weeks ago, when the war had but just begun, Mr. Eliot wrote me a long and earnest letter arguing that we should actively join the Allies against Germany. I was amazed and distressed then, because I so sincerely respect Mr. Eliot and had thought that he might so confidently be counted on to serve always as part of the balast of the nation, and utter what would be its sober second thought; but that shock has passed. The speeches he makes now add nothing. They come to me like a thing already discounted, an experience that is past and has faded a bit. I school myself to *look on* as impersonally as possible. I do not really read the newspapers: I merely glance at their headlines to get an impression of what the public is thinking about and getting what it takes for information about. And so I manage most of the time to hold excitements at arm's length and escape their contagion. *Somebody* must keep cool while our people grow hotter with discussing the war and all that it involves! There seems to be this advantage in having suffered the keenest, most mortal blow one can receive, that nothing else seems capable of hurting you! *Suffering*, personal annoyance, seem out of the question, something you have outlived.

But, why talk about myself when there are so many more interesting things to talk about! And to tell you the truth, nothing seems to me so uninteresting as myself. I know all the details of that subject, and it is both tedious and uninspiring. What I do love to talk about, however, is things and persons very near to me, not as President (for I am merely administering the presidency) but as a human being, a traveler between life and death. Human friendship means an infinite deal to me; and I find my thoughts going out to my friends now as never before, trying to make a circle of them close about me no matter how far away in space they may be, and no matter whether they all know one another or not. I wonder if you feel free to make new acquaintances or not now, or free to seek people out at all? I have a friend now living at 49 Gloucester St. in Boston whom I wish

very much you might know. She has had a hard life, chiefly hard
because it denied her access to the things she really loved and
was meant to live by and compelled her to be (or to play at
being until she all but became) a woman of the world, so that her
surface hardened and became artificial while her nature was of
the woods, of hearty unconventional friendships, and of everything that is sweet and beautiful: a born democrat. Her name
is Mary A. Hulbert. She lives with a son about whose health and
conduct she is constantly anxious; and she has very few friends
in Boston. I met her in Bermuda. I would put real pleasures in
her way if I could: therefore I am wondering if I might some
time be instrumental in sending you to her.

We are looking forward to a family reunion at Christmas. My
sister will be here, and all the girls. May I confide to you that
Jessie is expecting to become a mother in early February? She
will stay here till after the little one comes. I am only sorry that
the baby should suffer the notoreity of being born in the White
House! It may follow her through her whole life!

When is it going to be possible for you to pay us a visit? We
shall count on one as soon as it is possible. All unite in messages
of deep affection. My warmest regards to Mr. Toy.

Your devoted friend   Woodrow Wilson

WWTLS (WP, DLC).
  [1] The most recent one was Nancy S. Toy to WW, Dec. 6, 1914, ALS (WP,
DLC).


# From William Jennings Bryan, with Enclosure

My dear Mr. President:      Washington December 12, 1914.

I am sending you a telegram which I have prepared in accordance with your instructions of yesterday. I have submitted
it to Counsellor Lansing and Major Heimke,[1] the head of the
Latin Bureau. Please send it back with any corrections that you
may see fit to make.

It is intended to present two ideas—first, that we do not insist
upon their making any agreement with us against their will;
and second, that we must be satisfied of the representative
character of the government and of its ability to conduct a
government before we recognize them.

With assurances of high respect I am, my dear Mr. President,
Yours very truly,   W. J. Bryan

Okeh W.W.

TLS (WP, DLC).
  [1] William Heimke.

ENCLOSURE

December 11, 1914.

Please say to the Government that this nation has no desire to assume responsibilities in regard to Haiti's fiscal system except in accordance with the wishes of the Government. In expressing a willingness to do in Haiti what we are doing in Santo Domingo, this Government was actuated wholly by a disinterested desire to render assistance. If for any reason the Government thinks it best not to consider this proposition further you will not press the matter. If the Government again intimates a desire to consider the subject you may proceed in accordance with the instructions already received. You may further say to the Government that the question of recognition will be considered on its merits and that recognition will be granted whenever this Government is satisfied that there is in Haiti a government capable of maintaining order and meeting the country's obligations to outside nations. Such a government is impossible however unless it rests upon the consent of the governed and gives expression to the will of the people. It will be necessary, therefore, for us to have information as to the fiscal standing and general plans of the Government and as to its attitude toward foreigners and the obligations which it owes to the citizens of other nations, including its attitude on the subjects relating to the Mole of St. Nicholas.[1]

T telegram (WP, DLC).
[1] This telegram was sent to Port-au-Prince on December 12, 1914 (SDR, RG 59, 838.51/379, DNA).

## From William Joel Stone

Dear Mr. President: [Washington] December 12, 1914.

In your recent message to the Congress you made particular reference to the convention entered into by the London Convention to promote safety of life at sea and urged speedy action by the Senate.

The Committee on Foreign Relations reported the Convention on Wednesday last, with a resolution of ratification. I shall endeavor to have the Senate hold executive sessions each afternoon from this time forth to consider this resolution. Senator John Sharp Williams, Senators La Follette and Sutherland have expressed a purpose to offer a substitute for the Committee Ratification Resolution. The resolution reported by the Committee and the substitute have been printed by order of the Senate

in parallel columns, and I enclose a copy herewith.¹ There will
be active opposition to the adoption of the Committee Resolution and there is imminent danger that the requisite majority
will not be obtained.

I spoke to Secretary Bryan about this matter on yesterday,
suggesting that he take it up with you, but because of the urgency
of the matter I am sending this note to suggest that if you feel
so disposed it might be well for you to discuss the matter with the
senators named above. Also, I call attention to the pendency
of what is known as the Seamen's Bill before the Committee on
Commerce, of which Senator Fletcher is the acting chairman in
the absence of Senator Clarke of Arkansas. I apprehend some
opposition to the convention from members of the Committee
on Commerce. It would, no doubt, improve the situation if you
could have a talk with Senator Fletcher, Senator Simmons, Senator Martin, Senator Chamberlain and others, perhaps of that
Committee.                          Very sincerely,   Wm J Stone.

TLS (WP, DLC).
  ¹ The enclosure is missing. The committee, however, recommended an amendment which would reserve to the United States full rights to legislate for the
repeal of existing laws for the arrest and return of sailors deserting from
foreign ships in American ports. The substitute reserved to the United States
the right to abrogate existing treaties, conventions, and agreements, and to
impose upon all vessels in the waters of the United States such higher standards
of safety, health, and protection of passengers, seamen, and immigrants, as the
United States might enact for vessels of the United States. The latter opened
the way, not only for legislation relating to the arrest and return of seamen,
but also for more sweeping legislation. *New York Times*, Dec. 10 and 17, 1914;
Hyman Weintraub, *Andrew Furuseth, Emancipator of the Seamen* (Berkeley
and Los Angeles, Cal., 1959), p. 127; Link, *The New Freedom*, p. 272.


## A Memorandum by Herbert Bruce Brougham

*Memorandum of Interview with the President, Dec. 14, 1914.*

The President hopes for a deadlock in Europe. During the half
hour I was with him he talked mainly on this subject. He praised
the Times for its fair spirit in printing the chief documents of the
war, and for its editorial analysis of them. He said he could not
forsee what will come out of it all, but he thought the greatest
advantages for all concerned in the war, including the neutral
nations, would accrue from a deadlock that "will show to them
the futility of employing force in the attempt to resolve their
differences." The rest of what he said I will give as nearly as I
can recollect in his own words:

"The Powers are making the most tremendous display of force
in history. If the result of it all is merely to w[e]ar each other
down without coming to a decision, the point will be at length

reached when they will be glad to say, we have tried both bluff and force, and since neither could prevail, there remains this alternative of trying to reason out our differences according to the principles of right and justice. So I think that the chance of a just and equitable peace, and of the only possible peace that will be lasting, will be happiest if no nation gets the decision by arms; and the danger of an unjust peace, one that will be sure to invite further calamities, will be if some one nation or group of nations succeeds in enforcing its will upon the others.

"It may be found before long that Germany is not alone responsible for the war, and that other nations will have to bear a portion of the blame in our eyes. The others may be blamed, and it might be well if there were no exemplary triumph and punishment. I believe thoroughly that the settlement should be for the advantage of the European nations regarded as Peoples and not for any nation imposing its governmental will upon alien peoples. Bismark was long-headed when he urged Germany not to take Alsace and Lorraine. It seems to me that the Government of Germany must be profoundly changed, and that Austria-Hungary will go to pieces altogether—ought to go to pieces for the welfare of Europe.

"As for Russia, I cannot help sympathizing with its aims to secure natural outlets for its trade with the world, and a proper settlement should permit this.

"If the decision is not to be reached wholly by the forces of reason and justice after the trial of arms is found futile, if the decision by arms should be in favor of the nations that are parties to the Triple Entente; I cannot regard this as an ideal solution; at the same time I cannot see now that it would hurt greatly the interests of the United States if either France or Russia or Great Britain should finally dictate the settlement. England has already extended her empire as far as she wants to—in fact, she has got more than she wants—and she now wishes to be let alone in order that she may bend all her energies to the task of consolidating the ports [parts] of her empire. Russia's ambitions are legitimate, and when she gets the outlets she needs her development will go on and the world will be benefited."

He expressed himself as grateful to The Times for its general support of his Administration "even if in the case of certain measures it has not gone so far in support of them as I should like." I asked him about the Government shipping bill, and he explained at some length that it was introduced only after he has ascertained that private capital would not go in and accomplish the same thing, for which it was intended. As the bill is framed he said, it will not be in form or in spirit a Government merchant marine. The precedent for it was the United States Bank, in which private individuals owned 60 per cent. interest, and the Government had 40 per cent. Private individuals are now invited to subscribe freely for stock, and just as fast as it becomes profitable the United States will own less and less and private individuals more, this process being entirely within their judgment and desire to invest. "I told the gentlemen who came down here to reason with me about it, 'Very well, if you will go into the business the Government will stay out,' and they said that they would not go in. I said, so long as it does not pay and when we can get cargoes both ways and the business can become profitable you will have every opportunity to invest in it. Could that be fairer?

"It is not intended to compete by means of unreasonably low ocean freight rates, and the rates will be fixed on a fair estimate of the cost of transportation, with an allowance for risks and profits. But they will not be placed prohibitively high in order to make the business pay on a trade that is not enough developed. I think it is a great deal better scheme than for the Government to establish the system of regular ship subsidies.

"The Times has objected that the capture of a Government ship by a belligerent nation might raise delicate questions in a foreign prize court. To this there are two replies: First, it will not be a Government ship, but the ship of corporation in which the Government has only the relation of investor. I will admit at once that the Government will be a heavy, and, at first, a controlling investor, and that there is danger that the form of incorporation will not prevent the public from regarding it as a Government-owned ship. So far as there is danger of this it is sought to remedy it in the form of the bill.

"The second reply is that the trade routes chosen are not those with any nation engaged in this war, and the danger of capture is so little as to be almost negligible. But should a capture ever be made the case in the prize court would not be against the United States, but against the corporation in which the Government stands wholly in the relation of an investor."

T MS (L. Wiley Papers, NRU).

## To Robert Lansing

My dear Mr. Lansing:      The White House December 14, 1914

Thank you very warmly for the trouble you have taken in sending a full reply to my inquiry about the telegram from

Messrs. Fuller, Tracy, and Coudert. I now feel fully fortified in the matter.

Cordially and faithfully yours, Woodrow Wilson

TLS (SDR, RG 59, 763.72111/1333½, DNA).

## To William Joel Stone

My dear Senator: [The White House] December 14, 1914

Thank you warmly for your letter of December twelfth. I shall certainly try to see at least some of the gentlemen you mention, for I am deeply interested in the adoption of the Convention.

With warmest messages,

Faithfully yours, Woodrow Wilson

TLS (Letterpress Books, WP, DLC).

## To Shailer Mathews

[The White House]

My dear Doctor Mathews: December 14, 1914

I greatly enjoyed our interview of the other day[1] and find myself deeply and genuinely interested in the mission you are undertaking to Japan.[2] Everything which can bring about a better and cordial understanding between the people of this country and the people of Japan has, I need not tell you, my earnest approval.

That the feeling of America towards Japan is one of genuine friendship I think you believe as strongly as I do, and any message of friendship and cooperation and mutual good will is undoubtedly from the American people themselves.

Cordially and sincerely yours, Woodrow Wilson

TLS (Letterpress Books, WP, DLC).
[1] He met with Mathews on December 10.
[2] The Federal Council of Churches of Christ in America was sending Mathews and Sidney Lewis Gulick as a "Christian embassy" to Japan to "foster cordial relations between the United States and Japan." *New York Times*, Jan. 29, 1915.

## To Robert Underwood Johnson

My dear Mr. Johnson: [The White House] December 14, 1914

Thank you for your note of December tenth.[1]

I certainly did mar my letter to President Poincare by repeating the word "warm" too often, but now that the letter has been sent I am helpless to change it.

Upon thinking the matter over, I believe that it would not be wise just at present to publish the letter. I think you can hardly realize how extremely careful I have to be about the susceptibilities of those of our fellow-citizens whose sympathies are engaged on the one side or the other in this dreadful war across the seas. Perhaps this is not the time, therefore, to publish correspondence even of this sort, far removed as it is from anything that could possibly touch the war or its issues.

Cordially and sincerely yours,   Woodrow Wilson

TLS (Letterpress Books, WP, DLC).
  [1] R. U. Johnson to WW, Dec. 10, 1914, ALS (WP, DLC).

## To Edward Mandell House

My dear Friend:          The White House December 14, 1914

Thank you for your little note sent just before you started for Boston.

I am going to send this to await your return, in order to beg that you will set an early date when you can come down and pay a little visit that will be less anxious than the last one. Send me some intimation of your plans in the near future.

In haste        Affectionately yours,   Woodrow Wilson

TLS (E. M. House Papers, CtY).

## To Elsworth Raymond Bathrick

My dear Mr. Bathrick:    [The White House] December 14, 1914

Thank you for your letter of December tenth and its suggestions.[1]

I am heartily in favor of pegging away at work on a rural credit bill. The real trouble is at least one feature suggested by the subcommittee during the last session was so radical a departure from the policy of the Government hitherto[2] that it seemed impossible to go forward with the bill on those lines.

Cordially and sincerely yours,   Woodrow Wilson

TLS (Letterpress Books, WP, DLC).
  [1] It is missing.
  [2] That is, the provision for governmental underwriting.

## From Edward Mandell House

Dear Governor:          New York City. December 14th, 1914.

I have had a long conference with Seth Low this morning.

I think they have thought out the problem you have given them in regard to Colorado along pretty sane lines. The matter will have to be threshed out a little further and then I will present it to you for your approval before anything final is done.

Affectionately yours,   E. M. House

TLS (WP, DLC).

## Remarks at a Press Conference

December 15, 1914

Mr. President, are you formulating any plan looking to the enactment of legislation which will give the United States—the federal government—greater authority in the enforcement of treaty obligations wherever state laws conflict?

No, I don't see that there is any occasion or room for legislation. The whole thing is a question of treaty obligation and of the relative authority of treaties and state laws. In other words, nothing that could be put in legislative form would affect the matter one way or the other.

Are you formulating any plan that would look to a more satisfactory relationship between the federal government and foreign governments in matters of that kind?

No, sir. It is a mere matter of handling the case in the most satisfactory way. No plan, it seems to me, could be worked out.

Isn't it true that, if a state insists upon what it regards as it own sovereign rights, it can embarrass the government, and the government is practically without any recourse in the matter?

Yes, theoretically, that is true. You will notice, if you have the California case in mind, that the California legislation explicitly states that nothing in that is to be considered in derogation of the treaty obligations of the United States. . . .

Mr. President, have you taken any stand with reference to the proposed legislation concerning an embargo on munitions of war?

No, sir.

Did you notice that Mr. Ridder makes rather a savage attack in that connection—Mr. Herman Ridder?

No, I did not.

Have you expressed an opinion on the immigration bill that is pending?

Very often. Not in public though.

Have you anything to say in public now on it?

It is so full of items, good, bad, and indifferent, that I could not give a blanket opinion about it.

How about the literacy test, Mr. President?

> It is very well known that I think the literacy test is a bad test. I mean it is a test that does not test quality.

Is that objection so serious, Mr. President, as to overweigh the value of the good features of the bill?

> I don't know. I have not got to that yet.

Mr. President, has the Secretary of State asked you to use your influence to get his Nicaraguan and Colombian treaties passed at this session?

> No; I have several times expressed the hope that they would pass to the members of the committee—not since this session began, but in the last session. Yes, I did write to the chairman of the committee this session.

Have you decided yet, Mr. President, whether to withdraw the federal troops from Colorado?

> No, sir; we are going to let things settle down there.

I understand that Governor Ammons is coming here during the latter part of the week. Will you see him?

> I hope I shall. I think he is not coming for the purpose of seeing me, but coming on some other errand. . . .

Mr. President, do you favor any change in the London convention so that the seamen's bill should be enacted?

> I am just now seeking advice from legal quarters as to whether any change is necessary for the passage, at any rate, of most of the provisions of the seamen's bill. I have not yet got that advice. I have an idea that that convention is properly construed so as not to prevent additional legislation in the same spirit by any of the contracting parties. It is merely meant to establish a minimum, that each nation will see that at least those provisions are lived up to. Because they are above the standards of some of the nations who were present at the conference, though they are somewhat below our standards.

T MS (WP, DLC).


## Remarks on the Race Question[1]

[Dec. 15, 1914]

I am very glad to express my sincere interest in this work and sympathy with it. I think that men like yourselves can be trusted to see this great question at every angle. There isn't any question, it seems to me, into which more candor needs to be put, or more thorough human good feeling, than this. I know myself, as a southern man, how sincerely the heart of the South desires the good of the Negro and the advancement of his race on all sound and sensible lines, and anything that can be done in that direction is of the highest value. It is a matter of common understanding.

There is a charming story told about Charles Lamb. The conversation in his little circle turned upon some man who was not present, and Lamb, who, you know, stuttered, said "I h-hate that fellow." His friend said, "Charles, I didn't know you knew him." He said, "I-I don't; I-I can't h-hate a fellow I-I know." I think that that is a very profound human fact. You cannot hate a man you know. And our object is to know the needs of the Negro and sympathetically help him in every way that is possible for his good and for our good. I can only bid you Godspeed in what is a very necessary and great undertaking.

T MS (WP, DLC).
1 To members of the University Commission on the Southern Race Question, who had come to pay their respects. The commission, made up of representatives of eleven southern colleges and universities, was an outgrowth of the first Southern Sociological Congress, which met in 1912. Among the leaders of the University Commission were James Hardy Dillard, president of the Jeanes Fund and director of the Slater Fund, and Willis Duke Weatherford, International Student Secretary of the Y.M.C.A. See Ronald C. White, Jr., "Social Christianity and the Negro in the Progressive Era, 1890-1920" (Ph.D. dissertation, Princeton University, 1972), pp. 240-241.

## To Oscar Wilder Underwood, with Enclosure

My dear Underwood:        The White House December 15, 1914

Here is a letter which I wish you would read. Yager is a fine fellow. I have known him for twenty years or more.

I am earnestly interested in this Porto Rico bill and would esteem it a very fortunate thing for the party and for the country if it could be brought out. If your judgment approves, I would appreciate it very much if you would show this letter to Mr. Henry and express to him my conviction that this is a matter of the highest importance upon which it seems to me it would be very wise for the Rules Committee to take favorable action.

Cordially and sincerely yours,   Woodrow Wilson

TLS (O. W. Underwood Papers, A-Ar).

E N C L O S U R E

## From Arthur Yager

My dear Mr. President:        Washing_   December 12, 1914

It seems impossible at present to make any progress at all with the new Organic Act for Porto Rico, unless we can secure its early consideration and passage by the House. The Senate committee have promised to take it up for immediate consideration as soon as it passes the House, but its present position on the Calendar makes it evident that unless we can secure a special rule it will not be reached until quite late in the session.

Mr. Henry, Chairman of the Committee on Rules of the House, stated that he had no doubt that he could secure a special rule if you would write him a letter indicating your desire to have the bill considered by the House at this session.

There seems to be no opposition to the bill, and Mr. Jones tells me that he is confident that it could be passed in the House in three or four hours, if it could only be called up for consideration.

It is so important, from every viewpoint, that we should at least give this bill a fair chance at this session that I am writing to ask you to write a letter to Mr. Henry requesting him to secure a special rule for its consideration. It would produce a very discouraging effect in Porto Rico to have the bill die through mere neglect. Moreover, as it would require at least two years to put the new Organic Act into complete operation in the Island, I am naturally anxious for an opportunity to set up the new government under this bill during my administration as Governor of Porto Rico.

I hope, therefore, you will pardon me for asking your aid to this extent, in securing consideration for this important measure. If it should pass the House at an early date it is then assured of getting through the committee of the Senate, and even if it should fail, at the last, of consideration by the Senate, it would nevertheless be very encouraging to the people of Porto Rico to have it get so far toward its passage.

With the highest regard and esteem, I am,

Sincerely your friend,   Arthur Yager.

TLS (O. W. Underwood Papers, A-Ar).

## To Benjamin Ryan Tillman

My dear Senator:          The White House December 15, 1914

I am obliged to you for your frank letter of December fourteenth[1] and you may be sure will get busy in every direction that will do any good.

I am glad to tell you that the Federal Reserve Board has already authorized a lower rate of interest and I believe that the money will now begin to come out from the banks more readily.

I fear that you are under a misapprehension, my dear Senator, in saying that the "Secretary of the Treasury loaned the New York bankers the government's resources when he formed the gold pool." As a matter of fact, he merely did the same thing that he has done in connection with the cotton pool, and you will notice that after the conference yesterday, in which the Southern men who had come up to confer began by criticising the conditions of the cotton pool loans, they ended by endorsing the scheme unanimously and without qualification. I think I can say with entire confidence that no favorites have been played and I hope at the bottom of my heart that things will be worked out as well as it is possible to work them out in the present extraordinary conditions.

With the warmest regard and appreciation,

Faithfully yours,   Woodrow Wilson

TLS (B. R. Tillman Papers, ScCleU).
    ¹ B. R. Tillman to WW, Dec. 14, 1914, TLS (W. G. McAdoo Papers, DLC).


## To Walker Whiting Vick

My dear Vick:                [The White House] December 15, 1914

I have your letter of December twelfth. I must say that it does not seem to me that you are taking just the right attitude towards the Secretary of State. Nothing that he has done justifies that attitude, for I personally know he has tried to act with the greatest care and fairness and candor in all this matter.

I think it would be wiser on your part, therefore, if, rather than seem to wait to determine whether you yourself approve of the choice of an investigator before sending the documents in the case to the Secretary, you should frankly send the Secretary of State the documents to be in his care until the investigator is chosen and authorized.

Cordially and sincerely yours,   Woodrow Wilson

TLS (Letterpress Books, WP, DLC).


## To Thomas Watt Gregory

My dear Gregory,          The White House 16 December, 1914.

As the Secretary of State requests, I am handing you the enclosed papers.¹

The subject-matter is evidently of the most sensational kind. I hope that you will have it looked into thoroughly, but that, at the same time, you will have all possible precaution taken that no hint of it may become public unless and until it materializes into something upon which we have no choice but to act. But I need not give you such a caution.

Whenever you get a note in this handwriting (?) you may know that it has been written by me on my own machine.

With warmest regard,

Faithfully Yours,   Woodrow Wilson

WWTLS (T. W. Gregory Papers, DLC).

[1] These papers have not been found. However, about their subject matter, see the House diary, entry for Dec. 16, 1914.

## To Edward Mandell House

The White House Dec 16, 1914

Not crowded at all shall expect you with great pleasure.

Woodrow Wilson.

T telegram (E. M. House Papers, CtY).

## From the Diary of Colonel House

The White House, Washington. December 16, 1914.

I took the 12.08 for Washington and found Eleanor McAdoo on the train. McAdoo met us at the station. I went immediately to the White house.

As usual there was no one at dinner excepting the family. After we had finished the President read a few minutes from Stephen Leacock's "Arcadian Adventures of the Idle Rich."[1] We then proceeded to business.

I told of my interview with Harvey[2] and of Harvey's outlining the kind of work he wish[ed] to do in both Europe and the United States. I laughed and told the President he was evidently trying to take my job away from me. I was afraid I had not done the work very well, but Harvey had outlined just what I had been trying to do. The President was generous enough to say I had been invaluable in my services.

He spoke of my going abroad in order to initiate peace conversations.[3] He desires me to take charge of it and to go whenever I think it advisable. He thought Page could not do it because his influence is local. Gerard could not do it, neither could

[1] Stephen Butler Leacock, *Arcadian Adventures with the Idle Rich* (London and New York, 1914).

[2] That is, Colonel George B. M. Harvey.

[3] About the causes of the revival of Wilson's and House's hopes for mediation and the immediate dénoeument, see Link, *Struggle for Neutrality*, pp. 208-14.

Mayre [Marye] nor Sharp, for the same reason, even if they had the ability, which he felt they had not. He felt that I was the one to undertake it and asked if I would be willing to go at this season of the year. I said I would be glad to go at any time and under any conditions.

It was agreed that I should see Bernstorff tomorrow and start conversations with him. I told the President of my letters to Page,[4] and that I had cabled him to disregard them.[5] He thought I need not have done this as he approved what I had written. I replied that I could release them at any time but, for the moment, it was best to hold them. He agreed to this.

I then explained the purpose of my visit to Washington. I thought he might or might not have an opportunity to play a great and beneficent part in the European tragedy, but there was one thing he could do at once and that was to inaugurate a policy that would weld the Western Hemisphere together. It was my idea to formulate a plan to be agreed upon by the Republics of the two Continents which, in itself, would serve as a model for the European Nations when peace is at last brought about.

I could see that this excited his enthusiasm. My idea was that the Republics of the two Continents should agree to guarantee each other's territorial integrity and that they should also agree for government ownership of munitions of war. I suggested that he take a pencil and write the points to be covered.

He took a pencil and this is what he wrote:

[4] He referred, most particularly, to the following (EMH to WHP, Dec. 4, 1914, CCL [E. M. House Papers, CtY]):

"The President desires to start peace parleys at the very earliest moment, but he does not wish to offend the sensibilities of either side by making a proposal before the time is opportune. He is counting upon being given a hint, possibly through me, in an unofficial way as to when a proffer from him would be acceptable.

"Pressure is being brought upon him to offer his services again., for this country is suffering, like the rest of the neutral world, from the effects of the war, and our people are becoming restless.

"Would you mind conveying this thought delicately to Sir Edward Grey and letting me know what he thinks.

"Would the Allies consider parleys upon a basis of indemnity for Belgium and a cessation of militarism? If so, then something may be begun with the Dual Alliance.

"I have been told that negociations between Russia and Japan were carried on several months before they agreed to meet at Portsmouth. The havoc that is being wrought in human lives and treasure is too great to permit racial feeling or revenge to enter into the thoughts of those who govern the nations at war.

"I stand ready to go to Germany at any moment in order to sound the temper of that government, and I would then go to England as I did last June. This Nation would not look with favor upon a policy that held nothing but the complete annihilation of the enemy. Something must be done sometime, by somebody, to initiate a peace movement, and I can think of no way, at the moment, than the one suggested.

"I will greatly appreciate your writing me fully and freely in regard to this phase of the situation.

[5] EMH to WHP, Dec. 11, 1914, CC telegram (E. M. House Papers, CtY).

"1st. Mutual guarantee of political independence under republican forms of government and mutual guarantees of territorial integrity.

2nd. Mutual agreement that the government of each of the
contracting parties acquire complete control within its jurisdiction of the manufacture and sale of munitions of war."

He wished to know if there was anything else. I thought this
was sufficient taken in conjunction with the Bryan Peace Treaties
which had already been concluded between the Republics of the
two Continents.

He then went to his little typewriter and made a copy of what
he had written and handed it to me to use with the three South
American Ambassadors with whom it was thought best to initiate
negotiations. We discussed the method of procedure and it was
agreed that it should be done quite informally and without either
himself or the Secretary of State appearing in it, until after I
had sounded the different governments at interest. We did this
for another reason and that was not to hurt Mr. Bryan's sensibilities.

It was agreed that I should explain the matter to Mr. Bryan
and should tell him why it was thought best for me to do it rather
than the President or himself.

I asked the President how he would suggest my reaching the
Ambassadors in a way to make my word potential with them. He
had no suggestions, but thought I would find a way, although the
Brazilian Ambassador is the only one of the A.B.C. representatives I know. We discussed whether it was best to see them
individually or collectively, and concluded it would perhaps be
best to see them collectively, a plan which I later decided not
to do.

The President was evidently somewhat nervous about Mr.
Bryan's attitude. It was easy to see that he did not want him to
interfere in any way with my procedure, and yet he was afraid
he might be sensitive regarding it. I thought I could work it out
satisfactorily, for Mr. Bryan is generous and big minded in matters of this sort.

We talked of the religious issue which is lifting its ominous
head in many parts of the country. The President was very firm
in his determination to strike the Catholics a public blow, provided they carried their arrogance too far. It appears they are
angry because the President did not force the country into war
with Mexico on account of the supposed persecution by the Constitutionalists of the Catholic clergy and missionaries of Mexico.
This feeling has been fanned into a flame by such political agita-

tors as Mr. Roosevelt.[6] At this moment a dispatch came in from the State Department which Ambassador Morganthau had sent from Constantinople in regard to the situation in Turkey and Asia Minor.[7]

It seems that our Consul at Beirut[8] had raised no end of a row with Turkish officials concerning the care of Americans and foreigners now under our protection. The President wished to know whether I thought it would be advisable to warn all Americans out of Turkey. He said Mr. Bryan thought this should be done. I advised doing nothing for the moment, but to get a better insight into the true situation.

He said they had information regarding a company which was putting out fraudulent naturalization papers by the wholesale. Some German, acting either from a patriotic motive or for the German Government itself, has undertaken to buy up naturalization papers to give to German reservists who are in this country in order that they may proceed abroad. The Attorney General has been instructed to investigate the matter at once and report.

He then wanted my advice concerning the making of speeches throughout the country outlining democratic policies, both as to what has been accomplished and what is proposed. I thought he should make but one speech, and we agreed this should be made on Jackson day. We also agreed it was best to have it made at Cleveland, if that were possible, since there were objections to Chicago or St. Louis.

Bedtime came and we parted for the night.

[6] About the beginnings of this campaign, see Link, *Struggle for Neutrality*, p. 468.
[7] H. Morgenthau to the Secretary of State, Dec. 12, 1914, received Dec. 15, printed in *FR-WWS 1914*, pp. 776-77.
[8] William Stanley Hollis, Consul General at Beirut.

# A Draft of a Pan-American Treaty[1]

[Dec. 16, 1914]

### I.

That the contracting parties to this solemn covenant and agreement hereby join in a common and mutual guarantee to one another of undisturbed and undisputed territorial integrity and of complete political independence under republican forms of government.

### II.

That to this end, and as a condition precedent to the foregoing guarantee of territorial integrity, it is convenanted and agreed between them that all disputes now pending and unconcluded between any two or more of them with regard to their boundaries or territories shall be brought to an early and final settlement in the following manner, unless some equally prompt and satisfactory method of settlement can be agreed upon and put into operation in each or any case within three months after the signing of this convention and brought to a decision within one year after its inception:

Each of the parties to the dispute shall select two arbiters and those thus designated and commissioned shall select an additional arbiter or umpire; to the tribunal thus constituted the question or questions at issue shall be submitted without reservation; and the decisions and findings of this tribunal shall be final and conclusive as between the parties to the dispute and under the terms of this convention as to the whole subject matter submitted. The findings of such tribunal or tribunals shall be arrived at and officially announced and accepted within not more than one year after the formal constitution of the tribunal; and the tribunal shall be constituted not more than three months after the signing and ratification of this convention.

### III.

That the high contracting parties severally pledge themselves to obtain and establish by law such control of the manufacture and sale of munitions of war within their respective jurisdictions as will enable them absolutely to control and make them responsible for the sale and shipment of such munitions to any other of the nations who are parties to this convention.

### IV.

That the high contracting parties further agree, first, that all questions, of whatever character, arising between any two or more of them which cannot be settled by the ordinary means of diplomatic correspondence shall, before any declaration of war or beginning of hostilities, be first submitted to a permanent international commission for investigation, one year being allowed for such investigation; and, second, that, if the dispute is not settled by investigation, to submit the same to arbitration, provided the question in dispute does not affect the honour, independence, or vital interests of the nations concerned or the inter[e]sts of third parties; and the high contracting parties hereby agree, where this has not already been done, to enter into treaty, each with all of the others severally, to carry out the provisions of this Article.

WWT MS (WP, DLC).
¹ It was sent to the Argentine, Brazilian, and Chilean governments on Feb. 1, 1915, and is printed in *FR-LP*, II, 472-73. There are also WWsh and CLST copies in WP, DLC.

## From William Jennings Bryan

My Dear Mr. President:       Washington December 16, 1914.

I gave you yesterday a memorandum of a matter brought to my attention by Mr. Lansing and you sent the papers to my house last night.¹ I think the memorandum fully explains why Mr. Lansing thought it best to make the preliminary inquiries before bringing it either to your attention or mine, namely, that he was able to speak personally and unofficially in a sense that he could not have done had he been following instructions. He has today seen the British Ambassador, who was seen by the other party, and the British Ambassador has strongly advised the course suggested in a confidential communication to his own Government. It seems to me that if this understanding can be reached without any commitment on our part as to anything else, it would be wise to undertake it and possibly the present moment is an opportune time to make the arrangement. If we wait until the final conclusion of the war, conditions might or might not be favorable to such negotiations. As soon as you have had time to reach a decision in the matter I shall be glad to know your opinion.

With assurances of high respect, I am, My dear Mr. President,
Very truly yours,    W. J. Bryan

TLS (WP, DLC).
¹ R. Lansing, TS memorandum of a conversation with the Russian Ambassador, Dec. 7, 1914 (SDR, RG 59, 711.612/263, DNA). Lansing had sounded out the Russian Ambassador on the possibility of negotiating a new commercial treaty. The Ambassador had demurred at first because of the so-called "passport question," which had led the United States to abrogate the previous treaty in 1912 (see WW to H. Bernstein, July 6, 1911, n. 2, Vol. 23). However, he grew more interested when Lansing pointed out the advisability of Russia's regaining the friendship of the influential American Jewish community through a satisfactory settlement of the passport problem. Lansing then proceeded to discuss the problem with the British Ambassador, in order that the British government might influence its Russian ally to agree to a new treaty. See R. Lansing, TS memorandum of conversation with the British Ambassador, Dec. 8, 1914 (SDR, RG 59, 711.612/264, DNA). The Russian Ambassador informed Lansing on December 14 that he had communicated with his government on "the advisability of negotiating a treaty at this time." R. Lansing, TS memorandum of conversation with the Russian Ambassador, Dec. 14, 1914 (SDR, RG 59, 711.612/265, DNA).

## From Oscar Wilder Underwood

           Washington, D. C.
My dear Mr. President:         December 16, 1914.

I am in receipt of your favor of the fifteenth instant, in reference to the Porto Rico bill now on the calendar of the House. The bill meets with my cordial approval and I am anxious to aid Mr. Jones in securing an opportunity for its consideration in the House. The difficulty that confronts us at present is the pressure of the appropriation bills and if we sidetrack them for one measure it is hard to hold others back, but it will give me pleasure to take the matter up with Mr. Henry, show him your letter and endeavor at an early date after the Christmas Holidays to try and secure an opening where we can bring the bill up for consideration.

With kindest regards, I am

Cordially yours,   O W Underwood

TLS (WP, DLC).

## From Seth Low

Dear Mr. President:        New York December 16th, 1914.

I hand you herewith copy of a letter which our Commission is proposing to send to the Governor-Elect of Colorado, and also of the letter of transmission which will accompany it.[1]

You will observe that this letter refers to a letter of instructions from you to the Commission. In accordance with your request I venture to hand you a memorandum of suggestions as to the lines which we hope your instructions will follow.[2] I have ventured to go over the matter very carefully with Colonel House, who tells me that he will be with you to-morrow, so that he may be able to explain any point which may not be quite clear to you.

Our plan is to forward the letter to the Governor-Elect with a copy of your instructions as soon as I receive them. After this has been done I propose to enter into informal conference with the gentleman of whom you spoke,[3] showing him the letter to the Governor-Elect and your instructions. We think that in this way a good foundation will be laid for any future action that may be called for. Soon after January 1st. Mr. Mills and Mr. Gilday will go to Denver, while I will remain here unless telegraphed for. This will give the Commission representation at both ends of the line, so that the details of an agreement may be intelligently worked out, if an agreement is possible.

The Commission is wholly at a loss to determine how large a sum will be necessary for its expenses. If your idea is to have us perform this specific duty and then retire, we suppose that only a small sum will be necessary. On the other hand it is not improbable that your Commission will have to maintain a fatherly oversight over any agreement that may be worked out, if we are so fortunate as to secure an agreement. Such agreements are like laws. They do not always execute themselves; and it may be necessary for us to be in a position to employ someone to go to Colorado from time to time on behalf of the Commission. Under all the circumstances, therefore, we hope that it will not seem to you unreasonable to ask for an appropriation of $10,000., which we hope may be placed at your service to be administered under your instructions. I have been over this aspect of the question very fully with Colonel House who will explain to you the feeling of Mr. Mills and myself. Since I saw Colonel House I have had a further talk with Mr. Gilday, who will be well pleased to retain permanently his position as a Conciliator connected with the Department of Labor. This is because he is serving the Department all the time in this capacity in other connections as well as in this.

I cannot close this letter without saying to you how well I think Mr. Mills and Mr. Gilday are qualified for the work to be done. Each has had wide experience in the technical aspects of the problem with which we have to deal, and I like the spirit displayed by both of them in the several conferences that we have had.

I am, dear Mr. President,

Respectfully and sincerely, yours,    Seth Low

TLS (WP, DLC).
 1 [S. Low *et al.*] to G. A. Carlson, n.d., T draft L; [S. Low] to G. A. Carlson, n.d., T draft L, both in WP, DLC.
 2 [S. Low], T draft "Suggestions for Letter" (WP, DLC).
 3 John D. Rockefeller, Jr.

## From Oswald Garrison Villard

PRIVATE

Dear Mr. President:                 New York December 16, 1914.

May I call your attention to the fact that in the press of this city last night General Wood was reported as having advocated conscription at the luncheon of the Merchants' Association? It seems to me that this is in direct contravention of your letter of instructions to Secretary Garrison of last winter forbidding this talking of Generals, but whether it is or not it seems to me that it is an outrageous state of affairs that men like General Wood are advocating increased armament day in and day out. I do not think I do him an injustice when I say that he appears to be speaking at least three or four times a week. Is he not employed for other purposes than this; has he not duties to keep him at Governor's Island? Personally, I consider him one of the most dangerous men in the country today. I have had a deep mistrust of him ever since I became acquainted with the circumstances attending his career as Governor-General of Cuba. I may, therefore, be prejudiced against him, but I take the same attitude toward every talking General.

If I am right in thinking that General Wood is violating the spirit of your instructions will you not issue an order preventing his propaganda? General Scott, by the way, with General Wood, has been stirring up the undergraduates at Princeton with a view to arming, etc.

Sincerely yours,   Oswald Garrison Villard

TLS (WP, DLC).

## From William Jennings Bryan, with Enclosure

My dear Mr. President:        Washington December 17, 1914.

I am sending you a draft of a proposed instruction. This was prepared by Mr. Johnson and revised by Mr. Lansing and afterwards by myself.

I think, in view of the increasing tension there is on the subject it is well for us to put this Government's views in definite form so that in case inquiry is made as to what has been done it will be manifest that we have exerted ourselves to the utmost to bring about a lessening of the hardships imposed upon neutral countries.

It is a matter of such importance, however, that we are anxious to have you go over it carefully and suggest any changes in phraseology or any additions or subtractions that you may think wise.

It does seem as if they could do everything required for the protection of their rights without the great and constant injury which has been done to shipping.

We have had a similar experience in regard to communication by cable. We have many complaints of innocent cables being undelivered and the senders have not even been notified of the failure to deliver, so that great loss has been occasioned. This we have recently brought to the attention of the Government in another telegram, but the proposed telegram which I am enclosing goes over the whole subject more fully than we have heretofore done.

The enclosed clippings[1] indicate the public criticism that is being directed toward the policy of the British Government.

With assurances of high respect I am, my dear Mr. President,<br>Yours very truly,   W. J. Bryan

TLS (SDR, RG 59, 763.72112/545A, DNA).
[1] They are missing.

E  N  C  L  O  S  U  R  E[1]

December 16, 1914.

Draft of a Proposed Instruction to the
Ambassador at London.

The injurious effect upon the trade of this country with neutral countries of Europe produced by continued seizures by Great Britain of American cargoes, as exhibited by the number of vessels detained or seized, including the ALFRED NOBLE, BJORNSEN, FRIEDLAND, STRINDA, SIGRUN, FRAM, CANTON, KIM, SANDEFJORD, GEORGE HAWLEY, STALGHERN, EDWARD PIERCE, TYR, SIF, RAN, TABOR, ELLEN, and others, ⟨challenges⟩ *excites* the deep solicitude of this Government and ⟨,in behalf of American commerce, calls for⟩ *seems to justify a very* earnest ⟨resistance to⟩ *protest against* the present British practice. The occasion and cause must indeed be extraordinary when the Governments of an entire hemisphere are taking counsel of each other to avert disaster to their commerce from war in another hemisphere, and when neutral countries near the scene of hostilities join in reprobating assertions of rights by belligerents which are incompatible with the long accepted rights of neutrals. It becomes the duty of the Department to advert more at length to this interdiction of trade. The grounds brought forward to justify Great Britain's course announce a policy not hitherto advanced in recent times; and, if yielded to by the neutral countries concerned, would sacrifice the work of a century toward the greater security of neutral commerce from the evil resulting from the activities of belligerents.

Peace, not war, is the normal relation between nations and commerce built up between nations not at war should not be interfered with unless such interference is manifestly necessary to protect the rights of belligerent nations, and then only to the extent that it is necessary.

The bulk of the cargoes seized consist of foodstuffs and other articles of common use, admittedly relative contraband only, bound from one neutral country to another. It does not appear that these detentions and seizures, called provisional detentions in some cases, are based on possession of facts justifying a reasonable belief that the shipments arrested have in reality a belligerent destination, as that term is understood in the accepted rules of international law and in conventions declaratory of those rules.

To uphold a policy which would starve the enemy largely at the expense of neutrals, the novel ground is advanced that shipments

1 Words in angle brackets deleted by Wilson, those in italics added by him.

of absolute contraband articles to consignees in neutral countries will be intercepted by belligerents because those countries have not prohibited the exportation of such articles. Furthermore, the application of this policy by Great Britain appears to be arbitrary and inconsistent. For example, a shipment of copper from this country on the steamer [blank], consigned to a specified consignee in Sweden, was detained because Sweden had no embargo on copper, while on the other hand the Foreign Office is unwilling to state what Great Britian's course will be toward shipments to Italy though the Italian Government has issued its decree that shipments to Italian consignees or "to order," reaching Italian ports, will be denied exportation or transshipment to Great Britain's enemies.

In case of foodstuffs and other conditional contraband it is fair to assert that seizures have taken place from a belief that goods might ultimately reach the territory of belligerents through subsequent means or measures not comprehended in the original venture of their shipment. Such a belief is reduced to the merest suspicion in view of embargoes placed by neutral countries on the exportation of nearly, if not all, the articles involved. Admittedly most of these seizures are in pursuance of the Order in Council of October 29, namely, that conditional contraband on neutral vessels bound for neutral ports will be subject to seizure "when consigned to order or where ship's papers do not show the consignee, or where they show the consignee in enemy territory." The essential element of contraband, namely, enemy destination, is thereby destroyed, and a presumption of guilt is substituted in all cases, for which no authority exists, while in case of relative contraband the whole principle on which it is distinguished from absolute is ignored. Great Britain championed a contrary doctrine, when Lord Salisbury said during the South African war, "Foodstuffs, though having a hostile destination, can be considered as contraband of war only if they are for the enemy forces; it is not sufficient that they are capable of being so used, it must be shown that this was in fact their destination at the time of their seizure." It cannot be said with reason that consigning "to order" goods bound for a neutral country rightfully subjects them to seizure as relative contraband, on the presumption that they are destined for the territory of a belligerent and on the further presumption that they are for enemy forces.

The doctrine of continuous voyage cannot be invoked in support of Great Britain's course, for in the present cases goods are en voyage from one neutral to another, in accordance with long established custom for usual centers of trade, in some cases passing from American concerns to their branch houses in neutral countries; seizures are made upon mere presumptions, while embargoes by the Governments of neutrals upon exportation or transshipment destroy any possible idea of continuous voyage to enemy territory. There is not wanting evidence that the neutral countries to whose territories the goods are bound complain that their ability and freedom to secure supplies are seriously crippled and that neutral concerns to whom goods are destined have, in certain cases, offered guarantees that the goods are intended for domestic consumption. In later shipments as those on the ELLEN and TELLUS, copies of manifests exhibited to the Department show that those shipments were to specified neutral consignees. Copies of manifests were submitted to the British Consul and affidavits taken from all shippers that goods were intended for consumption in neutral countries. In spite of this, these ships and cargoes were detained. Whatever may be the purpose of Great Britain in practice, it operates directly to the advantage of her people and to the disadvantage of neutrals engaged in this trade.

The exercise of the right of visit and search results in vessels being taken into British ports and detained indefinitely while search is made for evidence of possible contraband on board, and in some cases in the cargo being unloaded. As a consequence, shippers and shipowners suffer such losses that ocean carriage is now often refused to manifestly innocent cargoes and unprecedented requirements and guarantees are demanded by shipping lines and insurers.

The Government of the United States does not desire that in the present conflict lists of contraband shall be restricted to such narrow limits as would not include modern instruments for waging war. It insists, however, that the doctrine of contraband be confined within reasonable limits which the present course of Great Britain appears to transcend.

The right of visit and search is not denied and reasonable detention on the high seas is not objected to in cases where there is evidence to justify a belief that contraband is involved; but indiscriminate detention in search of evidence of contraband or upon presumptions which the Order in Council would create cannot possibly be acquiesced in as reasonable. It is not sufficient for the protection of neutral rights that unwarranted detentions will impose liability for damages on the captor, or that in prize proceedings owners may show innocent destination. By such means is commerce destroyed, for ship owners will not assume the risks involved. A course in keeping with the well recognized principles of international law and usage will, it is believed, in the end better serve the interests of belligerents as well as neutrals.

The situation is critical, and the necessity for an understanding, if one is possible, is pressing.

In the discussion of these questions with the Foreign Office or in the note which you will present to the British Government in the sense of the foregoing, you may think it advisable to suggest that arrangements which have been proposed by the British Government will receive more favorable consideration and be less difficult of acceptance if Great Britain would release the shipments now detained, as it is believed that Great Britain must be convinced that, in most cases, valid evidence is wanting to show that the shipments in question have in reality an enemy destination.                                          Johnson

T MS (SDR, RG 59, 763.1112/545A, DNA).


## From William Jennings Bryan

My Dear Mr. President:          Washington December 17, 1914.

Mr. House will call your attention to a suggestion which was made to me by one of the South American Representatives[1] and I am inclined to think there is some force in it. You have not failed to notice the increasing urgency with which the neutral nations are presenting the idea of mediation or of some form of protection from the burdens of this war. The sentiment is unanimous among the South Central American countries that something ought to be done to protect the neutral nations if the war is to continue. The same idea has been presented by some of the neutral nations of Europe. A recent dispatch says that the kings of Norway, Sweden and Denmark are to meet for the purpose of considering what can be done to lessen these burdens. The Venezuelan Minister yesterday handed me a suggestion to the effect that you call a meeting of *all of the neutral* nations to be held in Washington for the purpose of considering a proposition to be submitted later to a convention in which all the nations, neutral and belligerent, will be represented. I think, however, that the idea of Mr. House, which I have mentioned, is the most feasible one, namely, that you invite all the nations, belligerent and neutral, to send representatives to a conference to be held in Washington for the purpose of considering ways and means by which the burdens borne by the neutral nations may be minimized with the consent and agreement of the belligerent nations. The belligerents could not take exception of it, were it understood that the changes were to be made through agreement with the belligerents, and I am sure it would appeal to all the neutral nations. The one who suggested this plan had in mind the possibility of its opening the way to mediation. He thinks that it would give you an opportunity to make an address of welcome which might be helpful in advancing the cause of mediation without directly referring to it. He thinks that the coming together of these representatives, even for the consideration of questions growing out of the war and yet not involving the subject of mediation, might lay the foundation for some coming together of the belligerent nations. I am very much impressed with the idea and with its possibilities for good. It seemed to commend itself to Mr. House also, although he only had time to think of it for a moment. It is at his suggestion that I bring the matter up this evening in order that you may talk with him about it more fully and let me know your impressions.

With assurances of high respect, I am, my dear Mr. President,
Very sincerely yours,   W. J. Bryan

TLS (WP, DLC).
1 Dr. Santos Anibal Dominici, Venezuelan Minister to the United States.


## From the Diary of Colonel House

December 17, 1914.

I arranged for an interview with Mr. Bryan at 9.30 this morning. I outlined the plan the President and I were preparing for the linking of the Western Hemisphere and showed him what the President had written, explaining why it was thought best that I should do it. He acquiesced in a most generous way, which proved my forecast to the President was correct. He did something which is characteristic of the man. After but a few minutes conversation upon the subject of this proposed League, he began to discuss the Ven[e]zuela Minister's proposal concerning the calling of a convention of belligerent and neutral nations for the purpose of securing the rights of neutrals. He also discussed the Russian Treaty which has been tentatively suggested as being possible at this time. After that he got off on prohibition and I was glad to take him to his office and proceed to other business. . . .

There was no one present again at dinner excepting McAdoo. After we had finished I reported to the President what I had done in the South American proposal. We discussed the Colorado strike, Seth Low's letter and other matters incident thereto.

We talked of the Senate's rejection of some of his nominations. He asked what I would do. I advised him to make an issue with them. I thought the Senate was determined to make itself even more unpopular with the country than it already was by arrogating to itself the exclusive power of making appointments. That it was a ridiculous attitude to assume and one which the country would not tolerate. The country would see clearly that the several Government departments could not be run if they were filled with political henchmen of the Senate. I advised him, however, not to get angry, but to go at it with determination and good humor. I advised not sending in a name they had rejected, but to continue sending in others just as often as he cared to do so, and to let them reject them at their peril. I counseled making the highest class appointments possible and leaving the Senate with the responsibility of turning them down because they were not of their own political following. The President thought well of this advice and said he would follow it.

He then read for an hour, A. G Gardiner's sketch of the Kaiser, one of Sir Edward Grey and one of Asquith.[1] After that we went to bed.

[1] The sketches of the Kaiser and of Grey appeared in Alfred George Gardiner, *Prophets, Priests and Kings* (London, 1908), which also contained an essay on Asquith. However, a much revised sketch of Asquith appeared in Gardiner's *Pillars of Society* (London, 1913), which Wilson was reading also at this time.

## From William Jennings Bryan, with Enclosures

My dear Mr. President:          Washington December 18, 1914.

I am sending you a copy of a telegram which we have prepared for transmission to the Hatien Legation, together with a copy of the telegram which it answers.

I submitted to you a telegram a few days ago to the effect that our recognition would *not* depend upon their making a treaty with us giving us the control of the customs, and that in deciding upon the question of recognition we would want to know it was a stable government, capable of performing its duties and giving promise of stability.

Before receiving this they have sent us a counter proposition—that is, counter to our original proposition—in regard to trade. It is so evidently an attempt to negotiate for concessions that I think it is well for us to let them distinctly understand that this Government is not disposed to make a bargain of that kind.

I would like to have the benefit of your suggestions before sending this telegram.

With assurances of high respect I am, my dear Mr. President,
Yours very sincerely,   W. J. Bryan

TLS (WP, DLC).

ENCLOSURE        I

Port au Prince December 12, 1914.

In the course of Foreign Minister's[1] interpellation in the Senate reported in the telegram of December 4, 9 a.m., the interpolator, on the refusal of Minister of Foreign Affairs to give any information as to the negotiations at that time which he considered premature, produced and read a draft of our convention for the customs control[2] as well as the counter-project referred to in my telegram of December 2, 3 p.m. which contemplated financial control and had appeared to me as possibly acceptable. This was the cause of the manifestation against the Minister for Foreign Affairs resulting in his resignation and the abandonment of that counter-project by the Government.[3]

On receipt of your wireless message on December tenth in reply to my December 1, 9 a.m. *Period.* December 2, 3 p.m. I at once asked for a private audience with Theodore[4] which was granted me last evening.

At this interview which Doctor Bobo,[5] Minister of the Interior, Acting Minister for Foreign Affairs, Minister of Public Works, Chief of Protocol and several Generals attended, I stated the conditions on which recognition as President would be granted expressing regret that interruption of the cable had caused a delay in receipt of my Government's instructions as to this.

I recalled the offer previously made to the former Minister for Foreign Affairs of the good offices of my Government with the Bank[6] for a loan for the traveling expenses of the Commission and the running expenses of the Haitian Government during the negotiations in Washington which offer I stated my Government might be compelled to withdraw should the contemplated issue of paper money be made. I protested as to this issue as being in violation of the contract with the Bank and a matter which it was contemplated should be taken up by the Commission and asked the decision of the President as to the appointment of desired Commission in conformity with stated conditions.

Acting Minister for Foreign Affairs, upon the request of Theodore who talks very little, replied. He regretted it was impossible for the Haitian Government to send a commission authorized to negotiate in any manner a control of customs and added that a second counter-project which had been approved by the entire Cabinet had been prepared and which he thought had been submitted to me on November twenty-fourth by Mr. Justin in accordance with a decision of the Cabinet which I assured him I had never seen. He admitted that this project did not comprise customs control but contemplated greater concessions and advantages to Americans and upon their most urgent and pressing appeal I finally consented to submit this counter project to my Government when the same should be presented to me by Dr. Bobo stating however that if it did not provide for all the conditions set forth in your November 12, 2 p.m. and November 16, 11 a.m., I greatly feared it would prove unacceptable.

This afternoon Dr. Bobo delivered to me this counter project and during our interview I again impressed upon him your instruction December 4, 11 a.m., and December 7, 5 p.m., which latter I had previously made the subject of a note to the Foreign Office and had communicated to my French and German colleagues.

Below is a resumé of the proposed convention which contains no provision for either financial or customs control but to which it is agreed that Article Five of your November 12, 2 p.m. will be added which, in fulfillment of my promise, I submit to the consideration of the Department respectfully requesting an early decision.

Haitian Government's counter project to Department's proposed convention.

Provides for the appointment of three commissioners to the United States to negotiate as to:

One. Appointment of three American and three Haitian engineers for the prospecting etc., of mines in Haiti.

Two. Salaries and expenses of the engineers to be borne by Haiti during preliminary investigations.

Three. The Haitian Government will concede to the Government of the United States or to Americans or American companies approved of by the Government the exploitation for twenty years of the mines designated by the engineers.

Four. Exploitation by a corporation. All expenses of installation, exploitation etc., of the same to be borne by the concessionaire.

Five. One third of the stock to be the property of the Republic of Haiti.

Six. The shares of the Government of Haiti to be registered and inalienable during the life of the concession.

Seven. Assistance from the United States in obtaining for Haiti a loan the amount to be determined, to enable it to consolidate its debt, meet its obligations past and future and reform its monetary system.

Eight. In return for advantages granted by Article Seven the Haitian Government will grant preference to the Government of the United States and citizens in commercial and industrial affairs while giving full protection to foreign interests in Haiti. A. Under equal conditions in a concession to be awarded, to give preference to the United States should it desire it. B. Settlement at the earliest possible moment by arbitral commission appointed in accordance with commercial law of Haiti of all questions pending between the United States Legation at Port au Prince and the Department of Foreign Affairs of Haiti.

Nine. Good offices of the United States to Haiti to secure modification of contract between Haitian Government and Bank.

Convention to continue in force for a period of (blank) years from and after its ruling [ratification] by the contracting parties in accordance with their respective laws.

The bill for the issue of sixteen million paper money has passed the Chamber of Deputies and has been sent to the Senate and by it referred to its finance committee. I now learn that Dr. Edmond Heraux has been appointed Minister of Finance vice Montreuil resigned and Louis Borno has been appointed Minister of Foreign Affairs vice Justin resigned. Borno Minister of Foreign Affairs and Minister to Dominican Republic under President Nord Alexis.                Blanchard.

1 Joseph Justin.
2 See W. J. Bryan to A. Bailly-Blanchard, July 2 and Nov. 12, 1914, *FR 1914*, pp. 347-50, 359.
3 About this incident and the background, see Link, *Struggle for Neutrality*, pp. 520-525.
4 Davilmar Thédore, President of Haiti.
5 Rosalvo Bobo, M.D.
6 The National Bank of Haiti, controlled by French and American banking interests.

ENCLOSURE II

Port au Prince. December 15, 1914.

New Minister for Foreign Affairs[1] cabled [called] by appointment at the Legation yesterday evening and after a two hours interview during which the points of your November twelve two P.M. and your November sixteen, eleven A.M. were discus[s]ed and their adoption pressed by me, the following conclusion was reached.

He had no knowledge of Doctor Bobo's counter-project cabled under date of December twelve, eleven P.M.

As to one. Customs Convention. It was an impossibility; two, National Railroad Company of Haiti. Stay of proceedings to December twenty-eight could be extended and question settled at Washington through the good officers of the Department between the Company and Menos,[2] Haitian Minister, who would receive full power to that end in lieu of a commission of three members. Three, Bank. The Haitian Government has no desire to issue paper money but it was compulsory, a case of force majeure. The bill would be adopted but would contain a clause specifying that in case of agreement with the bank the issue would not be made. This was confirmed by Minister for Foreign Affairs during my visit this afternoon to return his call. Proposition of agreement had been made by the government to the bank. Should they fail the Haitian Government would be willing through the good offices of the Department to have the question settled in Washington by the bank and Minister Menos specially accredited above. Four accepted. Five accepted. Six accepted.[3]

The above was confirmed in a lengthy note verbale received late this afternoon.

In view of your wireless of December twelve, five P.M. intercepted and communicated this afternoon by the HANDCOCK the Department seeming disposed not to press Customs Convention I respectfully submit the above to its favorable consideration and request instruction as to recognition under changed conditions.

Blanchard.

T telegrams (WP, DLC).
  [1] Louis Borno.
  [2] Solon Menos, Haitian Minister to the United States.
  [3] These articles stipulated that Haiti would give full protection to all foreign interests, would not lease any territory to a European government for use as a naval or coaling station, and would arbitrate the claims of American citizens against Haiti.

E N C L O S U R E     I I I

Washington, December 18, 1914.[1]

Your December twelve, eleven p.m., and your December fifteen, eleven p.m. Counter proposition seems based upon a misunderstanding of this Government's position. While we desire to encourage in every proper way American investments in Haiti, we believe that this can be better done by contributing to stability and order than by favoring *special*[2] concessions to Americans. American capital will gladly avail itself of business opportunities in Haiti when assured of the peace and quiet necessary for profitable production. Capital will not flow into Haiti except upon exorbitant terms and for speculative profits unless there is an assurance of peace and orderly government. If United States can, as a neighbor and friend, assist the Government and people of Haiti as it has assisted the Government and people of Santo Domingo, it will gladly do so provided that assistance is desired; but, as stated in our telegram December twelve, five p.m., this Government does not care to assume these responsibilities except on request of the Haitian Government. The Government of the United States does not deem it proper to enter such arrangements as those outlined in the proposition just submitted. The counter proposition does not give any assurance that the Government of Haiti is stable or any promise of a reign of peace and prosperity. When American investors seek to secure concessions we should be informed of the name and address of such Americans and of the terms or advantages asked, so that we may acquaint ourselves with the whole subject. Our obligation to the American people requires that we shall give all legitimate assistance to American investors in Haiti, but we are under obligations just as binding to protect Haiti, as far as our influence goes, from injustice or exploitation at the hands of Americans. Therefore, in order to perform our duty completely we must be fully informed as to the facts in each case.[3]               Bryan

T telegram (SDR, RG 59, 838.00/1065, DNA).
  [1] This telegram was sent at 4 P.M. on Dec. 19, 1914.
  [2] Word added by Wilson.
  [3] Wilson returned this telegram with the following note: "The enclosed has my entire approval W.W."

## From William Joel Stone

Dear Mr. President:               [Washington] December 18 1914.

I will leave Washington at 3:00 o'clock Sunday for Florida. I shall take Mrs. Stone[1] with me with the idea of getting her established down there for the winter. I will not return until after the holiday recess.

There are two or three matters that I have very much desired to talk with you about, but I have been so engaged that I have not been able to find time to see you; nor have I been able to see when my business would make it convenient for me to seek an appointment for any particular date. But now if I am to see you before I leave I must do so at some time between this afternoon and 2:00 o'clock Sunday. It may be that your engagements will not permit you to make an appointment such as I wish for during that interval. I am sending this note to inquire.

There are three things I wish to talk with you about:

1. I want to talk with you about the question of patronage solely with respect to the attitude of the President and the Senate

respectively. I do not think that official patronage is a thing big enough to estrange the President and the Senate and from every point of view I would regard that condition, if it should be created, as most unfortunate.

2. I want to talk with you about our neutrality laws and the duty of our Government with respect to contraband.

3. I want to talk with you about what appears to be a rapidly growing tendency in the direction of injecting religious prejudices into our political and public policies.

I would like to confer with you respecting these matters, all of which give me great concern, and to have the benefit of such views as you may feel at liberty to express. I want to get your viewpoint for my own information and use. If you care to go over these subjects as I suggest, and can find time within the limit stated, I will be glad to conform to your convenience. Please have me advised as speedily as possible by letter or phone.[2]

Sincerely yours,   Wm J Stone.

TLS (WP, DLC).
   [1] Sarah Louise Winston Stone.
   [2] Stone saw Wilson at the White House at 5:30 P.M. on Saturday, December 19.


## From Frank J. Hayes

My Dear Mr. Wilson:                    Denver, Colo., Dec. 18, 1914.

We officially terminated our coal strike on December 10, in line with your suggestion. We were of the opinion that when we took such action the operators would immediately make every endeavor to give our people employment. However, we have been keenly disappointed in this respect and but very few of the several thousand men we had on strike have been reemployed; in fact, several of our people have been driven out of the camps by armed guards when they applied for work.

We feel that this arrogant position of the operators is very unfair and inexcusable. They can employ a large number of our people at this time if they so desire, but it seems to be their present policy to take advantage of the helpless condition of the strikers and to belittle the peace plan you proposed and our earnest desire to meet requirements of the same.

If you will kindly call the attention of the operators to this unfair attitude we feel sure it will have a good effect and that within a short time permanent peace and quiet will prevail in all the coal fields of Colorado.

Very sincerely yours,   Frank J. Hayes

TLS (WP, DLC).

From the Diary of Colonel House

December 18, 1914.

The President asked me to see the British Ambassador this morning and I arranged to meet him at Billy Phillips' residence at eleven. The President desired me to tell him that he was anxious for the British Government to release the ships which are being held because of their supposed contraband cargoes. The President and I had gone over a despatch which Johnson of the State Department had prepared under the direction of Mr. Bryan to be sent to Ambassador Page at London. The despatch was crudely written and he said, "I can see we will have to re-write this." He took his pencil and began to make corrections. Before he had finished one page he became thoroughly out of patience and threw his pencil down saying, "It is not right to impose such a task upon me. They have not written good and understandable English, much less writing it in a way to avoid offence." He sent the document back to the State Department, requesting me to see Spring-Rice and attend to the matter verbally, telling him that the despatch would follow later.

I saw Spring-Rice and explained the matter to him and told him the President was anxious for the release of the ships. He promised to cable Sir Edward Grey and advise him to do so. I mentioned the crudity of the message referred to and asked him to explain to Sir Edward that the intentions of the State Department were of the best, but they did not understand the delicate phrasing of important diplomatic messages. The Ambassador was pleasant about it and said he liked Johnson and Lansing very much. He thought them both fine fellows and he had no trouble in getting along with them.

He said if Sir Edward agreed to the President's request, it would make two diplomatic triumphs for him, the first being his request regarding the Declar[a]tion of London. He thought when these papers were published, if they ever were, they would be considered great accomplishments. But the British Government would be careful as to their publication since the English people would think their Government had been weak in maintaining their position. How much of this was compliment and how much fact, I do not know.

He was distressed over the German bombardment of the coast towns and denounced it in unmeasured terms as being barbarous and cruel. I asked whether there was any danger of Russia weakening in her support of the Allies. He seemed to think there was a possibility. I cautioned him about sending his cables to Sir Edward, and asked him to protect both the President and me in order that the State Department should not know that messages were being sent in that way. He was certain there was no chance of the information getting back to the Department, for he had a method of reaching Sir Edward which would entirely protect us.

We then came to the most important part of our interview. I told him practically what I had written Page to say to Sir Edward Grey, that is, Germany was asserting her willingness to listen to peace proposals upon a basis of indemnity to Belgium and disarmament looking to permanent peace, and I thought the Allies would be placed in a bad light if they refused to consider peace upon these terms.

I asked him to kindly let me have a reply from his Government upon both proposals as soon as possible. I wondered whether Sir Edward Grey knew where he was getting his information and how. He replied, of course he knew that I was the one he was communicating with, and that he had a special code which covered me personally.

I found the Ambassador distressed and pessimistic regarding the situation in general and the attitude of the United States in particular. . . .

There were no visitors at dinner. After dinner he [Wilson] read for awhile. We again discussed the Senate and their rejection of appointments. I brought to him the request of one of the editors of the Delineator to write an article for that magazine giving a word to the mothers of the country that they were not rearing their sons to be ruthlessly slaughtered without any high purpose to be accomplished. He said while he sympathized thoroughly with that sentiment, it was difficult to write such an article. He could not bring himself to express his emotion coldly in writing; that it was something that welled up from the heart to be said at the moment, and not ground out.

We then went into a general discussion of science and religion, he doing practically all the talking. It was an illuminating discourse. He contended there was no borderland of science now, that one science had merged itself into another so there was a general continuity, and to understand one it was necessary, in a way, to have an understanding of all.

## From William Jennings Bryan, with Enclosure

My dear Mr. President:        Washington December 19, 1914.

I am sending you a letter just received from Secretary Redfield in regard to the safety of life at sea treaty.

It seems that the Senate has ratified the treaty with an amendment which reserves the right of this Government to impose conditional requirements upon all foreign ships entering our ports.

It is the opinion of Secretary Redfield and Congressman Alexander that this amendment so materially alters the treaty as to jeopardize its acceptance by other nations. They advise, therefore, that you ask the Senate to strike out that portion of the resolution.

I concur with them in this advice for the following reasons:

First: The substantial advantages gained by the treaty are so numerous and so important that we can afford to surrender for five years the right to impose—or, rather, to attempt to impose—additional requirements upon foreign ships. I say the right to *attempt* to impose, rather than the right to impose, because it is not at all certain that we would be successful in imposing any important requirements upon foreign ships. The right which is reserved in the ratification resolution is one which has existed heretofore but which has not been employed to any considerable extent, if at all. And there is no reason to believe that we could succeed in compelling other nations to materially change their requirements.

There are two obstacles in the way of the successful enforcement of any such additional requirements:

(a) We would be involved at once in diplomatic controversies, in which our position would be difficult to sustain in view of the great advance that the contracting nations have agreed to.

(b) Even if in diplomatic correspondence we insisted upon the justice of these requirements the other governments would have it in their power to punish us severely by simply refusing to conform to our requirements. We could exclude them from our waters, but we need their ships as much as their ships need our business, and more. They could suspend their trips to us much easier than we could do without the ships which we need, and unless we are prepared to at once supply American ships for all our commerce we may be compelled to abandon our position for the protection of our commerce.

Second: We must consider the proposed reservation in connection with the proposed legislation which the reservation has in view,[1] and I think we would find it difficult to defend this legislation.

We have, of course, the right to make any additional requirements of our own ships, but those who advocate the proposed additional requirements recognize that our ships would be at a great disadvantage if we by law compelled a large addition to the expense of operating the ship, unless we at the same time compelled our foreign competitors to make the same addition to their expenses.

In other words—it is an application of the protective idea. In the case of the tariff the price of the foreign article is increased by an import duty in order that the protected manufacturer may charge a higher price for the domestic product.

In the case of the proposed shipping requirements, the foreign ship is compelled to employ additional seamen in order that the domestic ships may be able to employ additional help. And it is believed that the demand for the employment of additional men does not arise entirely upon the actual need of these men for safety of life at sea, but in part at least upon the desire to increase the demand for this kind of labor.

If it can be shown that the additional requirements asked for is actually necessary for the protection of life at sea we would, of course, be justified in insisting that foreign ships, as well as our own, conform to the requirements. But no one can say with accuracy what is absolutely necessary for safety at sea,—it is largely a matter of opinion and opinions differ.

The treaty contains a number of requirements which are new and which greatly increase safety at sea. We are not in a position to say that we, only, give sufficient consideration to safety, or that the requirements agreed to by the other thirteen nations are so insufficient as to justify us in rejecting the treaty and staking our all upon the success of an effort to compel the other ships to accept this specific demand.

If, as is alleged, the demand rests not upon a fairly proven necessity, but upon a desire to increase the demand for this particular kind of labor, I do not think that we are in a position to stand sponsor for the demand either as against our own ships, and much less as against foreigners.

Our party has stood firmly against the doctrine that the legislative power should be used to impose a pecuniary burden upon one class for the benefit of another class—and this would be the effect of such a requirement as is proposed, if it rests not upon a desire to promote safety at sea but upon a desire to increase the demand for a particular kind of labor.

I do not know how fully the members of the Senate have considered the subject, but I agree with Secretary Redfield and Congressman Alexander that it is worth while to try the effect of a strongly stated message from yourself before giving it up. If you fail, we can urge the acceptance of the amendment by other nations, explaining that the *reservation* of authority does not necessarily mean the *exercise* of that authority, and you can use your influence to prevent the exercise of it in any obnoxious way; but I think we take great chances of losing the advantages of the entire convention by insisting upon reserving a right when it is extremely doubtful whether the right can be practically exercised to an extent that would be valuable.

With assurances of high respect I am, my dear Mr. President, Yours very sincerely,   W. J. Bryan

TLS (WP, DLC).
1 That is, the seamen's bill.

## E N C L O S U R E

## William Cox Redfield to William Jennings Bryan

**PERSONAL AND URGENT**

Sir:                            Washington December 19, 1914.

Replying to your letter of the 17th instant inquiring whether I see any reason why the International Convention on the Safety of Life at Sea should not be ratified by the President subject to the proviso in the resolution adopted by the Senate, it seems to me that the objections are insuperable and that you should advise the President to hand the resolution to the Senate with a request for further consideration and action before the end of the month. I believe the President should ask the Senate to strike out that portion of the resolution which reserves to the United States the right "to impose upon all vessels in the waters of the United States such higher standards of safety," and I believe the words "protection" and "seamen" should also be stricken out to remove all ambiguity. The words I have quoted seem to me in effect to nullify the resolution of ratification.

The Convention provides international standards of safety, and, like all treaties and conventions, is in some respects a compromise to harmonize views of participating nations. Article 74 of the Convention provides for the method of improvements in its provisions at any time through diplomatic channel and by common consent. For this procedure the Senate resolution substitutes the will of the Congress of the United States alone and thus destroys the principle of the international agreement while professing to ratify it. We shall take large risks by accepting this form of ratification in return for nothing but the remote possibility of successfully forcing upon other nations relatively small gains.

The whole world gains by the establishment of standards of construction for ocean passenger steamers, and to bring our own ships to the standards of the Convention in this respect will require time and effort. The world gains by the application of international rules for radio telegraphy, which have already been adopted by the United States. The value of the ice patrol and patrol for the destruction of derelicts heretofore maintained exclusively by the United States is recognized by the willingness of nations to contribute to the cost of that patrol. The Convention makes better provision for sufficient and efficient men to man lifeboats than is now made by any nation. The greatest gain of all is in the affirmation of the principle of international cooperation for humane purposes. The Convention, as the President has stated, "marks a most hopeful and decided advance in international civilization."

It is clear to my mind that the health and comfort of passengers, seamen and immigrants are not embraced in the Convention. The Senate seem to be of opinion that they are, or at least there is great doubt of their not being included in the Convention. There may be ambiguity in the language of the Convention upon which there may be a basis for the contention of the Senate that these subjects are included in the Convention, and it would meet my view if the resolution, amended as I have suggested, should be adopted, because I am advised by an inspection of the Convention itself and by representations made to me by the American Commissioners to the Conference that those subjects were not intended to be included in the Convention, and are not.

Article 68 of the Convention expressly provides as follows:

"It is understood that, the subject of this Convention being safety of life at sea, questions relating to the well-being and health of passengers, and in particular of emigrants, as well as other matters relating to their transport, continue subject to the legislation of the different States."

While it seems perfectly clear to my mind that the provision for the health and comfort of passengers and immigrants is excepted from the terms of the Convention and the United States will be free to enforce the provisions of existing law and if occasion require to provide other provisions for the health and comfort of passengers and immigrants, I see no reason why the Senate by the resolution ratifying the Convention should not construe the provisions of the Convention in that regard and

make it clear that the Convention is ratified with that understanding. So with reference to the provisions of our treaty relating to the arrest and return of deserting seamen. Some Senators
have taken the view that the following language in Article 68 is
ambiguous: "The treaties, conventions and arrangements concluded prior to this Convention shall continue to have full and
complete effect, as regards—

"(1) Vessels excepted from the Convention;

"(2) Vessels to which it applies, in respect of subjects for
which the Convention has not expressly provided"; and have
reached the conclusion that if the Convention is ratified it would
prevent us from enacting into law that portion of the seamen's
bill which stipulates that so much of the provisions of our treaties
relating to the arrest and return of deserting seamen shall be
abrogated, should the seamen's bill become a law. While the
language is not perfectly clear, yet to my mind any reasonable
construction would be that the Convention does not undertake
to interfere with existing treaties in that regard, but leaves each
of the signatory States free to continue such treaties in force or
abrogate them in the manner provided for in the treaties themselves. No suggestion has been made to me that the ratification
of the Convention would in any way conflict with the enactment
into law of that provision of the seamen's bill. On the contrary,
it is my opinion that we would be left entirely free to do so. In
fact, if the seamen's bill, S-136 as amended in the House, should
be enacted into law, I do not understand that it would conflict
with the terms of the Convention, and hence, while there may
be other questions, economic and diplomatic, which might arise
with reference to the advisability of enacting this bill into law,
yet they are outside of the Convention itself, as I understand the
Convention.

It may be that Article 68 of the Convention is ambiguous and
may be construed to mean that if the Convention is ratified we
will bind ourselves for the period of five years not to abrogate
so much of our treaties with the other signatory States as provide
for the arrest and return of seamen; and it may be that said
Article is not perfectly clear that the signatory States reserve
to themselves the power to make provision for the well-being
and comfort of passengers and immigrants and enforce them
alike on their own and vessels of the other signatory States in
our ports—if so, there cannot be any reasonable objection to so
much of the Senate resolution making it clear that the Convention is ratified with the understanding that these matters are not
included in its provisions and if we choose to legislate upon

them we will not be violating the terms of the Convention; but to go further and stipulate that we may violate all the other provisions of the Convention at will by providing other and higher standards of safety for life at sea than those embraced in the Convention and make those provisions applicable to foreign vessels as well as our own, is obnoxious to all the principles of international comity and effect, if not in terms tantamount to rejecting the Convention itself.

Respectfully,   William C. Redfield

TLS (WP, DLC).

## From Brand Whitlock

Dear Mr. President:                    Brussels. 19 December 1914.

As one grows older, less and less, I fear, has one the temerity to employ such words as "merry" and "happy"; less than ever this year, in a world gone mad! But I can not let the old year go to its close without sending you my best wishes for the new, with all the good will of a heart that has been with you in every step of your public career. I hope that the new year will bring you many enduring satisfactions and many beautiful compensations. Surely you deserve them, for you have borne your great burdens so bravely, and held on your high course so nobly, and surely you shall have them!

Believe me, my dear Mr. President,

Your ever devoted   Brand Whitlock

ALS (WP, DLC).

## To William Bayard Hale

My dear Hale:           The White House December 19, 1914

Just a line to say that I am very sorry that it will not be possible for me to see Dr. Bernard Dernburg.[1] I feel that it is imperatively necessary that I should decline interviews with any special agent of either side in the present struggle in Europe, for I am diligently and, I believe, consistently maintaining an aloofness and impartiality in the matter which I cannot venture to depart from.

Cordially and sincerely yours,   Woodrow Wilson

TLS (photostat received from W. H. Hale).
[1] Wilson was replying to W. B. Hale to WW, Dec. 16, 1914, TLS (WP, DLC).

## From the Diary of Colonel House

December 19, 1914.

Justice Lamar telephoned that the Argentina Ambassador was back. I made an engagement with him at half past eleven. I hurriedly gathered together what data I could get concerning Argentine and upon Naon himself. When the Justice introduced me he excused himself for a moment and took Naon aside to inform him how thoroughly I represented the President. He then took his leave.

I began the conversation by complimenting Naon upon the advanced thought in his country, particularly in regard to penal reform. I considered the Argentine fifty or one hundred years ahead of Europe and the United States in that direction. I marveled at the statesmanship that saw as long ago as 1864 when they had their war with Uraguay, that a victorious nation had no moral right to despoil the territory of the vanquished. After I had made these few remarks, I had fertile soil upon which to sow the seeds of my argument.

Naon took the typewritten memorandum which the President had given me and warmly approved both sentences—one and two. He was tremendously impressed with the significance of the first article and said it struck a new note, and would create an epoch in governmental affairs. When I told him the President had written the memorandum on the typewriter himself, he asked permission to keep it, saying it would become a historical document of much value.

I urged him to communicate with his Government by cable and to give me an answer by Monday or Tuesday. He felt confident the reply would be favorable. He took my address in New York and said he would communicate with me without delay. I let him understand that when the South American Governments had acted upon the matter, and it had been pretty well buttoned up, I would step aside and have the President and Mr. Bryan act officially. When I left, he followed me to the door and said he considered it a joy to work toward the consummation of such a policy as "your great and good President has promoted." I insisted upon haste since our country like others had a large military party, and they were not [now] clamoring for a greater army and navy. I hoped his country would understand what a propitious moment this was for such an understanding, for we now had a President with idealism. On the other hand, we might soon have a President with an ambition for territorial expansion, and there might be another story to tell.

At lunch I reported to the President the substance of my conversation with the Ambassador from the Argentine, and he was delighted. Naon thought I would have more difficulty with the Brazilian and Chilean Ambassadors, giving as his reason that they were imper[i]alistic in their tendencies, and that Chile had, at one time, tried to arrange with Argentine a war upon Bolivia and a division of her territory.

The President said in talking with the Brazilian and Chilean Ambassadors I could go very far, and he was emphatic in the statement that the United States would not tolerate such an aggression upon other republics.

In the afternoon I saw both the Brazilian and Chilean Ambassadors. Da Gama was easy of conquest and with practically the same argument I used with Naon. Suarez was more difficult because he is not so clever in the first instance, and in the second, Chile has a boundary dispute with Peru. He asked if I knew of this and I told him I did, but we would arrange in the final drawing of the agreement to cover such cases, since there were other boundary disputes which would have to be adjusted, like that between Costa Rica and Panama.[1] They both agreed to cable their Governments and strongly recommend the ratification of the proposal.

The President congratulated me warmly upon the day's work and said I had done a consummate piece of business. I answered that it was easy of accomplishment and I did not feel as if I had done anything at all. I had keyed myself up for a supreme test, and rather felt let down because it came with so little effort.

The President began to reflect and wondered whether we had moved too quickly. What he had in mind was the possible action of the Senate Committee on Foreign Affairs. We discussed the best time to take the matter up with the Senate Committee, and it was agreed it should be done immediately after the Christmas recess. He would first see the Democratic Members and later, perhaps, take the entire Committee into his confidence. Because this important matter might come up for ratification by the Senate, I wanted to change my advice as to how he should treat the Senate regarding the confirmation of his appointments. This policy might be of such importance, not only to the two Americas but to the world, that it would be folly to let a wrangle over patronage defeat such a measure.

As usual no one excepting the family was present at dinner. After we had finished the President read aloud for nearly two hours, "The Adventures in Arcadia of the Idle Rich."

Wallace telephoned to say that Bernstorff wished to see me

tomorrow. This determined my remaining over. I had hoped to leave for home tonight.

1 For a long account of this conversation, see the memorandum printed as an Enclosure with WJB to WW, April 21, 1915.

## Sir Cecil Arthur Spring Rice to Sir Edward Grey

Private.                              Washington. 19 December 1914.

Your friend sent for me to-day, and said that the President had received from the Department the draft reply to your proposals on contraband. The wording was unfriendly, and he did not approve it. After attempting corrections, he decided on ordering a complete new draft.

I presume that the draft is generally in the sense which I have already communicated, namely that the United States Government cannot enter into a bargain binding themselves to put difficulties in the way of legitimate trade in contraband. The President thinks that, while the new proposals are being drafted, it would help matters greatly if you could expedite the cases against the ships in court, and if possible liberate one or more (? of the innocent and) pay compensation at once. This would, he thinks, satisfy Congress for the moment. What causes irritation is detention of ships at great cost, because some contraband is suspected.

As soon as some measure of this nature is announced, we could probably arrange formally for the voluntary publication of sworn manifests under United States guarantee, but this is not certain.

I said most positively and in the strongest terms that you would never abandon the belligerent right of search for articles necessary for war equipment of enemy, and that if there was not sufficient guarantee that the ships did not contain such articles they would be detained and searched thoroughly.

T telegram (E. Grey Papers, FO 800/84, PRO).

## From the Diary of Colonel House

December 20, 1914.

Although Sunday, it has been the busiest day of all. I first went to call on Senator Culberson, Chairman of the Senate Judiciary Committee, in order to get his advice as to straightening out the controversy with that body. I took the Senator with me to Secretary Bryan's and had him wait in the motor until I could tell Mr. Bryan what I had done yesterday with the three South Americans. The President thought it advisable for me to keep him informed so there would be no hurt feelings. Mr. Bryan seemed pleased with what had been done but drifted off into the question of patronage and the best way to "do up Senator Hitchcock" in Nebraska. He followed me all the way to the automobile bareheaded in the cold bleak wind to get in as much as he could upon that subject.

I took Culberson home and called at Wallace's to meet the German Ambassador. Bernstorff was much exercised. He had information from his Government that the Allies intended bringing Japanese troops to Europe. If they should do this, he wanted me to know that all peace negotiations were ended as far as Germany was concerned. He was wrought up upon the subject, but I did not express an opinion. I promised to look into the matter and determine what was best to do. What I really did do was to tell the President and express the opinion that I [it] was entirely legitimate for the Allies to get Japanese to fight for them in Europe or elsewhere. The President concurred in this view.

I did not believe it was true that Japanese troops were going to Europe but even it [if] this were true, I attached no importance to Bernstorff's statement that Germany would not be glad to start peace parleys. I thought as a matter of fact, they would be more anxious for peace than ever. . . .

After leaving Gregory and Burleson I had another conference with Culberson. I reported to the President at lunch and told him I would take the three o'clock train for New York. He asked if I would not remain and discuss the Trades Commission appointments with him in the evening, to which I readily assented.

The President, Miss Bones and I took a long drive in the afternoon. When we got back, the Secretary of the Interior came for an hour's conference. It was mostly concerning the personel of the Trades Commission and the Senate controversy.

There was no one at dinner excepting the family. Later the President called Davies in, and we went into the personel of the Trades Commission.

At 9.45 Phillips of the State Department telephoned to say the British Ambassador desired to see me in the morning about a matter of importance. I told Phillips I was leaving for New York tonight and to ask the Ambassador to come immediately to his house, and I would be over within five minutes. I excused myself to the President and went to Phillips' and met Spring-

Rice. He had word from Sir Edward Grey concerning our peace proposals and thought it would not be a good thing for the Allies to stand out against a proposal which embraced indemnity to Belgium and a satisfactory plan for disarmament. Sir Edward wished me to know that this was his personal attitude. He also asked whether it would be advisable for the Duke and Duchess of Connaught, the new Governor General of Canada and his wife, to pay their respects to the President sometime soon.

I advised against this, but promised to consult with the President. Spring-Rice has an invitation to go to New Orleans for some exercises in the celebration of the Peace Centenary, which I advised him to decline. In my opinion, the best thing to do was to remain quiet, and do nothing which would give the German-Americans or other anti-English element an excuse to cause trouble in this country. This, he said, was in line with his own judgment.

I returned to the White House. The President excused himself from Davies and I told him the news. He was much elated, and wanted to know whether I could go to Europe as early as the coming Saturday. I stated that I could go at any time. He said he needed me on two Continents, but thought before I left we could button up our South American matters so as to leave me free. He spoke in feeling terms, and expressed again and again his gratitude for my assistance. He was fine enough to say that I had suggested two great things, and the manner of doing them. I have never known him so appreciative or more affectionate. I insisted that I was as grateful to him for giving me opportunities for public service as he could possibly be to me for anything I had done in the way of accomplishment.

Mr. Bryan telephoned at this moment to discuss some international incident, and then immediately drifted into the patronage question, and as to the best means of "putting Hitchcock in a hole." It amused the President greatly and we both laughed heartily. When he had finished the President said "damn" with force, and said he must relieve himself of such unimportant and futile talks at a time when the great world tragedy was uppermost in his mind.

He asked if I thought it would be well to say anything to Mr. Bryan about what I had done with the British and German Ambassadors. I thought it might be well to do so the first thing in the morning, and to do it with all the emphasis possible in order that Mr. Bryan might feel the import of it and keep the matter secret. This was finally agreed to, and I parted with the President at eleven.

## To Sir Cecil Arthur Spring Rice

Personal.
                                                 [The White House]
My dear Mr. Ambassador:                    December 21, 1914

    May I not thank you for the courteous message conveyed to
me through my friend, Mr. House, concerning the Governor-
General of Canada? I write to assure you that I will perfectly
understand the course pursued by the Duke of Connaught, and
I appreciate very sincerely the motive which has prompted the
inquiry and which will govern his action in the matter.
            Cordially and sincerely yours,   Woodrow Wilson

TLS (Letterpress Books, WP, DLC).


## To Lindley Miller Garrison

Personal and Private.
                                                 [The White House]
My dear Mr. Secretary:                     December 21, 1914

    Of course, I do not subscribe to the judgment of General Wood
contained in the enclosed letter from Mr. Villard (which I would
be very much obliged if you would return after reading it), but
I do think that General Wood is pursuing a questionable course
hardly consistent with the right spirit of the service and much
too individualistic. I would very much like your judgment as to
the proper way in which to handle the matter, for I really think
it ought to be handled.
            Cordially and faithfully yours,   Woodrow Wilson

TLS (Letterpress Books, WP, DLC).


## To Oswald Garrison Villard

Personal.

My dear Mr. Villard:    [The White House] December 21, 1914

    I ought to have acknowledged sooner your letter of December
sixteenth, but was prevented by a sudden rush of tasks that would
not be postponed.

    I had not seen a report of General Wood's address to the
Merchants' Association. I am going to look into the matter very
seriously and am warmly obliged to you for a little note of warning as to what is going on.
            Cordially and sincerely yours,   Woodrow Wilson

TLS (Letterpress Books, WP, DLC).

## To Seth Low, with Enclosure

My dear Mr. Low: The White House December 21, 1914

I warmly appreciate your letter of December sixteenth and regret that a sudden rush of tasks has prevented my replying sooner.

I will act upon your suggestion about the amount of the appropriation.

I take real pleasure in enclosing the letter suggested, and thank you sincerely for having thought it out for me so carefully.

As for the official to whom the letter should be sent, I think that your own judgment is right. It probably should be sent to the Governor-elect, particularly if, as I am informed, he is to be installed in office the first of the year.

Cordially and sincerely yours, Woodrow Wilson

TLS (S. Low Papers, NNC).

## ENCLOSURE

## To Seth Low and Others

My dear Sirs: The White House December 21, 1914

May I not again express to you my appreciation of your willingness to serve the country in the matter of the labor difficulties in the coal fields of Colorado? I believe that your striking exhibition of public spirit in this matter will in itself play an important part in inducing a course of action in the future in that state which will go very far towards producing an industrial peace.

I understand that the miners' organization has not only called off the strike, but has agreed to look after such of its members as do not secure early employment where they are. I am glad to learn that they have taken such action.

The plan of temporary accommodation which I have proposed to the mine operators and the striking miners did not involve a recognition by the operators of the miners' organization. It is the more interesting in view of that fact that the plan was assented to by the representatives of the striking miners. The situation has recalled to my mind the findings of the Anthracite Strike Commission. In that case also the union was not dealt with as such, and while many of the findings of that commission, of course, refer to local conditions connected only with the controversy it involved, certain of the findings of the commission seem to me to embody principles which might apply in one field as well as in another. For example, Finding IV provides for a Board of Conciliation on which both the operators and the miners are to be represented; Finding V secures to the miners the right, at their own expense, to check the weights upon which they are paid; and Finding IX provides "that no person shall be refused employment, or in any way discriminated against, on account of membership or non-membership in any labor organization; and that there shall be no discrimination against, or interference with, any employee who is not a member of any labor organization by members of such organization."

I would very much appreciate a report from the commission on the question whether these principles which have served to secure peace by agreement in Pennsylvania for twelve years in the anthracite coal industry are not now suitable and applicable to the conditions in Colorado, whether it would not be possible to obtain their acceptance there. If it is not, in the opinion of the commission, possible, it would throw a great deal of light on the situation if the commission would state the reasons why they do not find it possible.

I do not mean, of course, to confine the inquiries of the commission to these points. I would suggest that they also report as fully as the circumstances permit on any other question that may seem pertinent to this particular situation.

In my judgment the plan of temporary accommodation which I proposed contains all the elements of a just solution of the difficulties which have arisen in the Colorado coal fields, but I do not think that the commission need feel themselves bound to hold to the exact lines of those proposals if better and more satisfactory working agreements can be obtained. My conception of the duty of the commission is that it should act as a friend of all parties in an effort to bring about a mutually acceptable agreement. I have called attention to the anthracite coal settlement only for the purpose of suggesting that it affords a very useful and convincing precedent so far as the conditions in Pennsylvania at that time and the conditions in Colorado at the present time are similar or parallel.

Cordially and sincerely yours, Woodrow Wilson

TLS (S. Low Papers, NNC).

# From Sir Cecil Arthur Spring Rice, with Enclosures

Personal

Dear Mr President                    Washington. 21 Dec. 1914

I venture to enclose two telegrams which I have received from Sir E Grey one about Prize Court Proceedings and one about commercial telegrams.

The delays of the law are trying to the layman and I fully sympathize. In these cases there is a remedy, for any one who has been a sufferer without due reason has a claim to compensation. Perhaps an immediate payment in a specially hard case could be arranged and if so I should be very glad to be the medium or one of the mediums in such an arrangement. But I have no indication from London or Washington as to this.

I am glad to hear that of about 300 cases decided in the U S Prize Courts during the civil war only one is stated to have been disputed in England: and that one not seriously. This shows how great a similarity there is in the views taken in the two countries as to Prize Court Law.

The commercial telegram question is naturally very exasperating to the small percentage of sufferers. But the German spy system is on such a scale, and has such important branches in this country that some precautions are inevitable.

I have the honour to remain with the deepest respect, dear Mr President,

Your obedient servant   Cecil Spring Rice

ALS (WP, DLC).

## ENCLOSURE I

### MEMORANDUM.

Telegram from Sir E. Grey.

The number of neutral vessels now in the Prize Court is seven; the number of those detained for examination is ten, of which some will certainly be released. About twenty ships of those voluntarily sent into Court for examination or brought into port by British cruisers have already been released for every one which has been detained. The British Government will consider claims for compensation in all cases where the detention has not been justified.

Prize Court proceedings with regard to cargo necessarily take some time. If the Prize Court does not condemn the cargo as contraband it will be released or paid for but unless evidence is produced of the innocence of the cargo the decision of the Prize Court must be awaited. If such evidence is produced the cargo will be released immediately. In very many cases this has already been done. Appeal lies against all decisions of the Prize Court. It has perhaps not been sufficiently realised that the Prize Court of Great Britain as of the United States, is not a branch of the Executive and that it has already decided, as for instance in the case of the "Miramichi" that the claim of the neutral was good although the Crown had asked the Court for condemnation. The decision of the Court in this case has been accepted by the Government who in future cases will give effect to it. It will be observed that our procedure does not differ from that of the American Government.

It might become a matter of consideration whether it would not be advisable to forego certain rights as regards conditional contraband in return for a free hand as regards absolute contraband. This of course would be a matter for negotiation.

## E N C L O S U R E   I I

Telegram from Sir E. Grey.

Censorship of Commercial Cables between America and Europe.

Not all cables between Europe and the United States pass through British censor. About fifty thousand telegrams a day pass through the commercial cable censorship and of these very few are delayed or stopped.

Whenever the date and rate of despatch and addresses of sender and destined receiver are given the censor will inform the United States Ambassador in London whether the cable has been stopped by the British censor and what was the reason for such action.

T MSS (WP, DLC).

## From Lindley Miller Garrison

My dear Mr. President:        [Washington] December 21, 1914.

I have just received yours of even date, containing a letter from Mr. Villard, which, at your request, I herewith return.

I deprecate any voluntary expressions from Army Officers at this time about the military policy of the United States. I had so informed General Wood, and there is no doubt that he will not hereafter make any further public expression of opinion in this connection. I think the matter had much better be handled by the administrative and legislative authorities.

Sincerely yours,   Lindley M. Garrison

TLS (WP, DLC).

## Remarks at a Press Conference

December 22, 1914

Mr. President, there has been more or less discussion in the newspapers recently about appointments. Can you tell us anything about them?

So I see. It has been chiefly in the newspapers, let me say. I have learned with a great deal of interest that there is a fight between me and the Senate. I wasn't aware of it. The Senate has a perfect right to reject any nominations it pleases. I have no criticism. You may be sure that nobody can get up a row on the matter of patronage. We are engaged in very large affairs in this government, much larger than patronage. You won't find any arguments in this office on that subject.

Well, Mr. President, isn't it a fact that the stories discussing a row between the Senate and the President are based on what it is expected you will do, rather than what has been done?

Exactly. Anybody is at liberty to speculate what I will do, but I would advise you to wait and see. I don't know of any fight. It often gives me a very good idea of what not to do.

Mr. President, it is understood in the House that the ship purchase bill is ready to be put on the track and be slipped through when the proper moment comes. Do you know anything about that?

Perhaps it would be more appropriate to say "put on the ways." No, I don't know, speaking seriously, just what are the details of the plan of handling the bill in the House, but I am glad to hear that it is ready to be launched.

There was a statement that you had a conference with Mr. Gregory last night over some of these appointments that are being discussed in the papers?

That is not true. It was about future appointments.

In that connection, Mr. President, what is the status of the Maryland appointments?

Why, simply that I haven't gotten them all ready.

You are waiting to send them in all at once?

I prefer to do that in every case, so as not to leave any speculation. . . .

Mr. President, some in the House and Senate have stated that the Adamson clause on the Safety-at-Sea Convention has practically nullified it.

I sought advice on that myself and have received it, but I have not had time to look it over. It got to me late last night. I mean, as to whether it does nullify it. . . .

Mr. President, some of the members of Congress are urging a larger navy, presenting the argument that, because Congress last year and the year before provided one battleship, and the Secretary of the Navy urged a program of two battleships, now there is a shortage of two battleships, and they would like to have four next year or three this year or next year. How do you view that suggestion?

I view it from afar. . . .

Mr. President, have you taken any interest in the question of the Chinese loan, one way or the other?

How do you mean, taken an interest in it?

China is trying to get a loan.

I know that.

And some of the interests there are trying to prevent her from getting a loan. I understand that they appealed to you to strengthen the military service there against revolution.

They must have been absorbed in the State Department. Not all the protests that are made reach me.

Mr. President, have you told any members of Congress your position on those bills to prohibit exports of ammunition?

No, sir.

JRT transcript (WC, NjP) of CLSsh (C. L. Swem Coll., NjP).


## To Edward Mandell House

The White House Dec 22nd 1914

It will be both convenient and delightful to see you tomorrow.

Woodrow Wilson.

T telegram (E. M. House Papers, CtY).

# Paul Samuel Reinsch to William Jennings Bryan

STRICTLY CONFIDENTIAL

Sir:                                    Peking, December 22, 1914.

No. 478. I have the honor to report on developments in the Sino-Japanese situation since my confidential despatch (No. 460) of November 28th, and to submit some considerations in connection therewith.

A controversy of serious import has arisen with respect to the management of the Tsingtau customs. Under the arrangements with Germany, the customs remained an integral part of the Chinese Maritime Customs Service, although it was agreed that a German was to hold the position of Commissioner of Customs and that the foreign administrative personnel was to be composed of the same nationality. All these officials were, however, appointed by, and subject to the control of, the Inspector-General of Customs at Peking. When the question of the control of the customs arose, after the fall of Tsingtau due to the combined attack of Japanese and British troops, the Chinese Government first suggested that there should be appointed at Tsingtau a British Commissioner of Customs and that the staff should be half British and half Japanese: this was refused by Japan. The Chinese next suggested the appointment of a Japanese Commissioner with a staff half British and half Japanese: this also was refused. The Chinese Government next designated the Acting Commissioner of Customs at Dairen (a Japanese) to be Commissioner of Customs at Tsingtau, with the understanding that the rest of the personnel would be Japanese and British. The Japanese Government declined to recognize this appointment. The Chinese indicated their willingness to have the entire staff Japanese, but the Japanese Government still refused. The latter is now demanding that the Commissioner and staff of the Tsingtau customs shall not be selected by the Chinese Government and the Inspector-General, but will be supplied directly from Japan, to the number of forty-nine officials.

This demand, if successful, would place in the Chinese Customs Service a group of men not chosen by the Chinese Government: men who would most likely feel that their sole allegiance was to the authority that had selected them. If this demand is enforced by the Japanese it will constitute a precedent threatening the demoralization and disruption of the Maritime Customs Service. Consequently, all treaty powers are affected. I am informed from reliable sources that the British Legation has already indicated to the Japanese Minister that in this matter his

Government is getting into a brambly path. Mr. Aglen, the Inspector-General of Customs, is deeply concerned over this move, which would deprive his organization of unity and cohesion.

Incidentally, also, the manner in which the Japanese customs officials in Manchuria, although under the authority of the Chinese Government, have managed to extend advantages to their own nationals may be taken as an indication of what would be done were the service organized as it is now proposed to do at Tsingtau. It has been confidentially reported to me that Japanese officials here are already discussing the possibility, in consequence of the increased volume of Japanese trade with China, of being able, in the not distant future, to displace the British Inspector-General of Customs through a Japanese subject. The Japanese are in their action in Shantung following Manchurian precedents, as indicated by many details, among them the use of Japanese military currency along the entire Shantung railway and at interior points held by the Japanese. . . .

The unfriendly or suspicious attitude of Japanese individuals and officials with respect to American enterprise in China continues. The Japanese are prone to draw the inference that American business activity in China is conducted with a view to embarrassing Japanese plans and combating Japanese influence. An official of the Peking-Mukden Railway recently stated to a member of the Legation that a Chinese mining enterprise near Chinchou, in southern Manchuria, encountered a great deal of covert opposition on the part of the Japanese; finally rather truculent inquiries were made as to what American capital was invested in these mines. There being none, the obstruction ceased. . . .

The persistent campaign of hostility against America in the Japanese press may be to some extent accounted for because the United States is the only bugaboo which the militarist party in Japan can at the present time use to stir up militant sentiments for the purpose of gaining larger appropriations for warlike purposes. We are familiar with these devices in other countries and nearer at home. But the situation is somewhat different in that the Japanese people are unusually interested in foreign affairs and take them rather more seriously than other nations do; so that these press campaigns, by constant irritation of the public mind, leave behind them a dangerous deposit in the popular consciousness.

The recent declarations of Count Okuma and Baron Kato have not been reassuring either to Americans or to the Chinese. Indeed, these men find themselves in a difficult position: the easy success at Tsingtau and the remarkable gains which seem to be in the grasp of Japan make a policy of moderation and restraint unpopular at the present time. But Baron Kato's categorical denial that any pledges whatever have been given with respect to the return of Tsingtau or with respect to the Marshall Islands suggests the fear that in the last resort the Japanese Government may rely on the quibble that Tsingtau was to be returned to China only in the event of being peacefully and immediately delivered up by Germany. While there may be valid reasons for postponing the ultimate disposal of the German possessions now held by Japan, till the end of the war, the attitude and action of the Japanese Government seems to suggest rather that the interval is to be utilized to create a *fait accompli*, which will secure an enormous extension of power to Japan.

It is needless to say that this prospect is not entirely cherished by the temporary allies of Japan. The situation is that Japan has taken advantage of a conflict, which is primarily European and into the rigor of which Japan does not enter, for the purpose of gathering up the possessions of Germany in the Far East and the Pacific which could only be weakly defended. As these conquests of Japan would have been impossible under ordinary conditions and as they are due not to the power of Japan, but to the exertions of Great Britain, Russia and France in Europe, it is not considered just that Japan should thus easily gather the fruits of other peoples' sacrifices. On the contrary, it seems that the occupation of the position vacated by Germany in the Far East and the Pacific is a matter for all the powers to decide. While these things are, of course, not officially said, it is perfectly plain that especially the British in the Far East realize this aspect of the situation quite keenly. The results of this intelligence can not be looked for in any immediate action on the part of Great Britain, which must maintain the good relations now existing with Japan, but the results will inevitably come after the war has closed, when, however, the position of Great Britain in the Far East may have been changed irrevocably to her disadvantage. With great diplomatic shrewdness the Japanese Government is utilizing the Anglo-Japanese Alliance at the present time. British papers are prevailed upon to suppress news and comments unfavorable to the ally. The burden of official pronouncements in Japan is Anglo-Japanese friendship. At the same time every detail of Japanese policy in the Far East is diametrically opposed to British interests.

These matters affect the United States in that, while we have no such important interests in China as has Great Britain, nevertheless the traditions of American policy, the efforts and sacrifices of two generations of Americans at work in China, the trusteeship of intimate confidence which the Chinese place in America and, above all, the need which our country will have in the future of continued free access to China and of mutual friendship with its people—all these considerations make the future disposal of Shantung a matter far from indifferent to Americans.

The expressions of Count Okuma contained in the interview reported from Tokyo on December 11th, and therefore known to the Department, also had a disquieting effect here. The thinly veiled threats against the United States which it contains are not considered a good sign. The Japanese official interpretation of current events amounts in effect to the theory that Japan, having loyally and valorously come to the assistance of her ally —Great Britain—and having taken part in the great European struggle, can now no longer tolerate any question as to her absolute equality in all and every respect with the greatest nations of the world; and that the anti-Japanese sentiment in the United States is a blind prejudice of quality similar to the militarism of the German Emperor which must be "attacked without mercy." No matter how metaphorically the Premier of Japan understood these expressions, there can be no question as to the interpretation lent to them by the public. The Japanese are also inclined to draw the inference that as the friendship between Japan and Great Britain has now been sealed by the solemn baptism of alliance in war, Japan would have nothing to fear from the side of Great Britain were she forced to vindicate what she considers her rights against the United States. Thus the Japanese interference in the war, which they entered against the desire of the British Government, is made the basis not only of acquiring a position very unfavorable to British interests in the Far East, but of persuading the Japanese public that the Anglo-Japanese friendship is unalterable. This latter is a dangerous hallucination, as it is apt to encourage the Japanese public to favor unwarranted enterprises.

The attitude to be taken by the United States toward the continental Asiatic policy of Japan at the present time is a matter of great moment. Thus far it does not appear that the United States has received any credit on the part of Japan for the forbearance and good will shown towards the development of Japanese interests on the Asiatic mainland during the past years. On the contrary, as pointed out, the Japanese are rather apt to look upon

the American position in China as being intentionally opposi-
tional to their own plans.

If the United States should really enter upon a policy of trying to block the development of Japan, and should utilize the
hostility of China and the latent but serious fears of Great Britain,
Russia, and more especially of Canada and Australia, the results
might indeed be very damaging to Japan. Now that America is
following a simple, direct, open and straightforward policy and
is entirely abstaining from using her influence and power for the
weakening of Japan, the feeling is nevertheless still held alive
in Japan that the sole afterthought of American enterprise in
China is to embarrass Japan. Of all this the Japanese mind should
disabuse itself and recognize that Americans are in China for
their own purposes and of their own right, and that they expect to
remain there and develop their interests, but that their presence
is in no sense unfavorable to Japan.

No matter how generous the good will of America towards
Japanese efforts in economic and industrial development and
progress may be, the indications are that American rights and
just opportunities in China will receive further limitation unless
the situation is closely watched and every lawful interest is consistently asserted and defended. It is also necessary that Americans should realize the unusual opportunities which now exist
and which, unless utilized, will pass away forever; and that there
should [b]e established a strong, active American participation
in China's economic life, constituting a concrete interest in the
affairs of China, such as can not readily be ignored or brushed
aside by competitors desirous of preoccupying the field through
political action. It is also not improbable that the United States
Government would be able to obtain concerted action on the
part of several nations to the end that a solid front may be presented against the Manchurianization of Shantung and for the
purpose of enforcing the treaty engagements concerning equal
opportunities of trade, even in those small details, which seem
negligible, but which make and mar such opportunities.

I have the honor to be, Sir,

        Your obedient servant,  Paul S. Reinsch

TLS (WP, DLC).

## From Seth Low

Dear Mr. President:        New York December 22nd., 1914.

I thank you for your personal note received this morning which
I appreciate highly, and also for the letter to your Colorado Coal

Commission which is altogether admirable. I think it will enable us to be useful to the country in the important field in which you have asked us to serve.

Respectfully and sincerely, yours, Seth Low.

TLS (WP, DLC).

## To Sir Cecil Arthur Spring Rice

The White House

My dear Mr. Ambassador, 23 December 1914.

I am sincerely obliged to you for your note of the twenty-first and its enclosures. I hope and believe that all these matters, handled in this frank and reasonable way, will be worked out without serious or lasting embarrassment. If the threads get tangled we must patiently disentangle them.

With cordial regards

Sincerely Yours, Woodrow Wilson.

TCL (E. Grey Papers, FO 800/84, PRO).

## To Mary Allen Hulbert

Dearest Friend, The White House 23 December, 1914.

Just as I was about to sit down to write you a Christmas letter when your letter was handed to me in which you tell me of Allen's losses. I need not tell you how the news affected me. I thank you with all my heart that you have told me all about it; it is another evidence, which I welcome, that you believe in my friendship to the utmost. The distress of the news is little less than overwhelming. It has been on my heart all day like a great chilling cloud. But not in any way that would justify you in regretting that you told me all about it; what else could you have done? What is my friendship for if I may not share your distresses and at least be given a chance to think out what it may be possible for me to do? It would have cut deeper, if you had *not* told me, when at last I found it out! And I will think with all the earnestness there is in me what it is possible for me to do. At present, with the shock of the thing fresh upon me, I am only confused. My thought gropes and gets nowhere. But it ought to clear up, presently. I *ought* to be able to think of something to suggest and aid in! Need I tell you that I will try?

Meantime, this is just a line of sympathy. You will know how deep and genuine it is. Your note is touching to the last degree, but chiefly, I think, because it is so brave; because all the fine, indomitable spirit in you comes out so beautifully in every line of it, when you are least aware that you tre [are] showing me anything but the distress and fear. I admire you afresh for the quality which shows through it all.

How sad it is, when I wished only to send you the greetings of a happy season, to know that no wishing will bring you happiness and cheer! I can only send unmeasured sympathy; beg you to tell me of any plans that you can think out or even suggest; and tell you that you can count on anything possible from

Your devoted friend,   Woodrow Wilson

WWTLS (WP, DLC).

## To Nancy Saunders Toy

Dear Friend,               The White House 23 December, 1914.

It was very sweet of you to have Mrs. Hulbert out to take tea with you. I hope you liked her. She has just written me how intensely she enjoyed it, poor lonely lady. But what prompts this letter about her is the news I have just received from her of complete and all but overwhelming misfortune. Just before she went over to Cambridge to take tea with you her son had told her of his complete dissipation of his fortune! It was not a large one. On the contrary, it was small, only enough to keep them in moderate comfort. He was trying to make it big, and did not know what he was about! The result is, that they are penniless, and he has very little capacity for earning a living.

I have been wondering this: could anybody you know in Boston guide me to helping her to earn a living? She has a really extraordinary taste and knowledge in the matter of furniture and house furnishings of all kinds; an equally unusual knowledge of china, old and new; and a taste in interior decoration and a practical skill in making the contents of a room tell for the most that is in it, artistically, that I have never know[n] excelled. She can transform a room by merely moving the furniture about. You see what I am driving at. If there were some firm which dealt in all sorts of house furnishings, or some department store which dealt in everything, and which made it a part of its business to advise its customers about the decoration or furnishing of houses, or supplied its customers with an expert buyer in such lines, or did or advised concerning interior decoration, Mrs. Hulbert could in a short time make herself invaluable to them. I could, out of my own knowledge of what she knows and could do, give her a most unqualified endorsement, if I were given the chance: for what I want is the chance to help. I have the deepest sympathy with her, and greatly admire her gifts and character.

If I am inposing on you, my dear friend, or suggesting anything that it is impossible for you to give me guidance in, I know that you will feel free to tell me so. If I could not take that for granted, I would not have written what I have. The news from Mrs. Hulbert of her misfortune came to me only to-day, and I am keenly affected by it. I am thinking of writing also to my friend Arthur Tedcastle, of Boston,[1] to Mr. Olney,[2] and perhaps to Major Higginson,[3] much as I hate to do so; simply because I feel that I must help her (though she has not asked or even hinted at it, brave lady that she is) if it is possible, whether I like to appeal to comparative strangers such as two of these gentlemen are or not. What are friends for? And I have only too few opportunities to do anything for the people I know and admire!

All this, when I thought that to-day I should be writing you only messages of Christmas cheer and New Year hope! Forgive me! I know that you will; for I am trying to be a friend in need. My little family will be gathered about me by to-morrow evening. That will ease my heart; although in a way it will make my loneliness all the more poignant. God help me! I do not know yet how to carry this grief that has come to me. It has weakened me at the very sources of my life. But it has also made my feeling for my friends so much the more comprehending, I think. It makes me the more eager to reach out to them and try to help them. It enables me to know, I think, what you are suffering since your dear mother went away. I used seldom to think (the more shame upon me!) of writing frequently to even dear friends. I allowed the tasks and the fatigues of the day to make me selfish. Now I know what a heart needs, and would so like to give and help.

May I send many messages of affectionate friendship, then, as a Christmas offering? May I tell you how much I hope that the New Year will bring cheer and strengthened hope and courage when and whence they are least expected? And may I include Mr. Toy in these messages. I send them with all my heart, and am        Your affectionate friend,   Woodrow Wilson

WWTLS (WP, DLC).
  [1] This letter is WW to A. W. Tedcastle, Dec. 24, 1914, TLS (WP, DLC).
  [2] WW to R. Olney, Dec. 24, 1914, TLS (Letterpress Books, WP, DLC).
  [3] WW to H. L. Higginson, Dec. 24, 1914, TLS (Letterpress Books, WP, DLC).

## From Lindley Miller Garrison

My dear Mr. President:          Washington. December 23, 1914.

I have just been visited by Governor Ammons, Governor-elect Carlson, and Congressman Taylor,[1] all of Colorado. They informed me that they, or some of them, had seen you today.

Governor Ammons stated, and Governor Carlson did not dissent, that what they wished us to do was as follows:

At any time after Sunday next, which is the time when the Governor expects to get back to Denver, we can remove the troops from Routt County; very shortly thereafter we can remove them from Lewisville; very shortly after this move, we can move them from Freemont County. He desires to see Colonel Lockett and talk over with him when it would be best to move them from Trinidad. This is the large district where most of the troops are, and the one where they expect trouble, if anywhere.

Please let me know whether this general arrangement meets with your approval, so that I may act accordingly.

Sincerely yours,   Lindley M. Garrison

TLS (WP, DLC).
[1] Edward Thomas Taylor, Democrat.

## From the Diary of Colonel House

The White House Washington, D. C. December 23, 1914

The train was late and I did not reach Washington until 6.45. The President was eager to hear what I had to say, and came to my room and kept me from dressing for a few minutes which delayed dinner.

I told of young Spring-Rice's[1] visit to New York with messages from the British Ambassador, about which I in turn, wished to consult with him and also to discuss how far it would be advisable at this time to bring pressure upon the Allies to meet the willingness of Germany to start peace parleys.

There were no outside visitors at dinner excepting Dr. Grayson and myself. Afterward we went to the study and discussed the best means of action.

In the meantime, I had wired Phillips from New York to make an engagement with the British Ambassador at his home at nine o'clock. The President suggested that I telephone Phillips to find if this had been done. I did so, and found that Spring-Rice had a dinner engagement and desired to meet me at 10.15 but I did not wish to keep the President up so late since he would want to hear the result of the interview. Therefore, I asked Phillips to please communicate with the Ambassador again and ask him to come at 9.45, and it was arranged that way.

The President and I went into every phase of the situation, and it was decided that I should ask Spring-Rice to send another despatch to Sir Edward Grey and have him feel out the Allies as to Bernstorff's proposal.

In the meantime, we discussed the Trades Commission, the row with the Senate over the confirmation of appointments and other matters of current, though not permanent interest.

When I met Spring-Rice he said he had received another cablegram from Sir Edward Grey,[2] and while he was personally agreeable to the suggestion made, he had not yet taken it up with his own Cabinet, much less with the Allies. He felt there would be difficulties with France and Russia, and great difficulty in effecting a plan by which a permanent settlement might be brought about. Sir Cecil wanted to go into a discussion of what such a settlement would entail. It seemed to me footless to undertake such a discussion at this time, for it would probably cover a period of weeks, if not months, even after the powers had begun parleys. I told him it was not my idea that they should stop fighting even after conversations began, and that an armistice need not be brought about until at least a tentative understanding as to what would constitute a permanent settlement was well within sight.

He thought France would probably desire the French part of Lorraine, and he thought Russia would like Constantinople. He wondered if Germany would accede to the former request. I thought that was something to be threshed out later, and that the conversations should begin upon the broad lines of an evacuation and indemnity for Belgium, and an arrangement for a permanent settlement of European difficulties, including a reduction of armaments.

I was surprised to hear him say that the indemnity to Belgium could be arranged, for all the powers might be willing to share the damages done that brave little nation. I was also surprised to hear him say that he saw signs of what he called "a general funk among the European nations, and he thought perhaps most of them feared revolutions." He suggested that I say to Bernstorff that Germany was in possession of a large part of Belgium and a portion of France, therefore it would be to her advantage and to the disadvantage of the Allies to begin parleys now. In my opinion it would be a mistake to concede that Germany had any advantages whatsoever, and it seemed to me the proper attitude to assume was one of absolute confidence in the ultimate defeat of Germany.

He could not understand why Germany would consent to peace parleys now when they seemingly were so successful, and he did not believe the German military party or the German people as a whole, would permit such conversations being brought to satisfactory conclusions. That was also my opinion, as far as those two elements were concerned, but I thought the Kaiser, the Chancellor, the Foreign Secretary, and their entourage knew that the war was already a failure and did not dare take the risk involved, provided they could get out of it whole now. He thought if the Kaiser should seriously propose peace at this time, he would probably be assassinated and the Crown Prince become Emperor.

I admitted to Sir Cecil that it was a difficult and dangerous thing to handle, but I felt it must be handled sometime by somebody, and we might just as well begin to face the difficulties and undertake a solution. Sir Cecil said he would cable Sir Edward Grey tonight and tell him of our conversation and ask him to feel out the Allies, and let us know as soon as possible whether it was advisable for me to come to London.

I asked him to explain that we had no disposition to force the issue, but it would be inadvisable to let the Germans have the advantage of having expressed a willingness to begin parleys upon such terms, and then have the Allies refuse.

Sir Cecil thought he would have something definite for me within a week. Returning to the White House, I found the President anxiously awaiting me. After telling what had passed, we discussed what was best to do regarding Bernstorff, and we came to the conclusion that it would be well to leave him alone until I had heard something direct from the Allies, and then we could put the question squarely up to Bernstorff by telling him I was ready to go to London, but he must not let me go, only to find Germany repudiating what he had said.

It was now after eleven, and I insisted upon the President going to bed. On the other hand, he insisted upon sitting with me until I had changed my clothes and was ready to say goodbye. He again expressed gratitude and affection for the trouble I had taken and the manner in which I am trying to serve.

1 Thomas Aubrey Spring Rice, third secretary of the British Embassy in Washington and a cousin of Ambassador Spring Rice.

2 E. Grey to C. A. Spring Rice, Dec. 22, 1914, T telegram (E. Grey Papers, FO 800/84, PRO), which follows in full:

PERSONAL & SECRET. [London] 22 December 1914. 3.40 P.M.
Your private & secret telegrams of December 18 & 20.

I can only give my personal view which is that there are two main objects to be secured:

(1). Evacuation of Belgium, compensation for the wrong done to her and re-establishment of her independence. If Germany agreed to this the barrier to peace discussions as far as we are concerned would be removed, for it is the one thing that is a point of absolute right and of honour for us to secure.

(2). A durable peace that will secure us and our Allies from future aggression.

German views aim at a durable peace by placing the west of Europe under German domination. Even a German pacifist Professor said the other day that "the principle of the absolute sovereignty of the individual nations must be given up." We would rather perish than submit to that.

On the other hand the crushing of Germany is in the long run probably as impracticable as the domination of Germany, and secure peace is not to be obtained that way.

An internal change that made Germany a democratic State emancipated from the rule of the Prussian military party would be one solution of this problem, but it cannot be imposed directly from outside, though it might be the indirect result of defeat of Germany in war.

An agreement between the Great Powers at the end of this war with the object of mutual security and preservation of peace in future might have stability if the United States would become a party to it and were prepared to join in repressing by force whoever broke the Treaty. We should be quite willing that Germany should have future security by any condition that would also give it to us.

Such are my own personal views. Great Britain I consider is bound to fight on till the Belgian point is secured, even if we had to fight alone. That is an absolute minimum.

But there are also the views of the Allies to be considered. We have not yet discussed terms of peace with them and we are bound to do so when the time comes. Both will have to state their own conditions for themselves and what those will be will largely depend upon the progress of the war.

You can tell the President's friend the substance of this if you think it useful, but on condition that all knowledge of it is kept strictly to himself and the President only. It must on no account become known to the State Department.

## To Thomas Davies Jones

My dear Friend:          The White House December 24, 1914

I thank you from the bottom of my heart for your letter.[1] Of course, you are right in saying that when I am forgetful enough of my duty to think only of myself my heart is very heavy indeed, and I can hardly lift it to the level upon which it should move during this season, but, happily, a great deal of the time I simply can't think of myself and then there is added the infinite satisfaction and comfort of having friends who think of me as you do with generosity, trust and affection. That is enough to sustain any man and it does sustain me splendidly. There is nothing I would dare complain of, there is nothing I would be justified in complaining of. I can be and shall be happy in the thoughts which such letters as yours bring me.

Please accept from us all the warmest and most affectionate greetings of the season, and please be kind enough to convey them also to your brother and his dear household.

Faithfully and affectionately yours,    Woodrow Wilson

TLS (Mineral Point, Wisc., Public Library).
[1] T. D. Jones to WW, Dec. 22, 1914, ALS (WP, DLC).

# Two Letters from William Jennings Bryan

My dear Mr. President:          Washington December 24, 1914.

I am sending you a redraft of instructions to the American Ambassador at London.[1]

Mr. Lansing went over the text a second time and smoothed out such harsh places as he discovered and then I went over it after him, making some other modifications and inserting on page 7 that "mere suspicion is not evidence, and that doubt should be reserved in favor of neutral commerce, not against it."

We have tried to soften the expression without modifying or impairing the strength of our protest.

You have doubtless seen the (enclosed) despatch from Page in which he mentions a change in sentiment in Italy, due to the vexations caused by restrictions on commerce.[2] We are sure, from what we have heard, that this same irritation is growing in other neutral countries. I think that Great Britain, looking at the matter from her own standpoint, is making a mistake in imposing restrictions to the extent that she does. She is unnecessarily arousing resentment among those interested in neutral commerce.

I think that it is the part of friendship to bring this matter to the attention of Great Britain in such a way as to lead to a careful consideration of the whole matter.

Will you let me know whether we have made the text conform with your views—or, if not, what suggestions you desire to offer?

With assurances of high respect I am, my dear Mr. President,
Yours very sincerely,   W. J. Bryan

TLS (SDR, RG 59, 763.72112/545A, DNA).
[1] See the Enclosure printed with WW to WJB, Dec. 26, 1914.
[2] T. N. Page to the Secretary of State, Dec. 23, 1914, printed in *FR-WWS 1914*, p. 156.

My dear Mr. President:          Washington December 24, 1914.

I am sending for your judgment a rather important communication to the German Ambassador.[1]

You will notice in the papers enclosed a translation of the note received from the German Embassy in which they admit the right of belligerents to buy arms, ammunition, etc., in this country, but complain of the inquiries which we make in regard to ships carrying coal to war vessels.[2]

Mr. Lansing and I have gone over this very carefully and you will notice first that we call attention to the recognition of the right of belligerents to buy our arms. (See the last sentence on the first page.)[3]

In the next place we call attention to the distinction between the rules applicable to the purchase of ammunition and the rules applicable to ships carrying coal.

We also take occasion to assert that these principles have been enforced by this nation with impartiality.

We are wondering whether it might not be well, in view of the criticism we have received, to ask the Germany Embassy to permit us to give to the public their protest and our answer. It will meet the criticism which has been directed against us by some who seem to be ignorant of the rules of international law.

Please let me know whether you have any changes to suggest in the phraseology, and also whether it is worth while to try to secure publication.

With assurances of high respect I am, my dear Mr. President,
Yours very sincerely,   W. J. Bryan

TLS (SDR, RG 59, 763.72111 EM 1/1, DNA).
    [1] The Secretary of State to Ambassador von Bernstorff, Dec. 24, 1914, printed in *FR-WWS 1914*, pp. 647-49. Bryan summarizes this letter below.
    [2] Ambassador von Bernstorff to the Secretary of State, Dec. 15, 1914, *ibid.*, pp. 646-47.
    [3] "I take note, therefore, of your Government's statement that 'under the general principles of international law no exception can be taken to neutral states letting war material go to Germany's enemies from or through neutral territory,' and that the adversaries of Germany in the present war are, in the opinion of the Imperial Government, authorized to 'draw from the United States contraband of war, especially arms, worth several billions of marks.'"

## Sir Cecil Arthur Spring Rice to Sir Edward Grey

PERSONAL & SECRET.          Washington, 24 December 1914.

Your telegram of December 22.

I saw the President's friend to-day, who at once agreed that no one but the President should be informed of what passed. I learnt your telegram by heart, but gave nothing in writing.

He assured me most positively that the German Ambassador said in clear terms that his Government would agree to evacuation and compensation of Belgium, and to security against renewed attack in future. He said that he had no doubt that your standpoint, expressed in your telegram, would command the assent of practically every one, and added that he was ready to start at once for London if you wished.

I pointed out your views were personal, and that there were also the views of the Allies to be considered, and that both will have to state their own conditions for themselves. If he went at once, before you had consulted them, the journey might, I said, be taken in vain. He agreed, and also pointed out that the United States could never become an active party to an agreement to join in repressing by force whoever broke it.

Finally, he suggested that you should consider the matter and ascertain from the Allies if they were prepared to consider terms while continuing hostilities. If so, and there was a visible basis to negotiate on, he would start for Europe as soon as you gave him a hint. He would communicate in that case with Zimmermann, with whom he had previously negotiated and meet him in Germany after seeing you.

He seems convinced that both the German and Austrian Ambassadors desire peace, and that both have been instructed by their Governments to say so.

Meanwhile, there is not the least diminution of the anti-English ferocity of the German agents here.

T telegram (E. Grey Papers, FO 800/84, PRO).

## To Edward Mandell House

The White House Dec 25 1914

All our household join in sending Christmas greetings laden with real affection to you both. I wish I could see brought into your life some happiness and blessing equal to those you have brought into mine by your wonderful friendship. You have kept faith and strength in me.　　　　Woodrow Wilson

T telegram (E. M. House Papers, CtY).

## Two Letters from Edward Mandell House

Dear Governor:　　　　New York City. December 25th, 1914.

Seth Low telephoned me late last night and told me that Gilday and Mills want to go to Colorado at once.

He thinks it would be unwise to do this just now. If you concur in this view, he requests that you telegraph me immediately expressing the hope that they will not go to Colorado until the situation has been somewhat clarified.

The point is this: He has had an interview with John D. Jr. and he is very hopeful that everything can be adjusted provided no false move is made. He said he considered it now "a matter of tact," and he fears if the Board should go to Colorado at this time, something might happen to prevent an early settlement.

Affectionately yours,　E. M. House

He hopes I may receive the telegram by Saturday (tomorrow) noon.

Dear Governor:                New York City. December 25th, 1914.

I am enclosing you a letter from Lane[1] which explains itself.

If there is any change in the situation it might be well for me to see Curtis[2] and to look up Calloway[3] for you.

The papers state that the sensibilities of the Senate are hurt because you are not consulting any of them in regard to the appointments on this Commission.[4] This, taken in connection with what Culberson told me, indicates that they will hesitate to confirm any member of this board to whom there may be any possible objection.   Affectionately yours,   E. M. House

TLS (WP, DLC).
  [1] It is missing.
  [2] Cyrus Hermann Kotzschmar Curtis, head of the Curtis Publishing Co. of Philadelphia.
  [3] Fuller Earle Callaway, cotton manufacturer of LaGrange, Ga.
  [4] That is, the Federal Trade Commission.


## From Josephus Daniels

My Dear Mr. President:          Washington. Dec. 25th, 1914.

Close association for nearly two years has ripened my esteem into affection. Your example of having always an eye single to the public weal has been an inspiration in the tasks to which, by your partiality, I have had the privilege of addressing myself. My wish for you to-day is that a portion of the happiness you give to others may sweeten and brighten your own life.

My wife and boys join in love and Christmas greetings.

Cordially and sincerely your friend,   Josephus Daniels

ALS (WP, DLC).


## To William Jennings Bryan, with Enclosure

My dear Mr. Secretary,     The White House 26 December, 1914.

This paper is much improved and I am glad to give it my sanction.

I think it might be wise to send our Ambassador in London a cipher copy of the despatch from our Ambassador in Rome which speaks of the change of sentiment which is taking place in Italy; and to suggest to him that he might, in his discretion, make unofficial and confidential use of it in his conversations with the British Foreign Office. Very likely the British representative at Rome has apprised his government of these things, but Walter Page ought to have the information in his possession.

Cordially and faithfully Yours,   Woodrow Wilson

WWTLS (SDR, RG 59, 763.72112/545½, DNA).

ENCLOSURE[1]

December 24, 1914.

*Second Redraft of Instruction to*
*American Ambassador at London.*

The present condition of American foreign trade resulting from the ⟨continued⟩ *frequent* seizures and detentions of American cargoes destined to neutral European ports has become so serious as to require a ⟨frank⟩ *candid* statement of the views of this Government in order that the British Government ⟨have no misapprehension⟩ *may be fully informed* as to the attitude of the United States toward the policy which has been pursued by the British authorities ⟨since the commencement of⟩ *during* the *present* war.

You will, therefore, communicate the following to His Majesty's Principal Secretary of State for Foreign Affairs, but in doing so you will assure him that it is done in the most friendly spirit and in the belief that frankness will better serve the continuance of cordial relations between the two countries than silence, which may be misconstrued into acquiescence in a course of conduct which this Government ⟨considers⟩ *cannot but consider* to be ⟨a needless⟩ *an* infringement upon the right of American citizens.

The Government of the United States has ⟨seen⟩ *viewed* with growing concern the large number of vessels laden with Amer-

1 The following document went through several revisions. Cone Johnson made the first draft on December 16 (it is printed as an Enclosure with WJB to WW, Dec. 17, 1914). Bryan and Lansing had completed their revision of it, entitled "Redraft of Instruction to American Ambassador at London," by December 21. Bryan sent this redraft to Wilson on December 24. Wilson immediately made extensive revisions and returned his emended draft to the State Department on that same day. A new version, incorporating Wilson's changes and entitled "Second Redraft of Instruction to American Ambassador at London," was immediately typed in the State Department. It was returned to the White House, and Wilson made a few final changes on the document on his own typewriter. Wilson's revision of the first redraft is missing. All other documents herein referred to are in SDR, RG 59, 763.72112/545A, DNA.
The vocabulary and phrasing of the changes made in the first redraft clearly indicate that they were Wilson's. We have followed our usual method of using angle brackets to denote words deleted by Wilson and italics to denote his substitutions and additions. This telegram was sent to Page on December 26.

ican goods destined to neutral ports in Europe, which have been seized on the high seas, taken into British ports and detained ⟨often⟩ *sometimes* for weeks by the British authorities. During the early days of the war this Government ⟨believed⟩ *assumed* that the policy adopted by the British Government was due to the unexpected outbreak of hostilities and the necessity of immediate action to prevent contraband from reaching the enemy. For this reason it was not disposed to judge *this policy* harshly or ⟨resist⟩ *protest it* vigorously ⟨a policy which was so manifestly injurious⟩ *although it was manifestly very injurious* to American trade with the neutral countries of Europe. This Government ⟨relied⟩ *relying* confidently upon the high regard which Great Britain has so often exhibited in the past for the rights of other nations ⟨to amend a course⟩ *confidently awaited amendment of a course* of action which denied to neutral commerce the freedom to which it was entitled by the law of nations.

This expectation ⟨was heightened⟩ *seemed to be rendered the more assured* by the statement of the Foreign Office early in November that the British Government were satisfied with guarantees offered by the Nowegian, Swedish and Danish Governments as to non-exportation of contraband goods when consigned to named persons in the territories of those Governments, and that orders had been given to the British fleet and customs authorities to restrict interference with neutral vessels carrying such cargoes so consigned to verification of ship's papers and cargoes.

It is, therefore, a matter of ⟨keen⟩ *deep* regret that, though nearly five months have passed since the war began, ⟨there has been no indication on the part of the British Government of a purpose to change their policy or to treat less rigorously⟩ *the British Government has not materially changed their policy and do not treat less rigorously* ships and cargoes passing between neutral ports in the peaceful pursuit of lawful commerce, which belligerents should protect rather than interrupt. The greater freedom from detention and seizure which was confidently expected to result from consigning shipments to definite consignees, rather than "to order," ⟨has not materialized⟩ *is still awaited.*

It is needless to point out to His Majesty's Government, ⟨so often⟩ *usually* the champion of the freedom of the seas and the rights of trade, that peace, not war, is the normal relation between nations and that the commerce between countries which are not belligerents should not be interfered with by those at war unless such interference is manifestly an imperative necessity to protect their national safety and then only to the extent that it is a necessity. It is with no lack of appreciation of the momentous nature of the present struggle, in which Great Britain is engaged, and with no selfish desire to gain undue commercial advantage that this Government ⟨has reached the conclusion⟩ *is reluctantly forced to the conclusion* that the present policy of His Majesty's Government toward neutral ships and cargoes exceeds the manifest necessity of a belligerent and constitutes restrictions upon the rights of American citizens on the high seas which ⟨find no justification in international law or in the principle of self preservation⟩ *are not justified by the rules of international law or required under the principle of self preservation.*

The Government of the United States does not intend at this time to discuss the propriety of including certain articles in the lists of absolute and conditional contraband, which have been proclaimed by His Majesty. Open to objection as some of these ⟨are⟩ *seem to this Gov't.*, the chief ground of present complaint is the treatment of cargoes of both classes of articles when bound to neutral ports.

Articles listed as absolute contraband, shipped from the United States and consigned to neutral countries, have been seized and detained on the ground that the countries to which they were destined have not prohibited the exportation of such articles. Unwarranted as such detentions are, in the opinion of this Government, American exporters are further perplexed by the apparent indecision of the British authorities in applying their own rules to neutral cargoes. For example, a shipment of copper from this country to a specified consignee in Sweden was detained because, as was stated by Great Britain, Sweden had placed no embargo on copper. On the other hand, Italy not only prohibited the export of copper, but, as this Government is informed, put in force a decree that shipments to Italian consignees or "to order," which arrive in ports of Italy cannot be exported or transshipped. *The only exception Italy makes is of copper which passes through that country in transit to another country.* In spite of these decrees, however, the British Foreign Office has thus far declined to affirm that copper shipments ⟨so⟩ consigned *to Italy* will not be molested on the high seas. ⟨As a result⟩ *Seizures are so numerous and delays so prolonged that* exporters are afraid to send their copper to Italy, steamship lines decline to accept it, and insurers refuse to issue policies upon it. In a word, a legitimate trade is being ⟨destroyed⟩ *greatly impaired* through uncertainty as to the treatment which it may expect at the hands of the British authorities.

⟨Certainly neutral nations are entitled to know the exact way⟩

*We feel that we are abundantly justified in asking for information as to the manner* in which the British Government propose to carry out the policy which they have adopted, in order that ⟨they⟩ *we* may determine the steps necessary to protect ⟨their⟩ *our* citizens, engaged in foreign trade, in their rights and from the serious losses to which they are liable through ignorance of the hazards to which their cargoes are exposed.

In the case of conditional contraband the policy of Great Britain appears to this Government to be equally unjustified by the established rules of international conduct. As evidence of this, attention is directed to the fact that a ⟨great⟩ number of the American cargoes which have been seized consist of foodstuffs and other articles of common use in all countries which are admittedly relative contraband. In spite of the presumption of innocent use because destined to neutral territory, the British authorities made these seizures and detentions without, *so far as we are informed*, being in possession of facts which warranted a reasonable belief that the shipments had in reality a belligerent destination, as that term is used in international law. Mere suspicion is not evidence and doubts should be resolved in favor of neutral commerce, not against it. The effect upon trade in these articles between neutral nations resulting from interrupted voyages and detained cargoes is not *entirely* cured by reimbursement of the owners for the damages, which they have suffered, after investigation has failed to establish an enemy destination. The injury is to American commerce with neutral countries as a whole through the hazard of the enterprise and the repeated diversion of goods from established markets.

It also appears that cargoes of this character have been seized by the British authorities because of a belief that, though not originally *so* intended by the shippers, they will ultimately reach the territory of the enemies of Great Britain. Yet this belief is frequently reduced to a ⟨vague⟩ *mere* ⟨suspicion⟩ *fear* in view of the embargoes which have been decreed by the neutral countries, to which they are destined, on the articles composing the cargoes.

That a consignment "to order" of articles listed as conditional contraband and shipped to a neutral port raises a legal presumption of enemy destination appears to be directly contrary to the doctrine previously held by Great Britain and thus stated by Lord Salisbury during the South African War:

"Foodstuffs, though having a hostile destination, can be considered as contraband of war only if they are for the enemy forces; it is not sufficient that they are capable of being so used, it must be shown that this was in fact their destination at the time of their seizure."

With this statement as to conditional contraband the views of this Government are in entire accord, and upon this historic doctrine, consistently maintained by Great Britain when a belligerent as well as a neutral, American shippers were entitled to rely.

The Government of the United States readily admits the full right of a belligerent to visit and search on the high seas the vessels of American citizens or other neutral vessels carrying American goods and to detain them WHEN THERE IS SUFFICIENT EVIDENCE TO JUSTIFY A BELIEF THAT CONTRABAND ARTICLES ARE IN THEIR CARGOES;[2] but His Majesty's Government, judging by their own experience in the past, must realize that this Government cannot without protest permit American ships or American cargoes to be taken into British ports and there detained for the purpose of searching generally for evidence of contraband, or upon presumptions created by special municipal enactments which are clearly at variance with international law and practice.

This Government believes, and earnestly hopes His Majesty's Government will come to the same belief, that a course of conduct more in conformity with the rules of international usage, which Great Britain has strongly sanctioned for many years, will in the end better serve the interests of belligerents as well as those of neutrals.

Not only is the situation a critical one to the commercial interests of the United States, but many of the great industries of this country are suffering because their products are denied long-established markets in European countries, which, though neutral, are contiguous to the nations at war. Producers and exporters, steamship and insurance companies are pressing, and not without reason, for relief from the menace to transatlantic trade which is gradually but surely destroying their business and threatening them with financial disaster.

The Government of the United States, still relying upon the deep sense of justice of the British nation, which has been so often manifested in the intercourse between the two countries during so many years of uninterrupted friendship, expresses confidently the hope that His Majesty's Government will realize the obstacles and difficulties, which their present policy has placed in the way of commerce between the United States and the neutral countries of Europe, and will *instruct its officials to* re-

[2] The capitalized words were in the first redraft and were italicized by Wilson.

frain from all unnecessary interference with the freedom of trade between nations which are sufferers, though not participants, in the present conflict; and will in their treatment of neutral ships and cargoes conform *more closely* to those rules governing the maritime relations between belligerents and neutrals, which have received the sanction of the civilized world, and which Great Britain has, in other wars, so strongly and successfully advocated.

In conclusion it should be impressed upon His Majesty's Government that the present condition of American trade with the neutral European countries is such that, if it does not improve, it may arouse a feeling contrary to that which has so long existed between the American and British peoples. Already it is becoming more and more the subject of public criticism and complaint. There is an increasing belief, *doubtless not entirely unjustified*, that the present British policy toward American trade is responsible for the depression in certain industries which depend upon European markets. The attention of the British Government is called to this possible result of their present policy ⟨with no purpose of threat but solely⟩ to show how widespread the effect is upon the industrial life of the United States *and to emphasize the importance of removing the cause of complaint.*    Bryan

RL.

T MS (SDR, RG 59, 763.72112/545A, DNA).

## To William Jennings Bryan

My dear Mr. Secretary,    The White House 26 December, 1914.

I think the enclosed reply to the memorandum of the German Government both sound and conclusive, and I sincerely hope that you will be able, as you suggest, to obtain the consent of the German Government to the publication of this correspondence.

Cordially and faithfully Yours,    Woodrow Wilson

WWTLS (SDR, RG 59, 72111 EM 1/11½, DNA).

## A Telegram and Two Letters to Edward Mandell House

White House Dec 26 [1914]

My judgement concurs with that suggested with regard to the mission to Colorado.    Woodrow Wilson.

T telegram (E. M. House Papers, CtY).

My dear Friend,          The White House 26 December, 1914.

I fear I am very stupid. I do not even remember discussing any Mr. Curtis for the Trade Commission. I would be delighted to have you do anything you think wise about this or any other case. I have done nothing since we talked, because I have been waiting for the information Davies was to get for us.

I remember what has been told me about Calloway, but it was told me by persons in whose judgment and in whose ability to know a man when they see him I have no great confidence. If Lane really knows him and if you have means of making intimate inquiry about him, I would be greatly indebted to you if you would.

I dare not say see Curtis till I am reminded who he is: for I assume that the minute you spoke to him he would form definite expectations, no matter what you said.

In haste (I am grinding out my own letters to-day), and with warmest messages,

Affectionately Yours,   Woodrow Wilson


My dear Friend,          The White House 26 December, 1914.

I saw my nephew, Wilson Howe, just for a moment yesterday. He said something about seeing you concerning a "proposition" he had made to the C. & O. about trade, in coffee one way and coal the other, with South America. If he opens the matter to you, I hope that you will see that he incures no personal responsibilities, no financial responsibilities in particular, for he has invariably failed when he struck out for big things on his own hook. His line of success is as a man under employment and direction.

You have been exceedingly generous in advising and helping him. I feel almost as if I had imposed on you in the whole matter. You have put him on his feet.

Affectionately Yours,   Woodrow Wilson

WWTLS (E. M. House Papers, CtY).


## To William Cox Redfield

My dear Mr. Secretary,     The White House 26 December, 1914.

Your letter was just the tonic I needed.[1] It was prompted by a great generosity on your part. It should strengthen and give confidence to any man to be so thought of and sustained.

I need not tell you how I value such friendship or what it means to me. I am proud to have excited such sentiments in a colleague; and I want you to know how completely the confidence is reciprocated. One of the things that makes me hope that this administration is blessed of God is that such a remarkable band of friends and of disinterested public servants should have been gathered together in this little family which we call the cabinet. It is a presage of fine things; and I thank God for such support and such associations.

My daughters join me in all the best wishes of the season to Mrs. Redfield[2] and yourself.

Your sincere friend   Woodrow Wilson

This little machine is my pen.

WWTLS (W. C. Redfield Papers, DLC).
  [1] W. C. Redfield to WW, Dec. 25, 1914, ALS (WP, DLC).
  [2] Elise Mercein Fuller Redfield.


## To Nancy Saunders Toy

Dearest Friend,          The White House 26 December, 1914.

The horn spoon pleases me deeply. I am Scots very deep down in me, and porridge in a horn spoon seems to me like a thing of (minor) religion. I had broken the only one I ever had, and shall rejoice in this one, the more because you thought of it and sent it. And the lines I relish greatly.[1] They are not only of the right flavour themselves, but they speak a lightness of heart in the writer (if only for the nonce) which makes me happy.

I am paying to-day for a holiday yesterday by having a great pile of work to run through; but there is always time to speak to you; and this little note carries from all of us the most affectionate Christmas greetings.

Your sincere friend,   Woodrow Wilson

WWTLS (WP, DLC).
  [1] Mrs. Toy's "lines" (HwMS [WP, DLC]) were as follows:

*Christmas 1914*

Porridge is a goodly thing,
Smacks of Scotland's 'banks and braes'—
Be it added to its praise—
Smacks of health and strengthening.
Yet if gusto we would bring,
We must fetch from 'bonny Doon'
The really, truly, old, bone spoon—
(The only thing to use, on dit).* [pronounced English]
Let your own heart mend my wit.
And here's the end—a timely boon!

  *This *ought* to be ten lines of seven syllables—I *couldn't* make it! N.T.

## To Josephus Daniels

My dear Friend,          The White House 26 December, 1914.

Thank you with all my heart for your letter of Christmas greetings, handed me yesterday. It helped not a little to keep the cloud from descending on me which threatened me all day. And, by my stocking in the morning I found the delightful cake Mrs. Daniels had made for me. You are both of the sort that make life and friendship worth while. It is fine to have a colleague whom one can absolutely trust; how much finer to have one whom one can love! that is a real underpinning for the soul! And when marriage has united two of the same quality one can only wonder and be thankful that Providence has made them his friend.

Affectionately Yours,   Woodrow Wilson

WWTLS (J. Daniels Papers, DLC).

## From William Jennings Bryan, with Enclosure

My dear Mr. President:          Washington December 26, 1914.

I am gratified that you approve of the letters to Bernstorff and the instructions to the British Government. I am enclosing a note from Mr. Lansing calling attention to the importance of making some statement.

I thought when I sent you the answer to the German Embassy that it might be well to make that public but it occurs to me on reflection that there would be one objection to it, namely—that in publishing a protest which we answer the German-Americans might be so impressed by our refusal to agree with the German Embassy on the point presented, as to overlook the admissions made as to the right of belligerents to purchase arms.

I am inclined to think, therefore, it might be better for the statement to be made in a little different way. Now that we have this admission from the German Embassy you might make a statement in an interview, when it is opportune, that "the right of belligerents to purchase arms and ammunition in neutral countries is so well settled that we have had no protest or complaint from any belligerent as to purchases made by any other belligerent in the United States." This would answer the question without mentioning Germany and, at the same time the statement would include Germany, and those desiring to elaborate on the answer could use the statement as a basis for answers to the criticisms made by German-Americans. They could point out that if our country was doing anything unneutral the German

Embassy would call attention to it; the fact that it has not called attention to it being an admission that no just complaint has been made. If you do not think it wise to give out the statement yourself I could do it if you think best for I agree with Mr. Lansing that there ought to be some statement made which could be used as a reply to the criticisms that are directed against us.

With assurances of high respect I am, my dear Mr. President,
                         Yours very sincerely,    W. J. Bryan

TLS (WP, DLC).


E  N  C  L  O  S  U  R  E

## Robert Lansing to William Jennings Bryan

Dear Mr. Secretary:            [Washington] December 26, 1914.

I prepared sometime ago, as you will recall, a memorandum for the President upon a letter written by Professor Munsterberg setting forth in concrete form the complaints of Germany's sympathizers in this country as to the policy and conduct of the Administration in relation to neutral rights and neutral duties. I believe that these complaints are entirely unjustified and can be answered conclusively, and that the memorandum, which I hastily prepared, forms a basis for such answers.

These complaints are still being widely circulated among our people of German birth and descent and are undoubtedly alienating many of them from their political allegiance to the Democratic Party. This hostility is largely the result of false statements as to the course pursued by the Government and of ignorance of the rights and duties of a neutral nation. However unjustified the complaints may be, there can be no doubt of their political effect. Thousands of former friends of the Administration are being converted into bitter adversaries; and this is going on day after day by reason of the propaganda which is being carried on in an apparent effort to force the Government to adopt a policy favorable to Germany regardless of the fact that to do so would be a breach of neutrality.

It seems to me that as a matter of political expediency some steps should be taken to refute the unjust charges which are being made against the Administration and to explain to the public, particularly the pro-German element, the actual situation and what the Government can do and cannot do as a neutral power.

Furthermore, it seems to me that these steps should be taken as soon as possible. The movement has gained much headway, and, like a snow ball rolling down hill, is increasing in size and impetus as it advances. The longer it goes on the more difficult it will be to check it.

I have already spoken to you of this matter in a casual way, but, as I am becoming more and more impressed with the strength of the movement and with the serious political consequences which will follow if nothing is done to interrupt it, I venture to call the matter more definitely to your attention.

Very sincerely yours,   Robert Lansing

TL (WP, DLC).

## From Edward Mandell House, with Enclosures

Dear Governor:            New York City. December 26th, 1914.

I am enclosing you a copy of a letter from Da Gama which I have just received and which I know will please you as much as it has me.

As you know, I had a telephone talk with Naon, but he spoke such broken English and the connection was so bad, that I could not gather the sense of his message. He promised to write, but I have nothing from him yet. I gleaned enough to know that he wanted to have another conference, therefore I told him I would be in Washington early next week.

This is a matter of such far reaching consequence that I feel we should pay more attention to it just now than even the European affair, for the reason that if brought to a successful conclusion, the one must have a decided influence. upon the other.

Then, too, the European situation is not quite ready for us. The best, I think, you can do there, for the moment, is to keep the threads in your hands as now and not push unduly. I feel there is more danger in overdoing than in waiting the opportune time.

I am also enclosing you a copy of a letter I received from Gerard and which you will find interesting. The points that attract my attention most are, the Chancellor's remark that he could not see any peace in sight, that they are sending fifteen year old boys to the front, and that the pinch would probably be felt first in the lack of horses. I have thought from the beginning that this last would be their first serious trouble.

I have a long letter from Page, but he says nothing new.

Affectionately yours,   E. M. House

TLS (WP, DLC).

ENCLOSURE I

## Domicio da Gama to Edward Mandell House

My dear Colonel House:    [Washington] December 24' , 1914.

I have just received the answer from my Minister of Foreign Affairs to the telegram I sent him on Saturday 19th transmitting the two propositions of the President's project of Convention.

The answer was delayed pending further information that I sent on Monday and then consultation with our President who gladly authorizes me to declare that both points of the President's proposal are agreeable, it being understood that only American territories are contemplated in the first of those paragraphs.

I suppose that the sounding having proved favorable, the formal ouverture of the negociations will soon follow. This will be an epoch making negociation.    Yours sincerely,    Gama.

ENCLOSURE II

## Rómulo Sebastian Naón to Edward Mandell House

My dear Mr. House:    Washington, D. C. December 26th, 1914.

I called at the White House on Sunday in an endeavor to see you and talk on the subject which you called to my attention. It was so very difficult to speak with you over the telephone the same day, and I wished to tell you that I would like to know when you would be in Washington again.

We ought to talk a little further on the same matter, but my first impressions are in general confirmed. Hence I would appreciate it very much if you would be kind enough to advise me of the exact day on which you will be here, and how we may be able to meet each other.

With kind regards, I remain,

Very sincerely,    R. S. Naon.

ENCLOSURE III

Berlin, Germany.
No date—Sent by Cong. Metz

* * * I had a long talk with the Chancellor today, who sent for me as he was here a few days from the front. He says he sees no chance of peace now.

Germany is much worked up over America selling munitions of war to France and England. Also over the condition of German prisoners in other countries particularly Russia. The hate here against England is phenominal, actual odes of *hate* are recited in the music halls.

The people are still united and determined and seem to be beating the Russians in spite of the reports from the Allies press. On the French front there is nothing to report. The Reichstag voted another large credit and then adjourned. Only Leibnetz[1] objected and since then his own party has renounced him.

Life seems perfectly normal and provisions are only slightly higher. Women send their only sons of fifteen to fight, and no mourning is worn and it is etiquette to congratulate a family who have lost a son on the battlefield.

The losses to date here are about 4500 officers and 83,000 were killed, about 280 000 wounded and about 100 000 prisoners. Not great by any means out of a possible twelve millions.

The finances are in perfect order and the country can continue the war indefinitely—a war which is taken quite calmly by the people at large.

We still have lots of work. I have been especially engaged in getting cotton and chemicals and dyestuffs out. We have to have cyanide to keep our mines going, and dyestuffs to help endless industries and the Germans know this and want to use it as a club to force us to send cotton and wool in. So they only allow us to have about a month's supply at a time. Also they fear lest we should re-sell to the English.

If the war keeps on the Germans will probably suffer most for lack of horses for guns, as the average life of a horse in war is only about ten days.

My job is made harder by these sales of munitions by U.S.A. to France and England and by the articles and criticisms in American papers, but I still seem O.K. with the Government and the Kaiser has intimated he wants me to visit him at the front.

Copy of part of letter from Ambassador Gerard.

Information of the President.

TCL (WP, DLC).
[1] Karl Liebknecht, leader of the radical element of the Social Democratic party.

## To Mary Allen Hulbert

Dearest Friend,                The White House 27 December, 1914.

Your little note of the twenty-third has touched me very deeply. It unconsciously expresses your character, as I have known and deeply admired it. It shows the stoutness of heart, the gallant spirit in the face of disaster, the thoughtfulness of others, the indomitable courage (in spite of a certain touch of feminine dismay) that quickens my pulses and shows you to me as I have all along divined you to be: so that it actually sent my spirits up. You were *right* to tell me everything, and to tell me at once. You ought not to chide yourself for that for a moment. It was not cruel, as you characterize it, for what would I have thought my friendship worth to you if you had *not* told me? But that you should have thought it selfish on your part and thought more of me than of yourself in looking back upon your first letter is so true an interpretation of yourself that I value this last note of yours as one of the loveliest I ever received.

I must immediately confess what I have done. I know how intensely you want to get to work and *earn* something; and what came into my mind just so soon as the first shock and confusion of the misfortune had left my mind was that it ought to be possible for you to turn your unusual knowledge and taste in interior decoration, in furniture, and in china to profit. The day after I received the news, therefore, I wrote to five friends in Boston, telling them of what I wanted to help you to, if I could, and asking them to advise me where thereabouts to turn to make the try. There ought to be some large general furnishing house or some house in a special line, or even some great department store in which they would welcome such service as you could give better than any professional I have ever known.

I have not heard from any of my friends yet: maybe I shall not hear,—for one never knows *any*body until he puts them to some such test as this; but there has been no time to hear yet, and I am hoping for some kind of a lead. If not there, it must be sought elsewhere. Do you approve, or have I gone too far and too fast without your sanction or permission? I am so anxious to do something. I have thought of little else since you sent me the note. If there is any other line of inquiry or effort that you have thought of, please suggest it to me, and let me see if I cannot find some way to be of service in carrying it out. I have an idea that in some line of work such as I have suggested, where you would feel sure of yourself, you would get a kind of happiness and zest you have never yet had. Am I right, or am I on the wrong tack?

You are meeting the trial very nobly, very beautifully. You are meeting it just as I would have predicted you would. When there is anything to be borne with spirit and fortitude, when there is anything to *rise* to and do, you can be counted on to the limit, as you showed in Bermuda. God help you, help us, to find the way in which you can show your mettle to the utmost and win a new kind of happiness!

Your devoted friend,   Woodrow Wilson

WWTLS (WP, DLC).

## Jean Jules Jusserand to the French Foreign Ministry

Washington, le ? décembre 1914

N. 621 Réponse à votre télégramme 276.   reçu le 27 à 4 h. 50

Dès le premier mot et sans hésitation Président Wilson m'a dit: "Le Président Poincaré a toute liberté pour lire ma lettre à l'Académie et en faire tel usage qui lui paraitra convenable. Elle n'explique qu'à peine la vivacité et la chaleur des sentiments que j'éprouve."

M. Wilson a ajouté qu'il ressentait pour la personne et le caractère de M. le Président, au milieu de la terrible lutte actuelle, autant d'amitié que d'admiration. Il m'a ensuite longuement interrogé sur l'état de notre pays, l'esprit des troupes et du public. Les renseignements satisfaisants que j'ai pu lui donner ont paru lui faire grand plaisir. Je lui ai marqué combien on était touché en France de l'élan généreux avec lequel les américains de toutes classes manifestaient leur bon vouloir aux si nombreuses victimes françaises de la guerre et secouraient nos réfugiés et nos blessés.                    Jusserand

T telegram (Guerre 1914-1918, États-Unis, Vol. 490, FFM-Ar).

T R A N S L A T I O N

Washington, ? December 1914
received the 27th at 4:50

No. 621 In response to your telegram 276.

From the first word and without hesitation, President Wilson said to me: "President Poincaré has full liberty to read my letter to the Academy and to make such use of it as would seem most proper to him. It scarcely conveys the depth and warmth of the sentiments which I feel."

Mr. Wilson added that he felt for the person and the character of the President, in the middle of the present terrible struggle, as much friendship as admiration. For quite a while he interrogated me about the condition of our country, the spirit of our troops and of the people. The satisfying information that I was able to give him seemed to afford him great pleasure. I pointed out to him how much they have been touched in France by the generous spirit with which Americans of all classes have manifested their good will to so many French victims of the war and have helped our refugees and our wounded.   Jusserand

## From Edward Mandell House, with Enclosure

Dear Governor:              New York City. December 27th, 1914.

I am enclosing you a copy of a letter which has just come from Zimmermann.

It again gives us an opening, but just how best to use it, is the question. It should now be easy to test "Maine's["] sincerity in regard to "Jones' "[1] statement as to her willingness to begin parleys.

I shall leave here on the 12.08 Tuesday and will go to Doctor Grayson, being with you in the evening if that is convenient and agreeable.

We should have answers from both Argentine and Chili by then as well as from "New Jersey,"[2] so we can go forward with that work as well.   Affectionately yours,   E. M. House

TLS (WP, DLC).
[1] Wilson and House had prepared a code for confidential exchanges. Maine was Germany; Jones, Bernstorff.
[2] The Allies.

## ENCLOSURE

## Arthur Zimmermann to Edward Mandell House

My dear Colonel:              Berlin, December 3rd, 1914.

Please pardon me for allowing so much time to elapse before answering your letter of September 5th which was besides long delayed in reaching me. I read what you wrote with great interest, but it seems to me that considering the turn events have taken so far and the apparently unabated zeal of our opponents, the question of mediation has not yet reached the stage for action.

When I say "unabated zeal of our opponents" I have in mind

such utterances as appeared for instance in the London Correspondences of the New York Sun of October 9th and the New York Tribune of October 16th announcing that "to no voice of that kind (i.e. mediation) will England, France or Russia now listen."

On the other hand, you are fully aware of the fact that we have greatly appreciated the President's and your own good offices. You may be perfectly sure that the President's offer of mediation was received exactly in the spirit in which it was meant and that it was not for a moment considered an empty one.

Germany has always desired to maintain peace as she proves by a record of more than forty years. The war has been forced upon us by our enemies and they are carrying it on by summoning all the forces at their disposal, including Japanese and other colored races. This makes it impossible for us to take the first step towards making peace. The situation might be different if such overtures came from the other side. I do not know whether your efforts have been extended in that direction and whether they have found a willing ear. But as long as you kindly offer your services in a most unselfish way agreeing to act upon any suggestion that I convey to you, so it seems to me worth while trying to see where the land lies in the other camp.

Needless to say your communications will always be welcome and considered confidential.

When these lines reach you Christmas will not be far distant, so please accept my heartiest wishes for a Merry Christmas and a Happy New Year, and believe me, my dear Colonel,

Sincerely yours,   Zimmermann.

TCL (WP, DLC).


## To Edward Mandell House

The White House Dec 28th 14

Beg you will come here      lots of room and lots of welcome

Woodrow Wilson.

T telegram (E. M. House Papers, CtY).


## From Sir Cecil Arthur Spring Rice

Dear Mr President      Washington. 28 December 1914

In the name of my Sovereign and my government as well as of myself I venture to offer you the very best wishes for the coming year, on the occasion of your birthday. You know the very particular interest which we have throughout Great Britain and the dominions over seas in all that concerns the United States—and nothing concerns them more than their President—and we are very proud to think that their President comes from the same mixed stock as ourselves.

You know that there are great numbers of people who living far off will probably never see you or hear your voice, who yet follow with a personal interest and almost family feeling everything which you say or do. There is no politics in this, but it is a natural feeling which I am sure you will understand.

Begging that you will accept for yourself and your family the expression of our best wishes

I remain with the deepest respect    Dear Mr President
your most obedient humble servant    Cecil Spring Rice

ALS (WP, DLC).

## From Felexiana Shepherd Baker Woodrow

My dear Tommy:                Greensboro, N. C., Dec. 28, 1914.

It has often been in my heart to write you a short note to let you know how intensely interested I am in all that affects you, and how my sympathies are always with you.

For the last few days, however, I have been thinking more especially of the first time I saw you. I was being introduced to the family as the "new Aunt," when you were brought, and I was told "This is Tommy." I looked up and saw a lovely, fair Baby, about seven months old, in a white dress and blue ribbons.

How little I thought then, that I was being introduced to a future President of the United States!

In spite of all your greatness and high position, you have always been "Tommy" to me.

I am not now in the dear old home, so full of the memories of the past, in which your Father and Mother have so large a share with the dear Uncle who watched with such interest and pride your growing development and success.

I am quite sure that no one would rejoice more in your later triumphs than he.

Last year I was very ill, and Lottie and Mr. Clark brought me to their delightful home, where they are watching over me with the most tender, loving care.

And now, at the beginning of a New Year, I pray that our

Heavenly Father's richest blessings may rest upon you. May He guide and direct you in all things. May your life and health be precious in His sight, and may you be kept from all evil.

With love to the girls,

As always, Affectionately, "Aunt Felie."

ALS (WP, DLC).

## From William Eaton Chandler[1]

My dear Mr. President　　　　Washington Decr. 28 1914

On my birth-day and yours I send you my good wishes and my hopes for your prolonged life and health amid all your burdens and trials.

I must confess that it seems to me as if some newspapers (not all) appear to think that you know as much on your 58th birth day as I do on my 79th.

Please tell me if you think this is really so.

Very Truly　Wm. E Chandler

ALS (WP, DLC).

[1] Former Secretary of the Navy (1882-85) and Republican Senator from New Hampshire (1887-1901).

## Remarks at a Press Conference

December 29, 1914

Mr. President, what time did that note of protest go to Great Britain yesterday?

I wasn't informed just when it went. I supposed that it went on Saturday last.

You have had no reply to it?

No, we have had no reply to it. You understand, of course, that each case that has been called to our attention has been the ground for protest also, and the way the thing works out is that if the government concerned is in the wrong, damages have eventually to be paid.

Then this is not the first protest, is it?

No.

Made public?

They were protests of individual cases. If we made public everything we do, you wouldn't have space for anything else.

Is there any question of treaty violation entered into this in any way?

No, it is just a question of the rules of international law.

Does it have any bearing on former protests that we have made in other times; I mean, for example in 1812?

> Oh, no, the protest itself refers to precedents, but not to any former controversy between this government and that.

Is there a possibility of extended correspondence on this subject, Mr. President, or does this protest which we have sent represent fully our final position in the matter?

> It represents fully our position, and really so far as the theory of the position is concerned, there is no debating it, at least in our judgment.

I understand, Mr. President, that in theory—

> It has in former wars, yes. Rather, it would be more correct to say that we have taken our position in former wars.

Mr. President, the note as published this morning[1] contains a sort of threat in it; that is to say, we say, as I read it, that we want England to give us her position so that we might take steps to protect American interests.

> There is nothing of that kind in the note. The text of the note was not published. Diplomatic correspondence isn't conducted that way. . . .

Our position would apply naturally to any neutral country, wouldn't it?

> Yes, it would apply to any neutral country. There is nothing in it peculiar to our view of international law. The great embarrassment to the government in dealing with this whole matter is that some shippers have concealed contraband under cargoes of non-contraband articles, for example, under a cargo of cotton. So long as there are *any* instances of this kind, suspicion is cast upon every shipment and all cargoes are liable to doubt and to search. This government can deal confidently with this subject only if supported by absolutely honest manifests. . . .

Mr. President, can you say anything about whether or not the reports are true that there are strained relations between you and the Senate?

> No; it is quite the contrary. Strained relations seem to afford more public interest than normal relations; that is the only way I can account for the newspaper accounts. There are no strained relations between me and the Senate.

Mr. President, the story says there is danger of your legislative program not getting through at this session?

> You will recall that that has been said about every piece of legislation that has gone through, and it is no more true this time than then.

There was no time limit on the others?

    No, but the time limit acts as a spur.

Have you sent any telegram, Mr. President, about the withdrawing of troops from Colorado?

    No. Governor Ammons and Governor-elect Carlson were here the other day, and they had a conference with the Secretary of War about that and I suppose laid out a general plan.

They told us that they would begin withdrawing the troops as soon as the Governor got back to Colorado; and he got back Sunday.

    Did he? I dare say that they have started to carry out their plan then. Our only object is to keep them there as long as they need them.

Anything new from Mexico, Mr. President?

    Nothing at all.

I noticed in one of the morning papers a statement that this government had requested a general amnesty down there.

    We did advise it, yes, sir.

Well, does it seem to be pretty well established that there are to be no callous executions?

    I haven't noticed any great callousness. I don't think there has been a large number of executions. Many of the executions are strictly private, and so I don't know.

Mr. President, it has been said that the administration is behind the move in the Senate to sidetrack the immigration bill; is that true?

    No, sir, I am not engaged in any Machiavellian schemes. It is true this far: It is well known that there is one provision in the bill which I am opposed to.

JRT transcript (WC, NjP) of CLSsh (C. L. Swem. Coll., NjP).
  [1] About the premature publication of the note, see the House diary, entry for Dec. 29, 1914.

## To William Jennings Bryan

My dear Mr. Secretary:     The White House December 29, 1914

    I have your letter of December twenty-sixth enclosing the letter from Mr. Lansing, which I herewith return.

    I hope you will exercise your own judgment entirely as to the method and subject matter of publicity in regard to the German protest and our reply. I agree with you that the essential matter is to get before the public the admission of the German Government with regard to the sale of munitions of war.[1]

    Cordially and faithfully yours,   Woodrow Wilson

TLS (SDR, RG 59, 763.72111/1335½, DNA).
    [1] For further discussion of and the decision reached on this matter, see RL to WJB, Jan. 1, 1915, and WW to W. J. Stone, Jan. 7, 1915.


## To William Jennings Bryan, with Enclosures

My dear Mr. Secretary:    The White House December 29, 1914
    I return the enclosed letter merely as a brief way of refer-ring to it and in order to express my entire agreement with the judgment which it embodies.
        Cordially and faithfully yours,   Woodrow Wilson

TLS (SDR, RG 59, 793.94/218½, DNA).


E N C L O S U R E      I

## From William Jennings Bryan

Dear Mr. President:          Washington December 26, 1914.
    I enclose a paraphrase of a telegram which we have received from Peking. Mr. Williams, who was for twenty-five years in China, and is now head of our Far-Eastern Bureau, thought we ought to bring the matter to the attention of the British Govern-ment in the hope it's influence might be used to prevent the change which Japan contemplates.
    I have talked the matter over with Mr. Lansing and am in-clined to think it would not be wise for us to bring this matter to the attention of the British Government at this time for the rea-son that Ambassador Guthrie reports there is a great deal of feeling in Japan due to the belief there that we are opposing Japan's course in China. If Japan asked our advice I think we would be justified in pointing out the natural and necessary consequences of such a change, namely, that it will irritate China and create a feeling that ought not to exist between neighbor-ing nations. But under present conditions volunteer advice of this kind would not, I think, be acceptable and if we brought the matter to the attention of the British Government our action might cause irritation.
    I submit, therefore, for your approval or disapproval the sug-gestion that we telegraph to our Minister in China, saying that we are glad to be informed as to this but do not feel that we should, at this time, take up the matter with the British Gov-ernment, suggesting that the Chinese Government could ap-proach the British Government through their Minister there, in

case they desire to avail themselves of Great Britain's influence with Japan.

With assurances of high respect I am, My dear Mr. President, Yours Very Sincerely, W. J. Bryan

TLS (SDR, RG 59, 793.94/218½, DNA).

ENCLOSURE II

PARAPHRASE.

December 26, 1914.

The American Minister at Peking telegraphed the Department of State under date of December 23, 1914, stating that the appointment to Tsingtau Customs of forty nine officials taken from the Japanese Customs Administration has now been demanded by the Japanese. The Minister also states that the treaty powers would be affected by such action which would break up the organization of Maritime Customs Service.

T MS (SDR, RG 59, 793.94/218½, DNA).

## To William Jennings Bryan

My dear Mr. Secretary: The White House December 29, 1914

I have so often discussed the subject matter of Senator Shafroth's speech on the leasing system for the public domain with Senator Shafroth himself that I find I am familiar with the things that he says in the speech you were kind enough to send me, but I do not find myself at all convinced by them. The facts are assembled altogether from the point of view of those who wish the Federal Government in effect to turn over these great properties to the states themselves, and my conviction is that that would be a very difficult step to justify in any circumstances.

Senator Shafroth is sincere and impressive, but I must admit he has not convinced me.

Cordially and faithfully yours, Woodrow Wilson

TLS (W. J. Bryan Papers, DNA).

## To Lindley Miller Garrison

My dear Mr. Secretary: [The White House] December 29, 1914

Yes, so far as I can see, there is no serious objection to following out the plan of withdrawing the troops suggested by Governor

Ammons, and it was at my request that he saw you. I think that there will be the greatest safety and the least difficulty in following out his suggestions.

Cordially and faithfully yours,    Woodrow Wilson

TLS (Letterpress Books, WP, DLC).

## From Seth Low

*Confidential*

Dear Mr. President:                    New York Dec. 29. 1914.

I have had two conferences with Mr. John D. Rockefeller, Jr., which have been altogether satisfactory. He asks me to say to you that he will coöperate to the utmost with your Commission in bringing about a good result. He thinks, naturally, that the technical details must be settled in Colorado; but I am sure that he is personally in sympathy with what we want to do, and that we shall have his help in every proper way.

Our Commission has decided not to go to Colorado, just yet; but we are quietly at work paving the way.

Very respectfully and sincerely,    yours,    Seth Low.

ALS (WP, DLC).

## From the Diary of Colonel House

The White House, Washington, D. C. December 29, '14.

I took the 12.08 train down as usual. Davies met me at Baltimore and we went over in detail the personel of the Trades Commission. It is a difficult proposition to find the right men who will accept the position.

Dr. Grayson was at the station and we went immediately to the White House. A number of the family who had lingered over the holidays were still there. The President and I went into his study and had a conference for the half hour or more before dinner.

We agreed upon a plan of action concerning the South American adventure, and one in the European peace proposals. I arranged to meet Naon at 8.30 and Spring-Rice at 9.15. This left me but little time after dinner, and I went almost immediately to the home of the Argentine Ambassador. He endeavored to translate into understandable English the despatch which his Government had sent him in answer to this Government's proposals. The translation follows:

"The Government receives with simpathy the proposition

with the understanding that such a proposition tends to transform the one side character of the Monroe Doctrine into a common policy of all the American countries."

The despatch also asked for more information upon the second article of the Convention in regard to government ownership of munitions of war. Naon said he had sent four pages of cable concerning the first proposal and had merely mentioned the second, and that was the reason they were calling for additional information.

I explained the reason for government ownership of munitions of war was to prevent manufacturers from inflaming popular sentiment and influencing governments to maintain excessive armaments. Also because if the governments own armament factories, the question of the shipment to belligerent nations of munitions of war would be settled.

Naon was very enthusiastic over the entire proposal and said "it will not only insure the re-election of your President, but it will be such a great accomplishment that there will be nothing he can ever do afterward that can approach it in importance."

He thought Chile would hesitate to come in because she had dreams of expansion. He had talked with the Chilean Ambassador since I was in Washington and had not received much encouragement. I told him that the United States would not favor the acquisition of territory by the other Republics, either by war or otherwise, and that Chile might as well accept that condition in a formal convention. He replied that Argentine held the same view, and would not willingly permit territorial aggrandizement in South America.

I went from Naon to the home of Billy Phillips to meet the British Ambassador. I found him nervous and excited because of the premature publication, and a garbled account of the protest made by the President to the British Government concerning the holding up of neutral vessels. He did not mind the note, for he and I had already threshed that out and settled it long before it was sent. He had even received a reply from Sir Edward Grey indicating that the President's request would be granted. The note was merely a formal matter of routine after the real issue had been met, but what he objected to was the way in which it had been given publicity and the manner in which our press had treated it.

The President had talked with me about this before dinner, and had told me the leak had occurred in the State Department, though Mr. Bryan thought it had occurred through Tumulty. I asked the President if Tumulty knew anything about it. He replied that the other day Tumulty had stated we were being criticised by the pro-Germans for not taking a firm stand against Great Britain regarding to these contraband seizures, and that he, the President, had then told him of this note, but not mentioning its contents, therefore, Tumulty could not have given it out.

I asked what newspaper man got it and he said, David Lawrence of the Associated Press. That settled it in my mind that Tumulty had given it out, although I did not express this view to the President for he is so averse to believing anything derogatory to Tumulty, and I did not wish to disturb him.

I tried to explain to Spring-Rice how badly the President felt. He accept[ed] that part, but blamed the State Department most unreservedly, and said it was impossible to conduct diplomatic negotiations of a delicate nature through the newspapers. He claimed that it was not the first time, and that he hesitated to take up further matters with them, in fact he intended to absent himself from the Department in future. He had no doubt we would all be pro-Germans within six months, that the Germans were strong and had a thorough organization, and they would finally break down any anti-German sentiment which now existed.

I discussed peace overtures with him, although I knew the time was not opportune for such a subject, but I got nowhere. He began a tirade against the Germans which included Bernstorff and the German official family generally. He said if we would guarantee a permanent settlement, they would begin negotiations at once, but they would not accept anything Germany might propose. He talked so many different ways, in almost the same sentence, that I concluded he was too upset for me to have any profitable discussion with him and I therefore took my leave. He saw by my silence that I was not pleased with his conversation.

As a matter of fact, if I could properly get at Sir Edward Grey's ear I would advise him to replace Spring-Rice with a man of more robust health and a more equable temperament. In the work I did last year to bring Great Britain and the United States closer together, it was largely through Sir William Tyrrell that it was made possible.

When I returned to the White House and reported the substance of my two interviews, the President was p[l]eased with the one and disappointed with the other. He said "we had better give Spring-Rice ten days or two weeks to simmer down," and in the meantime he would undertake to see that there was no further leakage in the State Department.

He suggested that affairs of this nature would have to be conducted between himself, Mr. Bryan and Mr. Lansing alone, and not even a stenographer should be brought in. I disagreed with this, and thought there would be no danger in bringing in a private stenographer of either Mr. Bryan or Mr. Lansing, provided he would have the documents sent directly over to the White House proper, and not allow them to pass through the White House Office. I said this would be a protection to Tumulty because they could not accuse him then of telling something about which he knew nothing. He agreed to this method of procedure in the future.

We then discussed the best means of buttoning up the South American proposition, and it was agreed that he should see Senator Stone immediately upon his return, and we again discussed whether it would be advisable to bring the matter before the entire Senate Committee on Foreign Relations, or before the democratic members of it. He would not discuss anything of importance with Senator Alden Smith of Michigan for the reason that he immediately gave it to the press. That, in this instance, it was necessary to have the matter presented to the country properly when they first heard it, and not get a garbled or distorted account from a political opponent.

I told him Naon desired to know whether it was out [our] purpose to make twenty-one different treaties or a single convention. I had replied that it was the intention to make a single convention, which the President thought was right. Naon suggested, I told him, that the A.B.C. Powers and ourselves should first thresh out the terms to a satisfactory conclusion before bringing in the smaller republics. This, too, the President agreed to.

## To William Eaton Chandler

My dear Senator:                [The White House] December 30, 1914
Thank you very warmly for your gracious letter written on my birthday.

As for my own feelings, I can assure you that I do not feel as I should like to feel, that my wisdom grows with my years. I think that anyone who finds himself in my present situation, face to face with so many questions of capital importance, must, if he has any sense at all, grow more humble every day and less sure that he "knows the whole thing."

With best wishes and sincere appreciation,
        Cordially and sincerely yours,    Woodrow Wilson

TLS (Letterpress Books, WP, DLC).

From the Diary of Colonel House

December 30, 1914.

We had breakfast as usual at eight. The President and I talked a few minutes afterward and laid out the business that I should attend to. I made an engagement with the Chilean Ambassador for eleven o'clock.

I found he had not heard from his Government. He gave a change of ministry as the reason and was sure he would receive a favorable reply. I could not see how he could fail to do so. This was not really in accordance with Naon's statement to me, but I found Naon wrong in the first estimate of the manner in which Brazil and Chile would receive the proposals.

I saw Franklin Lane and discussed the Trades Commission appointments with him and also some matters concerning political procedure. He said he had proposed, and the President had agreed, to do away with the formal Cabinet meetings on Fridays, and substitute in lieu thereof an informal Cabinet meeting at the White House proper on Friday evenings, when political questions should be discussed. This is in line with my endeavours of last week to coordinate action between the President's immediate entourage and Congress.

Upon my departure I found J. P. Morgan waiting to see Lane.

I went from Lane to Gregory. We had a general talk about the New York situation, and he told me what he and Frank Polk had done the day before. From there I went to see Hugh Wallace to find whether he had any further information from Bernstorff. The German Ambassador has been away since I was last in Washington, and was still absent in the Adirondacks. Wallace still believes the Germans "are open, candid, and trustworthy, and that the British act with much duplicity toward me." I did not argue the matter with him.

At lunch the President and I had no opportunity to discuss matters, but just after lunch, I told him of my morning adventures and what the Chilean Ambassador had to say. We spoke of the Trades Commission personel for a few minutes, and I gave him some data I had gathered from different sources.

I called up Phillips at the State Department and told him I was sorry Mr. Bryan was out of town, because I desired to suggest to him that he sooth the ruffled feelings of the British Ambassador. I asked Phillips to take part in this laudable endeavor. I said my trip to Washington had been largely nullified by the premature publication of the President's protest to the British Government and I hoped they would get the Ambassador in a normal frame of mind before I returned, for he blamed the State

Department for the leak. Phillips said they had found exactly where the leak was, that it was not in the State Department, and indicated as nearly as he could over the telephone that it was Tumulty, a fact which I already knew as well as I could know anything that had not happened under my own eyes.

## From Edward Mandell House, with Enclosure

Dear Governor:          New York City. December 31st, 1914.

I am enclosing you a copy of a letter which I have just received from Brown.[1]

You will notice that he has gotten in a good humor again. The last thing I did, before leaving Washington, was to ask Billy Phillips to get on the job of smoothing him down. His efforts and the polite tenor of your note to his government, evidently did the work.

I had a delightful hour with John R. Mott today. He impressed me as being both sensible and powerful. There were two things that I got from him of value. One was that he believes the Germans are pretty well permeated with the philosophy of Treitschke. The other is that because of this he does not believe the war can be profitably ended for the good of mankind until it has been fought out more nearly to a finish.

                    Affectionately yours,   E. M. House

Thank you and dear Margaret for your never ending hospitality to me.

TLS (WP, DLC).
[1] Spring Rice.

### E N C L O S U R E

"Brown's" letter—It came just this way.

I have just received copy of the note that is the telegram to Page and it seems to me a very fair, just and courteous and firm presentment of the case to which no objection whatever could be raised on the ground of its form. I am sure it will create a very lasting impression and will remain on the records as an honorable effort to solve, in an amicable manner, the question at issue.

T MS (WP, DLC).

## To Arthur W. Tedcastle

My dear Tedcastle,        The White House 31 December, 1914.

I thank you with all my heart for your letter.[1] It was characteristic of Mrs. Tedcastle and you to respond so immediately and so generously to my suggestion about Mrs. Hulbert. You are proposing to do much more than I asked or expected, and I am correspondingly grateful.

It would be fine if either or both of you *would* call on Mrs. Hulbert, as you suggest; and I hope that you will feel at liberty to use my name as her friend, and as ready to vouch for what I have written you about her. She has unusual ability and extraordinary energy, and more tact and facility in dealing with all sorts of persons than any other person I ever knew.

This is just a line of answer to your letter and of gratitude. You are doing just what I would try to do were I there.

With warmest regards to you both,

Faithfully Yours,    Woodrow Wilson

WWTLS (WP, DLC).
[1] A. W. Tedcastle to WW, Dec. 27, 1914, ALS (WP, DLC).

## Furnifold McLendel Simmons to Joseph Patrick Tumulty

PERSONAL

My dear Mr. Tumulty:        [Washington] December 31st, 1914.

The Committee on Commerce at its session this morning voted to send the Seamen's Bill to conference.

Senator Fletcher is the Acting Chairman of the Committee and will appoint the Senate Conferees and will himself be Chairman of the Senate Conference Committee.

Without regard to my personal views as to the wisdom of legislation to better the condition of American Seamen, I am strongly of the opinion that the passage of this bill at this time will be full of embarrassment, not only to our relations with foreign governments but also to the programme of the Administration looking to the rehabilitation of our merchant marine. I am writing this to suggest that you call the matter to the attention of the President with the suggestion that he send for Senator Fletcher at the earliest convenient opportunity and discuss this bill with him. The Senator is right much in favor of the bill but he is also in favor of other legislation that to my mind would be embarrassed by the passage at this time of this measure. I feel that this legislation might very well, in conditions we now have, be held, temporarily at least, in abeyance.

Very truly yours,    F M Simmons[1]

TLS (WP, DLC).

[1] Attached to this letter is the following handwritten note: "Dear T. Please tell Senator Simmons that I have seen Senator Fletcher as he requests in this note. W.W."

# ADDENDA

## From Jessie Woodrow Wilson Sayre

[Williamstown, Mass.,
Dearest, dearest, Father,                               c. Sept. 10, 1914]

We have arrived safely in Williamstown, and as our coming galvinized the workmen into something more like life we have every prospect of really getting in soon. The papering will be finished today.

I spoke to Margaret about what you and I were speaking of and she said that though of course she had thought of it she had considered it as the problem of another person, because the possibility of falling in love seemed so remote that she would not consider it as really affecting herself. She *certainly* isn't any where near in love now. "Music," she said, "is my husband." Like me, she thinks you too wonderful and thoughtful for words, and how we love you for it! If she does fall in love your wishes would mean every thing to her, but I could not get her to seriously consider such a possibility.

Frank talked with Dr. Grayson about Cousin Helen. The Doctor had spoken quite frankly about her to Frank once before, and Frank felt very confident from what he said this time that he had *no doubt* about Cousin Helen's getting entirely well in time. I *hope* this is the truth.

Give my love to the dear little cousin, and for yourself a whole overflowing heartful from your devoted

Daughter    Jessie.

ALS (WP, DLC).


## From Edward Keating

Sir :                               Washington, D. C., Sept. 19, 1914.

I am taking the liberty of enclosing you marked copies of two Colorado papers. The articles I have indicated are significant as showing the reception given your "tentative proposition for the settlement of the Colorado coal strike" by the coal mine-owners and the striking coal miners.

The Pueblo Chieftain is the recognized organ of the coal mine-owners of Colorado. From the moment your proposal was given to the public, the paper has been printing inspired but anonymous articles calculated to discredit the plan. The one I have marked is typical, but by no means the most vicious.[1]

The Denver Express is as friendly to the miners as the Pueblo Chieftain is to the coal mine-owners. It is in close touch with the leaders of the strikers organization, and it has consistently urged the acceptance of your proposition.[2]

In this connection, permit me to particularly call your attention to the remarks of "Mother" Jones as reported in the Express.

I submit these papers to you for your information. If you desire to pursue the subject further, files of the Pueblo Chieftain—the mine-owners' organ—may be obtained from the Library of Congress.

My advices from Colorado clearly indicate that the vast majority of our citizens earnestly approve your proposition. Our state needs industrial peace, and you have submitted the only workable plan so far proposed.

With best wishes, I remain

Yours sincerely,    Edward Keating

TLS (WP, DLC).

[1] An undated clipping from the *Pueblo Chieftain* with the dateline "Denver, Sept. 15." This report said that, when the operators met next Saturday to consider Wilson's proposal, they would probably appoint a committee to wait on the President and tell him their side of the strike story. They would take the position that the Secretary of Labor and other officials of the Department of Labor had failed to confer with them and had listened only to labor's side of the story. The operators, the story went on, would ask the President "in all fairness to either hear their side or to appoint some one who will at least call on them and get their side."

[2] An undated clipping from the *Denver Express* bearing the dateline "Trinidad, Colo., Sept. 15." This was a news report about a meeting in Trinidad of 125 delegates and officers of the United Mine Workers of America to consider Wilson's three-year "truce" plan for industrial peace in Colorado. The headline of this report highlighted the arrest of John R. Lawson, one of the strike leaders, for the alleged murder of twelve persons. It also quoted "Mother" Jones as follows:

"One year ago today I told you boys it was necessary to strike to obtain your rights under Colorado laws and free yourself from industrial oppression. None could have fought the battle for liberty more bravely.     .

"Industrial oppression must die. The time has come when to accomplish those results, the sword must disappear. The pen must take its place. We must read, study, think. We are the bulwark of the nation. We have it within our power to rid this country of industrial tyranny, but we must be calm and deliberate to do so.

"We have in Washington today another Lincoln. He does not rush into things haphazardly. He has submitted you this proposition for a truce after long and calm deliberation. We must consider it in the same manner it was prepared, not with any great rush, but carefully weighing every point and every interpretation."

# From Elias Milton Ammons

*Denver*

Sir:    SEPTEMBER TWENTY-EIGHT NINETEEN FOURTEEN.

After considerable unavoidable delay I am at last able to write you more definitely concerning the Colorado situation. In a general way Senator Thomas will probably be better able to explain when he sees you more fully than I can write.

I have now so far completed arrangements that the state can, by the time the Federal Troops are removed—presuming they will be taken out gradually—take charge of the situation. The change, however, should be made with great care and I seriously doubt if the last of the men should be removed before the middle of November and until after the result of the election is known. There are some localities from which the troops might be taken sooner. I doubt if they will be needed in Routt County for so long a time and in both the no[r]thern field and Fremont County they might be removed sooner. The two districts in which they should be left last would be Huerfano and Las Animas counties.

We have available about six hundred men in the National Guard. By the middle of November this number could be increased to one thousand. The unjust criticism and even abuse heaped upon the men of the National Guard during the past trouble has created a feeling of bitterness among the men that is hard to overcome. Many of them upon returning to their homes were unable to secure employment and while still members of our Guard are widely scattered, some of them beyond the boundaries of the state. In the estimate of six hundred men available I do not include the organizations in the strike districts. These, of course, would not be called out on this duty except in cases of extreme emergency.

The information I get from the more troubled districts indicates a very threatening attitude. A priest who has just spent some considerable time among them informs me they are threatening to fight it out as soon as the Federal Troops go and declare they will in addition to what they have in the state bring in enough from the outside to arm ten thousand men for the purpose of destroying property, and shooting those who have been opposed to them. I do not believe they will attempt to carry out this threat but I most earnestly urge that your Excellency warn any of them against invading the state. I am led to believe that most of the guns to be used, if another outbreak shall occur, are already hidden in the strike districts. I have most reliable information that both guns and ammunition have constantly been shipped in and that not less than thirty-five hundred to four thousand guns are now hidden in the southern district and ready for use when wanted.

When the Federal Troops are removed there should be the fullest understanding with the local authorities in order that ample provision might be made to prefent unexpected outbreaks by small bands of lawless men intent upon revenge by burning property or shooting mine employes. It has been my purpose to put mounted police forces under the organization of the Guard in the counties of Huerfano and Las Animas, issue a proclamation under the new law against carrying and using arms and to do my utmost to see that no lawless efforts of considerable size are organized. It will be necessary to take unusual precautions because the operators have given up their guns while the strikers have not.

Of course, if the truce should be accepted either in its present or modified form by both sides to the controversy the local authorities would probably be able to control the situation.

If the suggestion which I make can be carried out you will not need to make preparations for winter and can, therefore, save that expense. We rarely ever have any severe weather until near December 1st.

I shall be glad to have any suggestions you may wish to make.

In closing, Mr. President, I want most earnestly to assure you of the gratitude of our people for your timely assistance in this most unfortunate affair and that personally I appreciate it more than I can express in words.

Yours sincerely,   E M Ammons

TLS (WP, DLC).

## An Appeal

[Nov. 14, 1914]

The present distress of the people of Belgium, their immediate need for food and clothing and shelter, has excited the deepest sympathy throughout the United States. Many committees have been formed to collect money and supplies for their relief, and there is pressing need for their action if the relief is in any measure to suffice; for in spite of munificent liberality in many quarters, only a tithe of the necessary means has been supplied. But great confusion has arisen for lack of cooperation,—lack of coordination of effort on this side the water not only, but between the committees here and the committees formed for the same purpose in Europe. Because of these circumstances, I have been appealed to by representatives of many of the American committees to suggest some means of effective cooperation. I am, of course, glad to be of service in such a matter and feel free to act because I have been assured by the representatives of the German and Austrian Governments that such efforts to succor the suffering in Belgium are viewed with entire acquiescence and approval by the governments which they represent.

I, therefore, take the liberty of suggesting and urging that all committees in this country and all individuals who wish to be of service in this appealing benevolence put themselves in communication with Mr. Hugh C. Wallace, 1800 Massachusetts Avenue, Washington, D. C., who has kindly consented, at my request, to undertake to act as the common agent of all in effecting the quickest and most efficient cooperation, supplying information as to what is most needed, and making the arrangements for the shipment of supplies and the rapid remittance of moneys. He is generously willing to act as the representative of all parties and their agent in every matter common to them all.[1]

T MS (C. L. Swem Coll., NjP).
[1] This appeal was not given to the press. See WW to EMH, Dec. 1, 1914.

## From Charlotte Everett Wise Hopkins

My dear Mr. President.          [Washington] November 4th, 1914.

I have written the enclosed[1] to be published in the Bulletin, the official organ of the Women's Dept of the National Civic Federation.

I shall be gratified if you will look over it & if anything in it does not please you I will gladly omit or change it.

I am to send it to the New York office as soon as you return it to me.

May I also ask your approval my [of] my appeal to the Women of the country for the model block of houses here—in loving memory of all your dear wife did?[2]

The appeal will be made through the Associated Press & the publications of all Women organizations, & from the interest I hear expressed on all sides I hope it will meet with prompt & great success.

Believe me, Very Sincerely Yours

Charlotte Everett Hopkins

ALS (WP, DLC).
[1] It is missing; the Editors have been unable to find it in published form.
[2] Mrs. Hopkins was organizing a movement to build a model block of sanitary homes in Washington to be called the Ellen Wilson Memorial Block. *New York Times*, Oct. 14, 1914. About the fate of this project, see Charlotte E. W. Hopkins to WW, June 21, 1915, n. 6.

## To Charlotte Everett Wise Hopkins

My dear Mrs. Hopkins: [The White House] November 10, 1914

I owe you an apology for not having replied sooner to your note of November fourth and returning the enclosed interesting manuscript.

I see nothing in the manuscript to change and want to say to you how very much touched I have been by your appreciation of the incomparable lady about whom it is written.

You certainly have my approval for the suggestion you make in the latter part of it. It would indeed be very gratifying to me to have such a block of buildings devoted to such a use bear her name. Cordially and sincerely yours, Woodrow Wilson

TLS (Letterpress Books, WP, DLC).


## A Speech Accepting a Statue of Philip Kearny[1]

[Nov. 11, 1914]

Mr. Chairman, Governor Fielder, ladies and gentlemen: It is with a sort of sober pleasure that I find myself here today. It was my privilege as Governor of New Jersey to assemble the group of men who have so admirably discharged the duty imposed upon them of preparing a fitting memorial statue of General Phil Kearny. I feel that it was a privilege to play some part in accomplishing this result.

I, of course, never knew General Kearny. But every story I have heard told about him makes me realize the charm and the power which the man exercised. There is no charming human being who does not make his fellow man feel the touch of comradeship and sympathy. I take it that General Phil Kearny at once made you feel that he was a likeable and trustworthy man, to begin with; and that his power consisted in the performance of his duty in such fashion that he knew that, if you were in his position, you would perform the duty in the same way. Soldiers do not resent severity if that severity wears the handsome garb of duty. A good disciplinarian is not hateful if he be an admirable man. And I take it that these qualities were combined in Phil Kearny.

It is always a good sign if a man's comrades abbreviate his first name. There is almost the touch of the hand in the mere familiarity of the designation. If soldiers speak of their chief as "Phil," you may know that they feel that he is of the same stuff that they are, and that he feels that in his own heart, and moves amongst them as one of themselves. I have always been sorry that I did not myself bear a first name that easily yielded to that process. I would rather be of bronze[2] than of wood. And yet I know that the quality of this man is constantly revealed in all other things that are known about him.

There is nothing noble or admirable in war itself. But there is something very noble and admirable occasionally in the causes for which war is undertaken. And there is something very noble and admirable in some of the characters which war develops. For if a man's character can go through the fire and come out resplendent, then you know that it is of the true quality, of the best human stuff. This is a character that was evidently tested by fire. It apparently coveted the test of fire. There was no need that Kearny should fight in the French army,[3] but when there was sacrifice at hand, and gallantry to be indulged in, he wanted to be in the game.

I take it that he had nothing against the Algerians. I take it that he had nothing against the Italians.[4] I take it, for that matter, that he had nothing against the Mexicans.[5] But when there was this challenge to a spirit that felt the zest of that kind of service, he could not resist the challenge.

And so I feel a touch of pride that this man should have been identified with New Jersey. New Jersey is not a big state, but it is filled as full of the heroic qualities of human nature as its territory will permit. Every inch of it counts. And I like to think that it recognized the quality of this man and took hold of him and said this is the kind of stuff we need to lead the First New Jersey Brigade.

Governor Fielder has told you how prompt or completely premature the Jerseymen were in arriving at the field of action. It was the promptness, the directness, the gallant thrust of this man that tied his comrades to him, even when he set a pace which they perhaps with reluctance followed. It is very awkward to have a commander that enjoys the front position, but after the fight is over you have a solid satisfaction, if you are in a condition to enjoy satisfaction, that you stood alongside of so gallant a figure and shared in so notable a service.

In accepting this statue for the Government of the United States, perhaps I may express for all of you our pride that there have been so many gifts, speaking of such qualities, for the Government of the United States to accept. Much as we admire General Phil Kearny, unstinting as our praise of him is, and should be, there has been many another man who has stood alongside of him with the same qualities and the same distinction of service.

This is not a single or isolated or singular gift to the Government of the United States. The government of a great people can always count upon great services, and the beauty of our government, the pride that we all feel in it, is that it is a government of a great people prodigal in their gift of services, always ready to provide those things which constitute the stuff of heroism and elevate a nation in the annals of mankind.

JRT transcript of CLSsh (C. L. Swem Coll., NjP).

1 The remains of General Philip Kearny (1814-62) had been moved in 1912 from Trinity Churchyard in New York to Arlington National Cemetery. Meanwhile, the State of New Jersey had commissioned an equestrian statue of him. A delegation from New Jersey, headed by Governor James Fairman Fielder and Colonel Charles F. Hopkins, chairman of the New Jersey Kearny Commission, had come to the cemetery for unveiling and dedicatory ceremonies. (Their special train carrying 300 Civil War veterans from New Jersey was late, and Wilson waited in the cold for more than an hour. He spent the time looking at the graves.) Fielder unveiled the statue (none of the news accounts mentions the sculptor) while a field battery from Fort Myer fired a major general's seventeen-gun salute. The Governor, in a moving speech, presented the statue to Wilson as the representative of the United States government.

2 A reference to the bronze statue.

3 The Secretary of War in 1840 sent Kearny to observe French cavalry tactics in the third and last French campaign in Algeria. Kearny not only observed but also fought under the Duke of Orleans with the Chasseurs d'Afrique. King Louis-Philippe awarded him the Cross of the Legion of Honor.

4 Kearny returned to France in 1859, served again in the French army in Louis-Napoléon's war against Piedmont, and again won the Cross of the Legion of Honor.

5 Kearny was commander of General Winfield Scott's bodyguard in the march to Mexico City.

## Cary Travers Grayson to Edith Bolling Galt[1]

My dear Mrs Galt,          The White House   25 August 1914.

You are truly a real friend. It was more than good of you to write me when you did. Your letter came just at the "psychological moment"—for I was feeling lonesome and all the other things that go with it; and every word of your kind letter did me good.

While I miss you much, I am doubly glad that you are away from Washington; first, because you are with Miss Gordon,[2] and, secondly, to escape the dreadful heat and humidity which has been so trying and persistent for the past ten days, or, so.

I had hoped to get a breath of the Northern Zephyrs, so to speak, at this time, and a glimpse of Miss Gordon and you, but unavoidable conditions prevented. I had succeeded in persuading the President to go away for three or four days—and to go [to] Prides Crossing, Massachusetts with Col. House. Japan misbehaved, and the President deemed it wise to remain here and handle the case himself. All's going well, so far, I am happy to relate. It would be a terrible thing for the United States to get into war at this awful time.

This is is [*sic*] a very trying and hard time with the President. So many complications to deal with both international and at home: He is now feeling the loss of dear Mrs. Wilson keener than ever. For several days he has not been well. I persuaded him yesterday to remain in bed during the forenoon. When I went in to see him, tears were streaming down his face. It was a heart breaking scene. A sadder picture, no one could imagine. A great man with his heart torn out.

Well, I hope the automobile trip was a success. I sent Miss Gordon a night letter but it was returned.

Where are you two going? Please let me know. While I cannot make any plans just now—but I am going to make a sudden and quick move the moment an opportunity presents itself to get away from Washington. The outlook is poor, but not hopeless. I am going to try to get the President away this week end. Unfortunately, I could not hold Dr Axson here. The President wanted him to be with the other members of the family at Cornish, N. H. Had he remained here I was planning to go away for a week, or, more. . . .

As ever, Your Sincere friend, Cary T. Grayson

ALS (EBW Papers, DLC).

[1] Identified in Edith B. Galt to Annie S. L. Bolling, March 23, 1915.

[2] Alice Gertrude Gordon of New York, close friend of Mrs. Galt's. Grayson was courting her at this time.

# INDEX

## NOTE ON THE INDEX

THE alphabetically arranged analytical table of contents at the front of the volume eliminates duplication, in both contents and index, of references to certain documents, such as letters. Letters are listed in the contents alphabetically by name, and chronologically within each name by page. The subject matter of all letters is, of course, indexed. The Editorial Notes and Wilson's writings are listed in the contents chronologically by page. In addition, the subject matter of both categories is indexed. The index covers all references to books and articles mentioned in text or notes. Footnotes are indexed. Page references to footnotes which place a comma between the page number and "n" cite both text and footnote, thus: "624,n3." On the other hand, absence of the comma indicates reference to the footnote only, thus: "55n2"—the page number denoting where the footnote appears.

We have ceased the practice of indicating first and fullest identification of persons and subjects in earlier volumes by index references accompanied by asterisks. Volume 13, the cumulative index-contents volume is already in print. Volume 26, which will cover Volumes 14-25, will appear in the near future.

The index supplies the fullest known form of names and, for the Wilson and Axson families, relationships as far down as cousins. Persons referred to by nicknames or shortened forms of names can be identified by reference to entries for these forms of the names.

All entries consisting of page numbers only and which refer to concepts, issues, and opinions (such as democracy, the tariff, the money trust, leadership, and labor problems), are references to Wilson speeches and writings. Page references that follow the symbol Δ in such entries refer to the opinions and comments of others who are identified.

# INDEX

## WOODROW WILSON

talk of second term, 23, 59, 94, 101, 290, 301; compares situation of Madison in 1812 with his own, 109, 118; disturbed over Republican victories, 264, 265; typing, 270; and Trotter affair, 305-306, 309n2, 311-12, 328,n2,3; photographs, *illustration section*

### APPEARANCE

Blythe on, 392

### APPOINTMENTS

507-508; to Federal Trade Commission, 269, 353,n1,2,3, 524,n4, 531, 548; to Interstate Commerce Commission, 269, 356; New York, 274-75; ambassador to France, 283; against appointing relatives, 377; finds patronage most disagreeable aspect of presidency, 399-401; and diplomatic and consular service bill, 448-49,n1; and Senate's rejection of WW's choices, 481-82, 490, 498, 507, 524; *see also* patronage

### CABINET

283, 319, 350; and shipping bill, 101; possibility of Bryan leaving, 384-85; WW's opinion of, 532; informal Friday evening meetings, 552

### FAMILY AND PERSONAL LIFE

on loss of EAW, 3-4, 4-5, 118-19, 157, 274, 320, 454-55, 564; retirement plans, 95; a typical day's routine, 141-42; on EAW memorial fund, 259-60, 260; I especially shrink from dwelling upon anything personal to myself. My instinct is to seek some occupation that will take my thoughts far afield where there is nothing that can concern me . . . I want to run away, to escape something, 289; lends money to P. W. Pope for his wife's operation, 310-